RUSSIA'S CRIMEAN WAR

Tsar Nicholas I (1796–1855). Courtesy of
Novosti from Sovfoto.

Russia's Crimean War

John Shelton Curtiss

DUKE UNIVERSITY PRESS   DURHAM, N.C.   1979

© 1979, Duke University Press
L.C.C. card number 76–28915
I.S.B.N. 0–8223–0374–4
Printed in the United States of America
by Kingsport Press, Inc.

TO THE MEMORY OF
GEROID TANQUARY ROBINSON

CONTENTS

MAPS

ILLUSTRATIONS

PREFACE

For Russia, as well as for Europe, the Crimean War was a landmark. As Professor Paul Schroeder has shown in *Austria, Great Britain, and the Crimean War,* it brought an end to the Concert of Europe, which had existed since the Napoleonic wars, and in its place left a situation in which the great powers operated without rules, without principles. Far from bringing peace by humbling Russia, it ushered in a series of European wars: the Franco-Austrian War in Italy; the war over Schleswig-Holstein; the German civil war of 1866; and the Franco-Prussian War. The French intervention in Mexico also can in part be ascribed to the international lawlessness that followed the Crimean War. Great quantities of blood and treasure were spent between the Treaty of Paris in 1856 and the Treaty of Versailles in 1871. Moreover, the Russo-Turkish War of 1877 showed that the Crimean War had not permanently solved the Eastern Question by weakening Russia, but had merely postponed conflict there. Thus the war of 1853–56 replaced an uneasy system of conservative control with a period of violent anarchy among the great powers.

To Russia also the war brought important changes, without achieving lasting solutions. Russia's presumed military supremacy was destroyed and could not be restored. This led to a search for allies—with France, then with Prussian Germany, and finally with the entente powers. But Russia could never feel secure.

The internal effects of the Crimean conflict were even more important. The empire's inability to develop an effective army based on serfdom led to the Emancipation of 1861, which freed the serfs from the feudal control of the nobility but left them in hopeless economic bondage to the regime. Hence the revolutionary movement grew in intensity, although the monarchy survived until 1917. The rapid development of the railways and of industry were outgrowths of the economic difficulties of the Crimean conflict, but instead of solving Russia's problems it merely changed their form and scope. The revolution continued to advance until its climax in 1917.

The historians have not properly elucidated Russia's role in this war. The English, strongly influenced by the Whig hatred of Russia propagated by Palmerston and his followers, with rare exceptions have blamed the war on Russian aggression and bad faith and have disregarded the repeated efforts of Nicholas I and Nesselrode to avoid war. Palmerston and Clarendon felt that Europe could have peace only if Russia's power was broken by stripping it of the Crimea, Georgia, and the Caucasus, as well as Poland and Finland. This, of course was impossible, and hence the British continued to blame Russia for starting the war and for threatening the stability of Europe. The French, who had never been so emotionally committed to this war, accepted their limited victory and wrote relatively little about it, especially since the Franco-Prussian War bulked much larger in their thinking. Several German historians have written about it, but with limited success, and the Germans seem to have been more interested in the rise of the German empire than in the senseless contest of 1853–56. Several Russian historians—M. I. Bogdanovich, N. F. Dubrovin, and A. A. Zaionchkovskii—have written sound studies. Eventually Eugene Tarle, after writing about Napoleon's invasion of Russia, wrote a major history of the Crimean conflict based on exhaustive research, especially on the diplomatic aspects. His two-volume study shows much understanding of the Russian situation during the war years, although his dislike of Nicholas I and his regime color his treatment of the subject. It is my hope to make additional contributions to the knowledge of this conflict.

I have approached the Crimean War—its genesis, its diplomacy, its campaigns, the making of the peace, and its most significant results for Russia—as an important aspect of nineteenth-century Russian history and have not attempted to treat it as a problem of European diplomacy. Since this is my first venture into diplomatic history, I probably have committed sins of omission and commission in this genre. So be it. In dealing with the Russian scene, at least, I feel that I may have been able to contribute something of value.

My research on the Russian army under Nicholas I aroused my interest in the Crimean War and gave me insight into the military scene. This interest led to the present effort to present a broad diplomatic, military, and social study, which was encouraged by the grant of a Senior Fellowship from the Social Science Research Council and the American Council of Learned Societies. Because of the grant, the Academy of Sciences of the USSR accepted me as a visiting member of its Institute of History, which provided access to Soviet archives and the riches of the Lenin State Library and other repositories. Academician M. N. Druzhinin and Professor E. I. Druzhinina gave me valuable advice on source materials, and Professor I. V. Bestuzhev was extremely helpful to me during my stay in Moscow. In Vienna Hofrat Rath and the staff of the Haus-, Hof-, and Staatsarchiv gave me invaluable assistance in orienting myself to their voluminous holdings and were unfailing in their courtesy and patience.

It is a pleasure to acknowledge several individuals who have aided me with advice and suggestions. Professor Paul W. Schroeder of the University of Illinois, by permitting me to read the manuscript of his book *Austria, Great Britain, and the Crimean War,* helped clarify my ideas about Austrian diplomacy of the period. Professor Peter K. Christoff of San Francisco State College provided valuable ideas about the Slavophils and also obtained copies of despatches for me from the Nederland Algemeen Rijksarchief. Mr. Charles E. Walker of the University of West Virginia furnished copies of despatches from the Archive diplomatique Français, Correspondence Politique.

Materials for this study have come from many of the leading libraries in the United States: Harvard, Columbia, New York Public, Library of Congress, University of North Carolina, and the Hoover Institution at Stanford. Duke University, which made this undertaking possible by granting a year of sabbatical leave, supplied much of the research materials from its Perkins Library and, through Mr. Emerson Ford, was able to obtain many needed items on interlibrary loan. To all of them I extend my thanks.

While, as mentioned above, many persons have given advice and other assistance, the responsibility for the ideas expressed is solely mine, and blame for mistakes or omissions belongs to me alone.

A NOTE ON THE CITATION OF DATES

In the nineteenth century Russia still used the Julian Calendar, which was then twelve days behind the Gregorian Calendar generally used in Europe and the West. French, British, Austrian, and Prussian despatches to their envoys in St. Petersburg were almost always dated by the Gregorian calendar, known as New Style. If, however, the despatch was intended to be delivered to the Russian chancellor, the date might be given in both the Old Style (O.S.) and the New Style (N.S.), thus: May 2/14, 1853; or June 24/July 6, 1854. Russian despatches to Western capitals almost always used both the Old Style and the New Style dates. Occasionally in my text it has been necessary to cite a despatch whose date does not clearly show whether it is in the New or the Old Style. In such a case the use of the proper indication (O.S.) or (N.S.) should make it clear which calendar was originally used.

ABBREVIATIONS USED IN NOTES

ADF, CP:	Archive diplomatique Français, Correspondence Politique. Paris
AVP. f. Kants., D. No. 161:	Arkhiv Vneshnei Politiki, fond Kantseliarii, Delo No. 161. Moscow
E.P., I:	Great Britain, Parliament, British Sessional Papers, 1854, LXXI, Eastern Papers, Pt. 1. London
HHSA, IX, 42:	Haus-Hof-und Staatsarchiv, Section IX, Carton 42. Vienna
Miliutin MS.:	D. A. Miliutin, "Moi starcheskie vospominaniia, 1816–1873 gg. Tri goda voiny, 1853–1856." Otdel Rukopisei, Biblioteka im. Lenina. Moscow
NRA:	Nederland Algemeen Rijksarchief. 's-Gravenhage
TsGADA:	Tsentral'nyi Gosudarstvennyi Arkhiv Drevnykh Aktov. Moscow
TsGAOR, f. 828, D. No. 602:	Tsentral'nyi Gosudarstvennyi Arkhiv Oktiabr'skoi Revoliutsii, fond 828, Delo No. 602. Moscow

PART ONE. THE COMING OF THE WAR

CHAPTER 1. THE BACKGROUND OF THE CRIMEAN WAR

The Crimean War was the first large-scale conflict after the Napoleonic wars, although there had been tension and minor wars between 1815 and 1853. The following survey of the developments that finally produced the explosion in 1853 will help to explain the origin of the conflict.

In 1815 Great Britain, guided by able statesmen, occupied a unique position, with its great navy and an army that had won glory against the French. Its flourishing trade and unrivaled industry created the financial strength that was the envy of the world. In spite of the rebellious Irish and hard-pressed peasants and workers at home, Britain was moving ahead on all continents with amazing success. Although it was rarely warlike, it was the most aggressive of the great powers.

India was the keystone of the British edifice. During the Napoleonic wars the British East India Company, with the aid of the navy, held out against the French and the Russians and a largely hostile population. After 1815 it rapidly expanded, conquering unsubmissive areas to the north, east, and south. In Afghanistan the British overreached themselves and after a year had to make a disastrous retreat. But by 1853 they controlled a territory from the Himalayas to Burma. The Russian threat to India had not materialized and it had become a fabulously rich market for British manufactures.

Elsewhere the Union Jack pushed forward. It was planted in Cape Colony to provide a haven for shipping to Bombay, although it proved costly and troublesome. Australia, at first merely a convict station, by 1854 had developed into a possession rich in sheep and gold; New Zealand, however, developed under anarchical conditions, which resulted in a troublesome Maori war before order was established and a stable system developed in 1852.

Canada, conquered in 1763, in 1815 had perhaps half a million people, many of them French. Although London was not greatly interested in Canada, the Canadian economy forged ahead and the population grew to almost three million by 1853. Railways were built and exploration of the North and West had made great strides, in spite of minor rebellions in 1837. The Act of Union had solved some of the political problems and the future seemed bright.

Elsewhere in the Americas England gained little territory, but it gained commercial supremacy in Brazil and the Spanish-speaking areas. Britain strongly opposed aggression by the United States in Cuba and in Mexico, but failed to prevent its expansion into Texas, California, and Arizona. Quarrels with the Americans arose over the Canadian boundary and the isthmus of Panama, but they were compromised without strife.

Economic motives were the driving force behind the British, along with humanitarian efforts to combat slavery and to protect African blacks, Polynesians, and Circassians, although in Ireland, India, and China they were not always compassionate. The British bullied the Persians and extolled the Turks, with whom they had a favorable trade, although they opposed the more modern Egyptian regime of Mehemet Ali, perhaps because it had a high tariff. Many Britons, indignant at the Russian blockade of the Circassians, hailed the latter as noble fighters for freedom, overlooking a Turkish traffic in Circassian girls, who were shipped to the slave markets of Istanbul.

China was a flagrant example of British commercial aggression, for the East India Company smuggled opium into China to pay for tea and silk. When Peking made a special effort to bar opium, Admiral Sir Charles Napier, British envoy to China, refused to obey the laws. The Chinese barred all trade with the British and seized over twenty thousand chests of the drug. Friction mounted, with some Chinese killed in a brawl. Finally Napier crushed Chinese resistance and, by the Treaty of Nanking in 1842, obtained wide trade privileges and the cession of Hong Kong and other treaty ports.

The French also were expansive during these decades, conquering Algeria and setting up a protectorate over Egypt. France also took control of Tahiti, the Marquesas, and New Caledonia. These gains caused friction with Britain, but no conflict arose.

The Russians also had their distant colony in Alaska, with outposts near San Francisco and in the Hawaiian Islands. But their communications were so difficult that they could hang on only with American help, and they considered selling Alaska to the United States even before the Crimean War. The Russians also were fighting the natives of the Caucasus Mountains, where they were making very slow progress.

While the British were thus expanding on five continents and a dozen seas, they were also active in European diplomacy, since they feared that the reactionaries of Europe would provoke their subjects to revolt. When there was a revolt in Portugal, British troops went to Lisbon and later Admiral Napier led a Portuguese fleet to prevent a coup. An uprising of the Belgians against their Dutch king threatened to bring on a general war. After the French and the British had joined to drive out the Dutch, they were close to war about what should become of Belgium. The French were very eager to annex it, but finally they had to accept Leopold of Coburg, uncle of Queen Victoria, as its king.

The Greek revolt against Turkey also affected Britain, since Britain sympathized with the Greeks but feared that Russia would destroy the Turkish empire. In 1827 Britain, France, and Russia joined to destroy the Egyptian fleet at Navarino to save the Greeks from extermination. The British soon decided that this was a mistake and withdrew, while French troops occupied the Morea. In 1828 Russia went to war with Turkey and in 1829 won a great victory that brought its army close to Constantinople. But the tsar showed marked restraint in the Treaty of Adrianople, and the crisis passed. The three powers agreed on a new Greek government, which was founded in 1833.

Lord Lyons, British minister at Athens under the able and aggressive foreign minister Henry John Temple, Viscount Palmerston, a Whig, demanded that the king grant a constitution and bullied him mercilessly when he refused. Lyons also was at odds with the French, and Prussia and Austria demanded his recall. Palmerston further angered France and Russia by backing the outrageous claims of Don Pacifico, a Portuguese adventurer, against the Athens government. Palmerston actually blockaded Greece, but had to back down in the face of French and Russian protests.

England also intervened actively in Spain, joining France in backing Queen Christina against the reactionary Don Carlos, with a Spanish Legion under Lacey Evans and with its fleet. Finally, when Isabella, Christina's daughter, became queen, with her sister as Infanta, the two powers tried to preserve a balance of influence by arranging suitable marriages for the two girls, which led to absurd intrigues, with each power sure that the other was betraying it. In the end the whole matter faded out, with neither having gained.

Palmerston was popular in England, where many enjoyed seeing him bully presumptuous foreigners. Some of his colleagues disliked him intensely but dared not clash with him, and Queen Victoria detested him and tried vainly to deny him the Foreign Office. He was also heartily disliked by many European cabinet members, who regarded him as a troublemaker. He greatly distrusted Russia and wanted to humble it in the Levant. He was constantly at odds with the Austrians, condemning them for their repression of the Italians, and the Prussians felt that he was a bad influence.

Many of Palmerston's clashes were with France—a proud and powerful nation, which resented its isolation after 1815. It set about restoring its commerce in the Levant, forming close ties with Mehemet Ali, pasha of Egypt, and aiding its economy and its army and navy. France bought much Egyptian cotton and helped set up munitions factories in Egypt, hinting that it would be glad to see Egypt independent of Turkey. London was troubled by this development and concerned about French naval development under Paixhans, a French naval officer who advocated small, armored steamers firing large shells and boasted that France would gain a naval supremacy that would reverse the verdict of Trafalgar. The French did little to carry out the Paixhans plan, but their talk troubled the British.

It is also significant that when the Russians defeated the Turks in 1829, Count Polignac, a reactionary premier under Charles X of France, offered a sweeping plan for partitioning Turkey, the Principalities of Moldavia and Wallachia and most of Armenia to go to Russia. The new Greek government was to obtain the Straits and France was to receive Belgium. This plan, which Charles X approved, was never presented to the Russian cabinet, for Russia made a moderate peace with Turkey at Adrianople before it could be broached. Charles X, who was dethroned in 1830, was replaced by Louis Philippe, who usually cooperated with England, although Palmerston often made it difficult. Nicholas I was an enemy of the Citizen King, whom he held to be a traitor to the principle of divine right. Louis Philippe's foreign policy was largely traditional, included a keen interest in Italy, opposition to the Holy Alliance, and support for Mehemet Ali.

The pasha of Egypt became an issue in 1830 when he demanded hereditary title to Egypt and Syria for having aided the sultan against the Greeks. Late in 1831 the Egyptians attacked the key fortress of Acre and took all of Syria. When the sultan moved against them, the Turkish army was routed and the road to Constantinople was open to the Egyptians.

The sultan now asked help from Britain, but only the Russians would aid him. With the Egyptians still advancing, the sultan called for the Russian fleet, which arrived in February 1833. Soon after, Russian troops were rushed by sea to the Bosporus and a peace was arranged granting Egypt and all of Syria to the pasha. The Russians then withdrew, thus easing the crisis. After they had gone, however, Russia induced the sultan to sign the Treaty of Unkiar-Skelessi, whereby Russia and Turkey became allies and the Porte promised to close the Straits to warships in time of peace. Thus, to the dismay of France and England, Russia had gained a great strategic advantage.

Since Nicholas I did not exploit his success, the British calmed down and Palmerston now feared that Mehemet Ali, backed by France, might cut England's communications with India via Egypt and Syria. The tsar promised not to attack India, and Palmerston, believing him, was sure that Turkey could now survive. But the sultan, furious at his rebellious vassal, attacked him in the spring of 1839 but again was routed by the Egyptians. The sultan suddenly died, and the fleet went over to the Egyptians. Mehemet would not return the fleet until he had received hereditary title to both Syria and Egypt, and France supported him. Russia, however, would make no bargain with the pasha, but, with Prussia and Austria, joined Palmerston in a coalition against him. Paris, furious at this turn of events, talked of war and increased its armaments, but the coalition held, and Louis Philippe accepted a compromise. The British fleet and the allied troops forced the Egyptians out of Syria in return for hereditary control of Egypt, and the French grudgingly accepted and signed the Straits Convention of 1841 stipulating that Turkey would control the Straits. Palmerston had won, but at the cost of infuriating the French and of angering the two German powers.

English relations with France remained strained under the moderate Tory premier Sir Robert Peel, and George Hamilton-Gordon, Lord Aberdeen, Peel's foreign minister, for French anger was still strong. Russia, however, remained pro-British, and in 1844 Nicholas visited Queen Victoria at London and Windsor. He charmed his hosts by his suave manners and his promise to maintain the Turkish empire as long as possible, although he induced them to sign a secret pledge to negotiate a peaceful settlement when the collapse of Turkey should finally occur. Nicholas and some of the British leaders took this agreement seriously, although most of the English paid little attention to it.

Peel and Aberdeen, while gratified by this entente, urgently sought to restore good relations with France and found Louis Philippe willing to offer a reasonable settlement of the question of Tahiti. Queen Victoria invited the king and queen to Windsor, where they were warmly received.

Palmerston, realizing that his conduct had hurt his career—for in 1845 the queen had helped to deny him the foreign ministry—now sought to show the French that he was not an enemy. But in 1846, after again becoming foreign minister, he clashed with France over the Spanish Marriages and then called for rearming against the French. The French entente was ruined, leaving Louis Philippe in a weakened position.

Foreseeing revolution, Palmerston took steps to avert it by urging the rulers to make timely concessions. He protested strongly against Austrian annexation of the Republic of Krakow, but to no avail. He succeeded in preventing interference in the Swiss civil war of 1846 long enough for the liberal Swiss Federation to win, thus averting Austrian intervention. His chief concern was Italy, where he saw revolution brewing. Palmerston actively supported King Charles Albert of Sardinia against Austrian threats and urged Pius IX and the Duke of Tuscany to support reforms. His fear was that if Austria should intervene in Italy that might involve France and bring on a general war.

When King Louis Philippe had to flee Paris, Palmerston was not upset but welcomed the moderation of the Second French Republic. He quickly responded to the appeal of Nicholas I of Russia for cooperation in stabilizing Europe. Although not friendly to Russia, he asked the tsar to persuade Austria to give up its Italian provinces and to develop its own lands. The Italians, however, were not satisfied with Austrian promises and invaded Lombardy. But before the French could act, Marshal Radetzky won a great victory for Austria and imposed peace on the Italians. Palmerston, still hoping that Austria would cede Lombardy, was furious when Prince Felix Schwarzenberg, the new Austrian premier, adopted a policy of repression instead of concessions.

While Palmerston disliked Austria as a center of reaction, he did not want to see it destroyed because he felt that it was "the pivot of Europe," and he would do nothing for the Magyars. Like Wellington, he urged the Russians to act against the Magyars, telling them to "finish as quickly as possible." He was furious at the Austrians for their vengeance on the captured generals and dignitaries, terming them "the greatest brutes that ever called themselves . . . civilized men." When Russia and Austria demanded that the Porte surrender Hungarian refugees, Palmerston backed Turkey's refusal by a naval demonstration with the French at the Dardanelles. Russia and Austria soon compromised the matter and Palmerston let it drop.

Palmerston's headstrong conduct reached its peak in the affair of Don Pacifico in Greece, which led Prince Albert of England to say that his recklessness had endangered England's safety. This remark touched off a general attack on the noble lord in the House, with William Gladstone, a noted Whig, making a highly effective indictment. After a vote of censure, however, Palmerston's appeal to public prejudices carried the day. Palmerston continued to cause trouble by indiscretions regarding General Haynau of Austria and Louis Kossuth, the Magyar nationalist. Finally, after Louis Napoleon's coup d'état in December, 1851, he rashly expressed his warm approval without consulting the cabinet. This action led to his dismissal from the government, to the rejoicing of Count Karl Nesselrode, chancellor of Russia, and Prince Felix Schwarzenberg, premier of Austria.

Edward Stanley, Lord Derby now took power, with James Howard Harris, Lord Malmesbury at the Foreign Office. Since the French were in an aggressive mood, there was real danger of war, for the French army was eager to scrap the Treaty of 1815. Malmesbury, however, was conciliatory and induced the French to drop their hostility toward Britain. When in December 1852 Louis Napoleon took the title of Napoleon III, the queen, accepting this, addressed him as "Sire, my Brother" and signed herself "Your Imperial Majesty's good Sister." Thus the Anglo-French entente was revived, and as Nicholas I had taken a stiff attitude toward the new emperor, France and England gradually drew together.

Thus the decades after 1815 had been filled with suspicion and tension that had more than once threatened to result in war, with the British, confident and at times even bellicose, repeatedly risking conflict. There had been no war, however, because the French, frustrated though they were, realized that they were isolated, and the Russians wanted to keep the status quo. But as France and Britain drew together in 1853, the stage was set for war when Nicholas I proved stubborn during the crisis over the Holy Places in Palestine.

Chapter 2. The Rise of the Eastern Question

From very early times the Russians had had an Eastern Question, for they were repeatedly attacked by nomads from Asia driving across the wide steps. Scythians, Huns, Avars, Magyars, Polovtsy, and Mongols harrassed their settlements, killing or enslaving their people. The Mongols conquered them, dominating them for two centuries, and it was only in 1480 that the Russians gained their freedom. They still had to fight the Tatar succession states and the Turks, who controlled the Black Sea and the Balkans. Only in the eighteenth century did the Russians, under Peter the Great, begin to drive back the Turks, and under Catherine II they threatened Constantinople. In 1808 Napoleon and Alexander I planned to partition Turkey, with Russia to get most of the Balkans. But this scheme failed, so that by 1815 Russia had reached only to approximately its present Rumanian boundary, and somewhat less in Asia Minor. Alexander was no longer seeking to destroy Turkey.

Thanks to its gains in the south, where it had ports like Odessa, Sevastopol, and Taganrog, Russia made great economic strides after 1815. With the right to use the Straits for commerce, it had a flourishing grain trade, with the export of wheat increasing almost 600 percent in three years.[1] Freedom for exports through the Straits was as essential for the Russians as the mouth of the Mississippi was to the young American republic.

The outbreak of the Greek revolt against Turkey in 1821 disturbed the prosperity in the Black Sea. It began in Moldavia, where it was soon put down, but quickly spread to Greece itself, where thousands took up arms. Alexander I, who did not favor it, cooperated with Prince Metternich of Austria against it. But after mass killings by the Turks, the Russian envoy at London warned that his cabinet could

1. A. V. Fadeev, *Rossiia i vostochnyi krizis 20-kh godov XIX veka* (Moscow, 1958), pp. 27–29.

not permit the slaughter of its coreligionists, to which Robert Stewart, Lord Castlereagh, the foreign minister, voiced strong objections.[2] Metternich, who hated the Greek revolutionaries and urged Alexander to let matters run their course, noted in his diary that the "incalculable" consequences of the revolt did not matter greatly, because in eastern Europe "three or four hundred thousand persons hanged, strangled, or impaled do not count for much." [3]

The Turks reacted to the uprising with mass fury against the Greeks of Smyrna and other ports and on Crete, Rhodes, and Cyprus. In Constantinople they hanged the Greek patriarch in his vestments in front of the cathedral. Stroganov, the Russian ambassador, wanted a collective protest against these outrages, but his British colleague at once refused.[4] Vicomte Chateaubriand, ambassador to the court of St. James, wrote to the Duke de Montmorency: "All England seems to be Turkish in its hatred of Russia." [5]

The Turks also vented their wrath on the Russians, stopping Russian ships going through the Straits, seizing their cargoes, and selling the grain for low fixed prices. Russian sailors and merchants were beaten, persecuted, and imprisoned. Alexander, much concerned, sent an ultimatum to the Porte to withdraw its troops from the Danubian Principalities of Moldavia and Wallachia (now Rumania) and to cease violating Russian commercial rights. It did not intercede for the Greek insurgents, but called on the Porte not to mistreat Greeks who had remained submissive. The great powers, it stated, would have to act, for they could not "calmly look at the annihilation of a whole Christian people." This was the first step by any of the powers on behalf of the Greeks. When the Porte failed to give a satisfactory reply, on July 29/August 10, 1821, Russia broke off relations with Turkey.[6]

Russia tried to reassure London that this action resulted from the outrages of the Turks and would be settled quickly when these ceased. If not, Russia would go to war—not to gain territory or influence, but to fulfill its duties to its peoples and their coreligionists as listed in its treaties. It did not seek the ruin of the Ottoman empire but

2. F. F. Martens, *Recueil des traités et conventions conclus par la Russie avec les puissances étrangères* (15 vols., St. Petersburg, 1874–1906), XI, 323.

3. Prince Clemens L. W. Metternich-Winneberg, *Mémoires, documents et écrits* (2nd ed., Paris, 1880–84), III of Amer. ed., 495.

4. Fadeev, p. 50.

5. C. K. Webster, *The Foreign Policy of Castlereagh, 1815–1822* (London, 1925), p. 400.

6. Fadeev, pp. 57–59.

was acting to end the massacres and pillage.[7] Britain, however, objected vehemently, believing that if Russia should fight it would be to make gains. Or if it sought to compel the Turks to make reforms in its Christian areas, Russia would then have the right to interfere in Turkish affairs, thus infringing on Turkish sovereignty. Prince C. A. Lieven, the Russian ambassador at London, tried hard to refute these arguments, but Castlereagh was unyielding.[8]

Austria also was horrified by the actions of Russia and by its hints of war. Metternich would not state what his policy would be, but kept warning that any Russian military action to help the Greeks would encourage the spread of revolution, so that Italy, Germany, and France would soon be lost.[9] The tsar heeded these urgings, for he valued the conservative alliance so much that he took no action for the Greeks and late in 1822 promised Metternich that he would not do so. He continued to appeal for collective action of the great powers but to no avail. And as the Greeks were holding off the Turks, he and Nesselrode, his foreign minister, did nothing, trusting Metternich and the Holy Alliance.[10]

In 1825, however, the sultan called in the powerful army and fleet of his vassal Mehemet Ali of Egypt, which subdued Crete and then the Morea, with the disunited Greeks helpless before them. A wave of sympathy for them swept Europe, and many young Russian army officers ardently backed them. Moreover, Russian landowners and commercial interests demanded restoration of commerce through the Straits. Alexander, faced with a defeat for vital Russian interests, frantically tried to compel collective mediation of the conflict, only to meet a flat refusal from Metternich. The tsar now decided to pursue an independent policy.

At this point George Canning, British foreign secretary, to prevent separate action by Russia, moved toward joint action with Russia and France. In the summer of 1827 the three countries signed an agreement providing for an autonomous Greece, tributary to the sultan. When the Turks rejected this proposal, a joint fleet under a British admiral sailed to Greek waters to force the Egyptians to withdraw their army. They fought the battle of Navarino in October, where

7. Martens, XI, 325.
8. Ibid., pp. 325–26.
9. Ibid., IV, pt. 1, 308–09.
10. Fadeev, pp. 86–91.

the Egyptian fleet was destroyed, thus greatly aiding the Greeks.[11]

While much of Europe rejoiced at this victory, England, in dismay, refused further action as demanded by Nicholas I of Russia. The latter, in anger, announced that he would occupy the Principalities, since Russia had to restore its trade and uphold its position at Constantinople. Russia would carry out the agreement made but sought no territory or other gains.[12] It also demanded that Turkey grant autonomy to Serbia.

Russian intervention, however, was delayed by a surprise attack of the Persians, who, believing that Russia was weak and unwilling to fight, suddenly invaded in force in 1826. The Russians believed that the attack was inspired by the British, who paid an annual subsidy to the shah and were training and equipping his troops. John MacDonald, the British envoy, had great influence over the ruler of Persia.[13]

The Russians, unprepared and dispersed, faced disaster, but their veteran troops fought off the first attacks and held. Then, reinforced under General I. F. Paskevich, the tsar's favorite, they quickly captured Erivan and in October took Tabriz without a fight. The crown prince was now ready for peace, but the shah, pressed by the Turks, refused, probably hoping that winter would halt the fighting. Paskevich, however, pushed through the snow almost to Teheran, and the Persians quickly accepted the Russian terms.[14]

This war was important solely because it delayed Russian action against Turkey and gave the sultan two years to prepare for war. After Navarino he repudiated all treaties and agreements with Russia and called for a holy war against it. Nicholas, who now was aiding the Greeks with money and arms, occupied the Principalities and in April 1828 declared war. He was careful to pledge that he would not destroy Turkey and would take only trifling gains in territory, although the Turks must accept peace proposals for Greece. He also asked England and France to represent Russian interests at Constantinople.[15]

Thus Russia avoided a break with the other powers, although relations were strained. The latter soon saw that Turkey was not in immedi-

---

11. Martens, XI, 335–43, 358–65.

12. Ibid., pp. 366–71.

13. Fadeev, pp. 145–47.

14. J. S. Curtiss, *The Russian Army under Nicholas I, 1825–1855* (Durhan, N.C., 1965), pp. 23–26, 36–38.

15. Fadeev, pp. 175–77, 180–83; Martens, XI, 377–93.

would have troubled the British "a thousand times less than such a result." [25] In time, however, the British anger subsided.

Nesselrode reacted sharply to the British fulminations, which he said must disturb the emperor "by their unfairness and impropriety." The British envoy hastily replied that the cabinet had made the protests merely "to satisfy Parliament." This answer did not satisfy Nesselrode, who retorted that while the British cabinet alleged that the annexation of some Turkish towns and districts would upset the balance of power, the vast and repeated conquests in India from 1814 on had systematically altered it. Nevertheless, he expressed Russia's sincere wish to preserve "the very best relations" with the Court of St. James. [26]

The Russians noted that Austria also was dismayed by the Russian victories, although Vienna was more restrained in its comments than London. When Emperor Franz I congratulated Nicholas on his successes, he hinted that Russia's actions had been partly to blame for the spread of the revolutionary spirit in Europe. The tsar, however, retorted that Austria, by consistently opposing the conservative alliance and supporting Turkey, had brought about its full collapse, which had encouraged the radicals. [27] But the Revolution of 1830 made the two empires realize that they needed each other, and in January 1831 Metternich agreed that they and Prussia should stand together to maintain order. [28]

The year 1831 was a troubled one for Russia, for most of it was spent in putting down the Polish insurrection of 1830, in the face of strong sympathy for the Poles in France and England and violent hostility toward the tsar. [29] Then came the conflict between Sultan Mahmud II and Mehemet Ali of Egypt, which has already been discussed. The pasha, angered by the sultan's refusal to give him Syria as well as Egypt, crushed the Turkish armies and invaded Asia Minor. The helpless sultan, unable to get aid from England, France, or Austria, ~~ly asked the tsar for help. Nicholas at once sent a strong Russian ~~ to Constantinople for action against the Egyptians, and when ~~tter still advanced, a sizable force of Russian troops sailed to ~~ntinople and landed on the Bosporus. The French and the Brit-

~~ens, XI, 415–17.
~~pp. 421–22.
~~V, pt. 1, 418.
~~p. 420–21.
~~leason, *The Genesis of Russophobia in Great Britain* (Cambridge, Mass., 1950),

ate danger, for the armies commanded by the emperor in the field won no victories but bogged down before Varna and Shumla. Lack of forage ruined the cavalry and forced the Russians into a disastrous retreat. Severe losses from disease made matters worse, and only the belated capture of Varna partially redeemed the situation. [16]

The emperor now put his army, much reinforced, under General I. I. Diebitsch, his chief of staff, who crossed the Danube in May 1829 and besieged Silistria, with the main Turkish army at Shumla. When the Turks tried to relieve Silistria, Diebitsch forced a battle at Kulevcha, where he routed them. The way to the "impassable" Balkans was now open, and after Silistria fell the troops pushed through the mountains in four days and made contact with the Russian fleet by capturing Burgas as well as an important crossroads in Bulgaria on July 12, routing ten thousand Turks. The inhabitants were cordial, supplies were plentiful, and communications by sea were good, while the Turks were demoralized. Disease was the only problem, for the men sickened badly in the summer heat. But no Turkish opposition occurred, and after reserves had arrived, Diebitsch moved against the key city of Adrianople, which surrendered without a fight. The Russians pushed ahead, in contact with their fleets in the Black Sea and the Aegean, until Russian cannon were heard in Constantinople. [17] At this moment the collapse of Turkey was so near that Count Polignac of France made his proposal for redrawing the map of Europe with a partition of the Turkish empire included (see Chapter 1, p. 6).

In Transcaucasia the Russian army under Paskevich had also been successful, quickly capturing the strong fortresses of Kars and Akhaltsikh. When the Turks tried a counteroffensive, the Russians repulsed it and in June Paskevich took the offensive. In a series of battles near Kars he routed much larger Turkish forces and on June 27 occupied Erzerum, major Turkish base in the area. But although the way was now open for advances into the heart of Asia Minor, Paskevich felt that the risks were too great. [18] Nevertheless, he, like Diebitsch, had revealed the innate weakness of the Ottoman empire.

The Russian forces, in spite of their small numbers, probably could have taken Constantinople, for their fleets controlled both the Black Sea and the Aegean, and the Turkish army hardly existed. More-

16. Curtiss, pp. 55–65.
17. Ibid., pp. 66–72; L. S. Stavrianos, *The Balkans since 1453* (2nd ed., New York, 1958).
18. Curtiss, pp. 39–43; Fadeev, pp. 255–73, 304–11.

over, the Russians could have obtained numerous volunteers from the Bulgars, Greeks, Armenians, and Georgians. But Diebitsch forbade the Bulgarians to rise, and rejected offers of cooperation from the Greek insurgents and did not ask for Serbian support. Paskevich did not encourage an Armenian uprising.[19] Thus, when there was a real possibility of expelling the Turks from Europe, the tsar turned his back on potential allies and hastened to make a lenient peace at Adrianople, to the amazement of friends and enemies. This was not because of any danger from the major powers. Prussia on the whole was sympathetic to Russia, and England and Austria were so sure that Russia would not win a big victory that Diebitsch's crossing of the Balkans took them by surprise and they were not mobilized. As for France, it was ready to join Russia in redrawing the boundaries of Europe, but Russia made peace so quickly that Polignac never had a chance to propose his scheme to the tsar.

The emperor apparently believed that if his generals pushed on, Turkey would collapse, which would lead to a frantic rush by the other powers to seize as much territory as possible and to deny Russia the key position at the Straits that geography offered it. On August 28, 1829, the tsar ordered Diebitsch to make "a good peace at Adrianople." [20] A week later he called together a secret meeting of the best minds of official Russia, to which Nesselrode read a memorandum on the need to keep the Turkish empire intact. Count D. V. Dashkov's warning that the destruction of Turkey would bring on a general war was followed by similar opinions. A letter from Count John Capodistria, president of the new Greek government, calling for an end to Turkish power in Europe and the formation of five new states, met with no support. Instead, the conference agreed that Turkey should be maintained as a barrier to keep the European powers from the Straits. If Turkey should collapse, however—which appeared quite possible—Russia should negotiate with the other powers concerning the fate of the Ottoman holdings.[21] For decades these principles guided the Russian government.

After the fall of Adrianople, Lieven and Matushevich, Russian diplomats at London, called for the capture of Constantinople and the

destruction of the Ottoman empire. Count Nesselrode, however, sharply rebuked them, saying that while the dream of Christianity again dominant at Constantinople was noble, it would bring Russia nothing but glory and would lose "all the positive advantages" of "having as a neighbor a state weakened by a series of unfavorable wars and of inevitable clashes with the chief European powers." As it was to Russia's interest to keep Turkey intact, they should drop all schemes for "an event which would be a real misfortune" for it.[22]

The Treaty of Adrianople reflected this thinking, for in Europe Russia acquired only some islands at the mouth of the Danube, but obtained the important guarantee that the Straits would be open to commercial shipping of all states at peace with Turkey. In Asia, Turkey ceded the whole Caucasian coast except for Batum, as well as Georgia and eastern Armenia. Russia annexed the town of Akhaltsikh and the fortress of Akhalkalaki, which greatly improved its position south of the mountains, but it returned Kars, Erzerum, and Baiazet—important strategic and commercial centers—although the local Armenians were very pro-Russian. The treaty also provided for virtual autonomy and more economic rights for the Principalities, a legal status for autonomous Serbia, and definite frontiers and autonomy for Greece.[23]

The Treaty of Adrianople did nothing for the Bulgars, whose hopes had been aroused by the Russian victories. By order of the tsar Diebitsch had to arrest and imprison their leaders, to prevent an uprising. Many Bulgars emigrated to Russia, while those who remained could only dream of freedom.[24] The events of 1829–39, however, set Bulgaria on the long road to independence.

In view of the prostrate condition of Turkey in 1829, the moderation was striking. Nonetheless the British cabinet sent to St. Petersburg declaring that Russia's acquisition of the coast and of Akhaltsikh was contrary to the interest powers and hence would "infringe on the balance of Aberdeen termed it "a deadly blow to the Ottoman could survive for only a short time. He declared ferred to have Constantinople captured by the peace. Wellington said that the capture and

19. Fadeev, pp. 322–25, 347.
20. Ibid., p. 326.
21. Martens, IV, pt. 1, 438–40.

22. Ibid., XI, 412–13.
23. Fadeev, pp. 337–39, 353–54.
24. Ibid., pp. 354–58.

25. Mar
26. Ibid.
27. Ibid.
28. Ibid.,
29. J. H. C
110–31.

ish were furious over this Russian triumph, but neither could act, and the tsar calmed their fears by removing the troops as soon as possible. Count A. F. Orlov, a special envoy, convinced the sultan that Russia was his only friend and that they should have an alliance. Thus the Treaty of Unkiar-Skelessi of July 8, 1833, pledged peace and friendship between the two rulers and cooperation in maintaining peace and security. A secret article reduced the sultan's help to Russia in case of war to the duty to close the Straits to all foreign warships, based on a traditional rule of the Porte.[30]

France and Britain, angered by this treaty, made a strong joint protest to Russia, and England, greatly troubled over the growth of Russian influence over Turkey, prepared its fleet for action and sought allies against Russia, but found none. Palmerston, having learned of the secret article, had a heated discussion with Prince Lieven, the Russian ambassador, who finally convinced him that it did not give Russia the right to send its fleet into the Mediterranean. While they remained angry, the British, without allies, had to cease their protests.[31]

British hostility and the emperor's anger at Louis Philippe made the tsar welcome the overtures of Emperor Franz I of Austria. The two rulers met at Münchengrätz in July 1833 for weighty political conferences, followed by meetings of the rulers and the crown prince of Prussia. Palmerston was sure that they were plotting the partition of Turkey. He was far off the mark, for Nicholas told Metternich that if the sultan asked for aid, he would sacrifice his religious feelings and grant it. He declared, however, that if Turkey ever collapsed, it would not be possible to revive it, and that the best solution would be to restore the former Greek empire.[32]

The crowned heads easily agreed to ward off the aggressive designs of France and Britain and to hold down their restive minorities. The stipulations of the Münchengrätz Convention, however, dealt only with Turkey, pledging that the powers would support the Ottoman empire under the present dynasty with influence and force. If it should fall, they should seek to avert the resulting dangers. Several articles dealt with Mehemet Ali, whom they would prevent from gaining the

30. Martens, XII, 43–44; P. E. Mosely, *Russian Diplomacy and the Opening of the Eastern Question in 1838 and 1839* (Cambridge, Mass., 1934), p. 10.
31. Martens, XII, 44–51.
32. Ibid., IV, pt. 1, 436–37, 443.

European provinces of Turkey. If the sultan should be overthrown, they would cooperate in complete harmony to set up a new order in Turkey. They would also try to prevent any changes that might occur from affecting the safety of their possessions, their treaty rights, or "the European equilibrium." [33]

Palmerston and the British were now persuaded that Russia would absorb Turkey unless Britain and any allies it could find should prevent it. The fanatical David Urquhart, who toured Turkey and gained a detailed knowledge of the Caucasus, published a book, *Turkey and Its Resources,* stating that Turkey, with its low tariff and weak government, offered splendid trade opportunities, while Russia threatened Turkey's very existence and England's trade prospects. [34] Palmerston, who agreed with this analysis, contrary to the views of his ambassador at St. Petersburg, in December 1833 sent "an extremely bellicose dispatch" to Lord John Ponsonby, the ardently Turcophil ambassador to the Porte, saying that, in spite of its peaceful assurances, Russia's acts proved the contrary. Hence England must "consider how Russia can be prevented from pushing her advantage further, and see whether it be possible to deprive her of the advantage she has already gained." Ponsonby should warn Turkey that England would prefer to see Mehemet Ali at Constantinople rather than the tsar. Palmerston even empowered the British Mediterranean squadron to pass through the Straits to counter a Russian attack on Constantinople, if "the violently Russophobe Ponsonby" felt it necessary. [35]

A review of Urquhart's book in the *Edinburgh Review,* which J. H. Gleason calls "a semiofficial pronunciamento in defense of Whig policy," shows how seriously the cabinet viewed its relations with Russia. It termed Russia aggressive and not to be trusted. If it gave cause, "from that very hour she will be made to feel the power of Britain even to the core of her huge empire." Russia was vulnerable because of the hostility of the Poles and other oppressed peoples. "We have small doubt," the review stated, "that the damming up of the Baltic and the Black Sea with our fleets, the destruction of her navy, and the annihilation of her commerce, which would be the easy and not expensive result of one campaign, would bring her to reason"—

33. Ibid., pp. 435–37, 441–48.

34. David Urquhart, *Turkey and Its Resources* (London, 1933), as discussed in Gleason, pp. 154–55.

35. Gleason, pp. 145–49. Sir Charles Webster holds that Ponsonby might call in the fleet only if the sultan requested it to guard against a Russian attack. Sir Charles Webster, *The Foreign Policy of Lord Palmerston, 1830–1841* (London, 1851), I, 333.

especially as the outbreak of hostilities would bring about the restoration of the kingdom of Poland.[36]

This was essentially Palmerston's program, for Palmerston believed that Turkey could ensure its survival by reforms, while Russia would be kept at bay by threats. Until 1849 he did not apply the program to Russia, which did not pick up the challenge. But reform was not enough to remedy the widespread failings of Turkey, although under Reshid Mustapha pasha valuable steps were taken. The Christians of Turkey were still largely exposed to exploitation and the corruption of local magnates, in spite of Reshid.[37]

The excitement over the Münchengrätz Convention waned in 1834, since Russia gave no offense. There was friction over the rejection of Stratford Canning as ambassador to Russia because he had offended Nesselrode, but in other respects Russia was conciliatory. When John George Lambton, Lord Durham, was ambassador he pleased the Russians and soothed the English by his accurate and reassuring analysis of Russian intentions and power, which he held were not aggressive, in spite of great strength at home. Unfortunately these views, close to those of his predecessors, had little lasting effect, for the passionate Urquhart managed to capture the minds of the British.

Urquhart's book, *England, France, Russia, and Turkey,* published in 1834, stated without evidence that Russia's great desire was to capture Constantinople and absorb Turkey. This victory, in turn, would lead to the annexation of Persia, which would then join in the conquest of India. Urquhart became secretary of the embassy at Constantinople, where he and Ponsonby collaborated in pro-Turkish, anti-Russian efforts. In late 1835 he began *Portfolio,* an organ for his Russophobe utterances. He campaigned ardently for the noble Circassians, who were fighting the Russian tyrant for freedom. Urquhart saw Circassia as the key to the situation, for if Britain aided the mountaineers, Turkey would be saved and Russia would recede beyond the mountains. His demand for the fleet in the Black Sea was echoed in the British press, and J. B. Fraser, active in Central Asia, and John McNeill, who became minister at Teheran, supported him. Urquhart strongly emphasized trade opportunities in the Near East, with Circassia an especially important area.[38]

At the same time, from the embassy Ponsonby was urging both

36. Gleason, pp. 149–51.
37. Stavrianos, pp. 315–18.
38. Ibid., pp. 173–90.

Palmerston and the sultan to defy the tsar and Mehemet Ali and called for a British fleet at Constantinople and in the Black Sea to enforce a *Pax Britannica*. Ponsonby told Mahmud that London would give vigorous aid "if he acted like a sultan and not as a vassal of the tsar." To Palmerston he wrote that if Britain had a fleet on the Bosporus it could "dictate terms to both Russia and the Pasha of Egypt" and insisted that Russia's apparent moderation was merely to gain time to crush the Circassians, after which it would again push to the Straits.[39] But Palmerston did not heed this advice, and in 1834 Wellington accepted the pacific assurances of the tsar and reduced the tension.

In 1835, with Palmerston again in the Foreign Office, Ponsonby sought to move him against the tsar and Mehemet Ali. But the minister was sure that reform would save Turkey, while war would mean its ruin. And since Lord Durham had convincingly shown that Russia lacked both the will and the strength for aggression and was moderate toward Turkey, Palmerston rejected the sultan's plan for revenge against Mehemet, but encouraged the reform movement and sent British officers to train the Turkish army. The British navy was told to avoid demonstrations. Ponsonby now was sure that his superior had been duped by the tsar with the aid of Austria, especially when he compromised the case of a British subject whom the Turks had jailed for wounding a local child.[40]

This trifling matter was followed by the incident of the brig *Vixen*, which Gleason regards as a plot to embroil England and Russia in war. Urquhart induced the Bells, merchants of Glasgow and London, to send the vessel laden with salt—a contraband cargo—to a small Caucasian port, in hopes of having the Russian navy seize it. Then, Urquhart hoped, London would have to send the fleet into the Black Sea, which might lead to war. Bell had actually tried to get Ponsonby and Palmerston to declare the Russian blockade of the Caucasus illegal, but they had refused. The *Vixen* sailed to the Caucasian coast, where late in November a Russian cruiser seized it and its cargo.[41] The Russian account asserts that the cargo consisted of gunpowder and other munitions and not harmless salt. The Russian envoy at London reported that in his presence Palmerston had raged against Russia

39. G. H. Bolsover, "Lord Ponsonby and the Eastern Question (1833–1839)," *Slavonic Review,* XIII (July 1934), 101–05.
40. Ibid., pp. 107–10.
41. Ibid., p. 111; Gleason, pp. 181–93.

and had sought war, but by holding firm, the envoy had compelled the foreign secretary to take a moderate tone.[42]

While this episode did not bring war, it inflamed the British press and public against Russia. Urquhart, furious at his failure, accused Palmerston of having betrayed him for Russian gold. This absurd charge was aired at length in Parliament and did much to intensify the anti-Russian feeling that led to the Crimean War. Palmerston, however, removed Urquhart from the diplomatic service.[43]

Another reason for British hostility was fear that Russia might cut the trade routes across Turkey to India. The flourishing caravan road from Trebizond on the Black Sea through Baiazet, Tabriz, and Teheran to the Persian Gulf ran close to the Russian border, and in 1829 Paskevich's army had cut it in several places. There was less danger from the Mediterranean to Damascus, Bagdad, and the Persian Gulf, but this territory was not entirely secure. Only the Red Sea route was far enough from Russia to be safe.

British trade with Turkey was highly important to British statesmen and the public. The rapid growth of commerce after 1825 brought a real need for markets and for sources of raw materials and food. Turkey was very valuable on both counts, for it had a much lower tariff than most of the countries of Europe, and in 1838 the Balta-Liman Convention further improved the terms of trade. Hence British exports to Turkey soared, from £1,080,000 in 1825 to £8,489,000 in 1852. British imports from Turkey rose much more slowly, from £1,207,000 in 1825 to £2,252,000 in 1852. As the balance was largely paid in bullion, this was a highly valuable commerce.[44]

Turkish exports also were useful, for they consisted of foods and raw materials. The Corn Laws were repealed in 1846, and by 1851 Britain was importing as much grain from Turkey (chiefly from the Principalities) as from Russia. Moreover, Turkey, unlike Russia, was not industrializing, so that British manufactures had a secure market there, while Russia was building competing industries, often with British machinery and steam engines.[45]

Thus Turkey had become a valued trading partner, while Russia,

42. Martens, XII, 62–66.

43. Gleason, pp. 193–204; R. W. Seton-Watson, *Britain and Europe, 1789–1914: A Survey of Foreign Policy* (Cambridge, Eng., 1937), pp. 187–88.

44. Frank E. Bailey, *British Policy and the Turkish Reform Movement 1826–1853* (London, 1942), pp. 72–74.

45. V. J. Puryear, *England, Russia, and the Straits Question, 1844–56* (Berkeley, Calif., 1931), p. 91.

once a top customer, had lost its primacy. In 1849 Palmerston told the Commons: "If in a political point of view the independence of Turkey is of great importance, in a commercial sense it is no less important. . . . It is quite true that in no country is our trade so liberally permitted and carried on as in Turkey." [46]

Thus the British equated Turkey's existence with their prosperity. And as British opinion was increasingly sure that Russia was the only threat to Turkey, it is no wonder that it was regarded with enmity.

Even India—fabulously wealthy and weakly held—appeared to be menaced. Every Russian move in Persia or Central Asia alarmed the English, who suspected intrigues against India. Russia, however, did not want trouble and at times did not support its agents in inner Asia. When Palmerston told the Russian ambassador that seemingly harmless Russian moves were like reconnaissances and outposts before a great fortress,[47] Nesselrode, by order of the tsar, prepared an answer. He stated that Palmerston's remarks "ascribed to Russia serious designs upon British India" which had a harmful effect on their relations. The tsar's policy in Asia, like that in Europe, "far from any thoughts of conquests, has as its purpose only the protection of the rights of Russia and esteem for the lawfully obtained rights of all other powers."

He added that the emperor had no thought of assaulting the safety and peace of British India. *"He only wants what is just and what is possible"* and would not permit any scheme against British power there. This not only would be *unjust,* it would not be *possible,* "because of the wide distances . . . the losses that it would cause, the difficulties that would have to be overcome"—and all for carrying out a risky, irrational plan. Study of the map would convince objective observers that no hostile intent dominated Russian policy in Asia. Russia had not urged the shah of Persia to attack Herat but had tried to arrange a compromise between the Persians and Afghans. Furthermore, Russia was willing to open all Central Asia to the commerce of the European powers, as there was opportunity for all. Russia had sought commercial relations with the Afghans, but this was permissible. Nesselrode, in turn, voiced *his* complaint against the numerous British agents trying to incite the people of Central Asia near the Russian frontier. England,

46. V. J. Puryear, *International Economics and Diplomacy in the East* (Stanford, Calif., 1935), p. 213.

47. Pozzo di Borgo to Nesselrode, Oct. 11/23, 1838, Martens, XI, 75.

like Russia, should seek peace in the heart of Asia and try to avoid a general explosion.[48]

William Lamb, Lord Melbourne, the Whig premier, was much pleased with this note, which he was willing to implement. Even Palmerston after some delay accepted it as "fully satisfactory." [49] But although Russia recalled its agent from Kabul and ceased its march against Khiva in 1838, the British continued their anti-Russian intrigues. The British public was being taught to think of Russia as a menace. The Russian envoy at London wrote that almost all Britons were convinced that Russia was aggressive, and the British cabinet was following a plan of systematic hostility to Russia.[50] Nesselrode felt that this picture was too gloomy, however. The emperor, while largely agreeing with the chancellor, added that they should be on guard and, if British insanity should lead to war, "I shall trust in God and the bravery of our troops to make them repent of it." [51]

On the whole the Russians were not concerned, as the government felt secure and few voices were raised against Britain. Nesselrode usually managed to calm his master's excited moments. In 1838, when the emperor wanted to send two battleships with auxiliaries from the Baltic for maneuvers in the Mediterranean and then sail them into the Black Sea, his minister warned against it, arguing that this action would violate the principle of closure of the Straits, which was generally accepted. Russia's violation of it now would anger the Turks and might lead to war. Russia should work to conserve peace and to avoid troubling Turkey. "To maintain instead of shaking this political barrier that the Dardanelles establish between us and the maritime powers"— these were "the real interests and the true needs of Russia." [52] Nicholas agreed. Russia still favored keeping the Straits closed to all warships, including its own, for its leaders realized that if they sent their fleet through the Straits they would meet far stronger British and French armadas in the Aegean.

Storm clouds were already gathering, however. In 1838 Mehemet Ali decided to proclaim his independence from the sultan, which would probably bring war, with Russia as Turkey's ally. England and France

48. Ibid., pp. 75–77. Italics are in the original.
49. Ibid., pp. 78–79.
50. Gleason, pp. 205–20.
51. Martens, XI, 78–79.
52. Mosely, pp. 71–89.

would then probably turn on Russia. Palmerston proposed a conference in London, which Russia and Austria refused, and France, which favored Mehemet Ali, also balked. Palmerston was furious at Russia for refusing, but the tsar held firm. Russia now was on the defensive.[53]

In 1839 when the sultan, encouraged by Ponsonby, moved to strike at Mehemet Ali, the new Turkish army collapsed and fled in panic. Moreover, even before this, Mahmud, sickly and alcoholic, died, leaving an ineffectual youth to succeed him. To complete the disaster, the Turkish fleet surrendered to Mehemet at Alexandria. But since the pasha failed to act decisively, England, with Austria and at first France, moved against him. Russia also was ready to cooperate. Nicholas I sent Baron Philip Brunnow, his best diplomat, to London in September, where he amazed Palmerston by stating that Russia would not renew the Treaty of Unkiar-Skelessi and would cooperate against Egypt. The Briton, much pleased, declared that he had no wish to force entry into the Black Sea—a mere temporary triumph. Each side should consider the Straits closed forever. Palmerston even agreed to recognize the influence of Russia in Turkey as "natural and legitimate. It results from your geographic position." [54]

Russia's proposals were that the powers should not guarantee all the sultan's possessions. They should keep the Straits closed to warships in peace and in war, and the British and French fleets should not enter the Sea of Marmora. Russia would join in guaranteeing an agreement between the sultan and Mehemet Ali, it would not renew Unkiar-Skelessi, and it would enter the Bosporus to save Turkey only as an agent of the European powers. Brunnow strongly urged a firm agreement among the powers on these points in order to compel Paris to accede to this proposal. While Nicholas did not trust France, he assured London that Russia would not interfere in French internal affairs.[55]

England, however, did not want to offend Paris, which strongly backed Egypt, and it was only after six months of futile talks that the four powers signed the London Convention, without France. If Mehemet refused to accept hereditary rule of Egypt and life control of Syria, their fleets would cut Egyptian communications and force his army to retire to Egypt, with the loss of all right to Syria. The rule of keeping the Straits closed to warships was affirmed.[56]

53. Ibid., Appendix A, pp. 141–46.
54. Martens, XI, 110–11; Bolsover, 113.
55. Martens, XII, 110–13.
56. Ibid., pp. 146–47.

When Mehemet rejected these terms, the allied forces drove his army back into Egypt. France was furious at its isolation and armed for conflict, while the British, preparing for war, sent word that they were counting on Russian support. Nicholas spontaneously pledged that a Russian squadron would at once sail to aid England if France should attack, and Palmerston was warm in his gratitude.[57] France cooled down, however, and in 1841 it joined in signing a five-power convention providing that the Straits would be closed to non-Turkish warships in times of peace. While Russia thus gave up its special position under the Treaty of Unkiar-Skelessi, its cabinet was pleased, for it gave the Black Sea coast security against attack, and Russia's relations with England were cordial.[58]

The Anglo-Russian entente continued after the Whigs fell in 1841 and Sir Robert Peel became premier, with Aberdeen as his foreign minister. Although Peel, Aberdeen, the queen, and Prince Albert earnestly sought French friendship, France was still angry and war seemed near, so Peel and Aberdeen welcomed Russian friendship. Nicholas regarded Louis Philippe as a troublemaker because of his sympathy for the anti-Russian Polish exiles of 1831. Russia and England cooperated in Persia, and as London was disappointed by Turkish reform efforts, there was little to keep them apart. A trade treaty in 1843 also helped. Mutual hopes for a visit by Nicholas to Queen Victoria resulted in the tsar's arrival in London in May 1844. He then went to Windsor Castle, where he charmed the royal couple and the court. Soon after he had gone, Nesselrode arrived.[59]

The emperor found time amid the social affairs to talk politics with Peel, Aberdeen, and Arthur Wellesley, Duke of Wellington, and also with Melbourne and Palmerston, who were out of office—with France a leading topic. Nicholas was sharply critical of Louis Phillippe, who, he felt, had tried to undermine and ruin him, which he could not forgive.[60] Then he turned to Turkey—"the dying man." When it would fall, there would be a crisis, for France, aggressive in Algeria and Italy, would move to take Crete or Smyrna. This attack would involve the British fleet, and the Austrian and Russian armies would also take a hand. Thus the danger would be great.

Peel replied that England's position was similar to Russia's, except

57. Ibid.
58. Ibid., pp. 154–60.
59. Puryear, *England, Russia, and the Straits Question,* pp. 36–83.
60. Ibid., pp. 43–45.

that it also felt Egypt was vital. Supported by France, Egypt's government was strong and could close the Red Sea or refuse to handle the mails.[61] It had twice threatened the peace of Europe and both Russia and England felt it might do so again.

After this exchange of views Nicholas offered his armies to England in case of war with France over any issue. He readily discussed mutual problems such as Persia, Poland, and Belgium, agreeing to settle them jointly with London.[62]

Turkey was the main subject of discussion, since the tsar had consistently held that its days were numbered and that the great powers must be ready to prevent a general war when its collapse should come. In 1829 he had agreed to preserve Turkey as long as possible, although with no real hope of success. Turkey had survived, however, but the challenge of Mehemet Ali made its survival again seem doubtful. In 1833 the tsar frankly said to Count Ficquelmont, the Austrian ambassador, that he would try to keep it alive but could do little. "I lack the power to give life to a corpse," he said, "and the Turkish Empire is dead." While the inevitable might be postponed, "I have no confidence in the maintenance of this ancient body; it is breaking down on all sides; a little sooner or a little later, it will collapse." [63]

The emperor urged Austria and Russia to discuss the matter frankly, adding that he had renounced the policy of Catherine II to destroy Turkey and sought no Turkish land. The two empires must arrange matters beforehand, to prevent Britain and France from making trouble. Perhaps a Greek empire at Constantinople under King Otto might be the answer. But Metternich was cool toward the whole idea and delayed action. When they met at Münchengrätz the tsar, feeling that Turkey might survive, dropped the question. Ficquelmont felt sure that Nicholas did not want Turkish land for Russia.[64]

Many Europeans, like Nicholas, foresaw the collapse of Turkey because of the obvious weaknesses of the regime—administrative, financial, judicial, military—and the rebellion and general helplessness of the Christian subjects against extortion and oppression. In 1829 Prince Polignac had proposed that the Turks be expelled from Europe

---

61. Baron Ernst von Stockmar, *Memoirs* (London, 1872), II, 106–09; Martens, XII, 236–37.

62. Puryear, *England, Russia, and the Straits,* pp. 46–47.

63. G. H. Bolsover, "Nicholas I and the Partition of Turkey," *Slavonic Review,* XXVII, no. 68 (1948), 116.

64. Ibid., pp. 117–20.

and confined to inner Anatolia. In November 1829 Aberdeen had held similar views about Turkey, declaring that "this clumsy fabric of barbarous power will speedily crumble into pieces from its own inherent causes of decay. . . ." England then should seek to replace it "in a manner most beneficial to civilization and to peace. . . ." [65]

But Turkey had survived and Reshid pasha, a minister of vision and ability, began wide reforms known as the *Tanzimat*. After Sultan Mahmud's famous decree (the *Hatti Sherif* of Gulhané, November 3, 1839), Reshid pushed through specific reforms, pledging the security of all, Christian and Moslem alike, against violation of their honor and economic rights. Criminals would be tried in public. Taxation should be equalized and collected by more tolerable means. The recruiting of soldiers should be more equitable. Reshid provided that official salaries would be paid regularly and promotion would be based on merit. A new penal code prohibited torture and limited the use of the death penalty. He created mixed tribunals of Moslems and Christians, where the testimony of *rayahs* (Christians) would have the same value as that of Moslems. The government also sought to expand and strengthen education.

These remarkable measures, which stimulated Turkish life, delighted Lord Palmerston. They had many opponents, however. When Khosrew pasha was removed for embezzlement in 1840, he and other Old Turks, aided by Lord Ponsonby, conspired against Reshid, who resigned in 1841. [66]

As the reaction against the reforms mounted, doubts arose regarding the stability of Turkey. The position of the Christians worsened and their discontent increased. In 1842 many Serbs revolted, and although the uprising failed, it was an important sign. Stratford Canning, an ardent Turcophil, warned his government in December 1843 of "an approaching crisis and the multiplying of those chances of disaster to which a decaying empire is ever liable." [67]

In September 1843 Nicholas again assured Austria that when Turkey collapsed he did not want Constantinople. They must prepare for the worst, or the catastrophe would catch them by surprise. He declared he would never cross the Danube and that Austria should have the Balkans south of it as well as Constantinople. While Metter-

---

65. V. J. Puryear, *France and the Levant* (Berkeley, Calif., 1941), p. 102.
66. Bailey, pp. 192–201.
67. Bolsover, "Nicholas I and Partition," p. 122.

nich felt that such talk was useless and wished to end it, the tsar would not be put off and in March 1844 sent Count A. F. Orlov to continue the talks. Russia did not want Constantinople and would not let either England or France have it, but would permit Austria to control it. The three eastern monarchs—Francis I of Austria, Frederick William IV of Prussia, and Nicholas I of Russia—should stand firm on this matter. Once more, however, nothing came of it.[68]

Thus Nicholas was consistent in his view of Turkey, which was widely shared at the time, although few diplomats drew the same conclusions. In England in 1844, however, he felt that he had a sympathetic audience, to which he presented his usual views: Turkey would soon collapse; Russia did not want more land and above all realized that it could not have Constantinople, but it would not permit any other power to have it either. Instead of suggesting Austria as keeper of the gate, however, he proposed that Constantinople should be a free city. He repeatedly insisted that he wanted to preserve Turkey as long as possible, but as this would be only temporary, he emphasized the need to consult when it should fall. He thus hoped to avoid a general war.

The emperor apparently established very good relations with Queen Victoria, Prince Albert, Peel, Wellington, and Aberdeen, winning their confidence by his frankness and honesty. Thus he felt that he had reason to hope for continuing goodwill for an indefinite period. Unfortunately, he did not realize that many Englishmen thought his openness was intended to deceive. Nicholas, who had a liking for personal diplomacy, may have done harm by stating his outspoken views and he probably would have been wiser to have been more reserved.[69]

After he had left, Nesselrode visited England, discussing the political relations of the two countries in more conventional fashion, especially with Peel and Aberdeen. Again the premier and the two ministers stressed the need to preserve Turkey as long as possible, although they agreed that its collapse was highly likely and that the two powers must then confer to decide on a course of action that would remove the danger of a general war. Neither party proposed that this agreement should take the form of a treaty because this would have infuriated the French and probably would have aroused opposition in England. The Turks would have been highly offended by such a treaty, and

68. Ibid., pp. 128–31.
69. Martens, XII, 234–37.

Metternich would have been very hostile. So it remained a secret understanding. For the record, Nesselrode wrote a memorandum summarizing the arguments and discussions and the agreement that they had reached. Aberdeen approved this without reservation as stating accurately the ideas exchanged, and accepted the correctness of its principles and the proposed course of action. Nicholas I approved it, except that he wanted the two cabinets to confer *before* the collapse of the Porte, if this seemed imminent. When Nesselrode sent the amended memorandum to London, Aberdeen replied in January 1845 that the statement was entirely accurate and hoped that they might continue to be in agreement "during all our negotiations with the Levant." [70]

Thus Russia and Britain reached an entente which, although it was not formally a treaty, was, both sides felt, essentially an alliance. In 1845 Russia supported Britain against France in the crises over Tahiti and Morocco and encouraged Britain to conquer the Punjab so as to have more troops available for the Mediterranean. Aberdeen had become such a warm friend that St. Petersburg believed that it could fully rely on him. This erroneous belief probably caused the tsar to act more confidently in 1852 and 1853 than he should have— [71] a misapprehension that helped to lead him into the Crimean War.

The emperor also felt confident of Austria. In December 1845 he had a long discussion with Metternich concerning Turkey, whose demise, he asserted, could not long be delayed. When it occurred, Austria should replace Turkey at Constantinople, and if Britain and France opposed this, he was ready to fight them if need be. As usual, however, the Vienna cabinet was not interested in this proposal, probably feeling that the scheme was really a cover for Russia's desire to have Constantinople for itself.[72]

On the whole the tsar felt comfortable in his dealings with the European powers. He enjoyed remarkably good relations with England, and with Austria and Prussia his rapport was good. France was another matter, for he would have nothing to do with Louis Philippe, although Nicholas Kiselev, his ambassador, was on good terms with him. Moreover, the Polish emigrés in France inflamed the irritations so that in 1845 the two powers had merely routine

70. Puryear, *England, Russia, and the Straits Question*, pp. 57–71, 444.
71. B. Kingsley Martin, *The Triumph of Lord Palmerston* (London, 1924), pp. 29–30.
72. Bolsover, "Nicholas I," pp. 134–35.

dealings with each other. Later in the year, however, they ratified a commercial treaty and their relations improved greatly, since the French, again at odds with Britain, were eager for friendship with Russia. When Austria, with Russian permission, annexed the free city of Krakow in 1846, France made only a *pro forma* protest.[73]

Palmerston was again at the Foreign Office in 1846, with the Whigs in power. In spite of the emperor's special courtesy to him in 1844, he remained unfriendly and made a strong protest over Krakow, which he termed a violation of the Treaty of Vienna. Parliament took it up, with Urquhart seeking to incite British opinion against Russian and Austrian tyranny.[74] The uproar was brief, however, for England was more concerned about France and the Spanish Marriages than about the Poles. London showed no concern when Russia set up two small outposts on the Central Asian steppe south of Orenburg in 1845, nor when it founded Raimsk on the Aral Sea in 1847.[75]

When the Revolution of 1848 swept Europe, both Nicholas I, in spite of his initial dismay, and Palmerston were sensible in their reactions. Both were pleased when the French did not seek Italian conquests and approved Lamartine as leader of the French. Both urged the Austrians to compromise with the Italians. Palmerston even asked the tsar to urge the Austrians to give up their Italian holdings and to concentrate on their own domains.[76] Neither England nor Russia was sympathetic to the Magyars, for when the Magyars declared the Hapsburg monarch deposed, Palmerston called for summary Russian action against them. Wellington, on hearing of Russian intervention in Hungary, told Brunnow that the force used should be strong enough to crush the revolt with one blow.[77] The English feared, however, that Austria would become "a Russian vassal." When the Russian troops withdrew from Hungary with no demands for compensation, the British ministers were overjoyed and told Brunnow of their astonishment at the generosity of his master. Palmerston wrote to Brunnow that the tsar had won great glory, not by military success, but by moderation and magnanimity.[78]

73. Martens, XV, 191–220.
74. Ibid., XII, 242.
75. R. A. Pierce, *Russian Central Asia, 1867–1917* (Berkeley, Calif., 1960), pp. 18–19; *The New Cambridge Modern History* (12 vols., Cambridge, Eng., 1957–60), Vol. X, *The Zenith of European Power, 1830–1870*, ed. J. P. T. Bury, p. 387.
76. Martens, XII, 250–51.
77. Ibid., pp. 254–55.
78. Ibid., p. 255.

The English were soon furious, however, over General Haynau's harsh punishments to the Magyars, and part of the wrath fell on the Russians. When Austria and Russia demanded the surrender of revolutionaries who had fled to Turkey, the British flared up, with Stratford Canning at Constantinople calling for forceful action. Palmerston remained cool, however, ordering "friendly and courteous" representations at Vienna and St. Petersburg, while the fleet moored in Turkish waters. British ships actually passed the Dardanelles, which annoyed the tsar. Russia and Austria, however, settled the matter peacefully with the Porte, and Palmerston even admitted that it had been a mistake to send the ships into the Straits and promised it would not happen again.[79]

Palmerston also did not object when Russian forces occupied the Principalities to suppress a revolt against the sultan and grudgingly kept silent when Russia and the Porte signed the Balta-Liman Convention approving the Russian intervention. Both Palmerston and Disraeli defended the Russian right to restore order there.[80]

While the two empires were natural rivals in Asia, an Anglo-Russian entente existed, "which Nicholas furthered by every courteous attention to Great Britain." Much suspicion of Russia, which had been nurtured for decades, still existed in British minds, however. Russia was viewed as bent on expansion at the expense of Turkey and in the inner reaches of Asia. A few wise Britons saw that its relations "with Circassia, Georgia, Persia are the same as ours with Rangoon, Scinde, the Sikhs, and Oudh." This expansion was not based on a master plan, for "they encroach as we encroach in India, Africa and everywhere—because we can't help it." The objectivity here displayed by Sidney Herbert, secretary of war, was rare, however, and most Englishmen wanted to check Russian expansion. But for the time being this feeling was latent, as France seemed much more dangerous.[81]

In 1852 France and England were again at odds—over French refugees in Switzerland, over confiscation of the property of the Bourbons, and French designs on Belgium. The French army was chauvinistic and wanted revenge for Waterloo. Late in the year Aberdeen, expected to be the next premier, told Brunnow that he feared a French invasion

79. Seton-Watson, pp. 267–69; Martens, XIII, 256–60.
80. Martens, XII, 252–53.
81. Sir Adolphus William Ward and George Peabody Gooch, eds., *The Cambridge History of British Foreign Policy, 1783–1919* (Cambridge, Eng., 1922–23), II, 359.

of England, as their steamships gave the French an advantage. Lord
Derby, the prime minister, and Lords Russell and Landsdowne all
thought the same. When Brunnow suggested closer Anglo-Russian
relations, Aberdeen agreed, saying that if Napoleon felt that England
and Russia were not together, "he will fall upon us." The emperor,
while scornful of such timidity, unworthy of the men of Trafalgar
and Waterloo, approved closer bonds between them.[82]

The Anglo-Russian entente still held. The tsar thought it was im-
probable that Britain and France, almost at swords' points, could
settle their difference and interfere with his intention to play a strong
role in the Levant. He believed that Austria, with its evident weakness,
would continue to look to Russia for support against France, and
Prussia would probably do the same. Nicholas, confident of his military
strength and the favorable diplomatic situation that he enjoyed, saw
no reason to draw back from the contest over the Holy Places in
Palestine that France had gratuitously begun.

---

82. A. A. Zaionchkovskii, *Vostochnaia voina v sviazi s sovrememnoi ei politicheskoi obstanovki*
(4 vols., St. Petersburg, 1908–13), *Prilozheniia*, I, 277–78.

CHAPTER 3. THE GENESIS OF THE FRANCO-RUSSIAN CONFLICT

The period between 1815 and 1853 saw the rise of new colonial empires, with Britain as the leader, followed by France, Austria, and the United States, while the Spanish and Portuguese empires had declined greatly. The Russian empire, at least in Europe, had almost ceased to expand and had refrained from taking Turkish territory on several occasions when it might have been possible. It was expanding in the Caucasus region, to crush the wild mountaineers, who frequently raided border settlements to seek plunder, including prisoners for the slave markets of Turkey. South of the Caucasus the Russians were invited to defend Christian Georgia from devastation by Turkey and Persia. But so difficult was the terrain and so fierce the mountaineers that the Russian advance was very slow and costly. David Urquhart and Lord Ponsonby rejoiced over the successes of the "noble Circassians" in withstanding Russian tyranny.

In the whole vast region between India and Russia the Russians made almost no progress, for the terrain was so forbidding and the opportunities so meager that they made only tentative advances and by the 1850s had hardly moved ahead. While the British were pushing into Persia and Afghanistan, the Russians pulled back. The alleged Russian threat vanished.

Russia lacked the basis for imperialism, for its economy was weak, with little for export. Its agriculture barely fed its own people, and its rising industry—a small cotton cloth production, some beet sugar manufacture, and iron foundries using charcoal fuel—could not compete with British production except in remote parts of Asia. In addition, Russia had no accumulated capital to finance industry, and the finance minister made useless loans to landowners rather than to manufacturing interests. Russia's financial position was bad and only foreign loans prevented collapse.

Transportation was extremely backward, for there were few hard-surface roads and during the rainy season movement was painfully difficult. Rivers and canals were much used, when they were not frozen. Nicholas I, over considerable opposition, started a railway system, but by 1855 Russia had only 653 miles of railway in operation. Furthermore, Russia had almost no efficient merchants with a knowledge of world trade, and the counting-houses of foreign firms in Russia's ports handled the exports and imports. In the Black Sea area Greek and Armenian merchants predominated. Russia lacked a strong merchant marine to nurture commerce on a world scale, for most of its Black Sea exports were carried in Greek bottoms, and foreign ships thronged its ports.

The Russian army, large as it was, was not a suitable instrument for conquest, as Lord Durham observed. Even minor campaigns revealed logistical weakness, because of the long lines of supply, with hauling by oxcarts or one-horse wagons. A suitable munitions industry was lacking, with gunpowder in short supply. The army also had personnel problems, for the fifteen-year term of service provided almost no healthy reservists, and the training of new levies was very slow. Most of the officers had limited education and were not suited for modern warfare. Russia's victorious campaigns were usually over greatly inferior foes, often with much difficulty. The resources for aggrandizement did not exist.

Furthermore, before 1853 there were no significant popular movements or intellectual currents calling for conquests. Those who espoused "Official Nationalism," the ruling ideology, with its slogan, "Orthodoxy, Autocracy, and Nationality," were essentially defensive; they were against revolution, liberalism, constitutional government, and socialism, and in support of the Orthodox church, the autocratic ruler, and the nobility. The more enlightened elements thirsted for modern ideas and institutions in order to get rid of backwardness and ignorance. Neither group sought expansion, for the vital problem was to end serfdom without a terrible peasant revolt that would bring ruin to all. Another group, the Slavophils, rejected Western civilization and its individualism, holding that before Peter the Great a special Russian culture had flourished. Its essence was community spirit *(sobornost')*, found in the village commune, the Assembly of the Land, the Orthodox church, and other early institutions. The Slavophils stressed Russian dress, music, folklore, and art and emphasized the common cultural traits of the Slavs in contrast to those of the Germans.

At least until 1850 they were not warlike and their influence was limited.

While the Slavophils were chiefly interested in internal matters, they were greatly opposed to German influence, especially in the Baltic states. A. S. Khomiakov, a nobleman of Moscow, was one of the few who knew and admired the Czechs and the South Slavs, for he had traveled widely in eastern Europe. He was very hostile to the Turks and passionately disliked the Austrians, to the point of wanting war against them to free their Slavic subjects. The Emperor Nicholas, however, frowned on such anti-German views and denied him the right to publish. Khomiakov had little political influence, because he was involved in so many diverse activities that he could not organize any sort of movement.[1] So, while he favored war with Turkey and Austria, his effect on foreign policy, like that of the other Slavophils, was almost nonexistent.

Michael P. Pogodin, professor of history at Moscow University went much further than the Slavophils, for in his Panslav frenzy he raged against the Turks, the Magyars, and especially against the Germans, who stood in the way of Russia's march to greatness. Since he tutored the heir to the throne in Russian history, he was obviously important. Nevertheless, his newspaper, the *Moskvitianin (Muscovite),* had few readers and limped along for years, apparently on the verge of collapse.[2] Pogodin also wrote impassioned memoranda on international affairs, copies of which he circulated in handwritten form. When, late in 1853, the tsar found himself facing war with Turkey, France, England, and even Austria, he began to consider encouraging a sweeping Slavic movement against Turkey and Austria. Early in 1854 Pogodin sent the sovereign a letter urging a complete reorganization of Russia's foreign policy toward support for all national revolutionaries who would fight against these enemies of the Slavs. The letter pleased the emperor, who sent his official approval to Pogodin.[3] In June Pogodin sent His Majesty another letter, claiming that Serbia and the Slavs of Austria were seething with hatred of their masters and would rise as one man if Austria broke with Russia. He sent copies of these

1. P. K. Christoff, *An Introduction to Nineteenth-Century Russian Slavophilism: A Study in Ideas,* Vol. I, A. S. Xomjakov ('s Gravenhage, 1961), pp. 99–117.

2. N. V. Riasanovsky, *Nicholas I and Official Nationalism in Russia, 1825–1855* (Berkeley, Calif., 1959), pp. 53–58.

3. E. V. Tarle, *Krymskaia Voina* (Moscow, 1944), I, 457–58.

missives to his adherents in St. Petersburg, Moscow, Kiev, Khar'kov and other centers.[4] But because he was domineering and extremely tactless, he alienated many of the Slavophils and other potential supporters.[5] Moreover, just at the time when he was urging active backing for the Czechs and the Balkan Slavs, Nicholas was about to have his armies withdraw from Bulgaria and the Principalities, under the urging of Paskevich, Nesselrode, and Orlov.

The Slavophil poet F. I. Tiutchev, brilliant and inspiring, probably aroused more enthusiasm than Pogodin by his ardent verses praising Russia and stressing the kinship of the Russians and the Balkan Slavs. His political views, however, were so reactionary that they had only a limited following and held no interest for the radicals, who looked to Michael A. Bakunin, a violent anarchist, and Vissarion Belinskii, a socialist journalist, or to the more moderate idealists who revered Professor T. N. Granovskii, a historian at Moscow University. Even the Slavophils themselves were relatively indifferent to the affairs of the other Slavs, since they were philosophers and folklorists, men of letters rather than men of action.[6]

Russia, then, was not seeking aggrandizement, for there were no powerful influences that demanded it. Nicholas I was devoted to legitimist monarchy in Europe and until 1853 would brook no suggestion of inciting the Slavs of Turkey or Austria to revolt. He opposed Panslav fantasies, and the Russian Orthodox church, of which he was head, was too inert to sponsor a crusade in the Holy Land.

Russia, however, was feared and hated by the liberals of Europe because of its reactionary orientation. Nicholas was closely aligned with Metternich, even though he did fight the Turks in 1828 and 1829 and thus helped the Serbs and the Greeks to obtain their freedom. Otherwise, however, he upheld divine-right monarchs. He wished to support the Dutch king against the Belgians, stood behind the Austrians in Italy, gave active aid to the sultan against Mehemet Ali, and sent help to Don Carlos, the reactionary claimant to the Spanish throne. In 1848 and 1849 he helped to suppress revolutions in Hungary and in Moldavia and Wallachia. When the king of Prussia attempted to unify Germany in opposition to the Austrian emperor, Nicholas

4. Ibid., pp. 458–59.
5. Riasanovsky, pp. 56–58.
6. M. B. Petrovich, *The Emergence of Russian Panslavism, 1856–70* (New York, 1956), p. 39.

intervened forcefully at Olmütz to compel Prussia to return to the Germanic Confederation, and further infuriated Prussia by frustrating the German effort to take Schleswig and Holstein from Denmark. Because he detested Louis Philippe as a traitor to the monarchical principle, he was not greatly upset by his fall, and he approved of the July Days and of Alphonse Lamartine, president of the French Provisional Government in 1848. He was gratified to see Louis Napoleon elected president in 1849 and warmly applauded his coup d'état as a victory over dangerous radicals. But he was annoyed by French pressure concerning the Holy Places in Palestine, and when France seemed about to challenge Britian over Belgium and other issues Nicholas, as has been mentioned, spontaneously offered to send his Baltic fleet to help repel the French menace.

In 1852 the tsar was confident of the soundness of his position. He realized that he was known as "the Gendarme of Europe" and was cordially hated in many countries. Such views did not trouble him, however, for he had the ardent sympathy of conservatives. In Austria Marshals Alfred, Prince Windischgrätz and Count Joseph Radetzky and almost all the high nobility admired and trusted him. The lesser Italian rulers relied on Russia to keep the French and Joseph Mazzini, Italian republican activist, at bay. Most of the German princes believed that without Russia the French would again dominate the Rhineland. While many Prussian magnates were still bitter over the "humiliation of Olmütz," others viewed France as a grave threat and felt that Russian protection against their Gallic neighbor was vital.

The Russian cabinet counted on its good relations with England, for Nicholas was sure that the understanding of 1844 was still in effect, and his support for Britain against France in 1852 caused him to believe that the British also valued the bond between them. He also felt that his cordial relations with Queen Victoria, Prince Albert, Lord Derby, and Lord Aberdeen ensured that the Anglo-Russian entente would endure. And since the suave and skillful Baron Brunnow maintained close rapport with the British statesmen, the tsar accepted his encouraging reports and felt that the opposition of Palmerston and his followers could be disregarded.

Thus he believed that France was completely isolated, with no chance of gaining allies to challenge Russia and its powerful friends. He was annoyed that France was demanding that Turkey restore

French privileges at the Holy Places in Palestine, claiming rights allegedly based on half-forgotten treaties like that of 1740. But Russia would insist on its rights by treaty and by usage, and the British were sympathetic and regarded the French demands as trifling, and Austria, a Catholic power, viewed the French claims as not really religious but motivated by political ambitions. Hence Nicholas trusted that the Turks as usual would find a way to dispose of the absurd French pretensions.

The French cabinet apparently viewed the matter in much the same way. France was isolated and denied the place to which it felt entitled, largely as a result of the Russian alignment against it. Britain, with its Russian ties, barred France from Belgium. Prussia and Austria and the other German states, allied with Russia, blocked French access to the Rhine, while in Italy, Austria, again with Russian backing, barred the way. In 1812 Russia had started Napoleon on his way to defeat in the Moscow campaign and had led the march of the Allies that ended at Paris in the spring of 1814. Russia had been a chief factor in preventing France from gaining a massive triumph through its protégé Mehemet Ali. Wherever Louis Napoleon turned, Russia was the insurmountable obstacle.

Russia had no grievances against France and it would not have mattered greatly to St. Petersburg if the French had gained part of Belgium or Luxemburg or had moved toward the Rhine. But Nicholas I was so committed to the doctrine of legitimacy that he would not cede anything from the Treaty of Vienna and thus was marked as Louis Napoleon's archenemy. And when the French president began to move toward the declaration of the Second Empire, the tsar called on Austria and Prussia to join him in taking action to prevent an explosion.[7] *The Cambridge History of British Foreign Policy* flatly states that Napoleon III "wished . . . to displace the Tsar as central sun of the European system; to wipe out memories of the Moscow disaster of 1812; to break up the Holy Alliance, and to rescind the Treaties of 1815. For reasons such as these, he wanted war—and a war in which that respectable Power, Great Britain, would be on his side." [8] It is not possible to document this allegation. Nevertheless Napoleon began and intensified the contest over the Holy Places, although his

---

7. A. H. Jomini, *Diplomatic Study on the Crimean War* (London, 1882), pp. 66, 77–79; Ward and Gooch, II, 356.
8. Ward and Gooch, ibid.,

religious convictions do not seem to have been strong, and the result was war with Russia, with England as France's ally.

The French case was historically weak, for from the Council of Nicaea in 333 to the eighteenth century the Greek church was dominant among the Christians of the Holy Land. The Crusades and the French alliance with the Ottoman empire in the sixteenth and seventeenth centuries did little to change the situation. Although capitulations of the sultans gave the Latin clergy control of many of the Holy Places of Jerusalem and Bethlehem, the Latins had only a small following in Palestine, where the Greeks and the Christian Arabs greatly outnumbered the Catholics who lived there. The Turkish authorities repeatedly issued decrees restoring to the Latins rights that the Greeks had gradually gained from them. In the eighteenth century French pilgrims to Palestine declined, while Russian and other Orthodox Christians came in increasing numbers.[9] Russian victories over the Turks compelled the latter to treat the Orthodox with respect, and the Treaty of Küchuk-Kainardji in 1774 provided that the Russian government might make representations to the Porte about the rights of the Orthodox clergy.

In the 1840s, however, English and Prussian Protestants founded a joint bishopric for missionary work and established schools and missions in Palestine. In addition, the French Catholics obtained a Latin Patriarchate of Jerusalem (previously a purely honorary title). Joseph Valerga, the Patriarch, was a dynamic, experienced missionary, and the Catholics founded twenty monastic orders, built schools, and won numerous converts.[10] The Turks, while angered by French support for Mehemet Ali, probably feared and distrusted the Russians even more. The Greeks of the Patriarchate of Constantinople, who enjoyed wide power over the Orthodox subjects of the sultan, strongly opposed increased Russian influence in church affairs in the Levant, as they well knew that Nicholas I exerted strict control over the Russian Church and had confiscated the property of the Georgian Orthodox Church. The Patriarchates of Alexandria, Antioch, and Jerusalem were more cordial to the Russians, since they needed donations from

9. Émile Bourgeois, *Manuel historique de politique étrangère* (Paris, 1892–1905), III, 361–62; Louis Thouvenel, *Nicolas I et Napoleon III: les préliminaires de la Guerre de Crimée, 1852–1854* (Paris, 1891), pp. xx–xxxix; Jomini, pp. 121–27.

10. T. G. Stavrou, *Russian Interests in Palestine, 1882–1914* (Thessaloniki, Greece, 1963), pp. 27–30.

St. Petersburg, although they did not want Russian control.[11] The thousands of Russian pilgrims and Russian donations to the Greek hierarchy brought increased standing for the Russians in Palestine.

In 1841 the Russian Church proposed a Russian ecclesiastical mission in Palestine, to found hostels for pilgrims and to set up a Russian school. The emperor, however, ordered that this mission be put under the Foreign Ministry, to avoid friction with the Greek clergy. In 1842 Nesselrode called for an active Russian policy in the Holy Land, including the sending of a reliable, cultured Russian churchman to encourage the Greeks. The churchman was to go as a simple pilgrim, so as not to attract attention, although he would be a secret diplomatic agent under Bazilii, the Russian consul.[12]

The man chosen was Porfirii Uspenskii, an unfortunate choice. Although this educated monk from St. Petersburg was an avid scholar, he quarreled fiercely with the Greek Patriarch of Jerusalem and the Greek clergy, while devoting himself to the humble, neglected Arab Orthodox priests. He proposed to channel Russian donations to these priests directly in order to eliminate what he charged was the flagrant corruption of the Greeks. He eventually became a friend of the Patriarch of Jerusalem and with him donated small sums to the Orthodox Arabs, founded schools, established a seminary at Jerusalem, and printed books for the Arabs. On the whole, however, because of his combative nature he probably weakened Russia's standing in Palestine.[13]

The overall position of Russia in the Levant was not strong, for the Turks naturally regarded it as an enemy, even though it had on occasion supported the Ottoman empire. The rigidly conservative policy of Nicholas I alienated the progressive elements in Turkey, so that only a few reactionaries favored Russia. The reform party looked to Lord Ponsonby, British envoy to Turkey and an ardent supporter of the sultan, and to Palmerston and Stratford Canning, Ponsonby's successor at the Porte, who believed that by its reform program Turkey could get rid of its ills and win the loyalty of its Christians. Indeed, many of the latter had found that Russia would do nothing for them,

---

11. Mikhail Volkov, "Chto dovelo Rossiiu do nastoiashchei voiny," in Zaionchkovskii, *Pril.,* I, 175–80.

12. Stavrou, pp. 31–34.

13. Ibid., pp. 34–38; Derek Hopwood, *The Russian Presence in Palestine and Syria, 1843–1914: Church and Politics in the Near East* (Oxford, 1969), pp. 19–30, 33–38.

while the efforts of British diplomats often brought improvement of their lot. Ponsonby and Stratford had great influence in Turkey, whereas the Russian diplomats were mostly ineffectual. Of the three Russian consuls in the whole Balkan area, only one was fairly capable. The Greeks, the Serbs, and the Bulgars all felt that they could get no help from Russia, while British pressure for reform had brought tangible results.[14]

Moreover, Russian military prestige had declined greatly, for by failing to act against Mehemet Ali in 1840 Russia had permitted Britain and Austria to gain the credit. Russia's difficulties with the Caucasian mountaineers and Russian compromising in the crisis over the Magyar and Polish refugees in Turkish service also appeared to be signs of weakness.[15]

The rivalry between Catholics and Orthodox Christians took a new turn with the Latin request for the right to repair the cupola of the Church of the Holy Sepulcher. In the spring of 1850 this request expanded into a general demand for recovery of some of the Holy Places held by the Greeks. In May the French ambassador sent a stiff note to the Porte asking it to restore to the Latins their rights under the Treaty of 1740. To avoid the issue, the Porte turned the problem over to a joint commission of Latins and Greeks, who quarreled fiercely and produced no agreement. At this point the French government chiefly wanted to placate the Catholic clergy in France, since it repeatedly told the Russian envoy at Paris that it did not regard the question as important.[16]

In 1851 the Marquis de Lavalette, an ardent and aggressive Catholic, arrived at Constantinople as French ambassador and presented a memorandum to the Porte based on the Treaty of 1740. V. P. Titov, the Russian ambassador, countered with a memorandum insisting on the Russian position. The Divan, however, ruled in favor of the French, after Lavalette had put pressure on the Turkish ministers and handed autographed letters from Prince Louis Napoleon and the Pope to the sultan.[17] Titov now stressed the right of Russia to make representations on religious matters as provided for by the Treaty of Küchuk-Kai-

14. Volkov, in Zaionchkovskii, *Pril.,* I, 180–82.

15. Ibid., pp. 182–83.

16. "Précis historique de la question des Saintes Lieux," ibid., pp. 333–34. This memorandum, by the Russian Ministry of Foreign Affairs, cites pertinent despatches from Russian diplomats in Turkey.

17. Thouvenel, pp. 6–8.

nardji, and on October 25, 1851, Prince Gagarin suddenly arrived at Constantinople with a personal letter from the tsar. In the letter Nicholas stressed his benevolent feelings toward the sultan and promised his moral support. He also expressed his painful surprise at the support given by the Turkish ministers to the French position and hoped that His Majesty would keep inviolable the rights of his Orthodox subjects. This demarche, upheld with much vigor by Titov (including a threat to leave Constantinople in twenty-four hours), was supported by a petition of the Greek clergy and laymen living at Constantinople, who cited the historic legal position of the Greeks and the recent official documents in their favor. These arguments impressed the sultan who, in spite of Lavalette's threats of a blockade of the Dardanelles, rejected the French proposal for equal sharing of the Holy Places and turned the problem over to a commission of *ulemas* (Moslem religious and legal experts). In November 1851 this body, after a study of the archives, pronounced in favor of the Greeks and rejected most of the claims of the Latins.[18]

At this point Lavalette intervened strongly at the Porte, even threatening bombardment of a Turkish port by a French squadron. The ministers sought to appease him by granting the Latins the right to officiate in one of the Greek shrines, with the Greeks to have a similar right in one of the Latin ones. The Divan also proposed to define the rights of both parties with precision so that no further crises would arise. The Russian government, in accord with the Patriarch of Jerusalem, agreed, even though the Latins gained thereby. It insisted, however, that the Greeks also should have the right to repair the cupola of the Church of the Holy Sepulcher, without Latin participation. A draft *firman* (decree) embodying these terms was sent from St. Petersburg, along with a draft letter from the sultan to the tsar agreeing to them. Titov and the Ottoman ministers discussed these documents together and, after they had been approved, the Porte solemnly handed them to the ambassador, who took official note of the transaction. The sultan, moreover, by a special autographed notation at the head of the firman, with his full authority recognized and upheld the previous grants to the Greeks. Furthermore, the sultan's personal reply to Nicholas I confirmed and corroborated the Greek privileges in most

18. Ibid., pp. 10–12; Harold Temperley, *England and the Near East: The Crimea* (London, 1936), pp. 287–89; "Précis historique," Zaionchkovskii, *Pril.,* I, 334.

explicit fashion.[19] This engagement thus was a personal pledge of the sultan to the tsar, any violation of which would seriously affront the latter's honor. Nothing now remained but the official promulgation of the firman in order to carry out its provisions.

Before he left on vacation, however, Lavalette had learned of the firman to the Russians and protested strongly, insisting that the Treaty of 1740 was still in effect. The French chargé d'affaires also told the Porte in very strong terms of the displeasure of his government at the Porte's decision. Probably as a result of these criticisms, the Porte wavered and delayed carrying out the pledges to the Russians. As to the cupola of the Church of the Holy Sepulcher, on which the Russians had laid great stress, it finally decided that the repairs would be done at the expense of the Turkish government by Greek workers and architects of the Patriarchate of Jerusalem, but it repeatedly postponed the work on a variety of pretexts. Moreover, the promised instructions to the local official at Jerusalem were so vague and allegedly so favored the Latins that the Russians were highly dissatisfied.[20]

In July 1852 Lavalette returned on the huge French battleship *Charlemagne.* Since this was a violation of the Straits Convention of 1841, Russia protested, and the Turks at first refused to let the ship dock. But with strong French support the Porte admitted it on the pretext that the Turkish admiralty had invited it. Lavalette thus arrived on the enormous vessel with great effect, menacing Turkey with violent action unless it satisfied the French demands.[21]

Lavalette at once undertook to settle the issue of the Holy Places, in which he was favored by a change in the Turkish ministry. Reshid pasha, who was not anti-Russian, fell from grace over a minor scandal and was supplanted by young, progressive men who admired Louis Napoleon and his dynamism. Mehemet Ali pasha and Fuad effendi, strongly anti-Russian, who greatly admired Napoleon's coup d'état and believed that Russia, which was having trouble in the Caucasus, counted for little, were in the key posts.[22] Secretly the Turkish ministers arranged with the French embassy not to publish the Russian firman and to give the Latins the key to the main door of the Church

19. "Précis," Zaionchkovskii, *Pril.,* I, 334–36.
20. Ibid., pp. 336–37.
21. Ibid., p. 337; Jomini, pp. 139–40.
22. Jomini, pp. 136–37, 140.

of the Nativity in Bethlehem (locally regarded as signifying ownership). The cupola of the Church of the Holy Sepulcher would be rebuilt at the expense of the sultan, without Russian supervision. In the meantime, to balk the schemes of Louis Napoleon, Nicholas I was working to revive the Quadruple Alliance of 1814, which, together with the urgent requests of Lavalette, induced Napoleon to push France's demands in the Holy Land with great energy.[23]

Hence in October 1852 the Porte sent a commissar to execute the settlement in the Jerusalem area, who ruled against the Russians and in favor of the Latins. The repairs to the cupola would be supervised by delegates of the Greek, Latin, and Armenian denominations rather than by the Orthodox Patriarch of Jerusalem. Nothing was said about registering the vital firman given to the Greeks and signed by the sultan. When the Russian consul-general asked about reading and registering it as law, the commissar claimed ignorance of it and sent the consul to the Patriarch of Jerusalem, who sent him back to the commissar. Therefore it was evident that the French had managed to prevent the reading of the Russian firman, which the sultan had promised the tsar he would grant and make the law of the land.[24] The Russians viewed this Turkish conduct as an act of bad faith toward their emperor, who regarded it as an insult.

The Russian diplomats did what they could to change the pro-French trend in the Turkish government, both by expressing the emperor's indignation at the lack of Turkish good faith and by making vigorous efforts to reassure the Turks that Russia would support them if the French made an unjust attack on them. These arguments, however, had little effect.[25]

A new act of bad faith by the Turks soon followed. In the autumn of 1852 Lavalette called for the carrying out of the secret agreement stipulating that the Latins should receive the key to the Great Door of the Church of the Nativity in Bethlehem, which would imply Latin ownership of the building. In November the Porte held a council to discuss the issue, at which Fuad effendi made a strong speech insisting that Turkey side with France, since Louis Napoleon was a great leader with a powerful army. An alliance with France would permit Turkey to settle all its problems: the Principalities, Montenegro, and the Le-

23. Ibid., pp. 138–39.
24. "Précis," Zaionchkovskii, *Pril.,* I, 338.
25. Nesselrode to Ozerov, Nov. 22, 1852, Zaionchkovskii, *Pril.,* I, 345–46.

vant. If Turkey refused, there was danger of a French invasion of Syria. Fuad sneered at Russia, claiming that it was too cautious to risk a war in which all Europe would be against it. Now Turkey could eliminate all Russian influence over the Orthodox of Turkey. After his speech, Fuad continued to threaten the sultan with danger from France.[26]

Finally Sultan Abdul Medjid had to give a firman to the Latins, which Lavalette rushed to Jerusalem, where crowds of Greek supporters had gathered to witness the triumph of *their* cause. In fact, so strong was the pressure that the commissar had to read the Russian firman—not publicly but merely to a select audience of churchmen and officials. Since this reading had no legal significance, the Latins were the victors, to the great anger of the Russians and the Greeks. Then the firman to the Latins was read, nullifying the one to the Russians. The Latin Patriarch of Jerusalem now went to Bethlehem, where on December 22, 1852, he installed in the grotto the Silver Star given by the French government. The keys of both the inner and the outer churches were taken from the Greeks and given to the Latins—a sign that the latter were now superior. The Latin Patriarch insisted on installing a special altar in the Grotto of Gethsemane and in other ways showed that he had won the contest.[27]

These actions by the French and the Turks were an open political challenge to Russia, since they stripped from the Orthodox of Turkey the rights they had enjoyed for centuries while favoring a mere handful of foreigners. According to A. H. Jomini, Nicholas I held that Turkey, incited by France, had attacked the Russian position in the East and had violated the rights of the Orthodox church, in spite of the Porte's pledges in treaties to maintain them. By his firman of January 30, 1852, the sultan had promised to maintain the status quo; but through trickery this firman had not been published, and new French threats had led to fresh attacks. The establishment of the Second Empire; the great prestige of the French and their influence over the Turks; the vast importance of political questions in the East; the hostile speeches in the Divan—"All concurred to make of these questions a direct struggle for political influence." [28]

The Orthodox of Turkey realized this, for the Patriarch of Jerusalem

26. Jomini, p. 142.
27. Ibid., pp. 143–44; Temperley, pp. 207, 297; Bourgeois, III, 376–86.
28. Jomini, pp. 148–50.

hastened to Constantinople to protest against the developments. But the Porte convened the Greek clergy and laymen and told them that a protest on their part would be regarded as equivalent to rebellion. It also gave the governors of the provinces extraordinary powers to deal with protests.[29]

France thus was engaged in a power struggle with Russia, ostensibly over rather trifling religious matters but actually over political influence at Constantinople—a strategic center of little direct interest to France but one that Russia regarded as vital. More and more France seemed to be moving to challenge Russia in a contest for supremacy in Europe. Another aspect of the contest—apparently not related to the drama in the East but certainly closely connected with it in terms of great-power politics—was also taking place in the West, over the apparently trivial matter of the form of recognition that would be granted to Prince Napoleon when he assumed the imperial title.

Louis Napoleon, who had twice risked his life to obtain this title, returned to France in June 1848 and in December he had been elected president by a huge majority. In spite of his oath of allegiance to the Second Republic, it was well known that he wished to be emperor. Standing as defender of universal manhood suffrage against the increasingly reactionary Assembly, on December 2, 1851, he seized power by a coup d'état attended by ruthless violence against the urban masses. Claiming to be a friend of the people, he restored the Napoleonic eagles to France's standards and rigorously repressed opposition. He also gave increased privileges to the Catholic clergy.

The Russian government was quite friendly to him and hailed his severity against "the revolutionary conspiracy." When on January 12, 1852, he wrote a cordial letter to Nicholas I declaring that he stood for order and stability, peace with Russia, and "new prosperity for Europe," he received a warm response. The tsar, addressing him as "Monsieur le Président, grand et bon ami," hailed the prince's support for "the principles of order and authority" and hoped that Providence would "aid you to close the era of revolutions in France." Nicholas declared that Russia would do everything possible to tighten the bonds between the two countries and would always be ready to join France in defending "the sacred cause of the social order, of the repose of

29. Ibid., p. 144.

Europe, of the independence and territorial integrity of its states . . . and to make respected the existing treaties." He signed his letter "your very affectionate Nicholas." [30]

In Austria Premier Prince Felix Schwarzenberg urged the great powers to agree on their policy if, as expected, Napoleon should make himself emperor. While the existing treaty banned the Bonapartes from the French throne, it could not be applied without causing a war. If the new emperor should avoid aggression they should accept him, since the treaty's purpose had been to keep France from plunging Europe into a new conflict. If, as he claimed, he stood for peace, they should accept his new status. There was no visible alternative, as the Bourbons could not be restored by force. Hence the powers should recognize the Second Empire, but insist on its pledges of peace and be ready to act as one if it should break them. [31]

Prussia's position was stronger. While changes might be made in the Treaty of Paris, this could be done only by unanimous action of the powers and until then they should stick by the treaty. Berlin felt that Schwarzenberg was too ready to give up the ban on the Bonapartes and legitimate rights and "solemn engagements that cannot be broken unilaterally." Berlin also held that Vienna did not attach enough importance to the British position. [32]

Britain, however, had no wish to challenge France. Under a series of weak governments and no longer sure of its navy, the British public, Ambassador Brunnow reported, would not risk war over the title of the French ruler, any more than when Charles X had fallen. (Here the tsar's marginal comment expressed disgust.) Thus, while the Cabinet of St. James would be willing to consult with the Russian cabinet, it would probably not give it effective support. [33]

Early in 1852 Nesselrode, in a summary of the situation, held that it was gratifying that the three empires wanted an understanding about Louis Napoleon's future title. Nicholas, however, disagreed with Austria, insisting that the powers must stand by the Treaty of 1815 banning the Bonapartes from rule in France and upholding the Bourbon dynasty. Louis Napoleon could not be ousted from power without risking

30. Zaionchkovskii, *Pril.,* I, 191.
31. Schwarzenberg to Lebzeltern, Dec. 29, 1851, ibid., pp. 194–99.
32. Budberg to Nesselrode, Dec. 28, 1851/Jan. 9, 1852, ibid., p. 202.
33. Brunnow to Nesselrode, Dec. 26, 1851/Jan. 7, 1852, ibid., pp. 192–94.

conflict in France and probably in all Europe. To avoid such a conflict, the tsar was willing to recognize the new imperial title, but only temporarily. This would not in any way prejudice the principle of exclusion of the Bonaparte family in general, which must be "part of the public law of Europe." Nicholas insisted on the permanent rights of the House of Bourbon, so that recognition of the prince would be only "recognition of an accidental and transitory fact."

Hence, while the powers should recognize Napoleon's government de facto, because of its preservation of law and order and its promises to keep the peace, recognition would be only transitory and could not prejudice the rights of the House of Bourbon. Napoleon should never have a recognized right to found a dynasty in France and to transmit power to it. The exclusion of the Bonapartes by the treaty should remain in full force.[34]

For almost a year Napoleon skillfully aroused enthusiasm for the empire and appealed to French patriotism and self-interest. The French cabinet also sought to win the support of Europe by blandishments and threats, while Nicholas I led the opposition to the French effort. When France threatened Belgium, Nicholas promised Lord Derby that Russia would support mediation and, if need be, give military assistance. In May 1852, as proclamation of the Second Empire drew nearer, he visited Vienna and Berlin to consult his allies. They agreed that they would not object to a simple proclamation of the empire and if Napoleon promised to accept the existing treaties, they would recognize him as emperor. The three powers would not, however, accept the Bonaparte dynasty.[35]

At this time Baron Georges Heeckeren, an envoy of Napoleon's, interviewed Emperor Franz Joseph and then, in Berlin, talked with Nicholas I. His task was to inform them of the coming proclamation of the empire and to find out the attitude of the monarchs of the three eastern powers—Austria, Prussia, and Russia. Heeckeren said that while his master was in a satisfactory position and had no foreign ambitions, he might have to change the form of the French government. He wanted to make explanations to the other powers and to satisfy them as to his peaceful intentions and his firm determination to observe the existing treaties and boundaries. In return, he asked for frank recognition and good will. The emperor replied that he had already

34. Ibid., pp. 199–202.
35. Jomini, pp. 83–87.

shown good will by his approval of Napoleon's suppression of radicalism in France. He felt, however, that the prince's position was so
strong that there was no need to alter it. He added that if a change
did take place, he would formulate his attitude toward it only after
receiving the guarantees that Baron Heeckeren had promised. Nicholas
politely refused to go into the matter of dynastic succession.[36]

Thus Russia clearly stood out as the center of opposition to the
Second Empire. While the other powers shared its dislike of it, their
attitudes were less rigid and they were willing to make concessions.
The British, for example, were inclined to accept Napoleon's pledges
of good faith, whereas the others insisted that the French should make
them spontaneously rather than through negotiations, which would
permit the raising of other questions, like that of the dynasty. On
this point the three Eastern powers declared their full reservations.[37]
Moreover, St. Petersburg insisted on treating the acceptance of Napoleon's imperial title as an exceptional, temporary relaxation of the Treaty
of 1815 rather than as a permanent precedent. Nicholas I consistently
held that only the Bourbon dynasty had a sound claim to rule France,
even though he was willing to accept Napoleon's temporary possession.
The Russian cabinet tried strongly to induce the prince to renounce
the imperial title, and Ambassador N. D. Kiselev urged him to be
satisfied with his presidential office, without risking trouble by change.
Kiselev was so insistent on this point that Napoleon became violently
angry, charging him and Russia with "hostility." As a result the envoy
went on leave in September 1852.[38]

Nicholas seems to have been obtuse in this matter, for he lectured
the king of Prussia ("cher et bon Fritz") on the need to avoid irritating
the French ruler. They should stay quiet, shunning all provocation,
while persistently stressing "our respect for the Treaties and our unshakable resolution not to depart from them. . . ."[39] This did little
to calm the Napoleonic ire.

As Napoleon's triumphal tour of France progressed, it became clear
that the die was cast, for shouts of "Vive l'Empéreur!" "Vive Napoléon
III!" filled the air. Napoleon made alluring promises, insisting that,

---

36. Zaionchkovskii, *Pril.,* I, 228–30.
37. "Resume peregovorov Russkago, Avstriiskago i Prusskago poslov s Lordami Derbi i
Mal'msberi . . . po povodu soglasheniia o priznaniia Lui-Napoleona Imperatorom," attachment
to desp., Brunnow to Nesselrode, Apr. 4/16, 1852, ibid., pp. 231–33.
38. Martens, XV, 253–62.
39. Zaionchkovskii,*Pril.,*I,214–15.

far from wanting war, "the Empire means peace," and the only conquests he sought were pacific ones. Glory would attach to a hereditary title, but not to war: woe to him who would start one! He himself would seek to conquer the minds of his opponents and the problems of prosperity, railways, economic security for the masses, and the like.[40]

Such utterances reassured many who feared new wars. In addition, in October 1852 Napoleon made an overture to Nicholas I to settle their problems, sending Prince Napoleon-Joseph Bonaparte to discuss the situation with Prince Alexander Gorchakov, Russian minister to Württemberg. The prince's suggestion was that the recognition question could easily be solved and that the quarrel over the Holy Places in Palestine could be settled. If Napoleon should change his course, could an alliance be arranged between the two countries? Gorchakov was skeptical, but Napoléon-Joseph kept stressing the value of an alliance and asked if Nicholas I would receive a confidential envoy of Napoleon at St. Petersburg. Gorchakov reported the conversation to his government and the tsar replied that he would gladly receive such an envoy. By that time, however, the recognition crisis was so severe that nothing came of the overture and Russia and France drifted into war.[41]

Although the peaceful utterances of Napoleon allayed the fears of war, the insistence on a hereditary empire and the name of Napoleon III was disturbing, for this indicated repudiation of the ban on Bonapartes. Moreover, the prince, in announcing the proposal to establish the empire, stated that it would give a "peaceful revenge" for the defeats of 1814 and 1815. Almost at once a Russian cabinet memorandum stated that to recognize such a regime would amount to repudiating the Congress of Vienna, the whole effort to unseat Napoleon I, and the restoration regimes. While the cabinet members could recognize Louis Napoleon personally, if they recognized him as Napoleon III, the whole foundation of Europe would be destroyed. The tsar could not recognize Napoleon III, and they must take action, lest he win his point by common consent. Unless Napoleon made the matter of the title a crucial issue, Russia would recognize him as "Emperor of the French." [42]

40. Ibid., pp. 237–38.
41. S. Goriainov, "Les étapes d'alliance franco-russe, 1853–1861," *Revue de Paris* XIX (1912), 5–11.
42. Zaionchkovskii, *Pril.*, I, 231–45.

The British and the Russians were close in their positions, with both ready to send troops if France invaded Belgium. But Lord Derby's government fell and, although Nesselrode strongly urged the Aberdeen government to stand fast, it felt that Parliament and British opinion would not permit a breach over the figure III, especially as the French sent gratifying assurances on this point. So the British quickly gave in and recognized the regime fully.[43]

On the eve of the announcement of the empire, Nicholas I made a last attempt to persuade Louis Napoleon to renounce the title of Napoleon III. His personal letter, couched in friendly, even warm terms, urged the French ruler not to take this step for, while it would not do harm in France, for the rest of Europe it would mean repudiation of the preceding thirty-eight years and hence would sow the seeds of discord in Europe. "We all wish to live with you in bonds of harmony and good intelligence," he said. "Do not voluntarily deprive us of the means for it." Kiselev developed the Russian argument at even greater length and with vigor, but without swaying the triumphant Napoleon.[44]

Nicholas now decided that his principles prevented him from giving this emperor of the French, who derived his power merely from the people, what was owing to one who was emperor by divine grace. According to Peter von Meyendorff, a veteran Russian diplomat, in the summer of 1852 Austria had persuaded the tsar not to address the new emperor as *"mon frère"* but as *"mon ami."* This advice dismayed Nesselrode, who saw trouble ahead, as did Prince A. F. Orlov. But since both German powers opposed the full title, Nicholas stood firmly beside them. Later Count Karl von Buol-Schauenstein, the new Austrian foreign minister, feared that this slight might cause an explosion, as did the Prussians. So they changed their letters of credence, hailing Napoleon as *"Monsieur mon frère."* As they failed to notify Nicholas, he, who had used *"mon ami"* instead of *"mon frère,"* was left isolated by his allies. But the tsar, who felt that his dignity would not permit him to change, stood firm.[45] Kiselev, in a long report, told of first presenting to Edouard Drouyn de Lhuys, French foreign minister, the letter raising Kiselev to Envoy Extraordinary and Minister Plenipotentiary, to show that his master wanted excellent relations

43. Ibid., pp. 245–48; Jomini, pp. 99–105.
44. Zaionchkovskii, *Pril.,* I, 248–49, 265–71.
45. Otto Hoetzsch, ed., *Peter von Meyendorff: Ein russicher Diplomat an den Höfen von Berlin und Wien.* (3 vols., Berlin, 1923), III, 3–5.

with Napoleon. Next came a note setting forth the Russian reservations concerning the number III. Drouyn, though displeased, did not comment. Then Kiselev handed over his letters of credence, which Drouyn read calmly, although he remarked that they were not in proper form and must be submitted to the emperor, and stated his opinion that they would not be accepted. Kiselev, realizing that he was in trouble, told his story to his colleagues from Austria and Prussia, who called on Drouyn as a sign of the unity of the three powers. While Count Joseph von Hübner, the Austrian, appeared irresolute, Count Maximilian von Hatzfeldt, the Prussian, took a strong stand and refused to present his letters at once as Drouyn urged. Both felt that Kiselev's credentials would be rejected. Kiselev also informed Lord Henry Wellesley, Earl of Cowley, the British envoy.[46]

Shortly thereafter Charles, Duc de Morny, an old friend of Kiselev's, called to offer his services. The envoy told Morny his story, pointing out that the tsar had been friendly to Louis Napoleon, who had not been tactful to Russia, which also had its sensibilities. The reservations over Napoleon's title and the salutation *"mon ami"* were based on principle and there was nothing at all personal about them. Kiselev appealed to Morny as a friend of peace to impress on Napoleon the value of Russian friendship, for with Austria and Prussia standing with Russia, a break with one would be a break with all. Morny promised to do what he could, and Cowley also supported Russia. But for two days there was no reply.[47]

Finally Napoleon received Kiselev with much cordiality. The Russian was greatly relieved, for he reported that if a break had occurred, the other powers would not have supported Russia, and real trouble might have ensued, with the world probably allotting some of the blame for it to Russia. He declared, however, that the outcome had been very beneficial, for it was generally known that the Russian emperor had taken the lead in the crisis and had been successful: "For us the game is won, and it is not France . . . but Russia with Her energetic and glorious Monarch which is now at the summit of greatness, power, and dignity." [48]

Drouyn de Lhuys was especially angry over the outcome, for he, along with Jean, Duc de Persigny, a confidant of Napoleon III's, had

46. Kiselev to Nesselrode, Dec. 29, 1852, Zaionchkovskii, *Pril.*, I, 299–301.
47. Ibid., pp. 302–04.
48. Ibid., pp. 309–10.

strongly advised against accepting Kiselev's credentials. When he found that Napoleon had done so without notifying him, he offered to resign, but the offer was not accepted.[49] Napoleon and his entourage had apparently believed that to tolerate a lesser salutation than *"mon frère"* might antagonize the French public to a dangerous degree. Drouyn kept sounding this note to Hübner, who warned Buol of the danger. Later, however, both England and Prussia, which could not afford to provoke France into hostility, failed to back Austria in its position, so that Buol gave in on the salutation, to the annoyance of Nicholas I. Russia, which did not have to face a French invasion of Belgium, the Rhineland, or Lombardy, could take a stronger position.[50] Kiselev's skillful use of Nesselrode's arguments succeeded, through Morny's mediation, in making Napoleon see that Russia had taken pains to be conciliatory to him, and since Austria, Prussia, and England urged him to accept Kiselev's credentials, he agreed to do so.

This incident, trivial in itself, had much significance. For one thing, it confirmed the tsar in his hubris. In his annual report for 1852 Nesselrode stressed that in this central problem Russia had taken the lead in Europe, thereby consolidating "the union of three great Powers" and bringing England closer to them. Russia's final recognition of the Second Empire was conditional upon its recognition of the status quo, and Russia made strict reservations against hereditary rights for a Napoleonic dynasty. Prussia and Austria did the same, but in a less categorical manner, so that Paris could see that there was no real unity among them. Moreover, the two Germanic sovereigns addressed Napoleon as "Monsieur mon frère," whereas Nicholas used "Monsieur mon bon ami." While Napoleon and his advisers were reluctant to accept the Russian formula, the firmness of Russia and the support of Austria, Prussia, and England made him agree to it. Nesselrode gloated that this had forced him to bend before Russia and had publicly reduced his fictitious strength. "It was necessary that Louis Napoleon should bear the penalty for his insolent message . . . proclaiming himself the most legitimate Sovereign of all." [51]

---

49. Hübner to Buol, Jan. 24, 1853, Haus-, Hof-, und Staatsarchiv, Vienna (hereafter cited HHSA), Section IX, Carton 41.

50. Friedrich Engel-Janosi, *Der Freiherr von Hübner, 1811–1892* (Innsbruck, 1933), pp. 104–05.

51. Zaionchkovskii, *Pril.,* I, 310, 312, 316–18.

This victory—if such it was—proved costly, for it marked Russia as the chief obstacle in the way of Napoleonic greatness. It also showed that the three northern courts were by no means solid, with Austria and Prussia following the Russian lead only when it suited their interests. Napoleon III believed that Russia had to be humbled and that Austria and Prussia might not act to prevent it. The tsar himself helped to weaken Russia's ties with Vienna and Berlin, for he was angry at their "cowardice, defection, betrayal" during the crisis, and expressed his feelings in harsh words to their envoys.[52] General Count Mensdorff, the Austrian envoy, reported that the emperor had expressed annoyance to him over the salutations of Austria and Prussia to Louis Napoleon, although "he was calmer than before." Three weeks later Baron Eduard von Lebzeltern, who replaced Mensdorff at St. Petersburg, stated that the monarch's irritation over the recognition was only temporary and that its "painful impression" had already vanished.[53] The stern language that the tsar used to the ambassadors of his allies probably did not endear him to their cabinets.

In France storm signals were flying. Kiselev had warned that if the tsar snubbed Napoleon, he would make an alliance with England against Russia.[54] Baron Hübner on January 26, 1853, warned his court that Napoleon III, in spite of his suave behavior, evidently had a hostile attitude toward Europe. His vanity was hurt by the recognition incident, and his failure to arrange a marriage with the Swedish Princess of Vasa, who married the Prince Royal of Saxony instead, added to his grievances. His marriage to Eugénie and his public reference to himself as a "parvenu" made a great impression. Hübner felt that, instead of a sudden negative action on his part, he would probably sink into "profound dissatisfaction," which, in the light of his adventurous nature, would be dangerous. For as he had been "within two inches of war" over a matter of politeness to which he believed he was entitled, he would certainly show no restraint if a real crisis arose.[55]

Nesselrode, for all his fulsome praise of the wisdom and courage of the tsar in the recognition question, had grave forebodings, which he revealed in a private letter to Brunnow in London. He prophesied trouble from Napoleon, who would feel that he must do more for

52. Hoetzsch, III, 5.
53. Mensdorff to Buol, Jan. 13, 1853, Lebzeltern to Buol, Feb. 5, 1853, HHSA, X, 36.
54. Martens, XV, 269.
55. Hübner to Buol, Jan. 26, 1853, HHSA, IX, 41.

France than the Bourbons had. Since only the East seemed to offer him a chance of success, he would probably seek to embroil Russia and Turkey by his demands. Russia would probably lose patience with the Porte and war would come. This time there would be no coalition against France in the Levant, and Russia would be isolated, for Austria and Prussia would not support it. The combined British and French fleets could penetrate the Black Sea, destroy Russia's naval establishments, and help the Caucasian mountaineers. Nesselrode added that if these were Napoleon's objectives, Russia could do little to prevent him from achieving them.[56]

F. F. Martens interjects a comment that if Nesselrode could predict Napoleon's actions with such accuracy, why did he not seek to prevent Russia from arousing Napoleon to action by refusing him parity with other monarchs and the title that he sought? [57] The point is well taken. The answer seems to be that the tsar was so confident and domineering that it was almost impossible to induce him to change his mind and Nesselrode did not have the strength of character to persuade him to reconsider. So Nicholas I, proud of the strength of Russia and sure that Austria, Prussia, and England were with him, continued along the course that would lead to disaster.

56. Martens, XI, 301–02.
57. Ibid., p. 302.

Chapter 4. The Seymour Conversations

In late 1852 and early 1853 the Russian diplomats faced a complex situation, as rapidly changing developments compelled them to reconsider some of their basic assumptions. By threats and intimidation the French had obtained sweeping concessions from the Turks concerning the Holy Places in Palestine, which greatly reduced the prestige of the Greek Orthodox and their friends and protectors, the Russians. Most of the Turks saw these threats as offering an opportunity to get rid of the hated Russian influence and to gain the protection of the strong, progressive French, in spite of the Porte's obligations to Russia. Much angered by the attitude of the Turks, Nicholas I was determined to compel them to make amends, for he felt sure that Russia's military and diplomatic strength would bring him success.

His confidence largely came from the Russian cabinet's good relations with Great Britain, which he had carefully nurtured since 1844. In 1852 the English were troubled by reports that the French had built a powerful navy, with which they planned to invade England and burn the towns on the Channel. The tsar reassured the British that if a crisis arose he would send a strong squadron to help them.[1] He also sent a delegation of high army officers to the funeral of the Duke of Wellington in November 1852.[2] In December Nicholas promised the Derby government that if the French attacked Belgium, as they threatened, Russia would at once put sixty thousand men in the field, with more to follow immediately.[3]

The Derby government, however, fell early in December, just when Russia needed support to restrain Lavalette on the Eastern Question and to keep Colonel Hugh Rose, the British chargé d'affaires, from backing him. But the change of governments brought Lord Aberdeen, who greatly admired Nicholas, to power. Lord John Russell, who

1. Zaionchkovskii, *Pril.,* I, 324–25.
2. Ibid., p. 327.
3. "Report of the State Chancellor for 1852," ibid., pp. 324–25.

expected soon to become premier in place of Aberdeen, was temporarily foreign minister, with Clarendon to succeed him. Palmerston had to take the lesser position of home secretary, on sufferance. The emperor believed that he could convince and impress Aberdeen, the queen, Russell, and George William Frederick Villiers, Earl of Clarendon of his honesty, as one gentleman to another, and thus retain their friendship for Russia. On January 9 he began his famous talks with Sir G. Hamilton Seymour, ambassador to Russia, and Brunnow skill-fully wooed Aberdeen, stressing that Napoleon III had sent Lavalette to Constantinople on the *Charlemagne*—an open violation of the Treaty of 1841. Baron Brunnow also announced Russia's final recogni-tion of Belgium, which had not been done under Lord John Russell and Palmerston.[4]

Aberdeen agreed with Brunnow, believing that Nicholas I was hon-orable and worthy of trust, and Nesselrode had equal confidence in him.[5] The premier regarded Napoleon as a tricky opportunist and a threat to England, and secretly approved of the tsar's refusal to address him as "Sire and good brother." [6] In January 1853 many Englishmen were disturbed by a rumor that the French ruler was about to seize the Channel Islands, and in February Palmerston wrote that "the French might by steam easily throw a large body of troops into these islands." The danger, however, never materialized.[7]

Because of the tension with the French, Aberdeen, who despised the Turks, wrote to Russell that they should be very careful in drafting the instructions for Stratford, Lord Redcliffe, as ambassador at Con-stantinople. Lord Redcliffe had asked for the power to assure the Turks of "prompt and effective aid" if danger appeared, which, Aber-deen said, "would in all probability produce war." While they probably should give the Porte moral support and try to keep Turkey from collapsing, Aberdeen felt that to fight for the Turks would be "the greatest misfortune." Above all, they should not trust control of "the Mediterranean fleet (which is peace or war) to the discretion of any man." [8]

4. Temperley, p. 299.

5. F. F. Martens, "Rossiia i Angliia nakanune razryva (1853–1854 gg.)," *Vestnik Evropy* (Apr. 1898), p. 564.

6. Ibid.

7. Martin, pp. 119, 103–04.

8. Sir Herbert Maxwell, *The Life and Letters of George William Frederick, Fourth Earl of Clarendon* (London, 1913), II, 2.

Thus, although Nicholas I was at odds with the Turks and the French, he believed that the British government, with his warm friend Aberdeen as premier, was friendly. Queen Victoria admired him and he hoped by his recognition of Belgium to strengthen his good relations with her. And since he had promised speedy aid if France should attack England or Belgium, he was sure that he had won the gratitude of the English and that they were hostile to France and would not support it in the quarrels over the Eastern Question.

The autocrat also drew confidence from his handling of the recognition crisis, in which he had opposed Napoleon's dynastic plans and had refused to use the customary salutation "Sire et bon frère." Napoleon at first had rejected the Russian greeting, but finally accepted it. The tsar failed to realize, however, that this triumph achieved nothing and left much bitterness in Paris, with Russia marked as the obstacle in the way of French prestige. He also did not see that the support of the other powers had been hesitant and could not be relied on in the future.

The Russian diplomats—among them Baron Brunnow—were far from hopeful of the future. In December Brunnow wrote that the French were obviously out to make trouble, for by threats they had forced the sultan to violate his word to the tsar. Now, if Russia reacted sharply, they would charge it with infringing on the independence of the Porte and say that they were obliged to come to its aid. They would then try to involve England, on the pretext of preventing Russian encroachments, and if the Porte also asked for help, England would be in a difficult position. In order "at all costs" to prevent this, Brunnow proposed that Russia should try to show that it would take strong measures to protect the sultan against the predominance of France, which had forced Turkey to affront Russia and to anger its Greek subjects. France thus was infringing on both the external peace of Turkey and its internal repose, while Russia stood for the rights of the sultan and the internal calm of his empire. The English ministers "must persuade themselves," Brunnow said, "that we want to defend the Sultan and not attack him, to sustain him in his rights . . . in short, to conserve Turkey, but not at all to hasten its fall." The emperor agreed that Brunnow was right and that Russia must agree to this course of action.[9]

In his letter of January 5, 1853, to Brunnow, Nesselrode prophesied

9. Brunnow to Nesselrode, Dec. 8/20, 1852, Zaionchkovskii, *Pril.*, I, 347–48.

that, in spite of Russia's moderation, Napoleon would force it into war with Turkey, by bullying the Turks into angering and insulting Russia. If it swallowed the insults, its prestige would be ruined. If, however, Russia should go to war, it would have no allies, for Prussia and Austria would not support it. Such a war would involve few French troops, and its fleet, probably with that of England, could dominate the Black Sea and aid the Circassians. It would be an inexpensive and successful war.

While a Russian counterattack might capture Constantinople and destroy the Turkish empire, Russia could not hold all of its conquests, and France would certainly gain much in the Levant. If not, Napoleon might demand Belgium, the Rhine, or Savoy—thus gaining territory and prestige, and if he did, Russia could do little to prevent the conquest. "At Constantinople distrust and suspicion of Russia were so deep-seated," Nesselrode said, "that the latter would not be believed even if it disavowed the intention to ruin Turkey and alleged that France wanted it."

Only the English could awaken the Turks to their peril, by showing the dangers into which France was leading them. They should speak strongly at Paris. "It is essential," Nesselrode continued, "that the French government does not count too firmly on an alliance with Great Britain in a war that its mind had gratuitously kindled." [10]

In his official Report for 1852, written in March 1853, Nesselrode asserted that France sought a protectorate over all Catholics in the East, "to make its influence predominate over ours. . . ." He added that perhaps Napoleon, blocked in Belgium, wanted to have a complication in the East. Certainly his intimidations of the Turks, which risked the dissolution of their empire, seemed rash and Russia could expect little forbearance from him at Constantinople. [11]

Nicholas became convinced that the British were indeed restraining Napoleon, for Brunnow reported an alleged change of opinion regarding the Turks, with English liberals and philanthropists concluding that it was hopeless to try to civilize Turkey and that all Turkish reforms were nonsense. Aberdeen told Brunnow with feeling: "I hate the Turks, for I regard their government as the worst and most despotic in the whole world." While the British public did not share this outlook, Brunnow cited a pamphlet that advocated letting Turkey collapse and referred to the speeches of Richard Cobden and John Bright, who

10. Ibid., I, 319.
11. Ibid.

favored Russia and scorned Turkey, mentioning that *The Times* approved this attitude.[12] Brunnow failed to realize, however, that Cobden and Bright, the liberals who had achieved the repeal of the Corn Laws in 1846, had lost most of their influence, and that *The Times,* like British opinion in general, was on the point of turning sharply against Russia. Even Aberdeen soon found himself unable to retain control of his ministry, which had begun to favor Palmerston's anti-Russian policy. Thus Brunnow's optimism helped to confirm Nicholas in his self-delusion that England could not join France.

In an undated memorandum of late 1852 the tsar listed various objectives to seek, including "reparation" for the affronts of the Turks; unspecified guarantees for the future; and maintenance of the previous situation, with the query, "Is this possible?" He cited various means of obtaining his objectives: by direct negotiation, by letter, or by negotiation through an embassy; by intimidation through the recall of diplomats; and by force. The last possibility included a declaration of war, surprise occupation of the Principalities, and a surprise attack on Constantinople. Some of the "probable results" he mentioned were that Turkey would give in; that it would not give in and Constantinople would be destroyed; that the French would send a fleet and an expeditionary force. He optimistically gave as the probable outcome a Russian victory, with the Dardanelles and Constantinople occupied and Turkey in collapse.

The last section of the memorandum dealt with the final solution. The tsar felt that the Turkish empire could not be restored, and ruled out Russian annexation of all European Turkey or Constantinople, with or without the Dardanelles; a restoration of the Byzantine empire; and the appropriation of Constantinople and the Straits by Greece. "The least bad of all the bad plans" was that Russia should keep the Principalities and the Dobrudja; Serbia and Bulgaria should be independent; the shores of the Archipelago and the Adriatic should go to Austria; Egypt, and perhaps Cyprus and Rhodes, should go to England; and France should have Crete. The islands of the Archipelago would go to Greece. Constantinople should be a free city, with a Russian garrison on the Bosporus and an Austrian force on the Dardanelles, and complete freedom of commerce. The Turkish empire should exist in Asia Minor.[13]

12. Martens, "Rossiia i Angliia," p. 567.
13. Ibid., p. 354.

This apparently was the emperor's basic plan, for he restated it repeatedly. It is striking that he blandly assumed that neither England nor Austria would raise objections.

Nesselrode, however, in a lengthy memorandum of December 20 (O.S.), 1852, begged his master not to reveal his views, reminding him that "the maintenance of the Ottoman Empire is closely tied to the true interests of Russia" and that since 1829 the emperor had zealously preserved the Porte against its internal weakness and the demands of other powers. Russia must "avoid everything that might compromise its existence." [14]

The chancellor stated that since the Porte had broken the sultan's pledge to the tsar, the best way to secure a peaceful solution would be to send a trusted aide of the tsar with wide latitude "as to the language, now threatening, now friendly" that he would use, and also as concerning reparation that Russia would accept. He was hopeful that the Porte would accept the terms of reparation, which would be backed by military steps. "Fear threw it into the arms of the French; it is likewise fear that must bring it back to us," he said.[15]

If, however, "the blindness and obstinacy of the Porte" should lead to war, which would be rather against France than against Turkey, Russia would have no allies. France would probably gain wide support by alleging that Russia had ulterior motives in starting the conflict over the key to the church at Bethlehem. In England, especially, France would arouse "a blind and ignorant public, which . . . had always showed itself jealous of Russia." Thus Britain would not be an ally of Russia, since it would either be hostile or an armed neutral. Austria, a Catholic power, would probably do the same, and Prussia would give Russia only moral support.[16]

Russia, by stressing the honest and peaceful views of the tsar and his desire to maintain the Ottoman empire, should bring the British and the Austrians to urge both France and Turkey to be more just to Russia and to protect the true interests of Turkey, which might lead to a settlement without war. If not, at least Russia would have proved that it wanted peace and had no hidden designs on Turkey. On the other hand, if Russia now suggested partition, "prejudiced and jealous minds would . . . see . . . proof that we want, not the

14. Ibid.
15. Ibid., pp. 354–55.
16. Ibid., pp. 355–56.

conservation, but the fall of the Ottoman Empire" and that it was using minor grievances to bring it about.[17]

Finally, Nesselrode appealed to the tsar not to reveal his ideas to the British cabinet. Such a disclosure would be not only dangerous but useless as well, for the fixed policy of the British was to make no commitment for an uncertain future.[18]

A few days later Sir Hamilton Seymour, ambassador at St. Petersburg, reported that the authorities were putting the 5th Corps on a war footing, probably as a result of a French threat to send an expedition to Syria. He estimated that if this corps and the 4th Corps marched against Turkey, they would total 144,000 men.[19] On January 9 Seymour read a memorandum to Nesselrode expressing concern that moving a strong force to the frontier would worry France and cause it to react strongly. It would also disturb the Moslems of Turkey and might cause the Christians to rise. Hence this sudden Russian move would lead to grave trouble. Russia's allies did not ask it to give up its lawful rights, but to gain them by negotiation rather than by force.[20]

At this point Nicholas I decided to renew the entente that he had established with England in 1844. At a formal dinner on January 9 (N.S.) he took Seymour aside for a chat about the harmony between the two cabinets with Aberdeen as prime minister, which, he said, reassured him about western Europe. Turkey, however, was a serious problem: "That country is in a critical state and may give us all a great deal of trouble." The highly disorganized country was on the verge of collapse—an event that would be a great misfortune. Hence it was vital that England and Russia should reach an agreement not to act on these matters without consulting each other.[21] After some remarks about "the sick man," the discourse ended.

In his commentary on Russian diplomacy Martens states that while Nicholas did not want war, his actions aroused fears and ill will that he should have avoided. He had offended Napoleon III during the recognition crisis. Now, thanks to the overly optimistic reports of Baron Brunnow, he had a mistaken view of British public opinion which led him, in spite of Nesselrode's warning, to raise the question

17. Ibid., p. 357.
18. Ibid.
19. Seymour to Russell, Jan. 6, 1853, Gt. Brit., Parliament, *British Sessional Papers,* 1854, LXXI, Eastern Papers (hereafter cited as EP), pt. 1, p. 56.
20. Seymour to Russell, Jan. 9, 1853, ibid., pp. 57–58.
21. Martens, *Recueil des traités,* XI, 305–06; EP, V, 1–3.

of the partition of Turkey, thereby suggesting that this was his real desire. He was sure that his remarks would not be misunderstood, for this was what he had said in 1844,[22] and his auditors had been charmed by his frankness and his "knightly honor." Even now Aberdeen and Russell were not horrified, although they felt Nicholas's views were incorrect. But since the tsar returned again and again to the partition theme, many in England were sure that this was his real objective.

The view that the collapse of Turkey was inevitable was widely held in Europe. In 1829 Polignac, the French foreign minister, and Charles X had actually proposed that France and Russia join forces to bring it about. In 1832 Mehemet Ali, with French backing, was close to dismembering Turkey and only armed Russian intervention had prevented it. Again, in 1839 Turkey's collapse was all but complete, and Russia and France could have made it certain. Turkey survived this crisis, however, thanks to the cooperation of the powers in defeating the Egyptians and bolstering the Porte. Sultan Mahmud and Reshid pasha now had pushed through Tanzimat a program of reforms that seemed to offer hope that Turkey could eliminate its deep-seated failings. By 1841, however, Reshid had fallen and some of the reforms had been rescinded. The position of the Christians had worsened, bringing a revolt of the Serbs in 1842. The omens were so bad that in 1844 the Turcophil Stratford Canning had warned that Turkey might collapse, because of weakness resulting from "the Porte's adoption of a policy of enforcing at every risk its authority where it has fallen into decay—or originally had been incomplete; from the state of the Turkish army and finances; from the general corruption of the Turkish official authorities; and from the excessive power which Riza pasha, present favorite of the sultan, has concentrated in his person. Each of these causes might suffice to overthrow a better consolidated regime than Turkey." [23] Hence when Nicholas I had preached in England that Turkey was about to fall, and that the two powers should be ready to cooperate to prevent a catastrophic war, he had received a respectful hearing.

Now, nine years later, the tsar again sounded this note. Aberdeen also retained his views on Turkey. In June 1853 he wrote to Lord Clarendon that the great powers were drifting fast toward war over

22. Martens, *Recueil des traités*, XI, 305–06.
23. Puryear, *England, Russia, and the Straits*, p. 38.

Turkey. He added that he was sure that any war, whether successful or unsuccessful, "will speedily lead to the dissolution of the Turkish Empire as at present existing, although we may continue to talk with grave faces of its integrity and independence." [24] In April Nesselrode wrote that direct word from Constantinople had confirmed Austrian reports "on the fanaticism of the Moslems and the strength of the war party, side by side with an empty treasury, an undisciplined army, continual desertions, and complete anarchy in the provinces of Asia." He added that in such a case one would expect the Porte to accept a compromise with alacrity, but apparently "an irresistible fatality pushes the Turks to their ruin." [25]

During the 1850s it was widely believed in Europe that Turkey would soon crumble. In the spring of 1852 Colonel Rose, British chargé at Constantinople, had stated that the diplomats and much of the European press were openly discussing this prospect, all agreeing that Turkey had too many inherent weaknesses to survive much longer. On March 10, 1853, Rose informed Lord John Russell that Turkey's friends hoped that it might survive as a Moslem country in Asia, "but it is a hope that is giving way before the reality of the facts." [26]

At the end of 1852 Ambassador Seymour reported that Count Mensdorff, the Austrian ambassador to the Russian court, feared that Turkish collapse was imminent, and that Russia was alarmed at the uprising in Montenegro against the Turks.[27] As for King Frederick William IV of Prussia, his fervent dream was a crusade to drive the Turks from Constantinople and restore the city to Christianity. Since this was not possible, however, in 1853 the king proposed a five-power treaty with the Porte, incorporating the basic principle that the sultan should not lose more of his sovereignty and autonomy. Somewhat inconsistently, however, he also proposed the liberation of the Christian populations of Turkey. The British at once rejected this proposal, fearing that such interference with the sultan's powers would hasten the collapse of Turkey.[28]

B. Kingsley Martin avers that before the Crimean War the big question was "the extent to which any European Power, or group

---

24. Maxwell, II, 15.
25. K. V. Nesselrode, *Lettres et papiers du chancelier Comte de Nesselrode,* ed. A. de Nesselrode *(1760–1856)* (Paris, 1904–12), X, 268.
26. Puryear, *England, Russia, and the Straits,* p. 207.
27. Ibid., p. 206.
28. Kurt Borries, *Preussen im Krimkrieg* (Stuttgart, 1930), pp. 58–59.

of Powers, might exert influence over the policy and administration of Turkey. It was almost axiomatic . . . that internal dissensions would break up the Ottoman Empire in the near future" unless it had real support. The politicians debated whether the outside backing should depend on promises of Turkish reform, or whether the most satisfactory solution would be partition. The "independence and integrity of the Ottoman Empire" was a phrase that was rarely used except in public speeches. George, Duke of Argyll, a member of the Aberdeen cabinet, wrote that there were no words "more grotesquely inconsistent with the facts of the case." The phrase, if it had any meaning, implied Turkey was so weak that its integrity and independence could exist, even nominally, only on condition that the powers "agreed to abstain from separate attacks," and "acknowledged among themselves that this should be a common and binding obligation." [29]

Inasmuch as the idea of the imminent collapse of Turkey was common currency in 1853, it is not strange that the British cabinet did not show consternation at the mention of such a possibility. Sir Hamilton Seymour himself, in reporting on his talk with the emperor, stated that it was greatly to England's interest to have it understood that no decision regarding Turkey would be taken without consulting Great Britain by "a sovereign who controls several hundred thousand bayonets." The envoy hoped that the tsar would not insist on partition, for if England refused to agree to it, it would then have no voice in the matter if it should occur later on. Any agreement with Russia, however, would appear to give British approval and would probably hasten Turkey's demise.[30]

On January 14 (N.S.) the emperor received Seymour cordially and the talks resumed. The monarch said that there had been dreams of conquest in the days of Catherine II, but now Russia had so much territory that it did not need more; indeed it would be dangerous to have it. Turkey was a very suitable neighbor because it was not aggressive, although it could protect itself. It had millions of Christians, over whom Russia watched, since Russia's religion came from the East. At times this was a very inconvenient obligation. Turkey, he added, had fallen into such decay that, while all wanted it to survive, "he may die suddenly on our hands." If Turkey should fall, "it falls

29. Martin, pp. 28–29. Quotation from Duke of Argyll, *Autobiography and Memoirs* (London, 1906), I, 441.
30. Seymour to Russell, Jan. 11, 1853, EP, V, 1–3.

to rise again no more." Nicholas suggested the wisdom of making plans for this event beforehand rather than to face the "chaos, confusion, and the certainty of a European war" which would result if the end should come unexpectedly. He wanted the British government to know this.[31]

Seymour answered that Turkey was not yet at death's door and the British did not like to plan for the demise of an ally. Nicholas replied that while this attitude was wise, it was important not to be taken by surprise. He wanted a gentleman's agreement with England. He said flatly that he would not permit England to control Constantinople and that for his part he would not take it. He might occupy it temporarily, but not permanently. Seymour thanked him for his frankness, adding that the British government might make some arrangement to guard against contingencies. The emperor briefly mentioned the dispute about the Holy Places, which he thought probably could be settled. He added, however, that if France sent troops to Turkey, he would at once have to do the same, even if it led to Turkey's downfall, but so far his forces had not moved. The envoy replied that his government was pleased with his moderation, although it felt that Nicholas was exaggerating the weakness of Turkey, which was not in grave danger.

Seymour told Lord John Russell, the foreign secretary, that he felt that the emperor was frank and honorable but too sure of Turkey's collapse. The British cabinet should respond to Nicholas's overture by proposing measures to strengthen Turkey, for since the tsar had promised to work with Britain, if he could be persuaded to keep his promise, all should be well.[32]

The ambassador was not shocked at the idea of partitioning Turkey, for he wrote that the emperor's frankness had convinced him that "a noble triumph would be obtained . . . if the void left by the extinction of Mohammedan rule in Europe could be filled up without an interruption of the general peace," thanks to the precautions adopted by Russia and England, the governments "most interested in the destinies of Turkey."[33]

His cabinet shared these views, for on February 8, 1853, Aberdeen wrote to the queen that the tsar's remarks "were quite in conformity

31. Seymour to Russell, Jan. 23, 1853, ibid., p. 4.
32. Ibid., p. 5.
33. Ibid., p. 6.

with his previous declarations" in 1844.[34] According to V. J. Puryear, British diplomatic documents show that the government was not alarmed, for Russell began to work in full harmony with the understanding of 1844 by advising the French to adopt a moderate course. Late in January he sent a "vigorously worded dispatch," fully in keeping with the recommendations of Nesselrode, to the French cabinet, in which, while passing no judgment on the religious dispute, he expressed concern over the use of threats to Turkey. France had started the controversy and was the first power to send its fleet into Turkish waters; hence it should take the lead in making concessions.[35] In January the British cabinet declined a French proposal for an alliance. While Russell admitted the natural anxiety of the French, his government was sure that "the Emperor will not enter unwittingly, and certainly without the consent of England, into any schemes for the subversion of the Ottoman power. Her Majesty's Government have reasons quite satisfactory to them for this persuasion." At the same time Russell readily admitted that the Ottoman realm was in great peril and was a tempting prize to ambition "of another great and formidable empire" (i.e., France). The attitude of Turkey itself, he added, increased its own danger.[36]

While these British moves were not communicated to the Russians, the cordial relations between Brunnow and Prime Minister Aberdeen and the sympathy of the London cabinet, with which the emperor felt he had an understanding, encouraged him. He yearned for still greater harmony with England, and finally, when there was no reply from London, on February 20 (N.S.) he approached Seymour at a ball and asked what his government had replied. The envoy answered that a response had come, but it was not what the emperor wanted. The tsar expressed regret. "I am not so eager," he said, "about what shall be done when the bear dies as I am to determine with England what shall not be done. . . ." Seymour responded that England did not think that Turkey was dying and that although the demise of both Portugal and Turkey had often been predicted, they had survived. England did not want to stir up trouble by acting. Here Nicholas said that if the English thought Turkey would live, they were wrong:

34. Victoria, queen of Great Britain, *The Letters of Queen Victoria* (London, 1907), II, 532.

35. V. J. Puryear, "New Light on the Origins of the Crimean War," *Journal of Modern History*, III, no. 2 (1931), 230.

36. Russell, to Cowley, Jan. 29, 1853, ibid., pp. 230–31.

"I repeat to you that the Bear is dying, you may give him musk, but even this will not keep him alive, and we can never allow such an event to take us by surprise." He held it vital to come to an understanding, which he could surely do if he could but have ten minutes' conversation with the ministers—"with Lord Aberdeen, for instance, who has full confidence in me, as I have in him. And remember, I do not ask a Treaty or a Protocol; a general understanding is all that I require—that between gentlemen is sufficient. . . ."

Seymour, startled, wrote that these remarks were very important and should be considered carefully. He believed that the tsar was convinced of the collapse of Turkey, and was sure that Russia and Austria had an agreement on the matter.[37]

On the next day Seymour read Nesselrode Russell's long despatch of February 9 (N.S.), which expressed the pleasure of the queen at the frank and friendly attitude of the emperor. As for the expected dissolution of Turkey, the question was, would it be better to prepare for it in advance rather than to face without preparation the confusion and the danger of a general war?

Lord Russell began by stating that no real crisis had arisen to make the matter urgent. The disputes over the Holy Places were really between France and Russia and did not concern Turkey directly. (Nicholas disagreed in a marginal notation: "These disputes can bring war; this war could easily end with the fall of the Ottoman Empire, above all if it took place following the horrors being committed in Montenegro. . . .") While the Turkish attack on Montenegro had caused a break between Austria and the Porte, Vienna had treated it as a border problem instead of a threat to the sovereignty of the sultan. There was no reason to tell the sultan "that he cannot maintain peace at home or keep friendly relations with his neighbors." (The tsar objected that the Montenegro matter was very serious.)[38]

Russell held that the agreement for the partition of the Spanish possessions in 1700 or the one regarding Tuscany did not apply because the circumstances were very different. The dissolution of the Turkish empire "can occur twenty, fifty, one hundred years from now." ("It can also happen unexpectedly," wrote the tsar.) In this case, an agreement about partition would increase the danger, for the sultan, who

37. Seymour to Russell, Feb. 9/21, 1853, EP, V, 8–9; J. C. Hurewitz, *Diplomacy in the Near and Middle East, 1535–1914* (Princeton, N.J., 1956), I, 140.
38. Russell to Seymour, Feb. 9, 1853, Zaionchkovskii, *Pril.,* I, 359–60.

would surely learn of it, would be angry and alarmed, while his foes would be greatly encouraged. The sultan's army would feel doomed to defeat. Thus the agreement would cause the very anarchy that had been feared and the good efforts of the Sick Man's friends would bring about his death.[39]

Moreover, the carrying out of the partition would be dangerous. If Russia gained temporary control of Constantinople, traditional Russian ambitions would clash with the jealousy of Europe. Furthermore, the final owner of the Golden Horn might well be more ambitious and aggressive than Turkey and would have wide influence. A show of friendship to Russia might lead to war, and if the sultan tried to restrict Russia's power ("This the Emperor of Russia will not permit," wrote the tsar), conflict would result. Neither England nor France, nor probably Austria, would like to see Constantinople remain Russian. For its part, the British government "renounces all intention or desire to possess Constantinople, and His Imperial Majesty can be perfectly reassured on this point." It would also promise to make no definite agreements about the fall of the Ottoman government "without first having concerted ahead of time with the Emperor of Russia."

(Here Nicholas noted: "This is a precious assurance, for it proves the perfect identity of intentions that exists between England and Russia"; he held that this would make it easy to take the precautions to prevent "what neither England nor Russia can ever permit.")[40]

Russell went on to say that the British government felt that no policy "wiser, more disinterested, more advantageous for Europe" could be followed regarding Turkey than the one the emperor had long pursued with great success. This would require that the cabinets of the powers show the greatest moderation toward Turkey; that all claims of the great powers be settled by amicable negotiations rather than by peremptory demands; that the powers avoid all military or naval demonstrations as far as possible; that disputes or questions involving Turkish internal matters or the competence of the Porte be decided after mutual understanding among the powers and not be imposed on the weakness of the Turkish government. (Here the tsar wrote that he felt this was what he had been doing.)[41]

Lord John added that the British cabinet felt that it was essential

39. Ibid., p. 360.
40. Ibid., p. 361.
41. Ibid., pp. 361–62.

to invite the sultan to treat his Christian subjects "in conformity with the principles of equity and religious liberty generally adopted by the enlightened nations of Europe." (N. I: "This is being done, but uselessly, and this is what can bring war and all its consequences.") Russell continued that the more the Turkish government practiced impartiality in its laws and equality in its administration, the less the emperor of Russia would find it necessary "to make use of this exceptional protection that His Imperial Majesty finds so burdensome and painful, although it is imposed by duty and sanctioned by treaties." ("Certainly," noted the tsar.) [42]

Finally, the foreign minister authorized Seymour to read this despatch to Nesselrode and to give him a copy for the tsar. He would then make *"those assurances of friendship and of confidence on the part of Her Majesty the Queen that the conduct of His Imperial Majesty is sure to inspire."* (Emphasis of the tsar, who noted: "I am very much touched by it, for I see there the guarantee of the future, which I dread.") [43]

While this despatch revealed that Nicholas I and the British cabinet differed over the imminence of Turkey's collapse, it is significant that there was a large area of agreement. Russell did not object to the monarch's insistence that Turkey was the Sick Man, doomed to certain demise, and probably many of Lord John's colleagues also accepted this view.

Russell, however, refused to make an agreement about the actual terms of partition, which, if they became known, would hasten the sultan's doom. Nevertheless, England renounced all desire to hold Constantinople, and Russell stated that "His Imperial Majesty can be perfectly reassured on this point." He also promised not to make any agreement about the Ottoman government without having "first concerted beforehand with the Emperor of Russia." Moreover, the foreign minister also fully recognized Russia's right of "exceptional protection" of the sultan's Orthodox subjects, which was "doubtless imposed by duty and sanctioned by treaties." This language offered ungrudging support to the claim to protect the Orthodox derived from the Treaties of Küchuk-Kainardji and Adrianople. All this, along with the warm expression of "friendship and confidence" on the part of the queen, gave Nicholas reason to believe that Russia and Britain had an effective understanding.

42. Ibid., p. 362.
43. Ibid.

Only a few months later the British public and the government objected vehemently to the "right of protection," which they now held gave the tsar great influence over the ten million Orthodox subjects of the sultan and hence infringed on his sovereign rights. But in February Russell and the cabinet accepted this right as a natural and traditional reality.

Nicholas, however, talked too much, in spite of Nesselrode's warning. On February 10/22 he summoned Seymour to his palace to discuss Russell's despatch. He began by saying how anxious he was to prevent the collapse of Turkey, reminding Seymour that in 1829 he had prevented General Diebitsch from taking Constantinople, and in 1833 he alone had supported the sultan against Mehemet Ali. He went on to say, however, that the catastrophe might still occur as a result of a foreign or an internal convulsion. At this his auditor inwardly concluded that a ruler who discussed the dissolution of a neighboring state must have made up his mind that its end was near. Seymour also guessed that the tsar could not have decided on this without the support of Austria. If so, the plan must be to induce England to join the two eastern empires in a partition of Turkey without the participation of France.[44]

The emperor seemed to support this view by stating that as long as England and Russia were in harmony he had no concern about France. The envoy, while agreeing that neither would tolerate France at Constantinople, added that Austria had not been mentioned, and it would surely be interested. "Oh!" said the tsar, "but you must understand that when I speak of Russia, I speak of Austria as well; what suits the one suits the other; our interests as regards Turkey are perfectly identical." [45]

Seymour now said frankly that the main difference between England and Russia was that the tsar stressed the fall of Turkey and what to do when it occurred, while the British thought of keeping Turkey as it was. "Ah!" replied the monarch, "That is what the Chancellor is perpetually telling me; but the catastrophe will occur some day and will take us all unawares." [46] He went on to say that when the time came, the territorial settlement would probably be easier than was generally realized. The Principalities of Moldavia and Wallachia were in fact an independent state under the protection of the tsar

44. Seymour to Russell, Feb. 25, 1853, EP, V, 9.
45. Ibid., p. 10.
46. Ibid.

and might remain so. Serbia might have the same sort of regime, and likewise Bulgaria: "there seems to be no reason why this province should not form an independent state." Egypt, Nicholas recognized, was important to England and if the British should occupy it during the partition of Turkey, "I shall have no objections to offer. I would say the same about Candia [Crete]. . . . I do not know why it should not become a British possession." Seymour replied that Britain merely wanted safe and ready communication with India via Egypt and nothing more.[47]

Seymour apologetically admitted to Russell that he might have failed to report some parts of the emperor's discourse, "especially the precise terms employed by him with respect to the commercial policy to be observed at Constantinople when no longer held by the Turks. The purpose of the conversation was that England and Russia had a common interest in providing the readiest access to the Black Sea and the Mediterranean." [48] It is understandable that in such an extensive interview the ambassador was unable to remember all that was said, but it is regrettable that on this highly important point his memory proved unreliable, especially as he later charged that the emperor was "intentionally inexplicit" as to the temporary occupation of Constantinople.

Nesselrode, who probably wished to moderate the effect of these disclosures, composed an oral note to Seymour on February 21/March 5, 1853 stating that the tsar had not proposed partition of Turkey, but had held the talks so that each side could say what it did *not* want, so they could avoid acting at cross-purposes. There were no plans for a partition or a binding agreement, but a simple exchange of opinions. By holding an informal conversation with Seymour, the tsar had chosen the most intimate, confidential means of communicating frankly with Her Majesty, since he desired that these talks should remain secret between them.[49]

Thanks to the informality, Nesselrode continued, there was no need to inform the other powers, so that there was little danger that these opinions would hasten the fall of Turkey, which was only a remote and uncertain contingency, now not especially imminent. But it could occur unexpectedly. The deteriorating moral, financial, and administrative state of Turkey, and the question of the Holy Places might bring

47. Ibid., pp. 11–12.
48. Ibid., p. 12.
49. Zaionchkovskii, *Pril.,* I, 362–63.

it about. While the latter issue might be easily settled, if the vanity and threats of France should cause the Porte to refuse satisfaction to Russia, war might come. Moreover, the sultan's concessions to the Latins might outrage the immense Orthodox majority. This was not a mere hypothetical question, for the Moslem atrocities against the Montenegrins and earlier in Bulgaria, Bosnia, and Herzegovina, made other Christians fearful and might bring on a general insurrection.[50]

The British cabinet, because of Turkey's feebleness, had asked that Russia should show great forbearance. The emperor felt that he had never ceased to do so, as the British cabinet had stated. But Russia could continue its moderation only if the other powers did the same. France had not done so. It had used threats to send a warship through the Dardanelles, in violation of the treaties. It had made claims and demands at the point of a cannon—at Tripoli, and again at Constantinople. By intimidation it had obtained the annulment of the firman and the solemn promises that the sultan had given to the tsar. Since England had kept silent regarding these cases of *force majeure* and did not offer support to the Turks, the Porte naturally decided that France was the dominant country and that it could disregard Austria and Russia. Hence the latter felt that they, too, had to use threats, since the Porte never gave in except before a stern demand. England should seek to make the Turks hear reason, refraining from any sign of supporting Turkey against the just claims of Russia. The Turks thus would learn to treat their Christian subjects more justly, which would be the surest way to avert the crisis that both monarchs wished to avoid.

Nesselrode stated that Nicholas I was pleased with the exchange of views, for now the two cabinets knew what they could not accept. They both recognized that neither could permit a strong power to gain control of Constantinople, and each renounced the idea of possessing it. They also agreed not to make any arrangements about actions to be taken after the fall of the Ottoman empire without first consulting with each other. Since the tsar believed that he could also count on Austria, he now had less concern over "the catastrophe that he always desired to dispel and to ward off as far as he is able."[51]

Sir Hamilton Seymour ventured to take issue with Nesselrode on

50. Ibid., p. 364.
51. Ibid., pp. 364–65.

one point. Feeling that both the emperor and the chancellor had misunderstood England's attitude toward France on the Eastern Question, he wrote to the latter stating that the British government, as far as a neutral could, was supporting the just claims of Russia and had not failed to press France to moderate its language to Turkey. Nesselrode quickly summoned Seymour to an interview on March 10, 1853, at which they discussed the memorandum. The chancellor said that Russia only wanted Her Majesty's government, while appealing to the magnanimity and equity of Napoleon III, to "strive towards opening the eyes of the French Ministers" to the mistakes into which Lavalette had led them. Seymour proved that that was precisely what his cabinet had been doing by reading part of a despatch of January 28, 1853, from Lord John Russell to Ambassador Cowley at Paris. Russell, expressing regret that the issue of the Holy Places had not been settled, refused to make a judgment on the merits of the case, since each side quoted treaties, conventions, and firmans. "But Her Majesty's Government," he said, "cannot avoid perceiving that the Ambassador of France at Constantinople was the first to disturb the status quo in which the matter rested."

Nesselrode expressed to Seymour his "warm satisfaction" at finding that the British government had given such excellent advice to France and only regretted that he had not received earlier "the conclusive evidence" concerning the action by Her Majesty's Secretary of State for Foreign Affairs upon the question of the Holy Places.[52]

Thus Seymour convinced both Nesselrode and Nicholas I that the London cabinet was supporting Russia against France—which must have encouraged the tsar to continue his strong measures against Turkey. Neither Russell nor Clarendon was really hostile to France, however, and many of their colleagues were pro-French. Furthermore, there was much latent Russophobia, which was beginning to reappear in England. Aberdeen was finding it difficult to keep the support of the other ministers. The tsar, and to a lesser degree Nesselrode, were blissfully ignorant of this hostility and remained convinced that the two Western powers could not overcome their ancient hostility and become allies. This realignment, however, was taking place, and the Seymour conversations helped to bring it to pass.

At first Seymour had not been greatly upset by the emperor's stress

52. Seymour to Clarendon, March 1, 1853 (N.S.), EP, V, 17–18. Russell's despatch to Cowley, Jan. 28, is in EP, I, 67.

on Turkey's imminent dissolution and actually stated that the Ottomans' removal from Europe without a conflict would be a real achievement. But the tsar's insistence that Turkey would soon crumble and
that a peaceful succession was needed made the envoy feel that these
remarks reflected wishful thinking and that Nicholas no longer wanted
to preserve Turkey. The suggestions for a post-Ottoman regime
strongly confirmed Seymour's belief that his host intended to oust
the Turks from Europe. While the Briton took note of the pledge
not to annex Constantinople, after studying Nesselrode's memorandum
he wrote to Clarendon that "the wording of this engagement, coupled
with the conversation which I had with the Emperor" made him
think that "whilst willing to undertake not to make himself the permanent master of Constantinople, His Majesty is intentionally inexplicit
as to its temporary occupation." [53]

Also important was the contradiction between Nicholas I's remarks
about the need to maintain the Turkish regime and his much greater
insistence on its approaching collapse and the need to prepare for it
beforehand. He had advanced that view in 1844 and now he pushed
it even more strongly. This time Russell and Clarendon were disturbed
by the tsar's inconsistency and began to doubt his "knightly honor"
that had so impressed the British statesmen. Palmerston, of course,
regarded Russia as England's real enemy. Even Aberdeen, close friend
of the tsar's, gradually lost faith in him. [54]

But Nesselrode and the tsar apparently had no inkling that the
English leaders were cooling toward Russia and drawing closer to
France. They were both convinced of the friendship of Aberdeen and
somehow expected him to dominate the cabinet. The optimistic reports
of Baron Brunnow, who was on cordial terms with many British political leaders, also helped soothe Nesselrode and Nicholas. Part of the
blame for the misreading of portents rested, however, with Lord Clarendon, the new foreign minister, who continued to stress the closeness
of the two cabinets and the strength of their entente. On March 23,
1853, Clarendon stated to Seymour that the cabinet believed "that
Turkey still possesses the elements of existence" and that Russell had
rightly stated that there was no reason to intimate to the sultan that
"he cannot keep peace at home or preserve friendly relations with
his neighbours." He expressed pleasure that the emperor was even

53. EP, V, 12–13.
54. Martens, *Recueil des traités*, XII, 305–08.

more eager to preserve Turkey than England was, for his policy would probably be decisive. He politely advised Nicholas I to stop predicting Turkey's demise, as such prophecies were the surest way to bring it to pass.[55]

Certainly the British agreed with the Russian cabinet that neither power could control Constantinople and a revived Byzantium or an expanded Greek state was not the right solution. Clarendon prophesied that any attempt to decide on the partition of Turkey's domains would fail and would probably cause anarchy. A conference of the powers would be a rational approach to the problem, but France would probably try to revise the whole treaty system of 1815, which could not be tolerated. Hence the only solution was to uphold the Turkish empire, since any great question in the East would become a source of discord in the West, which might lead to revolution and general chaos.

Fortunately, Clarendon continued, Turkey had energy and wealth and was trying to reform its failings. The great powers should be forbearing in dealing with it. Britain hoped to cooperate with Russia in such a policy and had "entire confidence" in the tsar's intentions. Believing that "the interests of Russia and England in the East are completely identical, they . . . hope that a similar policy there will prevail, and tend to strengthen the alliance between the two countries, which it is . . . the object of . . . Her Majesty's Government to promote." [56]

Clarendon added that he would be glad to discuss the matter further, for "the generous confidence" shown by the emperor entitled him "to the most cordial declaration of opinion" by the Court of St. James, which was well aware that in the event of any crisis concerning Turkey "the word of His Imperial Majesty would be preferable to any convention that could be framed." [57]

Nicholas I, who greatly wanted England as an effective ally, accepted these honeyed assurances at face value. In reality, however, Clarendon was saying that there was now no danger that Turkey might crumble and that the best course was to stop talking about it and to treat it with a gentle hand. The emperor, however, who still held that Turkey had treated Russia badly, was determined to compel the Turks to make reparation for their fault and to give guarantees for the future.

55. EP, V, 19.
56. Ibid., 19–20.
57. Ibid., p. 19.

And as the British were becoming distrustful of Russian intentions and were drawing closer to France, the whole basis for the tsar's policy—a loyal British ally, opposed to France—was deteriorating. The monarch, however, failed to realize this and followed the same course as before, with dire results.

The emperor's attitude was clearly revealed in his final talk with Seymour. On April 20 the latter reported that he had again talked with Nicholas about Clarendon's despatch of March 23. The tsar said that he was delighted that his overtures to the British cabinet had been received "in the same friendly spirit" in which they had been made and that he had the utmost confidence in "the word of a gentleman." He asserted that they now had a clear understanding on the main points, for which he thanked Seymour for making it possible. He declared that his promise would be equally binding on his successors, for he had left instructions for them and they would carry them out. Nicholas took issue, however, with Clarendon over Turkey's treatment of its Christian subjects, for he felt that the reports of British consuls and other agents were not always reliable. He added that while he had used no force against the Turks, he would not be trifled with and "if the Turks did not yield to reason, they would have to give way to the approach of danger." [58]

Finally, on April 5, 1853, Clarendon sent a despatch expressing "sincere satisfaction" with Nesselrode's memorandum "as a renewed proof of the Emperor's confidence and friendly feeling." He then responded to the chancellor's assertion that England had not done enough to restrain French aggressiveness. It had dealt with Paris over the sending of the *Charlemagne* through the Straits and, in spite of the Porte's permission, had induced the French to agree that the vessel should carry their ambassador to his post. The British then would cease their protests, on the understanding that a precedent would not be established.[59] Also by its instructions to Colonel Rose at Constantinople and its despatch to Lord Cowley at Paris the British cabinet had sought to restrain the French. And, when sending Viscount Stratford de Redcliffe to Constantinople, the cabinet had advised him that the government was "not insensible to the superior claims of Russia, both as respected the treaty obligations of Turkey, and the loss of moral influence that the Emperor would sustain throughout his domin-

58. Ibid., pp. 23–24.
59. Clarendon to Seymour, Apr. 5, 1853, ibid., p. 22.

ions if, in the position occupied by His Imperial Majesty with reference to the Greek Church, he was to yield any privileges that it had hitherto enjoyed to the Latin Church, of which the Emperor of the French claimed to be the protector." London hoped that by sending the famous Redcliffe, armed with an autographed letter of the queen to the sultan, the Turks might be induced to hear "moderate counsels." Redcliffe was to advise the Porte to treat its Christian subjects with the utmost leniency.[60]

The despatch even asserted that the Turks had apparently seen the light, for they had sent a pasha to Bosnia to redress the grievances of the people and gave very strong instructions to Omer pasha "to act with unvaried moderation" toward the Montenegrins, his foes. Actually, the latter had been the aggressors in attacking a Turkish fort. Also the reports of Turkish atrocities apparently were unreliable.

Finally, Clarendon said that as the two monarchs had now renewed their pledges to uphold the independence and integrity of the Turkish empire, Her Majesty's Government earnestly desired that henceforth their respective envoys should cooperate in "giving similar advice in the same friendly spirit to the Porte." [61]

A final despatch came from Seymour in St. Petersburg, who on April 21 wrote that he had communicated Clarendon's despatch of April 5 and had received a memorandum from the tsar stressing the cruelties of the Turks in Bosnia, which had driven many families into Austria. The monarch said that he would continue, as always, to be moderate and forbearing toward the Turks, in order not to trouble and humiliate them, always provided that the other powers would do the same and that none of them "abuses the weaknesses of the Porte to obtain concessions that work to the detriment of others." [62]

In these talks the two cabinets revealed their attitudes on the Eastern Question. At first the English welcomed the Russian overtures, not from a wish for the partition of Turkey, but because they feared it was inevitable and held that an agreement with Russia and probably with Austria would reduce the danger. Britain agreed that the tsar had a claim to reparation for the Porte's duplicity, and Russell conceded that the monarch had a right sanctioned by treaty to protect

60. Ibid., pp. 22–23.
61. Ibid., p. 23.
62. Seymour to Clarendon, Apr. 21, 1853, ibid., pp. 24–25.

the Orthodox church. As powerful France still seemed to be the enemy, Russia was a valuable ally in time of need. The British rebuffed French overtures and worked to secure Russia its claims from the Turks. The entente of 1844 appeared to be restored and in full vigor.

Nicholas, however, in spite of the warnings of Nesselrode, insisted on putting his cards on the table before Seymour, who became convinced that the emperor was determined to partition Turkey and seize Constantinople. The French, by adopting a more moderate policy, reassured the English and gave pro-French attitudes a chance to develop. Moreover, Seymour kept emphasizing the predatory designs of the tsar. The British cabinet now stressed the viability of Turkey and the need for forbearance toward it. The emperor paid lip service to this idea, although he refused to rule out the use of force. Moreover, Menshikov's threatening conduct at Constantinople (to be discussed later) led the British to doubt that Russia's intentions were peaceful. Colonel Rose requested the British fleet to sail from Malta, but, although the French fleet moved to Greek waters, the British cabinet refused to send its squadron. This rebuff to France delighted the tsar and Nesselrode, and Clarendon's despatch of April 5 emphasized that England had repeatedly sided against France on the Eastern Question. This confirmed Nicholas in his conviction that an Anglo-French alliance was impossible—a theory that was the basis for his whole policy. He thus saw no need to moderate his actions and continued to drive ahead to obtain his objectives, by force if need be. It proved to be a bad mistake.

By the end of 1852 the emperor must have decided on war with Turkey, for a memorandum written by him on January 7/19, 1853, stated that a break with Turkey would probably come very soon. He did not expect to have to fight the French in the early stages, although he was sure that they would quickly intervene with their fleet and perhaps with land forces. To him it seemed essential to strike a sudden, decisive blow, in complete secrecy. He proposed to move sixteen thousand men with thirty-two guns, a few Cossacks, and a minimum of horses, from Sevastopol directly into the Bosporus for an attack on Constantinople. If possible, a similar force would sail from Odessa.[63] In February Vice Admiral V. K. Kornilov of the Black Sea Fleet supplied a list of twenty-eight war vessels and thirty-three

63. Zaionchkovskii, *Pril.,* I, 582–83.

transport vessels, which would carry twenty-six battalions, six batteries of artillery, and two hundred Cossacks. Once they had established a beachhead, preferably at Büyükdere, the warships, if necessary, would take a force of troops to the Dardanelles to repulse a possible French attempt to force an entrance.[64] In the meantime, an army of about 100,000 men would march overland as soon as the weather permitted.[65] The emperor sent copies of his plans to Field Marshal I. F. Paskevich at Warsaw. He expressed a hope, however, that "it will work out without this; I shall decide on this only in extreme circumstances. It does not take long to begin a war, but it will end as it ends . . . God knows how." [66]

By March 22/April 5, however, the autocrat's plans had changed, for he wrote that Menshikov had reported that the Turks were fortifying the Bosporus, so that "a naval undertaking, in case of war, against Tsargrad [Constantinople] would be either extremely difficult or impossible." Now he believed that it would be best to take Varna by sea and then to occupy the Gulf of Burgas with its fortifications, while the land forces marched to join them. An advance on Constantinople would follow.[67]

Paskevich, however, strongly advised against an effort to take Constantinople, for as the army advanced deep into the Balkans it would be reduced by leaving garrisons in captured towns, by disease, and by battle attrition. Adrianople would be costly to take, and by this time the army would be too small for the difficult task ahead. Moreover, if Russia should become involved in a European war it would be in trouble, with so much of its strength in the Balkans. The field marshal advised Russia to be satisfied with the occupation of the Danubian Principalities with two or three divisions. This operation would cost little, while putting severe pressure on the Turks, and Russia could expand its influence among the Balkan Christians.[68]

Since the emperor greatly admired Paskevich, under whom he had served as a grand duke, he apparently accepted his arguments. Much as he would have liked to teach the Porte a severe lesson, he realized that there would be danger of a general war, while occupation of

64. Ibid., pp. 583–84.
65. Report of minister of war, early 1853, ibid., pp. 585–94.
66. "Iz pisem imperatora Nikolaia Pavlovicha k I. F. Paskevichu," *Russkii Arkhiv*, XLVIII, pt. 2 (1910) 165–70.
67. Memorandum of Nicholas I, March 22/April 3, 1853, Zaionchkovskii, *Pril.*, I, 597–98.
68. Report of the Prince of Warsaw, March 24 (O.S.), 1853, ibid., pp. 599–600.

the Principalities would probably not be a *casus belli.* If France attacked Turkey he probably would have rushed to seize the Bosporus, but as France did not, he could content himself with holding Moldavia and Wallachia. In doing so he believed that England would not make trouble, as he thought he had won it by his talks with Seymour. He was to be sorely disappointed. But as he did not want war, before resorting to force he awaited the outcome of the extraordinary embassy of Prince A. S. Menshikov to the sultan, in hopes that he might be able to achieve a resounding diplomatic triumph. If this came to pass, the tsar would have gained the prestige and influence that he felt was necessary to enable him to withstand the challenge of the French. If not, military action might then be tried.

CHAPTER 5. THE MENSHIKOV MISSION

By late 1852 Russian prestige in the Levant had sharply declined when the Turks, urged by the French, granted France its demands for more rights and privileges for the Latins—the Catholics—at the Holy Places at the expense of the Greeks or Orthodox Christians and Russia, their protector. Fuad effendi, a progressive Turk, openly urged alignment with France, the rising star in Europe, with its powerful armed forced and dynamic leadership, in order to eliminate Russian influence in Turkey.

The alignment presented a grave challenge to Russia, for its prestige and its vital economic and strategic interests depended on the flow of Russian grain through the Straits and a lesser tide of imports. Russia would be vulnerable to attack by the strong French army and navy aided by the Turks and the Caucasian mountaineers, which might bring disaster. Furthermore, if the tsar failed to react, his imposing position in Europe might crumble, for he had a host of enemies. St. Petersburg felt that the moment was propitious for a riposte, for it still counted on Austria and Prussia. England and France were at odds and Nicholas was convinced that they could never be friends. Hence, feeling that he could rely on British neutrality, the tsar began the Seymour conversations, which made him sure that his assumption was correct. With France isolated and in some financial trouble, he hoped for success.

The Russian plan was to restore its strong position by sending an ambassador extraordinary to Constantinople, who by virtue of the monarch's special trust and his messages for the sultan would induce the latter to meet his demands. In a report to Nicholas on December 13 (O.S.), 1852, Nesselrode stated that the envoy should make the sultan and his ministers see the error of their ways and, if need be, promise them support against threats from France.[1]

1. Zaionchkovskii, *Pril.,* I, 351–54.

The emperor named as his envoy Prince Alexander S. Menshikov, although Nesselrode preferred Count Alexis F. Orlov, another aide, who was an excellent diplomat and was more moderate than Menshikov.[2] The envoy was a general of cavalry, who had done well in the Turkish war of 1828, until he was wounded by a cannonball. He had had some diplomatic experience, and then became governor general of Finland and minister of the navy. He had great wealth and was a dilettante. Peter von Meyendorff, a veteran Russian diplomat, wrote of him: "There is the wittiest man in Russia, a negative attitude, a mistrustful character, and a talent for clever sayings. It is a matter of the country escaping a war, even at the risk of losing popularity by it, of temporarily displeasing the Emperor." Menshikov failed in his mission to Constantinople, causing Meyendorff to exclaim: "How badly are sovereigns served!" [3] It is by no means certain that Orlov could have avoided the war, but his common sense, tact, and charm might have enabled him to do so.

Menshikov was to proceed to Constantinople early in January 1853, but illness detained him until the end of the month. In the meantime the Ministry of Foreign Affairs, with the personal help of the emperor, prepared a series of reports, position papers, memoranda, and instructions setting forth the purpose, tactics, and strategy of the mission. A report of Nesselrode to the tsar, apparently of mid-January, stated that Menshikov was to receive proper credentials, a letter from the emperor to the sultan, and instructions specifying the Russian grievances in the religious question and "the reparations that Russia has the right to demand." [4]

The envoy's first move was to be a categorical demand that the Porte publish the firman and the Hatti Sherif which had been given to the Russians and that these should be properly registered at Jerusalem. Then he could entertain proposals in the name of the sultan to bring into harmony the literal execution of the firman with the granting of a key to the Church of the Nativity to the Latins. At this time, the envoy should ask the Porte to publish a second firman stating that the granting of the key did not give the Latins any right of possession or priority at the high altar of the church, and that the previous rights of the Greeks to hold services there and to have a

2. Martens, *Recueil des traités,* XII, 310.
3. Hoetzsch, III, 15–16.
4. Zaionchkovskii, I, 369–70.

Greek churchman guard the entrance should be maintained. Further, the ambassador should ask that the repair of the cupola of the Church of the Holy Sepulcher should be immediately begun, without Catholic participation. And if it came to light that the Porte had made additional concessions to the Latins at the expense of the Greeks, the envoy should take steps to have them cancelled.[5]

After a settlement had been reached on these points, the ambassador should not be satisfied with the publication of the necessary documents, but should insist that the whole arrangement agreed to should be solemnized by a separate document, either published or secret, with the title of convention or *sened*.[6] Furthermore, if the sultan, in making the settlement, failed to remove the ministers who had led him into the errors mentioned, Menshikov should refuse to have dealings with Fuad effendi.[7]

Finally, if the reparations required of the Porte should bring upon it the hostility of France, the ambassador should be empowered to conclude a defensive alliance with the Ottoman government, to apply solely to this contingency.[8]

As opening gun in the campaign, Nicholas I wrote a letter "as a friend and real ally" to the sultan, to be delivered by Prince Menshikov, who was to express to him "the deep feeling of pain and surprise" caused by the sultan's actions in regard to the Holy Places. The tsar expressed the belief that these moves, which had violated promises made to him and wounded him as a friend, were the result of advice by "inexperienced or malevolent ministers" who had given the sultan a false view of the situation and "also dissimulated to You the consequences of the revocation or the modification of the firman adorned with Your Hatti Sherif. . . ." While the tsar did not ask the sultan to violate a treaty obligatory for Turkey, he strongly urged on him "the maintenance of rights consecrated by centuries, recognized by all Your illustrious predecessors and confirmed by You Yourself, in favor of the Orthodox Church, whose dogmas are professed by the Christian populations subject to You and by the great majority of my subjects." To this request he added that if the sultan's concessions to his Orthodox subjects should lead to "some serious complication

5. Ibid., p. 370.
6. Ibid.
7. Ibid.
8. Ibid.

or danger," the already existing alliance between them would be further tightened, thereby nullifying "claims and pretensions incompatible with the independence of Your government and the internal tranquility of your Empire." [9] Thus the tsar intimated that if the sultan did not mend his ways, there would be grave consequences. If, however, the monarch fulfilled his duty to Russia, Nicholas promised him firm backing against France.

Menshikov's illness hampered the Russian plan. In the meantime, Austria sent Count Christian Leiningen (Linanges), a soldier, to protest sternly to the Porte against Omer pasha's intention to crush the Montenegrins with bloodshed. As the Austrians massed troops on the Turkish border, with Russia also promising support,[10] the Turks had to give in to Leiningen's demands. Thus the tsar's hopes for simultaneous demarches by Russia and Austria were disappointed.

Finally, on January 28 (O.S.), Nesselrode sent instructions to Menshikov stating the background of the case and advising him how to act. His first step should be a stiff demand to the vizir (prime minister of the sultan) that the firman issued to the Greeks in February 1852 and the pledges to Nicholas I must be properly promulgated and fully carried out. Menshikov should declare that Russia wanted no new rights and concessions, but the rights and privileges that Russia had enjoyed for centuries, which the previous sultans had known and confirmed and which the reigning monarch had promised he would ensure to the Orthodox in Palestine. The Turks would probably try to excuse their conduct by calling attention to French threats of dangerous hostilities, which they would say left them little choice. To this Menshikov should reply that Russia now was clearly entitled to have the Turks correct their grave mistakes, give reparation for them, and furnish guarantees against similar wrongdoing in the future. First of all, the minister most to blame for the crisis, through mistaken or willfully wrong reports, should be removed. Second, the Porte should issue a new firman delimiting the rights given to the Latins in the Church of the Nativity and making it clear and definite that they had no right to possess the church or to exclude the Greeks from their right to the high altar or priority in saying prayers. Moreover, a Greek cleric named by the Orthodox Patriarch of Jerusalem should guard the main door and further, the repairs to the main cupola of

9. Ibid., I, 386–87; text also is in HHSA, X, 38.
10. P. Meyendorff to A. Meyendorff, Feb. 1/13, 1853, in Hoetzsch, III, 10–11.

the Church of the Holy Sepulcher must be immediately undertaken, without Catholic participation.[11]

It would not be enough, however, to obtain correction of the mistakes, because the Ottoman government had gone back on its solemn and pledged word. Hence Russia could not be satisfied with a new set of promises but must insist that these measures collectively should be converted into a separate solemn document [acte], public or secret, "to be called a convention or sened, having the force and value of a treaty."

Nesselrode added that in bygone days it would have been easy to obtain redress for grievances by force of arms, but now Turkey was an enemy "more embarrassing than dangerous," for the collapse of the Ottoman empire "would become inevitable at the first serious shock that our arms would give it." The emperor did not want to accelerate this event, "and if it must one day occur," it would be desirable that it should not embroil the Orthodox Church in the "complications and political conflicts that this . . . will produce in the Orient." [12]

It was possible, however, that the Turks would object to the Russian demands, "so moderate and so just," which would be either badly received or evaded. In this case, if the Turks, through ignorance or their fear of France, should even risk a rupture with Russia, it would be useless to prolong the negotiations. At this point Menshikov should demand of the vizir a solemn audience with the sultan to deliver a communication of the highest importance. Here the prince would present the documents stating the Russian grievances and the efforts made to secure redress, including the emperor's letter to the sultan. He would then declare that inasmuch as the Porte had not provided the satisfaction and the guarantees demanded, "The Imperial Court cannot, without impairing its dignity and exposing itself to new offenses, continue to have a mission at Constantinople and maintain . . . its political relations with the Ottoman government." Hence, as instructed, he would, with deep regret, leave Constantinople and after three days should leave for Russia with all his embassy personnel.[13]

If Menshikov should be questioned about the reports of Russia's military preparations, he should confirm them, saying that they were

11. Zaionchkovskii, I, 371–73.
12. Ibid., pp. 373–74.
13. Ibid., pp. 374–75.

precautions taken because of the attitude of the Porte toward Russia and of the Porte's massing of men and munitions in Rumelia.[14]

On the other hand, if the sultan seemed worried by French threats and demands, as well as by his duty toward Russia, with which he sincerely desired a rapprochement, the envoy might offer a treaty of alliance. This would be a secret and conditional treaty, for a limited term and only in case France should propose a protectorate over Jerusalem, which the Porte would have to refuse. If the treaty should lead to hostile acts by France against Turkey, a condition for the alliance would be established. Since the alliance would impose sacrifices on Russia and none on Turkey, Russia would agree to accept as an equivalent the separate convention on the Holy Places.[15]

A further secret message from Nesselrode described the convention, which should obtain from the Ottoman government "more explicit and more detailed engagements" than Russia's earlier agreements, especially that of Küchuk-Kainardji. It would consist of seven articles and a separate, secret document. The prince should note that all its propositions were founded on firmans issued by the Porte, established usages, and privileges that the church and the high clergy had at all times enjoyed in Turkey, and that Russia was asking nothing that could trouble or anger "other Christian communities or their protectors." Indeed, Nesselrode insisted that the latter had by no means been considerate of the Orthodox populations of the Orient and had sought sooner or later to make the Catholic religion the dominant one in Turkey, "if not in the number of its adherents, at least in the protection and the confidence that the Ottoman Government showed" to its supporters. He added that the Turkish ministers had readily furthered this ambition, becoming "blind instruments of this propaganda, more political than religious." The chancellor, however, hoped that Menshikov could induce the sultan to follow the example of his ancestors in respecting "the religious convictions of his own subjects." If that proved possible, he might be able to induce the sultan to accept the convention as drafted, except for minor changes. But in any case, it was very important to secure the execution of the firman concerning the Holy Places.[16]

Here the chancellor surveyed the international scene. France was

14. Ibid., p. 376.
15. Ibid., pp. 376–77. (Secret.)
16. Ibid., pp. 377–78.

Russia's opponent, with which it had dealt calmly, politely, peacefully, but also firmly. By standing fast on the salutation question, Nicholas I had lessened the prestige of Napoleon III and dimmed the luster of his glory. Menshikov should be calm, courteous, and friendly to the French envoy, showing neither desire for war nor fear of it. Nesselrode asserted that Napoleon was seeking prestige in the Levant because he was blocked on the Rhine and in Belgium. His highhandedness in dealing with the Turks, thereby risking the collapse of their empire, showed that he was ruthless and would not be considerate of Russia. Of late, however, he had offered to settle their differences, and the recall of Lavalette was a good sign.[17]

Russia's relations with England seemed good, with Aberdeen disposed to be friendly. While Britain had given in on the recognition of Napoleon, it disliked him and his political system and feared that he might upset the status quo. It was not interested in the religious question in the East, but it would dislike having France cause trouble there. Hence Russia had been careful to explain to Britain its grievances against Turkey and France and the purpose of the Menshikov mission and the accompanying military gestures. The Russian cabinet had reassured England that it, too, wanted to preserve the Ottoman empire and asked it to deal strongly with the French to convince them that they could not count on England in a war in the East. Aberdeen had already tried to get the Tuileries to follow a more sober policy, and presumably Colonel Rose would receive corresponding instructions.[18]

Finally, Austria and Prussia had common views with Russia regarding the East. While Catholic Austria could not support the Orthodox in Turkey, it would not want France to dominate the Catholics of the Levant, for French policy was far more political than religious. Russia had given Austria the same explanations that it gave to England, and Austria acted spontaneously to restrain the French. It realized fully what the French were seeking and also the harm that could come to Turkey if the Porte, out of fear, sided with France. Vienna, realizing that France wanted to weaken the Russian-Austrian bonds, refused to connive. It had promised to warn France and to oppose the strong pressure on the Turkish ministers, for it also had its grievances against Turkey. Like Russia, it was greatly concerned about

17. Ibid., pp. 378–79.
18. Ibid., pp. 380–81.

Montenegro and had sent the special Leiningen mission with a personal letter of Emperor Franz Joseph to the sultan, and also made troop movements to the Turkish frontier. All this, Nesselrode stated, showed "a conformity of views and interests in the Orient between us and the cabinet of Vienna," so that Menshikov would probably find close support from the Austrian ambassador at Constantinople.[19]

The Montenegrin crisis, while itself of slight significance, had an important effect on Nicholas I. Beginning with sporadic border conflicts in 1852, it had become more serious when the mountaineers stormed a small Turkish fort and killed its garrison. The Turks then massed about sixty thousand men under Omer pasha to crush Montenegro. Since the conflict threatened to spread to Bosnia and Croatia, Austria had felt forced to intervene to save the Montenegrins. Russia, which had long protected them, at first could do little but exert diplomatic pressure on the Turks.[20] The Austrians, learning of large Turkish troop movements and ambitious plans, had to put large forces in motion. Early in January 1853 the Leiningen mission went to Constantinople to demand that the Turks halt their campaign.[21] M. Ozerov, Russian chargé d'affaires at Constantinople, had supported the Austrian position, and the Russian cabinet sent word to Vienna encouraging it to take positive action. Nesselrode carefully explained that the massing of Russian troops on the Turkish frontier was to put pressure on the Turks, but not for conquest.[22] This Russian aid greatly pleased the Austrians, since the Porte, perhaps with British and French diplomatic backing, had refused the desired concessions.[23] Finally, after the Turks had disregarded his ultimatum, Leiningen had declared that his mission was ended and boarded an Austrian steamer, with the Austrian legation preparing to follow. At this point the Western diplomats urged the Turks to give in. Leiningen arrived at Trieste a few days later, bringing word that the Turks had satisfied all his demands and had ceased their attacks on Montenegro. Felix Fonton, Russian chargé d'affaires at Vienna, reported that Emperor Franz Joseph was very grateful to the Russian emperor for his aid in this

19. Ibid., pp. 381–82.

20. Lebzeltern to Buol, St. Petersburg, Jan. 12/24, 1853, HHSA, X, 36; Fonton to Nesselrode, Vienna, Jan. 16/28, 1853, Arkhiv Vneshnei Politiki, fond Kantseliarii, Moscow (hereafter cited AVP, f. Kants), Delo no. 143.

21. Fonton to Nesselrode, Feb. 10/22, 1853, AVP, f. Kants., D. no. 143.

22. Fonton to Nesselrode, Jan. 16/28, ibid.

23. Fonton to Nesselrode, Feb. 10/22, ibid.

matter.[24] Russia also had cooperated with Vienna by sending its agent
Colonel Kovalevskii to warn Omer pasha against severity toward the
Montenegrins and to urge the latter to be prudent and moderate and
not to take severe reprisals against the Turks.[25]

While the two eastern empires were thus cooperating in the Montenegrin crisis, the French government was expressing concern over
the Leiningen mission and the Austrian troop movements to the Bos-
nian frontier. Drouyn de Lhuys, on hearing of the Austrian ultimatum,
stated to Hübner, the Austrian envoy, that he had been "strongly
and painfully impressed" by Vienna's moves, which contradicted its
peaceful professions. While it was permissible to make demands, the
six-day term of the ultimatum was too brusque, and the massing of
troops and artillery suggested hostile intentions toward Turkey, especially as the Porte had declared its willingness to parley.[26]

The French protest was in vain, however, for the Turks had ceded
to the Austrian demands, and Austro-Russian unity seemed firm.
When Fonton showed Count Buol, Austrian foreign minister, Russian
despatches setting forth Russia's intended support, Buol was much
pleased and stated that it would be excellent if the Porte could know
about the "complete solidarity between the two Imperial courts," holding that this information would influence future Turkish conduct. Fonton naturally suggested that Austria, if need be, could display the
same solidarity regarding the issue of the Holy Places in Palestine.
Buol at once gave him "the most positive repeated assurances, and
most satisfying ones." [27] A few days later Fonton reported that Buol
had said more than once that the chief result of the crisis was precisely
that it "brought out clearly the identity of views and the political
solidarity of the two Imperial Cabinets" in the Orient.[28] These developments help to explain why Nicholas I was so confident of Austrian
cooperation with Russia. In addition, Leiningen's success in threatening the Porte made the tsar hope that similar tactics by Menshikov
would achieve the same result.

Because of these circumstances, then, Nicholas I and his cabinet
expected that Menshikov's mission would succeed. Menshikov arrived

24. Fonton to Nesselrode, Feb. 15/27, ibid.
25. Nesselrode to Kovalevskii, Jan. 16/28, 1853, ibid.
26. Hübner to Buol, Feb. 23, 1853, HHSA, IX, 42.
27. Fonton to Nesselrode, Feb. 18/Mar. 2, 1853, AVP, f. Kants., D. no. 145.
28. Fonton to Nesselrode, Feb. 23/Mar. 7, 1853, ibid.

on February 23, on a steam yacht, accompanied by a glittering suite, including Vice Admiral V. K. Kornilov of the Black Sea fleet, an adjutant of the tsar. A large and excited crowd of Greeks had gathered to watch Menshikov go to the Sublime Porte. He first stopped at the offices of the grand vizir where, after the usual politenesses had been exchanged, he announced that he could not discuss the subject of his mission with Fuad effendi, the foreign minister, in view of his "bad faith and duplicity," which he had shown in his dealings with the Russian legation. As a result, Menshikov felt obliged to ask for the nomination of a dignitary who enjoyed trust.[29]

On leaving the vizir's suite Menshikov went past the offices of Fuad, who was waiting to receive him. The prince passed calmly by, however, pretending that he did not see the minister. The slight was obvious and cutting, and rumor swept through the Porte and into the city. Fuad resigned almost immediately. The French and British chargés at once urged him to stay on in his post, insisting that Menshikov's action was an unprecedented "assault on the dignity of the Porte." Colonel Rose was extremely agitated, and feverish gatherings of Fuad's friends met. The minister of war's utterances were very violent and there was much hostility toward Russia.

Shortly thereafter the sultan named Rifaat pasha as minister of foreign affairs, and Menshikov at once paid him the official call that he had refused to Fuad. The prince, who knew little about Rifaat, stated that he felt the latter "envisages the interests of his country in their true light." [30]

Menshikov next sought an audience with the sultan, whose ministers tried to delay it, fearing that the envoy might display hostility. But since he had treated Rifaat correctly, the audience took place on February 24. At the ceremonial reception Menshikov, when presenting his credentials, expressed to the sultan the sentiments of friendship that the emperor held for the stability and prosperity of the Ottoman empire. At the private audience that followed, with the foreign minister and two dragomans present, the ambassador delivered the emperor's letter to the sultan, who was much upset. The prince sought to ease

29. Menshikov to Nesselrode, Feb. 25/Mar. 9, 1853, HHSA, X, 38.

30. Ibid.; see also circular despatch of Drouyn de Lhuys, *ca.* Mar. 1853, Ministère des Affaires étrangères, Archives diplomatiques Françaises, Correspondence Politique, Russie, Paris (hereafter cited ADF, Russie), vol. 208, pp. 62–86. Drouyn complained of the threats made by Menshikov and insisted that the Franco-Turkish treaties were superior to the firmans and other Turkish engagements to the Russian court.

the situation by saying that, while the tsar complained of the sultan, he did so as a friend who was interested in the welfare of Turkey and the independence of its empire. He added that, while some ill-intentioned ministers had tried to defame the tsar, he wished to see Turkey prosper and would even be pleased to see its defenses grow stronger. The sultan, still perturbed, mumbled some broken phrases about misunderstandings, which he had not wanted.[31]

Colonel Rose, the British chargé, reported the incidents in quite a different light, stressing the elaborate efforts to make the embassy imposing and then the calculated effrontery in refusing to see Fuad, although the credentials had been sent to him the day before. The snub had happened before a large crowd, largely Greeks, and a guard of honor, and in spite of the efforts of the protocol officer to lead the prince to Fuad's rooms, whose door was already open to receive him. Rose and Count Vincent Benedetti, the French chargé, saw the incident and decided that Menshikov wanted to show by a dramatic demarche that a minister hostile to Russia "would be humiliated and punished even in the midst of the Sultan's Court," without advance notice to His Majesty. Thus he could get the cleverest man out of the ministry, humiliate him, and replace him with one favorable to his views. "If this manoeuvre had succeeded," Rose commented, "a second Treaty like that of Unkiar-Skelessi, or something worse, would probably have been the result." [32]

Rose believed that he should act. After vainly seeking from the Russian embassy an explanation of Menshikov's conduct, he was pleased to say that the next day Menshikov sent his first interpreter to assure the grand vizir that he had no wish to offend the sultan. Rose decided that the treatment of Fuad, the disaffection that Menshikov's actions had aroused among the hitherto passive Greeks, and the massing of Russian troops along the Turkish frontier "had greatly discouraged the Grand Vizir, his ministry, and the Turkish party in general." The vizir held that the Russian government intended to win some important right from Turkey that would destroy its independence "and asked me to request the British Admiral to bring his squadron to Vourla Bay [near Smyrna] from Malta." Colonel Rose agreed because he was convinced that if the sultan were not given support

31. Menshikov to Nesselrode, Feb. 25/Mar. 9, 1853, HHSA, X, 38.
32. Rose to Russell, Mar. 7, 1853, EP, I, 86–87; Drouyn de Lhuys, circular, *ca.* March, 1853, ADF, Russie, vol. 208, pp. 83–89.

at this moment, he would form a pro-Russian ministry. "I informed his Highness," he said, "that I would tell his Lordship that I felt convinced that the safety of Turkey required the presence of the British squadron in those waters. Benedetti said the same as regards the French squadron." Since Admiral Dundas had planned to leave Malta on March 20 to call at Corfu, Athens, and Smyrna, Rose held that he was merely asking him to leave one week earlier and to go to Vourla first, instead of to Corfu.[33]

The Earl of Clarendon, who had replaced Lord Russell at the Foreign Office, thought differently. After acknowledging Rose's despatches about the Menshikov mission he briefly, almost curtly, rejected the call for the fleet. The government believed, he said, that the situation did not "render it necessary for you to request that the British fleet should come to Vourla, and they have entirely approved the conduct of Admiral Dundas in not complying with your request and not leaving Malta without specific instructions from Her Majesty's Government. Admiral Dundas has been ordered to remain at Malta." [34]

Benedetti's request for the French fleet was honored by his government, for Lord Cowley telegraphed from Paris on March 19 that it would go to Salamis, because of the attitude of Russia. After a discussion with Drouyn de Lhuys, Cowley said that Russia was using the dispute about the Holy Places as a pretext for attacking Turkey. The fleet would be ready for anything.[35] In his memoirs the Duc de Persigny declared that in the council that discussed whether to send the fleet everyone except himself advised against the action. Persigny, however, strongly urged sending it since it would encourage the English bourgeoisie, in spite of Aberdeen, to give ardent support against the Russians. Napoleon agreed with him and halted the debate. Drouyn de Lhuys advised that they should consult England; but Persigny was opposed, saying that Aberdeen would refuse to cooperate. The dispatch of the fleet would appeal to the English people over the heads of the government, so that the public would force the hands of the men in power.[36]

Clarendon was annoyed by the French move. On March 23, 1853,

33. Rose to Russell, Mar. 7, 1853, EP, I, 87–88.
34. Clarendon to Rose, Mar. 23, 1853, ibid., p. 94.
35. Puryear, *England, Russia, and the Straits,* p. 238.
36. Jean Gilbert Victor Fialin, Duc de Persigny, *Mémoires du Duc de Persigny* (Paris, 1896), pp. 226–34.

he sent a despatch to Seymour at St. Petersburg saying that the government did not think that Rose was justified in calling for the fleet and it fully approved the decision of Admiral Dundas not to go. While a spate of alarming reports from Constantinople about threatening Russian moves had caused concern in both France and England, the British government was not perturbed, "for on more than one occasion [it has] received the personal assurances of the Emperor of Russia that he planned to uphold the Turkish Empire," and if he changed his mind, "this would be made known to Her Majesty's Government." No such word having been received, it felt no concern for Turkey. Clarendon had discussed with Brunnow the alarming rumors of Russian military movements and great naval preparations at Sevastopol, as well as alleged dangerous Russian demands to the Porte. On all those matters Brunnow had given "satisfying and conclusive" assurances that confirmed the judgment of the British. Since the French government had not received information from Russia, they were nervous and had acted hastily. In fact, Clarendon wrote that France's interest and commitment in the matter of the Holy Places "are the only grounds for now apprehending embarrassment in the East." He hoped that Nicholas would order Menshikov to be moderate toward the French so that the Latins would not be subjected to conditions "hurtful to the honour or interests of France." [37]

Cowley, probably on his cabinet's orders, asked the French cabinet why it had sent the fleet. It replied that it was merely a matter of precaution, based largely on Rose's call for the fleet from Malta. Since the French government did not know what Menshikov's demands were, its action was premature. Cowley now urged the emperor to pause until he had full knowledge of the situation. But the next day Drouyn said it was too late to change course. Once an order was published in the *Moniteur officiel* it was impossible to recall it. Cowley then sought to make the fleet movement less threatening by having it stop at Naples and other ports. Drouyn agreed to speak to the emperor about this, while insisting that the sailing had no hostile purpose.[38]

Clarendon continued to assert that sending the fleet had been a mistake. On March 29 he wrote to Cowley that on the 25th Count Walewski, French ambassador at London, announced that the fleet

37. Clarendon to Seymour, Mar. 23, 1853, EP, I, 94–95.
38. Cowley to Clarendon, Mar. 24, 1853, ibid., pp. 95–96.

would go to Salamis and that the French cabinet had received satisfactory communications about the instructions of Prince Menshikov. By stopping at Salamis the fleet would not menace the Russians but would merely serve as a precautionary measure. With the situation in the Orient serious, at Toulon the fleet would be too far away, while Salamis, like Malta, was nearer. Walewski hoped that if need arose, the two squadrons could act together.

To this information Clarendon replied that he still felt that the fleet had sailed too hastily and without sufficient reason. While he trusted Paris and London to act together when they had the same interests, this had not been the case here, for "the fleet had been ordered to sail without consultation or communication" with London, although the French were about to receive their despatches from Constantinople and they knew that Dundas would not leave Malta. Moreover, in spite of Cowley's effort, the French would not delay their fleet nor change its destination. Clarendon added that England had been entirely sincere in dealing with France and had tried to get an amicable settlement in the East. It had stated the reasons why it trusted the Russian emperor and Clarendon had informed Walewski of Brunnow's assurances, which General Barthelmy Castelbajac, French ambassador at St. Petersburg, had fully confirmed. The French knew that England had always supported the integrity of the Turkish empire. Clarendon made these points, he said, not as a rebuke to France, but to make clear the British position.[39]

Again Russia was pleased with the British. Late in March Nesselrode wrote Brunnow that he was gratified that they had not sent their fleet and that their trust in the tsar remained firm. Brunnow should tell the British ministers that "the intentions of the Emperor are still the same" and that all the "idle rumors" about the aims of the Menshikov mission—the occupation of the Principalities, territorial expansion in Asia Minor, a Russian claim to nominate the Patriarch of Constantinople, and threats by Menshikov to the Porte—were unfounded; that, in brief, the prince's mission at no time had any objective "but that communicated to the British government." Russia wanted a "friendly understanding" with France, but the French would have to be reasonable, and the English government should once more urge the French to be moderate.

39. Clarendon to Cowley, Mar. 28, 1853, ibid., p. 98.

The chancellor told Brunnow to thank Aberdeen and Clarendon especially in the emperor's name for guiding the British cabinet along a proper course. By refusing to follow the French, England "has performed an act of wise policy," he said. Not to have done so would have been ruinous for the peace of Europe, for a common front against Russia would have encouraged French rashness and upset all Europe. If the two fleets had appeared in the Aegean together in "a demonstration of a threatening nature," the emperor could not have made concessions in the face of threats.

With France acting alone, the situation was inconvenient but not serious. "The Emperor accordingly attaches little importance to it and His Majesty sees no reason for changing . . . his previous views and intentions," as he felt that the attitude of England would be enough to neutralize "the rashness of the Turks." He was especially pleased with Lord Aberdeen and Baron Brunnow.[40]

Seymour sent equally reassuring despatches. On April 5 he cited Nesselrode's pleasure at the refusal to send the Malta fleet and his unconcern at the sailing of the French squadron. Nesselrode even termed Colonel Rose a worthy man who had been misled by false reports. There had been no demand for the removal of Fuad, no ultimatum, no other demands. Seymour replied that England hoped for a speedy settlement of the issue of the Holy Places, without offending French honor. The chancellor said that Russia did not want to deprive France of any rights—neither the key to the Church of the Nativity nor the Silver Star.

Seymour asked why military preparations were continuing, if the cabinet felt peace was not threatened. Nesselrode replied that the emperor was only waiting until a satisfactory settlement was certain before stopping "all warlike preparations." [41]

Two days later Seymour found Nesselrode even more euphoric over the news from Turkey. On comparing the firman of February 9, 1852, given to the Latins, with that of the Greeks, he had found the differences between them so minor that it was amazing that the French had raised a commotion over so trivial a matter. Seymour seized the opportunity to suggest that in that case the count could announce that Russia's military preparations were being cancelled. While Nesselrode did not do so, he stated his conviction "that the negotiations

40. Nesselrode to Brunnow, Mar. 27/Apr. 7, 1853, ibid., pp. 117–18.
41. Seymour to Clarendon, Apr. 7, 1853, ibid., p. 119.

at Constantinople would be brought, and speedily, to a happy conclusion." [42]

Colonel Rose, however, was still concerned over information from British merchants at Odessa and other Russian ports of alarming military preparations indicating that war was very close, even though the Montenegrin crisis was over and Lavalette had been recalled. Since the merchants were halting their business operations, Rose questioned Menshikov about this. The prince tried to pass off the matter lightly, saying that a few soldiers' biscuits had been baked and a few troops embarked. No wagons had been commandeered for the army, however, and the Black Sea warships could carry only a few soldiers. Only one corps had been put on a war footing.

Rose countered that large quantities of biscuits had been made for use *in Turkey;* there were many transport ships, which could carry large numbers of troops; and two divisions had embarked or were ready to embark. He added that reports from the capital stated that two corps were on a war footing. Menshikov, apparently not prepared for these questions, answered: "All I can tell you is that I have the most pacific intentions." [43]

Rose's informants seemed to have gotten wind of the tsar's preparations for a surprise landing in Turkey and naturally were much concerned. By this time, however, the crisis was past and the emperor had shied off from his plans for a coup de main. Lord Stratford de Redcliffe, who had arrived at Constantinople early in April, sent a brief message to London that, while the Turks still seemed alarmed, the Austrian legation, with close contacts with the Russians, was not, as it believed that the Russians were moderate in their attitude and "a friendly solution" was possible. The latest commercial advice from Odessa was said to agree with this view.[44]

The calmer outlook largely resulted from the greater moderation of the French government. In place of the fiery Lavalette, the Tuileries sent the mild and conciliatory M. de la Cour, who sought to compromise the dispute. Although St. Petersburg refused to handle the matter in direct talks with the French and insisted on dealing with the Porte,[45]

42. Ibid., Apr. 7, p. 121.
43. Rose to Clarendon, Apr. 3, 1853, ibid., pp. 122–23.
44. Redcliffe to Clarendon, Apr. 5, 1853, ibid., p. 124.
45. Lebzeltern to Buol, Feb. 26/Mar. 10, 1853, HHSA, X, 36; Buol to Mensdorff, Feb. 23, 1853, ibid., 37.

the negotiations went smoothly. The French cabinet, feeling that it was losing ground, was not happy with the trend. When Cowley had tried to reason with Drouyn and urge moderation, the French suggested a close entente between the two powers (which would have meant sending the British fleet to the Aegean), whereupon Cowley said that Britain stood by the concert of five powers formed in 1841 to maintain the status quo in Turkey. His government had confidence in the word of the Russian emperor. Baron Hübner, who reported the incident, obviously approved.[46] Thus France was isolated and therefore had to adjust its position. Similarly, when La Cour had tried to gain support from Baron von Klezl, the Austrian envoy at Constantinople, the latter replied that Austria, although a Catholic power, would not support the French concerning the repairs to the cupola of the Church of the Holy Sepulcher. As a result, La Cour's language had become milder, and Klezl decided that France, although unhappy about the coming settlement, probably would not reject it but would merely state its reservations.[47]

The moderation of the French was encouraging to the Russian diplomats. Late in March Fonton learned from Buol that Baron François A. Bourqueney, the new French ambassador at Vienna, had frankly said that his government greatly regretted that the issue of the Holy Places had arisen. Contrary to the wishes of his cabinet, Lavalette had pushed things too far, and now Paris wanted to settle the matter amicably, although without dishonor. Bourqueney was embarrassed by the sailing of the French fleet which, he said, had been ordered to go when it appeared that the British fleet would sail. Now the French ships could not return to Toulon without a loss of prestige. Bourqueney's remarks seemed to indicate a moderate, even mild attitude on the part of the French cabinet, which wanted to escape from its isolation.[48] Nesselrode replied that Fonton's despatch agreed with his information. Buol's calm support for the Russian position must have had a marked effect on Redcliffe and Bourqueney when they arrived in Vienna. The chancellor said his news from Paris confirmed Bourqueney's admissions of French regret at its rash involvement in the Orient by Lavalette's actions and by the sending of the fleet. Now Paris wanted to withdraw gracefully. Russia was willing to spare

46. Hübner to Buol, Mar. 28, 1853, ibid., IX, 42.
47. Fonton to Nesselrode, Vienna, Apr. 15/27, 1853, AVP, f. Kants., D. no. 145.
48. Fonton to Nesselrode, Mar. 17/29, 1853, ibid.

French vanity regarding the Holy Places as much as possible and did not want to insist on anything that might offend the honor and the interests of the French government. Russia did not want to take away any of the concessions that the French had obtained from the Turks, but merely to bring them into harmony with the privileges of the Greeks. Russia also wanted some compensation for the Greeks for the wrong done them, and above all to protect against the return of new prejudices.[49] The latter objective—the securing of guarantees against future trouble for the Orthodox of Turkey—later proved to contain the germ of the Crimean War.

There was wide agreement among informed diplomats that Russia did not want war. General Castelbajac, a close personal friend of the tsar's, asserted that Nicholas I, the heir to the throne, and Count Nesselrode all wanted peace, to permit Russia's development and the smoothing out of internal problems. To E. A. Thouvenel at the Quai d'Orsay Castelbajac wrote that the tsar would never permit a strong power to control the gates of the Bosporus and the Baltic, "but he has no desire to gain control of them himself, convinced that possession of Constantinople would result in the dissolution of the Muscovite [sic] (Ottoman?) Empire and would be the signal for a general war. Regard what I say as certain, and believe that above all Russia wants peace. . . ."[50] The general even reported to Paris an incident that he regarded as significant. Early in 1853, as the tension between France and Russia heightened, the Grand Duke Nicholas, the heir to the throne, had expressed pleasure that the war might be near. When word of this remark had reached his ears, his father was so annoyed that he gave the young man a severe lecture and even ordered an official inquiry to determine from what source he had learned of the possibility of war.[51]

His Majesty continued to have a high regard for England, especially after its cabinet refused to permit its fleet to sail. In an unusual gesture he invited Sir Hamilton and Lady Seymour to an intimate dinner, during which the empress proposed a toast to Queen Victoria—a most unusual move. Nicholas I warmly seconded the toast. He then said that, while the British had their special means of influencing the Turks, he did not, and hence had to use force to sway them. He had explained

49. Nesselrode to Fonton, Apr. 1/13, 1853, ibid.
50. Thouvenel, pp. 35–36.
51. ADF, Russie, vol. 208, p. 17.

his intentions frankly to the British and was a loyal man. He did not express hostility to France, however, and as usual went out of his way to be cordial to Castelbajac.[52]

Early in April Lord Redcliffe, after a conference with the vizir and the foreign minister, reported on the situation to Clarendon. The ministers had told him that Prince Menshikov's manner had ranged from angry complaints and intimidation to assurance of supporting the Ottoman empire and establishing cordial relations as in the past. Menshikov called for upholding the status quo on the Holy Places, backed by a written agreement. While he was willing to agree to the privileges given the Latins, he was determined to have the cupola of the Church of the Nativity at Jerusalem [sic] repaired according to the Greek forms. The Turkish ministers said that nothing had been settled yet, but that they were hopeful that an agreement would be reached.[53]

The Turks were troubled, however, by Menshikov's "ulterior views." While Menshikov no longer asked for an offensive-defensive alliance, he was suggesting giving the Greek Patriarch of Constantinople tenure for life, which would increase his independence from the sultan. He also was proposing a clearer definition of the Russian treaty right to protect the Greek and Armenian subjects of the Porte in religious matters, with a formal agreement to confirm it. The ministers, who wanted to avoid a confrontation, asked Redcliffe's advice on how to deal with these problems. Redcliffe suggested first of all that they should try to separate the issue of the Holy Places from the other problems, settling it fairly, in such a way as to satisfy both the French and the Russians. If the prince raised other issues, they should insist on knowing all details of the proposals, their scope, and the reasons for them. If the requests seems to increase Russia's influence over the Orthodox subjects of the sultan in such a way as to weaken his government and authority, they should decline them, taking pains, however, to remove any existing abuses and to carry out more strictly the treaty provision which had led to the Russian remonstrance.[54]

Redcliffe was hopeful that the personal character of Nicholas I, his obligations to the other powers, and his numerous assertions of

---

52. Thouvenel, pp. 218–19.
53. Redcliffe to Clarendon, Apr. 6, 1853, EP, I, 125. The cupola in question was on the Church of the Holy Sepulcher.
54. Ibid., pp. 125–26.

support for the Ottoman empire would ensure that he would not try to achieve his ends "by mere arbitrary force." Both moral and political considerations would restrain him. He could not openly use force and compel the Porte to submit without incurring severe censure and risking highly important interests. If, however, Menshikov tried to force the Turks to accept his demands, they should insist on consulting the powers that had signed the Treaty of 1841.

Redcliffe advised the Turks to satisfy the tsar on matters that were not of grave importance, especially as the Russian attitude now seemed more reasonable than before.[55]

On the following day Redcliffe was officially received by the sultan, who greeted him with great cordiality and expressed a warm desire for good relations with England and to have its "sympathy and support." The ambassador then had a private interview with the monarch, with Rifaat pasha, the foreign minister, also present. Redcliffe expressed pleasure that the issue of the Holy Places would soon be settled. England had urged both Russia and France to be reasonable, and he promised to use his good offices "for conciliation and friendly arrangement." The sultan replied that "he placed the fullest confidence in me."

As for Menshikov's secret demands, Redcliffe expressed "conviction that the Sultan, in making every reasonable concession for the sake of peace and good neighbourhood, would be careful to admit no innovation dangerous to his independence. . . . These questions, I added, if properly managed, would soon in all likelihood pass away, or be amicably settled."[56]

For a time even a settlement about the Holy Places proved elusive, although, according to Mensdorff, Austrian ambassador at St. Petersburg, even Seymour, "to whom Count Nesselrode has communicated the latest instructions to Prince Menshikov, spoke to me yesterday with entire approbation of the conciliatory spirit" of these documents. The emperor remained unyielding in his demands, which he was ready to back with force of arms. All the same, as Mensdorff said repeatedly, "there was no doubt of a peaceful solution of the issues."[57]

On April 11 Redcliffe reported that Menshikov's attitude had softened greatly, for, while he still wanted to strengthen Russia's influence,

55. Ibid.
56. Ibid., pp. 126–27.
57. Mensdorff to Buol, Apr. 9/21, 1853, HHSA, X, 36.

he had dropped the plan for a defensive treaty. He also had no thought
of military action, unless the French fleet should revive it. He still
was determined to carry out his main points regarding the Holy Places.
But Redcliffe was hopeful that the clouds would disperse without a
storm, although he saw anxious moments ahead.[58]

Support for this cautious optimism came from the British consul
at Odessa, who reported that, while the mobilization of the Fifth Corps
was complete, the Fourth, in Galicia and Poland, because of the state
of the roads, would not be able to support the Fifth for at least six
weeks. Also preparations in the rear areas did not seem to be progress-
ing. Hence, while the two divisions at Sevastopol and Odessa, respec-
tively, were trained and ready for landing attacks, the commercial
community, although uneasy, trusted "in the wisdom and moderation
of the Emperor" and believed that peace would be preserved.[59]

The cupola of the Church of the Holy Sepulcher proved to be a
difficult problem, since both the Greeks and the Latins insisted that
they had a right to supervise its repair. Also Menshikov demanded
that the Porte should put the agreement about the Holy Places in
the form of a convention, with the force of a treaty. But finally on
April 22 Redcliffe reported that he had had a talk with Menshikov
and La Cour together and induced them to compromise on the last
points. Both men were reasonable and wished a fair settlement. While
La Cour might reserve his rights, this reservation would be only for
the record.[60] From St. Petersburg Mensdorff reported that the cabinet
was gratified by the latest news: "Prince Menshikov was well pleased
with the attitude of Lord Redcliffe and cannot refuse to recognize
the moderation of . . . M. de Lacour. . . ."[61] Finally, Nesselrode
communicated to Baron Eduard von Lebzeltern, the new Austrian
ambassador, a report from Menshikov that all the differences had
been smoothed out and they "have reached an agreement on the details
of an arrangement on the subject of the Holy Places." The Porte
was drafting a firman, to be approved by the Russian embassy at
Constantinople. "Under these circumstances," the chancellor said,
"one can hope shortly for a definitive accommodation of the matter,

58. Redcliffe to Clarendon, Apr. 11, 1853, EP, I, 134.
59. Yeames to Redcliffe, Odessa, Apr. 11, 1853, ibid., I, 163.
60. Mensdorff to Buol, Apr. 9/21, 1853, HHSA, X, 36.
61. Mensdorff to Buol, Apr. 18/30, ibid.

and it is probable that Prince Menshikov will soon return to St. Petersburg." [62]

Word on the details of the settlement came via Paris. The agreement about the cupola of the Church of the Holy Sepulcher was that it was to be repaired by the sultan, with the two Christian factions effectively barred from interfering, although the Greek Patriarch of Jerusalem had the right to "make observations" about the work. Since only the wooden cupola, which had neither inscriptions nor images, was to be rebuilt, most of the problem was eliminated, for the main part of the building was to remain unchanged. The Greeks and the Latins also agreed about the use of the church: since the Greeks would use it during the morning hours, the Latins received a longer period for their services. Finally, Menshikov agreed to accept an imperial firman, adorned with the sultan's signature, to guarantee the permanence of the settlement, instead of the convention that he had previously demanded. Thus, with good will on both sides, the thorny problem of the Holy Places was settled. [63]

Doubts still remained, however, for Buol felt called on to ask Fonton about Russia's intentions regarding the patriarchate of Constantinople. When he received a vague but reassuring reply, he stated that no one denied the right of the Imperial Russian Government, and even its *duty*, to exercise moral influence over the way in which the Porte governed the rights of the Eastern Church. The Austrian government actually asked for this right for Russia in the interest of the Greek Christians. Moreover, it trusted the disinterested views of the Russian cabinet. Nevertheless, in order to convince the Porte and to strengthen the influence of the two imperial courts, Buol wished to have satisfactory explanations, which he asked Nesselrode to send, so that he could prevent the two maritime powers from seizing on this issue and claiming to protect the Porte against encroachment by its two powerful neighbors. [64]

While it was ominous to have vague issues still arise concerning the Orthodox church, by early May 1853 the atmosphere had improved greatly. France and Russia had resolved their differences "so that the wolf was fed and the sheep were unharmed." The Holy Places

62. Lebzeltern to Buol, Apr. 28/May 10, 1853, ibid.
63. Cowley to Clarendon, Paris, May 8, 1853, EP, I, 161.
64. Fonton to Nesselrode, Vienna, Apr. 24/May 6, 1853, AVP, f. Kants., D. no. 145.

were no longer objects of contention. The talk of the approaching collapse of the Turkish empire had died down and, while Russian forces were massed in the south and the French fleet was still moored at Salamis, neither seemed poised to attack. Russia as before regarded England as a friend and had cordial relations with Austria, while France was no longer so isolated. Apparently no one wanted war, and there was great relief that the threat of it had vanished. Actually, however, the peaceful signs were deceiving, for the French cabinet continued to regard Russia as its opponent, and the English, who did not really trust it, were about to draw closer to France and to look on Russia as a dangerous threat to peace. Likewise Austria, faced with grave dangers on several sides, no longer believed that its safety lay in a firm alliance with Russia, and was slowly sidling into a neutral and an anti-Russian stance.

CHAPTER 6. THE RUSSIAN BREAK WITH TURKEY

While by May 1853 the problem of the Holy Places was settled to the general satisfaction, still the Russians demanded an edict to guarantee that the Porte would not permit anyone to upset the status quo of the Eastern Orthodox church. Russia based this demand on the Treaties of Küchuk-Kainardji and Adrianople. Since France had its Treaty of 1740, Russia felt it needed treaties of equal validity. Moreover, because the Porte, after issuing a solemn firman upholding the Russian demands in favor of the Greek Orthodox, had given in to the French and granted a firman to the Latins supporting their contentions and refused to carry out the pledges to the Greeks, the Russians insisted on a binding agreement.

Until late April the diplomats paid little attention to the Russian requirement. Other demands for a provisional treaty of alliance with Turkey and for life tenure for the Patriarch of Constantinople had already been dropped. But this time Russia was in earnest, and when Prince Menshikov used threatening language there was an angry outcry in England and France, charging that Russia had suddenly introduced a new and dangerous pretension. This view, however, was incorrect, for in December 1852 Colonel Rose had informed London that Ozerov, the Russian chargé d'affaires, "has much prejudiced his position" by a formal declaration that under the Treaty of Küchuk-Kainardji Russia had the right to protect the Orthodox in Turkey. "The Turks had heard," he said, "this assertion of Russian protection of the religious interest of ten or eleven millions of her subjects with unmingled dissatisfaction." Rose thought that the Russian citation of Article VII of the Treaty had no validity.[1]

The Russian cabinet, however, still regarded Küchuk-Kainardji in 1774 as its basis, for Nesselrode's instructions to Menshikov called for a convention more specific and more detailed than the earlier

---

1. Rose to Malmesbury, Dec. 5, 1853, EP, I, 50.

agreements, especially the Treaty of Kainardji. The chancellor stressed that the demands were all based on firmans of the Porte, established usages, and privileges that the church and the clergy had regularly enjoyed in Turkey. Russia was asking nothing that would anger other religious groups.[2]

The Kainardji treaty was obviously important. While it resulted from a Russian triumph, Turkey had been far from prostrate at the time, and France and Austria had strongly opposed a great rise in Russian power. Moreover, the great Pugachev uprising of Cossacks and serfs in 1773–74 indicated that Russia was weak at home, and as Russia needed a speedy peace, it had moderated its demands in order to get the Turks to accept them. Most of the provisions dealt with territories, but there were several articles that dealt with religion.

Article VII was the most important one, for in it the Porte promised at all times "to protect the Christian religion and its churches" and also to permit the ministers of the Russian court to "make representations on all occasions" both in favor of the new church at Constantinople (mentioned in Article XIV) and of those who would serve it. In Article XIV, providing for the return of Bessarabia, Bender, Moldavia, and Wallachia to Turkey, the Porte promised in return not to prevent, in any way or manner, "the completely free profession of the Christian faith, as well as the building of new churches and the repairing of old ones." It would also return lands to monasteries and other persons, which "were most unfairly taken from them," and would recognize and respect "the clergy with the esteem proper to their calling."[3]

The Porte also promised that the *hospodars* (princes) of Moldavia and Wallachia should each have a Christian chargé d'affaires of the Greek religion, who would handle their business and would be well treated by the Porte.[4]

In Article XVII Russia agreed to restore to the Porte all the islands of the Archipelago, while Turkey agreed to observe solemnly the points about an amnesty and to see that the Christian religion would never be persecuted, that the repairing and rebuilding of churches would not be forbidden, and that no servitors of this religion would ever

2. Zaionchkovskii, *Pril.,* I, 376–77.

3. E. I. Druzhinina, *Kiuchuk-Kainardzhskii mir 1774 goda* (*ego podgotovka i zakliuchenie*) (Moscow, 1955), pp. 352–55.

4. Ibid.

5. Gabriel Noradounghian, effendi, *Recueil d'actes internationaux de l'Empire Ottoman* (Paris, 1897–1903), I, 326–28.

be insulted or oppressed.[5]

In other, supplementary agreements in 1770 and 1826 the Porte accepted additional obligations to the Christian religion in European Turkey.[6] Finally, the Treaty of Adrianople, made in 1829, after great Russian victories, declared: "The Principalities of Moldavia and Wallachia . . . will preserve all the privileges and immunities . . . given them by treaties, capitulations, or Hatti sherifs. As a consequence, they will enjoy full exercise of their cults. . . ." [7]

Thus, while the Russian claims to enjoy broad rights to protect the Orthodox church, based on treaty rights with Turkey, were somewhat exaggerated, Nesselrode's position that Russia was claiming accepted rights backed by treaties was not far from the truth. Lord John Russell's admission of this truth has substantial justification.[8]

While Russia thus had the right to make representations about the Orthodox churches, clergy, and believers of European Turkey, who were then estimated to number ten or twelve million, with the Turkish population of the area perhaps three million, the importance of this claim escaped general notice during the contest over the Holy Places of Palestine. Also the crisis over Montenegro and later the Seymour conversations occupied the center of the stage for several months. The excitement over Menshikov's arrival at Constantinople and the sailing of the French fleet to Salamis also diverted attention from the Russian demands.

The Russian cabinet carefully avoided raising the issue. It gave friendly explanations about the Menshikov mission to London and Vienna, but decided that Menshikov's full instructions contained points "of too delicate a nature" to be freely communicated. Above all, at London the idea of a direct Russo-Turkish agreement seemed sure to "arouse strong opposition and to alienate the sympathies of the Ministry." So Nesselrode merely gave the British and Austrian diplomats a verbal summary of the instructions, keeping silent about the convention that Russia wanted to make with the Porte, and simply stated that it sought to obtain *guarantees for the future* and also *a reparation for the past* to preserve "the status quo of the Orthodox Church in the East." He also withheld full information in answering

6. Ibid., II, 168 (Art. V).
7. Ibid., II, 168 (Art. V).
8. Russell to Seymour, Feb. 9, 1853, Zaionchkovskii, *Pril.* I, 362.

the pressing questions of the British and Austrian envoys at St. Petersburg.[9] The French received even less information.

The changeableness of British opinion was evident from December 1852 to May 1853. On the one hand, much of the press was hostile to France, especially as fear of the French navy mounted. On the other hand, the Duke de Persigny related that when he visited England late in 1852 he found that the financial circles of the City of London wanted peace and friendship with France. When he reported this to Napoleon III and the council, he met only amused incredulity. Not long after, a group of British merchants, who met to confer on the dangers of the situation, decided to protest against the Francophobia of *The Times* and to show sympathy for France. They drew up an address to Napoleon III, which was quickly signed by four thousand of the leading business magnates. The Lord Mayor and the chief figures of the City took it to Paris and congratulated the emperor solemnly on having preserved law and order and stressed their good will and sympathy for France and the new regime.[10] Under pressure of this sort the English press and parliamentary opinion began to turn in favor of France.

The British government, under Derby, Malmesbury, Russell, and Clarendon, remained sympathetic with Russia and opposed to France, which had started the trouble over the Holy Places and uttered threats of violent action. Nicholas I, who pledged military aid if France should attack and frankly explained his tactics in the Orient, gained the confidence of Russell and Clarendon, who declined French overtures and stressed their solidarity with Russia. Since Brunnow rejoiced in Lord Aberdeen's warm friendship for Russia, his dislike of Napoleon III, and his scorn for Turkey, the tsar concluded that there was no danger that France and England would unite against him. Sir Hamilton Seymour, to be sure, by March 1853, distrusted and suspected Russia's plans in the East, above all its intentions concerning the fate of Constantinople when Turkey should collapse, and occasionally Brunnow warned that opinion and the press were turning toward France.[11] But Clarendon's warm, loyal trust soothed the tsar and calmed his fears.

9. Jomini, pp. 162–63.
10. Duc de Persigny, *Mémoires,* pp. 159–204, 213–14.
11. Martens, *Recueil des traités,* XII, 310–11.

Menshikov's aggressive conduct at Constantinople produced a flood of sensational rumors regarding the dangerous intentions of Russia, which put increasing pressure on Aberdeen, whom Brunnow termed "Russia's one friend in the Cabinet." [12] In despair the premier told Brunnow that his position was becoming more and more unbearable. While his confidence in the tsar was unshakable, he was hearing all sorts of charges that he had sold out to Russia or had been unduly credulous. Since he knew little about what the Russians really wanted, his morale weakened. Brunnow made a point of bringing this information to the attention of his cabinet, insisting that any other minister would long ago have given in to Palmerston's bellicosity and the force of public opinion.

Brunnow's views on the Menshikov mission were calm and sensible. On March 21/April 3, 1853, he wrote to Nesselrode: "One should not pull the cord too much, or it might well end by twisting the neck of the Sultan, or else it might break in our hands." To avoid this possibility, they should satisfy themselves with a nice little compromise Sened, so that neither side would be hurt. A drastic solution would add nothing to "the reality of Russian influence over the Turks. *Elle est dans les choses, elle n'est pas dans les mots.* Russia is strong, Turkey is weak—this is the preamble of all our treaties. This epitaph is already written on the tomb of the Ottoman Empire." [13]

While Nesselrode and several other Russian diplomats shared Brunnow's views, the emperor and his close advisers were sure that Turkey could not defy Russia. The situation changed suddenly when, after Menshikov's demonstrative challenge to the Porte, Colonel Rose, the British chargé at Constantinople, and Benedetti, his French colleague, urged their respective squadrons to sail to the Aegean. While the British cabinet refused, Napoleon III immediately ordered the French fleet to go. It sailed from Toulon on March 22, in spite of the British refusal. France also escalated a latent quarrel with Belgium over publications hostile to Napoleon and pro-Bourbon French officers in the Belgian army. On the very day that the French ships sailed from Toulon, M. His de Butenval, the bellicose French minister at Brussels, threatened the Belgian Foreign Office with a French invasion if Austria and Russia won victories over the Turks. King Leopold at once sent

12. Ibid., p. 310.
13. Ibid., pp. 311–12.

word to his diplomats abroad asking for protection against the French. Clarendon told him to prepare for anything.[14]

At this point Clarendon told Brunnow that he felt the French demarche at Brussels was "a means of intimidation" to make the British cabinet "more amenable and more accommodating toward France" in order to prevent "the risks to which a foreign complication might expose . . . Belgium." Clarendon's suspicions were strengthened by the fact that both French moves were made on the same day. The British government felt that France was trying to destroy Anglo-Russian unity and to establish Anglo-French unity in its place.[15]

On the next day, March 23, Clarendon sent his despatch to Seymour ending the talks with Russia about the partition of Turkey, as it did not now seem to be in danger of collapse, and complications in the Orient would imperil the existing situation in western Europe.[16] Two days later he told Walewski, French ambassador at London, that the British cabinet was not siding with Russia in its dispute with France.[17] This did not at once mean that Britain was now in the French camp but that it no longer needed its entente with Russia, for with the collapse of Turkey unlikely there was no reason for their alliance, especially as France moderated its threatening language.

Clarendon did not, however, frankly inform St. Petersburg of the change in outlook. Indeed, in his despatch of April 5 to Seymour he was at pains to prove that London had repeatedly sought to restrain the French and to bring the Turks to grant the just demands of Russia. Clarendon emphasized that the instructions to Lord Redcliffe ordered him to support the "superior claims" of Russia and expressed the hope that the envoy might induce the Turks to hear "moderate counsels." [18] Nicholas I, still convinced that the understanding of 1844 was effective and that a Franco-British alliance was out of the question, was determined to obtain what he held was Russia's due. The British people, however, increasingly felt the emperor's expressed desire to maintain the Ottoman empire was a cover for the intention to partition it and to annex Constantinople. Thus their innate suspicion

14. V. J. Puryear, "New Light on the Origins of the Crimean War," p. 232.
15. Ibid., p. 233.
16. Clarendon to Seymour, Mar. 23, 1853, EP, V, 19–20.
17. Puryear, "New Light," p. 233.
18. Clarendon to Seymour, Apr. 5, 1853, EP, V, 22–23.

and distrust of Russia caused them to view the furor over the Holy Places as a Russian pretext for vast schemes of aggrandizement that would be ruinous for the British imperial position.

On March 31, 1854, this matter was debated in the House of Lords, during which the Earl of Derby declared that Nicholas I had never deceived the British concerning his intention of compelling the Turks to recognize his protectorate over the Orthodox of Turkey, as established by treaty. The emperor had frankly stated that he would not permit England to establish itself at Constantinople and that he was willing to promise not to establish himself there as owner, although he might have to occupy it temporarily. Lord John Russell had replied that the British cabinet could make no agreement about the fate of Turkey. He had added, however, that the better the treatment Turkey gave to its subjects, the less would the tsar "find it necessary to apply that exceptional protection that His Imperial Majesty has found so burdensome and inconvenient, though no doubt prescribed by duty and sanctioned by treaty [*sic*]."

Derby added that with such a letter in his hand the emperor, while seeing that England would not at the moment make any engagement about the final fate of Turkey, also had every right to believe that it recognized his right to a protectorate guaranteed him by a treaty. It followed that, having accepted the protectorate, the British "of course extended to him . . . the right of vindicating by force of arms that which is already secured . . . by treaty." The former prime minister also said that he was sure that "the Emperor of Russia is convinced in his own mind that throughout all these negotiations he has been perfectly frank, open, and unreserved with the British Government in regard to his intentions." [19]

Derby's statement was not entirely accurate, for the Russian cabinet had not informed London just what it would demand from the Porte. But Her Majesty's Government had been even less straightforward with the tsar, for in February and March 1853 it had accepted his views about the partition of the Ottoman empire and had given him strong support against the French, only to turn against the idea of partition in late March and to move much closer to the French. But in his despatch of April 5 Clarendon, far from giving definite warning of this reversal, went out of his way to stress efforts in support of

19. Gt. Brit. Parliament. *Hansard's Parliamentary Debates* (3rd ser.), CXXXII (1854), 159.

Russia against France. Certainly, if Nicholas I had understood the importance of the British press and the House of Commons he would have realized that he could no longer count on Britain. Baron Brunnow's despatches warned of the weakening position of Lord Aberdeen, but failed to convince the tsar. Nicholas continued to believe that the opposition was an irresponsible group headed by Palmerston and Urquhart, and Lord Redcliffe at Constantinople, supported by a pack of sensational journalists, while England's stable elements—the queen, Prince Albert, Aberdeen, Derby, and the conservatives—favored cooperation with Russia and opposition to France. This mistaken view led Nicholas I to continue on his perilous course.

Richard Cobden and John Bright of the Anti-Corn Law League of 1846 also opposed France and Turkey and favored cooperation with Russia. They tried hard to transform the Anti-Corn Law League into a Peace Society but found it impossible. Cobden wrote Bright that he was opposed to the aggressive, interfering, threatening foreign policy of the Palmerston school. "But . . . the evil has its roots in the pugnacious, energetic, self-sufficient, foreigner-despising and pitying character of the noble insular creature, John Bull." [20] The jingoistic movement swept all before it, so that Aberdeen, deserted by the other ministers and in despair, could do little but fight a forlorn delaying action.

British suspicion of Russia, bolstered by the belief that it sought to annex Constantinople, centered on the claim to protect the Orthodox church in Turkey and its clergy. Because under the Turks each *millet* or "nation" of non-Moslems had its own head, usually the leading ecclesiastic, the clergy had an importance far beyond its churchly role. The Patriarch of Constantinople was the ruler of the "Greeks" (Slavs and Rumanians as well as Hellenes), over whom he and his Phanariot subordinates had great authority. The Turkish authorities and most British diplomats insisted that if the Russian cabinet had a treaty right to protect the Orthodox church it would thereby gain control over the believers as well as the churches. This was an unprecedented demand, they asserted, and as the ten million or more Orthodox would far outnumber the three million Turks, to give in to it would raise the influence of the tsar above that of the sultan. Hence the sultan's independence was at stake—a matter of crucial importance for all Europe.

20. Martin, p. 48.

The Russians held that they did not seek a new right but merely the reassertion of an old one that was needed to protect the Orthodox from infringements on their accepted status. Far from encouraging them to rise in revolt, the treaty right would calm them by the assurance that they were protected against outrage and hence uprisings were not necessary. Russia asked no political rights and was not in any way infringing on the rights of other cults or interfering with the Porte's relations with other powers.[21] Moreover, the Russian cabinet pointed out that Austria had the right to protect Turkish Catholics who were subjects of the Porte. The Russians also cited evidence that the French protected the Syrian Catholics and the Maronites, although the French claimed that their protection covered merely their subjects in Turkey. In addition Baron Brunnow adduced a protocol of 1830 on Greek affairs signed by the French plenipotentiary at Athens, Count Morency-Laval, stating that for centuries France had been "in a position" to exercise a special patronage in favor of Catholics subject to the sultan. Now His Most Christian Majesty, about to relinquish this right to the new king of Greece, asked that the new regime should give guarantees ensuring the protection that France heretofore had given to the Catholics of the Greek mainland and the islands. Thus France formally declared its right of protecting Catholics who were Turkish subjects, and Britain and Russia approved, apparently feeling that this declaration did not infringe on Greek sovereignty.[22]

But while precedents apparently existed for the Russian claim to protect the status quo of the Orthodox church of Turkey, the Turks and the maritime powers, Britain and France, strongly opposed it, claiming that it would give Russia such influence over the majority of the sultan's subjects that the latter's independence and sovereignty would be gravely impaired. While this argument had some merit, the attitude of the Patriarchate of Constantinople toward Russia made it less convincing. The Greek hierarchs enjoyed great influence and power under the sultan and hence had little desire to change masters, especially as they knew that the tsars had not been gentle to the Russian church. Mikhail Volkov, a Russian diplomat at Constantinople, who spoke Greek freely, reported that the Greek bishops of Constantinople were horrified at the idea of Russian control, saying that it would turn "our Church from a mistress into a slave." They re-

---

21. Menshikov to the Porte, verbal note of Apr. 7/19, 1853, Zaionchkovskii, *Pril.*, I, 300.
22. Brunnow, "Notice," apparently of May 13/25, 1853, HHSA, X, 38.

counted how Peter the Great had "cast down the lawful head of the Russian Church" and replaced him with a Synod and took over the administration of the Church's properties, while "Catherine II stripped the Church of all its property and turned [it] from a rich one into a pauper." Upon reuniting the Uniats (Orthodox who were under the Pope) with Orthodoxy, "your Nicholas I took away from the reunited Church its landed property and set up a modest subsidy for it." Even as late as 1852 this same Nicholas I, so zealous for the good of Orthodoxy, "deprived the Georgian Church of its independence, taking away its estates and setting up its subsidy." He would do the same with the Patriarchal Church of Constantinople. "We are now rich and strong," the bishops said, "Nine million souls in the hands of the Patriarch, his synod, and seventy bishops. You, with the right of protectorate in hand, will deprive us of everything, will wipe out our significance, and will let us go with a pittance." [23]

On the other hand, Russia enjoyed great influence among the Orthodox of Turkey, who realized that whatever freedom they had gained had been won largely by Russian blood. Russian arms had brought autonomy to part of Serbia by 1815, and the erection of the Greek kingdom was a direct result of the Russian victories in 1829. The Moldavians and Wallachians had obtained limited autonomy from the Porte, thanks to Russia, and the Russian protectorate established there had freed them from some of the most burdensome of the Turkish exactions. The Montenegrin freedom from Turkish domination was almost entirely a result of Russian protection. Probably few of the Balkan peoples had illusions about Russian altruism, for St. Petersburg was guided by its own interests and often disregarded the hopes and aspirations of the subjects of the Turks. Russia was highly conservative and did not support the liberal nationalist movements and the reforms that they sought. Nevertheless the Balkan peoples knew that their only real hope of independence lay with Russia. "We and the Russians are fifty million strong," said the Montenegrins. In June 1853 Clarendon wrote of "that influence over the Greek subjects of the Porte that Russia must always exercise." [24]

The Orthodox of Turkey needed protection, for in spite of the famous reforms of Gulhané enacted in 1839, their status remained insecure. They had little protection from extortionate Moslem landowners, cor-

---

23. Volkov, "Chto dovelo Rossiiu," in Zaionchkovskii, *Pril.,* I, 187–88.
24. Clarendon to Seymour, June 8, 1853, EP, I, 233.

rupt officials, from policemen to governors, and from the soldiers and *bashi-bazuks* (Turkish irregulars) who suppressed uprisings with ferocity. The Turkish regime did not provide minimal public safety, and the Russian demands were an attempt to meet the need.

Palmerston and Redcliffe, who were increasingly dominant in London and Constantinople, thought otherwise. They were convinced that the Turks were moving toward real reform—albeit somewhat fitfully—and that their rule was the best method for governing this region. Any attempt to remove Turkish control, they felt, would bring general, bloody war and endanger British rule in India. Probably nobody, except perhaps some of the Turks, wanted war, but there was a sharp conflict of interests. Hence the numerous efforts at a compromise arrangement failed.

As stated earlier, by late March the question of the Holy Places seemed close to a settlement, thanks to the moderation of the French and the Russians and the eagerness of the Turks to end the senseless quarrel. Lord Redcliffe also urged the Turks to stop the dispute about the Holy Places. On April 11 (O.S.) he wrote to Clarendon that the Porte would make concessions on all points except that of Russian protection of the Orthodox Church. He enclosed the text of Menshikov's proposed convention, supplied by the Turks, which was to explain Articles VII, VIII, XIV, and XVI of the Treaty of Küchuk-Kainardji and that of Adrianople, and was to have the force of a treaty.[25]

Article I of this draft convention stated that the Greek religion should always be protected in all churches, and representatives of the Russian government should have the right "to give orders" in the churches in Constantinople and other towns, as well as to the ecclesiastics, and "they shall be well received." Article II stated that the four Patriarchs were to receive full rights of status from the Turks and might perform their functions "without impediment." Article III provided that the Patriarchs were to be named for life and might be removed only for malfeasance in office. The remaining provisions, which dealt with specific rights of the Greek Church, were of less significance.[26]

Redcliffe stated that the Turks would reject the proposals on the right of protection and the Patriarchs. Menshikov, he stated, seemed

---

25. Redcliffe to Clarendon, Apr. 11, 1853, EP, I, 134–36. Since the text of the convention came from the Turks, there may be some inaccuracies in the wording.
26. Ibid., pp. 136–37.

much milder than he had been and showed no inclination to use force, although his determination to gain influence over the Orthodox was unchanged. France and Austria appeared friendly to the British viewpoint, and although the Austrian envoy still leaned toward Russia, he would probably not support the strong Russian demands. On the whole, Redcliffe was optimistic, although he foresaw stormy moments ahead.[27]

Since Redcliffe, while advising the Turks to be conciliatory on nonessentials, strongly urged them not to sign any binding commitment such as a sened, Menshikov met resistance from the Porte. As a result, on March 29/April 9 he wrote to his cabinet that "the fear of pledging themselves by a formal convention is always very strong" and that the vizir had begged him "not to insist on a demand that was impossible for them to satisfy"/(marked N.B. and underlined by the tsar). The vizir offered to send a special letter from the sultan to the emperor, with an embassy to explain his position. Menshikov replied that the Porte must deal with *him*. He planned to try to reach agreement on the Holy Places, with the demand for a guarantee for the future to come later. Foreseeing refusal on this, he would then have to use "my last efforts to obtain a convention. Should I push my insistence as far as a recall of the Legation"? ("Yes," noted the tsar.) When Menshikov asked if an exchange of notes or some other pledge would be acceptable, Nicholas I said that either a treaty or a convention would do.[28]

Finally, the envoy asked whether, if a rupture occurred, he should warn the Porte that "all infractions of the immunities of the cult of the East" would lead to demands for reparations by forceful means? *"Yes,"* wrote the tsar, *"I shall . . . add here that without a crisis of constraint it would be difficult for the Imperial Legation to regain the degree of influence that it had exercised earlier over the Divan."* Thus the emperor authorized breaking off relations with the Porte in order to compel a binding agreement and seemed willing to use force.[29]

By order of the emperor Nesselrode now sent a dispatch approving Menshikov's actions. He passed over the question of the Holy Places as nearly settled, stressing the convention "that Russia asks of the Ottoman Government with the sole purpose of better defining and

27. Ibid., p. 134.
28. Menshikov to Nesselrode, Mar. 29/Apr. 10, 1853, Zaionchkovskii, *Pril.,* I, 400–401.
29. Ibid., p. 401.

guaranteeing the right that our former treaties give us, to protect the Church and the Orthodox religion in the East." Nesselrode added that the emperor's demands of Turkey had no political motivation, but derived from his duty as sovereign to defend the church to which he and his people belonged. Hence he was not seeking a new protectorate over the Christian population of Turkey, but a formal pledge of the Porte to respect the immunities that the Turkish Christians had enjoyed at all times under the Turks and which the Turks were now violating.

It made no difference whether this engagement took the form of a convention, an explanatory decree as Rifaat pasha proposed, or even an obligatory note. "But what His Majesty does not wish and cannot tolerate." Nesselrode said, "after all his proofs of . . . good friendship . . . is that his intentions should always be put in doubt and that his representative be put off, now by promises . . . and by negotiations uselessly prolonged and . . . without any satisfactory result." [30]

Although he had not yet received this instruction, on April 7/19 Menshikov presented the Porte with a verbal note complaining strongly of its lack of faith and demanding a solemn decree within a definite time limit. The first two parts of the proposal dealt with the Holy Places: the Church of the Nativity at Bethlehem; the Grotto of Gethsemane, and the cupola of the Church of the Holy Sepulcher. Since they had already been agreed on, they caused no difficulty. The third section, however, called for a sened or convention to provide a strict guarantee of the status quo "of the privileges of the Catholic Greco-Russian rite of the Eastern Church and of [its] sanctuaries. . . ." Menshikov added: ". . . Russia does not ask political concessions of the Porte. Its desire is to calm the religious consciences by the certainty of maintaining what is and always has been practiced up to now." Because of the hostile tendencies manifested toward Russia it was seeking "in the interest of the religious immunities of the Orthodox cult an explicit and positive Act of guarantees; an Act that would in no way affect either the other cults or the relations of the Porte with other powers." [31]

Lord Redcliffe, who had received a copy of Menshikov's secret demands, declared that only the third point remained unsettled. The Turks were greatly worried about the Russian demand for the right

---

30. Nesselrode to Menshikov, Apr. 11/23, 1853, ibid., I, 404–05.
31. Menshikov to Rifaat, Apr. 7/19, 1853, ibid., I, 402–03; also EP, I, 158–59.

to intervene for the Greek churches and their clergy, and also by the proposal that the patriarchs be appointed for life. These claims were ostensibly based on the Treaty of Kainardji, although their scope was much broader than the treaty itself. Redcliffe felt that St. Petersburg wanted much greater influence over the Orthodox of the Ottoman empire and wished to put the onus on the Porte when it tried to evade it. There was also perhaps the motive of simplifying the relations between the empires, and to provide more effective protection for the Christians. The Turks, greatly alarmed, feared that this would result in the partition of their empire.[32]

Although Menshikov had done well in settling the question of the Holy Places, he now faced stiff resistance from the Turks, supported by Redcliffe. As his earlier communication had brought no real result, the prince continued to press them. He reported to his cabinet that the Turks still scorned the Russians because they had no effective treaty like that of the French. When, however, he sought to obtain an act with the force of a treaty, "its foreign councillors, Lord Stratford at their head, encourage the Ottoman Government to this resistance. . . ." Redcliffe felt that the act was "dangerous for the security and the independence of Turkey," for "by giving Russia a new title to the sympathy of the Eastern Christians it would reenforce its influence at the expense of the sovereign rights of the Sultan." Europe, which constantly sought to reduce Russian influence in Turkey, certainly would not permit this. Menshikov had made special efforts to win the friendship of Redcliffe, who reciprocated but still was implacably opposed to a Russian convention with Turkey. The prince stated that he had learned that the Englishman had given the Turks a draft note to substitute for the one proposed by Menshikov, which should satisfy the Russians.[33]

Although Menshikov's note of April 7/19 had asked for a speedy reply, it was only on April 23/May 5 that it came, in the form of a note from the Ministry of Foreign Affairs, along with two decrees from the sultan on the Holy Places and the repair of the cupola of the Church of the Holy Sepulcher. Menshikov at once replied, stating that the answer met the first two of his demands but that there was no response on the third and most important point demanding guarantees for the future. As he had recently received orders to intensify

32. Redcliffe to Clarendon, Constantinople, Apr. 9, 1853, EP, I, 127–29.
33. Menshikov to Nesselrode, Pera, Apr. 14/26, 1853, Zaionchkovskii, *Pril.*, I, 401–02.

his efforts on this matter, he was sending a new communication to the Porte "setting forth his claims within the final limits of his instructions. . . ." [34]

His proposals were essentially the same, namely, that the "Orthodox rite of the Orient, its clergy, its churches, and its possessions" would continue to have the protection of the sultan for their traditional privileges and immunities and, as a matter of equity, would share in advantages granted to other Christian denominations. This, with the firmans on the Holy Places, would be incorporated in a sened that would show the harmony of the two governments. The sened would take into consideration the objections and difficulties raised by the Turks, as shown by the text of the draft that he enclosed.

Menshikov hoped that the Porte would put aside "all hesitation and all distrust" and give him a speedy reply. He begged Rifaat, Turkish foreign minister, to send the answer by April 28/May 10, since a longer delay would be considered "a lack of proper conduct toward his government, which would impose painful obligations on him." [35] The draft sened [36] offered a more moderate form of the Russian proposals, for there is no mention of a treaty of alliance between the two empires. Nothing was said about the nomination, election, or tenure of the Patriarchs of the Greek Orthodox Church, and there was no mention of a right of the Russian government to "give orders" or to make representations to the Church and its clergy. Moreover, the draft did not contain any statement that would give the emperor or his officials direct control over the Orthodox laymen who were subjects of the sultan. But such control was probably intended, for Menshikov's personal remarks indicate that Russia wanted the right to protect laymen as well as the clergy.

Article 1 of the draft sened stated that no change should be made in the rights, privileges, and immunities that the Orthodox churches, religious institutions, and clergy had long enjoyed under the Porte, which would assure these rights and privileges to them on the basis "of the *strict* status quo existing today." In Article 2 the Porte promised to extend any rights and privileges conceded to other Christian cults also to the Orthodox. The Turkish government further promised to protect, honor, and confirm the rights and privileges of the Greek

34. Menshikov to Rifaat, Apr. 23/May 5, 1853, ibid., pp. 407–08.
35. Draft of Sened, Menshikov to Rifaat, Apr. 23/May 5, 1853, ibid.
36. Ibid., pp. 409–10.

Orthodox church of Jerusalem and its patriarch and bishops and also the Orthodox believers of the city of Jerusalem and of the vicinity, without prejudice to the other communities of native-born Christians of Turkey (Article 3). Article 4 provided that the Porte would faithfully carry out the firmans of the sultan concerning the repairs of the great cupola of the Church of the Holy Sepulcher, in order to maintain the strict status quo of the sanctuaries possessed by the Greeks either exclusively or in common with other cults. The Ottoman government further promised to grant to the lay and ecclesiastic subjects of the tsar who might visit Jerusalem and other places of devotion equal status with the subjects of the most favored nations and on request to assign a suitable location in or near Jerusalem for a church and hospice maintained by Russian clergymen under the supervision of the Russian consulate general (Article 5). Finally, the sened provided that the existing agreements between the two courts, and all the earlier treaties, corroborated by the Treaty of Adrianople, would retain all their force and value (Article 6).

Immediately after the delivery of Menshikov's note of May 5 Lord Redcliffe asked to see the prince, with whom he had had friendly relations. The latter, however, sent word that because of illness this was not possible and instead sent Ozerov to pay him a call. There was some preliminary sparring over the conduct of the Russian agent at Belgrade, who had intervened to bar Peter Karageorgevich from becoming prince of Serbia. Ozerov apparently persuaded the Briton that on the whole the agent's conduct had been correct.[37] The conversation then turned to Turkish affairs.

Redcliffe, "with much animation," spoke of the dismay that the Russian actions were arousing in Europe. He insisted that Russia was fully satisfied regarding the Holy Places and opposed its effort "to acquire a new right," complaining that his cabinet had not been informed of the Russian claim to protect the Orthodox rite. He also touched on the increasing Russian armaments near the Turkish border. This military buildup, he said, disturbed the Turks, since they knew how eager the Russian court had been to act together with the Austrians during the Montenegrin crisis. Speaking with warmth, Redcliffe urged the Russians to drop the legal approach and "to associate ourselves with his disinterested and constant efforts in behalf of the Chris-

---

37. Private letter, Menshikov to Nesselrode, Apr. 24/May 6, 1853, ibid., pp. 413–14.

tians, drawn from the principles of humanity." He declared that his convictions on this matter were so deep that he would give up his diplomatic career rather than renounce them. Ozerov, after thanking Redcliffe for his friendliness, strongly asserted that, by following the policy of Nicholas I, his court, because of its special position regarding Turkey, would, like England, seek to preserve the Ottoman empire. But the emperor, while sympathetic to the interests of Europe, must act according to his lights in reestablishing his dignity and "his legitimate influence." Ozerov urged the foreign diplomats who advised the Porte to urge it to reform itself in order to eliminate completely "this leaven of discord that would have incalculable consequences if the struggle should exceed the limits of a diplomatic negotiation." By thus urging Redcliffe to induce the Turks to end the danger of an open rebellion of the Orthodox, Ozerov indicated that Menshikov would make a last, crucial effort to achieve his goal and asked Redcliffe to aid in obtaining this objective. Redcliffe hoped that before proceeding to extremes the Russian diplomats could consent to some changes in the agreement they were asking of the Turks. Ozerov felt that Redcliffe was now more realistic about the Russian intentions, and Menshikov ventured to think that he would not be as stiff in his opposition as before, "especially if we can capture him a little by means of his vanity." [38]

Redcliffe, however, had by no means been won over, for on May 6 he wrote confidentially to Menshikov stating that at first the Russian assurances and Menshikov's expressed support for the independence and integrity of the sultan had led the writer to help mediate the dispute over the Holy Places. England had reason to believe that the tsar merely wanted to settle the issue of the Holy Places and sought "no extension of right or power in this country beyond what was assured to him by the existing Treaties." So Redcliffe had done his best to solve the problem, in hopes of promoting a "happy understanding" between the Russians and the Turks.[39]

He had, however, found Menshikov's later moves to be contrary to what he had expected of him: "How insurmountable the objections to the voluntary acceptance by the Porte of the first Articles of the Project of Sened appear to me to be." Although the sened had dropped the demands respecting the protectorate and the patriarchate, Redcliffe

38. Ibid., pp. 314–15.
39. Redcliffe to Menshikov, Pera, May 8, 1853, EP, I, 179–80.

held that the latest text, "by means of an Act having the force of a Treaty," would strip the sultan of powers proper to the head of the state. This would restrict, "for the benefit of a foreign influence," the sultan's sovereign control over the Greek clergy of Turkey, who, in spite of their ecclesiastical status, had wide civil authority "and affect the interests—and especially the sympathies—of . . . more than ten millions of subjects depending in great measure on their clergy." Redcliffe added that "such an extension of the existing treaties" would be an improper innovation "little in accordance with the spirit of legality recorded by common consent in the Treaty of 1841." [40]

Finally, the ambassador, hoping that Menshikov's intentions were more moderate than they appeared, begged him, because of the great interests at stake, to do everything possible to bring "your negotiations to an amicable termination" in harmony with the dignity and independence of Turkish sovereignty. He assured Menshikov that he would still be able to help achieve a settlement in order to "place the friendly relations between Russia and the Porte on a solid and durable basis. . . ." [41]

In a letter of April 27/May 9 Menshikov replied that he had been charged with obtaining reparation for his master for the offense to his dignity by the Porte—which should be a solid guarantee for the future of the faith professed by the emperor—but had, however, met "the distrust and the ill will of the Ottoman Government." In order to establish solid and friendly relations with the Porte, the tsar had charged him to insist that it should pledge itself "by a formal Act to respect his solicitude for the Church of the Orient." Because of the sad experiences of the past, "promises and assurances" would by no means be sufficient.

Menshikov differed frankly with Redcliffe on the scope of Russia's requests, saying that the sovereign rights of the sultan and the independence of his government were respected. Far from infringing on the principles of the five-power treaty on the conservation of the Ottoman government, the imperial government was seeking to maintain what had existed *ab antiquo.* Thus it displayed "disinterested caution." This moderation and the generosity of its requests gave Russia "the right to a perfect liberty of action" in treating with the Porte on matters arising solely from "the interest of our sovereign for his religion

40. Ibid., p. 180.
41. Ibid.

and that of his subjects." Menshikov denied that he had failed to live up to the "loyal assurances" given to the cabinet of Her Majesty concerning Russia's views on Turkey. He asserted that he had been entirely sincere in dealing with Redcliffe and had counted on frank cooperation from him.[42]

In closing, the prince stated that the embassy could not remain at Constantinople in the unsatisfactory position that the Turks and their friends were trying to impose on it. "Far from claiming any right of superiority," he said, "the Imperial government seeks only to bring its situation in the Orient to the level of those that its allies of the West possess." Consequently he would await the reply of the Porte, in order to reach a decision according to the orders from his superiors. He expressed the hope that the Ottoman Government would remember its earlier intimate relations with Russia and would not compromise them by "a thoughtless decision grounded on the same spirit of calculated distrust" toward Russia that had brought on the trouble.[43]

Menshikov's rejection of Redcliffe's olive branch shattered the fragile harmony between them. This was almost inevitable, as Redcliffe was adamant against any Turkish recognition of a Russian right of protection over the Greek Orthodox Church. Menshikov was sure that he held the winning cards and was about to win a great triumph.

On April 28/May 10 Foreign Minister Rifaat sent an official note in answer to Menshikov, stating that his government had carefully considered all the Russian documents. The Porte was eager for peace and friendship with Russia and especially sought close relations between the two emperors. It was anxious to settle all Russian claims that did not infringe on Ottoman sovereignty or threaten its independence. It would grant a church and a hospice at Jerusalem, with freedom to the Russian clergy and pilgrims, and would scrupulously observe the religious immunities that all subjects of the Porte, Christian or not, enjoyed. While the Russian court had fears for the religious rights of the Greeks, the sultan was always devoted to maintaining their immunities and did not intend to alter them. As for a sened on such a delicate question, "that is not only completely contrary to the rights of governments . . . but destroys the foundation of sovereign independence." The Porte, which had observed with care the many religious privileges that it had bestowed on its Greek subjects and the clergy,

42. Menshikov to Redcliffe, Apr. 27/May 9, 1853, Zaionchkovskii, *Pril.*, I, 415.
43. Ibid.

would also continue to maintain them and to conserve them completely, in harmony with its rights of independence.[44]

Menshikov at once replied that, while the sultan's desire for closer relations between the governments was gratifying, he regretted that the Porte showed unjustified suspicion of the request for consideration for the Greek Orthodox rite, "of which the Emperor is the natural defender." Menshikov referred to "the faults committed by clumsy and malevolent counsellors of His Majesty the Sultan," which could only be effaced by "an Act emanating from . . . the Sultan, a free but solemn engagement . . . " which the prince was charged to negotiate. He declared that if this request were rejected, "if by a systematic opposition the Sublime Porte persists in shutting to him even the ways of an intimate and direct entente . . . the undersigned declares with pain: He will have to consider his mission as terminated, break his relations with the Cabinet of His Majesty the Sultan, and place upon it . . . all the consequences that might result therefrom."

The ambassador hoped that the Russian views would be given most serious attention by the Porte and that the minister of foreign affairs would realize "the motives that do not permit the ambassador to accept the note of April 28/May 10 as a reply in keeping with the dignity of his Sovereign." He therefore begged Rifaat to reply to him by May 2/14, which should give enough time "for reflection which the very gravity of the question demands."[45]

In the struggle for influence at Constantinople Stratford Canning, Lord Redcliffe, played a crucial part. With long experience in diplomacy and politics, strong-willed, decisive, handsome, and charming, he was respected and feared. He had spent many years in Turkey and, while he recognized Turkish weaknesses and backwardness, he firmly believed they could be remedied. He ardently supported the reforms of Gulhané and was greatly concerned when they failed, as he feared that the corrupt regime might bring Turkish collapse and arouse the despair of the Christian subjects, helpless under oppression. Stratford was convinced that it was his duty to uphold the Turks and bully them into basic reforms.

Austin Henry Layard, the discoverer of Nineveh, who for a time had been personal agent for Stratford at Constantinople, told of the latter's "overbearing and imperious" manner in dealing with Turkish

44. Rifaat to Menshikov, Apr. 28/May 10, 1853, ibid., pp. 417–18.
45. Menshikov to Rifaat-pasha, Apr. 29/May 11, 1853, ibid., I, 418–19.

ministers. Even devoted Turkish statesmen were in the utmost dread of him and eagerly sought to avoid a personal interview, for if some demand of his was not carried out, he would rise to his feet and pour forth "a torrent of invective, accompanied by menacing gestures." [46]

Stratford regarded Russia as Turkey's deadly foe. In 1834 Palmerston named him as ambassador to St. Petersburg, but Nesselrode, with whom he had already clashed, declared him *persona non grata*. Palmerston and Stratford refused to accept this rebuff, but the tsar held firm. Finally Stratford was sent to Spain, although he was still listed as envoy to St. Petersburg. When Palmerston fell from power the Conservatives could appoint Lord Durham to the Russian court and end the long hiatus in relations. These events doubtless had a lasting effect on Stratford. In 1849 he was at Constantinople when Austria and Russia demanded that Turkey should surrender or expel the Polish and Magyar revolutionaries who had fled from Hungary. War seemed near, with British and French fleets in Turkish waters, while Austrian and Russian armies threatened. Stratford even sent British ships into the Straits, in violation of the Treaty of 1841. While Nicholas I avoided war by accepting a compromise, Stratford was marked as an opponent of Russia.

When the crisis over the Holy Places arose, he was in England, but after Menshikov arrived in Turkey Aberdeen and Russell sent Stratford—now Lord Redcliffe—back, although they distrusted him. He was instructed to mediate, but not to get deeply involved. The Turks welcomed him as a savior. While he did not promise support, he induced them to compromise over the Holy Places, but warned them not to commit themselves on political matters. Redcliffe got on well with Menshikov, and since La Cour, the French envoy, was cooperative, the issue of the Holy Places was soon settled. By April of 1853, however, Redcliffe learned that Menshikov was demanding a firm agreement with the Porte to protect the existing rights and immunities of the Orthodox church, based on the Treaty of Küchuk-Kainardji, and he was determined to prevent this. Louis Thouvenel, a high official of the Quai d'Orsay, later referred to "the perpetual intrigues of Sir Stratford Canning, who gave the singular spectacle of an ambassador of a great country . . . taking account of the instruc-

46. A. H. Layard, *Autobiography and Letters* (2 vols., London, 1903), II, 84.

tions of the British cabinet only insofar as these . . . agreed with his personal plans, his rancors, or his ambitions." [47] Unsuccessful in attaining his dream of becoming premier, this headstrong figure—"the English sultan"—played a key role in the unfolding events.

Menshikov had asked Rifaat to answer his latest demands by April 28/May 10. Since the reply was vague and indefinite, he returned a stern warning of the consequences of failing to meet his request, although he agreed to a new delay until May 2/14. Rifaat promptly requested a conference at the vizir's villa on the morning of the 13th, an invitation Menshikov at once accepted.[48]

According to Thouvenel, who later heard a detailed account of the proceedings from Mehemet Ali, the grand vizir, Menshikov and Mehemet, working through Argyropoulo, first dragoman of the Russian Embassy, had about reached agreement on a note for the sultan to sign and hand to Menshikov. The plan for a sened had been dropped, and the note would contain a recognition of the validity of the religious provisions of the Treaty of Küchuk-Kainardji. Menshikov realized that this was the only hope of a settlement, for if it failed, Turkey, threatened by Russia, would come completely under the domination of England and France. Hence he had worked sincerely and with great frankness with Mehemet Ali, as *"Russia did not at all want a rupture."* On May 13 Mehemet was waiting in his villa for Menshikov, sure that success was in sight.[49]

Unfortunately for this stratagem, however, Menshikov fell victim to a Levantine intrigue. Reshid pasha, an extremely ambitious former premier, was very eager to return to power and in late 1852 had made contact with the Russian diplomats at Constantinople. Now, hearing of the imminent settlement between Menshikov and Mehemet Ali, he apparently foresaw that if it succeeded his hope of again holding office would be remote. In order to prevent a settlement he joined with a group of pro-Russian Greeks, who in 1852 had sent an appeal to Nicholas I to send a special mission to Constantinople to restore Russian influence there. They included the Greek Patriarch of Jerusalem; Nicholas Aristarchi, Grand Logothete of the Greek Orthodox church, and intermediary between the Porte and the Patriarchate of Constantinople; and several others. Ozerov, the Russian chargé, who

47. Thouvenel, pp. 52–53.
48. Menshikov to Nesselrode, May 4/16, 1853, Zaionchkovskii, *Pril.,* I, 423.
49. Thouvenel, pp. 150–51. The quotation is from Mehemet Ali as related by Thouvenel.

had taken a hard line against the Turks, supported this group and opposed Mehemet Ali's compromise proposals. Aristarchi, in order to gain influence over Menshikov, undertook to discredit Argyropoulo, the dragoman on whom the prince had relied in his dealings with Mehemet Ali. To do this, Aristarchi informed the sultan confidentially that the dragoman wanted a country house and induced the monarch to present him with a fine house on the Bosporous, even giving him the keys in secret. Argyropoulo naively accepted it, amazed at his good fortune. Now, however, Ozerov, informed of it, charged him with accepting a bribe from the Turks and, since Argyropoulo had the keys on his person, he was completely discredited in Menshikov's eyes. Aristarchi now proposed that Menshikov deal with Reshid, who, if he were returned to power, would accept the sened that Menshikov had sought earlier, without the limitations that Mehemet Ali had asked for.[50]

On April 28/May 10 Prince Menshikov sent a letter to Reshid pasha, whom he had apparently not approached before, asking him, because of his intelligence, experience, and patriotism, to try to present to the sultan the facts of the existing situation and the probable consequences, unless the ruler should take proper action.[51] As already mentioned, on April 29/May 11 Menshikov sent Rifaat a note refusing his vague promises and urging him to reconsider his answer. Rifaat was to give his final response on May 2/14. The vizir hastened to send an oral invitation to a conference at his villa on May 1/13, which Menshikov accepted. On the appointed day, however, having "lost all confidence in the attitudes of the Ottoman Cabinet," Menshikov sent a message to the sultan asking for an interview, and, instead of going to Rifaat's house, anchored his yacht to await a reply. At 11 A.M. the sultan said he was waiting for him, and received him at the palace "with a benevolence that I thought was real." His Majesty promised that he wanted to settle their differences amicably and would reply speedily to the Russian claims. He also informed the envoy

50. Ibid., pp. 149–50. Needless to say, there are no documents to reveal the motives of those involved. Thouvenel, who seems fairly reliable, obtained his information from Mehemet Ali, who seems to have been less trustworthy. Temperley gives a somewhat similar account, putting the blame on Aristarchi and on Menshikov's gullibility. Harold Temperley, "Stratford de Redcliffe and the Origins of the Crimean War," *English Historical Review,* XLIX (Oct. 1933), 613–17.

51. Menshikov to Reshid Pasha, Apr. 28/May 10, 1853, Buiukdere in Zaionchkovskii, *Pril.,* I, 416–17.

that Rifaat had been removed as foreign minister. On leaving the palace Menshikov sent word to Rifaat that the sultan's promises of a satisfactory settlement made their conference unnecessary. When he returned to his mooring at Büyükdere he learned that Reshid had become minister of foreign affairs, Mustapha-pasha had been named grand vizir, Rifaat was president of the council, and Mehemet Ali, the former vizir, was now *Seraskier* (minister of war). Most of the other ministers kept their posts. Thus, although Menshikov had managed to bring Reshid into the ministry, its general composition had changed little.[52]

Whether Lord Redcliffe was involved in this trickery seems doubtful. Emile Bourgeois in his *Manuel Historique de Politique Étrangère* states that "this was the work of a very powerful diplomat, Sir Stratford Redcliffe," who, learning of Mehemet Ali's readiness to compromise with the Russians, used this scheme to remove him "by means of the Russians themselves." [53] Thouvenel suggests the same, without stating it as a fact.[54] On the other hand, Menshikov, who says it was the opinion of the Turks that Redcliffe had put Reshid into the government, declared that Redcliffe, "ordinarily so well informed, learned only late at night of the dismissal of the Grand Vizir . . . in the morning. He experienced a fit of anger at this which approached madness." [55]

Although Lord Redcliffe did not cause Reshid's return to power, he played a very important role in the ensuing events. He already had great influence over the Turks, who knew him as a friend and as a convinced opponent of Russian influence. In order to encourage the sultan to withstand Menshikov's strong pressure Redcliffe visited the palace and, after some hesitation, admitted on May 10 that he was authorized to call the British fleet to Turkish waters. Although he warned that he could summon the fleet only if a direct Russian attack on Constantinople threatened,[56] the Turks were reassured, for with the French squadron and the British fleet on call, they felt that they had little to fear.

At first Redcliffe feared that Reshid might give in to Menshikov,

52. Menshikov to Nesselrode, May 4/16, 1853, Zaionchkovskii, *Pril.,* I, 423–24.
53. Bourgeois, III, 373–77.
54. Thouvenel, pp. 152–53.
55. Menshikov to Nesselrode, May 4/16, 1853, Zaionchkovskii, *Pril.,* I, 427.
56. Temperley, "Stratford," p. 609.

but decided later that he had not done so. Redcliffe now sent Reshid written advice about his reply to Menshikov, but centered his influence on the members of the Grand Council, whom the sultan had summoned to decide on the answer to give. He sent them a memorandum setting forth the limits of the safe concessions to Russia. "It gives everything required by Russia but a form of guarantee, which in principle . . . would eventually prove fatal to the Porte's independence," he said. The memorandum provided that the Orthodox Church and its clergy, as those of other denominations, "shall continue, as regards *spiritual* matters, to enjoy under the sovereign protection of His Majesty the Sultan, the privileges and immunities which have been granted to them . . . by the Imperial favour." Other provisions promised respect for their property and the Russian clergy and pilgrims. The arrangements concerning the Holy Places should become a formal engagement. All these points should be guaranteed by an imperial declaration and communicated in the most solemn form "to the Court of Russia and to the other Great Powers of Christendom." [57] Menshikov, however, refused to accept this pledge, which was to all the powers instead of to Russia alone, and insisted on a formal concession to the tsar.

The prince, who hoped that he had won a triumph, soon learned that he had not. The Grand Council, which would meet to decide the issue, consisted of the ministers, past and present, provincial governors, Moslem leaders, and other influential men, almost all of them filled with patriotic fervor and hostility to Russia. Redcliffe left nothing to chance, for on the night of May 14th he got in touch with the leading ministers and their predecessors and easily induced them to oppose Menshikov. Mehemet Ali, the Seraskier, and Rifaat pasha were especially active in arousing defiance. Even Reshid, although committed to Menshikov, leaned more and more on Redcliffe and on the 14th asked him to help gain time—which the latter was glad to do, as it not only permitted him to influence the Turks but also to align the Western diplomats with him. [58]

May 15 was the decisive day. Menshikov still thought Reshid, with the aid of the sultan, might be able to bring the others into line. Reshid called on him in the morning and Menshikov gave him strong encouragement to compel his colleagues to accept Russia's proposals.

57. Redcliffe to Clarendon, Constantinople, May 15, 1853, EP, I, 195–96. The word "spiritual" was used to rule out Russian *political* influence in Turkey.
58. Temperley, *England and the Near East,* pp. 324–25.

In a letter of May 3/15 Menshikov told Reshid that the Porte's answer was neither satisfactory nor proper, so that he felt called upon to break off diplomatic relations. Because of the Turk's recent entry into office, however, "and in the hope that the ray of light that you will bring there" would make clear "the amicable and disinterested intentions of the Imperial Government," he was ready to permit a delay before taking the final step. He urged Reshid to make every effort to obtain an answer from the Porte and hoped that it would appreciate his serious motives. A lack of such appreciation could only be regarded as an affront, of which "my departure, as well as that of the Imperial legation, would be the inevitable and immediate consequence." [59]

Reshid accomplished nothing at the sultan's council on May 14, for it was dominated by Rifaat and the fiery Mehemet Ali, and both the ancient foes of Russia and the more progressive younger men joined in opposing concessions. Reshid did not dare speak out. On the next day, ordered to inform Menshikov of the refusal, he had a heated altercation with the envoy. Menshikov broke off relations and sent Reshid a threatening note, which the latter at once took to Redcliffe, with whom he conversed for two hours. Reshid, who allegedly had promised Aristarchi that he would "sign the sened the day he became vizir," had disavowed him and told Baron Mollerus, the minister of the Netherlands at Constantinople, that "he would cut off his hand before signing such a treaty." He tried to lay the blame on Aristarchi and also on the "inexorable" Redcliffe. He was able, even so, to convince Menshikov that he still hoped for a favorable outcome.[60] Harold Temperley rightly calls this "the day of dupes," with Menshikov the victim. On the 16th Menshikov reported to Nesselrode that he still felt Reshid was acting in good faith, "insofar as a Turk is susceptible of it." He added that Reshid, aided by Ahmed Fethi pasha, had succeeded in winning over part of the members of the sultan's council and even agreed to a delay of several days, "in hope of arriving at a satisfactory entente." He reported that his open preparations for departure, made at the legation, and his taking up quarters on his ship in the harbor, ready to raise anchor, had caused much commotion and fear in financial and commercial circles, so that he saw a chance of success, although it was not certain. He had even been assured that Lord Redcliffe was getting ready to accept

---

59. Menshikov to Reshid, May 3/15, 1853, Zaionchkovskii, *Pril.*, I, 426.
60. Temperley, "Stratford," pp. 615–16.

the idea of the occupation of the Principalities if a break should occur. He had doubts on this last point, however.[61]

All this suggests that Menshikov was so eager for some sort of success that he was grasping at straws. When the Grand Council met on May 5/17 these hopes were quickly dispelled. Allegedly because of the feverish activity of Lord Redcliffe, who had visited most of the dignitaries "in order to persuade them to vote against us and to adopt the draft reply to us that had been devised at the British Embassy and already transmitted ahead of time to . . . Mehemet Ali," the majority voted in favor of Redcliffe's proposal, and the others were overwhelmed and accused of pro-Russian feeling. The vote forty-two to three.[62]

On the following day, May 18, Reshid, with some embarrassment, called on Menshikov to announce that the council had voted to proclaim a decision of the sultan that there would be no change in the status quo of the Holy Places at Jerusalem without a prior understanding with the cabinets of Russia and France. The Patriarch of Constantinople would receive a firman of assurances on the maintenance of the privileges of the Orthodox rite. A sened with the force and value of a treaty would be proposed to Menshikov to promise the granting of a site for constructing a church and a hospice at Jerusalem. And an explanatory note would be sent to him at the end of the negotiations. (The note soon followed.)

After hearing this, Menshikov curtly refused to accept this demarche and declared that he was finally breaking diplomatic relations and would leave Constantinople with all his mission.

According to Menshikov, Reshid had seemed ashamed of the terms that he was offering and declared that he had no power to change the outcome. Menshikov added that during this interview Redcliffe, who had already been at Reshid's home, was waiting in a caique in the middle of the Bosporus and saw Reshid again for a third time after the meeting of the council, "at which a British dragoman, standing nearby, observed the debates. There, M. le Comte," he said, "is what the British agents have the effrontery to call the independence of the Turkish government." [63]

61. Menshikov to Nesselrode, Buiukdere, on board the Gromonosets, May 4/16, 1853, in Zaionchkovskii, *Pril.*, I, 426–27.

62. Menshikov to Nesselrode, May 9/21, 1853, Buiukdere, ibid., p. 428.

63. Menshikov to Nesselrode, May 9/21, 1853, ibid., p. 428.

A second despatch from Menshikov emphasized the warlike spirit of several of the Turkish leaders, although the envoy declared that the real cause of the Divan's hostility was the readiness of the sultan and his advisers to accept "every assertion that heightened the systematic mistrust that our religious sympathies in the Orient provoke." He added that the Turkish leaders, "bewitched by . . . the passionate activity of the British representative, easily believe in the predominance of England and perhaps count on some rash action on the part of France. . . ." M. de La Cour, however, had done nothing to give rise to such expectations. Menshikov felt sure that the Turks had given a pledge to Redcliffe, for he had recently had a private audience with the sultan and was said to be promising the Turks that they would have the support of Europe. Redcliffe was urging them to promise full equality before the law to their Christian subjects and the power to protest against violence and abuses. Menshikov, however, felt that any such reforms, like those of Gulhané, would be "an object of hate for the Moslems and of bitter derision for the Christians." [64]

As for the new firmans, he saw little that was important in them. He noted, however, that the Turks had pledged to uphold the *spiritual* immunities of the clergy and the churches of the Orthodox. This pledge appeared intended to limit the status of the Greek Orthodox to mere performance of service and would deprive them of all *civil* protection, in spite of the Porte's stated desire to end all suspicions on matters of the Greek church.[65]

Menshikov now decided that the "evasive and deceptive assurances" his notes had produced were not enough. The two firmans about the Holy Places did not give the guarantee desired by the emperor, and because the Porte rejected his wishes with mistrust, it was lacking in regard for the tsar. Thus, the strong religious ties between Russia and Turkey, instead of being a bond of friendship, had become a permanent cause of a hostile attitude. Reshid's latest proposal merely repeated propositions that had been made earlier, and only the provision for a hospice at Jerusalem would have obligatory force. Thus Menshikov felt it was useless to make further efforts toward an entente which would satisfy the dignity of his master. He therefore felt obliged to declare his mission terminated and to state that the imperial court could not, without exposing itself to new offenses, retain a legation

64. Menshikov to Nesselrode, May 9/21, 1853, ibid., pp. 429–30.
65. Reshid to Menshikov, May 8/20, 1853, ibid., pp. 430–31.

at Constantinople. Hence he and all the legation personnel would leave, except for the director of the commercial chancellery as caretaker.

Finally, he warned that the emperor would now have to take such measures as his interests required and that any infringement of the spirit and the letter of the existing stipulations would be a hostile act, which would compel the adoption of measures that he would regret.[66]

Menshikov still had not completely given up hope, however, for even after breaking relations and rejecting the Turkish note of May 6/18, brought by Reshid's son, he sent another note to the Porte. This was because Reshid had again expressed a wish to renew negotiations and because Baron Klezl, the Austrian envoy, in the name of his colleagues and on the invitation of Lord Redcliffe, had begged him to reconsider his decision, if he could possibly do so. Menshikov therefore sent word to Reshid that he would be satisfied with the attached note, to be signed by the sultan and returned to him. Reshid, "who does not dare take a step or say a word without the consent of Lord Redcliffe," allegedly begged the English dragoman to plead his cause to his master. "Put me at the feet of Lord Redcliffe," he said, "beg him to consent, represent our position to him, it is he who by his resistance pushed us into this abyss, it is for him to pull us out of it. . . ." Later that day, however, from a confidential source, Menshikov learned that Redcliffe had sent his secretary to Reshid to inform him that Menshikov's draft note—his last concession—"has the force of a treaty and in this form the propositions were unacceptable." As his last delay had now expired, the prince now had his steamer fired to proceed to Odessa.[67]

Baron Mollerus, the minister of the Netherlands, who was on friendly terms with Menshikov, observed these developments with much interest. He held that Menshikov certainly did not want a breach with the Porte, as his repeated last-minute concessions showed. According to the baron, Menshikov, who did not sufficiently understand the situation at Constantinople, failed to take advantage of his opportunities. When he first arrived, the Turks, lacking the support of both the French and the British ambassadors, were terrified and would have signed almost any demand that he might have presented to them.

66. Menshikov to the Porte, May 6/18, 1853, ibid., p. 432.
67. Menshikov to Nesselrode, May 9/21, 1853, Buiukdere, ibid., pp. 433–34.

But he failed to take them by storm and delayed and made concessions, so that the Porte came to feel that he was not as terrible as they had believed. When Lord Redcliffe came, he encouraged the Turks and persuaded Menshikov to be more moderate. Thus the dispute about the Holy Places was settled by a compromise. When, however, the Russian advanced more far-reaching demands, the Turks, now relying on Redcliffe to save them, rejected what earlier they would have readily agreed to. And Menshikov accepted this rebuff without acting with the firmness worthy of a Russian envoy.[68]

Temperley presents Redcliffe's actions in the last moment of the drama much as does Menshikov. The British envoy made no official pronouncement about Menshikov's note but sent some written "reflections" to Reshid, saying that while the sened had been dropped, the note would give Russia a permanent hold upon Turkey, with "a distinct right to call the Porte to account" if it failed to live up to the pledge. It was an attempt to establish Russian influence on the basis of a legal right, which was unacceptable, but Reshid should try to keep the negotiation going.[69]

The chief provisions of Menshikov's note were as follows:

1. The Greek Orthodox church, its clergy, church, and possessions, and its institutions, would in future enjoy without infringement, under the sultan, its ancient privileges and immunities or those granted by the sultans, and would participate in concessions made to other Christian churches, as well as to the foreign legations.

2. This section dealt with earlier firmans of the sultan concerning the Holy Places in Palestine, including the repair of the cupola of the Church of the Holy Sepulcher. These two firmans would be faithfully observed, in order to maintain forever the status of the sanctuaries, possessed by the Greeks, exclusively or in common with other rites. This promise should also extend to the maintenance of the ancient rights and immunities of the Orthodox church, both in Jerusalem and outside.

3. This section, concerning the granting of a site in or near Jerusalem for a Russian church and a hospice for pilgrims, had been already agreed on.[70]

It is difficult to find in these apparently harmless provisions any

68. Mollerus to Foreign Minister F. A. van Hall, Constantinople, May 23–24, 1853, Nederland Algemeen Rijksarchief, 's-Gravenhage (hereafter cited NAR).

69. Temperley, *England and the Near East,* pp. 328–29.

70. Menshikov to the Porte, May 8/20, 1853, Zaionchkovskii, *Pril.,* I, 434–35.

threat to the independence and sovereignty of the sultan, for they merely ensured the safety and well-being of the Greek Orthodox church and its clergy, "under the aegis of the sultan." Redcliffe, however, held that they would limit the authority of the Padishah and irrevocably infringe on his sovereignty, although he wished the negotiations to continue. Menshikov, as his efforts indicate, was extremely eager to arrive at some reasonable compromise, but the Turks, angered by Menshikov's threats and encouraged by British and French support, refused further negotiation: thus the first step toward war was taken. The prince refused to change "a single letter" of his note, and, as he had announced, sailed for Odessa at noon on May 21.

Temperley seems correct in saying that Redcliffe did not want war and was much less bellicose than Palmerston. On the other hand, he is not justified in insisting that Menshikov was still demanding a Russo-Turkish alliance—which the British, with their memories of the Treaty of Unkiar-Skelessi, regarded as monstrous. To be sure, early in his mission Menshikov was told to offer the sultan a defensive alliance if France showed signs of hostility toward Turkey over its concessions to Russia. This plan, however, had been quickly dropped when the Turks showed dismay. On April 11 Redcliffe said that Menshikov was not urging an alliance on the Turks. Later in the month, however, Mehemet Ali and Rifaat were warning that Russia's real purpose was a secret treaty of alliance.[71] On the 26th Redcliffe warned Ozerov, Russian first secretary, against such an alliance, which would lead directly to war.[72] The Turks continued to report that Menshikov was pushing strongly for an alliance, even though they never produced any written evidence for their allegations, and none of Menshikov's written proposals to the Porte of the last six weeks mentioned an alliance. In fact, Temperley states that "the alliance was never officially proposed."[73] The many rumors in Constantinople about Russian threats, no doubt largely of Turkish origin, probably were the source of the reports about the Russian demand for an alliance. Temperley himself says, "The evidence of Mehemet Ali . . . is prejudiced and not to be trusted."[74] Mehemet and Rifaat, however, were his source for the stories about Russian demands for an alliance.

While Redcliffe did not want war with Russia and hoped for a

71. Temperley, *England and the Near East,* p. 319.
72. Ibid.
73. Ibid., p. 332.
74. Ibid., p. 472.

peaceful settlement, his strongly pro-Turkish and anti-Russian sympathies probably brought war nearer. He was implacable against an enforceable Russian right to intercede for the Orthodox Christians and thus encouraged the Turks to reject any compromise settlement. Far exceeding his instructions, which called merely for mediation, he ardently sided with Turkey. Moreover, by his despatches and letters and his influence with the press he rapidly induced British opinion to support the Turks against what he termed Russian aggression. His prejudice did much to renew anti-Russian feeling and to turn the cabinet away from Aberdeen's entente with Russia and toward Palmerston's anti-Russian policy.

Redcliffe quickly became dominant at Constantinople. The Turks knew he would support them against Russia, even though he warned against war. A more reasonable man might have been able to reach a compromise with Menshikov, but Redcliffe's passionate, unyielding attitude led the Turks to rule out concessions to the Russians, and since his inflexible position was matched by the determination and arrogance of Nicholas I, war became inevitable.

The French role was less obvious than that of Britain, although it was France that had started the dispute over the Holy Places, and the French fleet was the first to sail to Eastern waters. France proved reasonable about the dispute over the Holy Places, but it had again played a disturbing role by threats of force to Belgium in March 1853, which helped to induce the British cabinet to end its entente with Russia and to cooperate with France in the East.[75] Baron Hübner, Austrian ambassador to Paris, on a visit to his son in Brussels, talked with the Belgian minister of foreign affairs, who confirmed the belief that France's relations with King Leopold were highly strained. Hübner felt that Napoleon had no real reason for anger, but wanted "to have in his hands a reason to quarrel if he wanted to, first of all with Belgium, and later with others." In May 1853, after the marriage of the Belgian Duke of Brabant to an Austrian archduchess, Napoleon poured out his wrath to the envoy, regarding the marriage as a personal insult because *he* had been denied such a match. Hübner reported: ". . . he made on me the impression of a man almost driven mad. . . . At these moments I believe he is capable of anything." [76]

75. Alexandre von Hübner, *Neuf ans de souvenirs d'un ambassedeur d'Autriche à Paris* (Paris, 1904), I, 123.
76. Ibid., p. 135.

Although France was not a moderating factor and had played a part in bringing about the war against Russia, the French government, unlike that of England, was not pushed into the war by public opinion. The reports of the local French officials who were charged with analyzing local feeling found in the provinces almost no evidence of interest in the Holy Places or in the Menshikov mission. The battle of Sinop in November 1853 (to be discussed later) caused an outcry in government circles and the paid press, and the emperor was much excited, but the French provinces were almost completely apathetic. When France entered the war three months after the battle of Sinop, there was almost no desire for it locally and considerable opposition to it appeared. Lord Cowley, the British ambassador, was much upset over the public attitude, for he felt that the war was very unpopular and Napoleon III was trying to back out of it. There was also substantial opposition to the alliance with England, as the public largely felt that the war was in Britain's interest and not in that of France. If the war could have been avoided, the French public, on the whole, probably would have been glad.[77]

The instructions of his cabinet had limited Menshikov's freedom of action and largely determined his tactics. Menshikov did well in settling the issues of the Holy Places with the French. When, however, he sought recognition of a Russian right to protect the Orthodox church and its clergy, he made no progress. In fact, he steadily moderated his demands, until he was about to accept a mere note from Turkey recognizing Russia's right to intercede, which might have solved the problem and prevented war. But Menshikov fell victim to the intrigues of Reshid and Aristarchi, which ruined all chances of a compromise solution. Possibly a more skillful diplomat, such as Count Orlov, might have been able to achieve a satisfactory settlement.

The Turks also played an important part in the diplomatic failure. Although they easily settled the issue of the Holy Places by agreement between France and Russia, aided by Redcliffe, they were not ready to cede on important matters. After being forced to yield to Austria over Montenegro, they were increasingly opposed to concessions to Russia. When they learned that Redcliffe could promise British support, they became strongly aroused against their ancient foe and were

---

77. Lynn Case, *French Opinion of War and Diplomacy During the Second Empire* (Philadelphia, 1954), pp. 18–25.

quite willing to risk a confrontation. By that time not even Orlov could have won them to a compromise.

Thus by the end of May 1853 Russia had broken with Turkey, and England and France, while seeking a settlement, were definitely supporting the latter. So it was that the Christians of Turkey were sacrificed to the imperial interests of the great powers.

CHAPTER 7. THE NOTE OF VIENNA: A SOLUTION THAT FAILED

When Menshikov sailed from Constantinople on May 21, 1853, he had not entirely given up hope of obtaining the agreement he sought, for he had left a copy of his draft note with Reshid, for the sultan to sign and send to him at Odessa. The crucial part of the note was the pledge that the Orthodox church, its clergy, its possessions, and its religious establishments would thenceforth enjoy, under the aegis of the sultan, "the privileges and immunities that were assured to it *ab antiquo*" or had been granted at various times "by the Imperial favor," and that as a matter of equity it would share the advantages granted to the other Christian rites "by convention or special provision." The other provisions, which confirmed the settlement about the Holy Places and provided for a Russian church and a hospice at Jerusalem, were not under dispute. The Turks, however, were bitterly opposed to granting Russia, by a binding diplomatic document, the right to protect the Orthodox church in their empire, and Lord Redcliffe fully agreed with this decision.[1] Hence the Porte again rejected Menshikov's proposals.

On May 27 Sir Hamilton Seymour had an acrimonious interview with Nesselrode, in which he attempted to prove that Menshikov's demands had been far more sweeping than the assurances to the British cabinet had indicated they would be. Menshikov's draft treaty had included the provision that Russia would enjoy the right to protect the religion of ten million Orthodox subjects of the sultan and thus, in Seymour's view, would gain greater influence over them than the sultan would have. Nesselrode, however, declared that for one hundred years the Greeks (i.e., the Orthodox) had always looked to the tsar. "No, believe me, this convention . . . is perfectly inoffensive and anodyne [*sic*]; it changes nothing in the state of affairs; it does not weaken the sultan's authority"; in fact, the chancellor claimed that it would

---

1. Letter, Redcliffe to Seymour, May 23, 1853, EP, I, 253–54.

strengthen it, as it would make his subjects more loyal by removing their grievances.

Seymour admitted that the tsar already had much influence over the Greeks and "the practice of so interfering has long prevailed," although the right "to interfere generally on behalf of the Greek subjects of the Porte is not yet secured to her [Russia]." He again asserted, however, that the British government had grounds for surprise at Menshikov's demands.[2]

Seymour's views were those of Clarendon, Redcliffe, Palmerston, and probably of much of the British public, who readily admitted that Russia had great influence among the Greeks, Bulgars, Serbs, and other Orthodox subjects of the sultan as a result of their religious and ethnic ties. The Balkan peoples realized clearly that the freedom or concessions they had obtained from the Turks had largely been won by Russian blood shed on numerous fields of battle. But to the British and the Turks, as long as this influence was exercised de facto it was not very troublesome, for the Turks could oppose it by law and through the Orthodox church, which, by accepting the control of the Porte, had become part of the system of government. But if the Russian cabinet, through a treaty, convention, or note, obtained a solid right to protect the Orthodox church and its clergy, the ten millions of Orthodox in Turkey and the Orthodox hierarchy would look to the tsar as their ruler rather than the sultan. Russian influence would, they felt, dominate Turkey and the whole Levant and the balance of power in Europe would be greatly disturbed. The people of France, according to the reports of Napoleon's own officials, had shown almost no interest in the quarrels about the Holy Places and were strongly opposed to war with Russia. Nevertheless they seem to have accepted the official argument that if Russia obtained a legal right to protect the Orthodox of Turkey, its influence would increase greatly at the expense of France.[3]

Obviously, then, it was not the question of the Holy Places in Palestine—which had already been settled to the general satisfaction of the parties concerned—that was at issue but rather the Russian demand that the Porte give a solemn pledge to protect the traditional privileges and immunities of the Orthodox church and its institutions. Essentially it was a matter of limiting Russian influence and power in the Ottoman

2. Seymour to Clarendon, May 27, 1853, ibid., pp. 211–12.
3. Case, pp. 26–29.

empire rather than a religious contest. In arguing their case the European diplomats stressed the effects of the Russian claims on the balance of power and the peace of Europe and showed no real interest in the religious or spiritual aspects involved. Moreover, in late May 1853 even Protestant Prussia, which cared nothing about Orthodox or Catholics, was against Russia in this matter. The English ambassador reported: "All agree that it is impossible for the Porte to sign this treaty, without incurring the loss of its independence." [4]

But while Europe generally opposed Russia's claims, the ten million Orthodox of Turkey needed protection from the three million Turks who ruled the Ottoman empire, in full control of its government and its army. Many of the landowners were Moslems exploiting Christian peasants. The regime was run by and for the Moslems, while the Christian *rayahs* ("cattle") had few rights. Even the ardently Turcophil Lord Redcliffe stated: "It is but justice to admit that Russia had something to complain about in the affairs of the holy places; nor can it be denied that much remains to be done for the welfare and security of the Christian population of Turkey." [5] The Christians were often oppressed by corrupt police officials or other local authorities and could rarely obtain redress in the courts, where the testimony of a Christian hardly counted. The Greek Orthodox church, which represented the Christians and controlled their local affairs, could do little, since it was so dominated by the Turkish rulers that it rarely dared intercede for its flock. Consequently, although Russia had shown little readiness to intervene on their behalf, the Orthodox of Turkey tended to look on it as a possible protector. The other powers cared little about them and were concerned lest Russia should mobilize the potential strength that lay at hand. Fear of this danger did much to produce the anti-Russian coalition that took shape.

On May 20/June 1 Nesselrode, in a despatch to Brunnow at London, charged that the Menshikov mission had failed because of "the vehement opposition . . . chiefly on the part of the English Ambassador Redcliffe." Menshikov had been very conciliatory and granted extensions of time. After asking for a convention from the Turks, he proposed a sened instead, and finally a simple note. But because of the "blind obstinacy" that he met, the dignity of the tsar demanded a new policy. The sultan should accept and sign the Menshikov note,

4. Bloomfield to Clarendon, May 30, 1853, EP, I, 223.
5. Redcliffe to Clarendon, May 23, 1853, ibid., p. 235.

which his master would still accept, although there was only one week in which to decide. After that the tsar would with deep regret send Russian troops into the Danubian Principalities of Moldavia and Wallachia. He still wanted to maintain the Turkish empire; he wanted no territory; and he would not now support an uprising of the Christians.[6]

At first the British had urged the Turks to satisfy Russia and withheld their fleet. But Redcliffe, alas, had displayed "an incurable distrust, a vehement activity." Even after repeated Russian concessions, he refused to give "any kind of guarantee whatever for the future." When Menshikov was willing to accept a simple note, the Briton said this would be as bad as a treaty, and when Reshid begged him to approve it, he still refused.

Nesselrode insisted that Russia had a good case, based on the Treaties of Küchuk-Kainardji and Adrianople. Russia, he said, derived its rights from these treaties, but needed a solemn confirmation because in 1852 the Turks had said that France had a treaty with Turkey, while Russia had none. Russia had made one concession after another and now, having reached the limit, was bound by its honor to insist on this last demand. Russia hoped that the Turks would see the light and settle matters peaceably. If not, and war should hasten the dissolution of the Turkish empire, "the responsibility will rest with that policy of distrust which, by exciting the Porte against us, has already more than once brought her to the very brink of an abyss, in which only the moderation of the Emperor has prevented her from being swallowed up." [7]

Nesselrode argued at length that the Menshikov note would not endanger the sovereignty of the sultan, for it would provide nothing new which would in any way add to Russia's existing right to intervene, in the name of religion, in Turkey's internal affairs if, as alleged, it sought to do so. It was no more harmful to the rights of the sultan than the French capitulations or the Austrian treaties. Already, by the Treaties of Kainardji and Adrianople, Russia was entitled to watch over the rights of the Orthodox clergy in Turkey. It had broken off relations with Turkey during the Greek revolt when the Orthodox church was persecuted. One fact that must be accepted was the sympathy and the community of interests of the fifty million Russian Ortho-

6. Nesselrode to Brunnow, May 20/June 1, 1853, ibid., pp. 241–45.
7. Ibid.

dox for the twelve million and more of the majority of the sultan's subjects. Thus Russia had a substantial basis for its claims.[8]

In addition to sending this justification to Clarendon, on May 19/ 31 Nesselrode urged Reshid pasha to face the situation. In a few weeks Russian troops would enter the Principalities—not for war with the sultan, which would be repugnant for the emperor—but to obtain "material guarantees" from the Ottoman government. To avert this calamity, Reshid, with the consent of the sultan, should sign the note and send it within a week to Menshikov at Odessa. Nesselrode earnestly hoped that Reshid and the Divan would accept his advice and "that in the interests of peace, which we must all be equally desirous to maintain, it may be followed without hesitation and without delay." [9]

As has been mentioned, Nesselrode, like Menshikov, ascribed the failure of the negotiations to Lord Redcliffe, who had compelled the Porte to reject even the most moderate Russian proposals. In a conversation at St. Petersburg with Seymour the chancellor charged Redcliffe with preventing the Turkish ministers from accepting them.[10] For his part, Redcliffe sent a letter to Seymour stating that he had helped to settle the issue of the Holy Places, but when Menshikov had demanded the right to protect the Orthodox church, the Turks had refused without urging from him. The sultan rejected the note, and the Council did likewise, by a vote of forty-two to three. While the Turks doubtless knew how Redcliffe felt, *they* made the decision, not he.[11]

While the Turks refused to grant Menshikov's chief request, they readily conceded on other points. The Council of Ministers adopted two firmans approving the Russian petition concerning the Church of the Nativity at Bethlehem and the repairs to the cupola of the Church of the Holy Sepulcher.[12] A message from Reshid declared that "the honour of the Porte requires that the exclusively spiritual privileges granted by the sultan's predecessors and confirmed by His Majesty remain in force; any privilege granted to one class of Christians should not be refused to the Greek clergy." The sultan had approved the building of a Russian church and a hospice at Jerusalem, and

8. Ibid., p. 244.
9. Nesselrode to Reshid Pasha, May 19/31, 1853, ibid., pp. 245–46.
10. Seymour to Clarendon, May 31, 1853, ibid., p. 231.
11. Letter, Redcliffe to Seymour, May 23, 1853, ibid., pp. 253–55.
12. Redcliffe to Clarendon, May 25, 1853, ibid., pp. 247–51.

the Porte would conclude a sened "on this and the special privileges of the Russian monks at both places." [13]

The sultan also issued an imperial firman to the Greek Patriarch of Constantinople, confirming the special rights that his ancestors had granted to the Greek clergy, and ordering that the immunities and privileges granted to its churches and convents, and those which peculiarly appertained to the Greek clergy, "be forever maintained." [14]

These concessions, however, did not placate the Russian cabinet, which insisted on a pledge to *it* to maintain the ancient rights and immunities of the Greek church in Turkey. Redcliffe, who was adamant against this, on May 22 sent a grim despatch to Clarendon that Britain must decide how far it would support Turkey. The Turks, he said, had no choice. "It was not the amputation of a limb, but the infusion of poison into the system that they are summoned to accept." Unless Turkey got help, it would sooner or later fall into Russia's power.[15] This despatch and the alarming messages from Seymour carried the day, so that Palmerston won the support of most of the cabinet, and even Aberdeen gave in to the enormous pressure. As a result, on June 2 Clarendon wrote to the admiralty that the queen wanted the fleet to go to the Dardanelles and that Admiral Dundas should rush word to Redcliffe that it was at his disposal. The foreign secretary also sent word to Redcliffe to this effect, adding that he should make sure that the Turks would grant free passage through the Straits "in the event of your being called by the Sultan to call up the fleet to Constantinople." [16]

The matter was not yet urgent, however, for the Russians had not moved. On May 28 Nesselrode informed Seymour of the departure of Menshikov from Constantinople, adding that a continued rejection of Russia's terms by the Porte "would be followed by the issue of orders for the entrance of the Russian armies into the Principalities." [17] Word of the British decision was quickly sent to Paris, where on June 5 Drouyn de Lhuys wrote to Walewski, French ambassador at London, that Napoleon III was delighted with the identity of views and action of the two countries and hoped that this would "prevent

13. Ibid., p. 252.
14. Firman to Patriarch of Constantinople, Annex to desp., Meyendorff to Nesselrode, May 31, 1853, AVP, f. Kants., D. no. 146.
15. Redcliffe to Clarendon, May 22, 1853, EP, I, 235–36.
16. Clarendon to the Admiralty, June 2, 1853, ibid., p. 210; Clarendon to Redcliffe, ibid.
17. Seymour to Clarendon, May 31, 1853, ibid., p. 232.

the complications which might arise in the East." Drouyn had promptly instructed La Cour at Constantinople to act in common with Redcliffe, and the French fleet would anchor beside the British at Besika Bay at the Dardanelles. At the same time, France would "make at all times sincere efforts to reconcile the pretensions of Russia with the sovereign rights of the Porte." [18] On June 8 Clarendon wrote to Cowley in Paris of the similarity of British and French views on the East, where the main purpose was to work for peace and harmony. He stated that the government had told both Houses of Parliament that there was a complete identity of opinion between the two governments and that both wanted to uphold the Turkish empire.[19]

In the meantime the Russians had not acted, although the Turks had failed to sign Menshikov's note and send it to Odessa. On June 9 Nesselrode sent a letter to Reshid pasha by a Russian warship under a merchant flag, warning him that unless he signed the note without change and sent it to Odessa in eight days, the Russian army would cross the border. This would not be an act of war, but a step to secure "a material guarantee" from the Porte until Reshid should send the signed note to Odessa.[20] Five days later Reshid told Redcliffe that as the Turkish position had not changed, the answer would be negative. Nevertheless the Porte was willing to send an ambassador to St. Petersburg, although there would be no Turkish engagement inconsistent with the sovereign rights and independence of the Porte.[21] Nicholas I and Nesselrode were convinced that the imminent arrival of the Allied fleets had confirmed the Turks in their decision. But since the Porte had already sternly rejected the Russian proposals, it is quite likely that it would have refused in this case even if the squadrons had not been sent.

But while the sailing of the fleets may not have been decisive with the Turks, it convinced Nicholas I that he must enter the Principalities, lest it appear that this Western threat had made him back down.[22] Although the Russians had already announced their intention to enter the provinces and the maritime powers had given this announcement as their reason for ordering their fleets to sail, no Russian troops

18. Drouyn de Lhuys to Walewski, June 5, 1853, ibid., pp. 228–29.
19. Clarendon to Cowley, June 8, 1853, ibid., p. 234.
20. Redcliffe to Clarendon, June 10, 1853, ibid., p. 298.
21. Ibid., June 15, p. 309.
22. Jomini, pp. 194–95.

crossed the frontier until July 2 (N.S.), long after the fleets were anchored at Besika Bay. The British ships came on June 13–14, and
the French on June 20.[23]

When the Russian forces finally entered the Principalities, St. Petersburg insisted that this move did not mean war, nor was it an attempt
to destroy the Turkish empire; it was merely a temporary measure
of compulsion to force the Porte to give a satisfactory answer to the
emperor's just demands. Russia was not seeking conquests; it was
ready to halt its armies if the Porte "will bind itself solemnly to observe
the inviolability of the Orthodox church." [24]

A circular from Nesselrode to Russia's diplomats stated the case
in greater detail. It held that the Porte was demanding of Russia a
rule of conduct so strict that it would virtually mean the scrapping
of all Russia's treaties and the ensuing right to "watch effectively
over the safety of the Greek rite in Turkey." In spite of Russia's
highly conciliatory intentions, this issue was insoluble in a peaceful
way, "for it would be a question for us of our treaties, of our repute
(crédit), of our worldly influence, of our dearest sentiments, national
and religious." [25]

The chancellor added that Russia's opponents, including the press,
seemed to ignore the fact that Russia was not asking for a new right
but for an old one that it, "by its position and by its treaties, enjoys
of protecting its faith in the East and of preserving this right, which
it cannot renounce." Russia's adversaries held that this right implied
a completely new claim of a protectorate, both religious and moral,
"whose future scope and consequences are exaggerated."

This view, however, was not correct, Nesselrode stated. Russia was
only asking for the status quo for the Greeks—"only the maintenance
of the ancient privileges that they have held under the aegis of the
sultan." He admitted that this meant a religious protectorate, "which
Russia has at all times exercised in the East." But since in the past
a protectorate had existed without damage to the sovereignty and
independence of Turkey, why could it not continue to do so? Russia's
claims merely required a simple confirmation of this right.[26]

23. Temperley, *England and the Near East,* p. 339.
24. Russian Manifesto, June 14/26, 1853, EP, I, 323.
25. Circular of July 3, 1853, HHSA, X, 38.
26. Ibid.

Nesselrode repeated that the tsar had never wanted to destroy the Ottoman empire or to seize its territories. Russia's moderate peace terms in 1829, its saving of Turkey in 1833, and in 1839 its initiative in helping to avert Turkey's collapse and the creation of the Arab empire had clearly proved this. The emperor's policy had always been to preserve the status quo in the East, which, as Russia did not need more land, was clearly in its interests. "Because Turkey, prosperous, inoffensive, placed between powerful states," served as a buffer for their rivalries, which would certainly clash fiercely if Turkey should crumble, Russia wanted to maintain it intact. But Turkey must deal properly with Russia in order for co-existence to be possible. It must respect the special treaties and their consequences and must refrain from acts of bad faith, underhanded persecutions, and perpetual vexations against the Orthodox, which would create a situation that would in time be intolerable for Russia and would compel it to resort to arms.[27]

Shortly after his forces entered the Principalities, Prince M. D. Gorchakov issued a proclamation to reassure the inhabitants. He stated that the occupation was temporary, that it would end as soon as the Turks met Russia's demands, and that Russia would avoid an offensive war against Turkey as long as possible. The occupying power would not change the existing institutions and the political situation would remain as it was. No new taxes would be imposed, and Russia would pay for provisions for its troops at a rate fixed by agreement with the local rulers.[28]

Gorchakov ordered his troops not to fight with the Turks in the Principalities unless they crossed the Danube, and then only if they were in small units. If large forces of Turks appeared, the Russians should retire on their main body. They should protect Bucharest from the Turks and also hold the line of the Danube.[29] The general also wrote to Reshid pasha at Constantinople to inform him of the troop movement into the provinces, stating that the emperor had not declared war on Turkey and that as soon as the Porte had met his "just demands," his forces would return to their own territory. He added that he had been ordered to avoid all hostile and aggressive action

27. Ibid.
28. Circular of Prince Gorchakov, July 4, 1853, ibid., p. 598.
29. Zaionchkovskii, *Pril.,* II, 81–83.

against the Turks beyond the Danube and that the Porte should consider issuing similar orders to its commanders in order to avoid clashes between the two armies.[30]

On the eve of the Russian entry into the Principalities there had been a widespread belief that this would be only the first step in the conquest of Turkey. These pledges of a speedy withdrawal and the orders to the troops not to attack the Turks indicated, however, that Russia had no thought of conquest, a view that was strongly supported by Crown Prince William of Prussia, who was not friendly to Russia. His memorandum, "The Russo-Turkish Question," written at Weimar on February 15 and 16, 1854, held that the deployment and numbers of the Russians in the Principalities showed that they did not at once intend war but only a peaceful occupation. Of the six infantry divisions under Gorchakov, only four were stationed along the lengthy Danube line, along with two cavalry divisions. The other two infantry divisions were at Odessa and Sevastopol, and the latter unit was at once transferred to the Caucasus and replaced by half the division at Odessa,[31] which left Gorchakov with insufficient forces to hold his position properly, to say nothing of an offensive.

At the news of the Russian entry the Porte at once sent a protest to St. Petersburg, declaring that it was greatly pained by this action, which violated the spirit of 1841 and broke repeated promises of Russian friendship for Turkey. It had undertaken to settle the grievances presented by Prince Menshikov and had done so to their mutual satisfaction and had even promised that Russia might build a church and a hospital in Jerusalem. While the Porte held that it must refuse the Russian demand for a solemn engagement to guarantee the rights and immunities of the Orthodox church within the Ottoman empire, the sultan publicly confirmed these rights and offered his solemn protection in a state paper bearing his official seal, which was communicated to the friendly governments. In this way the Greek church received protection without infringement of the sovereign rights of the sultan. The Porte was still willing to make an arrangement that would satisfy the court of Russia without violating the sacred rights of the sultan, by sending an ambassador to St. Petersburg to work out the terms of a settlement with the Russian cabinet.

---

30. Nesselrode to Meyendorff, June 30/July 2, 1853, with copy of letter from Prince Gorchakov to Reshid pasha, HHSA, X, 38.
31. Borries, pp. 347–50.

Although the Porte was entitled to regard the Russian action as grounds for war, it was willing to confine itself to a protest against the Russian aggression and would refrain from all hostile action. It was still willing to meet the justified claims of the Russian court and offered the most explicit assurances to confirm the settlement that would satisfy all concerned.[32]

In England the Russian entry into the Principalities aroused a storm of indignation in the press. All political parties were strongly against Russia and demanded action in opposition to its aggressive plans against Constantinople. Most of the statesmen were agreed, except for Aberdeen and a few others. Aberdeen and Brunnow worked energetically to avoid a break and an open Franco-British alliance, through such expedients as a special envoy for personal talks with the emperor. The premier also suggested personal correspondence between the two monarchs to clarify the political questions. Nesselrode warmly approved the British recommendation of a Russo-Turkish convention. Unfortunately, Nicholas I disliked the text of the proposal and greatly preferred the Austrian scheme of sending an ultimatum to the Porte to send a signed note to St. Petersburg.[33]

The British government did not regard the occupation of Moldavia and Wallachia as grounds for Turkey to declare war and officially notified St. Petersburg of its opinion. Clarendon pledged that the fleet would not enter the Dardanelles unless Russia actually menaced Constantinople. He also advised the Porte not to declare war.[34]

Austria was critical of the Russian intention to occupy the Principalities and informed the other powers, to Nesselrode's annoyance.[35] Foreign Minister Buol told the Turks, however, that they should not make of the situation a *casus belli*, and should not attack the Russians when they crossed the Pruth. Turkey should make great efforts to reach a compromise with its neighbor and thus solve its problem, as Buol held that the Turkish army was no match for the Russians and that the Christians of Turkey might rise if war came.[36]

At the same time the Austrian cabinet made an earnest effort to induce Russia to be moderate by sending Major General Count Gyulai,

32. Note of Sublime Porte to Russian Cabinet, July 2/14, 1853, AVP, f. Kants., D. no. 146.
33. Martens, "Rossiia i Angliia," pp. 582–85.
34. Puryear, *England, Russia, and the Straits,* pp. 284–85.
35. Nesselrode to Meyendorff, July 9/21, 1853 (Very Confidential). HHSA, X, 38.
36. Westmorland to Clarendon, June 11, 1853, EP, I, 271–72.

governor of Milan, to attend the Russian reviews and inspections and to bear an autographed letter from Emperor Franz Joseph to the tsar. Gyulai was to emphasize to the tsar the "dangerous complications" that the occupation of the Principalities might cause and Austria's hopes that the intervention of the great powers might bring a suitable settlement. If, however, the anxious desires of the Austrian government were not realized, and the occupation had begun or was about to begin, Gyulai should "strongly urge" His Majesty not to send in a large force. To do so might arouse concern that he was seeking more than the guarantee of reparation that he wanted, and the objective could be accomplished as easily with a small force. While the tsar was displeased by this advice, Nesselrode and Seniavin, a high official of the Russian Foreign Ministry, persuaded him to rely on Austrian mediation at Constantinople.[37]

France took a stiff attitude toward the Russian occupation, for Drouyn de Lhuys issued a circular to the French diplomats saying that the Porte was entitled to regard the Russian demarche as an act of war. Hence it would not be a violation of the Straits Convention if Turkey opened the passage to British and French warships.[38] But since the Turks did not make a *casus belli* of the Russian entry, the French took no action at this time.

Prussia also was displeased by the Russian break with the Porte, feeling that Menshikov had gone far beyond what Berlin had expected. Both the public and the diplomatic corps felt that Menshikov's conduct had been deplorable.[39] Prussia made various suggestions for compromise settlements, but late in June Nesselrode replied that these proposals could only be entertained when the Turks had signed Menshikov's note.[40]

But while the four major powers disliked Russia's actions, none of them wanted to go to war over them and all were eager to find an arrangement that would satisfy the Russians without weakening Turkey's independence. The Porte also hoped for a peaceful solution, if one could be had without harm to its sovereignty. St. Petersburg

37. Ibid., June 30, 1853, p. 319. M. S. Anderson, *The Eastern Question, 1774–1923* (London, 1966), p. 125.
38. Circular of Drouyn de Lhuys, July 15, 1853, ibid., p. 362.
39. Bloomfield to Clarendon, May 30, 1853, ibid., pp. 223–24.
40. Lebzeltern to Buol, June 13/25, 1853, HHSA, X, 36.

was also eager for a favorable settlement. Hence there was a great deal of diplomatic activity in the summer of 1853.

At Constantinople Lord Redcliffe continued his efforts to settle the crisis. Late in June, before the Russians had crossed the Pruth, he called an unofficial meeting of the four ambassadors to determine their views. All wanted a settlement that would not be harmful for Turkey and were willing to lend moral support. Redcliffe, as usual, was not willing to grant "the diplomatic engagement required by Russia" and held that they should have in mind the position of the sultan's government toward its allies and its people. Above all he wanted a simultaneous and strong declaration "that real and comprehensive improvement of the condition of the sultan's non-Musulman subjects can no longer be deferred." The four ambassadors proposed to serve as an unofficial organ of mediation and conciliation, taking due care not to offend Russia.[41] Redcliffe strongly supported Reshid and the peace party in Constantinople, urging them to send a special envoy to St. Petersburg and to communicate the latest firman granting concessions to the Patriarch of Constantinople. When on July 8 the sultan dismissed both the grand vizir and Reshid and replaced them with members of the war party, Redcliffe intervened and induced the sultan to restore them. He persuaded the Porte to protest against the Russian occupation rather than to declare war. According to Temperley, he was eager to gain time, for many days had been lost by the Moslem fasts of Ramadan and the feasting of Bairam. Also the dismissal of Reshid had cost another week. Thus the Turks had wasted two months of highly precious time.[42]

Russia also was active, seeking Austrian support to force Turkey into accepting the Russian demands. Baron Meyendorff was sent to Austria as ambassador and during his audience with Franz Joseph on his arrival at Vienna he asked that Austria give full support, including massing troops on the borders of Serbia and Herzegovina, to be followed, if need be, by occupation of these areas. The emperor expressed grave doubt about this proposal, as he thought it might give Napoleon III the very pretext he needed for aggression in Belgium or in Italy. Meyendorff reassured him that the tsar was allowing plenty of time to negotiate, and reminded him that Menshikov had been

41. Redcliffe to Clarendon, June 24, 1853, EP, I, 331–32.
42. Temperley, *England and the Near East,* pp. 339–41.

kept waiting for several months, while Leiningen, the Austrian envoy
to the Porte, had obtained his demands in eight days. Menshikov
had extended his time limit three times, until finally he felt that his
dignity called for an answer. Meyendorff was unable, however, to
overcome the young emperor's fear of war. The ambassador's final
word was that if war should come, there would be only five Russian
army corps to face the enemies of Austria and Russia. Meyendorff
concluded that although Franz Joseph was worried, he trusted the
tsar and would support his views, without, however, making any agreements with Russia.[43]

Since none of the powers wanted to deal with the Russian occupation
by force, diplomacy was called into play and in the summer of 1853
there was a spate of activity, as each of the uninvolved powers devised
expedients to solve the problem. The British cabinet, for example,
suggested that, with the approval of the Western cabinets, Russian
and Turkish plenipotentiaries should agree to meet to discuss Menshikov's Note and Reshid's reply, in order to negotiate a convention.
By removing from the two documents anything offensive for the other
side, the remainder should provide the material for one document
that would settle the issue. Above all, everything contrary to the dignity
and sovereign rights of the sultan would be eliminated.[44] When this
scheme was presented to Nesselrode, however, he preferred to accept
mediation from Austrian hands, along the lines of the "Bourqueney
Note" or some other plan.[45] The British proposal never came up at
Vienna, for it was sent only as a last alternative "if other things fail."
Meyendorff also reported that the Turks had seen the British plan
and had rejected it.[46]

Bourqueney, French ambassador at Vienna, proposed that the Turks
should sign the Menshikov Note and send it to St. Petersburg, where
Nicholas I in return would give pledges of his intentions to satisfy
the Turks. The French claimed that this plan had originated in Russia,
and Napoleon III doubted its value. He felt, however, that if before
receiving the signed Note the Russian cabinet would "submit for previous consideration the answer which . . . would be made to the Porte,
and that answer contained satisfactory assurances" and its stipulations

43. Meyendorff to Nesselrode, May 26/June 7, 1853, AVP, f. Kants., D. no. 146.
44. Castelbajac to Drouyn de Lhuys, ca. July 17, 1853, ADF, Russie, vol. 209, p. 170.
45. Ibid.
46. Letter, Meyendorff to Nesselrode, July 16, 1853, cited in Hoetzsch, III, 54.

were fully binding on Russia, he would consult with the British and Austrian governments about recommending it to the Porte.[47] The Turks, however, rejected this proposal, as they had done with the British scheme for a convention.[48]

St. Petersburg favored the Bourqueney plan, but insisted that the Porte bring the signed Menshikov Note, unchanged, and no other. It also demanded that the Allied fleets must leave Turkish waters as soon as the Russian forces evacuated the Principalities. Lord Redcliffe also had a plan for putting the Principalities under four-power protection. Berlin proposed a five-power protectorate over the Christians of the East. Russia opposed this plan, insisting on its right to independent dealings with Turkey.[49]

Finally Drouyn de Lhuys drafted a note for the Turks to sign and bring to St. Petersburg, which Castelbajac showed directly to Nicholas I. While the tsar greatly preferred it to the Bourqueney scheme, he wanted to find out how Austria felt about it. Drouyn informed Buol of this, whereupon Buol stated that he would support the French plan at St. Petersburg, since the four envoys were still conferring at Constantinople. Hübner suggested to Buol that the talks should be concentrated at Vienna, as London, Paris, and St. Petersburg were directly involved in the dispute, and Redcliffe dominated the diplomats at Constantinople. The resulting Conference of Vienna reworked the Drouyn Note, which, with some changes, became the Vienna Note, with London, Paris, and Berlin taking part. Early in August the four powers sent orders to their envoys at Constantinople insisting that the Porte sign it. In the meantime, however, the four envoys, with Redcliffe at their head, had already drawn up a letter to Nesselrode, which Reshid signed. It was then sent on to Vienna. The Conference disapproved of the Constantinople note and refused to forward it, insisting on their own note.[50] The failure of the Porte and the diplomats at Constantinople to cooperate with the Conference of Vienna indicated that trouble lay ahead.

The Note of Vienna, which was the handiwork of Buol and Emperor

47. Cowley to Clarendon, July 6, 1853, EP, I, 331; Seymour to Clarendon, June 27, 1853, ibid., p. 324.

48. Letter, Meyendorff to Nesselrode, July 19/31, 1853, Hoetzsch, III, 54.

49. Jomini, pp. 204–05. Nicholas I, with his cabinet, knowing that most of the powers were unfavorable to Russia's position on the Eastern question, consistently opposed involvement of the Concert of Europe in Russia's dealings with Turkey.

50. Hübner, I, 143.

Franz Joseph, along with some of the leading diplomats of Europe, indicated the strong desire of the governments and the public of much of Europe for peace. While it differed somewhat from the Menshikov Note, it pleased the Russians by including a formal promise of the sultan to respect the rights and immunities of the Orthodox church, based on the treaties between Russia and Turkey. Nicholas I gave it full approval on August 5, to show his respect for the Austrian emperor and to prove that his own intentions were peaceful. His sole condition was that the Porte must sign without reservations *(pur et simple)*. If it refused to sign, Russia would not be bound by its acceptance. London and Paris accepted the Note as it stood, and Vienna gave it the form of an ultimatum: if Turkey refused, the powers would give the Porte no more support against Russia. The other cabinets and the European public felt the same and were grateful to Russia for having brought peace near.[51] Even Lord Palmerston was pleased and complimented Clarendon on the note: "it is a great comfort and satisfaction to know that the conduct of foreign affairs is in such capable hands as yours." [52]

The Vienna Note, which, couched in flowery terms, ostensibly emanated from the Sublime Porte and was to be taken to St. Petersburg by a special Turkish ambassador, was intended to satisfy the tsar, while not infringing on the sovereignty and independence of the sultan. Its full text is given in Appendix 2 at the end of this volume. The following paraphrase gives its significant passages:

The sultan is extremely eager to restore good relations with Russia, and the Porte is now communicating his decision to Count Nesselrode.

While the Russian emperors have always shown a strong desire to maintain the privileges and immunities of the Greek Orthodox church in the Ottoman empire, the sultan has always supported them by renewing the decrees in its favor. Now Sultan Abdul Medjid, wanting to show his most sincere friendship for the Russian emperor, is trusting him and paying serious attention to the representations made by Prince Menshikov.

Hence the undersigned ambassador officially declares herewith that the sultan's government will remain faithful to the letter and the spirit of the Treaties of Kainardji and Adrianople concerning the protection

---

51. Theodor Schiemann, *Geschichte Russlands unter Kaiser Nikolaus I* (Berlin, 1904–19), IV, 295–96; Jomini, pp. 207–08.
52. Martin, p. 135.

of the Christian religion and that the sultan, as a point of honor, will preserve fully the spiritual privileges of the Orthodox church in the Levant and will allow the Greek church to enjoy full equality with other rites.

The latest firman to the Patriarch confirming the privileges of the Greek clergy is proof of the sultan's good will toward the Greek church, of which the undersigned solemnly notifies the Russian court. The Porte has settled the issue of the Holy Places in Palestine by the firman of February 1852, which will be enforced. It promises that no change will be made in the present situation without agreement with the French and Russian governments.

If requested by the Russian government, the Sublime Porte will grant a site in or near Jerusalem for a Russian church and for a hospice for sick or needy pilgrims and will give a solemn deed for it.[53]

From this paraphrase it is clear that in the Note the Porte was promising to maintain the existing privileges and immunities of the Greek church in the Ottoman empire and would preserve the situation of the Holy Places without change. It also mentioned the Treaties of Küchuk-Kainardji and Adrianople, which the Russian cabinet regarded as the foundation of Russia's rights to protect the Greek church, and thus supported the Russian claim to protect the religious rights of their coreligionists in the Turkish empire. The Note, however, did not contain any language that would seem to justify Russian interference with the sovereign rights of the sultan to rule his lay subjects of the Orthodox rite.

Lord Redcliffe, who was ordered on August 2 to support the Note of Vienna, now found himself in a difficult position, for he had persuaded Reshid to sign the Constantinople Note, which the latter stated contained Turkey's utmost concessions. The Vienna Conference, however, rejected it, and now Redcliffe had to support the Vienna Note, which contained greater concessions, although he knew that the strong nationalist party in Turkey would bitterly oppose it. Officially he supported the Note of Vienna, although the Turks knew full well that in his heart he was against it.[54] The Turks were not willing to accept

53. Clarendon to Redcliffe, August 2, 1853, transmitting the Note of Vienna, EP, II, 26–27.
54. Temperley, *England and the Near East,* p. 343.

it, since it was imposed on them by the great powers. Reshid strongly protested against its drafting without the knowledge of Turkey and denied that he knew of it beforehand. (Perhaps the Turkish minister at Vienna, who *had* seen it, did not dare report that he knew of it.) The Vienna Note aroused the suspicions of the Turks and infuriated many of them with its demand for greater concessions, so that Redcliffe lost much of his earlier influence.[55]

The ambassador, whose sympathies with the Turks were strong, reported to Clarendon that Turkey was in a dangerous condition internally, for the strain of the occupation of the Principalities put great burdens on the people. He warned that the dissatisfaction of the Bulgarians was on the point of erupting into a general insurrection and that there was strong belief that one of the political parties in Serbia was looking for the first opportunity to strike for independence. All European Turkey had been stripped of regular Turkish troops, who had been replaced by Albanian hordes "habituated to turbulence and plunder." The Montenegrins, he had learned, were probably about to invade Turkey to gain the support of the Christian tribes there, and "a spirit of fanaticism, dangerous alike to the Rayahs and to the authorities" was arising elsewhere. Also the language and conduct of the Greeks showed "views of ambition, unrestrained by principles or treaties."[56]

When, on August 12, Redcliffe urged the Porte to accept the Note, he found the Turks highly unreceptive. The Egyptian fleet had just arrived with thousands of troops, whose tents were visible on the hills. Moreover, the British and French fleets were known to be not far off and all the Turks believed that the Allies would support them. Egyptian troops paraded through the streets and hostility toward Russia mounted, stirred up by Mehemet Ali, minister of war.

On August 14 the Ministers' Council considered the Vienna Note, with Reshid and the grand vizir urging amendments to it. Six others were neutral, and Mehemet Ali and seven more favored rejection. On the 10th, when the Note was again considered, Redcliffe refused any amendments, although Reshid begged him not to forsake Turkey at this hour. On August 20 Reshid and other ministers accepted the Note, but only with amendments Russia would not approve.[57]

55. Ibid., p. 345.
56. Redcliffe to Clarendon, July 4, 1853, EP, II, 371.
57. Temperley, *England and the Near East,* pp. 346–47.

The Egyptian show of strength encouraged the Turks to defy Europe and caused Redcliffe's influence at Constantinople to be gravely weakened. Redcliffe had favored the Note of Constantinople ("the Turkish ultimatum") and had said that Europe would accept it, but Europe had refused it and in the Vienna Note made stiffer demands, which meant to the Turks either that Redcliffe had tricked them or that he was less influential than they had believed. Turkish feeling had been aroused by the Menshikov mission, and the Grand Council, full of reactionaries, gained great influence. Reshid could hold out no hope of amendments and, because he was for peace, was suspect and many politicians, including his colleagues, sought his ruin. He told Redcliffe that no one in the capital favored the Vienna Note, which was why it was rejected.[58]

While Redcliffe was widely blamed for the failure of the Note, by the summer of 1853 the Turkish drift toward war was almost irresistible. On the other hand, if in May Redcliffe had been less flinty against concessions to Menshikov, possibly the dispute between St. Petersburg and the Porte might have been compromised without harm to either side.

In the meantime, after Nicholas had fully accepted the Note of Vienna, the Russian cabinet was waiting for the Porte to respond to the Note, sent to it as an ultimatum by the Conference of Vienna. By his prompt acceptance of it the tsar showed his readiness for peace and no longer was the enemy for those who wanted to avoid war. Baron Brunnow, Russia's clever ambassador at London, on June 1 (N.S.) wrote an analysis of the probable results of war for Russia, which, he believed, would probably destroy the Ottoman Empire and scrap the Treaty of Kainardji, on which Russia relied. It would produce a number of small, troublesome states, like ungrateful Greece and the troublesome Principalities, and others. In the aftermath Russia would have less influence than before and would be more hampered by the rivalries of France, England, and even Austria.

Thus the war would not be advantageous for Russia, for it would be costly in blood and treasure, in order that Greece, England, and France would gain, and in place of Turkey there would be small states, which would either be troublesome vassals or hostile neighbors.[59]

58. Ibid., p. 347.
59. F. F. Martens, *Recueil des traités,* XII, 325.

Baron Meyendorff, Russian ambassador at Vienna, was fairly hopeful that the Turks would accept the Note of Vienna—"a plan backed
by all the diplomacy of Europe"—but he felt some doubt. He held
that if war came, Russia would be denied the use of the Black Sea
and, in order to placate Austria, would have to stay out of Serbia.
Nevertheless Russia should be able to cross the Balkan Mountains,
which would make the collapse of Turkey inevitable. But because
Russia had nothing better to put in the place of the Ottoman empire,
"even our triumphs would become embarrassments." [60]

The chancellor, however, was less hopeful, for on August 2 he took
Castelbajac, the French ambassador, into a secluded spot in his garden
and unburdened himself on affairs in the East. He said he was not
worried about England or France, or Russia, "but only about Turkey,
which is in a deplorable state of exaltation, or disorganization, and
of weakness." After waiting for fifteen days for news about the Note
of Vienna, all the news he had was two highly alarming telegrams.
"One," he said, "announced that in a moment of drunkenness, to
which he is strongly subject, the Sultan had dismissed Reshid-Pasha
and the other ministers who favor peace; but that the next morning,
on the urging of Lord Redcliffe, he had reversed this measure." The
second telegram stated that the war party had again won out in the
councils of the sultan. If that was the case, said Nesselrode, "I fear
the rising of the Turks against the Christians, and as a result, a general
insurrection of all the Christian populations—i.e., anarchy, massacres,
the complete ruin of the Ottoman Government and for us all complications of which no one can foresee either the term or the results."
He did say, however, that he would continue to negotiate with the
Porte as long as possible. [61]

Finally an official Note of the Sublime Porte to the representatives
of the four powers arrived at Vienna, with a modified draft note of
August 20, 1853. The two notes stated that the Turkish Council of
Ministers had examined the Note of Vienna and was pained that the
four powers had not taken into consideration the note that it had
sent to them. The Note of Vienna contained superfluous paragraphs
which were incompatible with the sacred right of the government of
His Majesty the Sultan. The sultan alone, the sole judge of his rights

60. Letter, Meyendorff to Paskevich, July 24/Aug. 5, 1853, Hoetzsch, III, 58–59.
61. Castelbajac to Drouyn de Lhuys, Aug. 3, 1853, ADF, Russie, vol. 209, 264–68.

and independence, was not consulted on the wording of the new draft. The rights were those of the Porte, and it was the one to sign the Note.[62]

The Porte stated that the following paragraph was the first to trouble it: "If at all times Emperors of Russia have testified to their solicitude for the maintenance of the immunities and the privileges of the Greek Orthodox church in the Ottoman Empire, the Sultans have never refused to consecrate them anew by solemn acts."

The Turks admitted the interest of the Russian emperors, but to them this passage suggested that only by the active support of the tsars had these privileges in the states of the Porte been upheld. Many of the privileges, however, had been granted in the time of Mehmed the Conqueror (1451–81) and had been maintained without any outside participation. The passage thus offered and implied pretexts for Russian interference.[63]

The second point was the clause referring to the Treaty of Kainardji. This treaty existed, and was confirmed by the Treaty of Adrianople, and its provisions would be strictly enforced. It was not, however, the source of the religious privileges. "The real and precise provision of the Treaty," the Turks said, "is limited solely to the Porte's promise to protect the Christian religion." While the Porte could strengthen its arguments by citing paragraphs that would give assurances to satisfy the Russian government, these assurances would give the latter reasons to claim the rights of surveillance and interference, which would impair the sovereign rights and independence of the empire. The government of the sultan would find it completely impossible to assent to this paragraph *"without being forced to it."* It would be willing, however, to renew the engagement of the Treaty of Kainardji by a separate note. It was especially eager to have the paragraph referring to the treaty suppressed or to have the promise of protection in the Treaty of Kainardji separated from the question of religious privileges, in a most explicit manner, so that at a glance one "will see that they are two different things." [64]

As for having the Greek rite share in the advantages bestowed on other Christian rites, the Porte would do this of its own free will. It

62. Zaionchkovskii, *Pril.,* II, 61.
63. Ibid.
64. Ibid.

could not be bound by precise stipulations for the many millions of the Greek rite.[65]

This having been said, the Porte appealed to the equity and justice of the four powers concerning its sovereign rights and independence. If they accepted its note, or if they made the desired changes in the Note of Vienna, the Ottoman government would not delay in signing it and would immediately send an ambassador extraordinary, "on condition of the evacuation of the Principalities." It further awaited a guarantee by the powers against all future interference with and occupation of the Principalities of Moldavia and Wallachia, in order to avoid a new misunderstanding between the two empires, once the Porte had renewed its relations with the court of Russia.

The Porte completely accepted the points of the draft relating to the Holy Places and to the building of a church and a hospital at Jerusalem.[66]

This development caused much irritation throughout Europe. All had been sure that Russia's acceptance of the Vienna Note meant peace. The Turks would be delighted to escape from their difficulty so easily, especially as they had the support of the four powers. If they hesitated, the pressure of almost all Europe would make them see the light. Now they had rejected their salvation and had insisted on evacuation of the Principalities before they would accept any arrangement with Russia. They even demanded a guarantee from the four powers that Russia should never again be able to occupy the Principalities.

Almost immediately Nesselrode sent a despatch to Vienna stating that on July 23 Nicholas I had ordered him to insist that Russia would not accept any changes in the Note and would withdraw its own acceptance. Austria and the others must threaten to abandon the Porte in the face of Russia if it refused to accept the ultimatum. He added that the Turkish changes were very important, as they were introduced in order to deprive Russia of any grounds for claiming to protect the immunities of the Orthodox rite and also to invalidate "the letter and the spirit of the Treaty of Kainardji." [67]

From Russia Castelbajac told his cabinet that, while unfortunately neither the Turks nor the Russians would give in, the emperor's reasons

65. Ibid., pp. 61–62.
66. Ibid.
67. Nesselrode to Meyendorff, Aug. 26/Sept. 7, 1853, HHSA, X, 38.

and his formal pledge to evacuate the Principalities as soon as the Note was delivered still showed a desire for peace. He added that "the shortest and best way would be to insist that the Porte accept the proposal of the Four Powers, accepted by Russia." [68] Castelbajac mentioned that the four ambassadors at St. Petersburg had tried "by all possible means to get Nesselrode and the emperor to end the delay by consenting to the Turkish changes and to accept a four-power compromise," but it was out of the question.[69] As a result, there was widespread anger against the Turks for preventing peace and both Drouyn de Lhuys and Clarendon sent their regrets to St. Petersburg.[70]

There also was belief in England that Lord Redcliffe was to blame for the obstacle. Clarendon was convinced that Redcliffe had acted contrary to his instructions: he was "bent on war" and "animated by such a personal hatred of the Emperor" as to act "directly contrary to the wishes and instructions of this government." Aberdeen also spoke of "the dishonesty of Stratford." [71] This judgment, however, seems to have been mistaken, for, as mentioned, Redcliffe was earnestly striving to keep Turkey from going to war, but was not able to overcome the passionate feelings of the Ottomans.

Public opinion soon veered sharply, however. Nicholas I had asked Nesselrode to prepare an analysis of the Turkish changes in the Vienna Note, which was done by his Foreign Ministry for the eyes of the monarch. A copy of this analysis, however, marked "confidential," was sent to the Russian embassy at Vienna, and from there to other Russian embassies. By a mysterious indiscretion a copy of it fell into the hands of a Berlin newspaper, which promptly made it public. The press generally seized on this revelation with glee and, "passionately hostile" toward Russia, announced that the Note of Vienna, drawn up in Paris and amended in London and Vienna, held a snare for Turkey. The journalists insisted that Russia, far from having renounced its intention to dominate the Ottoman empire, on the contrary still cherished this design, which lurked in the elegant phrases of the Note. Only Nesselrode's revelation, they said, saved the Turks from

---

68. Castelbajac to Drouyn de Lhuys, Sept. 9, 1853, ADF, Russie, vol. 210, 70–71.
69. Ibid., pp. 75–76.
70. Pierre La Gorce, *Histoire du second empire* (15th ed., Paris, 1894–1904), I, 188–90.
71. F. A. Simpson, *Louis Napoleon and the Recovery of France, 1848–1856* (London, 1923), pp. 230–36.

the fatal trap. This was especially the attitude of much of British public opinion, where the dormant Russophobia again flared up. Clarendon and Drouyn (who had composed the Note of Vienna) now held that Nesselrode's interpretation was as bad as Menshikov's Note and from mid-September they ceased to press the Turks to accept the Note of Vienna.[72] Fonton, Russian chargé at Vienna, wrote to Nesselrode that the British were especially ready to believe the worst of the Russians. The French cabinet also reacted unfavorably to the Nesselrode analysis, although perhaps more to preserve solidarity with London than from a definite conviction. Count Buol, however, refused to go along with the Western powers, telling the French cabinet that after minute examination of Nesselrode's arguments he had found nothing to justify rejecting the Note of Vienna.[73] Nesselrode told Castelbajac that after racking his brains he could find no motive for the attitude of France and especially of England in this matter, for Nicholas I had no ambition to gain control of Turkey. He was still very eager to maintain peace and would exert fresh efforts to soothe the concern of the Porte.[74]

Nesselrode's commentary on the amendments to the Note of Vienna centered on three passages. In the first paragraph following the preamble, the original read: "If the Emperors of Russia have at all times evinced their active solicitude for the maintenance of the immunities and privileges of the Greek Orthodox Church . . . ," which the Turks changed to read: "If at all times the Emperors of Russia have showed their active solicitude for the faith and the Greek Orthodox Church. . . ." This change, the chancellor stated, was to make it appear that the privileges and immunities of the Greek church stemmed not from the tsars, who had shown a general interest in this church, but from the sultans, who had granted, maintained, and renewed these rights to their Greek subjects. If Russia accepted this statement, it would be agreeing that the Porte had been unvarying in support of the Greek rite and its privileges and that the tsars had done little of significance

72. Ibid., p. 236; Schiemann, IV, 298–99. According to more recent scholarship, however, the "violent interpretation" was a Russian leak to claim that Russia had gained an advantage over France and still retained a strong position at Constantinople. The Russian cabinet thus hoped to keep a powerful influence over the Porte. Anderson, p. 126; A. J. P. Taylor, *The Struggle for Mastery in Europe, 1848–1918* (Oxford, 1954), pp. 55–56; J. B. Conacher, *The Aberdeen Coalition, 1852–1855* (Cambridge, Eng., 1968), pp. 184–95.

73. Fonton to Nesselrode, Sept. 11, 1853, Zaionchkovskii, *Pril.,* II, 245.

74. Castelbajac to Drouyn de Lhuys, Oct. 14, 1853, ADF, Russie, vol. 210, pp. 114–15.

for it and its adherents. From that it would follow that the Greek rite had done so well under the Turks that Russia would have no grounds, no basis to intervene and its pressure on the Porte during the last few years would be merely unjustified bullying of a weak power by a vastly stronger one, for unrevealed but highly suspicious motives.[75]

In the second disputed passage the original text stated: ". . . the government of His Majesty the Sultan will remain faithful to the letter and the spirit of the Treaties of Kainardji and Adrianople relative to the protection of the Christian religion, and . . . His Majesty considers himself bound in honour to cause to be observed forever, and to preserve from all prejudice . . . the enjoyment of the spiritual privileges which have been granted by His Majesty's august ancestors to the orthodox Eastern Church. . . ." The Turkish version read: "the government of His Majesty the Sultan will remain faithful to the Treaties of Kainardji and Adrianople, and his Majesty considers himself bound in honour to cause to be observed forever, and to preserve from all prejudice now or hereafter, the enjoyment of the spiritual privileges which have been granted by His Majesty's august ancestors to the Eastern Orthodox Church. . . ." In this fashion the sultan confirmed the two treaties, but without linking them to the protection of the Christian rite, which, on the contrary, derived from the voluntary actions of the sultans and thus did not become a solemn engagement to the Russian government, as the latter still insisted. Thus the Porte again sought to deprive the Russian court of all rights to protect the Greek Christians of Turkey.[76]

Finally Nesselrode was especially exercised by the change introduced into the Note of Vienna which stated that the sultan considered himself bound "in a spirit of exalted equity, to cause the Greek rite to share in the advantages granted to the other Christian rites by Convention or special arrangements." In his commentary the count declared: "The change that they propose in the place of the Austrian Note is above all inadmissible." The Ottoman government, he declared, would pledge itself to have the Greek Orthodox participate only in the rights that it would bestow on other Christian communities "subject to the Porte." Since, however, many communities, Catholic or other, were formed *not* of native *rayahs* subject to the Porte but of foreign ecclesiastics

75. Nesselrode to Meyendorff, Aug. 26, 1853, HHSA, X, 38.
76. Ibid.

or laymen not under Ottoman jurisdiction (this was true of almost all the convents, hospices, seminaries, and episcopates of the Latin rite in Turkey), it would not be possible for the Porte to grant restricted religious advantages and privileges. The Orthodox communities, formed of Ottoman subjects, would not be entitled to claim these privileges and Russia would not have the right to intercede for them.[77]

Thus the Russian cabinet saw the clauses of the Turkish amendments as devious attempts to deprive it of rights which it had previously enjoyed under the Treaties of Küchuk-Kainardji and Adrianople. This would leave the Greek Christians at the mercy of the Turks, who obviously favored the Catholics over the Orthodox. The Porte, which pointed out that the Greek Church had managed to exist for centuries after the Ottoman conquest, even though without Russian protection based on treaties, assured the Russian emperor that the sultan's benevolence would continue to maintain its immunities and privileges unimpaired. Nevertheless the Russian cabinet, which knew of the perils that the Orthodox had undergone during the War of Greek Independence and which had seen the Turks show strong partiality to the Latins during the dispute about the Holy Places in Palestine, remained convinced that only the threat of Russian protection could ensure the Greek Orthodox the peace and tranquility that they needed. Nicholas I hoped that he could reassure the Porte as to the moderate and reasonable use that he would make of this right. The Turks, however, had no confidence in Russian promises and felt that it would be better to fight than to surrender. And since British public opinion was so outraged by alleged Russian duplicity as revealed by Nesselrode that they began to demand that Russian naval power in the Black Sea be drastically reduced, a reluctant government was impelled to move closer and closer to conflict. Napoleon III, who had no concrete objectives in the Levant, saw this crisis as a means of aligning France and Britain against Russia and thus of ending the isolation that had kept France from playing a suitable role as a great power. The result of these contending forces was the war into which the powers gradually moved in the next five months.

77. Ibid.

CHAPTER 8. TURKEY GOES TO WAR

Russian insistence on its right to protect the Greek Orthodox church in the Ottoman empire shows clearly that Nicholas I was determined to preserve his influence over the Orthodox of Turkey. British and to a lesser degree French observers have advanced various explanations for this determination, which are generally based on the alleged predatory or aggressive nature of the Russians. Russia, it was said, had an insatiable longing for Constantinople—for reasons of sentiment or prestige, or to provide the warm-water port for which the Russians yearned. To gain the allegiance of the Orthodox Greeks, Bulgars, Serbs, and Arabs would be the first step toward the far greater ulterior aims that Russia was presumably pursuing. Others laid the Russian moves to the Emperor Nicholas himself, who sought Constantinople as a preliminary to the conquest of India.

Russia had been predatory in the past, especially under Catherine II. But the historical argument would also apply to other countries, for Spain, France, Turkey, Poland, Austria, and England all had had dreams of empire, although most of them had renounced them. In the nineteenth century Russia's expansion had been small and after its war with Turkey in 1828–29 it had shown great moderation. Twice when Turkey had been on the verge of disaster Russia had not tried to profit by these opportunities. It showed no eagerness to send the Russian fleet through the Straits, which it was reputed to cherish, for without bases in the Mediterranean its fleet would be at the mercy of the powerful squadrons based at Malta and Toulon. In fact, as already stated, Russia's leaders in 1829 had decided that the country's interests would best be served by having Turkey in control of the Straits, for they knew that Europe would not permit Russia to have Constantinople.

On the other hand, the Menshikov mission, which demanded that the Porte guarantee the rights and privileges of the Greek church;

the occupation of Moldavia and Wallachia; and the Note of Vienna were all intended to maintain the Russian influence over the Orthodox. Russia did not want the Christians of Turkey to revolt against the Turks. Just as in 1849, when Russian troops had put down an uprising in the Principalities against the sultan, in 1853 Russia was pursuing the same policy. Moreover, when in 1852 the Montenegrins rose against the Turks, the Russians had discouraged them from further adventures.[1] During his mission at Constantinople Menshikov had found time to compel Prince Alexander of Serbia to dismiss his premier and several other officials, to the annoyance of the Serbs.[2] Fonton, counselor of the Russian embassy at Vienna, had gone to Belgrade to lay down the law to the prince, which Buol called fresh proof of the "peaceful sentiments of the Russian cabinet and its desire to reduce the embarrassment of the Porte in maintaining the status quo in these provinces" as far as possible.[3] Castelbajac at this time spoke to Nesselrode about the dismissal of the Serbian premier. The chancellor replied with unusual heat that the latter was untrustworthy, "animated by a dangerous political spirit, unfortunately too widespread in Serbia. . . ." Since Serbia owed its existence to Russia, the latter could not permit it to become Russia's enemy "and the enemy of conservative principles." Thouvenel added that this was the motive of the emperor Nicholas and the basis of his dealings with Turkey and its border provinces.[4] In a despatch to Meyendorff at Vienna late in July Nesselrode reported that Peter Karageorgevich, the ruling prince in Serbia, was no longer guided by "revolutionaries and adventurers," thanks to the joint efforts of Fonton and the Austrian envoy. While Polish and Magyar propaganda was still active, and the Turks were still encouraging the prince, he felt sure that the situation would now be satisfactory.[5]

Here, apparently, was the real motive of Russia's actions in the Levant. Nicholas I was, with Austria, a bulwark of reaction. He had put down revolutionary outbreaks in Russia, Poland, Hungary, and the Principalities and was determined to eliminate all uprisings that might stimulate his restless subjects to unseat him. As the greatest

---

1. Instructions, Nesselrode to Kovalevskii, Jan. 19/31, 1853, HHSA, X, 38; Nesselrode to Fonton, Jan. 26/Feb. 7, 1853, ibid.
2. Clarendon to Redcliffe, Apr. 18, 1853, EP, I, 121.
3. Buol to Lebzeltern, Aug. 10, 1853, HHSA, X, 37.
4. Thouvenel, p. 131.
5. Nesselrode to Meyendorff, July 24/Aug. 5, 1853, HHSA, X, 37.

landowner in Russia he, along with the other serfmasters, felt that the ground was quaking beneath his feet. Although he recognized that serfdom was an evil that must go, he was terrified that its demise might lead to a great jacquerie with fire and bloodshed, and this he had to prevent. In order to do so he felt it essential to keep strong control over the Christians of Turkey lest they, by revolting against the sultan, should unleash the revolutionary whirlwind over eastern Europe. England and France, while repressive in Ireland, India, and Algeria, still stood for progress and freedom of a kind. The tsar had set his face against change and wanted to use his influence over the Christians of Turkey to keep them from rebellion. He wished, certainly, to obtain a more bearable existence for them, but chiefly in order, as he repeatedly said, to remove the incentive for rebellion against the Ottoman rulers. He was not consistent in his utterances and his actions, but he was firmly against revolution and he did not want war.

Bulgaria proved to be troublesome for him, for its population, strongly pro-Russian for decades, had from time to time attempted uprisings, which almost always ended in terrible reprisals by the Turks. In the spring of 1853 the situation was again desperate, for in a personal letter to Count Buol, Meyendorff told of having just had a talk with Rossler, an Austrian consul in Bulgaria, who gave a very dismal account of the lot of the Christians there, where "Turkish fanaticism had reached its peak." His statements were shortly corroborated by reports from Bulgars in Belgrade. Meyendorff asked Buol if Austria could not warn the Porte that it would bring about its own ruin if it did not take more effective steps to prevent such outrages.[6] The firmans and other documents by which the Turks claimed to have corrected the situation were of little value, as the people saw that they were not properly executed.

With this letter Meyendorff enclosed a report from the Russian consul general at Belgrade to Count Nesselrode of June 5, 1853, in which the consul referred to the highly disturbing news coming in from different parts of Bulgaria. The inhabitants, he stated, were so exasperated by fresh persecutions by the Turks that they were ready to take up arms. Notable citizens from several districts in Bulgaria had written to refugee friends and relatives in Serbia presenting a

6. Letter, Meyendorff to Buol, June 23, 1853, HHSA, X, 38.

grim picture of the excesses of the Moslems. The consul supplied an exact translation of one such letter, which he promised to send to Count Nesselrode, although he urged the writer and his friends to avoid all confrontation with the Turks and not to get into an unequal struggle. The letter, written by Nikolai Serdak for four associates of the district of Pirot on May 16, 1853, told of bands of Turks, numbering sixty altogether, who were overrunning their villages, perpetrating murders, violations, and looting, and cited specific incidents, with names and locations. The letter begged Serdak to bring this to the attention of the Russian consul: "Implore him as best you can and tell him that we have decided to rise up, as long as one of us remains alive." Serdak also asked the consul to write to Tsar Nicholas: "We have only God and Him to protect us." [7] But the Russian authorities did nothing about these appeals, since Russia was not at war with Turkey and still hoped to compromise its difficulties with the Porte.

When the army under Prince M. D. Gorchakov moved into the Principalities, Russia promised that the occupation would be only temporary and that there would be no interference with the normal government. The hospodars in charge of the two provinces seemed to be cooperative and the opposition to Russia seemed slight, although some persons were ready to fight in the forces of the Western powers or even of the Turks. A secret Russian report said that these were people inclined toward revolution, chiefly young nobles educated in England and France, who formed the nucleus of a dangerous tendency and were supported and incited by foreign consuls and the Turks. The hospodars repeatedly spoke of a revolutionary spirit in the Principalities, and Gorchakov, after negotiating with them, had to punish the culprits "with exemplary strictness." A special Russian police surveillance was set up to watch for troublemakers.[8]

This harmony was brief, for the Russians began to interfere in local affairs, especially after the Turks declared war. General N. I. Ushakov, administrative officer under Gorchakov, blamed this breakdown of good relations on the fact that under the Turks the hospodars had enjoyed full powers over the people and juggled matters at their convenience, and now they found Russian control distasteful. Russian military demands met with delays and even concealed opposition.

7. Ibid.
8. S. Nikitin, "Russkaia politika na Balkanakh i nachalo vostochnoi voiny," *Voprosy Istorii,* no. 4 (1946), p. 10.

The Balkan Peninsula

When the Turks declared war, the hospodars resigned and went to Vienna. Here they and two former hospodars proposed that after Russia had been defeated, Austria should establish a protectorate over the Principalities. The Austrians looked into the matter but did nothing. In the meantime Nicholas named one of his aides to take control of the administration, with a number of Russian commissars under him. Thus St. Petersburg showed no signs of encouraging self-government in the two provinces,[9] but set up full Russian administrative control.

Greece was another problem area, for in April 1853 the British consul in Prevesa wrote to Lord Redcliffe at Constantinople that the rural inhabitants of Thessaly and Epirus, "oppressed by fiscal exactions and subjected to intolerable acts of violence and injustice," had "the most rancorous feelings toward their persecutors." Many families had secretly fled to Greece, and they and other Epirotes living in Greece would be eager to promote disturbances in Epirus.[10] The situation there grew worse, for late in July Nesselrode sent a despatch to Meyendorff citing several documents from King Otto of Greece about the troubles along the Greco-Turkish frontier. He mentioned incidents of brigandage and incursions, which the Greeks were powerless to stop. The Turks sent in militia forces, which at times shared in the loot, and bands of fierce Albanians were also present. All this produced numerous charges and countercharges between Athens and Constantinople. Nesselrode asked Meyendorff to inform the Austrian government and to ask its help in calming the situation.[11] Not long after, Buol sent word that he had instructed Baron K. L. von Bruck, the Austrian envoy at Constantinople, to bring the matter to the serious attention of the Porte.[12] Bruck's request had little effect, however, for the situation grew worse.

St. Petersburg still would make no significant concessions to the Turks. In mid-June Vienna proposed that it should agree to receive a special Turkish envoy to resume the negotiations that Menshikov had broken off, but Nicholas flatly refused to receive one unless he brought with him the Menshikov note properly signed and accepted. This answer was sent to both Paris and Vienna. Nesselrode also com-

9. Ibid., p. 11.
10. Consul Saunders to Redcliffe, Prevesa, Apr. 13, 1853, EP, I, 178.
11. Nesselrode to Meyendorff, July 25/Aug. 6, 1853, HHSA, X, 37.
12. Buol to Lebzeltern, Aug. 24, 1853, ibid.

municated the emperor's decision to London, with his own comment that Nicholas would not concede one word of the Menshikov note or discuss any of its points. "We have a religious protectorate in Turkey and loudly proclaim it," he said. "We enjoy this right de facto and by law and we shall not renounce it out of esteem for those who are pleased to cherish distrust of us. This would be equivalent to . . . renunciation of our own influence." [13]

For the emperor the Christians of Turkey were very important. In a letter of June 20/July 2, 1853, to Emperor Franz Joseph Nicholas communicated his plans in much detail, beginning with the occupation of the Principalities. It was possible that war might break out, in which case he could no longer keep the Bulgarian, Greek, and other populations, exasperated and impatient, at peace. It was possible that all of them would rise up, and as the fleets could not do anything against them, the Turkish empire in Europe would be destroyed. Nicholas, who again insisted that he did not want conquests, held that the simplest thing would be to recognize the independence of each part of the empire as it broke away from Turkey: Moldavia, Wallachia, Serbia, Bulgaria, and so on. Such recognition would protect Russia and Austria from the charge of planning conquests and would create small states ruled according to their customs by men of their own choice, which would only have need of Russian and Austrian protection in order to exist. If the Turks should lose Constantinople, the best thing would be to make it a free city under the guarantee of all the powers of Europe, with the forts of the Dardanelles and the Bosporus razed. But for the present the tsar would remain on the defensive on the left bank of the Danube.[14]

In September 1853 Marshal Paskevich, who had vast influence over the tsar, wrote a memorandum for him on the probable course of events. If the maritime powers did not intervene in the contest, Russia could deal with the Turks with relative ease. But if France and Britain entered the Black Sea they would doubtless deny it to Russia, which would then have to advance by land. In this case it would be of great importance to obtain the support of Balkan volunteers, who, filled with bitterness and armed and paid by Russia, could be highly useful. The Russians could use the troops of the Principalities as a nucleus, expanding them with volunteers from Serbia, Bulgaria, and

13. Nesselrode to Brunnow, June 3/15, 1853, in Tarle, *Krymskaia Voina,* I, 195.
14. Zaionchkovskii, *Pril.,* II, 243–44.

Greece, and later creating special ethnic units when the men were available. Once the Russians crossed the Danube, the flow of volunteers would increase greatly, so that a new army of from thirty to forty thousand men would strengthen the Russian forces, with almost the whole country behind them. "I very much count on the militia of the Turkish Christians." The emperor read this plan with interest, but as the time was not yet ripe for it, he filed it for future reference.[15]

By September, however, the Russian cabinet was increasingly concerned over the danger of war. As mentioned in the preceding chapter, Nesselrode was much dismayed by the stubbornness of the Turks, who, he feared, might provoke the Christian subjects of the Porte to a general uprising. In addition, the increasing hostility of British public opinion and the press and the less vehement attitude of the French had brought the Allied fleets to Besika Bay, and they were clearly directed against Russia. At first the acceptance of the Note of Vienna by the great powers had seemed like a hopeful sign, but the refusal of the Turks to accept it without amendments had shattered the illusion, and the angry reaction to Nesselrode's "violent interpretation" had made it clear that peace was not yet within reach. Nicholas, who did not want war, had become less arrogant and saw the need for a real effort on his part to achieve a settlement. Lord Clarendon, while still distrustful of both Russia and Austria, also hoped that they might hit on a solution to the difficulty, and Count Buol, as before, was eager for a settlement. France on the whole wanted peace. These factors led to the highly important conferences at Olmütz where, late in September, the Austrians held maneuvers to which the powers were invited. Emperor Franz Joseph and Count Buol received the guests, including the tsar and Nesselrode, Prince William of Prussia, Lord Westmorland of England, and General Count Goyon of France.

Although the events at Olmütz consisted of the usual fall maneuvers and the accompanying social activities, it was obvious that there would be much diplomatic consultation (to be discussed subsequently), as the Russo-Turkish negotiations were deadlocked. With Turkish feeling highly inflamed by the occupation of the Principalities and the Allied fleets in Turkish waters, the possibility of war was a real one. Austria, although not directly involved, was unhappy over the presence of the Russians in Moldavia and Wallachia and feared that war would

15. Ibid., pp. 102–04.

lead to uprisings among the minorities of Turkey, which would probably kindle revolts among *its* peoples. Indeed, France, and more subtly England, let Austria know that if war came the Western powers would not be averse to revolutions in northern Italy, Hungary, and Poland unless Austria renounced its alliance with Russia and sided with the West.[16]

When the Turks rejected the Note of Vienna, several additional proposals were made. Paris suggested that the sultan should send an autographed letter to the tsar specifying his objections to the Note and stating what he would agree to, whereupon Austria would then induce the tsar to make assurances on the points raised by Turkey. The four powers would then support Russia's reply on the meaning of the Note. Thus Turkey's honor would be protected and the powers would have a valid interpretation of the Vienna Note for the future. This proposal or slightly different ones received the approval of most of the statesmen of Europe, although the British refused to give a definite answer and would not discuss a reciprocal withdrawal of the armed forces from the Principalities and from Besika Bay. The British did, however, suggest the adoption of the Vienna Note with a four-power declaration to prevent Russian misrepresentation of it. Redcliffe, Cowley, and Palmerston all approved this suggestion, as did the French, since they felt that it would bind Russia to their countries and prevent any secret Russian deal with Austria and Turkey.

At this point the "violent interpretation" of the Vienna Note had appeared, creating great confusion among the diplomats. Lord Clarendon, who was almost dominated by British public opinion, wavered between supporting the Note of Vienna and a collective guarantee and ended by repudiating the Note, on the grounds that the Russians were not honest and the Turks would not have accepted it in any case. All in all, he was delighted with the "violent interpretation," which had put Russia in the wrong and enabled him to wriggle out of the embarrassing position of having to compel the Turks to accept the Note or of washing his hands of them and leaving them to deal with the Russians as best they could. Both alternatives would have lowered his prestige in the eyes of the British public.[17]

16. Hübner to Buol, June 9 and 11, 1853, HHSA, IX, 42; Meyendorff to Nesselrode, Jan. 27/Feb. 8, 1854, Hoetzsch, III, 120–21; Engel-Janosi, pp. 110–11; H. Friedjung, *Der Krimkrieg und die österreichische Politik* (2nd ed., Stuttgart, 1911), pp. 33–36.

17. P. W. Schroeder, *Austria, Great Britain, and the Crimean War* (Ithaca, N.Y., 1972), pp. 66–77; Clarendon to Westmorland, July 9, 1853, EP, II, 351–53.

Thus on the eve of the Olmütz meeting no solution had been agreed on. To make matters worse, the Turks, increasingly concerned about the situation, suddenly asserted themselves. On September 23 a telegram from La Cour, French envoy at Constantinople, stated that there was grave danger of an uprising in which the lives and property of the Europeans—so Reshid pasha and the grand vizir had stated—might be in serious danger. Redcliffe and La Cour, instead of summoning the fleets, felt two steamers from each power would be enough to meet the need, without violating the Treaty of 1841 by calling in the main squadrons. These four steamers, together with others stationed nearby or temporarily present, formed a force of nine or ten. It turned out that the revolutionary danger had consisted of a petition calling for war posted on a mosque, and later a petition by thirty-five theological students urging war.[18]

As Turkey was not yet at war, the summoning of the steamers was a violation of the principle of closure of the Straits as provided by the Treaty of 1841. Baron Brunnow, Russian ambassador at London, felt it his duty to present to Clarendon a note registering, in the name of his government, its protests and reservations. Since Turkey had not declared war when the Russian forces had occupied the Principalities, the Treaty of 1841, providing for the Straits to be closed to foreign warships except when Turkey was at war, was still in effect. Hence by requesting the Allied warships to come to Constantinople the sultan was guilty of a violation of that treaty. The British and French governments also knew that Turkey was not at war and hence the Straits must remain closed. Thus their action in sending their vessels to Constantinople in time of peace was improper conduct. Brunnow thereupon registered his government's protests and made no promises concerning Russia's future conduct.[19]

It was in this situation that the statesmen met at Olmütz on September 23. Both Buol and the Emperor Nicholas were eager to achieve a real solution. The tsar was very cordial to Westmorland and to

18. Redcliffe to Clarendon, Sept. 15, 1853, EP, II, 121; Cowley to Clarendon, Sept. 28, ibid., p. 120; Clarendon to Cowley, Sept. 23, ibid., pp. 114–15; Fonton to Nesselrode, Sept. 20/Oct. 2, 1853, AVP, f. Kants., D. no. 147.

19. Brunnow to Nesselrode, Sept. 9/21, 1853, HHSA, 38; Note, Brunnow to Clarendon, Sept. 12/25, 1853, EP, II, 118–20; Nesselrode to Fonton, Warsaw, Sept. 19/Oct. 2, 1853, HHSA, X, 38. About Sept. 8 Nicholas had said that he would not protest if the French fleet, because of the danger of storms, should enter the Dardanelles, but only as a safety rather than a political measure and only if it did not go beyond the castles. Castelbajac to Drouyn, Sept. 9, 1853, ADF, Russie, vol. 210, 79.

General de Goyon and ordered Nesselrode to talk freely to the Briton. The chancellor declared that his master "still stood by his statement that he sought no new right and no increase of power in Turkey, but only desired the maintenance of the existing treaties and the status quo in religious matters." He still adhered to the Vienna Note.

At a later meeting Nesselrode said that the emperor had stated his full satisfaction with Clarendon's views, although he was hurt and annoyed by the latter's doubts whether he still stood by his promises, which he declared that he would hold to. By his orders Nesselrode and Buol had drafted a note containing the above assurances, to be delivered to the Porte by the representatives of the four powers, with the understanding that the Porte should receive it "as a sufficient guarantee for the acceptation of the original Vienna Note," which an ambassador should bring, signed, to St. Petersburg. Nicholas told Westmorland of his desire "to meet every legitimate wish" the powers had expressed to him.[20]

Buol supported this demarche by a despatch to London in which he stated his conviction that Russia was not seeking to interfere in Turkish internal affairs and that the demands of the tsar were not derogatory to the sovereign rights of the sultan. Buol regarded the declaration of this conviction, as set forth in the draft note, "to be the exact and authentic expression of the meaning of the Emperor of Russia, especially as His Imperial Majesty has seen and approved this note as expressing his real intentions." The minister believed that the proper way to offer a guarantee "against any false interpretation being put upon the Vienna Note and of overcoming the scruples of the Porte" would be a simultaneous declaration of the four powers. As soon as the ministers received authorization from their governments, Buol was ready to authorize the Internuncio at Constantinople to make this declaration, upon notification that this note would be immediately followed by the signature of the Vienna Note and its transmission by an ambassador to St. Petersburg.[21]

Buol added that he hoped that the draft note would "efface the impression produced on the English and French Governments by the last communication from the Russian Government" (the "violent interpretation") and expressed his belief that as the Russian cabinet had disavowed all intention of interference in the internal affairs of Turkey

20. Westmorland to Clarendon, Olmütz, Sept. 28, 1853, EP, II, 128–29.
21. Clarendon to Westmorland, Oct. 5, 1853, ibid., pp. 132–33.

and had given a more satisfactory definition of the rights it wished to see guaranteed, as well as an unconditional adherence to the *projet de note,* the objections to the Vienna Note appeared groundless. He stressed the great importance of adhering to the Vienna Note, in spite of the Porte's opposition to it, and hoped that the "united and energetic representations" of the four powers would overcome the resistance of the Ottoman government.[22]

Thus at Olmütz Nicholas I agreed with Franz Joseph and Buol on a very important concession to the Turks and their British supporters, which it was hoped would settle the differences over the Russian claim to protect the religious rights of the Greek Orthodox church. He also sought to reassure Austria and Prussia that he would not try to crush Turkey, and in this way to induce them to maintain their alliance with Russia. During the meeting the tsar stated that as before he wanted the old Holy Alliance of Austria, Russia, and Prussia; they should stand together as one man. Such an alliance was intended as a league against the Western powers. If, however, this was not possible, at least Austria's benevolent neutrality should be made clear. Nicholas met with disappointment, for Count Buol talked, not of military cooperation, but of the inviolability of the Turkish frontiers and of not crossing the Danube.[23] At Warsaw on October 4 the tsar entertained Franz Joseph and the reluctant King Frederick William of Prussia. Here the Austrian monarch declared that he was convinced of the honesty of the Emperor Nicholas and believed his promises not to dismember Turkey. Franz Joseph did, however, warn his host against weakening the sultan's control over his lands, since an insurrection of the Slavs of Turkey would endanger the peace and security of Austria. He also refrained from promising any military support for his powerful neighbor if war should come,[24] and would promise neutrality only with the reservation of freedom of action if Austria's interests were affected.[25]

Nicholas also tried to persuade the King of Prussia, whom he had urgently invited to come to Warsaw on October 4, to uphold their alliance, but Frederick William, who was fearful of antagonizing France and England, would not promise more than neutrality, although

22. Ibid., p. 133.
23. Egon Corti, *Mensch und Herrscher* (Graz, 1952), pp. 129–30.
24. Schiemann, IV, 300–301; Martens, *Recueil des traités,* VIII, 431–32.
25. Corti, p. 130.

he insisted that the ties between the two monarchs were stronger than ever. The tsar, however, would not be denied, for shortly after the Warsaw meeting he appeared, uninvited, at Potsdam, where he stayed for two days. When he found that he could not win over the king, he conferred with Baron Otto von Manteuffel, the foreign minister, but without success, for the latter would promise nothing for the future. Manteuffel was reported to have said, however, that he was sure that the emperor wanted peace, and that he was returning home in a chastened mood.[26]

During the period of the Crimean War Prussia, which was in a very difficult position, was not at all interested in Turkey and the Eastern Question and above all sought to remain neutral. If it made the wrong moves it could find itself at war with dynamic France in the Rhineland, or with Austria, which resented Prussia as an upstart. If it aligned itself with the West war with powerful Russia might ensue, or if it sided with Russia it would have to fight France, possibly Austria, and certainly Britain, which could blockade the ports of Prussia and ruin its flourishing trade.

The Prussians were badly split, for there were two hostile parties. The Conservatives—chiefly high nobles and army officers—grouped themselves around the conservative newspaper the *Kreuzzeitung*. They were hostile to France and Catholicism and regarded Russia as their protection against France and the revolutionary movement. They disliked Austria for its domineering ways and its opposition to Prussia's rise. Against them was the *Wochenblatt* group, largely Liberals and Catholics and fiercely opposed to the Conservatives and Russia. King Frederick William IV was determined to maintain active neutrality and above all not to fight Russia. His brother William, the Prince of Prussia, hated Russia and the Conservatives and wanted an alliance with England. Otto, Baron von Manteuffel, the minister president, leaned toward the *Wochenblatt* party and hoped for an agreement with England about Prussian neutrality. Count Otto von Bismarck, an aggressive diplomat, worked energetically to oppose Austria and to support neutrality, in sympathy with Russia and to strengthen Prussia. Austria, leaning strongly toward France, wanted to draw Prussia into an alliance with the West and against Russia.

In 1853 the Wochenblatt party was in control, with Bonin as minister

26. Schiemann, IV, 310; Thouvenel, p. 249.

of war and anglophil Christian von Bunsen, a fiery foe of Russia, as envoy to London. Count Albrecht von Pourtales, a friend of the king's and an important diplomat, was of this group, and Baron von Manteuffel favored it. Prince William, the heir to the throne, lent the party much influence and was eager to fight Russia. King Frederick William, a nervous, almost hysterical person, leaned toward London, but did not want to fight Russia. With Austria exerting great pressure to join it in a four-power alliance against Russia, Prussia's course seemed decided. The king sent Pourtales to London to negotiate Prussia's relationship with Britain and also made him a high official in the Foreign Office.

Pourtales, influenced by the British, became convinced that Prussia should join an alliance against Russia. The king, however, rejected this scheme as nonsense. Pourtales made another effort to steer Prussia into British hands, calling on it to agree to an alliance with Austria against Russia and a firm alignment with the West. The monarch sharply rejected this proposal and dismissed Pourtales from his diplomatic post. At this juncture on his own initiative Bunsen, in London, attempted to tie his country to the West. He hoped for a general war against Russia, which would lead to the restoration of Poland. Prussia should obtain Austrian Silesia and Moravia, while Austria should obtain the Principalities. Prussia should reorganize the German Bund under its leadership. Bunsen vigorously pushed this scheme before the British leaders, with little success. When he reported his actions to his cabinet in March 1854, the king was horrified and quickly recalled him from London, replacing him with a Conservative. The monarch also removed Bonin from the Ministry of War when he sought to support Bunsen.[27]

At this point Prince William of Prussia, heir to the throne, reacted sharply in letters to Baron von Manteuffel. As "first soldier in the Army" he protested the removal of Bonin and urged the king to reconsider, stating that if Bonin were not reinstated in his position, he would go into voluntary exile in Baden, as he did not want to serve under the new system. The king rejected this proposal sharply. While the prince quickly stated that he was not speaking for the army and declared that he would obey the orders of the king and was not a rebel, the damage had been done. In answer to what he regarded

27. H.-J. Schoeps, *Der Weg ins Deutsche Kaiserreich* (Berlin, 1970), pp. 16–22; E. R. Huber, *Deutsche Verfassungsgeschichte seit 1789,* (Stuttgart, 1957), III, 233–36.

as threats, the king said: "One does not threaten a comrade thus. One does not threaten a brother thus. One does not threaten the King thus." He sent the prince into exile in Baden and suspended him from his military and other official duties. Probably only the apology of the prince saved him from imprisonment in a fortress. As it was, the *Wochenblatt* group, including Princess Augusta, daughter of Queen Victoria, talked of getting the king to abdicate. Bismarck and the Conservatives, however, were in strong support of the king and, calling for unity, rallied much of the country around them.[28]

By standing firm in this crisis Frederick William kept control of the situation, supported ardently by Bismarck and with some hesitation by Otto von Manteuffel.

When France and England declared war on Russia, Prussia was badly isolated and in danger, as Austria might easily slip into alliance with the sea powers. As a result, the Prussian king offered Austria an offensive and defensive alliance, which it warmly welcomed. In the negotiations in Berlin Prussia worked earnestly for a stronger neutrality, while Austria wanted to align Prussia firmly with the West against Russia. The treaty of April 20, 1854, provided protection for all German and non-German lands of the German powers, and the signers agreed to demand that Russia evacuate the Principalities. Other than that, the treaty did little but bring Austria and Prussia closer together and keep the former from entering the war. Thus, in spite of his emotional outbursts, King Frederick William aided in keeping the war from spreading, which proved helpful to both Russia and Germany.[29]

While the king was wrestling with the *Wochenblattpartei* and the Prince of Prussia, Otto von Bismarck was learning the facts of political life as Prussian delegate to the Diet of the Germanic Confederation. At first, as a member of the *Kreuzzeitung,* Bismarck trusted the Holy Alliance and Nicholas I and approved of Austria as head of the Bund. He soon came to regard Austria as hereditary enemy of Prussia, however, and was angry to see the tsar back Austria as the leading German state. In seeking support for Prussia, Bismarck thought of France as a possible ally, in spite of Napoleon's coup d'état, which he held had been necessary to restore order. He now sought to learn about the new French regime and the role of the army. Although he saw that

28. Schoeps, pp. 22–28; Huber, III, 237–39.
29. Huber, III, 239–40; Schoeps, pp. 31–32.

Louis Napoleon would have to favor the army, he guessed that he would want peace. Prussia, the envoy felt, needed good relations with France, which might help it to gain prestige. He strongly opposed the anti-French articles in the *Kreuzzeitung,* since he felt they would gratuitously arouse hostility. Prussia needed French friendship, for its hostility would condemn it to be eternally dependent on Austria. Prussia must preserve all of its options, while awaiting a favorable moment. With French friendship Prussia might oppose Austria and gain strength. Bismarck hoped to frighten the lesser states of Germany into fearing that Prussia, with French sympathy, might be a powerful factor in German affairs.[30]

Napoleon, learning from his envoys of Bismarck's sympathies for France, lavished favor on the count and indicated that he would favor an alliance of Russia, France, and Prussia. After the Crimean campaign, France would be ready to turn against Austria and would welcome Prussian aid. Bismarck intimated the French views to his cabinet and in October 1854 also informed Prince Glinka, Russian envoy to the Bund, adding that a Russo-Prussian alliance with France would be the only one to serve their interests. While Russia did not respond to the suggestion, Bismarck felt greatly strengthened by the French attitude and could hint to the lesser German states that he could offer them French aid against Austria.[31]

The Russian cabinet, however, showed no signs of allying with France, for its chief concern was to avoid a general war. Although at Olmütz the tsar had failed to strengthen his alliances, he had made important concessions in order to avert war. Nicholas was very conciliatory to England and even suggested that its fleet might enter the Dardanelles for shelter from the winter storms. He abandoned his demand for the Vienna Note pure and simple, and for the first time talked of evacuating the Principalities as soon as terms were agreed on. He did insist on two points: the maintenance of the treaties and of the status quo in religious matters. He would give "an additional guarantee" to the Porte, disavowing the "violent interpretation" of Nesselrode. He asked Austria to draw up a new proposal—the "Buol

30. Herbert Geuss, *Bismarck und Napoleon III: Ein Beitrag zur* Geschichte *der preussisch-französischen Beziehungen, 1851–1871* (Graz, 1959), pp. 9–13. The author's sources consisted of Bismarck's reports to Manteuffel, his letters to Leopold von Gerlach, reports of the French envoys at Frankfurt, and his rather sketchy statements about his visit to France in 1855.
31. Ibid., pp. 14–23.

project"—which presented the original Vienna Note, with a solemn explanation of the interpretation which the powers—Russia included—made of it. In this fashion he gave ground while avoiding war.

Harold Temperley, a careful and dispassionate scholar, terms these concessions "a most serious effort for peace." The Buol project's recommendation of adoption of the Note by the Porte was accompanied by the following pledge from the tsar: "The Cabinet of St. Petersburg gives a new assurance that it will in no way exercise for itself the protection of a Christian cult inside the Ottoman Empire, and the duty of protecting this cult and maintaining its religious immunity has devolved on the Sultan and that Russia only reserves to itself that of watching that the engagement contracted by the Ottoman Empire in the Treaty of Kainardji be strictly executed." As the Emperor Nicholas fully approved the proposal, it was an abrogation of the "violent interpretation" of Nesselrode, which the latter had already explained as an unofficial opinion. The Buol project would be a public document under the supervision of the four powers as witnesses. If England had accepted this proposal, the old Note of Vienna might have been adopted, or at least would have served as a basis for the negotiation of a settlement.[32]

Unfortunately for the cause of peace, both England and Turkey were opposed to a settlement. The Porte had rejected several compromise offers and, now that England and France were committed to support it, was increasingly determined to challenge Russia. And since Turkey's difficulties had grown after the occupation of the Principalities, many Turks, fearing that the Western powers would not take action until spring, were determined to strike before the Ottoman weaknesses could force a surrender. After the manifestoes calling for war late in September, the sultan summoned a council of 120 persons to consider the situation. On September 26 the members voted to reject forever the Note of Vienna in its original form, and then pronounced in favor of a declaration of war against Russia. The repeated efforts of Redcliffe and the other European diplomats to prevent this action were in vain, and the decision for war was unanimous. The procedure for declaring war was left to the sultan.[33]

Although the British cabinet ordered Redcliffe to call the fleet to Constantinople, he summoned only four steamers, in order to exert

32. Temperley, *England and the Near East*, pp. 354–56.
33. Tg., Redcliffe to Clarendon, Sept. 26, 1853, EP, II, 130.

some influence upon the Turks but not to encourage them to go to war. Redcliffe also induced the sultan to call in his chief advisers and had him seek to restrain the war frenzy. They disavowed the rebels, who were sent off to Shumla to serve in the army. This did not, however, end the demands for war.

The excitement again mounted, with the ministers threatening to resign if the sultan opposed war. Fearing to lose them, the sultan gave in to the demands and, under pressure from Mehemet Ali, on September 23 he belted on the sword of the Prophet and made a boastful speech to his ministers. He issued a call for a Grand Council—sure to be hostile to Russia—and this request, so soon after belting on the sword, meant that war was certain.[34]

Turkish belligerence now flared up, and Reshid talked back to Redcliffe. The Grand Council met in an atmosphere of war fever, with no one in favor of peace. Redcliffe ordered the steamers to leave, hoping that that would calm the inflamed minds, but he realized that the Turks were unmanageable and made no challenge to them or any appeal to the sultan, lest he be overthrown. The sultan had gone too far: he approved the decision of the Grand Council for war, backed by a ceremonial decree of the Sheikh-ul-Islam (the leading Moslem in Turkey), which made it final. On October 4 the sultan proclaimed the declaration of war.[35]

Redcliffe, still hoping that it would be merely a paper war, with no hard fighting, tried to have Reshid hold back as long as possible with the execution of the decision. The latter, however, answered that the decision, once taken, could not be delayed. Even when London ordered him to bring up the fleets, Redcliffe delayed, hoping that the Olmütz offer would succeed. Clarendon, Palmerston, and Russell destroyed that hope. Redcliffe still delayed calling for the fleet, until, sure that war was inevitable, he summoned it on October 22. According to Temperley, he was "like Aeneas, in tears." [36]

When a telegram from Clarendon on October 18 ordered him to make a new attempt at negotiation, with much difficulty Redcliffe and his colleagues induced the Turkish ministers to agree to hold up the orders for hostilities for ten or twelve days. But already Omer

34. Temperley, *England and the Near East,* p. 359.
35. Ibid., pp. 360–61; Fonton to Nesselrode, Sept. 21/Oct. 3, 1853, AVP, f. Kants., D. no. 147.
36. Temperley, *England and the Near East,* pp. 361–63; Conacher, pp. 188–195.

pasha, commander in Bulgaria, had sent a demand to Prince Gorcha-kov to evacuate the Principalities in two weeks. Although the prince replied that he would have to wait for orders from his government, Reshid, on October 18, declared that this response "was the beginning of the war." On the 19th Redcliffe learned that orders had been sent to Omer to begin. On October 23 the Turks crossed the Danube to occupy the town of Kalafat, killing a few Cossacks. Also, on the night of October 15–16 (O.S.), Turkish forces and irregulars in Trans-caucasia attacked and took the border post of St. Nicholas and others invaded the border areas, where the Russian forces were too weak to drive them off. By late October military activity was underway in both theaters of war, with the Turks on the offensive.[37]

On October 20 Nicholas I announced to his people that, in spite of Russia's efforts to obtain a peaceful settlement of its grievances, the Turks had declared war and attacked along the Danube. Now Russia would have to take up arms to secure satisfaction for its very moderate demands and for the protection of the Orthodox faith in the East. He was confident that his loyal subjects would unite with him in taking up arms for the sacred and just cause. *"On Thee, O Lord, have we put our trust, let us not be shamed for ever."* [38]

When the Turks crossed the river at Oltenitsa and dug in, on October 23 a Russian force under General P. A. Dannenberg attacked them under highly disadvantageous conditions. Although the Russians lost heavily, their discipline and courage dismayed the Turks, who made for their boats to recross the river. At this point, however, Dannenberg, fearful of heavy casualties from Turkish cannon on the far bank, halted the attack and recalled the troops. The Turks thus kept control of Oltenitsa, although, in spite of their claims of a great victory, a few days later they recrossed the Danube. On Christmas Day, 1853, a Turkish army of eighteen thousand attacked an isolated post at Chetati, held by Colonel N. K. Baumgarten with twenty-five hundred men and six guns. Colonel Baumgarten's troops fought desperately and repeatedly beat off the assailants with heavy losses, although they were almost on the point of collapse. At this point another small

37. Temperley, pp. 364–65; Jomini, pp. 221–22; D. A. Miliutin MS, "Moi starcheskie vospomi-naniia" (Lenin Library, Moscow), pp. 37a–38a; Fonton to Nesselrode, Sept. 24/Oct. 6, 1853, AVP, f. Kants., D. no. 147; Meyendorff to Nesselrode, Sept. 30/Oct. 12, ibid.; Annex no. 4 to desp., Meyendorff to Nesselrode, Sept. 28/Oct. 10, Report of Baron Schlechta, 2nd Dragoman of the Austrian Embassy, ibid.
38. Zaionchkovskii, *Pril.,* II, 72.

force of Russians attacked the Turks from the rear, but with heavy losses. At last the main Russian force made a belated appearance, whereupon the Turks withdrew to safety. Once more the Russian commanders had incurred severe losses by mismanaging their troops, and only the bravery and discipline of the units had averted disaster. General F. I. Soimonov, however, skilfully repulsed the Turks when they tried to cross the lower Danube.[39]

In the Caucasian area the Russian forces were scanty, because many troops were required to hold off Shamil and his fierce mountaineers. Prince M. S. Vorontsov, almost in panic, warned the emperor that he could only spare six battalions to hold the frontier, menaced by large Turkish armies and numbers of Kurds and other warlike irregulars. Finally, with "great reluctance," the tsar sent one division by sea to strengthen the army in the field, and named the veteran Prince V. O. Bebutov, in spite of his recent illness, to take command in Armenia. In November the latter inadvisedly permitted Prince Orbeliani to advance against the Kurds, who were ravaging the Armenian population. Orbeliani, proceeding without patrols or flank guards, stumbled into a force of twenty thousand foes at Baiandur, where for two hours his men suffered under heavy Turkish artillery fire, while irregulars attacked his flanks and rear. Finally Bebutov arrived to save him, whereupon the Turks withdrew.[40]

Soon the situation improved for the Russians. Late in October, when the Turks, with eighteen thousand men, attacked Akhaltsikh, the key to Georgia, Prince I. M. Andronikov, recently reinforced, attacked them from the front and flank. The Turks were severely beaten, losing about 3,500 men, with their camp, provisions, and thirteen guns, while the Russians lost only 361 men. Next Bebutov, with a small force of veterans, moved to save the Armenians from the depredations of the Kurds, only to be surprised by a vastly larger Turkish force, which threatened to capture them all. After hesitating, Bebutov had the center and right charge the enemy and with the help of effective artillery fire routed them. In the center there was a hard fight, until finally the Turks gave way and fled, with the Kurds

39. M. I. Bogdanovich, *Vostochnaia voina 1853–56 gg.* (St. Petersburg, 1876), I, 131–38, 167–83; A. N. Petrov, *Voina Rossii s Turtsiei: Dunaiskaia Kampaniia 1853 i 1854 gg.* (St. Petersburg, 1890), I, 136–45, 158–80.
40. M. Ia. Ol'shevskii, "Russko-turetskaia voina za kavkazom v 1853 i 1854 gg." *Russkaia Starina*, XLIV (1884), 179–82.

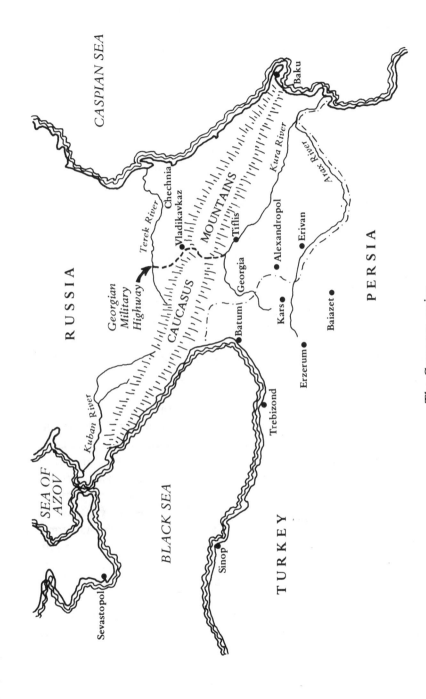

The Caucasus region

Labels on map:

CASPIAN SEA

RUSSIA

Baku

Terek River

Chechnia

Kura River

Araxes River

Vladikavkaz

CAUCASUS MOUNTAINS

Georgian Military Highway

Tiflis

Alexandropol

Erivan

Georgia

Batumi

PERSIA

Kars

Baiazet

Erzerum

Kuban River

SEA OF AZOV

BLACK SEA

Trebizond

Sevastopol

Sinop

TURKEY

looting them as they went. The Russians took twenty-six guns and two Turkish camps, although there were few prisoners. While they lost rather heavily, they had thoroughly beaten and demoralized the main Turkish army, which lost eight thousand men. Thus the region south of the Caucasus was safe until spring.[41]

Another problem for the Russians was the string of small forts along the shore of the Black Sea. In September 1853 Paskevich urged the tsar to evacuate them, since it would be impossible to hold them against a naval attack.[42] The emperor refused, but Admiral Serebriakov reported that it would be impossible to provision them, so that they could not hold out against the Turks. In addition, the Circassian mountaineers were said to be preparing to attack at the first appearance of a foreign fleet. Finally it was decided to evacuate all but the forts close to the Crimea. With some delay, by March, thanks to favorable weather, the navy was able to evacuate 3,849 men as well as most of the cannon.[43]

During the last three months of 1853 the Russians, who had expected an easy victory over their ancient foe, found that the Turks were troublesome opponents. Even so, the Russians, with better discipline and morale, were superior to the Turks, who were plagued by the usual defects of lack of confidence, inertia, and above all corruption that often deprived their soldiers of food, pay, hospital care, and other essentials. British and French officers had done much to train them and make them effective soldiers, and the Allies had sent large amounts of equipment, including firearms superior to those of the Russians, so that the Turkish army was on the way to becoming an effective force. Two advantages, however, were lacking: time to instil confidence and military skill in the Turkish officers, and an honest and competent administration to provide for the army. With these two vital elements missing, the Turkish army, even with foreign equipment and foreign officers to train it, was so far inferior to the Russians that the latter, in spite of often incompetent generals and a military machine that was also stained with corruption, were able to defeat far larger Turkish forces.

Although the Russian army was probably the largest in the world in 1853, it was always troubled by a shortage of strength on the battle-

41. Ibid., pp. 420–26.
42. Zaionchkovskii, *Pril.,* II, 106.
43. N. F. Dubrovin, *Vostochnaia voina 1853–1856 godov* (St. Petersburg, 1878), pp. 32–37.

fields of the south. The exposed Polish salient between Austria and Prussia, from which the major invasion route led to Moscow via Smolensk, was the most dangerous sector in the Russian defenses. And since the Polish population was hostile and much of it sympathized with France, both the emperor and Paskevich in Warsaw were convinced of the absolute necessity to keep a heavy concentration of the best troops to prevent invasion of Russia by the road that had been traveled by Polish warrior-kings, the tempestuous Charles XII of Sweden, and Napoleon's Grande Armée, and to keep the Poles in submission. The Baltic shore, from East Prussia to Finland, was another avenue of approach, for with British and French fleets controlling the sea, and a hostile Sweden waiting to recover Finland, Latvia, and Estonia, powerful forces had to be kept on hand to repel invasion by the Gulf of Riga or the Gulf of Finland. The armies had to be on the spot as soon as danger threatened, for the poor roads and great distances would make it impossible to move them from one part of the country to another. Similarly, the Black Sea was a danger zone, for British and French fleets and armies, allied with Turkey, were a real threat, and by late 1853 the Russians had learned that their "ally" Austria would give no support and might even join the enemy. Furthermore, Russia had to keep over two hundred thousand men in the Caucasian theater to keep the mountaineers from overrunning the far-flung defenses and to hold back the Turkish armies at Kars and Batum. Finally, the empire required several hundred thousand men to keep order in the fifty provinces of European Russia and to restrain raids from the Central Asian khanates. Nicholas I had correctly said that he did not need conquests, for his empire was large enough. Even though the Russian armies remained strictly on the defensive as he had promised, the Russians in Asia Minor and along the Danube were hard pressed to keep back the invaders. If major European powers entered the war, the Russians would have their hands full.

At the end of September 1853, however, the Russians were not thinking of broadening the war, for the emperor and Nesselrode now placed their hopes on the new compromise that had been worked out at Olmütz with Franz Joseph and Count Buol. The tsar had solemnly promised the powers of Europe that he had renounced all right of interfering in the religious relationships between the sultan and his Greek Orthodox subjects and wanted merely the status quo for his believers, over which he would have a general right of supervision. The agreement reached about the Holy Places in Palestine would remain unchanged, and the Greek Orthodox religious communities were to have the identical rights and immunities as other Christian communities composed of subjects of the sultan (the Armenians, the Copts, the Maronites, and the Assyrians). This agreement represented a substantial concession on the part of the emperor, for he renounced important claims that he had previously insisted on according to the terms of the Treaties of Küchuk-Kainardji and Adrianople. Also, for the first time he agreed to supervision by the other powers over Russia's relations with the Porte.

The Olmütz overture occurred at a most unfortunate time, for just when the emperor was offering these significant concessions, the Turks demanded a declaration of war and threats to the sultan appeared. There was excitement over the coming of the British and French steamers to Constantinople, followed by the British cabinet's order to Redcliffe to call the British fleet to the Sea of Marmora, which was duplicated by France. All this caught the attention of the British public, which, guided by Lord Palmerston, completely distrusted the Russians and the Austrians and expected them to arrange at Olmütz a perfidious partition of the Ottoman empire. The fact that Nicholas I made crucial concessions and gave a cordial audience to Lord J. F. Westmorland did not receive the attention of the British public, which tended to regard these overtures as a Machiavellian stratagem to reassure the people of Europe while the fate of Turkey was being decided in secret. Although Clarendon had made suggestions quite similar to those offered at Olmütz, his reaction to them was suspicious and unsympathetic.

The British cabinet was in no position to control the course of events, although the decisions that it made largely determined the outcome. It was headed by the honorable, sincere, peace-loving Lord Aberdeen who, as a personal friend of the Russian emperor and Count Nesselrode, sought desperately to prevent the drift to war. His main duty, he felt, was to keep the existing cabinet intact, lest it be superseded by one headed by Lord Palmerston, who wanted to settle the conflict by a direct confrontation with Russia to make it back down. And if Russia accepted the challenge and went to war, Palmerston was sure that England, with some help from the rest of Europe, could inflict crushing defeats on it and deprive it of the Crimea, the Caucasus, and the lands south of it, as well as Poland and Finland. To prevent this calamity, Aberdeen felt it necessary to make concessions to public opinion, so that his government could keep its majority and thus avoid war. But Palmerston, not Aberdeen, had popular support, and the latter, almost alone and under great pressure, was forced to make so many concessions that in the long run he was forced to take the fatal steps that led to conflict.

In this confused struggle the Earl of Clarendon, British foreign secretary, was a key figure. Like Aberdeen, in March 1853 he stood for peace and good relations with both Russia and Austria. As the Franco-Russian contest over the Holy Places developed, however, Clarendon, at first on excellent terms with Russia, gradually drew closer to France and became suspicious of both Austria and Russia. Like Aberdeen, Clarendon disliked the Turks, but fearing that Nicholas I intended to destroy the Ottoman empire, the foreign minister gave increasingly strong support to Turkey. The misunderstanding over the Russian claim to protect the Greek Orthodox church in the Levant and the mistrust aroused by Nesselrode's "violent interpretation" of the Note of Vienna made him very suspicious of the honesty of Nicholas I. Hence when Count Buol proposed the Olmütz Note as the solution for the impasse between Russia and Turkey, Clarendon was predisposed to reject it.

At its second meeting the cabinet adopted Clarendon's proposal concerning the fleet, to which it devoted much time, and also, almost as an afterthought, his rejection of the Olmütz proposal, on the grounds that the Turkish declaration of war had cancelled it. Aberdeen wrote the queen that he was unhappy about the reply to Olmütz for, while it would not have been adopted completely, it could have furnished a very useful background document.

It is surprising that there was no real opposition to the rejection, for there was a strong peace element in the cabinet. Aberdeen, however, was too concerned about preserving the unity of the cabinet to contest the matter, and William E. Gladstone, chancellor of the exchequer, did not take up the issue. If Gladstone had taken the lead, the Olmütz proposal might have been accepted as a matter for discussion. But with Gladstone failing to act and Sir James Graham, first lord of the admiralty, not present, Palmerston drove relentlessly for the policy that led to war. Also, no one thought to consider the views of the queen. So, almost inadvertently, this crucial decision took place without the consideration that it deserved.[44]

By his pledges at Olmütz Nicholas I had made a concerted effort for peace, which should have led to serious negotiations. The declaration of the Russian emperor that he fully renounced the claim to protect the Orthodox church within Turkey and merely reserved the right to observe that the sultan's pledge to protect it should be strictly enforced should have calmed the fears of the Porte with regard to Russia's intentions and guaranteed that the "violent interpretation" could no longer be regarded as valid. The fact that the offer of Nicholas would be under the supervision of the four powers as witnesses would prevent any possible evasion. Even Buol, who was not happy with a four-power guarantee of Turkey, stated that "the sympathy and support of the Powers is assured to the Porte for the future." [45] In early October Buol declared that if the Porte should remain stubborn instead of heeding the advice of its friends, Austria would not continue its support. If the Turks should be so rash as to take the offensive against Russia, "then the Austrian Government considers it time to declare openly to the Porte that it will be reduced to complete isolation, of which it can easily foresee the consequences." [46] France also supported the Olmütz proposal, for after Hübner had communicated the details to the Paris cabinet, Lord Cowley learned from Drouyn de Lhuys that Napoleon III was favorably inclined toward it. Drouyn said that it seemed to guard against the chief dangers of Russian interference in the internal affairs of Turkey and that he was sending word to this effect to London. Cowley, however, said that, while Buol's proposal contained valuable concessions by Russia, there was much that needed clarification. In particular, he asked what should be done by the maritime powers if Turkey refused to accept the proposal. He felt sure that the British government would not go as far as Buol had recommended: it would certainly not abandon Turkey to its fate, if it insisted on holding to its decision on this vital matter. Drouyn said that he had not asked Napoleon how he felt on this point, although he believed that he would not be willing to abandon Turkey. Drouyn thought they should submit the proposal to the Porte and if it rejected it

44. Conacher, pp. 197–200.
45. Temperley, *England and the Near East,* p. 355.
46. Clarendon to Westmorland, Oct. 5, 1853, EP, II, 133.

the Allies should reserve "perfect liberty of action" for themselves. Later Cowley learned that Kiselev, Russian ambassador to Paris, had just seen Drouyn, informing him that he could certify that the Emperor Nicholas had given to Austria the assurances referred to in Buol's Note.[47]

On October 4 Count Alexandre Walewski, French ambassador at London, told Clarendon that the assurances in Buol's note concerning Turkey were satisfactory to the French government, which was willing, if London concurred, to sign the four-power note and exchange it at Constantinople for the signed Note of Vienna, which should go to St. Petersburg. Clarendon replied that, while the British cabinet had not yet considered Buol's proposal, he knew that it would not approve a measure that it knew to be useless and would not be justifiable in any case. The Porte had rejected it categorically and would be sure to reject it again. Moreover, if London accepted it, that would certify that the British regarded the emperor's assurances to be "complete and satisfactory" and that they should not support any further opposition to his demands. Clarendon, however, declared that a despatch from Vienna giving these assurances would not provide "real security" to the Ottoman government "and would not neutralize the analysis of Count Nesselrode, which disclosed the views of Russia and justified the fears of the Porte." Hence the Turks would refuse the Buol note, and Britain and France would be in a difficult position.

After communicating Clarendon's arguments to the French cabinet, on October 6 Walewski told Clarendon that the French government was no longer supporting the Vienna Note.[48]

In spite of the fact that the Emperor Nicholas had offered a promising basis for negotiating a satisfactory peace, Clarendon returned again and again to his overriding concern that the British government might appear to be abandoning the Turks to the mercy of the Russians. He despised the Turks, but he knew that British opinion, especially in the House of Commons, would react strongly to any apparent betrayal of them. And this opinion mattered greatly to the foreign minister and to most of his colleagues.

For some six weeks before the crisis the cabinet had not met, and many important decisions, often vague and sometimes contradictory, had been taken by a handful of leaders—among them Palmerston,

47. Cowley to Clarendon, Oct. 4, 1853, EP, II, 131–32.
48. Clarendon to Cowley, Oct. 7, 1853, ibid., p. 140.

who wanted to send the British fleet into the Black Sea, and Lord John Russell, who often supported him. Aberdeen, the prime minister, and Clarendon were both averse to war and in opposition to the war hawks. On October 8, however, the full cabinet met and made a number of clear-cut decisions. It overruled Aberdeen, who felt that Olmütz had given a chance for peace, by rejecting it and authorizing a despatch to the effect that the tsar's assurances were not convincing, for the emperor might in future "assert a protectorate over the Greek Church . . . and over twelve million subjects of the Porte." The cabinet did not want war, for it submitted a counterproposal which Clarendon thought might have succeeded if the Turks had not declared war. It also commanded Redcliffe to bring the fleet to Constantinople, although he was opposed to it. It did not order it into the Black Sea, as Palmerston wanted, but had it stop at Büyükdere, a wide section of the Bosporus. Redcliffe was also to prepare a peace proposal to be made to the Turks. Both the summons to the fleet and the order to the anti-Russian Redcliffe to prepare the Turkish peace offer were steps that would offend the tsar. But as the cabinet was under the influence of the French, who wanted the two squadrons to enter the Black Sea, it cared little about the monarch's feelings. It was taking steps that led to war and rejecting the Russian compromise offer, but at the same time it would offer conciliation to St. Petersburg.[49]

In this way an important opportunity for peace was lost. Clarendon wrote to Lady Clarendon on October 3: "Things get worser and worser. The beastly Turks have actually declared war; so there is an end to the Olmütz arrangement, out of which something might possibly have been made; but it's all over now." [50] He gave other explanations for the breakdown of relationships, few of which were true. When on October 5 Baron Brunnow asked if the British cabinet had decided about Buol's proposal, the foreign secretary stated that in no case would Her Majesty's Government recommend the Note of Vienna to the Turks, because they had determined not to accept it; and also because an Austrian despatch with assurances concerning Russia's intentions "could not, in the eyes of Her Majesty's Government, neutralize the analysis of Count Nesselrode, in which those intentions were disclosed in a manner to leave no doubt" concerning Russia's

49. Temperley, *England and the Near East,* pp. 356–57.
50. Maxwell, II, 30.

subsequent interpretations thereof.[51] In like manner, on October 4 Clarendon told Walewski that a despatch from Austria "containing these [Russian] assurances would offer no real security to the Turkish government and would not neutralize the analysis of Count Nesselrode, which disclosed the views of Russia and justified the fears of the Porte." The Turks would certainly refuse the collective note drafted by Buol, and then the position of the English and French governments would be "false and embarrassing." [52]

Clarendon's justification for rejecting the Olmütz proposal was that Nesselrode's "violent interpretation" was still valid and hence the assurances that Nicholas I made at Olmütz had no force. This argument is obviously unsound, for Nesselrode himself had said that the "violent interpretation" was his own personal opinion and not binding on the Russian government. Furthermore, the Russian emperor had expressly declared that he was renouncing all claim to the right to interfere in the relations between the sultan and his Greek Orthodox subjects. Certainly the solemn declaration of a head of state repudiated and invalidated the unofficial statement of his foreign minister. Yet Clarendon repeatedly declared that the "violent interpretation" was still the recognized policy of Russia, when surely he must have known that this was not true. P. W. Schroeder gives ample proof that even before he saw the document Clarendon was determined to reject the Olmütz proposal and the reasons that he gave for doing so contradicted one another. He clearly did *not* believe that the violent interpretation destroyed the credibility of official Russian assurances. He expressly wrote to Seymour that at Olmütz the tsar "did eat dirt and went far to neutralize the dispatch of objections to the modifications." Seymour agreed, saying that Nicholas was obviously trying to back down, and "the Buol note was a clear example of it." [53] Lord Cowley, whose problem was to persuade France to oppose a project which Napoleon, Drouyn, and the other French leaders all had favored, had to explain to them that if the Western powers decided that the Olmütz proposal was safe and suitable for Turkey, how could they get the Porte to accept it against its will? Should they force it on the Porte, or abandon it if the proposal were rejected? "The difficulty for us," Cowley wrote to Clarendon, "appears to me to avoid getting again into *the fix* out

51. Clarendon to Seymour, Oct. 6, 1853, EP, II, 137–38.
52. Clarendon to Cowley, Oct. 7, 1853, ibid., pp. 140–41.
53. Schroeder, pp. 78–79.

of which we have just escaped—that is, finding ourselves advocating Russia against Turkey."

Clarendon expressed this view even more clearly to Walewski. If the British accepted the Olmütz proposal they would put Russia again into a favorable position and would at once risk being refused by the Porte. They would then have no grievance against Russia and would find it extremely difficult if later they decided to take active measures against it, in support of the Turks, who had twice refused to accept their advice. They decided that they would stick by Turkey, in spite of the weakness of their position, and would devise the most plausible argument to justify this conduct to Austria.[54] The French government agreed to this plan, largely in order to gratify the British and solidify their alliance.

Thus, although Clarendon repeatedly alleged that the violent interpretation made it impossible to accept the Buol proposal, his real reason for rejecting it was that if he did so it would put the cabinet in "a fix." To accept it would be to admit that Britain had no grievance against Russia and that it must then proceed to try to compel the Turks to accept the collective guarantee offered by the four powers. If, as seemed probable, the Porte should again refuse, England would then logically have to announce that it was withdrawing its support from the Ottomans, thus leaving them to face the Russians unaided. To do this would certainly arouse a storm of protest in England and might even cause the collapse of the Aberdeen government. On the other hand, if the cabinet tried to compel the Porte to accept the Buol proposal, British public opinion, long accustomed to regarding both Austria and Russia as treacherous and oppressive, would view such a course as outright betrayal of the noble and valiant Turks and a threat to British communications with India. Hence, although Clarendon knew better, he felt it necessary to placate political passions and to refuse a promising Russian concession upon a specious pretext. This was not the conduct of a frank and honest statesman.

Buol, however, still wanted to press the Olmütz plan on the Porte before it declared war, so that the Russian forces could be withdrawn from the Principalities before hostilities started. He held that the tsar had given sufficient guarantees to protect the Porte, for he merely wanted the maintenance of the status quo for the Greek church and sought no new right concerning it.[55]

54. Ibid., pp. 79–81.
55. Westmorland to Clarendon, Oct. 4, 1853, EP, II, 141.

St. Petersburg also did not wish to drop all negotiations, for on his return from Warsaw Nesselrode had learned of the Turkish declaration of war and of the Anglo-French rejection of the Austrian proposals made at Olmütz. In the light of this situation and in order to keep the negotiations unbroken, Buol had decided to try a scheme that he and Nesselrode had already discussed at Olmütz. This would be for the four powers to hand to the Divan a collective note much like the original plan worked out at the meeting of the heads of state. It would contain strong assurances of the real intentions of the emperor regarding Turkey and would now urge the latter not to sign the Vienna Note but to deal directly with Russia by sending a plenipotentiary to a place chosen for the negotiations by the two belligerents.[56]

Since Russia was now at war, it should not take the initiative in this matter. The Porte, however, would probably not be willing to act, especially in its present state of warlike excitement. If, however, Austria should feel able to make Turkey realize that the initiative must come from it, and could induce the two maritime powers to accept the proposal that Austria would make, the Emperor Nicholas would not stand in the way. If the Porte should send a negotiator to Prince Gorchakov's headquarters in the Principalities, Gorchakov, with a plenipotentiary supplied to him for the purpose, would receive the necessary instructions for treating directly with the Ottoman government. For his part, the emperor, in order not to spoil the success of such an effort at conciliation, would not change his attitude. The Russian troops would be ordered to remain on the defensive, merely repelling a Turkish attack if it should occur. The Russians would in no way oppose Buol's project of overtures, if he believed he could achieve a good result.[57]

The French and the British, however, were notably less eager to stress negotiations than the Austrians and the Russians. In a despatch of October 4 to Walewski at London Drouyn stated that the Western powers should honor Buol for his effort to keep alive the negotiations and should carefully consider all plans that might prevent the outbreak of hostilities. But as the situation was changing so rapidly, with Turkey calling for war, they should seek reconciliation of Turkey and Russia and also must preserve Turkey from the dangers of war. The Emperor Napoleon felt that M. de La Cour must receive more specific instructions concerning the role of the French naval forces, which must play

56. Nesselrode to Meyendorff, Oct. 5/17, 1853, HHSA, X, 37.
57. Ibid.

a big part by protecting Constantinople from attack and in case of need protecting the southwestern shore of the Black Sea as far north as Varna, at the end of the Balkan Mountains. He proposed that the fleets be distributed so as to protect Constantinople and thus to be prepared for action, although not to seek it. He hoped that the British would approve.[58]

Shortly thereafter Baron Brunnow, after his official interview with Clarendon, brought up a statement made by Clarendon in a letter in which he claimed the right of the British fleet to pass through the Straits and stated his own personal view that if it entered the Black Sea, "it might be regarded by the Russian government as a serious proceeding that would impart a new character to the question at issue." Clarendon stiffly replied that the passage mentioned referred to the right possessed by the British government as a consequence of the Russian occupation of the Principalities and the suspension of the Treaty of 1841; how Britain might exercise this right would depend upon the circumstances. Since Brunnow's inquiry was unofficial, Clarendon would not discuss the matter further.[59]

This rather ominous jousting was followed two days later by a despatch to Redcliffe at Constantinople, instructing him to have Admiral Dundas send word to the Russian admiral at Sevastopol that if the Russian fleet should leave this port to attack Turkey, land troops, or perform some other hostile act, Dundas was ordered to protect Turkey from attack, and he hoped that the Russian admiral would make no move to endanger the peaceful relations between Great Britain and Russia.

Clarendon expressed a hope that the French admiral would make a similar declaration.[60]

And so the maritime powers—chiefly the British—had rejected two Russian offers to negotiate, the latter of which was marked by real and substantial concessions which should have been used to serve as the basis for a compromise peace under the general supervision of the powers. In the meantime the Turks, full of fanatical zeal, and encouraged by the visible support of Allied warships at Constantinople, could not be restrained from declaring war and, when Redcliffe sought to have them postpone military operations, took the offensive against

58. Drouyn de Lhuys to Walewski, Oct. 4, 1853, EP, II, 136–37.
59. Clarendon to Seymour, Oct. 6, 1853, ibid., p. 138.
60. Clarendon to Redcliffe, Oct. 8, 1853, ibid., p. 143.

the Russians in both theaters of operations. Redcliffe was compelled to call the British fleet into the Bosporus, where it moored at Büyükdere halfway up to the Black Sea. Moreover, at the suggestion of the French, Admiral Dundas was instructed to notify the Russian admiral at Sevastopol that the Allied fleets would protect the southwest coast of the Black Sea and, if the Russian fleet should venture to attack the Turkish coast, the Allied fleets would drive it back into its harbor or destroy it. At the same time a French army of twenty thousand men was getting ready to sail for operations in European Turkey. Obviously the peace that still existed among the great powers was a fragile one. Indeed, the maritime powers gave considerable evidence of hoping that Russia would commit some overt act that would enable them to place the onus of having begun the war upon the Muscovites.

CHAPTER 9. FRANCE AND BRITAIN ENTER THE CONFLICT

By the second week in October 1853 the Russian court saw that the situation had taken a sharp turn for the worse. The Turks were about to declare war, and the British and, somewhat reluctantly, the French cabinet had decided that the striking concessions made by the tsar could not be accepted as a basis for compelling the Porte to negotiate for peace. While the Russians cared little about the Turks, they knew that the maritime powers were strongly committed to the Ottomans, and that unless the course of events changed, Britain and France would soon support them against Russia. The Russian cabinet was not afraid of the Western powers, but it could see that an expanded war offered little benefit and might bring painful surprises. If it should lead to the collapse of the Turkish empire, fierce conflict among the great powers might result—and this Russia did not want. Even if the Christian states—Rumania, Bulgaria, Serbia, and an enlarged Greece—arose spontaneously, they would probably prove unruly and might be downright troublesome. And if revolutionary movements got started there, who could tell how far they might spread? Finally, Russian finances were weak, and a large-scale war would strain them badly.

Austria also needed peace. Its position in the center of Europe exposed it to grave dangers, for France, under the ambitious Napoleon III, with an army eager to regain its former glory, was a menacing neighbor, which alternately wooed and threatened Austria. At times the French made suggestions that the Hapsburgs might, by supporting France, set up an Austrian protectorate over the Principalities. Then there were threats that if Austria backed Russia, it would lose its Italian possessions and France would encourage the revolutionaries of Hungary and Poland to take up arms. The British also were very hostile to Austria and favored Italy. In addition, Count Buol feared that if the Russo-Turkish war continued, the maritime powers would surely intervene and would put heavy pressure on Austria to join them against Russia. An Austrian alignment with the Western powers and Turkey would be extremely dangerous, for Russia would probably strike at Austrian Galicia from the Polish salient, with neither the British navy nor the French forces able to give much help. Austria's finances had been extremely weak ever since 1848 and 1849. Moreover, Austria feared that if Russia became desperate, it would urge the Balkan Christians to revolt against the Turks, which would probably destroy the Ottoman empire. This, the Austrian leaders believed, would encourage their large Slavic populations to revolt, with fatal results for the Hapsburg monarchy. For these reasons Buol was anxious to have the war brought to a speedy end, before the offensive of the Turks in the Danube area and in Asia Minor could draw in the British and the French.

Fortunately for Buol's hopes, Nicholas I had made a solemn promise at Olmütz to uphold the existence and independence of the Turkish empire, disavowing all efforts to interfere in the relations of the sultan with his Christian subjects, although he still expressed a general interest in the treatment of the Turkish Christians. As early as October 8 Buol sent a personal letter to Nesselrode asking if he thought he should make another effort for peace on the basis of the suggestions of the Russian cabinet at Olmütz. He would suggest, however, that Russia and Turkey should negotiate directly, in a place to be chosen, on bases agreed on in advance. He thought it very likely that the maritime powers would agree, especially as the British were now strongly opposed to the Note of Vienna, and he believed that they and the French would favor direct talks between the belligerents. Buol asked Nesselrode to consider the matter carefully: "Let us not neglect any possible means of halting a conflagration that might spread to Europe." The tsar made a notation on the letter that he believed the proposal was too strong and would lead "to absolutely nothing." He agreed to discuss it with Nesselrode, however.[1]

The emperor's skepticism was largely based on the attitude of the British government. Early in November the British cabinet held a deliberation on its policy on the Eastern Question, in which it was clear that it was not impressed by the Olmütz proposals. It also made a momentous decision regarding its attitude toward Turkey, declaring

---

1. Letter, Buol to Nesselrode, Oct. 8, 1853, HHSA, X, 371.

that it could not leave the Turks without support if they were in danger of being crushed by Russia. Hence it would first send the British fleet to cover the Turkish coast from attack, as a purely defensive action. As winter was approaching it did not feel that the danger was imminent, but it wanted to be ready, in case Russia should attack a Turkish port. This system had been provisionally agreed on between England and France. The French had even mentioned sending an expeditionary force to support the Turks, but the British regarded this suggestion as premature and apparently there was no agreement on this point. Nicholas I read Brunnow's despatch with interest.[2]

Immediately thereafter Brunnow had an interview with Aberdeen, who stated that after a lively debate he had prevented the cabinet from ordering the fleet to enter the Black Sea. Aberdeen believed that with winter near the Russians would not attack, so that probably the British would not have to defend the Turks as they had agreed. Nevertheless, he mentioned Varna and Batum as ports the British would defend, since he felt it his duty to let St. Petersburg know. To this Brunnow responded that Aberdeen, by preventing the entry of the fleet into the Black Sea, had probably avoided a clash between the two navies. After Brunnow's frank warning, the British government could choose between avoiding a clash or provoking one. Here Aberdeen claimed that the Black Sea was now legally open, since Turkey was at war. The Russian replied that legality was one thing, common sense another. A British squadron sent to cover Turkish ports would become an auxiliary of the Turks and hence hostile to Russia, although technically it might remain on the defensive. England should face the facts: if it did not want war, it should not provoke it by ostensibly peaceful measures. Brunnow commented that Aberdeen was being used by the Whigs in his cabinet, who would later ease him aside. This, he stated, was the tactic of Lord John Russell, who hoped to become premier when Aberdeen should go.[3]

Russell also talked to Brunnow, who said that probably winter would suspend hostilities, thereby giving those who sought peace a chance to achieve it. If not, he was ready for war. When Russell expressed a hope that the war would be short, Brunnow said he had no such hope, since this was a conflict in which the great powers felt their honor was involved. It would be longer than Russell thought, for in

2. Zaionchkovskii, *Pril.,* II, 66–68.
3. Ibid., pp. 68–71.

adversity Russia did not compromise. Lord John, after a pause, said that he no longer thought that it would be wise to rush things, although if war came, England could not leave Turkey without defense. To this Brunnow answered that if the British came to Turkey's aid, the war would be longer than Russell seemed to believe, for he did not think that England would maintain a war to a finish as it had against France from 1793 to 1815. Russell was apparently sobered by Brunnow's warning that a war with Russia would be long and difficult.[4]

In the meantime, even the Turkish declaration of war and the resulting attacks on the Russian forces in the Principalities did not cause the emperor to renounce his peaceful intentions, for the fighting proved annoying rather than dangerous. The tsar expressly declared that he would hold to his defensive policy and would not cross the Danube.[5]

Since this announcement seemed to offer an opportunity for a new strategy, Buol now proposed that the powers should try to induce Russia and Turkey to reach an understanding, based on Russia's concessions at Olmütz and the Porte's proposed alterations in the Note of Vienna. Buol urged this idea upon Drouyn de Lhuys, who, although skeptical, was willing to cooperate if a conference at Vienna had any chance of success. The representatives of the four powers, after hearing the views of the belligerents, should state in a protocol, couched in an inoffensive manner, the substance of the Note of Vienna and the changes asked by Turkey and Russia, and the promises made at Olmütz. This document would then serve as the basis for the peace talks.[6]

Buol sent a despatch to the Russian court in which he expressed his pleasure at the pacific attitude of the tsar and his wish to see peace negotiations continue. The Austrian government would lose no time in working for peace. Buol felt it better to work with the French, British, and Prussians rather than alone, as no other method offered any real chance for success. Hence he would call on the others to join, trusting that the recent trends toward peace in England and France would help to make them cooperative.[7]

Paris was much interested in the statement of the Russian cabinet

4. Ibid.
5. Buol to Lebzeltern, Oct. 16, 1853, HHSA, X, 37; Hübner to Buol, Oct. 26, 1853, ibid., X, 42.
6. Hübner to Buol, ibid.
7. Buol to Lebzeltern, Oct. 26, 1853, HHSA, X, 37.

that Nicholas I had decided not to cross the Danube, but merely to repulse Turkish attacks. Napoleon declared he would receive all proposals from any quarter, and if the Conference of Vienna had any chance of success, France would cooperate. Drouyn made a suggestion quite similar to that of Buol, calling for a protocol to state the substance of the Note of Vienna and the changes asked by Russia and Turkey, as well as the tsar's promises at Olmütz. Such a protocol, couched in a nonpartisan manner, might serve as the basis for negotiations.[8] Clarendon also sent two draft notes to Buol for consideration. The latter, however, telegraphed that the notes did not seem suitable, for they did not mention the evacuation of the Principalities nor did they speak of "pacification." Furthermore, since Russia and Turkey were at war, a diplomatic convention rather than a note was needed. Nevertheless, Buol thanked London for its interest and promised that the items sent would be considered. He also suggested that the note from the Porte should be addressed to the four powers, which then might present the documents to St. Petersburg as the basis for the preliminaries of peace.[9]

The working out of the arrangements for the peace talks was beset by various developments. On October 21/November 2 Nicholas I declared war on Turkey in what some seemed to think was unusually vehement and threatening language.[10] The choice of a site for the negotiations was not easy, for the British wanted to hold them in London, which Russia refused outright, and some proposed Constantinople. Buol, however, rejected the Turkish capital as too inconvenient, and also because the "presence of Lord Redcliffe . . . [would] make the work of peace impossible." [11] Also, the Western powers questioned the good faith of Russia and sought to insist on evacuation of the Principalities as an essential condition for negotiations. They also wanted the plenipotentiaries of the belligerents to appear before the conference, which would intervene officially. The Allies were eager to move their fleets into the Bosporus, or even to the mouth of the Danube. But by patient efforts Austria induced them to drop these demands and to work seriously for peace.[12]

Baron Eduard von Lebzeltern, the Austrian ambassador at St. Pe-

8. Hübner to Buol, Oct. 26, 1853, HHSA, IX, 42.
9. Buol to London and Paris, *ca.* Oct. 30, 1853, tg., HHSA, IX, 42.
10. Text in Hübner to Buol, Nov. 12, 1853, HHSA, IX, 42.
11. Buol to Lebzeltern, Dec. 14, 1853, ibid., X, 37.
12. Buol to Lebzeltern, Dec. 7, 1853, ibid.

tersburg, was able to learn much of Nesselrode's thinking from General Rochow, the Prussian ambassador, a close friend of the chancellor's. Nesselrode, while appreciating Austria's efforts for peace, was dubious about achieving it through the collective note and the Protocol, especially as he believed that the representatives of the powers at Constantinople would leave much discretion to the Divan concerning the Turkish proposals. The Turks were permitted to reject any of the conditions previously refused, and there was no real pressure put upon them, which, he felt, would make them less cooperative. He prophesied that if they refused the bases suggested by the four powers, the latter would end by menacing Russia. Both Nesselrode and his master declared firmly that Russia could never consent to negotiate with the Porte before the representatives of the other powers.[13]

In the meantime Drouyn de Lhuys kept constant pressure on Austria to take a stern attitude toward Russia. He intimated that if it supported Russia in the crisis, that would mean attacks from France in Italy, which, with England, would encourage the revolutionaries in Hungary and Poland. On the other hand, if Austria were willing to oppose Russia, along with France and England, Russia would have to withdraw behind the Pruth and war would be averted. If, however, the tsar's armies attacked Austria, the rest of Europe would come to the rescue. But if Austrian soldiers set foot on purely Turkish territory, that would cost Austria Lombardy and would give the signal for general revolution, which would bring down all the governments, with Austria falling first of all.[14]

Buol paid little attention to this hectoring, although occasionally he reacted. Later in November he declared that Austria would not enter the war because of threats, and if France inspired a revolution in Italy, it would at once join Russia. Austria would not fight for the Turks nor for the Greek church, but would take such action as its interests dictated. It would have much to say in the final settlement, but it would not fire the first gun.[15]

In spite of Drouyn's truculence, France proved helpful by inducing England to drop some of its unrealistic ideas and to cooperate in a serious way in arranging a new peace effort.[16] The progress of the

13. Lebzeltern to Buol, Dec. 3/15, 1853, ibid., X, 36.
14. Two despatches, Hübner to Buol, Nov. 13, 1853, HHSA, IX, 42.
15. Schroeder, pp. 105–06.
16. Hübner to Buol, Nov. 25, 26, 27, 28, 1853, HHSA, IX, 42.

negotiations was so rapid that on December 9 Ambassador Hübner sent Buol an editorial from *Le Moniteur universel* of Paris, which spoke of the successes and the unanimity of the views of the four powers, all of which offered hope for "solid peace between Russia and Turkey." When the news came of the acceptance and signing of the three documents (the joint protocol on the positions of Russia and Turkey and the notes to Russia and Turkey) at the Conference of Vienna, Drouyn was greatly pleased and made flattering remarks about the Austrian efforts.[17] As mentioned above, however, Nesselrode was by no means happy about these developments, from which he did not expect to obtain peace.

Unfortunately for the cause of peace, military events had already made a pacific solution vastly more difficult. By surprise attacks on the weak Russian position in Asia Minor the Turks had endangered the whole position of the tsar's armies south of the Caucasus, and although the veterans of the Caucasus Corps had defeated the attackers, the Russian situation was still shaky. So when the Turks formed a squadron to send munitions and troops to their forces in Georgia, the Russians moved to intercept it. From the end of October Admiral P. S. Nakhimov, in spite of severe storms, cruised with a substantial force along the Turkish coast from Sukhumi to Sinop, on the coast of Anatolia. Although he sent several of his ships back to Sevastopol for repairs, he persisted in his search for the Turkish squadron, and on November 23 (N.S.) discovered it moored in the harbor of Sinop. He immediately blockaded the port with the ships he had and sent an urgent message to Admiral Prince A. S. Menshikov at Sevastopol to send reinforcements at once, especially the steamers and ships under repair. Osman pasha, knowing that the Russians were nearby, sent a hasty letter to Constantinople for aid, but too late. Neither the Turks at Constantinople nor the British in the Bosporus had time to act.

On November 30 Nakhimov, who had received support, decided to attack. He had six big ships and two frigates, but no steamers. His fleet carried 716 guns, many of them heavy. The Turks, with no ships of the line, had seven frigates, three corvettes, two transports, and one sloop, with 472 guns, none of them heavy. The Turks also had good shore batteries to protect the harbor, but their value was

17. Ibid., Dec. 9 and 11, 1853; Conacher, pp. 202–13.

Admiral Pavel Nakhimov. Courtesy of
Tass from Sovfoto.

much reduced by the mooring of the Turkish vessels in such a way as partially to mask the fire of the forts.

When the Russian vessels entered the harbor and engaged the Turks, to whom they proved far superior, the well-trained Russian officers and crews functioned nicely, with the ships helping one another when in difficulty. The Russian fire blew up several Turkish ships, and others were beached and burned. In all some 3,000 Turks died on the ships or in the forts and the city, which were destroyed, while the Russian losses were only 38 killed and 240 wounded. Only one Turkish ship escaped—a fast steamer of twenty guns, commanded by Adolphus Slade, an Englishman known as Mushaver pasha. Quickly realizing that the Turks were doomed, Slade and his ship escaped from the harbor and fled to Constantinople, after a close chase by the Russians.[18]

In St. Petersburg, where the emperor hailed the victory in a public letter, there was great delight. A tableau, "The Battle of Sinop," was staged, with music, "captured Turks," and the like, with much of the imperial family present for the opening night. Balls and illuminations in honor of the event continued for some time.[19]

In England, where opinion had been turning against the Turks, the news of Sinop caused a sharp shift of feeling. The Russian attack, the public felt, was a violation of the emperor's pledge to stay on the defensive and not to take offensive action, and hence was an outrage. The fact that Turkey had fought several battles with the Russians and that the action was to prevent reinforcements from reaching the Turks in Georgia was disregarded. The Russian move was viewed as a defiance of England, which had sent its fleet to protect the Turks, although it had failed to do so in spite of a relative nearness to them. Palmerston's resignation from the cabinet, which had occurred before the news of Sinop broke, ostensibly over parliamentary reform, was quickly linked in disgust with Aberdeen's policy of mildness to Russia. Many Britons believed that the one true English minister had been forced out by traitors like Aberdeen, Prince Albert, and even the queen, who were strongly against Palmerston's pro-Turkish policy. There was a great wave of pro-war, anti-Russian feeling and, when Palmerston returned to the cabinet, he became the real leader of the war party, backed by most of the cabinet, Parliament, Tennyson, and the Church of England. There still were many who were not for war—

18. Tarle, I, 317–23. This is a fairly objective account of the battle.
19. Temperley, *England and the Near East,* p. 373.

Macaulay, Carlyle, Gladstone, and Argyll, as well as John Bright and the Quakers. But the peace society had collapsed, and both the Whig and Tory parties wanted war.[20]

In France the reaction was less violent, especially among the citizenry. Napoleon and Drouyn de Lhuys, however, were furious, regarding Sinop almost as an insult to France. Drouyn conferred with Lord Cowley, proposing that the two powers should protect Turkish territory, and Napoleon took the same tone. (As mentioned in the preceding chapter, the French had made a similar proposal on October 4, which had led to a warning to the Russian authorities at Sevastopol that the two fleets would not permit the Russians to attack Turkish territory.) Now Napoleon III, threatening to act independently, compelled the British cabinet, largely dominated by Palmerston, to agree that the English and French fleets would enter the Black Sea to protect the Turks and would force any Russian war vessel that they met to return to Sevastopol or retire to the nearest port. Any aggression against the Turkish flag would be prevented. The Turkish fleet, however, would not take the offensive against the Russians.[21]

Clarendon, who had been fairly moderate, now joined forces with Palmerston. Aberdeen, who was still for peace, again gave in as the war party promised that it would support the peace negotiations then in progress. This was a fatal decision, since it moved England much closer to war, and the flimsy restraint to full-scale conflict was soon overcome. Although Brunnow at once pointed out that Russia had the right to fight Turkey anywhere, since Turkey had declared war and its troops had attacked the Russians in Europe and in Asia, his remarks had no effect. Early in January 1854 the British and French envoys communicated to Nesselrode that their fleets had entered the Black Sea to protect Turkish cities and coasts from assault, because of the "unprovoked attack" at Sinop.[22] The count protested strongly, but the Russian cabinet did not declare war, although relations remained dangerously strained and the declaration of war came several months later.[23]

While these events were taking place, Nicholas I, who saw that

20. Ibid., pp. 371–72, 374–75; Martin, pp. 183–89, 193–244.

21. Hübner to Buol, Dec. 13, 1853, HHSA, IX, 42; La Gorce, I, 199–202.

22. Temperley, *England and the Near East,* pp. 376–78; Martens, "Rossiia i Angliia," pp. 599–600.

23. Martens, ibid., p. 600.

conventional diplomacy was not solving the problems between Russia and England, sought to deal with them through personal correspondence with Queen Victoria, with whom he was on friendly terms. In his personally written letter of October 18/30 he appealed to her on the basis of their friendship and mutual trust to settle the differences between their two states. Essentially he was asking her to disown her ministers and to return to the earlier harmony between their two peoples.[24]

The queen, who believed in the importance of good relations between monarchs, could not, however, disavow her cabinet. In a friendly and courteous letter of November 14 she tactfully stressed their common desire to preserve the existence of Turkey and the tsar's pledge to act with England in this endeavor. Gently she suggested that the emperor's claims, on the basis of the Treaty of Küchuk-Kainardji, were not justified and were unacceptable to the sultan. She also regretted the Russian occupation of the Principalities, closing with the hope that all troubles between them could "be removed or quickly conquered with the help of Your Imperial Majesty." This, of course, was all she as a constitutional monarch could say. It was not, however, enough to satisfy her exalted correspondent.[25]

In his final letter of December 4 Nicholas thanked Victoria for her trust in him, for "there are no more reliable foundations than the word and the personal character of the Sovereign, for on them, in the last analysis, depend war and peace." He again asserted his reasons for insisting that Turkey must respect the historic rights of Russia, based on Article VII of the Kainardji Treaty. He felt that respect for these rights was vital "for the existence and the honor of Russia." If war resulted, those who had exaggerated this simple problem must bear the blame. The occupation of the Principalities was merely a "measure of compulsion," and in no way an aggressive step toward annexation. He agreed that he could easily solve these problems—but only if his opponents acted in good faith and ceased to demand unacceptable conditions. The naval measures taken had the character of a threat, in the face of which he could not retire, as "the noble heart of Your Majesty must certainly understand." [26]

---

24. Ibid., pp. 595–96. The text of the correspondence is in Zaionchkovskii, *Pril.*, II, 195–98.
25. Martens, "Rossiia i Angliia," pp. 597–98.
26. Ibid., pp. 598–99.

While this unfruitful essay in personal diplomacy was taking place, the professional diplomats were organizing the Conference of Vienna, composed of the envoys of Austria, of France, Great Britain, and Prussia, with Count Buol presiding, to try to smooth out the differences between Russia and the Porte—a danger for all Europe. In a protocol drawn up by the conference of December 5, 1853, the envoys stated the pledges of the tsar that he would not infringe on the integrity of the Ottoman empire and its territories. Moreover, he sought no new rights of protection over the Orthodox church or over Turkey, but merely those rights established by the Treaties of Küchuk-Kainardji and Adrianople, whereby the Porte had promised to protect the Christian faith and its churches. The Russian court added that in asking the sultan to pledge to uphold its promises, it in no way sought to lessen his authority over his Christian subjects. For its part, the Sublime Porte declared that it was ready to recognize all of its contracted engagements and to take note, with its sovereign rights, of the Russian emperor's interest in the rite which he and most of his subjects professed.[27]

In view of these facts the members of the conference felt that it should send a joint communication to the Porte, stating the wish of the four powers to help reestablish peace by their mediation and their desire for Turkey to make known the conditions under which it would be willing to treat. For this purpose they were sending the collective note to the Porte and the identical instructions of the courts to their representatives at Constantinople.[28]

In the collective note the four representatives stated that their governments greatly regretted the beginning of the war and wished to have it end. As Russia had declared itself willing to negotiate and the four powers trusted that Turkey also was eager for peace, they asked the Porte to inform them of the conditions under which it would treat.[29]

Buol's successes in organizing the Conference of Vienna and getting the powers to agree to collective action were quickly followed by setbacks. The news of the battle of Sinop, which reached Western Europe about December 11, and the sharply hostile reactions in London and Paris, threatened the collapse of the peace efforts. By hard work and

27. Protocol of a Conference held at Vienna, Dec. 5, 1853, HHSA, XII, 199.
28. Ibid.
29. Collective Note addressed to Reshid pasha, Dec. 1853, ibid.

pressure on France Buol managed to avert a failure, for the French induced the British to continue their support for the conference. But almost at the moment that the delegates were signing the Protocol and the collective note, the maritime powers were forming an alliance to "sweep the Russian fleet off the Black Sea." On December 31, 1853, Hübner reported to Buol that Drouyn de Lhuys had informed him that the Allied fleets would enter the Euxine with instructions to force all Russian war vessels that they met to return to Sevastopol or other ports or face destruction. Drouyn expressed his *idée fixe* that this strong stand would force the tsar to moderate his attitude and would lead to a speedy peace. If the two German powers concurred by joining in the face of Russian blandishments, the peace effort would be a complete success.[30]

At this same time Kiselev, after receiving a despatch from Nesselrode, had a long interview with Drouyn. As he later told Hübner, Kiselev sought above all to show that the interests of France were by no means similar to those of England and that the French would be wrong to let themselves "be taken in tow" by the attitude of the British. Drouyn also told Hübner of the interview. He stated that the Russian spoke warmly and with emotion, insisting that the interests of France and Russia in the Orient were very close and that if, instead of following the lead of England, France would approach the Russian cabinet, the two countries could easily come to an understanding. Drouyn replied that France and Britain were now indissolubly linked and were pursuing European interests, while Russia sought its own special interests, which were far from those of France. France, which had spoken at Vienna, was linked with Austria, Prussia, and Britain in diplomatic action and had formed an intimate union with Britain, from which it would never separate. Drouyn reported this conversation to Napoleon, who agreed with him vehemently. The emperor held that Russia, after wooing England, was now trying to detach France from Britain and Austria, to wipe out the four-power effort, and to reach a special arrangement with France. Drouyn concluded that Russia, in spite of its peaceful words, would redouble its efforts at Vienna and Berlin to gain influence there. Now it was vital to have the two German powers stand firm. By adhering to the Protocol of Vienna, they had joined the action of France and Britain and would safeguard

30. Hübner to Buol, Dec. 31, 1853, HHSA, IX, 42.

peace. Here Hübner begged Drouyn not to be drawn along by England and not to exaggerate the unity at Vienna: Austria still sought peace without quarrelling with Russia.[31]

On January 7, 1854, Buol sent a despatch to Lebzeltern, Austrian ambassador at St. Petersburg, expressing his "painful surprise" at the sending of the fleets into the Black Sea, at a time when collective action was seeking to get the Porte to approach Russia about peace. Austria declined all responsibility for the movement of the fleets. Buol added that since so far the fleets had not yet entered the Black Sea, and Redcliffe was now "working ardently for peace," he hoped Russia would not react immediately, but for the moment would be satisfied to protest and to reserve action, which would still leave room for a diplomatic solution.[32]

Russia was decidedly against the Protocol of Vienna and the Collective Note to Turkey. When Lebzeltern read these documents to Nesselrode, the latter, although silent, was obviously displeased. He made a disparaging comment about the Protocol. He also was sharply critical of the efforts of Britain and France to draw Austria away from its Russian alliance into active cooperation with the West. In addition, he strongly opposed French attempts to use Prussia for its purposes if war should break out, terming this intimidation. While the chancellor admitted that Austria's position was extremely difficult, he did not believe that there would be a general war.[33]

General Rochow, Prussian ambassador, saw the tsar shortly before the *Te Deum* of victory for Sinop. The emperor had exactly the same pacific attitudes that he had had before the Turkish declaration of war and the Russian victories: he was ready to make peace if the Porte would agree to his demands, but if the Divan refused, he had firmly decided to use all means of coercion. Nicholas expected little result from the collective demarche at Constantinople. He also believed that Austria and Prussia, by drawing closer to the maritime powers, had made a bad mistake.

The Russian court was annoyed that it was informed of the documents drawn up at Vienna only after they had been signed, leading His Majesty to hope that Austria would not detach itself from the

31. Ibid.
32. Buol to Lebzeltern, Jan. 7, 1854, HHSA, X, 38.
33. Lebzeltern to Buol, Dec. 3/15, HHSA, X, 36.

Russian alliance. In contrast to the calm, firm attitude of the emperor, the ultra-Russian public was bitter against the four powers and accused Austria and Prussia of betrayal. There were even some highly unjust slanders of Nesselrode.[34] The attitude among higher circles and the general public was very critical of Austria because of its role in the four-power move at Constantinople. Lebzeltern found that they failed to appreciate Austria's efforts to promote peace and accused it of being unfaithful to the Russian alliance and of ingratitude toward Russia, allegedly because of French threats. War feelings were strong in all classes; Nesselrode seemed to be the only sane person in sight.[35] Even he, however, was irritated by the attitude of the Allies—especially the "absurd reasoning" of the English regarding the battle of Sinop. The British were furious at the successes of the Russians, holding that they should not have attacked the Turkish squadron. Apparently they disregarded the fact that the squadron was carrying soldiers and supplies to eastern Anatolia, where the Turks had captured Fort St. Nicholas.[36]

Finally, the Porte sent its reply to the Collective Note and to the urging of the diplomats at Constantinople. Since, basically, its proposals agreed with the advice given by the four powers, Buol presented it to the St. Petersburg cabinet. Its contents were:

1. Speedy evacuation of the Principalities should be the first matter for deliberation.
2. The Porte would be ready to renew its treaties with Russia.
3. The Porte would maintain forever the religious privileges granted to the non-Moslems on the basis of perfect equality among them and would give guarantees on these points to Russia as well as to the other powers.
4. The Russian proposal regarding the Holy Land and a church at Jerusalem would definitely be accepted.

If the Russian cabinet accepted these bases, the Porte would send a plenipotentiary to negotiate peace directly with Russia in a neutral place chosen by the powers, where the latter would be directly represented. At the peace conference the Treaty of 1841 would be confirmed

34. Ibid., Dec. 7/19, 1853.
35. Ibid., Dec. 14/26.
36. Ibid., two despatches.

and completed. The Porte promised to make a special effort to improve the Turkish administration to assure the greater well-being of all its subjects.[37]

Buol strongly urged the Russian court to accept the Turkish terms, as the members of the conference unanimously agreed that they were in harmony with the wishes of their governments and hence were worthy of being communicated to Russia. The representatives, more and more eager to settle the conflict, earnestly hoped that Russia would accept a revival of the negotiations, which seemed to promise success and would offer Russia and Turkey peace on honorable terms. The Russian response would decide the fate of Europe and, if it approved, would provide a fine guarantee for the Christians in the Orient, which would chiefly be of benefit to Russia. Austria did not think that Russia should reject this proposal.[38]

The Russian response, however, was highly unfavorable, for after Lebzeltern had communicated this despatch and had stressed Austria's great eagerness for peace, he wrote a private letter to Buol stating that they should cherish no illusions about "the slight chance of seeing the Emperor Nicholas accept the propositions of the Porte." He even reported that it was said that it was fortunate that he and not Count Valentin Esterházy, the newly appointed ambassador, had presented the despatch containing the Turkish terms, "for the impression produced upon His Majesty by its content would infallibly have rebounded on the person of this Envoy. . . ." Lebzeltern added that warlike enthusiasm remained strong in the capital, where captured Turkish flags were paraded through the streets.[39]

In spite of the tenseness on the banks of the Neva, Buol continued to display a friendly and conciliatory attitude toward Russia. On January 17 Hübner read to Drouyn de Lhuys a protest from Vienna against the action of France and Britain in sending their fleets into the Black Sea without first notifying Austria and Prussia. This might compromise the success of the Conference of Vienna and would separate Britain and France from the two German states. Drouyn, however, held that Austria and Prussia should join the west and not vice versa, since a strong and united stand against Russia was needed. Hübner, in addition

37. Buol to Lebzeltern, Jan. 13, 1854, HHSA, X, 38; Protocol no. 2 of Jan. 13, 1853, HHSA, XII, 199, and Annex to Protocol no. 2, Translation of Turkish Note of Dec. 31, 1853, ibid.
38. Buol to Lebzeltern, Jan. 13, 1854, HHSA, X, 38.
39. Lebzeltern to Buol, Jan. 11/23, 1854, HHSA, X, 39.

to reasserting that the action was "inopportune and dangerous," declared that the maritime powers did not pay enough attention to "the confidence" that the two German monarchs "put personally in the word of the Emperor of Russia." [40] And after the Russian cabinet had reacted moderately to the declarations by Paris and London about the sending of their fleets (without making it a *casus belli* as it had earlier threatened to do), Buol stated that Franz Joseph was greatly pleased with "the high wisdom and the moderation" of the tsar, which promised to bring a most happy result for the preservation of peace. Buol asked Esterházy to explain all this to Nesselrode and the emperor, confident that the Russian cabinet's acceptance of the Austrian overtures of January 13 would conclusively open the way to a friendly entente "to resolve the grave questions that hold the world in anxiety." [41]

When on February 2, 1854, the representatives of the four powers met to hear the Russian response, the result was very disappointing. The Russian cabinet declared that, provided the Porte had a sincere desire to reestablish relations with Russia on their old footing and to eliminate the causes of dissension, no treaty would be easier to negotiate and apply. This, however, would require agreement both on the form—the manner of negotiating—and the *fond*—the conditions of peace. As for the form, the Russian cabinet set "essential and irrevocable conditions" that the negotiation and signing of the treaty of peace must take place directly between Russia and the Porte, either at the Russian army headquarters or at St. Petersburg, by means of a plenipotentiary sent by the Porte. In the latter case, the representatives of the four powers might obtain instructions to direct, assist, and support the Turkish plenipotentiary, but without holding an ostensible conference. They could be sure that Russia would be most accommodating. [42]

As the bases for negotiations, as far as they could be defined in a rapidly changing situation, the emperor proposed the following:

1. Full and complete confirmation of the earlier Russo-Turkish treaties, starting with Küchuk-Kainardji and the conventions of Adrianople concerning the Danubian Principalities and Serbia.

40. Hübner to Buol, Jan. 17, 1854, HHSA, IX, 45.
41. Buol to Esterházy, Jan. 24, 1854, HHSA, X, 38.
42. Annex to Protocol no. 3, Feb. 2, 1854, HHSA, XII, 199.

2. The plenipotentiary should sign clarifications according to the attached protocol regarding the meaning and practical application of the earlier and more recent firmans of the sultan concerning the religious liberty and the immunities granted to the churches of the Eastern Orthodox rite.
3. Evacuation, after the briefest possible delay, of the Principalities and other Turkish territory occupied by the Russian armies, as soon as arrangements had been made.
4. Reestablishment of the government of the Principalities, as before.
5. Regularization of the right of asylum, and the conditions under which it would be granted in the respective states, to agitators and revolutionaries who, disguised as political refugees, would come to stir up trouble. . . .

As for the Treaty of 1841, Russia regarded it as never having ceased to be in effect; hence there would be no need to renew it or to complete it by a guarantee.[43]

In order to settle the issue of the Orthodox church, the Russian cabinet proposed that the Turkish plenipotentiary should declare the sultan's emphasis on the security of the clergy, church, and established religion of the Eastern rite. To support this intent and to assure "to the Eastern Orthodox rite the rights, privileges, and religious advantages that have been granted," the sultan had given a Supreme *Iradé* (decree) to the patriarchate and the Greek clergy by solemn documents and promised to observe them forever and would protect them against infringement. He also would give to the Greek clergy the rights given to other Christian faiths.

In return, the Russian plenipotentiary would declare that the emperor never had any intention to extend this general guarantee beyond that proceeding from the Treaty of Kainardji and hence there was "nothing contrary to the independence and rights of the sultan," and that the Greek rite and its clergy would continue to enjoy these immunities *"under the aegis of their Sovereign the Sultan."* On receiving this Supreme Iradé from the Ottoman plenipotentiary, the Russian plenipotentiary would declare it a new pledge of friendship.

Both sides would now agree to regard these acts as mutually satisfying.

Russian subjects both lay and clerical, would have the right to visit Jerusalem and other holy places on the most-favored-nation basis.

43. Ibid.

If the Russian cabinet requested it, Russia would be granted a site in Jerusalem or the vicinity for building a church and a hospice for needy pilgrims, which would be under the special jurisdiction of the Russian consulate general in Syria and Palestine.[44]

After having heard these Russian proposals, the representatives of the four powers stated that as a whole and in detail there were such essential differences from the bases of negotiation approved at Vienna on January 13 that they had not judged them suitable to transmit to the Porte. Hence these documents would be transmitted to their respective courts for further consideration.[45]

Thus the Conference of Vienna, convened by Buol to reach a compromise peace between Russia and Turkey, evolved into a grouping of France and England allied with Turkey against Russia, with Austria and Prussia at first in a posture of neutrality. The two German states, however, under heavy pressure from France and England, and finding the Russians insufficiently conciliatory, drew closer and closer to the Western powers in opposition to Russia. Essentially the differences between the two positions were slight and with good will it should have been possible to reach a satisfactory solution. Basically, however, there were such deep-seated divergencies that a solution proved impossible. The Russians wanted a return to the status quo, with their religious rights in the Holy Land firmly established and their right to a limited supervision of the observance of the privileges and immunities of the Eastern Orthodox church and its clergy throughout the Ottoman empire specified in the peace treaty. The tsar wanted recognition of the Russian right of protection over Moldavia, Wallachia, and Serbia and to have the Straits remain closed to foreign warships when Turkey was at peace. Russia refused to submit to the jurisdiction of the powers of Europe and was unwilling to have Turkey put under the protection of the public law of Europe by an expansion of the Treaty of 1841.

The British and French and the Turks wished to curtail the power of Russia in the Levant in various ways. They proposed to strip it of its protectorate over the Principalities and Serbia and to put the Ottoman empire under European protection. They would let Russia have the religious privileges in the Holy Land that had recently been agreed on and a limited supervision over the Turkish maintenance of the privileges of the Eastern Orthodox church under the aegis of

44. Ibid.
45. Protocol no. 3, Feb. 2, 1854, HHSA, XII, 199.

the sultan. Russia, however, would have to share this supervision with the other powers and not hold it as an exclusive right. In addition, the more extreme British leaders, headed by Palmerston, hoped to deprive Russia of the Crimea and the Caucasus, which should be returned to Turkey, and talked of curtailing the Russian Black Sea fleet. France, however, cared little for these specific changes, but sought to destroy the Holy Alliance of the three Eastern monarchies, so that France would be the foremost power on the continent, presumably in alliance with Austria.

Since the tsar observed the formation of the coalition against Russia, he was increasingly convinced of the need to hasten the collapse of Turkey by invading Bulgaria and encouraging insurrections of the Serbs and the Bulgars. With the allied fleets in the Black Sea, this would be the only means by which Russia could hope to destroy the coalition that was forming. This course of action could not succeed, however, without the neutrality of Austria and Prussia. (There was no possibility of their active support.) For this purpose Nicholas sent his close friend Count A. F. Orlov, one of his ablest men, to propose to the monarchs of Austria and Prussia an approval of the liberation of the Balkan Christians, lest England should decide to free them. In his plan, sent to Paskevich and Nesselrode, the tsar wrote: "And so we declare that our wish is to establish the actual independence of the Moldo-Wallachians, the Serbs, and Bulgars, the Bosnians, and the Greeks; that each of these nations shall receive the land where it has lived for centuries, that each of them should be ruled by a person of their own choice . . . from their own countrymen." [46]

Before Orlov approached Vienna, however, he ventured to suggest to his court that it accept the Allied terms in the Protocol of January 13, which would then be sent to the Turks, with minor changes. These terms would provide for an armistice and Russian withdrawal from the Principalities, while the Allied fleets would simultaneously leave Turkish waters.[47] Actually, the Russian position differed sharply from that of the Turks, since the Russians set the rigid condition that the final negotiations and the signing of the treaty must take place directly between Russia and a Turkish envoy at St. Petersburg or army headquarters.[48]

46. Tarle, I, 342.
47. EP, VII, 39, 70–80; Martin, pp. 38–40.
48. Nesselrode to Orlov, Jan. 8/20, 1854, HHSA, X, 39.

On January 22/February 3 Orlov had an audience with Franz Joseph, who received him warmly. The envoy stated that he had come to explain the basis on which his cabinet would negotiate peace, on very moderate terms. Since, however, the decisions of the maritime powers would be the deciding factor, peace was by no means sure, and his master had to prepare for war. Orlov's task was to explain this situation to both Austria and Prussia, with the help of letters that the tsar had given him. Earlier, Franz Joseph had written that his condition for maintaining strict neutrality was that the Russian army should not cross the Danube. Orlov said that, with the Allies now blockading the Black Sea, a restriction on Russian land operations was unacceptable, for Russia could not remain on the defensive in the Principalities while Omer pasha was free to attack. It would not help if the Porte promised not to attack there, for this would merely prolong the crisis and deprive Russia of a means of ending it.

The emperor said he could understand this, but Austria was fearful of a Russian offensive, because it would lead the Turkish Christians to take up arms, which could be very harmful for Austria's interests. "The emancipation of these peoples," he said, "would create a new order of things dangerous for Austria." [49]

Orlov replied that Nicholas's letter contained full and explicit explanations on this matter, to the effect that whether Russia should win or lose, Austria's interests would be safeguarded, provided Austria agreed to keep strict neutrality. If it remained neutral, the tsar and his cabinet would formally promise not to make any settlement about the Turkish provinces without a preliminary agreement with Vienna. Franz Joseph said he trusted the intentions of the emperor, but he felt that if the Turkish Christians rose it would be impossible to compel them to accept the conditions that one would seek to impose on them, and there would be great opposition from the maritime powers. While Orlov admitted that there would be difficulties, he held that they would be greatly reduced if the two empires were in full accord at this crucial moment, especially if backed by Prussia and the other German states. Russia would give support at Berlin for an Austrian proposal to renew the Treaty of 1851, for Prussian cooperation if France should invade northern Italy. The emperor thanked the tsar, but doubted if such a proposal would help, for Prussia seemed to be following the wrong

49. Orlov to Nesselrode, Jan. 22/Feb. 3, 1854, no. 1, AVP, f. Kants., D. no. 160.

course. He promised to meditate regarding the stipulations in the tsar's letter, and asked Orlov to confer with Buol.[50]

In his talk with Buol, Orlov explained in detail the message that he had brought. Buol was eager for Russian proposals that might aid the negotiation of peace and hoped that Orlov, Ambassador Meyendorff, and he might draw up a new proposal to the Porte. He said little about Orlov's proposals to the young emperor, except to express fear that a solemn agreement about Turkey's provinces, as proposed to his master, would, if it become known, lead to a general conflagration, and that in any case Austria could not engage itself without essential guarantees. Buol did not favor a similar proposal to Prussia, whose attitude did not seem favorable to Austria.

Orlov was by no means sure of the success of his mission, but, after talking with Austrian military men and other figures, he believed that Austrian neutrality, even if it were expectant, would not have a hostile character.[51]

To Orlov, Buol's fear of provoking war on the Rhine and in Italy and his demand for formal guarantees from Russia were signs that the Russian proposal faced grave difficulties. Moreover, word from Prussia indicated that it was arranging a deal with England and would not in any circumstances join Austria in firm neutrality. Thus "the terrain already mined by the maritime courts" offered no hope for the Russian proposals. On the other hand, the envoy warmly praised the attitude of all the top Austrian military men and their devotion to the tsar. He mentioned that he had used the good attitude of Prince Windischgrätz to act indirectly on the mind of the emperor by trying to show that the tsar's proposal for Austria was the only one suitable for Franz Joseph's dignity and interests.[52] This statement apparently was an effort to induce Franz Joseph to replace Buol with the prince.

Orlov had a second, two-hour interview with the emperor who, during it, showed no softening of his position, declaring: "Only if the Emperor Nicholas gives me a formal guarantee for the maintenance of the Ottoman Empire and an engagement to return the border populations to the conditions that they are now in" under the suzerainty of the Porte, could he consent to the tsar's proposals and declare armed neutrality.[53] The ambassador, who had been authorized by

50. Ibid.
51. Ibid., no. 2.
52. Ibid.
53. Ibid.

the tsar to agree that Austria should share in Russia's protectorate over Serbia and even, if need be, should have Austrian troops besiege the Turkish garrison in Belgrade, as well as to promise to discuss the effective dredging of the mouth of the Danube,[54] was unable to sway the emperor. Orlov's comment that the situation of the Christians of Turkey would not be changed was in vain, since Nicholas I had promised to share the protectorate with Franz Joseph. The latter, however, said that the religious ties linking these people with Russia would give it such preponderance that the Austrian protectorate would be only nominal and would cause endless friction with Russia. "God is my witness," said the emperor, "that my heart has never been so oppressed as it has been in the last two days, placed as I am between my sympathies and my duties. . . ."

When the Russian asked him what he would do, if he would not adopt armed neutrality, Franz Joseph replied that he would keep a watchful neutrality and send an army corps to the frontiers. Orlov countered with the remark that in that case a Russian corps would move to the frontiers of Transylvania, which might lead to war. The emperor hastily said that the maneuver would be merely a demonstration and he would promise that it would not have a hostile character. Orlov now felt that he should warn Franz Joseph of the dangers he would face in future, with Palmerston, Austria's worst enemy, soon to dominate British foreign affairs. The emperor said he realized it only too well, but perhaps he could count on Louis Napoleon. This would be a mistake, Orlov said, for France could offer less security than Russia could, by an alliance of the monarchies. His host agreed, but said that one could not count on Prussia. He was in a painful and dangerous position, but he had to do his duty. Without mentioning the Austrian debt to Russia, Orlov remarked that some day Europe might regret not having been friendly to Russia. Germany would be in real trouble, but Russia, instead of helping, might merely be guided by its own interests. Although the discourse between emperor and ambassador at times had been "very animated," when they parted Franz Joseph took very cordial leave of Orlov, saying how good it was to exchange ideas.[55]

Orlov stated that the emperor's opposition was based on fear for his southern provinces, although the real reason was fear of France.

54. Report, Orlov to Nicholas I, Jan. 7, 1854, Zaionchkovskii, *Pril.,* II, 257.

55. Orlov to Nesselrode, Jan. 22/Feb. 3, 1854, no. 2, AVP, f. Kants., D. no. 160; letter, Buol to V. Esterházy, Feb. 3, 1854, HHSA, X, 39.

Buol had said frankly that if Austria made the declaration asked by the tsar, it would bring France into Italy.

Orlov sent a letter about his mission to Nicholas I, saying that, as he had expected, it had been a failure. While he had been warmly received by the emperor and the military leaders, who spoke enthusiastically about the Emperor Nicholas, Franz Joseph had been gloomy and reluctant to talk about diplomatic matters. He also found Buol worried and demanding "guarantees," which was a sign of trouble. In his long interview with the emperor, Orlov thought he was really worried about France, although he would not talk about it. Franz Joseph would probably write a letter to the tsar giving assurances that Austria's position would not be hostile. This attitude was sincere, but Orlov felt it was only temporary. While Austria had not aligned itself with one of the maritime powers, as Prussia had, it had not kept its liberty of action. Fear dominated its thinking, and fear could easily sway its decisions.

Orlov believed that he had convinced the Austrians of Russia's "absolute necessity" to cross the Danube, and they had accepted it. If this should lead the tsar to change his plan of campaign, it need not restrain the offensive, but merely change its direction as might seem proper.[56]

Orlov injected a new note by suggesting that the Germans were so split and divided that they had no real leadership, and hence Germany floated at the mercy of events. Its friendship had not helped Russia at the Conference of Vienna, for its diplomats had merely followed the lead of France and Britain. In the light of the weakness and cowardice of Germany and of Louis Napoleon's proposal of mediation, would it not perhaps be better, if it contained honorable conditions, "to take them as basis for a direct understanding, leaving aside the friends whose good intentions fall before the fear that dominates them." Orlov was apologetically suggesting to his emperor that Russia should drop the Germanic powers and form an alliance with France.[57] Nothing came of this proposal, although as will be shown later, there were important influences on both sides working for a Franco-Russian rapprochement.

While Orlov was suggesting a Russian alignment with France, Emperor Franz Joseph and Buol were seeking another means of bringing

56. Letter, Orlov to Nicholas I, Jan. 23, 1854, AVP, f. Kants., D. no. 160.
57. Ibid.

peace between Russia and Turkey. The young emperor told Orlov that there was little difference between the Russian and the Turkish proposals, except the form—the method of reaching agreement—and that he should talk with Buol about this. When Orlov did so, Buol stressed the intense desire of his master for peace and his hope that, by a few minor changes to satisfy Russia, the Turkish proposals could be used as bases for an entente.

Buol proposed that after a request to St. Petersburg to reexamine the Turkish proposals immediately, the Russian cabinet would send to Vienna the preliminaries for peace, definitively drawn up. Vienna and the conference would then get the Porte to accept and sign them, with Meyendorff, Russian ambassador at Vienna, to receive instructions on the necessary changes in the wording of the proposal. With the preliminaries agreed on, the conference would send them to Constantinople for the Porte to accept and sign. Then the preliminaries of peace would be taken to St. Petersburg by a solemn embassy of the Austrian emperor, who, in the name of the four powers, would ask the tsar to approve them and have Nesselrode sign them. (Notation by the emperor: *A quel fin?*) [58]

Thereupon the tsar would order the evacuation of the Principalities and Paris and London would withdraw their fleets. Next, the plenipotentiaries of the combatants would meet in the agreed place to negotiate and sign the final treaty, according to the bases agreed on. Finally, the six powers would proceed to renew the Treaty of 1841.

Orlov replied that he had no instructions on this matter, but he would notify Nesselrode. He wondered how the French and the British would react to it. The tsar noted on the despatch: "It seems to me that since the rupture with England and France we could no longer talk of conferences; if Austria *alone* wishes to be responsible for negotiations this perhaps would be another matter." [59]

In spite of the skepticism of the Emperor Nicholas, the Russian cabinet, probably as a result of the urging of Nesselrode, Paskevich, and Orlov,[60] did draw up a new set of peace preliminaries and sent it to Vienna. The procedure to be used would be the one suggested by Buol: independently of the Conference of Vienna, Buol would send it to Constantinople for approval and signature by the Porte. There-

58. Orlov to Nesselrode, Jan. 26/Feb. 7, 1854, AVP, f. Kants., D. no. 160.
59. Ibid.
60. Letter, V. Esterházy to Buol, Feb. 25, 1854, HHSA, X, 39.

upon an Austrian Ambassador Extraordinary would bring the signed document to St. Petersburg, where the Russian court would sign it. This would then be the basis for the definitive treaty to be concluded directly by the two belligerents in a place on which they would have to agree. The first two articles, promising the reestablishment of peace and the confirmation of the earlier treaties, were noncontroversial. The third, however, relating to the guarantees of the privileges and immunities of the Greek rite, was a disputed point. It provided that the Turkish plenipotentiary would communicate officially to the Russian court the imperial firman to the Patriarch of Constantinople, adorned with the sultan's signature. The firman would be annexed to the treaty, as a testimony of the sultan's firm intention to maintain these privileges, rights, and immunities, and the court of Russia would receive it as a guarantee of sincere friendship. (This document would legalize the right of protection over the Greek Orthodox church in Turkey, which the tsar still claimed under the Treaty of Kainardji.) The Turks also promised to maintain the special rights granted to the Russians at the Holy Places in Palestine and the right to build a special church and a hospice for pilgrims in or near Jerusalem. Article VI provided for the simultaneous evacuation of the Principalities by the Russian forces and the withdrawal of the British and French fleets from Turkish waters, which the Porte should arrange beforehand with its allies. These events were to take place as soon as the signing of the preliminaries was complete. Finally, after the evacuation of the Principalities was complete, the governmental and administrative institutions there (based on the Treaty of Adrianople), which had been temporarily suspended by the occupation and the war, would be reestablished in full.[61]

Once the bases of the peace had been signed according to the above procedure and the orders sent to the respective military forces to withdraw from their advanced positions, the plenipotentiaries of the belligerents would meet in a place on which they would have agreed to negotiate directly and to sign the final treaty of peace.[62] The locale where they would write the treaty, however, was sharply limited by the tsar's insistence that the meeting would occur either "at Petersburg

61. Nesselrode to Meyendorff, Feb. 14/26, 1854, HHSA, X, 39 and Draft of Preliminaries, ibid.

62. Draft of Preliminaries, ibid.

or at Bucharest, or finally at a place on the Danube to be declared neutral," as in the past. Nesselrode added that he did not see how the Porte and its new allies could reasonably object to this, except "to push their distrust and their malice to the last limits." Finally, the chancellor instructed Meyendorff to impress firmly on the Austrians that these were the last concessions that the tsar could agree to. If they were not accepted, he would feel free to present new proposals, in case he had to extend greatly Russia's military operations.[63] It is important to note that Nicholas I refused to make peace with Turkey before a "tribunal" of powers, of whom two were hostile. Russia and Turkey must negotiate without an audience, although the Turks might consult privately with representatives of the four powers. Furthermore, Russia insisted that there was no need to renovate the Treaty of 1841, since it still existed and functioned. The Allies wanted to insert a guarantee of the Turkish empire into this treaty, but Russia could not accept it because it was felt that it would permit Turkey to misbehave toward its neighbors without fear of being punished.[64]

The Russian proposals arrived at Vienna at a most inopportune time, just as the conference was about to send an ultimatum to the Russian capital to evacuate the Principalities or face a declaration of war. Buol thought it vital to give careful consideration to the Russian document, and Bourqueney, the French delegate, proposed delaying the courier bearing the ultimatum. Westmorland, for Britain, concurred. So, although they all felt that the Russian proposals had no merit and should be rejected, they detained the ultimatum in order to have two or three days to consider them. Bourqueney termed the proposals "a snare, skillfully laid in order to produce division amongst us." Buol said he would be put in a bad light if he supported the ultimatum at the very moment when Russia's proposals had arrived.[65]

Quite possibly the differences between the Russian and Turkish proposals might have been compromised *if the desire had existed.* But the conference had decided on war unless Russia surrendered unconditionally. Lord Cowley, ambassador at Paris, said that Russia's terms were inadmissible, first because Russia was likely to attack Constantinople, and also because discussion of them "would destroy the Union

63. Nesselrode to Meyendorff, Feb. 14/26, 1854, HHSA, X, 39.
64. Nesselrode to Meyendorff, Jan. 13, 1854, AVP, f. Kants., D. no. 164.
65. Westmorland to Clarendon, Mar. 4, 1854, EP, VII, 74.

of the Four Powers." Thus the final Russian proposals did not receive careful consideration on their merits.[66]

The last episode took place on March 5, when Buol reconvened the conference to consider the Russian document and, if possible, to secure its acceptance by Britain and France. The maritime powers, however, which were on the verge of war with Russia, would make no concessions. They stated that the Russian proposal differed radically from the Protocol of January 13, which had been approved by the conference, in the following manner:

1. The evacuation of the Principalities would be dependent on the exit of the Allied fleets, not only from the Black Sea, but also from the Straits.
2. The assurances concerning the religious privileges of the Greek Orthodox, which the Porte had made to the five powers simultaneously, under the Russian plan would be included in the final treaty between Russia and Turkey and would be confirmed in a special official note addressed solely to Russia, which would be considered part of the treaty.
3. The members of the conference were expressly barred from proposing modifications and changes in the text of the treaty and were denied the right to pass approval on it.
4. While the Porte's proposals expressly asked revision of the Treaty of 1841, so that Turkey would come under the guarantee of European public law, this point was omitted in the Russian version and hence would not be considered during the writing of the treaty.

The Austrian and Prussian representatives agreed with the British and French concerning the "notable divergencies" between the Russian draft and the Protocols of January 13 and February 2: "Consequently the Conference has unanimously recognized the impossibility of following up these proposals." [67] Thus the peace negotiations came to a halt and much of Europe moved on to war.

The Emperor Nicholas had become more and more convinced that an expanded war was imminent. For a period in 1853 he had been certain that England was friendly, in spite of Redcliffe at Constantino-

66. Martin, p. 40.
67. Protocol no. 4, March 4, 1854, HHSA, XXI, 199; Buol to V. Esterházy, March 5, 1854, HHSA, X, 38.

ple and Palmerston in London. This illusion, however, had disappeared when the British supported the Turks and blamed Russia for the failure of the Note of Vienna. The Russian occupation of the Principalities greatly inflamed British public opinion, to which Lord Clarendon was very sensitive. The movement of the British fleet to Besika Bay and later its entry into the Sea of Marmora, together with the French, indicated that war was drawing nearer. Nicholas tried to refute charges of aggrandizement by his pledges of moderation at Olmütz, but the British would not listen. When the Russians won the battle of Sinop and Palmerston rose to power in England, war fever rose in both countries, and the French government, which had been more moderate than the British, became bellicose, although the French public was much opposed to war. Nicholas himself began to sketch plans for crushing the Turks, although his forces remained largely inactive on the Danube. Count Buol, however, hoped to promote a compromise between Russia and Turkey, with the backing of the four powers. Russia was skeptical, feeling that the Conference of Vienna was an attempt to destroy the triple alliance of the Eastern monarchs and to form a powerful grouping against it. To counter such an action, the tsar sent Orlov to Vienna to persuade Austria to maintain a friendly neutrality, but Orlov terrified the young ruler with his plans for inciting the Christians of Turkey against the sultan. Austria even talked of massing troops on the Russian border, while Prussia seemed to be leaning toward England.

France, however, seemed to be more pacific, although its fleet had moored in the Orient long before the British left Malta. Paris had accepted a settlement over the Holy Places that was less than it had sought. While France, like England, objected to the Russian occupation of the Principalities, Napoleon wrote a proposal for a compromise between Russia and Turkey which delighted the tsar.[68] Castelbajac reported in June 1853 that the tsar was using on him the same sort of cajolery that he had earlier used on the British, and that he was obviously seeking an entente, which might make "a permanent alliance." The envoy held that an alliance with Russia would be more advantageous than one with Britain, for it could be made without war, while an alliance with Britain might lead to revolutionary wars.[69]

For some time nothing came of this suggestion, for Napoleon be-

68. Nesselrode to Kiselev, July 4/16, 1853, ADF, Russie, vol. 209, pp. 160–61.
69. Castelbajac to Napoleon III, June 10, 1853, ADF, Russie, vol. 209, 84–87.

lieved that Britain had more to offer than Russia did. In the autumn of 1853, however, France showed real signs of interest in Russia. At the end of October A. M. Gorchakov, Russian representative at the German Bund, sent a coded despatch to Nesselrode reporting an overture from Prince Napoleon, who regretted the poor relations between the two countries. Napoleon III, he said, shared his feeling and always had sought a rapprochement. This was still his *idée fixe*. Gorchakov said that Nicholas I felt the same way, for he admired Napoleon III's work and respected France. The prince said that, because efforts to obtain cordiality from Russia had failed, he had turned to England, although he was not hostile to Russia. If now France should decide to change course, could it obtain a Russian alliance? Gorchakov could not make any promises, but stressed that Russia must have a dominant position at Constantinople, which its interest and geography demanded. The prince raised no objections to this request, but said that France would want Savoy and some small Italian duchies. Gorchakov, while promising nothing, said that Russia would welcome French friendship. He commented to the chancellor that this conversation did not seem to be a mere idle chat, for Prince Napoleon said that he would report their conversation to Napoleon III, who would be pleased.[70]

A few weeks later Baron A. L. Seebach, Nesselrode's son-in-law who was Saxon minister to Paris, returned to his post after a visit to St. Petersburg. When Seebach paid a courtesy call on Drouyn de Lhuys, the latter greeted him with great cordiality and asked if he could offer a ray of hope. Seebach replied that he could not see where it might come from, after France, playing England's game, had backed Russia into a corner. France cared little for the Turks, but was seeking a position of great power in Europe. Drouyn agreed, but said that France needed more than the "polite phrases of Russia" before it made a change. France had allied with Britain because the alliance that it really wanted had been denied it. Drouyn asked Seebach to inform Nesselrode of the conversation and to assure him that if the Russian cabinet wanted to make a confidential demarche, he would pledge his word that it would be kept completely secret.[71]

Shortly thereafter Nesselrode, with the approval of Nicholas I, wrote

70. A. M. Gorchakov to Nesselrode, Stuttgart, Oct. 20/Nov. 1, 1853, Zaionchkovskii, *Pril.,* II, 1–4.

71. Letter of Seebach to Nesselrode, Paris, Nov. 26/Dec. 8, 1853, ibid., pp. 173–74.

to Seebach to thank Drouyn for his message. He stated, however, that France, while professing peace, went out of its way to exaggerate Russia's differences with the Porte and to cast doubt on the emperor's intentions. Starting from these false premises, France had forced Russia to choose between a shameful peace or war to a finish. Russia wanted peace as much as any power, had high regard for Napoleon, and would be happy to welcome a special envoy from him. But this would be helpful only if France abandoned its dangerous policy leading to war and showed trust in the tsar: ". . . what we want is an honorable peace, based on confirmation of our former treaties and on a guarantee . . . of the immunities that the Orthodox church enjoys in the Ottoman empire. Let France use its influence to make this peace possible, and it will be made." [72]

On December 14/26 Kiselev paid an unexpected visit to Drouyn de Lhuys, after a period of coolness between them. The ambassador suggested a new political alignment, with France ceasing to strengthen England's position in the East. While Napoleon's position was strong, he could gain a stronger one by an alliance with two or three continental powers. Kiselev, who stated that he was speaking entirely without authorization, asked Drouyn to put the idea before Napoleon III. He had no great hopes of success, but if the idea were accepted, it might loosen the French ties with Britain.[73] Perhaps because of this overture, Kiselev received an especially gracious treatment from the imperial couple at Princess Matilde's ball on New Year's eve, where there was general talk that war was inevitable. Eugénie insisted on dancing with him, and Napoleon approached him twice. On the second occasion the monarch deplored the trend of events in spite of his efforts and hoped that the wisdom and moderation of Nicholas I would change the situation. Kiselev said that his master was moderate and desirous of peace and would remain so, but the situation seemed to be developing more for England's benefit than for that of France. He felt it would be unpardonable if war should come and hoped that the wisdom and skill of the French cabinet could avert it. Napoleon answered with vague, polite phrases, which the Russian felt meant little. The predominant opinion in French government and court circles was that war was inevitable.[74]

72. Letter, Nesselrode to Seebach, Dec. 23, 1853, ibid., pp. 174–75.
73. Tarle, I, 338.
74. Kiselev to Nesselrode, Dec. 22, 1853/Jan. 3, 1854, Zaionchkovskii, *Pril.,* II, 179–80.

These French gestures, however, troubled Lord Cowley, the British ambassador. Cowley also cited Napoleon's remarks at a state ball about his hopes for a compromise with Russia. The Prussian ambassador then asked what he would do if Turkey refused to accept the arrangement. The emperor answered that if the tsar made worthy proposals, he would take care of the Turks. Then the ambassador asked, What about England? The emperor replied, "L'Angleterre fera ce que je voudrai."

Cowley wrote to Clarendon that French opinion was turning strongly against England, even in the emperor's entourage. "What do we need an English alliance for?" Cowley quoted the French. "It has always brought us misfortune." He added, "In fact, I cannot repeat too often that the idea of war has become so unpopular that I do not wonder at the Emperor wishing to back out." [75]

While these flirtations were in progress, the actions of the great powers led on to war. The sending of the Allied fleets into the Black Sea early in January 1854 was accompanied by notification to Admiral Menshikov at Sevastopol that the Allied squadrons would protect both Turkish territory and Turkish warships. All Russian warships at sea would be compelled to return to a Russian port or face destruction. The Russian government did not at first regard this ultimatum as grounds for war, although it might well have done so. But since it was not clear whether the Turkish navy would also be prevented from attacking Russia, on January 4/14 Nesselrode expressed concern over the measure, which had been enacted because Turkish attacks in Asia Minor had aroused the Russians to attack in the battle of Sinop. If now the Allies would give Russia the same protection they would give Turkey, this understanding needed to be firmly established. On the other hand, if they would permit Turkey to attack, while protecting Turkey against Russia, Russia's belligerent rights would be violated, and the emperor would feel obliged to protest. Such action would bring general war much closer.[76]

This communication was quickly followed by despatches sent by the chancellor to Brunnow and Kiselev ordering them to ask their respective courts whether they would protect both Russia and Turkey on an equal basis. If the answer was negative, and therefore hostile

75. F. A. Wellesley, ed., *The Paris Embassy during the Second Empire* (London, 1928), pp. 37–39.

76. Nesselrode to Brunnow and Kiselev, Jan. 4/16, 1854, Zaionchkovskii, *Pril.*, II, 218–20.

to Russia, the ambassadors should ask for their passports and leave their posts immediately, and should order all Russians in each country to leave at once.[77]

Both Brunnow and Kiselev approached the cabinets they were accredited to, with the former dealing directly with Aberdeen. On January 11/23 Brunnow called on the premier and handed him a copy of Nesselrode's despatch protesting the intervention of the maritime powers in the quarrel between Russia and Turkey. Since Aberdeen did not deny the arguments of the note, Brunnow then politely asked him whether or not the Russian flag and coast would receive the same protection against attack as those of Turkey. Would there remain complete equality of communication between the ports of each belligerent country? Aberdeen had to admit that both powers intended to "favor the Turkish flag" and that their admirals had secret instructions to help the Turks in shipping their troops and war equipment. Armed with this information, Brunnow sent a protest note to Clarendon, demanding explanations on both questions. In a few days he received an answer confirming these facts, which was identical to that given to Kiselev in Paris (on January 20/February 1). Both envoys thereupon requested their passports.[78]

A few days later Brunnow made a farewell visit to Aberdeen, whom he found in a sad state of mind. Aberdeen at once began to pour out reproaches against himself because of his action in sending the fleet to Besika Bay and because, strongly wishing for peace, step by step he had led England to war. But he still insisted that there would be no war. "This is impossible!" he said in a raised voice. "I do not want to believe it. This would be a monstrous war and a calamity, which could benefit only the spirit of revolution and would sadden all proper governments."

Brunnow's farewell to Clarendon was unemotional: they merely shook hands and said goodby.[79]

In St. Petersburg, where diplomatic relations were also being severed, the emperor felt that Britain's conduct had been somewhat less hostile than that of France. On the other hand, he disliked Sir Hamilton Seymour, while he still warmly admired Castelbajac. He treated both envoys with courtesy, but in order to show his appreciation of the

77. Ibid., pp. 220–21; Martens, *Recueil des Traités,* XII, 338.
78. Martens, "Rossiia i Angliia," p. 603.
79. Martens, *Recueil des Traités,* XII, 339–41.

latter's efforts to preserve peace between France and Russia, Nicholas made the striking gesture of bestowing on him the Order of St. Alexander Nevskii and permitted him to stay as long as he wished.[80]

The rupture of relations was not, however, a declaration of war, for the emperor refused to issue it. Napoleon III, by an exchange of letters with the tsar, took the next step. Drouyn de Lhuys had repeatedly stated that Russia would back down if the Allies took a strong stand. Now, after the seizure of the Black Sea by the Allied fleets, Napoleon, in an autographed letter of January 29, made what he believed was a very conciliatory approach to the Russian sovereign, which Clarendon felt was far too gentle.[81] The emperor gave a fairly objective account of the diplomacy of 1853, although he charged the failure of the peace efforts to the occupation of the Principalities, the Nesselrode explanation of the Note of Vienna, and above all Sinop, which had offended the honor of France and Britain. Hence the Allies had occupied the Black Sea, with open partiality toward the Turks as a guarantee to match the Russian occupation of the Principalities, to make possible a fair exchange in a peace settlement.

Napoleon called on Nicholas I to choose between peace and war. If it was to be the former, it would be simple to arrange an armistice; all hostility would then cease, and the forces would retire to their bases. After the Russians had withdrawn behind the Pruth and the Allied fleets had evacuated the Black Sea, the tsar should name a plenipotentiary to negotiate directly with a Turkish envoy, with the resulting convention to be submitted to a four-power conference. Nothing in this plan was unworthy of him or wounding for his honor. If he should reject it, however, France and England would have to rely on "the fortunes of war" to settle what should be settled peaceably.[82]

This letter angered the Russian emperor. The summary of recent events was biased and unfair, passing over provocative Allied actions. Moreover, the letter was at once published in the *Moniteur* for all to read, which was tactless. Although Napoleon may have intended to be conciliatory, Nicholas I was incensed.

The historians by no means agree regarding Napoleon's intentions. Edmond Bapst [83] holds that Napoleon was trying sincerely to persuade

80. Zaionchkovskii, *Pril.,* II, 191–92.
81. Simpson, pp. 242–47.
82. Letter, Napoleon III to Nicholas I, Zaionchkovskii, *Pril.,* II, 184–86.
83. Edmond Bapst, *Les origines de la guerre de Crimée* (Paris, 1912), pp. 482–83.

Nicholas to accept the peace proposals already agreed on at Vienna. A. W. Kinglake, however, believes that he aimed to make his letter moderate enough to retain the support of Lord Aberdeen and the British cabinet, "and yet to give the alliance a warlike direction. . . . With his left hand he seemed to strive after peace; with his right he tried to stir up a war." [84] Bernadotte Schmitt notes that at that time there was a fierce clamor for war in England, which Nicholas I was to be brought to declare and which he refused to do. Napoleon's letter made no effort to appease the tsar's pride, but termed the battle of Sinop an outrage and an affront to the military honor of France and England. It was also a gratuitous violation of the Russian pledge to refrain from offensive action. Now, Napoleon declared, France and Britain must have a definitive understanding or a final rupture. If the answer was a refusal, "then France, as well as England, will be compelled to leave to the fate of arms and the fortunes of war that which might now be decided by reason and justice." [85] This language was certain to irritate the Russian ruler, and the notice that the Russian fleet would not be permitted to move provisions to Russian troops [86] added to Nicholas's wrath. Schmitt draws from these facts the conclusion that Napoleon, far from persuading Nicholas to agree to a compromise settlement, was actually trying to infuriate him and to bait him into a declaration of war against the West.[87]

On January 28/February 9, 1854, the tsar sent his reply to Napoleon, declaring that he, too, stood for peace and order and reminding the latter that France had started the trouble by challenging the rights and privileges of the Eastern church, although the French had soon accepted a compromise over the Holy Places. Unfortunately, the intrigues and animosity of Lord Redcliffe had inflamed the suspicions of the Turks against Russia and did much to lead them into war. To counter these aggressive actions, the tsar had to occupy the Principalities, to save them from Turkish rule. The French fleet then sailed into the Levant, thereby stimulating Turkish fanaticism, and the English fleet soon followed, while Redcliffe continued his intrigues. The Russian forces remained on the defensive even when the Turks attacked

84. A. W. Kinglake, *The Invasion of the Crimea* (6th ed., Edinburgh, 1877), I, 361–62.

85. Bernadotte E. Schmitt, "The Diplomatic Preliminaries of the Crimean War," *American Historical Review*, XXV, no. 1 (Oct. 1919), 51.

86. Julius von Jasmund, ed., *Aktenstücke zur orientalischen Frage* (Berlin, 1855–59), I, 235–36.

87. Schmitt, p. 53.

Russian posts in Asia and ravaged the country. The Russian army inflicted defeats on the Turks in Asia and the Russian squadron destroyed a Turkish squadron taking supplies to the eastern front. This was the battle of Sinop, in which the French, still at peace, were not directly involved.

Here Nicholas rejected the offer of an armistice and refused to withdraw from the Principalities, since this would have amounted to retiring in the face of a threat. He was sure that in his place Napoleon would have done the same. If France should decide on war, "I shall reply that Russia will be the same in 1854 as it was in 1812." He closed, however, with an offer to restore good relations on a cordial basis. If Napoleon would order his fleet to prevent the Turks from taking new forces to the Caucasus, he would restrain the Russian fleet. Finally, if the Turks wanted to send a plenipotentiary to negotiate, he would not refuse. His conditions were known and there would be no change in them.[88]

Whether Nicholas, by his mild defiance, missed a fine chance to win the French away from their alliance with Britain, as F. A. Simpson believes,[89] or whether Napoleon gave in to intense British pressure is not clear. But it should be noted that in spite of his boast about 1812 Nicholas did not rebuff Napoleon's overture but offered to restore good relations and make peace with the Turks. Perhaps the Emperor of the French decided to maintain the British alliance against Russia because he had already committed himself so far that the army and the militants like Drouyn and Persigny would not permit him to back down. The desire to escape isolation was apparently a leading motive for French conduct and Napoleon perhaps felt that Britain would be a more useful ally than Russia.

Now that relations had been broken off and the correspondence of the emperors had accomplished little, both Britain and France were eager to have an outright declaration of war. But as Nicholas I had refused to make this move, the Allies agreed to present a joint ultimatum for evacuation of the Principalities. They were encouraged in this decision by Austria's increasing opposition to the occupation of the two provinces and its demands for guarantees that Russia would

88. Letter, Nicholas I to Napoleon III, Jan. 28/Feb. 8, 1854, Zaionchkovskii, *Pril.*, II, 189–91.

89. Simpson, pp. 245–47.

not increase its empire in Europe, "to which Austria cannot consent, and that no change will be made in the political position" in Moldavia and Wallachia. Austria would stress to the Russian cabinet the "grave inconveniences" resulting from a crossing of the Danube and a campaign in European Turkey. If a general war should develop, Franz Joseph would have to think of his "sacred duties" and could not avoid taking forceful action.[90]

The Allies well knew of the increasingly anti-Russian attitude at Vienna and of Austria's refusal to pledge definite neutrality—and also of its efforts to induce Prussia to sign an anti-Russian agreement. Moreover, Buol actually supported the Anglo-French ultimatums to Russia on February 27, 1854, and was ready to declare war if Russia did not show a desire for peace.[91] Consequently the courts of the maritime powers felt safe in presenting their demands to St. Petersburg. They summoned the Russian cabinet to confine its contest with the Porte to purely diplomatic terms and to announce at once that it would order Prince Gorchakov and his army to recross the Pruth, so that Moldavia and Wallachia should be evacuated by April 30 (the French set the date at April 15). If there was a negative answer or continued silence, France and Britain would declare war.[92] The British ultimatum was delivered on March 19/31 by the British consul. Nesselrode promptly returned the Russian answer: "The Emperor does not judge it proper to give any reply to the letter of Lord Clarendon." He also stated: "We shall not declare war." [93] The French ultimatum was presumably delivered at the same time.

While Nicholas I refused to declare war, on February 9/21, 1854, he published a war manifesto written in his own hand. It gave a brief account of Russia's quarrel with the Turks and of the support that the British and French had given them, even sending their fleets into the Black Sea to protect the Moslems. They also were seeking to deny the Russians the use of this sea. Hence Russia had broken diplomatic relations with them. Thus, against Russia, warring for the faith, the British and the French had joined the foes of Orthodoxy.

90. Buol to V. Esterházy, Jan. 24, 1854, Supplementary Instructions, HHSA, X, 38.
91. Hübner to Buol, March 2, 1854, HHSA, IX, 45, citing Buol's despatch of Feb. 25 to V. Esterházy.
92. Clarendon to Nesselrode, Feb. 27, 1854, Zaionchkovskii, *Pril.*, II, 221–22; Letter, Drouyn de Lhuys to Nesselrode, Feb. 27, 1854, ibid., p. 192.
93. Consul Michele to Clarendon, March 19, 1854, EP, VII, 82–84.

Russia, however, would go forth to meet them as in 1812. The manifesto's final words were: "Forward for Christianity! May God arise and scatter His enemies!" [94]

In London war feeling was so strong that the public would brook no opposition. It was widely believed that the government would send Lord Aberdeen and the Prince Consort to the Tower as traitors.[95] In Paris, however, there was little war frenzy. The two governments, which regarded the Russian emperor's refusal to answer their ultimatum as defiance, declared war—Paris on March 27 and London on the 28th.[96] Austria did not declare war.

Bernadotte Schmitt terms the action of the British and the French "precipitate, injudicious, and disastrous." If they had not declared war, but instead had joined the German states in demanding that Russia accept the peace terms as stated in January 1854, Russia might have accepted. The Russian government was wavering, and later it admitted regret that it had not accepted these terms in the first place.[97] Schmitt continues: "But the truth is, the French and British governments in February, 1854, did not desire peace . . ." and, no matter how much Russia is to blame for raising the issue that led to war and its stubbornness in refusing concessions, "it is clear that she was not given a last opportunity to accept the terms of peace acceptable alike to Turkey and to the powers." Hence when the ultimatum of the Western powers merely insisted on evacuation of Moldavia and Wallachia without any reference to peace terms, the Russian government naturally said that the tsar "did not think it becoming to make any reply." [98] Thus, while all three of the powers, along with Turkey, were responsible for the coming of the Crimean War, the primary blame for it rests first of all with Britain and also with France, and to a lesser degree with Russia.

In this march toward war Palmerston was well in the vanguard, for on March 19, 1854, he presented to the cabinet a paper sketching his war aims—his "beau ideal." These aims included the restoration of Poland as of 1772; the union of Finland with the kingdoms of Sweden and Norway instead of with Russia; Austria's retention of

94. War Manifesto of Feb. 9 (O.S.), 1854, Zaionchkovskii, *Pril.*, II, 193–94.
95. Arthur Charles Hamilton-Gordon, Baron Stanmore, *Sidney Herbert, A Memoir* (London, 1906), I, 218.
96. Simpson, p. 248.
97. Jomini, I, 434.
98. Schmitt, p. 61.

the Danubian Principalities, with a surrender of Lombardy and Venetia; Turkey's enlargement through the acquisition of the Crimea and Georgia; and the enlargement of Austria and Prussia in a Germany freed from the domination of the tsar. Aberdeen warned that this was a plan for a thirty years' war.[99]

99. Donald Southgate, *The Most English Minister: The Policies and Politics of Palmerston* (New York, 1966), p. 346.

CHAPTER 10. RUSSIA WITHDRAWS FROM THE PRINCIPALITIES

As France and Britain moved closer to war, Russia's strategic situation changed, for obviously the Allied fleets would drive it from the Black Sea and would protect Constantinople. On the other hand, the Western powers could not bring sizable forces into the Danube basin for some time, so that the powerful Russian armies could expect to take the offensive against the Turks with little opposition until June or July of 1854. Moreover, a successful attack on the Turks would probably compel the Allies to concentrate their forces south of the Danube to save Turkey from collapse, thus preventing them from striking at Odessa, the Crimea, or in Georgia.

A successful Russian drive across the Danube, however, would be possible only if Austria did not intervene. Although it was still nominally an ally of Russia, Emperor Franz Joseph and Count Buol were gravely concerned by the tentative efforts of Russian agents to incite the Serbs and the Montenegrins. In addition, they feared that a Russian advance toward Serbia or a strong push through the Balkan Mountains would so encourage the Slavs from Bulgaria to Bosnia that a general insurrection against Turkey would occur, which might bring about its collapse. An uprising of the Slavs of Turkey would perhaps spread to the Austrian Slavs, and the Magyars of Hungary, still restive, might also rebel. This prospect was so grim that the Austrian leaders felt it essential to prevent its fruition, lest the Austrian empire also should crumble and vanish.

Austria, however, would find it hard to oppose a Russian offensive, for its armies were much larger and had strong forces in Russian Poland, threatening the Austrian flank. The Austrian commanders, with rare exceptions, were strongly pro-Russian and would be reluctant to fight the armies of the tsar. Most of them would gladly fight beside Russia against the Turks, in order to take Bosnia, Herzegovina, and Serbia, and they looked on England and Napoleonic France as their sworn enemies. And even if Austria should reluctantly make common cause with France and Britain against Russia, the maritime powers would not be able to exert much strength in Bulgaria until summer. So Austria alone would have to bear the brunt of a Russian offensive, unless it could gain the support of Prussia and the rest of Germany. For Austria, then, Prussian aid was vital. This, however, Prussia was most reluctant to give.

Nicholas I, who had been hopeful of the collapse of Turkey as early as 1844, was increasingly eager for insurrections of the Balkan Christians as his diplomatic situation grew worse. For much of 1853 he did little to stimulate unrest among the Greeks, Serbs, and Montenegrins, largely because he did not want to anger the Austrians, who strongly opposed nationalist movements. Nesselrode, however, who was usually ready to accept the emperor's views, in his report of November 8, 1953, expressed disagreement with his master's views about inciting the Christians of Turkey. He stated that it would be extremely dangerous for the Christians themselves, whom the Russians could not help against brutal Turkish reprisals. In addition, the tsar's latest plan ran counter to all his policies, for he had never approved of stirring up national minorities against their lawful governments, and would contradict his solemn promises not to seek the collapse of Turkey. Nesselrode stated that it would be better if the rising of the Christians was spontaneous and produced by the events of war, especially when Russia could not yet help them. He held that under no circumstances should Russia be responsible for inciting the Turkish Christians and their subsequent beating by the Turks.[1]

The chancellor's call for cautious dealing with the Balkan Christians, however, showed ignorance of the recent past of the Bulgars, who had made real gains in trade and handicrafts, in spite of Turkish repression. In 1835 uprisings occurred, and in 1841 outbreaks had taken place at Nish, Pirota, and Leskovats. Although the Turks had repressed them ferociously, fresh Bulgar uprisings took place at Vidin in 1850, which the Turks again crushed. Nevertheless, the Bulgars were not cowed, for they sought to escape their oppressors, and many vainly tried to flee to Serbia. Even though British agents in Bulgaria urged them to seek English help, they still relied on Russia.

The Turks, as always, still overtaxed them and drafted young Bulgars

---

1. Martens, "Rossiia i Angliia," p. 608.

for work on fortifications, where many died of privations. Turkish raids and violence, with murder, torture, looting, and rape infuriated the people. Hence, when Russia occupied the Principalities in 1853, a Bulgar delegation visited General Gorchakov, hoping in vain for aid. Late in the year a group of Bulgars from Brailov presented a new appeal, complaining of heavy taxes and trade restrictions. They cited a lack of Bulgar schools and printing, as well as the ban on the Bulgarian church. In spite of these grievances and the killing of 106 Bulgars of Brailov in 1852, they asked for self-government under the sultan. This petition brought them no relief, however,[2] and probably what they really wanted was independence. The persistence of the Bulgars in striving for freedom indicated that they were serious and would welcome Russian troops.

Nesselrode's cautionings greatly annoyed Nicholas I and did not cause him to change his views, for he insisted that Russia would soon drive the Turks back across the Danube and then cross over to the right bank, about April 1854. Nesselrode accepted this statement and he also agreed that the Russians must learn the actual attitude of the Christians. Nicholas, however, did not regard it as dangerous and premature to send in secret agents, holding that the British were doing this and by urging the Christians to free themselves were gaining the reputation of liberators. On the other hand, he agreed that Russia should send in agents only if its troops had crossed the Danube and if it was certain that the Christians wanted liberation enough to accept the cruel sacrifices that this holy cause would entail.[3]

The Russians thus saw that they could count on aid from the Balkan Christians only when their army held a strong position south of the river from which it could aid the insurgents. And as the emperor had great trust in Field Marshal Paskevich, victor over Persians, Turks, Poles, and Magyars, he turned to him for advice.

Paskevich, after doing well in the Napoleonic wars, had received a command in the Guards, with the then Grand Duke Nicholas serving under him as division commander. Nicholas greatly admired Paskevich, calling him "father-commander" to the end of his days. Because of this admiration, the general led Russia's armies and won glory in its wars, although he was very cautious and feared to tarnish his prestige by suffering defeat. Next in line was General M. D. Gorchakov,

2. Nikitin, "Russkaia politika na Balkanakh," *Voprosy istorii,* no. 4 (1946), pp. 12–15.
3. Ibid., pp. 608–09.

an elderly and indecisive commander. Some of the second-rank generals, such as F. V. Rüdiger and A. N. Lüders, showed promise, but Paskevich kept them in the background.

Late in December 1853 Paskevich proposed an early crossing of the lower Danube to take the forts there and then to push on to take Silistria in three weeks. Silistria would then serve as a base for a drive into western Bulgaria to encourage the Bulgars and the Serbs to rise.[4] The Allied fleets could do little, and the Russians should be able to capture Adrianople.

The situation soon changed, however, as France and England moved toward war with Russia, and Austria, while not actively hostile, sent an army corps to the Serbian frontier and advised Russia not to cross the Danube. Prussia showed signs of joining Austria. Hence the tsar urgently summoned Paskevich to a conference early in February. In his reply the field marshal stressed great danger from Austria and Prussia, each of which could field 150,000 men, which would make a Russian offensive impossible. He wrote that the large forces in Asia facing the Turks and the Caucasians could be reduced and that only a small force was needed to protect Odessa and the Crimea, for landing attacks, he said, could cause Russia little harm. Instead, a large army was needed along the lower Danube, where it would not excite the Serbs. The Russians should take Silistria and other fortresses, and if the Allies came to the rescue, they should crush them. But the crucial need was for a large reserve army in the center (i.e., Poland) to deal with Austria and Prussia.[5]

Paskevich held that the siege of Silistria would be possible with six divisions unless the Allied armies interfered. After Silistria's fall the Russian forces could take Rushchuk and Little Wallachia and then push on across the Danube to Tyrnovo to arouse the Serbs and the Bulgars. This plan, however, could be accomplished only if Austria remained neutral. But as Austrian neutrality appeared highly uncertain, they should postpone the siege of Silistria for a time. It would be best to establish a bridgehead across the lower Danube and to counterattack if either the Turks or the Austrians took the offensive.[6]

This cautious program did not suit the emperor, for on February

4. Letter, Paskevich to Gorchakov, Dec. 29, 1853, Zaionchkovskii, *Pril.,* II, 297–307.

5. A. P. Shcherbatov, *General-Fel'dmarshal kniaz' Paskevich, ego zhizn' i deiatel'nost'. Po neizdannym istochnikam* (St. Petersburg, 1888–1904), VII, 96–102.

6. Ibid., pp. 104–06.

1 he sent his new plan to General M. D. Gorchakov, in which he insisted on adhering to his offensive, although with changes to cope with the efforts of the Allies to help the Turks. Moreover, Austria, while giving "most friendly" assurances, had put an observation corps on the Serbian border and no one could say how long it would hold out against the urgings of the maritime powers. Nevertheless, Nicholas still intended to act forcefully.

While staying on the defensive in Little Wallachia, the Russian forces should speed up the crossing of the lower Danube and the capture of the local fortresses, in order *first of all* to begin the siege of *Silistria*. When Silistria fell, they should send the river flotilla upstream and begin the siege of Rushchuk. If the Turks should try to relieve Silistria, so much the better, since this should make it possible to give them a bad defeat and then finish the siege in quiet. Once the Russians had taken Silistria and began their push against Rushchuk, the cooperation of the Serbs and the uprising of the Bulgars would be possible. The emperor held that the Rushchuk offensive would be only "a useful diversion," which might draw off part of the Turks. If the Russians should take Rushchuk, they would have a strong position beyond the river, but perhaps they then should not go farther until it became clear what effect the insurrection of the Christians would have.

In the meantime, the emperor hoped that his armies might capture Kars and Baiazet in Asia, but he did not know what else they could do.[7]

The emperor again mentioned Silistria, stating *"I regard it as necessary* to begin the siege" so that the Russians could be secure on their left flank in case the British and the French landed on the coast. The landing would be less dangerous if Russia held the fortress. He also believed that they must besiege Rushchuk in order to gain full control of the river and thereby protect the Principalities and also help the Serbs if they started a real uprising. He stated that he was informed that the Serbs would cooperate "as soon as we are across the Danube."[8]

Shortly thereafter Nicholas learned that the Prussians were holding secret talks with the English. Also General Heinrich von Hess, the Austrian chief of staff, visited Meyendorff, the Russian envoy at Vi-

7. Nicholas I to Gorchakov, Feb. 1, 1854, Zaionchkovskii, *Pril.,* II, 312–13.
8. Ibid., p. 314.

enna, and warned against making an attack on Kalafat or doing anything else decisive south of the Danube. Hess also advised against
the Russians' drawing too close to Serbia, since if they did so, Austria
would occupy it.[9]

These factors led the tsar to draft a plan of military operations
against Austria. The best strategy would be to strike directly at Krakow, thus outflanking the Austrians in Galicia. But as it was doubtful
that Prussia would remain inactive, it would be better to avoid danger
to the Russian flank and rear by halting short of Krakow and by
penetrating Galicia. The Russian Guards, behind Warsaw and Novo-
georgievsk, could watch Prussia and form a reserve for Paskevich's
army in Galicia. But even if the Russians were successful in attacks
against Austria, Nicholas held that they should only occupy Galicia,
in order not to frighten Germany into entering the war to protect
Austria.

He also hoped for a Magyar revolution if Russia did well against
Austria. While Russia would not instigate the revolution, it would
benefit from it, as it would be so dangerous for the Hapsburgs that
it would compel them to accept Russia's terms.

As for Prussia, he did not believe it would remain neutral long,
for if Russia defeated Austria, it would probably enter on the latter's
side. Hence Russia should be on guard against it and not try to push
its successes too far.[10]

Whether the emperor expected to carry out this plan, or whether
it was mere wishful thinking, is hard to say. His conduct, however,
indicated that he was beginning to face the facts. Late in February
he drew up a new plan that reflected the growing danger of Allied
landings in the Caucasus, in the Crimea, and in Bessarabia. Also,
the hostility of Austria was clear, for it threatened Russia's right flank
and rear. While there was no immediate danger in Poland and Volhynia, the Russians in the Principalities were in peril. Hence they should
decide what to do, without running too great a risk, but also keeping
Russia's influence over the Balkan Christians and maintaining its
objectives.

The Russians would continue to drive against Silistria, while maintaining a readiness to strike at the Turks and destroy them if they
should attack; or they would try to repulse any Allied landings. By

9. Tarle, I, 364.
10. Ibid., pp. 364–65.

the end of June it should be clear whether Austria was really hostile or whether, restrained by Prussia and fearing Russia, it would remain neutral.

Furthermore, the Greek uprising might spread through the Balkans, in spite of Austria's opposition. Russia could still play a waiting game, collecting hay, preparing and hauling provisions, and training reserves, while the Turks struggled with supply problems. The decisive blow— the capture of Silistria and perhaps Rushchuk—would probably come in August and September, at the close of the campaign of 1854.[11]

The people of the Greek kingdom, who had obtained freedom after the Russo-Turkish war of 1828–29, always had hoped to free their fellow-Greeks of Epirus, Thessaly, and Macedonia. The Hetairia (secret society of the 1820s) was revived and in 1853 hoped for Russian aid to achieve its goal. Hence, as Russia and Turkey moved toward war, there was much eagerness to join in the fray. In September the Greek envoy in London told Baron Brunnow of the hopes of the Hetairia to free its brothers under Turkey. In December a Greek of Bucharest discussed with General M. D. Gorchakov the society and its hopes of Russian money and arms. It had only 9,000 men, however, and Gorchakov, while sympathetic, was loath to encourage it, as he knew that the tsar felt that the rising of the Greeks was treason against King Otto in Athens.

But the Greeks still trusted Russia and expected a mass uprising in the Turkish provinces. Although they knew that Russia was not sympathetic, they were sure that Europe, not Russia, would decide the outcome. In Greece itself army officers resigned and went off to lead former deserters against the Turks. The Hetairia thanked Gorchakov for his promises of aid, although he denied making them. But the society had only a few thousand men in the field and complained of a lack of money to buy weapons. Gorchakov would not help, and Meyendorff, ambassador in Vienna, urged his cabinet to restrain the Greeks, lest Russian influence in the Balkans would be weakened if they were quickly crushed. In Athens the frenzy still mounted, with seminary students removing cassocks and beards and following their rector against Turkey. Omer pasha, however, led a great Turkish force against them, and England and France threatened to blockade the Piraeus.

11. Zaionchkovskii, *Pril.,* II, 315–17.

Nicholas I would not be swayed and denied Gorchakov's plea for the Greeks.[12] In March Turkey broke relations with Athens; Britain and France sent forces to the Piraeus, and Austria and Prussia supported them. Russia was isolated.

With Austria keeping Serbia and Montenegro quiet and Russia doing nothing for the Bulgars and Greeks, the Balkan peoples could not achieve anything. Russia, which had to retreat back across the Pruth and stand on the defensive on its own soil, had lost its chance to win the war.

By early March, however, Paskevich was warning of Austria's threat to the Russian communications with almost 250,000 men (a gross exaggeration). In addition, the Allies were concentrating in the Black Sea area for a possible landing at Odessa or Akkerman, to strike at Russian communications in conjunction with an Austrian push from the north. While Paskevich was taking measures against these threats, with some justice he regarded the situation as difficult. Gorchakov was ordered to cross the lower Danube on March 7, to take the minor fortresses, and build a strong bridgehead. He was not, however, to take Girsovo. Paskevich expected little from this operation, for his main concern was an Austrian attack from Transylvania.[13]

General Gorchakov shortly reported to Paskevich that the crossing of the Danube had been very successful with three small fortresses taken. Also the Turks had apparently abandoned Girsovo, so that the Russians could take it at least fifteen days ahead of schedule. Gorchakov proposed to take Girsovo and build a strong bridgehead there, for the Allies probably would not make a landing before April and his advance would compel them to rescue the Turks, instead of a landing at Odessa or in Bessarabia. While the British would probably take the mouths of the Danube, the Russian river flotilla should be able to prevent them from coming up the river. Nicholas was delighted, as shown by his enthusiastic marginal comment.[14]

Paskevich, after a visit to the army, on April 4 reported it in good condition, although, because of the danger from Austria, he wanted to withdraw the troops to Moldavia. On learning, however, that the Austrians could not move for five or six weeks, he ordered an advance to Chernyvody and Silistria, although he warned that if Austria and

12. Nikitin, "Russkaia politika," pp. 26–28.
13. Ibid., pp. 317–19.
14. Report of Gorchakov, Mar. 16, 1854, ibid., pp. 328–31.

the Allies marched, Russia would have to evacuate the Danube valley. He saw little gain in taking Girsovo, except to trouble the Turks and the Allies. He did not seem to expect Silistria to fall.[15]

Paskevich's memorandum was more pessimistic than Gorchakov's, for he expected a French landing of some 40,000 men which, with perhaps 70,000 Turks, would drive the Russians from Bucharest. If Austria joined in, the combined forces could crush the Russian rear, so that the remnants would have to fight their way through the enemy, with the Turks in pursuit. Thus they might lose "half an army." Hence, "common sense would now demand that we leave the Danube and the Principalities" to take another, more secure position. The emperor marked this passage with three exclamation points.[16] Nevertheless, the field marshal ordered an advance to Chernyvody, a two days' march from Girsovo. There the troops stayed until April 30, waiting for orders to march to Silistria.[17] Obviously Paskevich was dragging his feet.

Nicholas I insisted on pushing the offensive. On April 17 he wrote to Paskevich that "with extreme vexation and astonishment" he had received his letter of the 11th, which was completely contrary to his hopes and "unchanging will." He minimized the danger from the Allies and said there must be no retreat—"it is certainly shameful to think of it." As for the Austrians, they were not moving, and Berlin reported that Prussia merely wanted to frighten the Russians and would not attack. The Prussians also feared an uprising of the Serbs. Meanwhile time was precious, for the French and the British could not help Omer pasha until June at the earliest. Yet Paskevich suggested abandoning everything. This, the tsar wrote, was painful to him. He could not agree with the field marshal's "strange proposals" and demanded that Paskevich carry out his "splendid former plan" in the most effective fashion, without troubling himself with ill-founded fears. "Here is shame and ruin, there is honor and glory!" he exclaimed.[18]

The following day he wrote again, urging Paskevich to push ahead, for his troops were invincible if well led. "Now I expect from you," he said, "that once more you will show this, for the honor and benefit of Russia and for new laurels for your brow. *Amen!*" He added that

15. Letter, Paskevich to Nicholas I, Apr. 15, 1854, Bucharest, ibid., pp. 395–96.
16. Memorandum of Apr. 15, ibid., pp. 397–98.
17. "Voina Rossii s Turtsiei," *Russkaia Starina,* XVI, no. 9 (1876), 89.
18. Ibid., pp. 91–92.

he was impatiently awaiting the report that General Lüders was near Silistria and had built a new crossing. He ended: "For God's sake, don't lose precious time!" [19]

Paskevich thus voiced his fears and begged the tsar to retire back across the Russian frontier, which Nicholas refused to do. The field marshal's view of the situation was partly correct, for an Austrian attack upon the Russian communications would have been ruinous. The Austrian mobilization, however, was much slower than Paskevich believed. The threat from the French and the British also was not immediate. Even so, Russia's situation was risky. But the field marshal lacked the courage to resign his command or to ask for a transfer to another post. Instead, he ostensibly agreed to carry out his master's orders, although he continued to warn against the danger from Austria and to state that if his forces captured Silistria, they would shortly have to give it up. In his letter and report of April 22 he again stressed the growing Austrian danger and the fact that Prussia would join in demanding evacuation of the Principalities. Paskevich proposed a voluntary evacuation, to prove to the Germans that Russia was not aggressive. As for the Christians of Turkey, the sultan had promised them sweeping concessions, and Russia could be satisfied with these. This, too, would mollify the Germans, and if Austria was still bellicose, Russia could defeat it by invading Galicia, and Austria would collapse. "In the meantime I shall not stop the movement of the troops to Silistria, but I await your command," the field marshal said.[20]

Thus Paskevich's leadership against Silistria was far from enthusiastic. Paskevich repeatedly delayed opening the siege on various pretexts. He had to wait for news from Austria; then he spent weeks inspecting the troops and the terrain; and when he heard of the Austro-Prussian convention of mutual support, he wanted to withdraw all his forces to Russia. Even as late as April 27 he wrote the tsar that the Austrians would attack on May 20 and by the 27th the Russians would be in peril, and he actually took some steps toward retirement. Only when the monarch wrote that the Austrians would not dare attack did he finally march to Silistria on May 4. Thus Paskevich took six weeks after crossing the river before he began the siege.[21]

19. Ibid., p. 92.
20. Letter of Paskevich to Nicholas I, Apr. 22, 1854, Zaionchkovskii, *Pril.,* II, 402–03; Shcherbatov, VII, 147–51.
21. Curtiss, pp. 322–23.

Before the siege began General K. I. Schilder, a talented engineer, had promised to take Silistria in a week. But as Paskevich refused to let him attack it along the river bank, but made him attack Arabtabia, a strong stone outwork a mile from the city, much time was lost. Paskevich refused to cut off all supplies to the city, although the Russians outnumbered the defenders five to one. He also did not make full use of the siege artillery, thus delaying the siege. Prince V. I. Vasil'chikov, an able soldier, stated that the field marshal, lacking the moral courage to refuse the emperor's demands for a siege, merely went through the motions, hoping that in some way he could abandon the operation. He held that while Paskevich had correctly opposed the tsar's policy, he should have resigned rather than pretend to carry it out.[22]

The threat of Austria was what terrified the field marshal. Vienna held that free navigation of the Danube, which was impossible with Russia in control of the Principalities, was essential for Austria's economy. Since Russia was apparently consolidating its hold there, the situation could not be tolerated. Another factor was Austrian pride, for the Austrians resented the fact that in 1849 Russia had to rescue their country from defeat at the hands of the Magyars. Probably more important was the existence of large numbers of Slavic subjects, restless and resentful, who were dominated by the Germans and the Magyars and who tended to look to Russia for liberation. While Nicholas promised that he would not support the Slavs of Austria, his wish to help the Serbs, the Bulgars, and the Greeks of Turkey seemed to the Austrians a real threat to their dominant position, for the revolution, if successful among the Turkish Slavs, might well spread to those of Austria. When Count A. F. Orlov delivered the tsar's proposal for freedom for the Serbs, the Bulgars, the Greeks, and the Rumanians, Franz Joseph was horrified and moved closer to Russia's enemies.

Even before Orlov's mission Russia was actively supporting the Serbs, for in November 1853 Nesselrode wrote to Meyendorff that Fonton, secretary of the embassy at Vienna, wanted to ship arms to the Serbs, which presented difficulties. If Austria would grant a transit permit for them, it would be simple to send them to Vienna by rail and then ship them down the Danube; a Serbian delegation could come to receive them and pose as purchasers of the weapons in Austria.

---

22. Ibid., p. 323.

Fonton could arrange matters if Franz Joseph would permit it, "which I permit myself to doubt." [23]

Franz Joseph certainly would not agree, for he knew that Fonton and Mukhin, Russian consul at Belgrade, as well as various Russian secret agents, were intriguing with the Serbs and the Bulgars. Shortly after Orlov's departure, Meyendorff, meeting the emperor at a ball, complained that the Austrian press and government were charging Russia with revolutionary politics just because it had some six hundred volunteers—Serbs, Greeks, or Bulgars—in its army in Wallachia. Since the Turks had accepted thousands of revolutionaries from all countries, including many Poles, why object when Russia accepted Christian volunteers? The emperor answered sharply that these volunteers were a danger to Austria, which greatly needed the status quo. He could not be indifferent to the extension of Russian protection to a large part of the Turkish empire. When Meyendorff reminded him of the tsar's offer to share protection over Serbia with him, the emperor stated that this would mean little, for because of its nationality and religion similar to those of the Serbs, Russia would have all the influence and Austria would have none.

The Russian then suggested that Austria was taking measures against a danger that hardly existed. The emperor's answer was that he knew that Russia was planning to cross the Danube and that sixteen thousand muskets had been brought to arm the Christians. When Orlov had come he had recognized that the Russians were determined to forge ahead, and he had to take measures which the vital interests of his empire dictated to him.[24]

Nicholas I himself wanted peace, for in a letter to "cher et excellent Fritz" (King Frederick William IV of Prussia) in March he stated that as soon as he should learn that the maritime powers had compelled the sultan "to grant to all Christians without exception the conditions that he refused to me" and he had been officially notified that the treaty had been concluded, he would be satisfied. He would immediately evacuate the Principalities as soon as he knew the guarantees obtained by the powers and that the Allied fleets would simultaneously depart from the Black Sea and the Straits.

The tsar hoped that the Greeks of Epirus and Thessaly would not be lured by the new concessions into laying down their arms and

23. Nesselrode, *Lettres,* X, 298–99.
24. Meyendorff to Nesselrode, Feb. 9/21, 1854, cited in Tarle, I, 362–63.

accepting the Turkish yoke again. He felt that if the Christian powers forced them to do so, it would be "infamy," and he himself would not do so. "It is enough that for the moment I have urged the Serbs to remain quiet." As for Austria's request that he would guarantee no change in the political regime of the Turkish provinces in Europe, he still felt that no one could promise that, certainly not he. But he had offered a pledge that if the Christian provinces of Turkey should free themselves, Russia would never permit them to try to gain territory from Austria. This he felt was the "really important pledge." [25]

Baron Meyendorff, who from his listening post at Vienna could observe the situation closely, believed that Russia's situation was very shaky. The Austrian generals, who were strongly pro-Russian, at the same time were talking about getting "their piece of the cake"—i.e., Bosnia and Herzegovina and perhaps Serbia. Meyendorff held that Russia must be very careful in dealing with Serbia and Montenegro and that the Russian agents in this area "are more harmful for us than helpful." While Russia had said that it did not want to incite the Serbs and Montenegrins against the Turks, still it hoped to gain from an insurrection and its agents were involved in the situation. He insisted "that the help of the Slavic populations will not do us as much good as a war with Austria would harm us," and he hoped to act so that "our real and durable influence over the populations" would not suffer.[26]

A week later Meyendorff wrote Nesselrode that Buol seemed a little less curt, perhaps because Mukhin and Kovalevskii were out of the Serbian areas, and also because the Russian operations in Bulgaria were going slowly. He believed that Austria would not go to war, provided that Russia did not go far beyond the Danube "and that you permit me to preach tranquility to the Serbs and Montenegrins." This was the price of Austrian neutrality. Also, if Russia had encouraged these Slavs to fight, how could it decently retire from the Principalities, as it had offered, and leave them to the punishment that the Austrians and the Turks would hasten to inflict on them? [27]

Paskevich had suggested letting "the Austrians enter Serbia," which would involve them in a bitter fight. But Meyendorff felt it would not be wise to push Austria into such action, for it would tell the

25. Schiemann, IV, 426–27.
26. Hoetzsch, III, 142.
27. Ibid., pp. 143–44.

Serbs, who would then detest the Russians as much as they did the Austrians. Moreover, Russia could not afford to seek the aid of the Slavs south of the Danube, since Europe would not permit Russia to destroy Turkey. To promise independence to the Balkan Slavs, which it could not carry out, "would be to kill Russia's influence in these countries, which Russia must save and keep for the future." [28]

Meyendorff continued to write to both Nesselrode and Paskevich that Russia must evacuate the Principalities. "The neutrality of Austria still depends on us," he said. "Let us not cross the Balkans, and say so! As passing them would not lead to anything, and would be very risky, what would we lose by giving it up? Everything else would work out if this were done." The problem was not one of making peace with France, England, and Turkey, but of not arousing Germany against Russia. He reported that Buol felt that Russia's peace offer brought by Duke George of Mecklenburg had little chance of success, for the moment, for the Allies wanted more than Russia would concede. Moreover, the Allied effort to improve the lot of the Christians of Turkey had brought nothing but a firman that provided in vague terms that Christians might be witnesses before Moslem courts.

One significant move by the Russians in mid-April was the evacuation of Little Wallachia, which was left for the Turks and the Austrians,[29] since Russia no longer hoped to gain the support of the Serbs. The withdrawal still left Austria dissatisfied and threatening and close to committing itself to the Western powers in order to force Russia from the Principalities. But because the French and the British could give it little direct help against Russia, Austria needed the promise of aid from Prussia, which it was reluctant to give. Prussia's decision proved to be a vital factor.

Since November 1853 Count Buol and the Austrian emperor had moved further away from Russia. Russia's refusal to accept the compromises worked out by Buol, its fierce attack on the Turks at Sinop, and its increasingly strong control over the regime of the Principalities seemed to them to indicate that its pledges of moderation and renunciation of territorial gains meant little. As Britain and France were putting strong pressure on Vienna to side with them against Russia, the Austrians had to make a vital decision. Consequently, on January 16, 1854, Buol made a report to the emperor, proposing alternative actions,

28. Meyendorff to Gorchakov, Vienna, Apr. 7–19, 1854, ibid., pp. 149–50.
29. Meyendorff to Nesselrode, Apr. 16/28, 1854, ibid., pp. 155–56.

depending on which of three possible courses Russia pursued. If Russia would promise not to make conquests and in reciprocity with the Turks would agree not to carry the war across the Danube, Austria would maintain an expectant neutrality. If, however, Russia pledged that it sought no conquests but crossed the river to attack Turkey, Austria would have to look after its interests by stationing an observation corps near the theater of war and to agree with the other powers that Russia must not be permitted to gain additional territory. Finally, if Russia should decide on an all-out war to destroy the Ottoman empire, Austria should join in a quadruple alliance against it to oppose its territorial designs and other aggressive moves.[30]

On January 23 the emperor called a ministerial conference, to which he presented Buol's proposal of the 16th. The members agreed closely with Buol's views, with suggestions that Russia should be asked not to cross the Danube unless the other powers did so. Austria and Prussia should work together at all times. Alexander Bach, the minister of interior, insisted that Russia must not cross the river, to avoid an uprising of the Serbs, Montenegrins, and Greeks. In such a case, Austria would have to occupy the border provinces. To avoid war with the sea powers, Austria must speak strongly and decisively to Russia, which was perhaps the only way to hold it back. There was general agreement that if Austria became involved in the war, it would have to seek either loans or subsidies from the West. The emperor agreed that it might have to occupy the border provinces of Turkey. He added that probably the sea powers would want Austria to enter the war, but he would decide about this on the basis solely of Austria's interests and not because of outside pressure.[31]

Shortly thereafter Count Orlov arrived on his special mission, asking Austria and Prussia to sign an agreement with Russia that if they would be neutral in the war, Russia would protect their territory. Emperor Franz Joseph said that Orlov had stated that Russia could not promise not to cross the Danube and that if an insurrection of the Slavs of Turkey occurred, the tsar would not prevent it, and would recognize their political independence. He would, however, promise that the two emperors would share a joint protectorate over the new states.

Buol pointed out that Prussia had already rejected the Russian

30. Buol's proposal to Emperor Franz Joseph, Jan. 16, 1854, HHSA, XL, 48.
31. Conference of Jan. 23, 1854, ibid.

offer and that an Austrian pledge of absolute neutrality would bring an attack of France and England on Austria. He also charged that Russia was not adhering to the Treaty of Münchengrätz concerning Turkey and hence its pledges had no value. Austria should decline the Russian offer, but without hostility. It should, however, preserve freedom of action and protect its interests. Baron Heinrich von Hess, the chief of staff, advised that if Russia crossed the Danube and aroused a revolution in Turkey's northern provinces, that would expose Austria to danger. Austria should then take a protectorate over Serbia and occupy it as soon as Russia crossed the river. General Karl von Grünne, the emperor's military adviser, said that Austria should occupy it *before* Russia crossed the Danube. All present opposed the Orlov offer—to combat revolution, to avoid war with the Allies, and to avoid financial ruin. The emperor said that in view of the unanimity of viewpoints Austria should immediately occupy Serbia.[32]

After the rejection of the Orlov proposals there was a period of apparent quiet which masked intense diplomatic activity. The Allies had decided on war against Russia, which they hoped it would declare against them. For his part, Nicholas I was convinced that his one hope of success was to attack the Turks across the Danube and to incite the Slavs to bring down the Turkish empire. Austria wanted to join the maritime powers in an ultimatum to Russia to evacuate the Principalities, but feared to risk war without the support of Prussia. England and France put great pressure on Austria to join them against Russia, but Austria hung back. Finally, on March 21, Buol presented a proposal to Franz Joseph to make the crucial decision.

Buol held it was now or never, for without Austria the maritime powers could not hope to defeat Russia, which threatened to destroy Turkey and kindle a revolutionary blaze from Bulgaria to Bosnia and Herzegovina, which would be ruinous for Austria's interests. An endless war would probably bring fatal results for Austria's financial position unless it joined France and England in forcing Russia to withdraw. Austria had little choice but to act, for this was the decisive moment, which might never return. But it still had to secure the most favorable conditions for its entry.

First of all, it must make sure that the sea powers would make a decisive attack in the Principalities, so that it would not have to bear

32. Conference of Jan. 31, 1854, ibid.

the brunt of Russia's anger. It should join them only when they and the Turks stood facing Russia on the Danube. It should then offer Russia new peace proposals and if it rejected them, it should demand the evacuation of the Principalities. Austria should also induce Prussia and the lesser German states to join the coalition for the same purpose, including the essential pledge to defend all territories of the German states against attack and to prevent the annexation of the Principalities. Austria should have the right to occupy certain Turkish territories (Serbia, Bosnia, and Herzegovina?), and the Bund must support this step.

The Allies also must promise to make no conquests. Further, they should compel the Porte to give full privileges to its Christians of all rites. Additionally, they should induce the Porte to give a protectorate over the Principalities to Austria instead of to Russia. And lastly, no member of the group should make a separate peace with Russia.

Buol again stressed that this was a uniquely favorable moment for Austria. If it did not seize it, it would never be able to realize its objectives.[33]

An imperial conference considered Buol's proposals on March 22 and 25. Hess, Bach, the emperor, and Grünne all picked flaws in his scheme, holding that Buol was risking all-out war with Russia, which would be far too dangerous without Prussia's sure support. Hess said Buol had put Austria in a situation where it had to join France and England to stop Russia or the Allies and the war would cause more devastation for it than Russia would. He held that both England and France were more revolutionary than Russia, which had fought the revolution for forty years. Some day Austria would need the help of Russia, while England would always be revolutionary, and France would be until it broke with England. Hess also emphasized the cost of a war with Russia. Austria would not be ready to take the field until the summer, and even then it would need 150,000 Prussian troops. If Russia won, it would ruin Austria. If Russia lost, there would be a general war against it, with Poland arising again—a second revolutionary center in Eastern Europe. Austria would be pushed to the east, out of Germany and Italy, and France would dominate Germany.

Austria, Hess said, must have a Prussian alliance. It must intervene

33. Buol's proposal of March 21, 1854, ibid.

only when it was ready, with Prussia and Germany, to stop the war and "impose our will on France and England as well as on Russia." It should not join the sea powers unless Russia became completely unreasonable.[34]

Buol and Hess argued hotly at the conference of March 25, for the former wanted to keep the Prussian treaty from restraining Austria, while Hess as well as Prussia wanted just that. Buol wished Austria to have the right to occupy the Principalities as well as Bosnia and Serbia.

Hess repeatedly interrupted Buol, saying that occupation of the Principalities meant war. Buol fiercely denied this, holding that it was in line with Austria's whole policy in the East. The crucial question was which alliance did the ministers want—one to protect Austria in the Principalities or one that would cover it in Serbia and Bosnia "but would be useless for protection of Austria's interests in the East"?

Franz Joseph found it hard to make a decision, as he saw merit in both positions. He agreed that intervention meant war with Russia, and he wished to assure Prussia that it would be used only as a last resort. Thus neither Buol's nor Hess's plan was adopted.[35]

The subsequent conference at Berlin to which Hess was sent was a vital one, for both Russia and the maritime powers were vigorously trying to line up Austria and Prussia in their favor. On March 14 the king of Prussia, concerned about his isolation, had sent a proposal to Vienna for an alliance of the two countries, which was warmly received. The king's willingness to have Prussia and the Bund support Austria if it had to occupy Serbia and Bosnia in order to force Russia out of Moldavia and Wallachia was very welcome.[36]

The Emperor Nicholas hastened to approach King Frederick William by sending Duke George of Mecklenburg with a letter urging the king to support Russia in its efforts to free the Christians of Turkey. An Austrian effort to restore the Turkish yoke over these sufferers would bring Austria into war with the tsar, who hoped that the king would be guided by his conscience to "defend the holy Cross." Specifically, the emperor was willing to accept Turkey's solemn pledge to

34. Schroeder, pp. 160–61.
35. Ibid., pp. 162–63; Protocol of Conference, March 25, 1854, HHSA, XL, 48.
36. Charles Hallberg, *Franz Joseph and Napoleon III, 1852–1864: A Study of Austro-French Relations* (New York, 1955), p. 60; Borries, pp. 166–67; Buol to Esterházy, Apr. 18, 1854, HHSA, X, 38.

grant equality with its Moslem subjects to its Christian populations, provided it did not invalidate the religious privileges enjoyed by the Christians and that the Porte maintained and confirmed Russia's treaties of Küchuk-Kainardji and Adrianople. If this were done, the tsar would have his troops leave the Principalities simultaneously with the withdrawal of the Anglo-French forces from the Turkish domains. He also urged the king to convene a conference at Berlin instead of Vienna, under his auspices.[37]

England promptly refused a conference at Berlin, and on April 9 the Conference of Vienna met as requested by France and Great Britain, at which the maritime powers formally testified that, since Russia had not responded to their demand to evacuate the Principalities, they now were in a state of war with it. The conference then stated that it stood for the integrity of the Ottoman empire and the evacuation of the Principalities and the consolidation, under the aegis of the sultan and his sovereignty, of the civil and religious rights of his Christian subjects. The four members, from England, France, Austria, and Prussia, pledged themselves to seek in common to attach the existence of Turkey to the general equilibrium of Europe and to deliberate and to agree on the best means to achieve this equilibrium. The four governments also pledged not to make any agreement with Russia or any other power contrary to these principles without having deliberated them in common. The Prussian adherence to the Protocol seemed to align it firmly with the anti-Russian camp. The king of Prussia, however, was a warm admirer of the tsar and believed Nicholas would liberate the Christians of Turkey. He disliked Napoleon III and, along with Gerlach, Dohna, the queen, Prince Charles, and the influential Bismarck, had no desire to follow Austria's lead.[38]

The talks at Berlin dragged on for some time, for neither side was unified. Prince William of Prussia wanted to join forces with Austria in an alliance with France and Britain against Russia. He and the Liberals were opposed, however, by the Gerlach-Bismarck group, who were strongly pro-Russian and heartily disliked Austria. The king and Manteuffel, the foreign minister, however, realized that if there

37. Nesselrode to Meyendorff, March 16, 1854, AVP, f. Kants. D. no. 161; Instructions to Prince George of Mecklenburg, March 16, 1854, Zaionchkovskii, *Pril.*, II, 344–45; Letter of Duke of Mecklenburg to Nicholas I, Mar. 23/Apr. 4, ibid., pp. 345–47; Martens, *Recueil des traités,* VIII, 434–36.

38. Protocol of Conference at Vienna, Apr. 9, 1854, Zaionchkovskii, *Pril.,* II, 338; A. Debidour, *Histoire diplomatique de l'Europe, 1814–1878* (3rd rev. ed., Paris, 1919–20), II, 110–11.

were no agreement with Austria, it would surely join the West against Russia. Hess and Thun, the Austrian representatives, were sympathetic to Russia and did not want the treaty to put it in peril. The conference therefore decided on an Austro-Prussian offensive and defensive alliance that provided for protection for all the territories of both powers, German and non-German. Both Austria and Prussia were obligated to mobilize part of their forces and, in case of need, to call on the Bund for its forces as well. The negotiators hoped that the Russian forces would soon be withdrawn from the Principalities, since Russia had expressed satisfaction over the concessions that the Porte had made to its Christian subjects. (The principle of reciprocal withdrawal of the Allied fleets from Turkish waters, which was dear to the hearts of the king and the tsar, was quietly dropped.) Further, a Separate Article was adopted providing for a communication from Austria to St. Petersburg calling for the evacuation of the Principalities, which would be strongly backed by Prussia. If the Russian court rejected this demand, action would be taken under the provisions of the offensive and defensive alliance, and any hostile attack on the territory of either Austria or Prussia would be repulsed by all the military forces at their disposal. On the other hand, no mutual offensive movement would be required unless Russia incorporated the Principalities or attacked or passed the Balkans.[39]

Nicholas I was unhappy about Frederick William's signature of the treaty, feeling that the king had given in far too much to Austria. According to Kurt Borries, the emperor talked of war against Austria and offering an alliance to France, thus abandoning Prussia and Austria. But Nesselrode and Orlov soon cooled him down. Realizing that he must save Russia's position, Nicholas followed Meyendorff's advice by making a concession to Vienna. He still insisted that Austria and Prussia must do nothing to bring the Balkan Christians back under the Turkish yoke, and that if Russia withdrew from Moldavia and Wallachia, Britain and France must withdraw their armed forces from Turkey. But he agreed to accept the three points of the Protocol of April 9 and secretly promised Frederick William that he would evacuate the Principalities. He was fully convinced that the intentions of the king were noble, but doubted whether the results of his efforts were sufficient. He also regarded Frederick William as erratic and

---

39. Text of the Austro-Prussian alliance, Apr., 1854, Zaionchkovskii, *Pril.*, II, 339–41, 348–51; Borries, pp. 179–81; Jasmund, I, 286–88.

unreliable.[40] The latter apologized for signing the alliance, but said that he felt it was necessary. He pointed out that the *casus belli* given in the Austro-Prussian treaty of April 1854 was an impossible one: "The incorporation of the banks of the Danube in the Russian Empire and a Transbalkan march on Constantinople." He added that while God did not permit them to fight side by side, "wait *in sancta patientia.* The day will come." Nicholas, for his part, wanted only one thing from Prussia: to hold onto its neutrality for the benefit of Germany and Russia. On April 29/May 10 he wrote the king: "Maintain yourselves, my dear friend, in a strong and independent position toward the Western powers and you will serve the cause of peace. . . . No attitude will be more in accord . . . with this old and good friendship that has existed between us for so many years." [41]

Austria, however, regarded the decisions at Berlin as granting it a free hand toward Russia. On May 15 the emperor sent a letter to Count Buol announcing the concentration of troops along the frontiers of Transylvania. He had ordered three infantry and one cavalry corps of 100,000 to 120,000 men to take up positions in Galicia to ensure that the empire would be secure against attack. Buol was to inform the Berlin cabinet of these troop movements and to send Major General von Mayerhofer to Berlin as liaison officer for military matters.[42] Mayerhofer was ordered to urge the Prussian cabinet to carry out its agreed mobilization of 200,000 men by the middle of June for readiness by the end of July.[43]

The reason for these Austrian military preparations was that Austria had decided to forward an ultimatum to the Russian cabinet. On June 3 Buol sent a series of very important despatches to Esterházy at St. Petersburg urging the tsar to end the crisis in the East, which had already caused damage to Austrian commerce and industry because of the prolonged occupation of the Principalities. These evils would increase greatly if the war expanded. Hence the Austrian monarch fervently wished to have Russian military operations south of the Danube cease and to obtain from the tsar "positive indications of the precise time . . . when he would put an end to the occupation of the Principalities." The emperor of Russia, who surely wanted peace,

40. Borries, pp. 198–99; Martens, *Recueil des traités,* VIII, 436–37.
41. Martens, ibid., pp. 437–48.
42. Letter, Franz Joseph to Buol, May 15, 1854, HHSA, XL, 48.
43. Instructions to Maj. Gen. Mayerhofer, May 31, 1854, ibid.

would certainly think about how to end this state of affairs and would not, by delay or setting up conditions for evacuation, "impose on the Emperor Franz Joseph the imperious duty" of taking strong measures.

In reading these despatches to Nesselrode, Esterházy should, Buol said, stress the need for receiving from him "prompt and precise explanations which . . . could . . . serve as progress toward limiting the horrors of war." [44]

Buol added that, while Austria and Prussia had made an agreement with France and Britain, Franz Joseph wished to solve the problem, not by aligning with Russia's foes, but by the spontaneous help of the Emperor Nicholas. Why could the tsar not accept the pledge in the Protocol of April 9 that the powers would assure the equality of the Christians of Turkey? Why would this pledge not serve as the guarantee that he had sought from the Porte? If an agreement was not possible, Russia should show good faith by retiring behind the Pruth, while the Allies and the Turks remained beyond the Danube. If Russia would come to a congress to agree on the bases of peace and to work out there the fate of the Orthodox Christians, the Allies would surely accept this proposal, and the result would be a general armistice and an agreement about the positions of the fleets.

Austria would use all its influence to produce a settlement satisfactory to Russia, provided Russia did not insist upon precise conditions for peace. It should not ask a formal document of the Turks and must not insist on immediate withdrawal of the fleets from the Black and Baltic Seas, which the Allies would reject. These matters could be worked out later.

Esterházy was advised to present these ideas informally, in confidential talks, emphasizing the wish of Franz Joseph to prove his benevolence toward Russia. Franz Joseph profoundly desired to eliminate everything that might alter the intimate relations between the two courts and hoped to find the same attitude "in Nicholas I, his most august friend." [45]

Finally, Buol discussed the possibility that Russia would not evacuate the Principalities peaceably. Austria was already proposing to the Porte that Austrian troops should occupy the two provinces and expected that the Turks would readily agree. In addition, the emperor

44. Buol to V. Esterházy, June 3, 1854, no. 1, HHSA, XL, 38.
45. Ibid., no. 2.

had ordered the movement of considerable forces of troops, so that there would be two large corps in Transylvania and Galicia by the end of July. Buol was pleased to state that occupation of the Piraeus by a squadron and by French troops had forced King Otto of Greece to declare neutrality and name a new ministry. As a result the revolution seemed on the wane, although the Montenegrins remained aggressive. These items were sent to Esterházy for his information, although he was to use the knowledge as he saw fit.[46]

Understandably, Nicholas I was furious at Austria for its ultimatum. Even though General Gorchakov lifted the siege of Silistria on June 23 and then retreated across the Danube, Russia's response to the summons promised to be uncompromisingly hostile. Although on the 26th Esterházy learned that Colonel Edwin Manteuffel, the Prussian envoy, was hopeful of a moderate reply, and Esterházy had heard also that Nesselrode had persuaded the emperor to have his troops retire from the Danube, the envoy was still not received by the Russian cabinet. In his letter to Buol, Esterházy stated that he was still waiting for his audience with the tsar and that "Count Nesselrode avoids speaking to me of affairs." [47] When the monarch finally had an audience with him on July 6 (N.S.), he denounced Austria in unsparing terms, and he later told the Prussian king he would rather fight Austria than yield to it. Nicholas's advisers persuaded him against an engagement with the Austrian troops as they entered the Principalities, but it seemed that the Russians would not recross the Pruth without a fight. Even the relatively moderate Nesselrode warned that Austria's taking over the Principalities as Russia evacuated them would mean war.[48]

The Prussians also were angry over the Austrian demands, for when Buol drafted his ultimatum he did not consult with the king of Prussia as he had promised to do, although he informed the latter of his intentions. He had conferred with Colonel Manteuffel on the demands, and the two were apparently in agreement as to the need for reciprocity in respect to evacuation. But while Manteuffel was waiting for word from Berlin, Buol sent off the summons, with all reference to reciprocity omitted.[49]

46. Ibid., no. 3.
47. Letter, Esterházy to Buol, June 26, 1854, HHSA, X, 39.
48. Schroeder, p. 185.
49. Letter, Meyendorff to Nesselrode, May 23/June 4, 1854, Hoetzsch, III, 171.

Buol also was at odds with the Bambergers, representatives of a group of eight middle states, headed by Saxony and Bavaria, who met at Bamberg on May 25 to confer on the situation. The Bambergers were much concerned that Austria and Prussia were leading Germany down a dangerous path to war. While they felt that the intentions of Prussia, although it was largely dominated by Austria, were good, they had no confidence whatever in Buol, whom they regarded as under the thumb of Bourqueney, the French ambassador. Russia appeared to be the only reliable support of conservatism in Europe, which they clung to. But they feared that under pressure Russia would come to an agreement with France, which would put the smaller states under French vassalage, with the dismal prospects of a new Confederation of the Rhine. So in despair and fear of war, they turned to Prussia.[50]

On June 3 the Bambergers sent a note to Austria and Prussia in which they demanded reciprocity in withdrawing the armed forces from the Black Sea area. They insisted on the maintenance of the European balance of power, complete freedom of navigation and commerce on the Danube and other rivers into the Black Sea, and an untroubled existence for the kingdom of Greece—a covert protest against the seapowers, which had occupied the Piraeus because of the Greek insurrection. They also called for the elimination of Turkey from all of Europe but Rumelia and Constantinople. In its place they wanted viable succession states: the Principalities; an enlarged Greece, including Epirus, Thessaly, and most of Macedonia; and a composite state to include Bosnia, Herzegovina, Serbia, Bulgaria, and probably Montenegro. In almost all respects this program was anathema to Austria, while it was favorable to Prussia and Russia. Needless to say, England, France, and Austria were bitterly opposed to it. In Prussia only Bismarck encouraged the Bambergers, and in Vienna the Russian envoys were warmly favorable to them.[51]

After sending its summons to St. Petersburg, the Austrian cabinet urgently appealed to the Prussian king to meet Emperor Franz Joseph at Teschen on January 8–9, to discuss a joint call to the tsar to evacuate the Principalities. Meyendorff had strongly advised the king to state that nothing could be asked of Russia without equivalent concessions by the West and to complain of Buol's action in sending the summons

---

50. Borries, pp. 216–17.
51. Ibid., pp. 218–19; Jasmund, I, 309–11.

without discussion with Berlin. The resolutions of the Bamberg conference were another reason why the king should stand firm against Austria, since the Bambergers demanded an armistice on land and sea and an equivalent withdrawal of the other belligerents. They also called for wide protection of the interests of Germany in the Black-Sea-Balkan area and of the Christians of Turkey.[52] Hübner, sharply critical of the Bamberg group, termed them "unofficial agents" of Prussia. The reports of these diplomats, the rumors they circulated, their feverish activity, "all devoted to the defense of the interests and the dignity of Russia," created turmoil in the salons and cabinets across the Rhine. "It is a secondary element," said Hübner, "if one wishes, but worthy of drawing the attention of the great governments."[53]

A few days after the Teschen meeting Meyendorff reported to his cabinet that there was no asperity there, for Franz Joseph used pacific language, while Frederick William was trusting and did not raise the issue of Austria's unilateral handling of the message to St. Petersburg. The king did not say that he shared fully the views of the Bamberg group, but merely stated that he felt that Russia had a right not to agree to evacuate the Principalities except on a basis of reciprocity. The principle of reciprocity was the basis of the instructions that were drawn up by Count Nesselrode and completed by the king for Colonel Edward Manteuffel at St. Petersburg. The Berlin cabinet ordered Manteuffel to ask Russia for evacuation and felt that thereby it had done its duty according to the Convention of April 8/20. Prussia and Austria would tell the German states that they stood for peace and that the convention would not cause trouble.

The difference between Frederick William and Buol became apparent during the latter's audience with His Majesty. The king declared his firm intention not to fight Russia and dwelt at some length on the grievous results of such a war for Germany. Buol, however, presented his opposing view in a rough manner, on the basis of the Treaty of Berlin. The monarch, however, who had a bad cold, cut him short.[54]

The Austrians thus felt that having Prussia on their side was of little real help, for the king was sympathetic with Russia and deter-

52. Meyendorff to Nesselrode, May 27/June 8, 1854, AVP, f. Kants., D. no. 161. Extract from reply of the German Courts, after meeting at Bamberg, ibid., annex.
53. Hübner to Buol, May 21, 1854, HHSA, IX, 46.
54. Meyendorff to Nesselrode June 1/13, 1854, AVP, f. Kants., D. no. 161.

mined not to go to war. While Buol insisted that Russia must evacuate the Principalities or face war, Prussia held that one could not expect evacuation without reciprocity—i.e., removal of the British and French fleets from the Black Sea and from Turkish waters back to Malta and Toulon. The Prussians did not speak sternly to the Austrians, for they feared to alienate them, which would cause them to join with the British and the French at once. But while the Prussians were mild to them, they refused to mobilize their forces as the Austrians were doing and sought to delay the latter in their effort to prepare to fight Russia. Austria needed Prussia, for the French and the British could not supply the large armies that it would need if war came, and only Prussia could field the forces that could protect Austria's flank against Russia. Only if the tsar would agree to retire across the Danube and the Pruth would Austria be out of trouble, and he would not agree, but insisted on pushing the campaign in Bulgaria as the sole way to strike an effective blow at the Turks.

In the meantime the siege of Silistria was moving slowly, for Paskevich was concerned about an Austrian attack out of Transylvania against the Russian communications and his retirement from Silistria. During May the emperor wrote him five times, urging him on and belittling the Austrian danger. On the 23rd he wrote that the news from Vienna was favorable: the Prussians and other Germans were restraining the Austrians, and the mobilization of the Russian reserves had been very successful. "Do not despair!" he urged his father-commander. Finally, however, on June 1 he sent word to the field marshal to ship out the wounded and the sick and all unnecessary baggage, even though the Austrians would not be ready to take the field until July. He advised that if Paskevich had not taken Silistria by the time he received this letter, and if he could not guarantee the date of its fall, he should lift the siege and retire across the Danube.[55]

Before the commander could receive this letter, however, a strange incident occurred. On May 29 Paskevich rode out with a group of aides to inspect the siege, only to draw Turkish gunfire. A projectile landed near him and, although he was not hit, he complained of pain in his shoulder and rode off in his carriage back across the river. There was much skepticism in the army concerning whether he had received a contusion or not.[56] Nicholas, however, believed the injury

55. Shcherbatov, VII, 170.
56. Curtiss, pp. 232–34.

was genuine, for he wrote Paskevich a letter full of sympathy, ordering him to take a good, long rest. M. D. Gorchakov would take command of the army.[57]

Gorchakov, who, although elderly, was a capable commander, set about the siege with a will. He realized the dangers threatening him, but was not alarmed by them and thought it best to continue the siege until the peril became great. His forces were mining the chief Turkish fortification. He did not feel that the Allied forces would be ready to strike for some time, and staying at Silistria would compel them to fight in the Danube area instead of making landings on Russian territory. It would force the foe to approach slowly and cautiously. He felt, however, that the Turkish Christians, while sympathetic to the Russians, were not eager to take up arms. If the Allies came in a haphazard manner, he should try to beat them in detail and then, if possible, renew the siege. If, however, they came in a sound, organized fashion, in great strength, the Russians should withdraw across the Danube and fight off attempts to cross, striking at small units that were able to cross the river. When the foe became exhausted by their efforts and lack of provisions, the Russian forces again should take the offensive, to take Silistria and Rushchuk and then winter there, hoping to spread the uprisings, which presumably, after the defeats of the Allies, would burst forth with great strength. But if war with Austria seemed probable, they should withdraw across the Danube and fight off the foe on all sides, as might be possible. The tsar was delighted with this scheme, which he said agreed completely with his views.[58]

Gorchakov moved ahead with his plans. Arab-tabia, the Turkish fort before Silistria, was successfully mined on June 7 and most of its defenses were destroyed. On the night of June 9 six regiments were in position to storm it, with more in reserve. But as the men eagerly awaited the signal, suddenly a special messenger from Paskevich ordered them immediately to cease all operations and to withdraw across the Danube. It was only with difficulty that the commanders were able to induce the troops to obey orders and to retreat from what they believed would have been certain victory. Nicholas wrote in a letter to Prince M. D. Gorchakov, "How sad and painful for me, dear Gorchakov, that I had to agree to the insistent arguments of

57. Zaionchkovskii, *Pril.*, II, 413–14.
58. Proposals of General Gorchakov, May 31 and June 1 (O.S.), 1854, ibid., pp. 409–13.

Ivan Fedorovich [Paskevich] as to the danger threatening the army from the faithlessness of Austria, whom we had saved." [59]

By June 11 the Russians were back across the river, untroubled except at Giurgevo, where a fiery Turkish commander overran a Russian outpost on June 21. The Russians counterattacked vigorously, which was costly, since the Turks had better firearms than they. In driving them back the Russians lost some eighteen hundred men, only slightly less than the foe. By June 23 the Turks had retreated. After holding their ground for several days, the Russians again moved slowly out of the Principalities.[60]

The retirement caused a sensation throughout Europe. The king of Prussia and the Bamberg states, feeling that evacuation should be reciprocal, held that the sea powers should be required to withdraw and an armistice should be arranged. Count Buol, however, who was close to France, did not agree. He now found himself in a less favorable situation than before, for when the Russians were behind the Pruth they would no longer be threatened by an Austrian drive from Bukovina into their rear. Russia could fight Austria on even terms or better, and as Prussia would not support Austrian aggression, the Vienna cabinet was suddenly in a dangerous position. What answer would Russia now give to Buol's ultimatum? Would it be war or peace? The Austrians were very eager to occupy the two provinces as the Russians withdrew and had actually made a convention with the Porte on this point.[61] The tsar had threatened war if Austria moved in. Would he hold to this resolution, or would he let Austria go ahead, *faute de mieux?* Buol also feared that England and France might not make their main drive west of the Black Sea and might attack the Crimea or the Caucasus. Thus the Russian withdrawal, far from solving all problems, not only left most of them unsettled but raised new questions.

Now that peace appeared to be somewhat nearer, the question of the bases for negotiations was increasingly urgent. Austria had said that Russia could not hope to reenter the Concert of Europe without sacrifices, which encouraged Bourqueney of France to state that any arrangement would have to settle the problems of the Principalities, navigation of the Danube and the Black Sea, and Turkey's ties to

59. Shcherbatov, VII, 184–87; Petrov, II, 172–84.
60. Curtiss, pp. 324–25; Tarle, I, 451.
61. Jasmund, I, 323–24.

Europe. France did not want to destroy Russia but to restore the balance in the Levant by limiting its power. The Black Sea was to be opened to Western naval power, and Austria should control Moldavia and Wallachia as a barrier against Russia.[62] The objectives of Clarendon and Palmerston were far more drastic than those expressed by France.

The Russian withdrawal from Silistria and its gradual retirement toward its lands beyond the Pruth thus eased the immediate crisis and cleared the way for a new approach to the problems troubling the powers. The problems themselves, however, remained unsolved.

62. Schroeder, pp. 182–83.

Chapter 11. THE WAR SHIFTS TO THE CRIMEA

When, shortly after the Russian army withdrew from Silistria, Prince A. M. Gorchakov went to Vienna as ambassador, Count Nesselrode sent him a despatch stating the Russian position on the Principalities. Nesselrode held that the Russian occupation had not been the chief cause of war, as the Austrian cabinet averred, for the Note of Vienna and the proposals at Olmütz had come after the occupation. It had been the hostile and provocative demands of France and Britain that had produced the break. Since then the conflict had spread far from the Principalities, to Russian coasts on the Black and Baltic Seas. The Russian position in Moldavia and Wallachia had become merely a strategic one, which could be relinquished, provided the great powers would compensate for the sacrifice this renunciation would entail. For the occupation of the two provinces provided the only real chance for Russia to take the offensive and without it it would be exposed to the assaults of its foes. Austria had promised the Western powers to do everything possible to obtain evacuation, which it had the right to do. It should also explain the guarantees it could give that Russia's honor and security would not suffer. In deference to the interests of Austria and Germany the tsar would be willing to begin negotiation concerning the precise time of departure.

Before Russia could evacuate, however, it would ask Austria to guarantee an armistice by land and sea, and to declare that, after Russia had gone, Austria's obligations to the maritime powers would be ended and that it would pledge its neutrality. Austria could not compel the Allies to end the war or to evacuate the Baltic and Black Seas and Turkish territory, but it could at least take these steps toward peace, as it would have fulfilled its obligations to the Allies.[1]

Austria then should explain to Russia the guarantees it could give, whereupon the tsar, in deference to the wishes and interests of Austria

---

1. Nesselrode to Gorchakov, June 17/29, AVP, f. Kants., D. no. 164; ibid., HHSA, X, 38.

and Germany, would be ready to negotiate regarding the precise time of evacuation. Nicholas was as anxious to end the crisis affecting all Europe as was the Vienna cabinet. He did not want to hold these provinces permanently or to incorporate them into his domains, and still less to overturn the Ottoman empire. He would be quite ready to subscribe to the Three Principles of the Protocol of April 9. Russia had always announced that it stood for the *integrity of Turkey,* as long as it was respected by the other powers. As for the *evacuation of the Principalities,* it would be ready to proceed, if provided with suitable guarantees. Concerning the *consolidation of the rights of the Christians in Turkey,* if both civil and religious rights were considered inseparable and guaranteed by the European powers, the emperor would sign an agreement.

In view of these attitudes of the emperor, it should not be difficult to arrive at the bases for peace, or at least to the negotiations for them by means of an armistice. In a reserved despatch of the same date (June 17/29, 1854) Nesselrode added that while Austria might be ready to offer the promise of an armistice, there would be no certainty that the sea powers would accept it. Moreover, even an armistice would be only temporary, and if the Allies would not make peace on acceptable terms, the war would resume, with Russia having given up its favorable position and having nothing to show for it.

While Austria might favor Russia's requests, it was not certain that it would continue to do so, for repeatedly it had given in to the pressure of France and Britain and had turned against Russia. Hence the St. Petersburg cabinet must ask Austria to guarantee the armistice on land and sea and, after the evacuation, to declare that its obligations toward the West were ended and that it would guarantee its neutrality. These guarantees should be given in a written agreement, which Austria's previous pledges had not forbidden.[2]

In his despatch of June 26/July 8 Gorchakov told of his interview with Buol in which he had communicated Nesselrode's answer to the Austrian summons, which the count curtly stated was no answer. The Russian said it was more than that: it was an overture that embraced the whole question at stake. Buol expressed annoyance about Esterházy's frigid reception at St. Petersburg, but Gorchakov replied that this was only a triviality and that the attitude of the Russian

---

2. Nesselrode to Gorchakov, June 17/29, 1854, AVP, f. Kants., D. no. 164.

court had changed. The real question was, Would Austria consider Russia's proposed plan for making peace?

When Buol expressed doubts that these proposals were real bases for peace, Gorchakov replied that they were, but he was offering them not to the enemy—France and Britain—but to Austria, Russia's former ally, with whom it had had untroubled relations, except when misunderstandings had occurred. If Buol thought that they were worth considering, he, on his own initiative, should sound out the attitudes of the adversaries. At this point Buol said that he would bring the proposals before the French and British representatives, who would probably want to add others. Gorchakov agreed to this plan, as it would clarify the position of Russia's adversaries, for they would have to show their true colors. The false colors were the references to "guarantees about the future"—a vague phrase that should be explained.[3]

Buol now volunteered that if the French and the British wanted to impose terms that "would tend to reduce or humiliate Russia, they can never count on us." His master the emperor had always said that and was sticking to it, and he himself felt the same way. His first duty was to uphold the interests of his country, but he had always valued an entente with Russia. Gorchakov answered that that was excellent and that they should clear up the nuances between the Austrian and Russian positions and return to the tradition of good relations. He would forget the past, would deal seriously with Buol, and only with him.

Gorchakov did not discuss the substance of the proposals, since he felt that the mild cordiality between himself and Buol was too fragile to endure ardent discussion. Buol did raise the question of reform of the civil and religious rights of the Christians of Turkey, under a European guarantee. The envoy gathered that this would not be a sweeping reform contrary to the Koran, but a moderate one, which would extend to all Europe, or at least to the five powers, the exclusive right of protection that Russia by its treaties had had in some Turkish provinces.

At first Buol's manner was cool, terse, and distrustful, although he gradually thawed and at the end of the discussion was fairly approachable. Gorchakov did not think that this amiability would last long and expected that Buol would soon revert to his earlier manner.

3. Ibid., June 26/July 8, 1854, AVP, f. Kants., D. no. 161.

It was good, however, to conclude without a clash. Buol seemed to be struck, even alarmed, by the trend of his talk with the Russian envoy, which he had intended to go quite differently. Finally, he told the prince that it was a conversation, not a negotiation, and he would have to confer with his master the emperor, to which Gorchakov did not object.[4]

Gorchakov's special audience with the Emperor Franz Joseph, which occurred shortly thereafter, revealed the monarch "as a man relieved of a heavy burden"—apparently the result of Nesselrode's despatches. He mentioned his happiness that now the bad feeling between him and the tsar, for whom he had the warmest affection, could end. He had felt great pain when his duties as sovereign had conflicted with his heartfelt sentiments. Gorchakov stated that Nicholas I had felt the same and that his mission had made this plain. He hoped that His Majesty had been satisfied with his proposals. While Franz Joseph did not say that he had been satisfied, he did say that he saw in them the "germ of an entente" and had sent word that he would support them. He rejoiced over the evacuation of the Principalities and the desire that had brought it about.[5]

At this point Gorchakov expressed a hope that the good feeling of the two rulers would not be troubled by minor questions and referred to the entry of Austrian troops into Wallachia without advance notice. Franz Joseph quickly said that there had been no hostile intent. He had been surprised by the rapid Russian retreat and had feared anarchy and a Turkish incursion, which would have been calamitous for his country. As soon as the Russian retreat slowed down, the situation changed, and hence he would send orders not to move, but to stay far from the Russian forces in Wallachia. When Gorchakov asked if he might send this assurance to his cabinet, the emperor said, "I count on it." [6] They parted on warm, cordial terms.

Gorchakov then called on Buol to learn what had been decided. He was told that Vienna would inform Paris and London concerning the Russian attitude and, since it contained the "germ of an entente," would sound them out about an armistice that might lead to peace. Buol expected that the two courts would demand guarantees that an armistice would not be just a device to gain time, but would signify that Russia really wanted peace. Vienna, after formulating its opinion

4. Gorchakov to Nesselrode, June 26/July 8, 1854, ibid.
5. Ibid., June 27/July 9, 1854.
6. Ibid.

as to the nature of these guarantees, would send it to St. Petersburg and await the Russian reply, while retaining freedom of action. It would not, however, make any demonstration until the question was settled.

Buol also wanted to send Paris and London the text of the Russian communication, even though it contained harsh words about them. Gorchakov did not object, feeling that the Russian reply showed honest anger. He hoped that the Vienna cabinet would express a favorable attitude toward the Russian despatches when they were sent, although there would be more chance of success if Austria would express agreement, as he felt Russia was entitled to expect. Buol, however, refused to do the latter, since Austria was merely an interested party.[7]

A period of anxious waiting, both at St. Petersburg and at Vienna, followed. Nesselrode wrote Gorchakov that if he could bring Russia the means to keep the peace with Austria and thereby with all of Germany, "it would be the best present you could make. . . ."[8]

In his despatch of June 30/July 12, Gorchakov was mildly optimistic in reporting the closeness of Prussia to Russia, which was based on the latter's deference toward it and supported by the rest of Germany, now rallying around Berlin. This harmony he termed a great embarrassment to Austria, which could not disregard it, and which probably could not weaken the support the Prussian king enjoyed. Hence Buol would have to reckon with King Frederick William. Another gain was that the raising of the question of war aims was forcing the Western powers to declare their true feelings. The counterproposals of Britain and France to the Austro-Prussian demarche concerning the Russian answer would give the first indication of the Allied position, and the more Russia forced the Allies to declare themselves, the more effective the Russian arguments to the German courts would be. If it should become evident that the Western powers wanted the political downfall of Russia and if they should make proposals in this vein, Russia could then go to Austria, proof in hand, saying, "Do you have the same goal? Do you want to continue with allies that admit it?" As difficult as he was, Buol would never dare follow them, and if he had wanted to, Franz Joseph would not let him.

During this period the French and British diplomats were not very active. Ambassador Alvensleben of Prussia told Gorchakov that since

7. Ibid., June 27/July 9, 1854.
8. Letter, Nesselrode to Gorchakov, June 27/July 9, 1854, Tsentral'nyi Gosudarstvennyi Arkhiv Oktiabr'skoi Revoliutsii, Moscow (hereafter cited TsGAOR).

Gorchakov had come to Vienna there had been a real upturn in the cause of peace, although he did not trust it. The tsar's marginal comment here was *"idem, idem, idem, idem!"*

In closing, Gorchakov added that he expected much trouble, but he was calm and trusted God and the Russian people.[9]

Late in June Buol read to Gorchakov his despatch to Esterházy, which laconically and in neutral phrasing said that since the Russian reply offered the germ of a solution, the Vienna cabinet would support it at Paris and London and would urge the Western powers to give serious consideration to the Russian overtures. Buol said to him, "Anyhow, it is a truce."

Buol stated that Austria and Prussia would agree on the text of the demarche to France and Britain. Gorchakov wrote that he hoped that it would contain a very strong dose of Prussian opinions, which would "leave nothing to be desired." On the other hand, Albrecht, Count von Alvensleben, a special emissary of Prussia, had told Gorchakov that Buol, "for the hundredth time," had trotted forth his suggestion of a Prussian military demonstration ("Canaille!" wrote the tsar), to which the Prussian gave his usual negative answer. Buol was not ready, however, to send special military negotiators to London and Paris.[10]

Bourqueney, the French ambassador, made special efforts to have Buol transmit the Russian overtures to Paris and London without supporting them, which resulted in lively scenes. Buol, under the direct orders of Emperor Franz Joseph on this point, could not disobey his master.

Informally, Bourqueney suggested ideas for the future peace: territorial integrity of both parties; neutrality of the Principalities, with both Russia and Turkey barred from sending their troops there; and the protection of Moldavia and Wallachia under the guarantee of the European powers. Further, Russia's right of protecting the Christians of Turkey should be abrogated and replaced by a collective guarantee of all Christians in Turkey. Finally, Russia should no longer station troops in the Danube delta, and there should be a broad application to the Danube of the rules of free navigation of rivers as set forth by the Congress of Vienna.[11]

9. Gorchakov to Nesselrode, June 30/July 12, 1854, AVP, f. Kants., D. no. 161.
10. Ibid.
11. Ibid.

Also on July 12 Gorchakov sent a coded despatch to General Count Rüdiger, commanding the forces facing Galicia, stating that, in spite of Austrian verbiage, a break in the relationships between Austria and Russia seemed near, and it was vital that the Russian troops should not fire a musket or take counteraction until it had been definitely verified that Austria had been the aggressor. If Russia seemed to be attacking Austria, Prussia would be drawn in against it. If the Austrians should attack, the first Russian action must be to telegraph the fact to the Emperor Nicholas and to inform the king of Prussia by courier. According to Colonel Edward Manteuffel, the latter would then immediately detach himself from Austria.[12]

Two days later in a letter to Nesselrode the prince stated that the Eastern Question could only be solved advantageously for Russia with the help of the Slavs, whose liberation must take place under the Russian banner. He was convinced, however, that any efforts to achieve emancipation at that moment would delay and might annihilate it. "Instead of raising crosses on mosques, we would plant them on tombs," he said. He held that Russia must keep alive among these populations "the living faith in the interest that we bear in them, confidence in our arms," and the conviction that they must patiently await the signal for liberation at a future date. Russia was condemned to coexist with Turkey, inevitably, although not too much longer. Peace would be made now without removing Turkey from the map of Europe—"an obligatory breathing spell."

Austria would insist on the evacuation of Moldavia and Wallachia, which was a point of honor for Franz Joseph. While both the emperor and Buol feared war terribly, "we shall infallibly have one," said Gorchakov, unless the question of evacuation, to which Russia was already committed, could somehow be settled. He suggested that Russia concede evacuation to the two German powers on the condition that they both accept the Protocol of April 9 as the basis for a future peace. While the Allies and the Turks would then shift their attack to Russian territory, they intended to do so anyway.

Gorchakov suggested that Prussia should take the initiative in this proposal, and perhaps Buol might go along, which might lead to a return of the old Triple Alliance.[13]

12. Gorchakov to Nesselrode, July 12/24, 1854, AVP, f. Kants., D. no. 161.

13. Letter, Gorchakov to Nesselrode, July 14/26, 1854, Tsentral'nyi Gosudarstvennyi Arkhiv Drevnykh Aktov, Moscow (hereafter cited TsGADA), fond 3, Delo no. 140.

So far the prince had taken pains to be mild and conciliatory to Buol, hoping to bring him to a better attitude. This approach had resulted in some progress, but as it was slow, Gorchakov had decided to use stronger language. On July 14/26 he reported to the chancellor that he had expressed dissatisfaction to Buol over the latter's failure to inform him of the response of Paris and London to the Russian proposals. What did the insistence of Britain and France on restoring the European equilibrium mean, and what guarantee did Austria require for it? Buol was greatly embarrassed and confused by this confrontation and could give no clear explanation of Austria's position. A discussion of the question of whether the two cabinets were turning against each other, which Buol said Austria would never do, followed.

At this point Gorchakov released his bombshell, saying that he frankly felt that Austria was on a slippery slope leading to war. The prince's opinion perturbed Buol, who said that Austria would never make war on Russia. The ambassador replied that the entry of Austrian forces into the Principalities while the Russians were there would mean war, even if General Gorchakov was asked to evacuate, for he would stand fast. Buol protested, saying that Austria would merely be compelling Russia to withdraw from territory where it did not belong and where the honor of Franz Joseph was involved. Austria would not invade Russia, and if Russia struck back, Austria would have the support of all Germany under the Treaty of April 20.

Gorchakov said that once firing began, the two countries would be at war. Russia would not attack, and the Diet and Germany would not support an offensive war.

Buol denied the last part of this statement, saying that the Additional Article provided for German support and the Germans had all agreed to it.[14]

The prince then declared that by the many concessions it had offered Russia had shown its desire for peace and friendship with Austria. If these concessions were not accepted but were answered by stern new demands, there would be conflict. From the beginning, he said, Austria had thought that it could frighten Russia into giving way—a course that would inevitably lead to war—and to avoid war Austria must abandon its policy of intimidation.

If Austria and Russia should become friends, Gorchakov continued,

14. Gorchakov to Nesselrode, July 14/26, 1854, AVP, f. Kants., D. no. 162.

and settled their differences, after which the Western powers threatened or attacked Austria in Italy, all Germany would rally to the latter's side, as would Russia. Austria, Russia, and Germany would win, and Austria would hold a position of honor. If, on the other hand, Austria gave in to pressure from the West and, with the Allies, fought Russia, Russia would surely suffer defeats, but not mortal ones. When the war ended, there would be peace, and the Allies would depart, leaving Austria facing the eternally hostile frontier of a nation of sixty million people. Could Austria survive such an outcome? Gorchakov was not making threats; he was stating the realities of the situation, based on history and geography.[15]

Buol was violently shaken by this frankness and declared that Gorchakov was right: they must avoid war. The latter said that if Buol could effect a peaceful solution, he would win the undying gratitude of the Emperor Franz Joseph. Buol agreed, but warned Gorchakov not to count on Prussia, which had no prestige and was inconstant. Russia should trust Austria. Together they should make France and Britain see the light. As soon as a reply came from London and Paris, Buol would inform Gorchakov of everything that was said and they could then work for peace, and he hoped the Western powers would also. Austria must insist, however, on the evacuation of Moldavia and Wallachia at a fixed date. Gorchakov promised that Russia would withdraw, which it had already pledged to do, but the date for evacuation would be determined by circumstances. Buol agreed, saying that when the moment came they would confer on the means to solve the problem.[16]

Gorchakov's comment on the discourse was that the general outcome seemed good, although Buol was so very changeable that one could not rely on him. At least, before Buol could act in a new crisis he would have to talk with Gorchakov. If he did not do so, the latter could appeal to Franz Joseph.[17]

The ambassador also mentioned that Count Albrecht von Alvensleben of Prussia had said that the Diet of the Germanic Confederation had *not* promised to support Austria in a crisis over the Principalities. Prussia and the German states were completely satisfied with the Russian response to the demands of Austria and Prussia. The Diet would

15. Ibid.
16. Ibid.
17. Ibid.

take up the special question of the Principalities only if Austria had declared it was not satisfied with the Russian response. This point had not even been touched on, much less decided. The attitude of the other German states was much closer to the Prussian position, and as soon as they formulated their views, the support that Buol claimed would vanish.

Alvensleben also stressed that if shooting occurred between the Austrian and Russian troops, the latter should be careful not to fire first, but to make it very clear who was the aggressor. He also urged that if fighting developed the Russian army should not counterattack in Galicia. The attitude of Prussia depended on it.[18]

Obviously the Russian cabinet had no confidence in Buol and wanted to avoid giving him any advantage. Gorchakov therefore sent along a memorandum with his letter to Nesselrode of July 22/August 3 on the problem of the evacuation of the Principalities, about which Franz Joseph was so concerned. The envoy believed that the maritime powers would compel Austria to raise this issue in a demand to Russia. If Buol did so with an offer of guarantees that could satisfy Russia, there would be no crisis, since the guarantees would form part of the bases for peace negotiations. If, however, he merely presented a demand, Russia's military honor would not be upheld. This second possibility would require prudent calculation.

Gorchakov ventured to suggest that if Buol did not offer acceptable guarantees, Russia should evacuate the Principalities *strategically* and mass its strength behind the Pruth. It should make no explanation to Austria and undertake no negotiation whatever, thereby leaving Vienna in uncertainty concerning Russia's intentions and giving it a free hand for its schemes with the Porte and the West. The resulting intrigues would be only a spider web, since Russia would have given them no sanction. He saw the following advantages from such a course:

1. It would put Russia in a defensive position "where we are invulnerable."

2. It would spoil the schemes of the courts of the maritime powers to drag Austria into war against Russia for their own interests.

3. Austria could hardly start war against Russia without putting itself into opposition not only to Prussia, but also to the rest of Germany.

18. Ibid.

4. The position of Austria would be worse "than after an unfortunate war." It could not disarm in the face of a hostile Russia and would steadily exhaust its scanty remaining resources. These limitations would widen the abyss before it, to say nothing of inviting dangerous European events which were obviously imminent.[19]

Russia, on the other hand, would be intact, with no real losses, its strong position, and the prestige of its arms. While this situation would impose a strain, the uncertainty should not last very long, and Austria, now its adversary, would succumb first of all. Russia would remain in a strong position and "we would remain the masters of the future, *because we have not compromised it by any concession whatever* [N.I's Italics]." Gorchakov felt that such a course might ruin Austria, but this eventuality should not deter them; "*The cabinet of Vienna would only be reaping what it had sowed!* [N.I's Italics]."

If, however, Austria should return to a reasonable course and to its own interest, Gorchakov would be delighted, but he felt Russia could not count on it. Moreover, at the moment Russia could not expect any negotiations except under highly unfavorable auspices. He held that with the force of inertia "an invincible rampart for Russia," a period of inaction without humiliation and without the restrictions of newly contracted engagements would give Russia a chance to prepare "the high hand to dominate events."

Nicholas I, who was delighted with this memorandum, adorned it with approving and often gleeful comments. In his instructions to the chancellor he wrote: "I adopt completely the plan in this note; and I urge you to meditate on it well and to prepare the execution of it, in the reply to Gorchakov." [20]

Early in August (N.S.) the French sent their reply to the Austro-Prussian demarche following the Russian overtures (the British reply was much the same). Drouyn de Lhuys said that his cabinet could not negotiate unless it knew that Russia would agree to the following:

1. Revision of the Treaty of 1841.
2. Removal of the Russian protectorate over the Principalities, with a European guarantee in its place.
3. Free navigation of the Danube.

19. Gorchakov, Supplement to letter to Nesselrode, July 22/Aug. 3, 1854, Letter B. Zaionchkovskii, *Pril.,* II, 365–67.
20. Ibid., p. 367.

4. Abolition of the powers of the protectorates over their coreligionists; placement of the rights and privileges of the Christians under a collective guarantee.
5. Reservation of the British and French cabinets of the right to make additional demands later in the war.

Buol asked the Allied powers if they would agree to negotiate if Russia accepted. Both France and Britain agreed, the latter with reluctance. Buol told Alvensleben that if Russia accepted the first Four Points and the Allies would not negotiate, Austria would part company with them and in future would align with Russia. (Point 5 was only conditional.)

Gorchakov believed that Buol's more reasonable attitude stemmed from Emperor Franz Joseph, with whom Buol had had a long talk. While the ambassador did not rely greatly on Buol's new position, he believed that Franz Joseph was more reasonable than his minister and wished for better relations with Russia.

France seemed more reasonable than it had previously, since it had already gained most of what it sought; the British, however, were reluctant to negotiate and seemed to hope that they might break off the talks on some pretext.[21]

Further clarification of the Four Points came when the *Moniteur* stated that the Third Point meant the end of Russian predominance in the Black Sea.[22] This interpretation, it soon appeared, indicated that the Allies were determined to destroy Sevastopol and the Russian Black Sea fleet.

Gorchakov, like his cabinet, seemed confident that Russia's position was very strong, with the evacuation of the Principalities almost complete. In a secret despatch of July 26/August 7 he wrote that the Russian position had been steadily improving since his long talk with Buol, who had been using the Four Points as a rampart against further demands of the Allies. Buol had insisted on explaining to the French and British the consequences of a Russian acceptance, which he held would of necessity lead to an armistice and peace negotiations. If the courts of the maritime powers refused to cooperate, he said that all Europe would be against them. Buol now seemed to be asking for a discussion with Gorchakov and seeking his support.[23]

21. Gorchakov to Nesselrode, July 22/Aug. 3, 1854, AVP, f. Kants., D. no. 161.
22. Miliutin MS, p. 134a.
23. Gorchakov to Nesselrode, July 26/Aug. 7, 1854 (Secret), AVP, f. Kants., D. no. 161.

The Russian cabinet now revealed its decision, first by a telegram to Ambassador Gorchakov that the tsar had approved the army's withdrawal from the Principalities, which he regarded as a strategic necessity and in no way a concession to Austria. Hence the necessity for the massing of large Austrian forces was removed. If Austria still continued its hostile attitude, Russia would regard it as a sign that Vienna intended to make war on Russia and would act accordingly.[24] On July 28th (O.S.) a coded telegraphic despatch informed the envoy that the emperor had approved and adopted Gorchakov's plan for "watchful waiting" (to be explained later), which he should follow at all points. His Majesty advised him to be on guard against any surprise and not to have any faith in the sincerity of the Austrian cabinet.[25]

When Gorchakov, as instructed, announced to Buol that Nicholas I had approved General Gorchakov's withdrawal from the Principalities, he reported to his cabinet that the result was a sensation—"favorable to the highest degree." Buol at once went to give an account of the matter to Franz Joseph, while Gorchakov informed Nesselrode that by his decisions the Emperor Nicholas had vastly increased "the force of our political and military attitude." [26] Two days later the envoy telegraphed in secret to Nesselrode that Franz Joseph had behaved "very well; Hess perfect." Buol, however, seemed much less happy. Gorchakov informed his cabinet that the Austrians seemed to consider it a political necessity for them to enter Wallachia. "In spite of the etiquette, in my opinion they will disregard us, if we refuse," he said. "That would play the game of the West." Why, then, he continued, should they make a point of a mere matter of form, when the chief question had been largely settled? If the Russian court was unwilling to make an actual agreement, it might be better not to give a definite answer.[27]

For a time Gorchakov hoped that Austria would return to its old policy of cooperation with Russia, especially since the Emperor Nicholas had offered Franz Joseph the opportunity to do so by his evacuation of Moldavia and Wallachia. Gorchakov both directly, and indirectly through Baron Hess, urged Buol to seize this opportunity. Buol re-

24. Ibid., July 24/Aug. 5, 1854, tg. AVP, f. Kants., D. no. 164.
25. Ibid., July 28/Aug. 9, 1854, tg.
26. Ibid., July 26/Aug. 7, 1854, tg., f. Kants., D. no. 161.
27. Ibid., July 8/Aug. 9, 1854, tg.

turned from an interview with the emperor with warm, flattering words for Gorchakov and an expression of Franz Joseph's hope that soon he would be able to restore his former cherished intimacy with the tsar. Shortly, however, these sentiments proved to be nothing but empty phrases. As for Bourqueney, when he heard of the Russian withdrawal, he exclaimed: "It is the shipwreck of our best hopes!" He soon recovered, however, and with Westmorland quickly set to work to draw Buol, by means of the Four Points, into the system of protocols and notes and away from Russia.[28] Thus Bourqueney hoped to lure Buol into pursuing his dream of gaining control of the Principalities without war, which he still feared.

Gorchakov wrote happily that Nicholas I's policy of watchful waiting was fine, since it meant peace with Austria without permitting it to reduce its forces; Prussia and Germany would be on Russia's side. There would be no more tiresome diplomatic subtleties, and Russia could benefit as the situation developed. Austria and the Allies could settle the Eastern Question as best they could, while Russia could probably stick to the Protocol of April 9. Russia should, however, keep strong forces on the Pruth and in the south. While the trial was not yet over, Gorchakov thought that the worst was past and Russia would win out in the long run.[29]

This conclusion proved to be overly optimistic, for the French and the British had already drawn up the Four Points as their basis for peace, which they adopted and sent on to Vienna for its approval. As these provisions had been worked out on the basis of the Protocol of April 9, the three powers held that the relations of the Porte with the Russian court could not be solidly established unless:

1. The Russian protectorate over Wallachia, Moldavia, and Serbia were replaced by a collective guarantee of the five powers, by agreement with the Porte.

2. The navigation of the Danube to its mouth were freed from all hindrance and were not put under the rules established by the Congress of Vienna.

3. The Treaty of July 13, 1841, were revised in concert by all the parties, in the interest of the European equilibrium.

4. Russia ceased claiming the right of protection over the Christians

28. Gorchakov to Nesselrode, July 30/Aug. 11, 1854, ibid.
29. Ibid.

of Turkey, and unless France, Austria, Great Britain, Prussia, and Russia jointly obtained from the Ottoman government consecration and observance of the religious privileges of the Christians, with no infringement of the dignity and independence of the sultan.

The above conditions formed the Four Points, the Allied war aims. Further, the French and British governments would reserve the right to make known their special conditions for making peace with Russia. For the present they would not consider any proposal of the Russian cabinet which did not imply complete acceptance of the above principles.[30]

The Austrian government at once exchanged its note with those of the other two powers, declaring that it accepted for itself the obligation not to negotiate except on these bases, while reserving for itself the right to advance additional demands if it should be forced to take part in the war.[31]

In his despatch of August 14/26 to Gorchakov, Nesselrode stated that in replying to Austria's request not to cross the Danube and to recall its troops from the Principalities, Russia, to satisfy the wishes of Austria and of Germany, had given up its only military position that could equalize its situation. Now the forces of France, England, and Turkey could throw themselves en masse on Russia's lands in Asia and in Europe, without Russia's being able to strike back. Russia had complied with this request and had renounced all reciprocity on the part of its opponents. It had, however, asked whether Austria, after the evacuation was complete and Russia's obligation to the other powers had been completed, would cease to make common cause with them, with their proclaimed goal of moral and political abasement of Russia. Austria, however, had referred this query to the other powers and asked them to decide questions that Russia expected it alone to answer. Thus it became evident that Russia's sacrifices had won it no consideration from its opponents, which intended to prolong the war in order to humiliate and enfeeble Russia and were not ready to talk peace. When it published its reply to the Austrian government, France showed that what it wanted was to destroy all of Russia's earlier treaties and to ruin its naval establishment, which, from lack of a counterweight, allegedly was a perpetual menace to the Ottoman

30. Draft of the French and British Notes, AVP, f. Kants., D. no. 162.
31. Ibid.

empire. France also sought to limit Russian power in the Black Sea.[32]

The Four Points, which Austria recommended to the Russian court, to be adopted without reservation, were by no means final, for the maritime powers would still retain the right to advance, at a suitable moment, changes in their demands according to the outcome of the war. And yet Austria had fully adopted these bases and pledged itself not to treat on any other terms.

It was superfluous for Russia to examine these conditions, which were not yet settled and which could only be enforced on Russia if it had been defeated in a long struggle. If Russia accepted them, they would not ensure a durable and solid peace but only one subject to endless complications. Since Austria, for which Russia had made a sacrifice, had bound itself to Russia's enemies, the Russian cabinet declared itself unable to make more concessions compatible with its honor, and, since its sincerely peaceful intentions had not at all been accepted, Russia, like its adversaries, could only rely on the fortunes of war for the further fixing of the bases of peace. Russia now would wait on its own territory, on the defensive, until just overtures should meet its wishes for peace, having decided resolutely to defend its lands against attack.[33]

Buol's role in these confused exchanges of notes angered the other powers, especially Russia, which, with some justice, felt that it had met the minister's demands, only to find Austria joining with its enemies. This was true, but there was no trap set for Russia, for Buol was anxious to avoid war with Austria's powerful neighbor. Buol's basic policy had been to get Russia out of the Principalities, by negotiations if possible, but by war in company with France and Britain if there was no other way. He did not want a long, general war, for Austria could not endure that without great suffering. So he was delighted when Russia retired across the Pruth. He still felt the need for support from the Allies, lest Russia should turn on Austria, and with Allied support he could occupy the Principalities. But he did not want war with Russia, and his alignment with the West was a nonfighting commitment rather than one for war, as his actions after the exchange of notes proved, for they were away from war rather than toward it.[34] This pacification naturally angered the French and

32. Nesselrode to Gorchakov, Aug. 14/26, 1854, HHSA, X, 38.
33. Ibid.
34. G. B. Henderson, *Crimean War Diplomacy and Other Historical Essays* (Glasgow, 1947), pp. 98–99; Schroeder, pp. 191–97.

above all the British; but Buol had gained what he wanted: Russia was out of the Principalities, and Austria held them.

Nicholas I was furious about the Four Points, not so much because of their content, but because to him they represented one more example of Austria's betrayal of Russia. Gorchakov felt the same, saying that Buol was as corrupt as Redcliffe, but without the latter's genius.[35]

Although his wrath remained strong, the emperor was in no position to act, especially since the Baltic Sea had suddenly become the scene of a threat to St. Petersburg and the major Russian fortresses of Kronstadt, within sight of the capital, and Sveaborg, the defense south of Helsingfors (Helsinki). All official Russia knew the enemy was in the Gulf of Finland, for their sails were visible from the tsar's palace at Peterhof. Now Moldavia and Wallachia and the Black Sea seemed relatively remote and unimportant.

Neither England nor France had any territorial objectives in the Baltic region and during 1853 neither showed any interest in military activity there. Vice Admiral Sir Charles Napier, who had had a long and successful career, wrote to Lord Aberdeen in July of danger from the Russian Baltic fleet and the need to prepare the defense of the North Sea, but without result. Finally, after steps had been taken to form a fleet for a Baltic campaign, in February 1854 Napier was given command of it. It included some excellent ships-of-the-line, a number of coast-guard ships of shallow draught, and a few steamers. As an *ad hoc* squadron, it was poorly manned, with very few trained men, except coastguardsmen, and few good officers and midshipmen. The training of seamen was pushed so the fleet could sail as soon as the Baltic ice opened, but Napier constantly complained of the lack of midshipmen.[36]

In London hopes were high that under Napier the fleet would not only be able to prevent the large and well-trained Russian fleet from sailing to British waters and destroying commerce, but that it would even capture Kronstadt, the naval base west of St. Petersburg, and bombard the capital itself. The admiralty did not encourage this view, but it was widely held. On March 7 there was a solemn farewell banquet to Napier at the Reform Club. In some of the speeches hope was expressed that the admiral would achieve miracles. One orator,

35. Gorchakov to Nesselrode, Aug. 2/14, 1854, AVP, f. Kants., D. no. 162.
36. Sir Charles Napier, *The History of the Baltic Campaign* . . . , ed. Butler Earp (London, 1857), pp. 1, 4, 5–14.

apparently after drinking a number of toasts, even stated that he would take St. Petersburg in three weeks! Napier himself had too much sense to believe such boasts.[37]

Napier's fleet soon encountered grave difficulties in getting through the straits between Norway and Denmark, where bars, reefs, fogs, and storms added to the hazards of a lack of skilled pilots and reliable maps. It is a tribute to the crew's seamanship that it passed these dangerous waters unscathed and reached Copenhagen. Here the men found a mixed welcome, for while the Danish merchants valued their profitable trade with England, the aristocrats sympathized with Russia, and many of the working people had bitter memories of British bombardments during the Napoleonic wars. The Danes permitted the fleet to moor in their waters, but the most that they would promise was a cool neutrality in the war.[38]

As more and more of his ships joined him, Napier sailed slowly up the Baltic and in April anchored near Stockholm. Like the Danes, the Swedes had declared neutrality in the approaching war. There was, however, considerable anti-Russian feeling in Sweden, led by the Crown Prince Oscar, with the press and liberal opinion openly in favor of Britain and hostile to Russia, the hereditary enemy. Moreover, the Russian government had suddenly closed the Finnish border with Norway in the Arctic because the reindeer of the Lapps of Norway had overgrazed the pastures in Finland. Some Swedes—probably incorrectly—viewed this action as a step toward setting up a Russian naval base in the north. King Oscar I, however, a friend of Nicholas's was strongly opposed to war and had little interest in regaining Finland. As Napier's fleet approached Stockholm the crown prince, in tune with the active war spirit of the people, made overtures to Britain and France for an alliance.[39] Napier tried earnestly to induce the king to join in the war against Russia with his fine fleet, including the gunboats so useful in the numerous *skerries* (rocks, reefs, and islands) in those waters. Colonel Blanchard of France, a military envoy, also tried to win over the king of Sweden, but his efforts were in vain, although he suggested that Sweden might obtain both the Åland

37. Ibid., p. 15.
38. Ibid., pp. 25–26.
39. Ibid., pp. 69–70; Albin Cullberg, *La politique du roi Oscar I pendant la guerre de Crimée* (Stockholm, 1912), I, 74–77; C. M. Runeberg, *Finland under Orientaliska kriget* (Helsingfors, 1962), pp. 81–82.

ATLANTIC OCEAN

Tromso

NORWAY

Kola

Tornea

RUSSIA

GRAND
DUCHY
OF FINLAND

SWEDEN

Abo

Vyborg

Kronstadt

Bomarsund

Sveaborg

Helsingfors

Stockholm

Aland
Islands

Reval

St. Petersburg

ESTLAND

LIVONIA

Riga

KURLAND

Copenhagen

BALTIC SEA

The War in the Baltic

Islands and Finnish territory. The king was cordial to Napier, whom he received in his home; but he insisted on maintaining neutrality, especially as the Swedish diplomats in Europe advised it.[40]

Baron Langenau, Austrian envoy at Stockholm, helped to fortify this decision, for he advised the crown prince to hold to neutrality and warned the king against giving in to a fleeting passion for war or grasping for the dangerous prize of Finland. Vienna sent word that, while Austria would welcome Sweden as an ally, the Swedes must make their own decision.[41]

France was eager to have Sweden as an ally. In May 1854 Baron Hübner at Paris reported that Drouyn de Lhuys had stated that the Allied navies would have done their work badly if by the end of the campaign Kronstadt and Sevastopol had not fallen.[42] In July and August Drouyn pressed Sweden strongly, although the Allies had achieved little in the Baltic. Drouyn also tried to get Austria to exert influence on King Oscar, hinting that his reward might be the Åland Islands as well as Finland. Late in July Drouyn received an apparent offer of a Swedish alliance and urged the British to accept it. The conditions set were a guarantee of possession of Finland and Austria's entry into the war. General Baraguey d'Hilliers, commander of the French troops in the Baltic, delivered the French offer of alliance to the king on July 29. Sweden now asked Langenau about Austria's decision. Buol replied honestly that Austria was not going to go to war, and Sweden refused to oppose Russia.[43]

One probable reason for the Swedes' refusal was their realization that the British fleet was not suitable for the dangerous waters of the Baltic and Finland. While its great ships were superb, they could not maneuver well in crowded waters and could not enter the shoal waters off Kronstadt and Sveaborg. Moreover, there were few steamers and almost none of the gunboats needed among the tiny islands. Bomb-ketches to lob eleven-inch bombs on the main fortifications also were lacking.[44] Swedish naval men could see that the British fleet could not command those waters or lead an attack on Russia's strong position. They knew that in September the British and French fleets would

40. Napier, pp. 123–28; Guichen, Eugène, Vicomte de, *La guerre de Crimée* (Paris, 1936), pp. 228–29; Runeberg, pp. 50–53.
41. Schroeder, p. 198.
42. Hübner to Buol, May 21, 1854, HHSA, IX, 46.
43. Schroeder, pp. 198–99.
44. Napier, pp. 4–10 *passim,* 40.

sail to the South and then when the Baltic froze in midwinter the Russian forces could cross the ice to burn villages near Stockholm, as in the days of Peter the Great. The war therefore did not offer an attractive prospect.

By the time Napier's fleet was ready for action in May the Russians had put their fortifications in good condition and were able to hold off the attackers, often with the help of newly formed Finnish battalions. The British were able, however, to capture many fishing vessels, although in some cases they were ambushed and men and ship's boats were lost. At Hangö and Åbo the attackers were driven off by the fire of the forts or by gunboats. Napier did not dare attack the naval base of Sveaborg and his fleet never came within range of Kronstadt, since the water was too shallow for the big ships, and the defenses, including mines, were too dangerous for the others.[45] But while the Allied ships could do nothing against the main defenses, they had a very important effect on the war. The St. Petersburg-Kronstadt area, the seat of the Russian government, was vital for the nation's functioning. Hence the emperor and his advisers massed great numbers of troops there which, if sent to the Crimea, might have ensured a Russian victory. If only a quarter of the 200,000 regular troops [46] with their vast supplies of ammunition and cannon had gone to Sevastopol, the Russians probably could have withstood the Allied attack there. Although the British and French fleets left the Baltic in August and September 1854, the authorities, because of the lack of railways, sent few of the Russian troops to the south, for they fully expected that in 1855 there would be another, stronger attack on their Baltic defenses.

The only concrete achievement of the Allied fleets in the Baltic was the capture of the old fortification of Bomarsund in the Åland Islands with a garrison of about two thousand men. Napier's forces were not responsible for the victory, for on June 21 the defenders beat off the British vessels, causing some damage. The admiral now decided that since he could not get close enough to the forts to destroy them, he would wait for the French fleet carrying a division of troops and siege artillery. Late in July the troops and the heavy guns were landed on the other side of the island, where batteries were built. The French siege guns and some heavy British cannon then reduced

45. M. Borodkin, *Voina 1854–1855 gg. na Finskom poberezh'e* (St. Petersburg, 1904), pp. 87–118.
46. Miliutin MS, pp. 182–83.

the works to ruins. On August 13 the defenders, unable to return the hostile fire, surrendered to the French. Soon the French sailed away with their prisoners, and not long after Napier's fleet left.[47]

The fall of Bomarsund did not greatly excite the Swedes, for the sailing of the Allied fleets showed the limitations of their power. The Swedes were largely anti-Russian and would gladly have taken Finland if it were possible without a costly war. The Allies continued to urge King Oscar to join them as the obvious victors in Europe's war against Russia, offering Bomarsund and promises of aid. But the king insisted on specific conditions for Sweden's entry: a formal agreement pledging the great powers to reduce Russia's power to less dangerous levels, with the recovery of Finland from Russia as a guarantee; the employment of sufficient forces to achieve this goal; Austria's incorporation into the coalition; peace terms dictated by the whole coalition; and subsidies for Sweden to cover its expenses.

Through the treaty, which should go into effect only when Austria had acceded to it, Sweden would employ its impressive navy, with about two hundred gunboats, and about seventy thousand troops.[48] These terms were so unlikely that Oscar's proposal amounted to a rejection.

The Allies, however, still hoped for Swedish participation in the campaign in 1855. Baraguey d'Hilliers, the spokesman, promised to station a French force in Sweden during the winter, which in the summer would be joined by large French contingents. The king, however, replied that these forces could take Finland only if Russia had been badly beaten elsewhere. Lord Clarendon also urged Sweden to join the Allies, although he would not promise Finland. The Swedes responded by asking if the Allies would destroy Kronstadt and the Russian fleet, take St. Petersburg and dictate peace there, and guarantee Sweden against Russian attacks in the future. Sweden, greatly exposed to Russian attack, realized that the Allies did not intend to commit their real strength in this northern region and dared not run the risk of entering the war unless Austria would join them and promise to fight until Russia was helpless. Since Austria had no such intention, Oscar clung to his neutrality.[49]

While the attention of Europe was thus concentrated on the events

47. Borodkin, pp. 118–77; Napier, pp. 362–80.
48. Guichen, pp. 229–30; Tarle, I, 496–501; Runeberg, pp. 107–09.
49. Cullberg, pp. 82–85.

in the Baltic and the Gulf of Finland, there was a breathing spell in the Black Sea area. The Russian pledge to evacuate Moldavia and Wallachia had eased the strain on Austro-Russian relations, and the Russians had permitted Austria to occupy the Principalities after their regiments had crossed the Pruth. Suddenly, however, the Austrians signed an agreement with the French and the British to adopt the Four Points as the obligatory bases for peace and not to agree to any other terms. Most of the Points were acceptable to Nicholas I, but the Third, which called for revising the Treaty of 1841 in order to end Russian dominance on the Black Sea, was not. The Allies held that this revision required the destruction of Sevastopol, the mighty naval base, and the reduction of the Black Sea fleet to a much lower level. Count Buol claimed that these provisions were much more moderate than most of the intentions of the maritime powers and that he supported them, not as obligatory requirements, but as subjects for discussion in the coming peace conference. Probably Buol was sincere in wanting to reach a reasonable settlement, but the tsar did not believe this. To him Buol's agreements with his enemies were dishonorable efforts to form a powerful coalition to impose their peace terms, to Russia's disadvantage and to Austria's benefit. He regarded Austria's call for unconditional acceptance [50] as an ultimatum and as proof that Austria was in league with Russia's enemies.

The emperor's ire against Austria continued to grow and finally, about the middle of August, he wrote out a note setting forth Russia's grievances against its neighbor. Austria had raised endless objections to Russia's just demands upon Turkey and had insisted on upholding Turkey's integrity as a basic point, which meant that the Christians of Turkey would be denied the opportunity to obtain their freedom. Gaining courage, Austria had made common cause with Britain and France, even though they were at war with Russia, and Vienna still claimed to be at peace. It had increased its armaments greatly and massed its forces to threaten Russia's flank and rear. It had tried to get Prussia to demand Russia's evacuation of the Principalities and then had gained permission from Turkey to occupy them. At the moment of Russia's withdrawal from the two provinces Austria, through an exchange of notes with France and Britain, had agreed on the terms for future peace talks, while still nominally at peace

50. Schroeder, p. 200.

with Russia. Finally, it put no obstacles in the way of Turkish occupation of the Principalities and of the Turks' use of them as a base from which to attack Russia.[51]

The tsar then drew up his conditions for settling Russia's grievances against Austria: demobilization of the armies massed on the Russian borders; evacuation of Moldavia and Wallachia, or at least expulsion of the Turks therefrom; reestablishment of the legal government in the Principalities under the hospodars; and recognition of all of Russia's rights under its earlier treaties with Turkey. Nicholas demanded annulment of Austria's notes exchanged with England and France and of its treaty with Turkey. He asked for an affirmative answer in half a month.[52]

This note was never sent, for Nesselrode and Orlov convinced the emperor that Russia could not afford a war with Austria at that moment. In addition, Prince A. M. Gorchakov persuaded him that Russia's defensive position was strong and that he could punish Austria by giving it no good grounds for going to war with Russia and by denying it all assurances of moderation that would permit it to disarm. Gorchakov had outlined this plan in a letter to Nesselrode, calling it Plan B, saying that Russia's defensive position was "invulnerable" and that it would prevent the maritime powers from dragging Austria into the war, for Prussia and the other German states would vehemently oppose its entry into the conflict. Austria's position would be desperate, for its finances were very weak; it could not long maintain a mobilized army and would soon be bankrupt.[53] The nature of its financial crisis had been made clear by the fact that in July (N.S.) Emperor Franz Joseph had consented to a forced loan of 350 million florins in five annual payments from the estates of the nobility, over the unanimous opposition of the Council of the Empire and its president, Baron Kübeck von Kübau, after His Majesty had previously promised to reject the loan. Now, apparently under the pressure of Buol, Bach, and Baumgartner, Franz Joseph approved it, disregarding the objections of the council.[54] Hence Gorchakov had grounds for

51. Draft of note by Nicholas I, n.d. [ca. Aug., 1854], Zaionchkovskii, Pril., II, 368.
52. Ibid.
53. Gorchakov, Supplement to letter to Nesselrode, July 22/Aug. 3, 1854, Letter B, Zaionchkovskii, Pril., II, 365–67.
54. Meyendorff to Nesselrode, June 21/July 3, 1854, AVP, f. Kants., D. no. 161.

expecting Austria's finances to collapse, especially as a budget deficit of 25 percent had been announced in May.[55]

To make matters worse for Austria, in mid-July the Prussian envoy at Vienna reminded Franz Joseph that two months before he had declared that if Russia evacuated Moldavia and Wallachia it should be rewarded with an armistice and with steps to remove the Anglo-French fleets from Turkish waters, whereas in July he refused to make these concessions. Buol, however, spoke harshly to Colonel Edwin Manteuffel of Prussia, saying that Prussia could not prevent Austria from entering the Principalities and from entering the war if it wished.[56]

Prince Gorchakov, whom Nesselrode regarded "as a General-in-Chief invested with unlimited power, whom one should let alone, if one wishes him to win victories," [57] read to Buol the despatch rejecting the Austrian proposal. It was contrary to the count's expectations. Buol had apparently promised the Emperor Franz Joseph that relations with Russia would become smoother, and now the word from St. Petersburg showed that the two cabinets were still locked in a fierce contest. This realization so shocked him that he hardly dared report to the emperor, and he asked Gorchakov to devise some expedient that would solve his problem. But the Russian said that the orders of his master were so precise that they needed no commentary, and hence he could not help him.[58]

When Gorchakov called on Buol the next day Bourqueney was in his office; he heard heated and angry tones and saw the French envoy leave in anger. He then had a long discussion with Buol, who insisted that the Four Points had not been presented as an ultimatum but as points for discussion that would lead to peace talks. Buol declared that "there can be no question of war" between Austria and Russia unless the latter should attack. He had just communicated this position precisely to the French and British; the Four Points were the maximum Austrian demands, he had told them, and it would never ask more. The next day, however, Buol refused to put into writing the promises he had made. He tried hard to prove that Gorchakov's position was

55. Ibid., May 9/21, 1854.
56. Borries, pp. 206–07.
57. Letter, Nesselrode to Gorchaov, Aug. 14/26, 1854, TsGAOR, f. 828, D. no. 602.
58. Gorchakov to Nesselrode, Aug. 24/Sept. 5, 1854, AVP, f. Kants., D. no. 162.

much stronger than that of the Russian cabinet, especially at Berlin.

Buol asserted vehemently that Austria and Russia would not go to war and that Austria, having fulfilled its task in the Principalities, did not have to act further. Austria's action in the Principalities would cost it money, but also would be costly to Russia. Austria did not support the extreme demands of the British and the French, "especially the absurd claim to regulate the number of war vessels that Russia could have on the Black Sea." Several of the Four Points had been accepted, and most of the Fourth. Gorchakov said that the Four Points would give Austria little advantage, since they would involve danger and an expense.[59] Both diplomats agreed that they had not reached any understanding and that the outcome of the war would be decisive. Gorchakov, expecting that Buol would make a great effort to win Prussia and the middle German states to his point of view, repeatedly stressed the need to exert influence over Prussia. On August 8/20 the prince advised Russia to hold to the bases of the Protocol, without examining the content of the Four Points, as a means of getting Prussia to return to its former pro-Russian position. Anything else, he feared, would encourage the adversaries to take new steps to draw Prussia to them. "Bismarck must point out in the Diet the differences between the positions of the two courts," he said. The foe would make fresh efforts to win Prussia to its side.[60] A few days later he wrote that Franz Joseph was eager to avoid a rupture with Russia and probably had urged Buol to help reactivate the negotiations. Gorchakov asked earnestly for a refusal of all such overtures, as any nuance in the present Russian attitude, no matter how feeble, would reduce the powerful impression of the Russian reply.[61] On August 25 he emphasized Buol's trickery and his hopes that events at Berlin might shake belief in Russia's resolution. Gorchakov opposed anything that might lead to a discussion of the Four Points until Buol might show by his actions that he had a real desire for an accord with Russia.[62]

Finally, Meyendorff paid a farewell visit to Franz Joseph before returning home. The monarch said he was much pleased with the evacuation of the Principalities and would never attack Russia. He had already ordered General Hess to spread out his cantonments for

59. Ibid.
60. Ibid., Aug. 8/20, 1854.
61. Ibid., Aug. 21/Sept. 2, 1854.
62. Ibid., Aug. 25/Sept. 6, 1854.

sanitary reasons. Meyendorff criticized the emperor for accepting the Four Points along with Russia's enemies. Franz Joseph protested, saying that he in no way wanted what Russia's foes wanted, and certainly not a war with Russia.[63]

As for the Allies, at first they had planned to fight only a naval war, but they soon found that they could do little at sea. When the French bombarded Odessa in April, they met stiff resistance from a four-gun battery on the mole. Although they burned a number of Russian ships in the harbor, they achieved no positive result. Some weeks later when some British ships made soundings near Odessa, the *Tiger,* a fine steam frigate, ran aground and could not be floated. Russian ground forces set it afire and captured its crew.[64]

The French slowly formed an army of three divisions at Gallipoli, although they had to send a brigade to the Piraeus to keep the Greeks from fighting the Turks. By May 29 there were about 30,000 French at Gallipoli, and about 25,000 British there and at Scutari.[65]

The Russian crossing of the Danube and the slow march to Silistria, however, upset this leisurely mobilization. The Turks felt sure that the fortress would fall and that Gorchakov's army could then push on to Constantinople. Marshal Armand Jacques de Saint-Arnaud and Fitzroy James Somerset, Lord Raglan now decided to try to hold Constantinople by landing two divisions at Varna, although they were far from ready. In June they landed there, to menace the flank of the Russians, who were slowly besieging Silistria. But, as already related, on June 23 the Russians, fearing an attack of the Austrians on their flank and rear, suddenly left Silistria and retired across the Danube. Eventually, by August, all the Russians were back across the Pruth on Russian territory, where they were safe from the Austrians. Nicholas I had hoped that the retirement from the Principalities would lead to an armistice, the departure of the Allied fleets, and peace talks.[66]

But the Allied governments and the British public were eager to settle accounts with the Russian troublemaker, and their armies wanted to fight. They did not, however, want to campaign along the Danube, and the French refused to fight in Asia Minor. But in December

---

63. Meyendorff to Nesselrode, Aug. 24/Sept. 5, 1854, AVP, f. Kants., D. no. 162.
64. Tarle, I, 514.
65. La Gorce, I, 220–24.
66. Ibid., pp. 225–30.

1853 George Levenson Gower, Lord Granville, who was not a militant, suggested an attack on the Crimea to take Sevastopol. In January 1854 Sir James Graham, first lord of the admiralty, circulated a memorandum from Sir John Burgoyne saying that Sevastopol could not be taken except by a land army, which meant the Turks could not take it. At this point Napoleon III assigned Barraguey d'Hilliers to investigate the possibility of a landing in the Crimea, and in March he named the Crimea a likely objective. Palmerston also thought it might be a good target. Others were rather pessimistic. By March 1854 Graham was eager to attack the naval base at Sevastopol, convinced that it was the best goal. By that time Graham's feeling was widely shared in England. In a long memorandum to the cabinet Palmerston advocated a landing in the Crimea, calling it the real objective, in order to destroy Sevastopol and the fleet. He lightheartedly declared that it could be taken before winter. Public opinion, led by *The Times,* favored the operation and Prince Albert greatly desired to destroy Sevastopol. On June 29 Lord Raglan was instructed not to bog down in Wallachia, since the Crimea was the objective.[67] Saint-Arnaud received similar instructions in mid-July and eagerly accepted the new plan.

The medical condition of the troops seemed good in mid-June. But cholera had broken out in southern France and was raging when the 5th Division sailed for Turkey, with the infection spreading in its ranks. The disease was also present at the Piraeus, Gallipoli, and Constantinople, although there were few deaths. But in July Saint-Arnaud made a fatal decision to send an expedition to hurry the Russians out of the Principalities. Late in July the 1st Division, with a number of *bashi-bazuks* (irregulars), set out in gay spirits, eager for adventure. They went through the Dobrudja—a dismal country, lacking in food, water, and firewood—fighting in two slight skirmishes with Cossacks on July 29 but sustaining few casualties. By the next morning, however, many were already dead or dying of cholera. The troops maintained their discipline, but the irregulars fled. The soldiers reached the sea and were taken by ship back to Varna, many of them near death. Over five thousand of the French troops died of cholera within a month, and those who survived were severely weakened.[68]

67. La Gorce, I, 231–35; Conacher, pp. 251–56, 451–52.
68. La Gorce, pp. 237–43; Tarle, I, 527–29.

The illness caused much gloom in the French camp. Worse was to follow.

On August 10 there was a great fire in Varna, which consumed much of the town. In the high wind vast stores of provisions and some powder magazines were lost, although a shift of the wind helped to save much of them. Saint-Arnaud was terribly dismayed by the disease and then by the fire, and longed for a great victory to improve the situation. Many of his advisers and some of the British were now against any undertaking, realizing the lack of preparations and the absence of essential information about the coast and the terrain where they planned to invade. The navies had been able to learn about the depths along the coast, but little was known about the conditions on land, and even maps were lacking.[69]

This was not the only choice available, for on August 11 Lieutenant Colonel A. Kalik of the Austrian army brought a message from Baron Hess, commander-in-chief of the Austrian Third and Fourth armies, that his armies would be ready in the first ten days of September to make a coordinated attack on the Russian army in Moldavia, if it did not retire across the Pruth. Hess hoped that the French, the British, and the Turkish forces would attack the Russian left while the Austrians attacked on the right.[70]

The reply to this communication, given on August 12 by Marshal Saint-Arnaud and Lord Raglan, the Allied commanders, was that, in the hope of avoiding war, the Austrian government had delayed for two months the entry of its armies into Wallachia, when it could have given powerful assistance to the French, English, and Turkish armies. At the end of June the latter had been in a position to strike a great blow at the Russian army, when the Russians were withdrawing from Silistria. If at that moment the Austrian forces had struck from Bukovina at the rear of the Russians, their army would have been ruined.

(Actually, at this time neither the Anglo-French nor the Austrians were in any condition to strike at Gorchakov's Russian army in the Principalities.) Since this opportunity had been lost, the French and British had to decide on another effective way to strike at the Russians

69. Tarle, I, 530–32.
70. Lt. Col. Kalik to St. Arnaud, 11–12 Aug., 1854 (from the Archive de la Ministère de la Guerre, Paris), Zaionchkovskii, *Pril.,* II, 431–32.

and chose as their objective the Crimea. Their preparations were now well underway and late in August they expected to land more than sixty thousand men there. It was then too late to change their plans.

The Allied commanders expressed confidence that the Austrians and the Turks would be able to strike a powerful blow at the Russians, aided by the Anglo-French drive into the Russian rear.[71]

And so the fateful decision was taken. On September 7 the Allied forces, numbering about 60,000 men, embarked for the Crimea.[72] The conflict had now become the Crimean War.

71. Confidential note to Cols. Kalik and Lowenthal in reply to their message sent by General Baron Hess (from the Archive de la Ministère de la Guerre, Paris) Zaionchkovskii, *Pril.*, II, 432–33.

72. Tarle, I, 542; La Gorce, I, 246–47.

Part two. The decisive
Developments, 1854–56

CHAPTER 12. THE BEGINNING OF THE CRIMEAN CAMPAIGN

The landing in the Crimea in order to attack Sevastopol, which took place on September 1/13, 1854, was not a new idea, for David Urquhart, Lord Ponsonby, and Lord Palmerston, the leaders of the anti-Russian movement, had long called for the destruction of the Russian Black Sea Fleet and its powerful base. The annihilation of a Turkish squadron at Sinop in November 1853 had made it plain that the Russians could let loose terrible destruction upon the Turks from their central position in the southern Crimea, and only the capture of Sevastopol by the Allies could prevent similar blows. When the Allied squadrons entered the Black Sea and demanded that the Russian fleet shut itself in its harbor or suffer destruction, the message was clear. Moreover, Palmerston continued to call for the capture of the Crimea and an end to the Russian fleet.

Napoleon III also demanded the capture of Sevastopol, although less openly. On April 14, 1854, a French vessel captured a Russian customs official at Eupatoria and took him to Admiral F. A. Hamelin, who questioned him eagerly about the Crimea. The admiral asked him about the number of troops in the Crimea, the number of soldiers, sailors, and cannon at Sevastopol, and the resources of the Crimea in horses and grain. He asked if the Russians knew that the Allies wanted to besiege Sevastopol by land and sea and inquired about the state of the roads between Sevastopol and other cities. The prisoner learned that the French had sounded and surveyed the coast near Eupatoria, so that he supposed that they intended to land there. Baron Meyendorff, the Russian ambassador at Vienna, said that this evidence agreed with the remark of Bourqueney, the French ambassador to Austria, about an occupation of the Crimea and about fortifications that the French would build on the isthmus of Perekop between it and the mainland, in order to keep Russian reinforcements from entering the peninsula.[1]

1. Meyendorff to Nesselrode, June 16–28, 1854, AVP, f. Kants., D. no. 161.

Admiral Prince Menshikov and his superiors foresaw an Allied landing in the Crimea, for in January 1854, after sighting Allied ships in coastal waters, he asked for reinforcements. In February the Ministry of War had so much evidence—talk of landing in the area in both the British and the French parliaments, a prediction in *The Times,* and other signs—that late in the month the Ministry of War urged that reinforcements be sent in haste to the Crimea. But Paskevich objected that the real danger was in Russian Poland rather than at Sevastopol, and the forces were not sent. The continued signs of Allied design on the Crimea, however, especially after Turkey was no longer in danger on the Danube, all pointed to an Allied landing. In June *The Times* specifically named Sevastopol as the objective.[2]

On June 20/July 2 Menshikov sent a memorandum to the capital indicating that an Allied landing would be made at Eupatoria for an overland attack on Sevastopol. He also listed the strength of his troops as twenty-six battalions, with only thirty-six light guns—rather less than twenty-five thousand men.[3] Since he expected that the Allies would land fifty or sixty thousand, on June 30 he sent an urgent letter to Prince M. D. Gorchakov, asking him to send to the Crimea the 11th division from the troops released by the evacuation of the Principalities.[4] Gorchakov hastened to grant the request, which infuriated Paskevich, who had expressly forbidden this and who held that Menshikov had enough troops, whereas the front against Austria would require vastly greater forces.[5] The emperor, however, warmly commended Gorchakov for his action and wrote Paskevich that the 11th division was needed to defend the Crimea—a matter of the highest importance.[6]

Menshikov was satisfied with the arrival of this division, as he seemed to feel that now he could prevent the Allies from succeeding in their venture. By the middle of August he had decided that probably they would not attempt a landing, since the current period of good weather would be too short to permit success. Actually, the danger remained, and the emperor should have sent three divisions to the Crimea, along

2. Dubrovin, pp. 74–75.

3. A. D. Krylov, "Kniaz' A. S. Menshikov, 1853–1854" *Russkaia Starina* (hereafter cited as *RS*), VII (1873), 853.

4. N. K. Schilder, *Graf Eduard Ivanovich Totleben: ego zhizn' i deiatel'nost'* (St. Petersburg, 1885–86), I, 248–49.

5. Ibid., pp. 249–52.

6. Ibid.

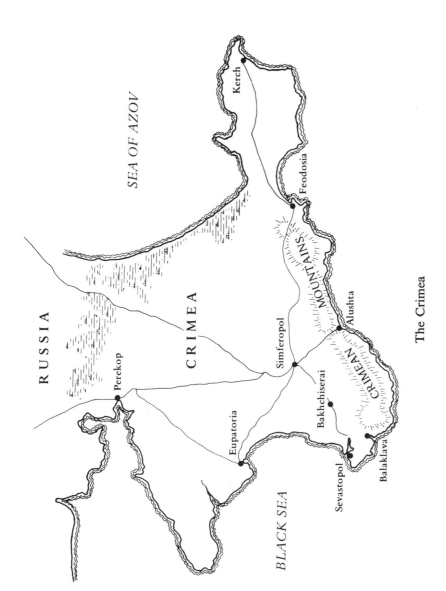

The Crimea

with a commander-in-chief with full powers. If that had been done, the Crimea probably would not have been lost.[7]

General M. D. Gorchakov, continuing to feel concern over the safety of Sevastopol, late in July called in Colonel E. I. Totleben, a fine engineer, who had taken command of the siege operations at Silistria after the death of General Schilder. Gorchakov sent Totleben to Menshikov, warning the colonel of the need to avoid antagonizing the suspicious prince. Gorchakov's letter to Menshikov stated that since there was danger that the Allies would land a big army in the peninsula, the Russians might have to defend Sevastopol from the rear by means of earthworks, and Totleben, who was experienced in field operations under fire, could be very useful. "This is the best pupil of Schilder," he said, "able, intelligent, brave as his sword. He is fully acquainted with all the stratagems of the deceased. . . ." [8] Menshikov told Totleben to return to Gorchakov's army after resting, but he stayed on, inspecting the forts. He reported to the commander that the seaward defenses were in superb condition, which pleased Menshikov, but he found that the landward fortifications hardly existed. The prince, while annoyed, let him remain although he did not assign him to work. Totleben made a detailed inspection of the situation, which disclosed that the lack of money had caused a grave shortage of entrenching tools; there were only enough tools for two hundred men. He also noted the running feud between Menshikov and the resident engineers. Totleben repeatedly urged the prince to push the work of building the fortifications and above all to buy the needed tools. The commander was irritated, but finally ordered the buying of the tools, although he did not think it was necessary, as it was too late in the year for an attack, and he felt peace would come in the spring.[9]

St. Petersburg was less optimistic than the prince, for it continued to urge him to push the fortification work. The minister of war on August 18 (O.S.), while agreeing that there would be no landing in 1854, stressed the need to hurry the building of the forts, giving Menshikov carte blanche in his dealings with the engineers and assigning money to cover the work. At about the same time—perhaps two weeks before the Allied landing—Nicholas I urged Menshikov to rush the

7. Ibid., pp. 252–54.

8. N. K. Schilder, "Priezd E. I. Totlebena v Sevastopol' v avguste 1854 g.," RS, XVIII (1877), 508–09.

9. Dubrovin, pp. 74–75.

construction of Bastions 3 and 4 and the defense line at Sevastopol, which should be completed by April of 1855—eight months later.[10] Menshikov's letters in midsummer to the minister of war repeatedly stated that the news from Varna all seemed to show that the Allies would postpone the invasion until 1855 because of the danger from the equinoctial storms in September. Menshikov cited the reports of the cholera and the fires in Varna as proof of the difficulties of the enemy and added that one sea captain had brought word that the British had moved their Highland regiments from Varna to Constantinople because they had suffered so much from the mosquitoes on the Bulgarian coast.[11] On August 26 he wrote to the minister that General Gorchakov, apparently convinced that the Allies would not abandon their plan, had sent him a special courier to bring word of the Allied landing when it should occur. Menshikov added: "I do not believe it, although I remain ready to receive the enemy."[12] Even Nicholas must have decided that the invasion would not occur for some time, for late in August he issued an order to remove the cavalry regiments from the Crimea because of lack of forage there and to send out the Black Sea battalions on the grounds that now, because of the lateness of the season, "one should not expect landings in the Crimea." One such battalion, which was actually on the way to the Caucasus coast when the Allies landed, was hastily sent back by the local commander.[13] Menshikov was also convinced that there would be no invasion in 1854, for two days before it occurred he wrote to General Adjutant Annenkov: "My suppositions have been completely borne out; the enemy could never dare to make a landing, and because of the present late season a descent is impossible." [14]

When on August 16/28 the emperor wrote ordering urgent work on the land fortifications of Sevastopol, which should be complete by April, "without sparing work," Menshikov replied that all this would take years, even in normal times. The whole matter required a technical study, as the terrain was difficult.

In the meantime, the southern side of the city was fortified with temporary walls and batteries, which would be strengthened in the

10. Schilder, *Graf Totleben,* I, 278–79.
11. Ibid., pp. 41–44.
12. Schilder, "Priezd Totlebena," p. 510n.
13. P. K. Men'kov, *Zapiski* (St. Petersburg, 1898), I, 199n.
14. Russia. Voennoe Ministerstvo. *Stoletie Voennago Ministerstva 1802–1902* (St. Petersburg, 1902), T. 3, Imperatorskaia Glavniaia Kvartira, Kn. 3, 342–43.

autumn months. The weakest part of Sevastopol was the northern side of the bay. While the walls were built as far as possible, there was little room for fortifications and the earth, largely shale, crumbled badly. The southern side was better suited for defense, since, in addition to the fortification walls, the buildings of the city could be defended by barricades manned by troops and by the inhabitants. Nicholas I, who was trying to run the whole war almost single-handed, could devote little thought to the Crimea. His marginal comment on Menshikov's report was that his recommendations were fine and he would leave it to Menshikov to carry out as best he could, without loss of time.[15]

The emperor probably had no idea of how little had been done to defend the city. Totleben's notebook of August 16 praised the seaward fortifications, which, built of stone and skillfully designed, were heavily armed with powerful cannon, howitzers, and mortars. In addition, the ships of the fleet were moored in the small bays, from which they could deliver telling fire. Totleben declared that the foreign press, which previously had been scornful, now stated that it was impossible to take Sevastopol from the sea. The landward defenses, however, left the city extremely exposed: "These fortifications consist of several batteries armed with guns of very small caliber, which could only give some opposition to Tatars." [16] By the time of the battle of the Alma the situation had improved only slightly. The northern part of the landward defenses was still very weak and little had been done to improve it. While the southern part was better prepared, only Bastions 6, 7, and 8 were in good condition. Bastion 5 consisted of only a stone barracks, with cannon behind it. The curtain walls for joining the works gave protection only against musketry fire. The Schwartz redoubt had been built, and there were three barricades leading to Bastion 4, which was far from finished, since its wall was thin and its batteries were weak. The Malakhov *kurgan* (hill) had only a stone tower containing guns. Bastion 3 was merely a battery of seven eighteen-pound guns, and Bastions 1 and 2 were only field fortifications. Thus to cover a perimeter of seven *versts* (four and one-half miles) there were only 145 cannon.[17]

15. V. D. Krenke, *Oborona Baltiiskago Priberezh'ia 1853–1856 gg.* (St. Petersburg, 1887), pp. 12–16.
16. Schilder, *Graf Totleben, Prilozheniia*, I, 43–44.
17. Ibid., I, 295–301.

Prince V. I. Vasil'chikov, a fine soldier, gave a gloomy description of the landward defenses early in September. There were almost no land fortifications, except three defensive barracks and three stone towers, which proved of little value. On the Russian flank Bastions 5 and 6 were set up with low walls, and between them a finely cut defensive stone wall with musketry loopholes. The wall, however, was so thin that it gave little protection. Likewise, the towers would soon collapse when their cannon were fired, and the barracks were vulnerable to bombs. The casemates in the fortifications were too narrow for effective gun action, and the stone facing of the embrasures soon fell in. Almost no trenches or earthworks had been built. On the Malakhov, in front of the tower, there were four twenty-pound guns, unprotected by earth works. On the northern side there was a fine fortification with bastion fronts, but dominated by the surrounding heights. Thus no effective preparations had been made, in spite of the Allied threat. Menshikov, always suspicious, had refused to permit Totleben to improve the situation, which appeared downright hopeless.[18]

While Menshikov was an intelligent man, he was a wretched administrator with no system of staff work. He was highly distrustful of his subordinates whom he regarded as enemies trying to undermine him, or as intriguers and grafters seeking to get rich at the expense of the treasury. Hence he made no regular provision for supplies and was constantly at odds with the engineers in charge of the fortification work. He tried to do everything himself and when he could not, he relied on Lieutenant Colonel Wunsch, whom he trusted. Wunsch, with no skilled assistants, ran affairs as best he could with a few aides and clerks. He acted as a one-man administration, functioning as chief of staff, general on duty, quartermaster-general, intendant, and director of the chancellery, and ran the hospitals, posts, and military police.[19] As a result, the administration was in chaos.

Menshikov repeatedly wrote to St. Petersburg for the needed staff officials, especially a general intendant for supplies and a quartermaster-general. He did not suggest candidates, as he had left the army thirty years before. Finally the Ministry of War announced the sending

18. V. I. Vasil'chikov, "Sevastopol'. Zapiski," *Russkii Arkhiv* (hereafter cited as *RA*), XXIX (1891), pt. 2, 182–83.

19. Ibid., pp. 177–78; A. A. Panaev, "Kniaz' A. S. Menshikov v razskazakh ego ad'iutanta A. A. Panaeva," *RS*, XVIII (1877), 126; Dubrovin, pp. 173–74.

of a leading commissariat official for the post of intendant general on his staff. Menshikov, however, sent word that he could not accept the man because of his advanced age (over seventy) and his poor physical condition (he was extremely fat).[20]

The assignment of Colonel A. E. Popov, chief of staff of the Guards' Reserve Corps, to Sevastopol turned out to be even more remarkable. Menshikov's aide had visited the colonel to say that the prince had asked the emperor to send him to the Crimea, for Popov had visited Menshikov at his request in 1844, and another of the latter's aides had spoken highly of him. Nicholas called Popov in, saying that he was sending him to the Crimea at Menshikov's request. Prince Radzi-will was to accompany him. When the colonel and Radziwill arrived at Sevastopol, Menshikov received him warmly and invited him to spend the night at his quarters. Early the next day, however, Menshikov called Popov in and told him that "as I don't need you, I am assigning you to Prince P. D. Gorchakov" (Gorchakov was an elderly second-rank commander). Popov refused the position and asked Menshikov for another assignment. On October 4 he received the post of chief of staff under the commander of the troops of Sevastopol, although he never was given the post that the tsar had assigned to him. Popov believed that Radziwill had turned Menshikov against him, even though the commander needed his services.[21]

Prince V. I. Vasil'chikov, who had a fine service record with the Southern Army, also experienced Menshikov's whims. After General M. D. Gorchakov had evacuated the Principalities, he sent Vasil'chikov to Menshikov, since the latter needed skilled men. The admiral received him coolly, and sent him away. In October, however, he suddenly summoned Vasil'chikov and made him chief of staff of the garrison, which involved him in arduous work, as the other staff officers had done little to improve the administration. The new chief of staff, how-ever, went out of his way to ease the tensions between the army and navy men. Later the young prince found that he owed his appointment to the heir to the throne, who had told his father of the general disorder and the absence of all system in meeting the needs of the garrison.[22]

Because of the lack of effective organization, the supply problem

20. Panaev, pp. 293–94.

21. A. E. Popov, "Moi priezd KKn. A. S. Menshikovu, Sentiabr' 1854 goda," *RS*, XIX (1877), 323–29; V. I. Den', "Zapiski," *RS*, LXV (1890), 563.

22. Men'kov, I, 322; Vasil'chikov, pp. 208–10.

was especially grave. A Colonel N. K. Batezatul, who arrived with some of the reinforcements, wrote on September 19 that "the bad thing is that he [Menshikov] had no provisions or ammunition and apparently there is no one who is exclusively occupied with this matter. Everything that we can find we haul with us from Kherson, both provisions and ammunition, and we, together with the uhlans, bring them to the admiral." [23]

With his pessimistic, distrustful nature, Menshikov could provide no leadership against the Allied forces. He held no conferences with his admirals concerning strategy or tactics and had nothing himself to suggest. As for the ground forces under him, he obviously regarded them as poorly trained and feared to lead them into battle against the French. He never showed himself to them or tried to win their confidence. He was not lazy, for he worked hard, trying to do everything himself, but he rarely revealed his plans or sent written instructions to his subordinates. When Vasil'chikov reported to him in camp preceding the battle of the Alma he discussed his troops in highly disparaging terms. In his view the soldiers did not want to fight and the cavalry was worthless. He had a very critical opinion of General P. P. Liprandi, who was bringing reinforcements, terming him a "Greek intriguer." As for his own generals, he regarded them as useless, expressing his scorn for each of them. He told Vasil'chikov that he could stay in camp for a while, and then he would be sent back to Gorchakov as a courier. He, too, was obviously viewed as an intriguer.[24]

When the Allied fleet passed by Sevastopol Menshikov had ample time to prepare for battle, for he marched out with his troops to a strong position on the banks of the Alma river, where he stayed almost inert for about a week. Characteristically, he held no conferences with his generals and issued no plans or dispositions, so that no one knew what was expected, or where the ammunition reserves or the field hospitals were. Little was done to improve the battlefield by clearing away vineyards and walls that would provide cover to enemy sharpshooters and only two earthworks were built, which offered little cover for the Russian troops. Moreover, during the four days that the Allies spent getting their troops ashore and organized, the Russians made no harassing attacks on them with their numerous cavalry and horse

23. Dubrovin, p. 173.
24. Vasil'chikov, pp. 177–78, 191–92.

artillery, which would have complicated the task of the enemy and encouraged the Russian soldiers. Menshikov also made no effort to evacuate the considerable quantities of supplies that were in Eupatoria, which were all taken by the invaders.[25]

Even more important, he did not reconnoiter the field of battle himself, but assigned it to a junior officer, who led the troops back and forth and finally stationed them well down on the slope, far from their reserves and with the skirmishers and the main units too close together. In this exposed position, with no cover, the Russians were compelled to retire up the hill before facing the foe, which led to substantial losses and discouragement. Orders were given by Menshikov's adjutants, over the heads of the divisional commanders; hence no chain of command existed. In fact, the two field commanders, Generals Kiriakov on the left and P. D. Gorchakov at the center and the right, had no clear idea of the limits of their authority so that two years after the battle they argued about which one had command over one of the regiments, although neither could produce any documents to prove his views. In fact, no disposition or written instruction for the troops has been found. Because of this disorganization, the commanders acted according to their best judgment, with a marked lack of coordination.[26] Some of the regiments saw no action at all during the battle.

While the Russians in the Crimea thus had significant weaknesses and failings, the Allied forces also had handicaps, which caused them to enter the conflict not in the best of condition. First of all, they were three separate armies, with no real unity of purpose or common objective. Because neither the French nor the British would accept a commander-in-chief from the other army, they did not name one, and the two armies operated side by side, but with almost no coordination. And no one even thought of considering the wishes of the Turks, who were under the command of Marshal Saint-Arnaud. The British had ambitious war plans, of which the taking and destroying of Sevastopol and its fleet would be only the first step. They hoped also to drive the Russians out of the Crimea and the Caucasus and to take Finland and Poland from their empire. Napoleon III had more modest aims, for he cared nothing about the Caucasus and Georgia but wanted

25. S. K. Gershel'man, *Nravstvennyi element pod Sevastopolem* (St. Petersburg, 1897), pp. 35–38.
26. Dubrovin, pp. 90–94.

to defeat Russia and limit its power and to destroy the Holy Alliance, leaving France as the diplomatic center of Europe. What the Turks wanted was unimportant; the two sea powers would decide the outcome, and the Porte would have to accept it. While the Allies were agreed about taking Sevastopol and destroying the Russian fleet, beyond that they had no common goal.

The French, who had been fighting in Algeria for decades, had a veteran army, a working military system, and several capable generals. Their infantry was well trained and armed with the deadly Minié rifle, supported by powerful artillery. Since, however, they expected to capture Sevastopol in a few weeks, after a brief campaign, they had no cavalry when they landed. Moreover, Marshal Saint-Arnaud, their commander, was already mortally ill and could offer little leadership.

The British forces were trained in line tactics, which offered ample scope for the devastating fire from their Minié rifles but was not suitable for a war of maneuver. They had effective artillery, but in small quantity, and about a thousand cavalry. The British commanders, who were mostly veterans of the Napoleonic wars, had little understanding of the needs of a modern campaign, and Lord Raglan, the commander-in-chief, had lost an arm at Waterloo. Like the French, they had no wagon train with them, and they had almost no tents for their soldiers.

The British government had never provided a workable military system for its army, with suitable provisioning, transport, medical and hospital care, and other needed services.[27] The Turks had almost no military organization, and most of their commanders were corrupt and cared little for their men, who died of disease and privation in great numbers.

One of the main weaknesses of the Allied forces lay in the haphazard, unorganized nature of the expedition, for they had never seriously planned the objectives and strategy of the campaign. At first they had landed at Varna to protect the Turkish army in Bulgaria, but after the Russians had retired to Bessarabia in July 1854 the Allies had finally decided to attack Sevastopol. They knew little about the Crimea, but finally decided to land at Eupatoria after a reconnaissance while the whole Allied armada waited. They had no maps of the interior and could only guess at the size of the Russian force. Fortu-

27. A. J. Barker, *The War against Russia 1854–1856* (New York, 1970), pp. 22–26.

nately for them, they had fine weather for their debarkation, although a heavy rainstorm drenched the British, who had no shelter-tents, while at night the French were dry and comfortable under canvas. The rain was followed by heavy work the next day, landing horses and cannon in rough water, which left them exhausted and chilled.

Disease plagued the soldiers from Varna to Sevastopol, for the French had brought cholera from southern France, and it spread quickly to the British and the Turks. Even after the troops were on the ships to go to the Crimea, men continued to die and were buried at sea. Unfortunately, some cadavers came loose from the round shot that had taken them to the bottom of the sea, and they rose from the depths among the hundreds of vessels, their grisly looks giving no comfort to the living. Deaths continued throughout the leisurely sail to Eupatoria and during the debarkation. Cold rain, a shortage of drinking water, and lack of fuel for cooking, plus the strenuous work of moving vast heaps of provisions, ammunition, and equipment, weakened the soldiers so that they could march only five miles a day, even without their knapsacks.[28] Fortunately, the Russians failed to trouble them in their encampments, but even so, the British, and to a lesser degree, the French, went into their first battle in weakened condition. The lack of coordination of the two armies was already visible, and there was little cooperation between them.

On September 8/20 the French and British forces began their advance against the Russians on the south bank of the Alma river, with their artillery massed on Kurganie Hill. Here the British faced the main Russian concentration and, as they could not match the Russian fire, they had to lie on the field, passively suffering their losses. The French were on the right, along the Alma to its mouth, with General Pierre Bosquet assigned the task of turning the Russian left. Menshikov had heard from Lieutenant Colonel P. V. Zaleskii, who had reconnoitred the mouth of the river, that the gully leading up from the sea was impassable, and satisfied by his report, did not personally inspect the terrain, but merely placed a battalion to watch the area, although it was nearly a mile from the river. This was a grave mistake, for there was a rough road running up the gully which the Tatars had used to haul melons to market. This fact was reported to Menshikov, who refused to accept it, although there was time to investigate and

28. Ibid., pp. 50–55; W. H. Russell, *The British Expedition to the Crimea* (rev. ed., London, 1877), pp. 89–91.

make the road impassable. He could easily have had his troops dig out the trail and throw up a breastwork to bar the enemy, which would have kept them from turning the Russian flank. But with the trail open Bosquet's forces easily climbed it. Although the Allied naval gunfire was ineffective because of the elevation of the plateau, once the French had reached the high ground and brought up their heavy guns, while the Zouaves struck down the Russian gunners, the Russian left was untenable. Now the French could turn their fire on the Russian center.[29] General Kiriakov learned of the French appearance, but failed to take effective action against the danger, and when Menshikov came he took what he thought were sufficient measures and left. Thus Bosquet's forces easily overcame the Russian defenses, successfully turning the Russian flank.[30]

At about the same time Lord Raglan decided to lead his troops into the teeth of danger. He had the men rise and dress their rank with great precision, and then, carefully preserving their alignment and keeping step, the line of redcoats, almost two miles long, advanced up the hill. After crossing the river, they marched up the heights, and a series of ferocious fights between British and Russian units followed, with the redcoats winning, thanks to their use of line formation against the Russian columns, which had much less firepower. Eventually the British drove the Russians off their central position, and with the French moving on from the left, the greycoats were forced to retreat. General Kiriakov, braggart and drunkard though he was, managed to assemble a strong force with considerable artillery, and neither the French nor the British undertook pursuit. At first the beaten army kept its discipline, but when it came to the Kacha river, with its one bridge, all cohesion vanished and the troops straggled back to Sevastopol as best they could. Many of the wounded died on the field untended, while some managed to return to the army. The Russians lost about five thousand killed and wounded, while the Allies lost about three thousand.[31]

In the battle the French and the British were fighting the least effective part of the Russian military system, for the Crimea was a

---

29. A. P. Khrushchov, *Istoriia oborony Sevastopolia* (3rd ed., St. Petersburg, 1889), pp. 9–10.

30. M. Enisherlov, "Srazhenie pri Al'me," *Voennyi Sbornik* (hereafter cited *VS*), no. 1 (1859), pp. 1–28; Khruschchov, pp. 9–10.

31. La Gorce, I, 267–68; Bogdanovich, III, 27–30.

remote region, weakly held. Menshikov had never commanded line troops and showed no sympathy with the army. Until just before the Allied landings he had only limited power and a scanty number of troops, while Paskevich hoarded manpower in an inactive region. Because of the improper military administration at Sevastopol and because attention centered on Poland and the Baltic, nobody cared enough about the situation in the Crimea to take the required action. With his inferior numbers, Menshikov should have avoided a pitched battle, although the position he picked was the best available, albeit over four miles long. More important, he failed to make use of the opportunities offered, especially on the left flank, where, as already described, he neglected to take action to deny the road to the plateau to the French. On the other sectors of the front he failed to build enough field entrenchments to protect his men against the superior firepower of the enemy. Also Menshikov made no use of his relatively large force of cavalry to threaten the British flank and throw their advance into confusion.

All these points have been made by numerous Russian critics, with considerable justice. Even more significant is the charge that, instead of risking battle on the Alma, Menshikov should have moved his army inland to a position threatening the flank of the Allies if they marched to attack Sevastopol or to pass around it, as they did. Because the Allies had almost no wagon train, they could not have moved very far from their base at Eupatoria and probably could not have attacked him, while he would have been able to receive reinforcements and supplies. If Menshikov had followed such a strategy, the French and the British, suffering from cholera and with Saint-Arnaud about to die and a lack of harmony at the top levels, would have been in an impossible position, with no suitable strategy available to them, and they might have been forced to evacuate the Crimea without a battle.[32]

In his *Report* Captain George B. McClellan, who was sent from the United States to investigate the war in 1855 and 1856, agreed with this view. He further contended that Menshikov should have blocked the harbors of Kamesh and Balaklava by sinking vessels at the entrances, which would have compelled the Allies to obtain their supplies solely from Eupatoria—an impossible position, as they had so few wagons.[33] It is doubtful whether this proposal was feasible,

32. Bogdanovich, III, 31–32; Khrushchov, pp. 17–18; Vasil'chikov, p. 178.
33. George B. McClellan, *Report,* Special Session, Senate, Ex. Doc. No. 1, 34th Cong., 1857

because of the complete control of the waters around the Crimea by the Allies, but a move to a strong flank position was possible and might have been highly effective.

After the battle Menshikov brought his army to Sevastopol, where most of the troops bivouacked on the outskirts of the city. After they had regrouped, received provisions, and replaced the expended ammunition, they were again ready for action. Menshikov, after looking over the situation, now decided to make a flank march to Bakhchiserai in order to save the army from capture and to threaten the enemy's flank and rear if they attacked the fortress. He was very secretive about his intention, although he did tell Admiral Kornilov of his plans. The latter was greatly upset, holding that the prince was abandoning the city to the Allies. Menshikov took almost no precautions against surprise, except to send General Kiriakov to scout north of the city. Kiriakov's report that the English were only two or three miles away, apparently satisfied Menshikov. Late on September 11/23 his army set off for Bakhchiserai, with an advance guard but no patrols or flank protection. General Kiriakov, following the advance guard, almost marched his troops into the British position and had to retire in haste. Later he lost his way and wasted a good deal of time, holding up the force of General P. D. Gorchakov. Then on the 13th he got ahead of the advance guard, becoming separated from the main forces, and again had to be recalled, so that in two and one-half days his troops had had to march over fifty miles. It was almost sheer luck that the Allies, who were also on the move, did not encounter the Russian forces and inflict deadly blows.[34]

The Allied armies, after resting and reorganizing, moved to the Kacha river, south of the Alma, where they considered their course. They were disturbed by the fierce fight that the Russians had made and believed that they would fight even harder behind their fortifications. Also, Saint-Arnaud was obviously close to death and Francois Canrobert, his successor, felt unsure of himself. Since they had heard reports from the Tatars that the southern part of the city was unfortified, they resolved to march around the fortress in order to assault it from the south, using the harbors of Balaklava and Kamesh as bases. So on September 24, when Menshikov's army was marching to the northeast away from Sevastopol, the British and the French began to march to the south. After a slow march from the Alma to

34. Bogdanovich, III, 43–44, 52; Khrushchov, pp. 21–24; Vasil'chikov, pp. 180–81; Gershel'man, 64–68.

Bel'bek, they halted for a day and a half to rest the troops. At noon on September 12/26 they began their flank march "by the curious arrangement of sending the English artillery in advance, without escort, through a woods." The French also found the march slow and dangerous, for they were hampered by the great amount of British baggage as they went, gropingly, in a single column through woods and defiles. At one point the French had to halt as the road went through a narrow defile with room for only six men abreast. All the French artillery was massed in a sort of crater at the entry into this gorge—"a most dangerous movement, not far from the enemy and almost under the guns of the fortress." The French were much disturbed at the folly of proceeding blindly through such dangerous terrain. Guérin spoke of "the imprudence of the chiefs." [35]

A special providence must have watched over both armies, for by chance they made no real contact with each other. Finally, as the Russians had almost gone, some English cavalry blundered onto a convoy of Russian wagons, of which they captured about a score. The Russian army continued on its way, and the British resumed their march to the south. They established themselves at Balaklava, with the French at the better harbor at Kamesh. [36]

In the meantime the Black Sea Fleet with its commanders, Lieutenant General Moller, commander of the garrison, Colonel Totleben, and several reserve battalions remained in Sevastopol, cut off from the outside world and ignorant of Menshikov's intentions. Many, like Kornilov, felt that Menshikov's departure with the army was treason. There were only some 5,800 men in the city, with almost no land fortifications, especially south of the bay. The inhabitants of the city were eager to help defend it, but had no arms or guidance. Kornilov put Totleben to work fortifying the northern sector, where he accomplished wonders. Batteries were erected and twenty guns were set up to repulse the expected attack. Totleben undertook the most pressing matters first, building field fortifications rather than formal defenses. [37]

On September 10/22 Kornilov ordered the crews of three frigates to work on the defenses of the southern side, where they soon found that there was no master plan. Admiral Nakhimov called a council

---

35. McClellan, p. 7; Léon Guérin, *Histoire de la dernière guerre de Russie* (Paris, 1858), I, 275–77.
36. Bogdanovich, III, 53–54.
37. Schilder, *Graf Totleben,* I, 313–15.

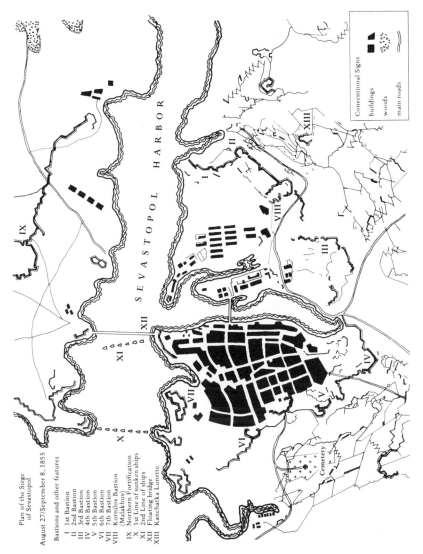

Plan of the Siege
of Sevastopol

August 27/September 8, 1855

Bastions and other features

I   1st Bastion
II   2nd Bastion
III   3rd Bastion
IV   4th Bastion
V   5th Bastion
VI   6th Bastion
VII 7th Bastion
VIII Kornilov Bastion
      (Malakhov)
IX   Northern Fortification
X   1st Line of sunken ships
XI   2nd Line of ships
XII Floating bridge
XIII Kanchatka Lunette

Conventional Signs

buildings
woods
main roads

SEVASTOPOL HARBOR

Cemetery

Plan of the Siege of Sevastopol

of war, which could provide little help. The admiral, feeling that if the Allies attacked in force all would be lost, gave orders that in case of an assault they should destroy the ships rather than let them fall into hostile hands. Kornilov, however, sensing that the northern sector was not in danger, took over the defense work with the help of Totleben and Admiral Nakhimov, and assumed the title of chief of staff of the garrison.[38]

These leaders now took urgent steps to improve the defenses of the city by shortening the lines, making them continuous, and mounting as many guns as possible. Totleben laid out the plans, making every effort to prevent the Allies from taking the city by storm. Great guns from the ships were moved into the new batteries, the ditches were deepened, the breastworks were thickened, the powder magazines were made more secure. In the frenzied work that ensued, the inhabitants took an active role, with women bringing food and water to the men or carrying dirt for the works in baskets. In one thirty-six-hour period they put over one hundred guns into position. Local Tatars had told the Allies that the city was undefended on the south, but when the Allies came they found it so well protected that they did not dare assault it, and hanged the Tatars for lying.[39]

In making this astonishing effort the defenders were operating under great difficulties, for Totleben had discovered that there were only enough iron shovels for about twenty men and no picks at all. He tried to get Menshikov to obtain the picks, and when this proved impossible, he turned to the local commander of engineers. At length, when the matter became urgent, they sent to Odessa for iron shovels and bought over four thousand of them; they were not able to obtain picks, however. They rushed the shovels to Sevastopol in twelve-horse wagons, which arrived on October 17/29, when the siege was already under way.[40]

In spite of these obstacles, the defenders were determined to fight to the death and, although the fortifications were far from sufficient, on September 15/27 Admiral Kornilov decided to consecrate them with the troops in battle positions, while the clergy, with ikons and banners, moved in processions singing *Te Deums,* sprinkling the sol-

38. Dubrovin, pp. 178–81.
39. Ibid., pp. 182–85.
40. Schilder, *Graf Totleben,* I, 274; E. V. Tarle, *Gorod Russkoi Slavy* (Moscow, 1954), p. 31.

diers with holy water, and blessing them with the sign of the cross. Kornilov then rode along the lines and encouraged the troops, who declared that they were ready to die with honor.[41]

By September 15/27 the British and the French were located south and east of Sevastopol, based on the two ports. Neither Lord Raglan nor General Canrobert, the new French commander, wanted to risk an assault on the Russian position, which at that time had 172 guns mounted south of the bay. Saint-Arnaud's fatal illness, and the need to reorganize their supply arrangements and to build defensive positions, caused the Allies to delay their attack and instead to prepare for a bombardment first. And, as before, thousands of men worked day and night on the Russian defenses, with women and children bringing dirt in baskets, filling sandbags, and carrying gabions and fascines to the places needed. "Daily fresh batteries sprang up as if by enchantment," J. G. Calthorpe wrote.[42] The Allied delay gave the Russians invaluable time to strengthen their shaky defenses by means of their greater energy and inspiration. Also the Allies had trouble in moving their guns and supplies up to the lines. The thin layers of soil were insufficient for field fortifications, and much dirt had to be laboriously brought in in baskets. Many of the Allied soldiers sickened from overwork and the difficult conditions. The Russians, however, were in good health, for there were only a few cases of cholera and no epidemic.[43]

As late as September 24 (O.S.) the defenses of Sevastopol were still very weak. Colonel V. I. Den' (Dehn), an engineer and son of General I. Den', the leading engineer under Nicholas I, reported that Bastions 5 and 6 were badly exposed and the fourth was merely an earthwork like a lunette, attached by a trench to a flèche, which was later called the Bastion 3. (A lunette was a field fortification with two faces and two parallel flanking walls; a flèche was a simple V-shaped entrenchment.) The Malakhov had merely a stone tower, which was being covered with an earth embankment, and Bastions 1 and 2 had almost nothing to stop a foe, which caused Kornilov to admit that the enemy might easily attack with cavalry with some chance of success. Den' added that in 1850 his father had told him that all his urgings to fortify Sevastopol by land were disregarded by Nicholas

41. Dubrovin, pp. 191–93.
42. S. J. G. Calthorpe, *Letters from Headquarters* (London, 1856), I, 267.
43. Dubrovin, pp. 236–38.

I, who had jokingly asked if these fortifications were to be used against the Tatars, who were submissive. "In this case, what has been done is enough," hc said.[44] The emperor completely failed to understand the great development of steam, which made it possible to carry large armies by sea.

Because of this earlier failure to complete the landward fortifications, the defenders now had to undertake it in haste, doing what was essential to hold off an assault. They set up field-type works to give protection against field artillery and to provide defensive fire against attacks, leaving the erection of permanent defenses against a regular siege and the building of secure powder magazines and dugouts for the defenders of the future. Fortunately, the Allies did not realize the weakness of the Russian defenses and did not dare make a general assault, although it probably would have succeeded. They began to erect batteries a long way from the Russian position, and at the end of September the French opened their first trench, over one thousand yards from the Bastion 5. This delighted the Russians, for it indicated that the French did not now intend to storm the position but were preparing for a full-scale siege. The British followed suit with a trench even farther from the Malakhov *kurgan* and Bastion 3. The Russians, guided by Totleben and inspired by Kornilov, to whom Menshikov left the erection of the defenses, now could strengthen their chief positions by building supporting batteries, digging trenches to protect the defenders, and replacing light guns with heavy ones from the fleet.[45] They opened fire on the new batteries of the Allies to harass their men and to learn the ranges, and made frequent sorties against them, both by day and by night. Sharpshooters also fired on the enemy workers, although in this the Allies had the advantage. In the meantime the garrison was building fortifications and powder magazines, bringing up supplies, and mounting heavy naval guns in the batteries. Naval vessels were moored where they could enfilade the ditches and ravines leading to the city. The earthworks, however, were not very effective, for the soil was largely shale, which did not hold its position when piled to form walls or embankments. The powder magazines were not properly protected. Fascines (long bundles of rods and brush) and gabions (bottomless baskets of brush to hold dirt) were often lacking, since the materials for constructing them were not abundant.[46]

44. Den', "Zapiski," p. 661.
45. E. I. Totleben, *Opisanie oborony g. Sevastopolia* (St. Petersburg, 1863–78), I, 245–80.
46. Ibid., pp. 281–301; Dubrovin, pp. 238–42.

Finally, the French and the British completed their preparations for an assault on the fortress, which would be preceded by a great bombardment on October 5/17. At the appointed time all the batteries opened fire, with the Russians replying "with a very lively and perfectly directed fire" which hit the French batteries with great effect. The Russian sailors especially, who manned many of the batteries, fired with great rapidity, with little attention to aim. They succeeded in gaining superiority over the French, blowing up several magazines, which compelled the French batteries to cease fire at eleven o'clock and to postpone the assault until the 19th. This delay permitted the Russians to repair their batteries and reorganize their gunners.[47] The British, however, did much better, for their huge guns wrought havoc in isolated Bastion 3, silencing many of its guns and laying low most of the gunners. By 3 P.M. only one-third of its cannon were still firing. Then the main powder magazine blew up, killing one hundred men. At this point the Russians expected that the bastion would be stormed, which would make it impossible for the Russians to hold the city. But the British delayed because the French were disheartened, and the Russians brought in more gunners and fresh ammunition and continued to fire. Although late in the day only two guns were still firing from Bastion 3, with five gunners working them, the Allies missed the opportunity to capture it and thus to dominate the city. The British and French fleets, moreover, achieved almost nothing. While they damaged one of the main Russian harbor batteries, the Russians inflicted heavy damage on their ships, which withdrew late in the afternoon.[48]

The Russian casualties were quite severe during the bombardment, for the reserves, massed close to the fortifications, suffered greatly from the Allied fire. In the day's fighting 1,112 men were lost, of whom 304 were killed. The Allies lost only 348 men, most of them French.[49]

A severe blow to the Russians during the bombardment was the loss of Admiral Kornilov, who enjoyed immense influence over the rank and file. At the height of the action Kornilov, as chief of staff, in spite of the appeals of the men, went to Bastion 3 to inspect the situation, and then to the Malakhov, where he lost a leg by a cannon

47. Charles Auger, *Guerre d'Orient. Siège de Sévastopol* (Paris, 1859), I, 106–07: Totleben, pp. 302–06.
48. Vasil'chikov, p. 195; Totleben, I, 307–29; D. V. Il'inskii, "Iz vospominaniia i zametok Sevastopol'tsa," *RA,* XXXI, pt. 1, (1893), 274–83.
49. Il'inskii, pp. 282–83.

shot. He died not long after.[50] His loss had a great effect on the men, who swore to follow his example by fighting to the death.

On October 19 (N.S.) the Allies reopened the bombardment, with two new French batteries. The Russians again knocked out one of these, and blew up the powder in three others. By midafternoon, however, the Allies had gained superiority over the Russian gunners, whose fire slackened, as many of their embrasures caved in. But the Russian fire, while reduced, was still strong, and once more that of the Allies died down and the bombardment ceased, again destroying hopes of an imminent assault.[51]

The French continued to press against Bastion 4, which was weak and isolated, and their approaches drew steadily nearer. Totleben added new Russian batteries, but they were in the rear of the bastion, whereas the French batteries were close to the front of it and their fire was concentrated. Many of the Russians feared that they would have to give up the bastion, which would make defense of the city untenable.[52] Also Menshikov was greatly worried about a shortage of powder, since the naval gunners used it lavishly, in spite of Menshikov's protests. (Later on the staff ordered the gunners to aim carefully and fire more slowly.) There was no system of reporting about the supply of powder and no central control over it, and this danger did much to make the admiral, now reinforced by the 12th division under General Liprandi, decide on a counterattack against the British.[53]

On October 11/23 Menshikov called a conference to consider the crisis. Colonel Popov proposed an attack on the British Vorontsov Battery on Green Hill, which later proved to be the key to Sevastopol. He hoped that it could be taken and held and that from there the Russians could direct their fire on other British batteries and drive them back. Menshikov fully approved the plan. Liprandi, however, while he praised the objective, held that the operation would be much too costly and he refused to carry it out, greatly preferring an attack on Balaklava, the British base port. General P. D. Gorchakov agreed with him. Menshikov, feeling that he could accomplish little with the opposition of his generals, asked Popov to try to persuade Liprandi

50. Totleben, I, 307–08.

51. Auger, I, 110.

52. Totleben, I, 337–57; A. E. Popov, "Zapiski o prebyvanii ego pod Sevastopole s 1-go Oktiabria po 1-e dekabria 1854 g.," *RS,* XXI (1878), pp. 321–22.

53. Dubrovin, pp. 252–62; Vasil'chikov, p. 194.

to attack the Vorontsov Battery, but Liprandi still insisted that Balaklava should be the objective.[54] He warned, however, that with his limited forces he would have no real chance of success and that the attack would awaken the Allies to the weakness of their flank; but Menshikov now insisted on attacking Balaklava.[55]

The resulting action on October 13/25 was a demonstration rather than a full attack. The Russians easily captured the four redoubts north of the port, since the Turkish defenders fled with almost no resistance. The Russian cavalry now advanced to wipe out a British supply park but encountered a considerable force of British cavalry and retreated. An attempt to break through to the port was checked by a regiment of Scottish troops. When a counterattack by British cavalry met with some success, Lord Raglan sent his vague order to the Light Brigade to attack, which produced the famous but costly charge of the Light Brigade into the center of the Russian position. The British did some damage, but were struck in flank by a Russian cavalry charge and were cut down by artillery and musket fire as they tried to escape.[56] Liprandi made no effort to pursue the matter further.

The effects of this reconnaissance in force were not very significant. The Russian soldiers were greatly heartened by their success in fighting the enemy and regarded the outcome as a Russian victory. Many of the officers, however, regarded it as a mistake, for it accomplished nothing important and actually aroused the Allies to strengthen their flank and rear to ward off a fresh Russian attack. If Menshikov had had the fortitude to wait for the arrival of the 11th and 12th divisions, which occurred about ten days later, a massive drive by these forces and Liprandi's troops probably could have captured the whole British base and supply system and might have ended the war then and there. Thus there was widespread belief that Menshikov had lost a highly promising opportunity for a real success.[57]

But as Balaklava decided nothing, and both armies were considerably reinforced, the siege went on and important events would occur before winter brought a halt to the operations in the Crimea.

54. Popov, "Zapiski," *RS,* XX, XXI (1878), 313–20.

55. Dubrovin, pp. 259–61.

56. Totleben, I, 367–77; Adolphe Niel, *Siège de Sévastopol: Journal des opérations du génie* (Paris, 1858), pp. 76–77; "Kniaz' Menshikov," *RA,* XIX (1877), 59–61.

57. Gershel'man, pp. 139–44; Stepan Kozhukhov, "Iz krymskikh vospominanii poslednei voiny," *RA,* VII (1869), 918–90; Bogdanovich, III, 111–22.

CHAPTER 13. INKERMAN: THE DECISIVE BATTLE

The battle of Balaklava had little significant effect on the course of events except to awaken the British to the weakness of their right flank. The French were pushing the siege of Sevastopol with vigor and, as they had put the vital Bastion 4 in danger, they planned to storm the city on November 6/18. Heavy Allied reinforcements were expected and the danger to the Russians appeared grave. Fortunately for the latter, about October 17 the 10th and 11th divisions arrived from the Southern Army, which gave the Russians temporary numerical superiority—90,000 to 71,000 for the Allies. Menshikov at once decided to attack from Chorgun, where he sent the newcomers.[1]

Lengthy conferences were held in Sevastopol about the coming attack, with the general opinion favoring an offensive from Chorgun toward Balaklava. Suddenly, however, Menshikov changed his mind, as the emperor had sent word that such an attack would be risky and that the push should be made in an easterly direction from the left flank of the Russian position before Sevastopol, against the right flank of the British, which lay on the Inkerman heights south of the Chernaia river. Menshikov's report of October 22 specifically mentioned the tsar's instructions. As a result, Menshikov's plans had to be hastily changed, and the staff officers drew up the new plan without consulting the generals who would carry it out, which caused confusion and uncertainty.[2]

The new plan was vague, calling on General F. I. Soimonov "to attack the English position," without stating where. No maps were supplied. Instead, Colonel Popov of Menshikov's staff visited Soimonov on the eve of the battle and discussed the details of the operation with him. Finally, at 2:30 A.M. Soimonov's aide awoke the troops and attempted to lead them to their positions, but because of the

1. Dubrovin, pp. 265–67.
2. Ibid., pp. 270–74.

lack of knowledge of the terrain and a heavy fog over the area they became lost.[3]

In the meantime General P. A. Dannenberg, commander of the newly arrived 4th Corps, took it upon himself to clarify the sketchy orders issued by Menshikov. He ordered Soimonov to begin the attack at 5:00 A.M. instead of 6:00, as stated by Menshikov, and told him to attack to the right after climbing up the difficult Kilen-balka (Carenage ravine), instead of to the left of the ravine, between it and the valley of the Chernaia river. Menshikov, however, had ordered him to attack to the left of the ravine, in order to protect the ascent of General P. Ia. Pavlov's troops from the river, where they would cross a bridge.[4]

The resulting confusion was largely caused by the fact that Menshikov and Dannenberg detested each other and the prince was determined to give Dannenberg as little part in the battle as possible. Menshikov instructed the latter to stay with the reserve until Soimonov's and Pavlov's forces should join, when he would take command of them. As commander of the 4th Corps, Dannenberg apparently felt that it was his duty to clarify the sketchy orders issued by Menshikov, but in doing so he only added to the uncertainty.

On the morning of October 24 (O.S.) Soimonov's forces, in spite of the fog and the mud, reached the rim of the ravine by 5:00 A.M., one hour before Pavlov was to arrive. They achieved a complete surprise and, even though only three regiments were there, with scanty artillery, they took a British battery and a camp. Soimonov's main forces remained in reserve with General O. P. Zhabokritskii, awaiting orders from his superior. Soimonov, in the face of desperate resistance, pushed slowly ahead, suffering heavy losses from the excellent British musketry. Both he and his second in command were killed in the early stages of the battle, so that the orders to Zhabokritskii were not received. Two more regiments arrived at the crest two hours later, but the pressure of the British was so great that they had to retire with heavy losses.[5]

In the meantime Pavlov's force of almost twenty thousand men, with much artillery, arrived at the bridge site, only to find that Admiral

3. A. Andriianov, *Inkermanskii boi i oborona Sevastopolia* (St. Petersburg, 1903), pp. 14–15; 70–71.
4. Popov, "Zapiski," *RS* XXI (1878), 494–502.
5. Gershel'man, pp. 167–68; Dubrovin, pp. 280–93.

P. S. Nakhimov's sailors, who had been ordered to build the bridge, had not done so—perhaps because Dannenberg had told Pavlov to do it. Hence the troops, unable to cross the river, had to wait for a considerable time until they could cross and climb the steep hill, and before they could get there Soimonov's force was cut to pieces.[6]

At length, after the British, in spite of heavy losses and several repulses, had driven the Russians back, Pavlov's troops reached the crest and Zhabokritskii's reserve regiments appeared on the scene. Colonel Popov got the latter to move straight ahead to back up the main force, which was standing in the central British position. But at this point Dannenberg arrived and sent Zhabokritskii to the right. Popov objected that they should push ahead and dig in on the key position that they had gained, but Dannenberg rode off without changing his order. Colonel Totleben also wanted the fresh regiments to dig in on the heights, but Dannenberg's order stood and Popov failed to get him to change it. Even so, Pavlov's regiments, under Dannenberg's command, pushed ahead to drive the British back and victory appeared in sight for the Russians. Dannenberg brought up much of Pavlov's artillery to Cossack Hill, where they were massed in a battery much stronger than anything the British had. Calthorpe, a British staff officer, spoke of "the terrible cannonade" that the Russians loosed upon the British from their artillery on Cossack Hill—twenty-four heavy and sixteen light guns, and three field batteries on high ground dominating the Kilen-balka. Two Russian frigates in the harbor also directed heavy fire against the enemy. Until the last moments of the action the British had only thirty-six nine-pounders.[7] A French account also relates the great effectiveness of the Russian cannon when they were turned on the British camp: "The cannonballs and the grape shot of the Russians spread death in all ranks; the latter were no sooner reformed than new volleys thinned them out again." [8]

The British, however, had one great advantage over the Russians in the vastly more effective musketry fire, for, while the Russian muskets were of little value at ranges over sixty paces, the redcoats, with their Minié balls, were deadly at two hundred, shooting down commanders and gunners. Calthorpe tells how the Russian troops repulsed a British counterattack and then advanced to recapture the Sandbag

---

6. Vasil'chikov; pp. 203–04, Popov, "Zapiski," *RS* XXI (1878), 503–05.
7. Calthorpe, I, 364–65.
8. Guérin, pp. 375–76.

Battery from the Coldstream Guards. The latter held the battery for a long time with determination and vigor, in spite of the Russian numbers, which were five times as great. The Guards "continued to fire on the Russian masses with such coolness and accuracy that the ground was covered with dead and wounded. But no amount of slaughter seemed to check the enemy's onward course; they showed reckless bravery and stolid determination for which we had never given them credit." In time the Russian numbers decided the issue, and "the Guards, after losing one-third of their strength and exhausting their ammunition, slowly retired from the battery." [9]

Not all the survivors of the Russian regiments retired to the reserves, however, for small groups of soldiers led by junior officers or sergeants continued to function, using extended order and maneuvering skillfully to attack British units in line formation. With both musketry and the bayonet, by sudden attacks on the flanks and rear of the enemy, they caused much destruction. So, although the British forces compelled the main Russian units to retire, in the meantime the British units were being cut to pieces, and they had to pull most of their troops from the siege lines to hold their camp. Finally, after the main Russian forces had reached the battle and with the aid of their artillery, began to push the British relentlessly back, Raglan, faced with ruin, appealed to Bosquet to send reserves from his observation corps to save the day.[10]

One important element in the battle was the Chorgun detachment of some 22,000 men under General P. D. Gorchakov, which was detailed to threaten the Observation Corps of the Allies along their exposed flank running from Balaklava to the cliffs of the Sapun-gora to the heights where the main battle took place. While the Sapun position was almost impregnable, between it and Balaklava there was a considerable expanse of rolling terrain which was not. This area was partially fortified and the French forces of General Bosquet held it, to prevent a Russian drive into the British rear. Originally Menshikov had specified that the Chorgun force should "attack" the Allied position along the Vorontsov Road, but, fearing that such an attack would be catastrophic, he altered the orders to require Prince Gorchakov to "distract" the Observation Corps from the main action. Gorchakov, a feeble old general, had no stomach for a bloody battle and

9. Calthorpe, I, 360.
10. I. V. Bestuzhev, *Krymskaia voina 1853–1856* (Moscow, 1956), pp. 108–10.

satisfied himself with a long-range cannonade against the French, who readily interpreted it as a mere feint. Hence Bosquet, after sending three battalions and some artillery to aid the British, soon decided to send the bulk of his troops to stop the advancing Russians on the Inkerman heights, leaving only a thin cover to hold against Gorchakov's army, whose infantry took no part in the battle.[11]

In his own defense Gorchakov claimed that an attack on the French position would have been ruinous, as their defenses on the Sapungora were impregnable, with cliffs of over one hundred feet. If he had attacked at Balaklava, Bosquet could then have sent his whole force to rescue the British, while Gorchakov's troops would be badly hurt, for Balaklava by that time was heavily fortified.[12] It should be noted that a large part of the Chorgun force consisted of cavalry, which was useless against fortifications, and its artillery was composed mostly of light guns which were not suited for a real battle. On the other hand, General N. D. Timofeev, as ordered, at 11:00 A.M. made a sortie from Bastion 6 at Sevastopol with four battalions and four guns, which overran two French batteries and spiked a number of guns. The French counterattacked vigorously, driving the Russians back with heavy losses, but came under the fire of the fortress, which cost them dearly.[13] This venture, however, occupied the French siege corps for several hours and prevented it from taking a direct part in the main battle. Conceivably, if the Chorgun detachment had made a real attack, with infantry and artillery, against Bosquet's position, even though the action would certainly have been very costly, it probably would have delayed the sending of Bosquet's troops to rescue the beleaguered British on the heights, who would then have been crushed by the Russians. The British army in the Crimea probably would have been destroyed, the siege lifted, and the Crimea evacuated.

But since the Chorgun detachment remained inactive all day, Bosquet soon realized that it was safe to send his troops to help the British. First he sent three battalions with artillery, which advanced in a broad formation against the Russians. On reaching the crest of

11. Popov, "Zapiski," *RS* XXI (1878), 496–99; Auger, I, 124–25; Niel, pp. 94–96; Den', pp. 675–76; McClellan, *Report,* pp. 9–10; Bogdanovich, III, 146–46; Vasil'chikov, however, who was a good soldier, held that it would have been impossible to attack from Chorgun (Vasil'chikov, pp. 202–03).

12. N. F. Dubrovin, ed., *Materialy dlia istorii krymskoi voiny* (St. Petersburg, 1871–1874), IV, 187–93.

13. Bogdanovich, III, 148–50.

the hill they came under the fire of the Russian guns on Cossack Hill and at once lost a number of men. In their confusion most of them panicked and retired down the hill, in spite of the bugles and drums calling them on and the efforts of their officers. They soon reformed their ranks and went back into action, only to receive "a most murderous discharge" of the Russian artillery, which again caused them to waver, until two British staff officers encouraged them. "I cannot describe to you," said Calthorpe, "the sinking sensation one felt on observing our allies give way; our first impression was that they had retired, beaten back by the overpowering masses of Russian infantry. . . . I confess myself that . . . I thought the day was lost." [14]

The first injection of French troops failed to halt the Russians, who, with the aid of their artillery, threw them back and slowly advanced. Pavlov's troops, led by Dannenberg, came up and, pushing the British steadily back, were on the verge of success. At this critical moment, however, Bosquet's reserves arrived and, with their devastating cannon, gained the upper hand. But the Russians retreated slowly, still fighting, and Totleben was able to establish a strong rear guard that protected the retirement of the Russian artillery to the river and to safety. [15] The Russians lost none of their cannon and there was no attempt at pursuit.

The battle of Inkerman was the crucial encounter of the Crimean War, for the Russians made no other major attack until the hopeless battle of the Chernaia River in August 1855. The Allied attempt to storm Sevastopol in June 1855 never had a chance. The Russians now had no hope of winning a great victory, and the Allies definitely decided not to try to attack the fortress, but to concentrate on siege tactics. The Russians also undertook intensive strengthening of their defenses under the guidance of Totleben.

The Russian army never really recovered from the catastrophe that it had undergone, for its losses were frightful. Both the British and the French with their deadly small arms concentrated on killing Russian commanders and also gunners. Almost all regimental and battalion officers of the divisions involved were put out of action, and the senior officers as well. Of the 55,000 Russian soldiers in action outside Sevastopol, the men killed, missing, and wounded numbered 11,959, although

14. Calthorpe, I, 373–75.
15. Totleben, I, 430–49.

probably some of the losses cited had taken place during the bombardment that had preceded the great battle. If one charges these losses solely to the troops actively engaged in the battle, the ratio becomes 1 to 2.5, or 40 percent—a staggering toll. Probably the total battle losses were about ten thousand.

The Allies lost many fewer than the Russians, although probably more than the official figure of 4,338. The British alone probably lost five thousand, including nine generals killed or wounded.[16]

Perhaps the most horrifying aspect of the battle was the suffering of the wounded. The Russian military system failed completely to deal with the problem, for it could only provide a field hospital of some 1,200 beds to care for ten thousand sufferers. Linen, vessels, and most important, bandages and compresses were insufficient for even half that number, and the miserable soldiers had to sit or lie under the open sky, covering themselves with bloody cloaks, stiff as boards. Shirts and trousers were used for bandages or lint. Fortunately for a time the weather was warm and clear, which probably saved many from gangrene infection. Many officers died of this scourge, jammed together in barracks by the medical authorities "in such crowding, filth, and stench that one could not pass through; and the air was so fouled that a healthy man could not breathe. God be your judge, messers medics and general-staff-doctors!" [17]

Even before Inkerman the wounded from the battle of the Alma had caused the hospital system to break down, and with the loss of 8,486 men killed, wounded, and missing during the next two months, the medical personnel were too scanty to care for the wounded properly. The fierce battle of Inkerman caused another breakdown, for there were almost twelve thousand casualties, mostly from troops in the field. Wounded men, untended for two or three days, lay in their uniforms, while the surgeons worked night and day at top speed. Dr. N. I. Pirogov, the great Russian surgeon, later wrote to a friend: "No one who has not seen with his own eyes can form any conception of the filth, the miserable condition in which our wounded and sick lay from October to December." [18]

The Russians were not alone in this failing, for the British had only a rudimentary, antiquated system of medical care for their sick and wounded, and as a result the conditions that Florence Nightingale

16. Andriianov, p. 31; Bogdanovich, III, 150–52; Totleben, I, 457–59.
17. Vasil'chikov, p. 206.
18. N. F. Edekauer, "Nikolai Ivanovich Pirogov v Sevastopole," *RS,* XLVII (1885), 294.

found in the base hospital at Scutari were deplorable. The French, who had a more effective military organization, provided much better care for their casualties, including sisters of mercy to nurse them in the hospitals and a system of moving them from the battlefield. In time both the Russians and the British, by introducing civilian volunteer personnel, substantially improved the care of their patients. But corruption and inefficiency continued to plague the Russian medical system until after the war was over.

The catastrophe at Inkerman came as a severe shock to the Russian public, both civilian and military. The Russians had finally attained numerical superiority over the Allies, and with the veterans of the 10th, 11th, and 12th divisions, commanded by good fighting generals like Soimonov, Pavlov, and Liprandi, on terrain of their choosing and enjoying almost complete tactical surprise, they had reason to expect success. When it did not come, there was heated discussion of the reasons for the failure.

One natural response to the question was the creation of a scapegoat in the person of Prince Menshikov. Certainly his preparations were done in great haste, to take advantage of the temporary Russian superiority in numbers before the heavy shipments of new French and British troops could arrive. The original plan was for a mass attack from Chorgun toward Balaklava, but, as mentioned above, a special message from the emperor had warned that such an attack was now perilous since the British had been warned of the danger during the battle of Balaklava. Hence the plan had to be completely revised by his staff officers, who drew up the new instructions without consulting the generals who would be involved. There was no effective reconnaissance of the terrain, and no detailed map of it was available. It turned out that the 5th Corps, when it was stationed in the Crimea a few years before, had made a fine, detailed map, of which a copy was sent to the Ministry of War. The original was in the files of the 5th Corps, which, in September 1854, was in the Danube area, and the map, stored in Odessa, could not be obtained from the guardian of its files. An appeal to the Ministry of War brought the response that by law it could send its copy only with the special permission of the emperor, which could not be obtained in time. Finally, the map arrived by special messenger, the day after the battle! [19]

19. M. P. Pogodin, *Zhizn' i trudy,* ed. N. O. Barsukov (St. Petersburg, 1888–1910), XIII, 182–83.

One of the causes of failure was that the complicated attack was not synchronized, for Soimonov, told to begin his drive at 5:00 A.M., was much ahead of Pavlov, whose forces did not move until 6:00. When Pavlov's regiments arrived at the site of the bridge, it had not been built, perhaps because Dannenberg had instructed Pavlov to have it constructed. Hence the 11th division was held up for an hour, while Soimonov's forces were locked in mortal combat with the British. Soimonov's reserves were in the rear under General Zhabokritskii, who had been ordered to wait for instructions. But as Soimonov had been killed and his subordinates had been put out of action, no orders came. Dannenberg, ordered to remain with Pavlov's troops until they joined with Soimonov, could not send them into action, and Menshikov, who was well in the rear, took no real part in the action. Thus the British had an hour's respite during which they could regroup their units and bring up reinforcements.

Finally Pavlov's regiments reached the summit, where they merged with Soimonov's units. Zhabokritskii sent the reserve regiments up also, and Popov directed them straight ahead to entrench on the central British position. But when the composite division began to fight, Dannenberg diverted it from the general line of advance and sent it to a most unadvantageous position, when it should have supported Pavlov's forces. He also failed to bring up the artillery until the last minute. Thus, according to Colonel Popov, "General Dannenberg by his orders ruined our attack; the commander-in-chief [Menshikov] at the decisive moment was not on the field of battle." Dannenberg failed to attack the left of the British line, and instead concentrated on the very difficult terrain on the British right. He also failed to use the composite division for a crucial period when Pavlov was struggling to hold the key position that his regiments had taken. 'Thus in the second phase of the fight," Popov commented, "the possibility of success was permitted to slip away." [20]

In the meantime the Chorgun force of 22,444 (sixteen battalions of infantry, as well as eighty-eight guns and fifty-two squadrons of cavalry), played no part in the combat, although it had enough strength to play a significant role. Also, probably from carelessness, no one thought to throw in the force of four thousand men, with considerable artillery, that stood idly by on McKenzie Hill throughout the battle

20. Popov, "Zapiski," *RS,* XXI (1878), 510–11.

to repulse the Allies if they should attack there.[21] As it turned out, there was no danger of an Allied attack and these troops could have been usefully employed in the main battle. If the Chorgun force had also been used, it is highly probable that the battle of Inkerman would have resulted in a great Russian victory.

The Russians also were operating under difficulties that even better generals could not have eliminated. The terrain was against them, for to reach the enemy their troops had to climb up steep heights, either by the Careening Ravine from the city, or, as in the case of Pavlov's force, by steep roads that led from the valley of the Chernaia river to the heights. Even Prince Gorchakov and Liprandi of the Chorgun detachment would have had to attack the enemy on the Sapun-gora or on the fortified hills around Balaklava. And even when the 10th and 11th divisions reached the heights held by the British, they found little room to deploy, but were confined by the ravines to narrow areas where they offered easy targets for the British. The Russian artillery, so important for supplying needed firepower, could not easily follow the infantry, for each position was separated from the next by deep gullies, which caused costly delays while positions were changed under deadly enemy fire.[22] The British, who were entrenched on the field of battle, had no such problems; their reinforcements and the French troops who came to their aid arrived by relatively easy approaches that did not hamper their movements.

Finally, the firepower of the Russian forces was greatly inferior to that of their opponents. As a result of the ingrained scorn for the bullet and trust in the bayonet, the Russians used smoothbore muskets, which had an effective range of only one hundred paces or less, while both opposing armies used the Minié ball, which greatly increased the range and effectiveness of their fire. Totleben states that in the decisive actions the British small-arm fire was much more destructive than the artillery fire.[23] And since during much of the battle the Russian troops had little or no artillery support, they were compelled to rely on short-range musketry and the bayonet, which was apparently the chief cause of the far greater Russian casualties compared to those of their adversaries.

Thus it is impossible to escape the conclusion that the Russians

---

21. Totleben, I, 423; Popov, "Zapiski," XXI, 514.
22. Andriianov, pp. 56–58.
23. Totleben, I, 436.

had little chance of success in this battle. The orders for it were hastily drawn up and far from clear and precise, with little done to explain to the troops or the commanders what was wanted. The plan was theoretically excellent, but it was very complicated and called for careful coordination of the attacks, which was sadly lacking, for Pavlov's force was delayed by the fiasco over building the bridge, Dannenberg could do little to synchronize the actions until the battle was half over, and Menshikov, the commander-in-chief, did nothing at all during the action.

The Russians fought bravely, in spite of their handicaps, repeatedly pushing the British back and forcing their way to the heart of their position. At length, after Pavlov's battalions came up and Zhabokritskii's division reached the scene, the English army was on the brink of ruin. But the delay in bringing up the reserves and the artillery, the crowding together of the Russian forces between the ravine and the river, made it impossible to bring their full strength to bear. In addition, the failure to make use of the Chorgun detachment, and the neglect of the troops and guns on McKenzie Hill, prevented success. In contrast to this ineffective use of manpower, Bosquet sent almost his whole force to rescue the British and did much to decide the outcome.

In the last stage of the battle, when Dannenberg had been able to take command, he displayed much activity and, in spite of his error in diverting Pavlov's troops to the wrong spot, did well. He maintained liaison between the various units, sent them where they were needed, organized flank attacks, and strengthened weak units. When his weary forces began to falter and their ammunition had been exhausted, he sought urgently for reserves, but Menshikov could not provide them and hence, at 1:00 P.M., Dannenberg reluctantly gave the order to retreat. Some of his subordinates were convinced that he sought death, for he had two horses killed under him and he repeatedly risked his life. He regulated the movement of the retreating troops. When the French tried to cut off some artillery units, Russian infantry charged and saved the guns.[24] The remark of the usually knowledgeable Colonel Men'kov in his diary that during the battle Dannenberg did nothing sensible [25] seems to have been unfair.

In this vital battle Prince Menshikov did little to achieve success,

24. Andriianov, pp. 83–84.
25. Tarle, *Gorod Russkoi Slavy,* p. 73.

for, as at the battle of the Alma, he gave no effective leadership. While he did provide an intelligent plan for the battle of Inkerman which, properly explained to the commanders and coordinated from above, should have brought success, it was vague as to details. Also he made no effort to synchronize the actions of Soimonov and Pavlov, to say nothing of Gorchakov of the Chorgun force. A capable commander-in-chief should have done much to eliminate the confusion and bring Soimonov's reserves into battle in time and in the right place. Moreover, no one—not even Menshikov—seems to have taken steps to move the powerful Russian artillery to support the infantry, which was winning almost entirely with the bayonet, at terrific cost. Although others were remiss in this respect, it was Menshikov's responsibility to see that the battle was fought properly. This he did not do.

Menshikov also must bear the blame for neglecting to have General Liprandi, in charge of Gorchakov's Chorgun command, use his infantry and artillery to probe for weak spots in the long Allied flank, which could have been done with enough vigor to prevent Bosquet from sending almost his whole command to rescue the British from disaster. This action would have been costly, but it probably would have won the battle and with it the war. As commander-in-chief Menshikov had full responsibility for controlling and guiding the Russian army, but he stayed in the rear and did nothing, while the army suffered defeat. His treatment of General Dannenberg also was unwise, for he denied him any power to act until the forces of Soimonov and Pavlov had joined. While Dannenberg was not a successful commander, he at least could have given some unity and cohesion to the Russian attack and brought the artillery into play to a greater extent. But Menshikov neither gave Dannenberg any real authority nor used his own to snatch victory from the jaws of defeat. His sole excuse for failure was that his soldiers had not fought with sufficient courage—although the British and French emphasized their stubborn determination, in spite of the terrible losses that they suffered.

Thus the blame for the defeat at Inkerman must above all be assigned to Prince Menshikov, with somewhat less to Dannenberg and Prince P. D. Gorchakov. On looking further, however, one sees that the Russian army had more than its share of incompetent generals, with Field Marshal Paskevich heading the list, and with Nicholas I also at fault. It also becomes clear that the whole military system, with its emphasis on massed bayonet attacks, its scorn of accurate musketry, its distrust of military scholarship and reliance on practical experience, as well as its training the cavalry for glittering parades and reviews rather than for scouting and outpost duty, was to blame. The Russians' artillery was very good and their engineers were excellent in siegecraft, mining, and fortification, but in the main the Russian army used tactics and weapons that were out of date, and it was this antiquated system that produced the incompetent commanders and the inferior weapons that caused the defeat at the battle of Inkerman.

As a result of this encounter the Russian soldiers firmly believed that they could stand up to the French and British troops, even with their inferior weapons. Their confidence in their commanders, however, had vanished, and with rare exceptions they fought the rest of the war behind their fortifications. The Russians now felt that they could not end the war by driving the foe into the sea, although they still felt that they could outlast them and win a stalemate. The struggle continued, bloody and unrelenting, until late in 1855.

The Allies also had lost some of their illusions, for on the eve of the battle of Inkerman they had still expected to renew the bombardment for a few days and then storm the fortress once and for all. But the loss of generals and field officers, to say nothing of noncommissioned officers and privates, had been so severe, and the closeness of a shattering defeat so imminent, that on November 7 the British army could not take offensive action. A grand council of war met, with both French and British generals present, to consider the scheduled plan to assault the fortress at Sevastopol. Lord Raglan still wanted to go ahead with it, but Canrobert was decidedly against it, as he held that the Allies were too few and the Russians might again attack their rear. Canrobert insisted that they must stay on the defensive, strengthening their position, until reinforcements should come. While Raglan was strongly opposed to this program, he had to accept it, "as the English army now was reduced to a little more than 16,000 bayonets." [26] Several of the British generals were so dismayed by the battle of Inkerman that they feared that the Russians would renew their attack and drive them into the sea. Sir George Lacey Evans, an experienced soldier, was one who advocated lifting the siege and evacuating, and the Duke of Cambridge took a somewhat similar posi-

---

26. Guérin, II, 1–2; Calthorpe, I, 398–99.

tion. Sir John Burgoyne, the noted engineer, was another who felt that the British position in the Crimea was very precarious. In fact, the British, while the victors in the battle, were by no means sure that they had won and they were deeply moved by a realization of the calamity that they had narrowly escaped.[27]

Similar feelings existed in London, for even before Inkerman Lord Clarendon wrote to Lord Cowley in Paris that he feared that with winter approaching the Allied position would be precarious, and when winter brought the military operations to an end, how could they reembark? While the British had reembarked at Corunna in Spain, he said, their position in the Crimea was vastly more difficult than it had been there. And after Inkerman he wrote in despair: "Everyone is downhearted about the victory (if it was one) and feels that another such triumph, or another such attack, would finally smash us, and then will come the monster catastrophe—a horrible compound of Afghanistan and Corunna." [28]

The Allied discouragement after Inkerman was greatly intensified by the logistical problem, for the British found it impossible to supply their troops in the trenches. The harbor at Balaklava was small and remote from the main British positions, so that all supplies had to be transported up a very difficult dirt road for a distance of eight miles to the front line. The road remained unimproved, and no significant stores of provisions were accumulated at the divisional camps. Worst of all, horse transport was impossible, for the hay and grain for the animals remained at the port, while the horses starved on the upland heights and died in great numbers. Even cavalry horses were used to haul supplies, but they too died. Suddenly calamity struck, for on November 14 (N.S.) a hurricane destroyed all tents and temporary shelters and wrecked or sank numerous ships carrying essential cargoes. One ship went down with medical supplies and seven hundred tons of warm clothing for the troops. Since little had been done to accumulate supplies at the army positions facing Sevastopol, the regiments soon found themselves forced to live on greatly reduced rations which, because of lack of fuel, they often were unable to cook. To make matters worse, the miserable soldiers had to stand guard in trenches filled with mud or water and had no proper shelter to return

27. Calthorpe, I, 385, 400; Camille Rousset, *Histoire de la Guerre de Crimée* (Paris, 1878), I, 395.
28. Wellesley, p. 63.

to when off duty. As the storm brought fierce winds and torrents of rain, followed by snow and intense cold, their clothes and boots were almost always wet. In addition, the soldiers had to carry up all supplies from Balaklava over roads that were "nothing more than deep tracks of mud, perpetually blocked by the carcases of animals that [had] died on the way. . . ." Calthorpe described the soldiers as "the care-worn, threadbare, ragged men, who form the staple of the English forces in the Crimea. . . ." [29] Because of the terrible privations, there were increasing desertions to the Russians. Those who remained fell sick in increasing numbers, and since most of the hospital tents had been carried away in the storm, most of the sufferers had to be sent, with a minimum of care, to the base hospitals at Constantinople, where the medical system had completely broken down.

Balaklava had become a pesthole, filled with dead and dying Turks, crowded into hovels without the least pretence at sanitation and in the last stages of scurvy, typhus, and cholera. "The sick appeared to be tended by the sick, the dying by the dying," said Calthorpe. By the end of 1854 there were 3,500 sick in the British camp at Balaklava, with about one hundred more stricken every day. As a consequence, the strength of the regiments was greatly reduced: the 63rd Regiment had only seven men fit for duty; and on January 7, 1855, the 46th had only thirty. The crack Scots Fusileer Guards had only 210 men on parade—less than one-seventh of their normal strength. [30] This desperate situation continued until the winter ended in February and the army could dry out. Also, in January, a contractor, using labor from England, built a railway from Balaklava to the army lines, which practically solved the logistics problem. Until then, however, the condition of the British army in the Crimea was deplorable and, with the loss of veteran soldiers and officers, its fighting qualities never returned to their previous high level.

The French also suffered from the storm of November 14, since their shelter-tents were blown away and, according to Calthorpe, four wooden huts used as hospitals collapsed on the wounded. But their military organization was able to overcome the worst effects of the disaster, and since they had good ports close to their military position, they had no logistical problem like that of the British.

The Russians apparently were not badly affected by the great storm,

29. Calthorpe, I, 408–43.
30. Russell, pp. 192–97.

since they possessed the city of Sevastopol, with its forts, barracks, and other buildings and because simple huts had been constructed to provide shelter for their field army, thanks to the skills of the soldiers and the resources of the area. Their logistical problems, however, were much more severe than those of the British and the French and they grew worse as the war progressed.

Before the Allied landing in September 1854 the Russian army had forces of less than fifty thousand in the Crimea, with an administrative structure to match. There was a small Provisions Commission to handle food problems, but it had little authority and no official with authority to act. Since the local officials did not expect an Allied invasion, they took no steps to accumulate provisions or to form wagon trains. The regiments in the Crimea had only the usual supply wagons for their own local needs. Because the peninsula produced little but grapes and cattle, almost all the provisions and forage needed by the greatly enlarged army had to be hauled in from neighboring provinces of southern Russia. Hay was essential to feed the thousands of draft animals that were brought in, but the army could obtain only a fraction of what it needed, chiefly in remote regions. To make matters worse, the Cossacks and foraging parties of cavalry looted the estates, consuming what they liked and wastefully destroying cattle, carriages, and other goods.

Fortunately for Prince Menshikov, General Prince M. D. Gorchakov, learning of the lack of all system for provisioning the Crimean army, hastened to send him three half-brigades of one thousand wagons each. These half-brigades—one of horse-drawn wagons and two of oxen—took in soldiers' biscuits and grits for the troops in the Crimea. Two more half-brigades were organized in neighboring provinces and entered the area in November 1854. Finally, Gorchakov sent in one more unit of ox-carts, bringing the total to six thousand wagons. But the movement of provisions was very slow. The animals, often poorly fed, were worn out by the heavy work on the bad roads and did not live long. By December 21 there were only two thousand left. Gorchakov now ordered the formation of four more units for March 1, 1855.[31]

To deal with the administration of supply problems in the Crimea Gorchakov sent his highly experienced Intendant General, F. K. Zatler, who managed to bring some order out of the chaos. Zatler was

31. Totleben, I, 666–69; Men'kov, I, 248–49.

able to set up an intendancy for the Crimean Army, with Menshikov's assistant, Colonel Wunsch, as intendant. Under him some of the worst evils diminished, and later on Zatler himself became intendant. But the prices for hauling supplies increased sharply, with the cost of hay soaring to unheard-of heights. To make matters worse, in May 1855, a joint British and French expedition penetrated the Sea of Azov, bombarding cities, burning shipping, and destroying great quantities of supplies. While these actions did not stop the flow of provisions and fodder to the Crimea, they made it much more costly and difficult.

Hay remained a crucial problem throughout the campaign, for on it depended the lives of the draft animals, who supplied the needs of the army. Dr. N. I. Pirogov, who did a tour of duty in the late months of 1854, wrote:

> The whole road . . . was crowded with transports of wounded, guns, and forage. Rain was pouring down as if from a pail, the sick, and among them amputation cases, lay two and three in a wagon, groaned and shivered from cold; and men and animals scarcely moved in mud to the knee; dead animals lay at every step; out of deep pools protruded the swollen bodies of dead oxen, which burst with a crash; and at the same time one heard the cries of the wounded, and the cawing of predatory birds, flying down in whole flocks to their prey, and the shouts of tormented drivers, and the distant roar of the cannon of Sevastopol.

All this aroused in him justified fears for his future patients.[32]

In the light of the problems of hauling and storing provisions, it is not surprising that there were reports of moldy biscuits issued to the troops. On December 2, 1854, Menshikov wrote to Gorchakov that three convoys of biscuits sent from the Southern Army had turned out to be so spoiled that even after superficial sorting the food could not be used.[33] This kind of waste apparently was not a unique phenomenon.

The feeding of the numerous cavalry and artillery horses in the Crimea was another insoluble problem, for the intendancy was completely unable to provide the vast quantities of hay that were needed. The result was that the army avoided trouble by a dishonest bargain

32. N. I. Pirogov, *Sevastopol'skie pis'ma i vospominaniia* (Moscow, 1950), p. 148.

33. A. S. Menshikov, "Oborona Sevastopolia. Pis'ma," *RS,* XII (1875), 318; Fedor Zatler, *Zapiski o prodovol'stvii voisk v voennoe vremia* (St. Petersburg, 1860), I, 239–40.

with the commanders of the regiments whereby the latter accepted payment in cash at extraordinarily high prices, for which they assumed the feeding of their animals. The food used for the horses was sailors' biscuits, with chopped scrub oak leaves for roughage. The commanders could pocket large sums from the amounts issued, and if the animals died of the substitute for hay they could be replaced.[34]

Prince Gorchakov was much troubled by the lack of transport facilities and the price of hay, which had risen to one ruble, sixty kopecks per *pud* (thirty-six pounds). He told the army units going to Sevastopol to buy wagons and oxen and to haul in what they could, and they could then slaughter the oxen for beef, which helped to keep the cost down. In addition, during the warm months a great amount of mowing took place in the Ukrainian provinces, which furnished hay at a cost of twenty-five to thirty kopecks per pud. But until the oxen could be fed grass en route, it was useless to send in wagon-loads of hay, for the animals would eat it all before they arrived. During the warm months, however, the grass grew and the roads improved greatly, and by drafting over 125,000 peasant wagons it proved possible to keep the army supplied and able to defend itself.[35] The cost of these emergency measures, which was extremely high, fell heavily on the population of the southern provinces, for few of the oxen survived a summer's hauling and many of the drivers died of disease and privations. While the provinces neighboring on the Crimea experienced almost no enemy action, they suffered severely from the losses of peasants and animals in hauling supplies.

A shortage of water was another difficulty that the Crimean Army encountered, for in places the water table was 300 to 350 feet below the surface. In order to cope with it, in 1855 some 250 old wells were cleaned out or new ones dug.[36]

Much more distressing was the hospital situation, for when the Allies landed, the Russians had only the normal peacetime facilities on hand. The battles of Balaklava and above all Inkerman brought a grave crisis, for lying exposed to the weather were great numbers of sick and wounded. Late in October there were almost eighteen thousand patients, mostly in Sevastopol and the vicinity. There was a great shortage of buildings suitable for hospitals, for many of those

34. ———."Iz pokhodnykh vospominanii o Krymskoi voine," *RA,* VIII (1870), 2049–50.
35. Bogdanovich, III, 197–200; Zatler, *Zapiski,* I, 252–70.
36. Zatler, *Zapiski,* I, 248.

in Sevastopol were vulnerable to enemy fire, while in Bakhchiserai and Simferopol few structures could be used. As for moving the patients, they were hauled chiefly in narrow, jolting, springless wagons that had brought provisions, with two or three sufferers crowded together. Little provision was made for their care, except that state peasants and Mennonites took over as attendants for 1500 of the number, under the supervision of doctors and medical assistants.[37] Hospital equipment was woefully insufficient, as were the supplies of woolen trousers, boots, and overcoats.

The most dangerous lack, however, was the shortage of projectiles and especially gunpowder to fire them. The fortifications had a great number of cannon, as Totleben could draw on the almost endless resources of the navy. There was not, however, a large supply of powder, and while the number of cannon in the Russian works greatly exceeded that of the Allies, after the first bombardment the Russians always fired far fewer rounds than the enemy. Moreover, they had none of the huge mortars that the Allies used so effectively and also no heavy bomb cannon. As a result, as the winter ended, the Russians were inferior to their enemy in manpower and in armaments. During the period of relative inactivity Totleben had been able to strengthen the fortifications greatly and, by building dugouts and traverses (partitions between the individual cannon) had made the garrison much less vulnerable to hostile fire. But the logistical problem remained as bad as ever; thus, in spite of the urgent demands of Nicholas I for offensive action while the Allies were still in a weakened position, the Russians could not mount a successful attack to end the war.

After Inkerman Menshikov had completely abandoned the idea of a new offensive and was above all concerned about surviving the attacks of the Allies. One of his worst fears was that the supply of powder would be exhausted during the coming bombardments and that he would be forced to evacuate Sevastopol. During the first bombardment the Russian gunners had fired about ten thousand rounds and the reserves were running low. The commander made frantic appeals to St. Petersburg for more gunpowder and sent aides to all likely points to have the supplies on hand sent to Sevastopol. Prince V. A. Dolgorukov, the minister of war, sensing the gravity of the situation, sent his adjutants all over Russia to order the sending of reserve supplies

---

37. Totleben, I, 673–76.

to the Crimea. But the reserves were not large, and other areas also were threatened, while Russia's powder factories had a limited output. So, while convoys of powder began to move toward the threatened city, the amounts were not great and especially during the wet season it was impossible to transport them with any speed. Fortunately, during the winter months the Allies also were still in difficulty and there was no new full-scale bombardment until the end of March 1855. But even then the Russians could only fire about half as many rounds as the enemy.[38]

While the Russians still had substantial strength in the Crimea, the fact was that for them this area was one of the most difficult parts of European Russia in which to fight, for almost everything had to be delivered in wagons over hundreds of miles of very poor roads. On the other hand, once the British had their railway from Balaklava to their front lines, the Allies had no real problem in supplying their necessities in abundance. Moreover, Britain and France could furnish plentiful amounts of provisions and munitions, as their production was much greater than that of Russia, and in addition, they could draw on the resources of the whole world. The Russians, with a much larger population than their foes, could bring only a fraction of their strength to the Crimean battlefields.

---

38. Panaev, pp. 53–58; Dubrovin, *Materialy dlia istorii krymskoi voiny,* IV, 308–11.

CHAPTER 14. THE STRUGGLE FOR AUSTRIA

The new, violent phase of the conflict that the Allied landing in the Crimea ushered in did not by any means halt the diplomatic efforts of the great powers to bring about a realignment of forces. Above all, the contest centered on the position of Austria in the midst of the warring powers and Prussia. Buol and the emperor felt that to accept Russia's dominance of the Principalities and the Black Sea was intolerable and that only by siding with France and in part England could Austria throw it off. England, however, was very hostile to Austria, which could get the necessary support against its giant neighbor only from Prussia and the rest of Germany. But Prussia—especially in the person of Otto von Bismarck—hated Austria and looked on Russia as the essential shield against France.

Austria thus had numerous enemies and only France seemed friendly, although it could not be relied on. Under such circumstances, it would take all the skill of Count Buol to improve its situation and to avoid disaster. Its chief concern was that Russia, furious with Turkey, would strike out at the Ottomans by invading the Balkans and encouraging the Serbs, Bulgars, and Greeks to rise against Turkey. To prevent this eventuality, Austria was willing to go to war with Russia, provided that it could induce Prussia to protect its flank against the Russian masses. In order to restrain Austria from throwing itself into the arms of the French, on April 20, 1854, Prussia had signed a treaty with Austria promising to protect it if Russia attacked it, or in case it annexed the Principalities or invaded the Balkans. This limited support was enough to encourage Austria to threaten to attack the Russian forces in Bulgaria and the Principalities. Nicholas I, while enraged over Austria's "ingratitude," realized that it was in earnest. Hence in August 1854 he announced that the Russian forces would withdraw from Bulgaria and the Principalities to Russian territory.

While this announcement removed much of the danger to it from

Russia, Austria still felt naked and alone in a hostile world, and it decided to adopt the Four Points, sponsored by France, as the basis for restoring peace. The Russian protectorate over the Principalities would be converted into a five-power supervision, and joint action of the powers would ensure the free navigation of the Danube. The powers also would induce Turkey to grant equal religious rights to all Christian denominations. Finally, to satisfy England and weaken Russia, the Third Point provided that the Treaty of 1841 must be revised to give Turkey the protection of the Concert of Europe and to end Russian predominance on the Black Sea. Russia's response to this and consequently to the other provisions was justifiably hostile. On the other hand, now that Russia was withdrawing from the Principalities, Austria could demobilize and await the outcome of the Allied invasion of the Crimea. It did not, however, turn against France and Britain, for on August 8 it agreed to exchange notes with them, which promised that the war would be for limited aims only and that Austria would seek to obtain peace by diplomatic means. Austria disappointed the Allies by refusing to sign an alliance with them, but it felt that it had served the cause of peace by compelling Russia to evacuate the Principalities.

Austria at once sent the Four Points to St. Petersburg, saying that it would vigorously urge the Allies to make peace on this basis, with an armistice as the first step. Franz Joseph would halt his armies and demobilize, and if the Western powers insisted on continuing the war, they would be to blame.[1] Nicholas I, however, was very angry and Nesselrode had to reason with him at some length to prevent him from declaring war on Austria.

Prince A. M. Gorchakov, although less irritated, also was annoyed. He wrote to Nesselrode that he had been wrong in trusting Franz Joseph to restrain Buol, for the emperor was thoroughly under the latter's influence and that of Alexander Bach, the minister of interior, and both men hated Russia. He stated that Austria even seemed ready to defy Prussia and the Diet and to align directly with France and England. Buol no longer bothered to preserve appearances toward Russia. Gorchakov saw war with Austria as likely to come at any moment and believed that Buol and Bach were leading Prussia and Germany to succomb to the French yoke.[2]

1. Henderson, pp. 167–71.
2. Gorchakov to Nesselrode, Sept. 25/Oct. 7, 1854, AVP, f. Kants., D. no. 162.

In this contest to secure German support Prussia played an inglorious role, for the king, while he was hostile to Austria and sympathetic to Russia, feared to risk war with the West. His chief concern was that a British blockade could ruin Prussia's seaborne commerce as it had during the Napoleonic wars. The Prussians had no great dread of the French army, for with much of it committed in the Crimea and Algeria they were confident that their own fine army, fighting beside Russia, could deal with the French and humble Austria as well. But Frederick William was so dismayed at his prospects that he made overtures to the British cabinet through his strongly anti-Russian ambassador, Baron Christian von Bunsen, and appealed to Napoleon III through his envoy, Count Maximilian von Hatzfeldt, and through various ambassadors on special missions.

Prussia and Austria both wanted to maintain neutrality and to avoid war with Russia, but each distrusted the other. As Prussian representative to the Diet of the Germanic Confederation, Otto von Bismarck was aggressively hostile to Austria and quarreled fiercely with the Austrian Count Anton Prokesch von Osten, who was accustomed to lording it over the lesser German states and tried to dominate Prussia. Bismarck kept urging his government and the king to take a strong stand against Austria, which was now hand-in-glove with France and, so the envoy prophesied, would help to ruin Russia and thereby deliver the Germans over to a new Napoleonic bondage. He emphasized bitterly that Austria, in its dealings with Russia, regularly completed diplomatic negotiations without regard for Prussian interests. When Prussia, at Austria's behest, asked Russia to accept the Four Points in return for concessions by Austria, only to have Buol refuse to make any effort to secure these concessions for it, Bismarck, on August 15, declared that this was Prussia's opportunity to break away from the Conference of Vienna, which had assigned to Prussia the role "of a money-and-recruit depot" for the West. Instead, he said, "We worry about being alone and hold fast to Austria's coattails," while Buol's newspaper scolded them for impertinence, "convinced that we will still run after them like a leaderless poodle." [3]

This anguished protest produced no apparent result, and Austria continued to ride roughshod over Prussia's objections as Buol once more supported the West. The news from the Crimea doubtless encour-

3. L. F. Leopold von Gerlach, *Briefwechsel des Generals Leopold von Gerlach mit dem Bundestages-Gesandten Otto von Bismarck,* ed. Horst Kohl (Stuttgart, 1893), p. 183.

aged the Austrian inclination toward supporting the sea powers, for the glowing reports about the battle of the Alma and especially the spurious message that the French and the British had stormed a Russian entrenched camp, aroused the enthusiasm of Franz Joseph. On October 2 the emperor wrote to his mother that these defeats were a well-deserved punishment for Prince Menshikov. "I am awaiting at any moment the news about Sevastopol, touted as impregnable, where then the whole Russian fleet has been lost," he said. When, however, the news proved to be merely a "Tatar report," originating with some local resident, he wrote to his parent that he still was cheerful, for he believed that "if we proceed forcefully and energetically, this Oriental business can produce only advantages for us, for in the Orient lies our future, and we shall force back Russia's might and influence" to those limits from which it had advanced "to bring about our ruin." It was hard, he said, to have to turn against former friends, but it was necessary, for "in the East at any time Russia is our natural enemy." He added: "Above all, one must be an Austrian, and hence I rejoice . . . over the weaknesses that Russia now displays." [4]

Austria's congratulations to France for its victory on the Alma publicly revealed its feelings, for its rejoicing went far beyond the limits of official politeness. Drouyn de Lhuys promptly published the Austrian felicitations in the *Moniteur,* whereupon Gorchakov made official representations to Count Buol over their clearly partisan spirit. After stating that he could understand how Buol personally could be pleased that the victory might hasten the end of the war, Gorchakov said he regarded it as slanderous to assert that the Emperor Franz Joseph could rejoice at a reversal of the Russian army, which had recently shed its blood for the monarch's cause. He asked that his observations on this matter be placed before the emperor, but Buol stiffly refused to commit himself. [5] The resulting unpleasantness caused quite a strain on the relations between the two diplomats. Nicholas I, by no means dismayed by this exchange, ordered Nesselrode to telegraph Gorchakov to maintain the position he had taken and to show himself "perfectly indifferent to the ill will of Buol." [6]

4. Franz Joseph I, *Briefe Kaiser Franz Josephs I an seine Mutter, 1838–1872* (Munich, 1930), pp. 230–32.

5. Buol to V. Esterházy, Oct. 8, 1854, HHSA, X, 38.

6. Nesselrode to Gorchakov, tg., Sept. 30, 1854, AVP, f. Kants., D. no. 165.

From September on, Austria, guided by Buol and Bach, seemed to be moving more and more into the orbit of France and slipping closer to war with Russia. Its policy, however, was too ambitious to be realistic, for it sought to dominate northern Italy; to control all Germany and the German Bund; to keep Galicia and Bukovina; to dominate Hungary and Transylvania; to expand down the Danube and down the Adriatic to Serbia, Bosnia, and Herzegovina; to control the Principalities and become mistress of the Danube valley. But Austria lacked the manpower and the financial strength to pursue such a policy, and there was no unity among its ruling circles. Prince Klemens von Metternich, former chancellor and foreign minister, and the high nobility had a tradition of close friendship with Russia, which had supported Austria against revolutionary influences, and they felt that this principle was still valid. It was also advocated by the generals—Hess, Radetzky, Windischgrätz, Grünne, and others—who were determined to hold on to Austria's domains in Italy, Poland, Hungary, and the South Slav regions, and even hoped to annex Serbia, Bosnia, and Herzegovina. They regarded France and Britain as threats to Austria as did the emperor. Baron K. L. Bruck, minister of trade and finance and General Hess wanted to develop central Europe, in alliance with Prussia and Bavaria, and to develop the Danube valley and the Balkans, while retaining Russian friendship. Buol and Bach, however, were eager to throw off Russian influence and, in alliance with France, to dominate northern Italy, the Danube valley, and the Balkan peninsula. They quarreled fiercely with Bruck, Hess, and the other generals and Metternich and the nobility, who still believed in the value of Russia's friendship. Diplomats Hübner and Prokesch were fervently pro-French and wanted Austria to enter the war on the side of the Allies. The Emperor France Joseph, who was jealous of Russia, tended to side with Buol and Bach, although he was much opposed to war with Russia.

While in July 1854 Vienna had refused the treaty of alliance that it was about to sign, it still did not reject the French overtures, for it feared to be left alone to face Russian hostility. On the other hand, it realized that in a war with Russia it would have to accept severe losses, and if the Allies should lose in the Crimea (as almost happened at Inkerman), they might leave Austria to the mercy of Russia. More than ever the Austrians comprehended that in order to fight Russia they needed the support of all Germany, which Germany would give only if Russia were clearly the aggressor. The Austrians wanted a short, limited war, in which France and Britain would do most of the fighting and Austria would escape with minimal losses. If Germany could be enticed into fighting Russia beside France and Britain, that also might save Austria from catastrophe. The Austrian cabinet feared, however, that Austria would incur Russia's undying enmity if such an alliance took place.

Russia, however, did not want a full-scale war with Europe, for it would be very costly. While in the spring of 1853 France had seemed isolated and the tsar regarded both England and Austria as allies, now Russia's big task was to avoid a general war, which meant keeping Austria from joining its enemies. This goal, in turn, depended on encouraging Prussia and the middle German states to stay aloof from the allies and from Austria.

Nesselrode used the information that Gorchakov supplied to him from Vienna to carry out this program, informing the courts of Berlin, Munich, Stuttgart, and Dresden of "the undoubted intentions" of the Austrian government, so that they could decide what action to take.[7] Similarly, Gorchakov, while not bothering to call on Buol, used his time to "stimulate and fortify," with considerable success, the German diplomats he met in Vienna. As most of the lesser German courts did not want to have Austria drag them into bondage to France, Gorchakov's arguments found ready listeners. In addition, most of the Austrian generals were unhappy over Buol's actions, and discontent over the "National Loan" was rising, with many localities unable to meet their assigned quotas.[8]

Late in October 1854 Ludwig Count von der Pfordten, the Bavarian premier, who had been conferring for some time in Vienna, stated his views of Austria's position to Gorchakov. He believed that Austria did not want to make a real commitment to the sea powers, since it very much desired to stay out of war and feared that if it pledged support to them and then did not enter the war, it would be open to French charges of bad faith. Franz Joseph had reassured him that he keenly wanted to avoid war with Russia and had no territorial gains in mind. While he had to protect Austria's interests in the Principalities, he would view "their possession as a calamity." Pfordten was hopeful that Russia and the Germans could gradually move Aus-

7. Nesselrode to Gorchakov, Oct. 4/16, 1854, ibid., D. no. 162.
8. Gorchakov to Nesselrode, Oct. 8/20, ibid., D. no. 162.

tria in the desired direction by a cautious approach. Gorchakov, while agreeing with this assessment, felt that the German courts should not be too docile or weak, for then there would be no limits to Austria's arrogance. The Bavarian left Vienna in a mildly optimistic frame of mind concerning the results of his efforts, which he regarded as a "supreme effort to obtain peace, at a menacing moment." Gorchakov also was moderately hopeful.[9]

While Austria still seemed on the brink of war, Gorchakov believed that the emperor was not ready for it, especially as his generals were against it. The ambassador believed that if only the German states did not give in to Austria, they could restrain it. Prussia and the other Germans felt that Russian acceptance of the Four Points would be a starting point for an agreement among the German states, Austria, Prussia, and Russia. Gorchakov suggested that if the German states could get Prussia to propose the Four Points once more, it would probably do so courteously rather than peremptorily, and the proposal could be made a definite basis for negotiations instead of a starting point for additional demands. He suggested that if Prussia and the Confederation revived these proposals as indicated, it might be wise for Russia, rather than to reject them, to enter into negotiations with Berlin and the lesser states but with Austria only if it used an identical language.

Since Nesselrode's despatch to Ambassador Andreas Budberg at Berlin seemed to suggest this plan, Gorchakov felt authorized to discuss the matter with von der Pfordten. In Gorchakov's view, if Prussia and Germany should take this approach, there might be a chance of negotiation, and Russia could take part without loss of dignity.[10]

On the following day Gorchakov sent off a coded message to Warsaw, which was then wired to St. Petersburg, saying that Buol had suddenly become more reasonable, for Prussia had decided to declare its neutrality pure and simple and, with the rest of Germany, felt strong enough to make it respected. Prussia felt that the Four Points were sufficient guarantee for peace and should be the definitive bases for it, and it would undertake to get them accepted by Russia in suitable form. Vienna had kept this a secret. Buol and his associates were now beginning to hesitate, especially since England refused to approve a secret article of the French treaty of alliance in which Austria asked

9. Gorchakov to Nesselrode, Oct. 27/Nov. 8, 1854, ibid.
10. Ibid., Oct. 16/28, 1854.

for a guarantee of its holdings in Italy and Poland. France was willing to grant the request, but Britain refused on a legalistic parliamentary pretext.[11]

Buol's position of helmsman of the Austrian ship of state was certainly a difficult one, as shown by a lengthy proposal that he made to the emperor, in which he asked permission to speak on the political situation. The minister's first point was a veiled charge that Baron von Hess, in addition to protecting Austrian interests in the Principalities, had the special duty of preserving the best relations with the commanders of the belligerent powers and of steadfastly pursuing the same purpose as they were, for "a breach between us and the sea-powers would be the real triumph of Russia." Unless Hess held to this rule and acted honestly along this line, he would not be able to save the emperor grave embarrassment. Buol acknowledged Austria's difficult relations with the sea powers and the increasing distrust of his nation in Paris and London, much of which was caused "by the slanders and insinuations" from Berlin and the "quite singular conduct and talk of our higher military functionaries." Unless this intrigue were ended, he warned, the Allies might compel Austria "before the right time and against our will, to push into open war." [12]

Buol insisted that Austria could obtain the peace needed only in union with the maritime powers, and sulking would not bring it. If it should fall out with the sea powers, "in that case we have definitely lost our game and Prussia and von der Pfordten can rightly rejoice." If the Allies should still continue the war, Austria would suffer; if they should withdraw from it, they would occupy the Black Sea and abandon the Danube, in which case the peace with Russia would be made at Austria's expense, and even after the war, France and Russia could unite to punish Austria. Buol could suggest no other policy than cooperation with the West, "for every other leads to isolation or to the old dependence on Russia." He termed those like Metternich, who sought restoration of the close Russian relationship, "fanatics or hypocrites" and promised that out of the present confusion would come a political recovery, with Austria in a strong position, provided it took a firm stand in the present crisis.[13]

This appeal to His Majesty, which had an air of desperation, did

11. Ibid., Oct. 17/19.
12. Memorandum, Buol to Franz Joseph, Sept. 26, 1854, HHSA, XL, 48.
13. Ibid.

not meet with full approval, for, probably at his demand, Buol, in a routine talk with Gorchakov early in November, told him that he ardently desired to attain peace that winter, by means of conferences. Gorchakov responded that it would be easy to obtain a solution if it were honorable on both sides. In the same despatch Gorchakov informed his cabinet that he was in indirect but steady contact with Hess, whose calculations of "the expense of an open war" in contrast to the present situation had terrified the minister of finance. Franz Joseph, Gorchakov declared, knew of his rapport with Hess and encouraged it! The tide seemed to be turning away from the West, for Buol stated that he felt that the demarche of the king of Prussia was a suitable means of reaching an understanding.[14]

Apparently the weakness of the Allies revealed by the battle of Inkerman and the great storm in November convinced Buol that France and Britain would not win a speedy victory and that peace talks were in order. On November 4/16 Gorchakov reported that he had had a talk with Buol, who wanted to discuss politics. The Austrian mentioned the powerful influence of Russia in the East—at Constantinople, in the protectorate over the Principalities, and in the religious authority over the Orthodox of Turkey. Gorchakov admitted this, but said that it was natural, just as Austria was strong in Italy. Certainly Russia was a less dangerous neighbor there than industrial England would be or revolutionary France. As for the Principalities, they were more trouble than they were worth and Russia had no dishonorable intentions there. As for the religious question, he said that Russia would gladly sign a protocol that would give the Christians of the Balkans real civil and religious protection under a European guarantee. The guarantee, however, must be sincere—"une affaire de conscience—" for Nicholas would not give way on this vital matter. Even so, Russia would still retain great religious influence, for "each sheep will still come to its shepherd." There were several millions of Orthodox, and only a few score thousand Catholics in Turkey.

Gorchakov stated that his interview with Buol—his first after six weeks of intentional silence—was a big event. Both Hess and the emperor knew of it, and His Majesty himself came to Buol to hear his report of it, which indicated his real wish for peace with Russia.[15]

On November 5/17 Gorchakov informed his cabinet of his commu-

---

14. Gorchakov to Nesselrode, Nov. 2/14, AVP, f. Kants., D. no. 162.
15. Gorchakov to Nesselrode, Nov. 4/16, 1854, ibid.

nication to Buol of the tsar's decision to accept the Four Points. Buol said that the news would overjoy his master, since it represented a pledge of peace, a sign of hope for the return to good relations. He expressed fear, however, that Russia would insist on excluding the Western courts from the parleys, but Gorchakov urged that they be invited and if they should come, they should negotiate together; if not, Austria and Russia should confer. Buol believed the Western diplomats would come but would make improper demands, which he would be ready to oppose. The prince, however, said that they should not ask France and England to explain themselves in advance, any more than Russia should be asked to. This concession greatly reassured Buol, who hastened to carry the news to Franz Joseph. On this same day Gorchakov received a telegram from his court expressing the emperor's pleasure with his conduct during the preceding weeks.[16]

Not long after, Buol stated his doubts concerning the wording of the Russian acceptance, which he believed would differ from that of Austria and the Allies. Gorchakov took the position that the Four Points should be accepted only as a starting point for a peace conference and that their real meaning should be worked out during the conference. Vienna accepted this view. Britain and France, however, which wanted to punish Russia, regarded the Four Points as a check to their plans and intended to evade them by all means. Moreover Buol had adopted the Four Points against his will, Gorchakov averred, under pressure from Franz Joseph, as the best way to get the support of Germany, and if he could find a pretext to withdraw from this position he would probably do so, because of his great fear of a rupture with the West. Russia should avoid furnishing the pretext. Gorchakov found Buol greatly changed from the preceding day, for he now declared that the Russian formula differed so sharply from that of the West and Austria that he would have to consult with the English and French before deciding. Gorchakov sought to prove that there was no difference by comparing the two texts, but Buol merely talked in generalities without committing himself. He also tried to prove to Buol that with the peace of Europe at stake they should not quibble over the wording of the preliminaries, which were a mere starting point.

Gorchakov expressed his opinion to Nesselrode that, to avoid trou-

16. Gorchakov to Nesselrode, Nov. 15/17, 1854, ibid.; Nesselrode to Gorchakov, tg., Nov. 5/17, ibid., D. no. 165.

ble, Russia should accept the Austrian Four Points and persuaded Buol, after some fussing, to write out a new formula for Russia's acceptance, as follows: "The Imperial Court of Russia accepts the four propositions of Austria as points of departure for the peace negotiations." Gorchakov personally accepted the formula and sent it to his cabinet for approval. He advised adopting it, as it would clear the air and "halt Austria on its fatal tendency toward the Western powers."

The envoy told Buol that this would not be a surrender to the West, as the main thing was to avoid with honor a struggle with all Europe in the spring and to wreck the plans of the French and the British by removing Germany and Austria from their influence. Buol was much relieved to hear this and said he would oppose all further demands upon Russia and would interpret the Four Points in a moderate way. Also he declared that he had no further ties with the West and hence could firmly oppose its demands. To prove his good faith, Buol gave Gorchakov a copy of his despatch to George Esterházy at Berlin. He said that if the arrangement were adopted, Austria could reduce its army and pull it back from the Russian frontier, and Russia could then use its troops elsewhere. This would mean Austrian neutrality.[17]

Thus Gorchakov had reason to feel that he had achieved a great triumph which would lead to peace negotiations and bring an end to the war. Buol's assurances were most specific: he would oppose all further demands on Russia and would interpret the Four Points in a moderate way. He had no further ties with the West and would firmly oppose its demands. Austria would reduce its armed forces and remove its troops from the Russian frontier. Only if these declarations were false could Russia regard Austria as an enemy.

But Buol, it turned out, characteristically had been far from honest, for Austria had been negotiating with France and Britain for a new alliance ever since Russia had announced evacuation of the Principalities in August. When the Allies decided to invade the Crimea they realized that they needed Austrian support to confine large Russian forces that otherwise would be sent to Sevastopol. The Austrians, however, no longer felt need of the West, for Russia could not attack the Hapsburg domains when it was facing invaders in the Crimea.

17. Gorchakov to Nesselrode, Nov. 11/23, ibid., D. no. 163; Drouyn de Lhuys to Bourqueney, Nov. 22, 1854, HHSA, IX, 49.

But the Allied victory of the Alma and the false report of the fall of Sevastopol convinced Vienna that it would soon have to deal with the victors of the Crimea, who might vent their spite against Austria's position in Lombardy and Venetia. Austria had proposed the Four Points to Russia, which was greatly angered, but that was not enough to mollify the sea powers, and Buol pushed his emperor to accept a new treaty of October 1. Lord Clarendon was very bitter about the Austrian refusal to enter the war, but both he and Drouyn de Lhuys soon realized that the treaty was the most the Allies could hope for. In mid-October Vienna rejected a French counterproposal, although in moderate terms. It also threatened Russia by mobilizing its forces. Finally, on November 1 a new French draft was gladly accepted by London. This proposal provided that, if, as expected, Russia again refused the Four Points, the Allies and Austria should confer to realize their aims. The war not going well in the Crimea, for the bombardment was not a success, and Balaklava was only a limited victory. The Germans in the Bund were on the point of taking action contrary to the wishes of Austria and the West, and the battle of Inkerman was almost a disaster. In the meantime Nicholas I accepted the Four Points officially on November 20. Also Prussia agreed to protect Austria in the Principalities and to support it in the Diet. Moreover, in order to secure Austria's signature, France had to sign a convention guaranteeing its position in northern Italy during the war. Consequently, on December 2, 1854, Franz Joseph reluctantly accepted the treaty.[18]

The new treaty confirmed the Four Points as the basis for peace, although it also reserved to the signatories the right to make additional demands, and the signatories pledged not to make any agreement with Russia without consulting the others. Article V provided that if by the end of 1854 peace had not been established, the powers would confer to decide the best means "of achieving the object of their alliance," which, to the French, who had drafted the treaty, clearly indicated warlike measures on the part of Austria following an ultimatum to Russia. The preamble to the treaty called for ending the war as soon as possible "by restoring general peace" by negotiation. But the British were intensely against negotiation, which they "resisted to the last," their statesmen refusing to face the implications of the

18. Henderson, pp. 167–85.

documents that they had signed on August 6 and December 2. Tacitly they had been trying to deceive Austria and draw it into the war by agreeing to projects that they were sure the Russians would never accept. But as the Russians proved conciliatory by accepting the Four Points on December 2, the limitations that the British had accepted ceased to apply. The British regarded this treaty as a nuisance and wanted to postpone it until Sevastopol should have fallen.[19]

For the French, however, the Treaty of December 2 was a real triumph, for Napoleon's objective had been not the Holy Places in Palestine or control of the Black Sea but the breakup of the historic Russo-Austrian alliance, which had now been accomplished by isolating Russia through linking Austria with France. Thus the treaty represented a real diplomatic revolution. Napoleon, who was at dinner when he received news of it, ran at once to the empress and warmly embraced her. Baron F. A. Bourqueney received high praise for his role in negotiating the treaty and was awarded the Grand Cordon of the Legion of Honor. Count Vincent Benedetti, a leading French diplomat, wrote that the Treaty of December 2 had overturned everything and revealed a new horizon; the Holy Alliance was now dead.[20]

In Vienna the general public hailed the treaty, thanks largely to the tight control of the press by Bach and Buol, who had planned it. The strong pro-Russian party—the generals and the high nobility—was angry, for it still felt that Russia was a necessary bulwark for Austria and did not trust revolutionary France. Hübner and Prokesch felt that the treaty did not go far enough, for they wanted war with Russia. Buol, however, did not want to fight Russia but sought negotiations for a limited settlement, which would succeed if the powers were honest in their support of the Four Points. He wanted neither a war of nationalities nor any serious weakening of Russia. Rather, he hoped for a reasonable peace that would protect Austria's interests in the Balkans. What he did not realize was that he had gone too far and had infuriated Russia. The resulting enmity between the two powers continued until World War I, which resulted in the fall of the Hapsburg monarchy.[21]

To Gorchakov and the Russians this development came as a real shock, for the envoy knew nothing of it until Franz Joseph sent Buol

19. Ibid., pp. 184–85.
20. Ibid., pp. 185–86.
21. Ibid., p. 186.

to inform him of the treaty of alliance just signed by the three powers. France and England pledged themselves to be limited by the Four Points as bases of peace and Austria would remain linked to them until they had been actually made the bases of peace. The Emperor Franz Joseph insisted that his feelings and hopes remained unchanged and that in the treaty he sought only to limit the demands of the Western powers. He asked Gorchakov to present these decisions to his cabinet in their true light.

The ambassador sent word to Franz Joseph of his profound surprise, for he had just informed his court of the assurances of the emperor and Buol leading to an honorable understanding beneficial to both countries. He thought he had made peace possible; now he was faced by this treaty, which he could not understand or justify to the tsar. Buol tried to explain that by the treaty he had sought to limit the demands of the sea powers, for which negotiations had been in progress since August, and that it had been agreed on beforehand; it was only a coincidence, he said, that the acceptance of the treaty and Gorchakov's note of November 16/28 came at the same time. It had been a question of an immediate break with the Western powers, and he had to choose the lesser of the two evils.

Gorchakov's comments were biting, for he said that the treaty showed that the Western powers could get anything they wanted from Austria. Now that Russia had accepted Austria's conditions, he could not understand why Austria had acted as it had. How would Prussia and the Bavarian von der Pfordten feel about this? Buol replied that Austria could never count on an alliance with Prussia and Germany because Russia's influence in Germany was too strong. Hence they would be less valuable as allies than the West. He also said that the treaty would be one more step toward peace since it would limit the demands of the Western courts. Gorchakov said that he had to be distrustful because of the French interpretations of some of these proposals, and he expected that the article on the revision of the Treaty of 1841 would be close to that of Drouyn de Lhuys, "which would make any agreement impossible."

According to Gorchakov, the preceding day Bourqueney and West-morland had gone to Buol's office to demand the signing of the treaty, whose text had already been set and copies made. Buol tried to turn them away, which caused a heated argument, during which the envoys threatened that if the treaty was not signed in twenty-four hours, they would at once demand their passports. Buol hastened to the emperor, warning him that if His Majesty would not agree, he would have to resign. So the emperor authorized Buol to sign.

Gorchakov stated that this incident showed the weakness of Austria, while Russia remained strong and unchanged. The conferences would take place, and the Four Points *alone* would be discussed. He begged the tsar not to withdraw his authorization to enter the conferences on the bases agreed on as the point of departure. If the other powers tried to lead Russia into improper directions, he would only need instructions to report His Majesty's decision. Unfortunately, this event would require new sacrifices by Russia, but Russia's loyalty and devotion would overcome the trials. Russia was strong and would survive.[22]

On December 3 Emperor Franz Joseph wrote a letter to Napoleon III, in which he stressed the value of their treaty of alliance and expressed the belief that, like himself, the emperor of the French wanted the return of a solid peace. The recent Russian overtures seemed to the writer to open an honorable way to achieve this end. Louis Napoleon's words to him, he said, were a guarantee that France would negotiate, and the Russian emperor was ready to treat on the basis of the Four Points as they had been formulated. He was also counting on Napoleon III to induce Queen Victoria not to refuse this gesture of conciliation. If the talks should fail, through the fault of Russia, the glory of Louis Napoleon would not have suffered. It would then be time for the energetic employment of the united forces of the alliance to bring about the solution of the crisis. He hoped for complete success.[23]

This alliance was Buol's chief act, toward which his whole policy had tended. He had turned steadily against Russia and when the clash came, he did not try to compromise with Russia but to humble it. This, as Metternich realized, gave rise to the Russo-Austrian conflict, which led on to the climactic events of 1917 and 1918. Buol lacked foresight and vision. Concentrating on the immediate present, he had little perception of the future. The German press was very favorable to him, for Prussia was now secure, and Austria was allied with France and Britain. The war seemed about to end, but if not, Austria had strong support.

22. Gorchakov to Nesselrode, Nov. 20/Dec. 3, 1854, AVP, f. Kants., D. no. 163.
23. Letter, Franz Joseph to Napoleon III, Dec. 3, 1854, HHSA, IX, 49.

Buol, however, had caused a diplomatic revolution, which had angered much of the army and the government. The emperor was not completely with him and was unwilling to be severe with the pro-Russians. He later felt that the break with Russia had been a great mistake, for Nicholas I was bitter over his "ingratitude." This was what had troubled Metternich. Austria thus had lost its two best allies (Prussia as well as Russia) and gained no permanent ones in their place. A Franco-Austrian alliance might have worked if Austria had insisted on a compromise with Russia, but the French demanded a triumph, and the Franco-Austrian alliance was infirm. France was too unstable to be a loyal ally.[24]

Prussia also was thoroughly alienated, for its sympathies were with Russia and it regarded Austria as arrogant and deceitful. Whereas earlier Russia had been haughty and domineering and had disregarded the interests of Prussia, after its withdrawal from the Principalities it had repeatedly taken steps toward peace. Austria, on the other hand, had disregarded German interests by aligning itself with France, the enemy of the Germans, and threatening war against Russia, the shield against revolution. Bismarck continued to preach to the Bamberg states that although Austria was playing fast and loose with them, at the "intimidation session" of September 30 they had all "put the chair before the door" and Prussia had found that it could not cooperate with them. Now, after the Treaty of December 2, they came to him to beg him to rally with them around a policy opposed to the treaty, for their sympathies were all with Prussia. His response was: "Very fine, but what can I do with sympathy?"[25]

Finally, on January 25 Prussia took a strong stand in the Committee of the Bund for firm opposition to French demands for the right to march across South Germany. Bismarck argued that to prevent this march, Prussia should demand mobilization of two army corps of the Bund and two Prussian corps. He actively lobbied among the delegates of Saxony, Wurttemberg, Mecklenburg, and Bavaria for support of this resolution. "If we do not grasp the helm of the German ship with decisive initiative," he said, "it will be driven by the wind of Austrian intimidation and the Austrian current into the French harbor, and we shall be in the position of a cranky ship's boy on

24. Henderson, pp. 187–89.
25. Gerlach, pp. 208–09.

it." [26] Shortly thereafter the envoy mentioned a letter from Foreign Minister Baron von Manteuffel, who agreed that if the French threatened to advance, Prussia should make a strong counterdemonstration, although he objected to Bismarck's suggestion of a mobilization of Prussian forces in answer to a French massing of troops. Bismarck regarded this decision as unfortunate, since it would show caution and indecision, which probably would bring the Austrians and the neutrals to lose respect for Prussia. "If, however, they are convinced that Prussia is determined to stand fast," he said, "they will not try anything but will remain quiet."

Austria was still trying to win over the lesser German states by frightening them with talk of an Austro-French military convention and a march by 200,000 French troops into Bohemia, decay of the Bund, and of a new redistribution of German territories. Also, there were all sorts of rumors, inspired statements, and even reports to the German princes declaring that Prussia was on the point of adhering, on Austria's urging, to the Western powers, so that the lesser states that stood behind Prussia would only gain the enmity of Austria and the sea powers for their pains. Bismarck asked General Ludwig von Gerlach, adjutant to King Frederick William IV, to take steps to help defeat this insidious pressure.[27]

Bismarck continued to counterattack, preaching that Prussia would not give in to Austria and to France, for it had a powerful army and, with help from Russia and the middle states, would be more than a match for Austria and any troops France could bring across the Rhine. He reminded his audiences how the Germans had fared under French domination after Austerlitz and Jena. He declared firmly that, in spite of the wavering of his king, Prussia would not adhere to the Treaty of December 2, which would be a sign of weakness. His efforts finally achieved success, for he had gained the confidence of the leaders of the Bamberg states. In the great debate in the Diet on Austrian Eastern policy on February 7, 1855, in spite of the threats and rumors from the Austrians and the adherents of France, the other Germans, with few exceptions, voted for Prussia as their leader. Bismarck had taken the lead in opposing Austria and France and he had become the bulwark against Austria.[28]

26. Ibid., pp. 224–25.
27. Ibid., pp. 227–28.
28. Ibid., 243–44.

Since his schemes for German aid—Prussian adherence to the Treaty of December 2 and demands for mobilizing federal contingents of troops against Russia—proved impossible, Buol made even less promising moves. In December 1854 General Hess, the Austrian chief of staff, who was very eager to avoid Austrian involvement in a general war against Russia, demanded the mobilization of 200,000 Prussians in six weeks and the delivery of two federal army corps to the armies of Prussia and Austria. With wide backing from the other German states, Prussia completely rejected this proposal.[29] Thereupon, apparently hoping to frighten Russia into making peace, Buol issued confidential circulars to several of the German states asking for federal mobilization against Russia, inviting the states to make secret alliances with Austria and to place part of their armies under Austrian command in case of war. In return, Austria would guarantee their territories and give them a share of any gains resulting from the war. The Germans almost unanimously rejected these schemes, and when the secret overtures to join Austria against Prussia leaked out, the latter had grounds for charging that Austria was trying to destroy the Germanic Confederation. Thus Prussia's position as leader of the anti-Austrian forces became stronger than ever, and Buol quickly abandoned the whole effort, including the call for German mobilization. As a result of Buol's scheming, Prussia turned against Vienna, calling for federal mobilization against *all* menaces to Germany from both East and West. This move was above all directed against France, to show that Austria could not drag the Germans after it. Thus Prussia, in spite of its flighty king, had gained greatly in prestige, and since it was pro-Russian, Russia's position was considerably improved.[30]

In the meantime the Russian cabinet on November 13 had authorized Gorchakov to accept the Four Points without comment, except to reserve the right of interpretation, as a starting point for negotiations. The controversy centered on the Third Point, which provided for the revision of the Treaty of 1841, to be carried out "with the purpose of maintaining the European equilibrium." Inasmuch as Drouyn de Lhuys had already declared that this must mean the razing of the fortifications of Sevastopol and a limitation of the Russian Black Sea Fleet to four ships of the line, as well as a guarantee of the Ottoman

29. Heinrich von Poschinger, ed. *Preussen im Bundestag, 1851–1859: Dokumente der königlichen preussichen Budestags-Gesandschaft* (Leipzig, 1882–84), II, 157–61.
30. Schroeder, pp. 239–42.

empire, Nesselrode reminded Gorchakov that his court could not accept such a proposal.[31]

When the plenipotentiaries met on December 16/28, Bourqueney read a much milder memorandum that he, Westmorland, and Buol had prepared, saying that the revision of the treaty "must have as its object the attachment of the existence of the Ottoman Empire more completely to the European equilibrium and put an end to the preponderance of Russia on the Black Sea." The application of this principle, however, would depend so much on the events of the war that it would not be possible to define it. Gorchakov, to the surprise of his colleagues, announced that he would consent to the phrase about attaching Turkey to the European equilibrium, but he refused to accept the obligation to put an end to the preponderance of Russia on the Black Sea. Bourqueney replied that the three courts did not intend to propose measures that would cause any dishonor to the emperor. His instructions, however, required him to insist on Prince Gorchakov's acceptance of the passage in question. After Emperor Franz Joseph had spoken on the matter, Gorchakov agreed to accept the Third Point, whose purpose would be to link the Turkish empire to the European balance. Gorchakov added that he would be ready to discuss at the formal peace conference the means that the three courts would propose to end Russia's domination of the Black Sea, on condition that he would never consent to anything contrary to the dignity of his master. Franz Joseph fortified Gorchakov's position by stating in an audience with him that "my name will never be attached to a condition which would wound his honor or his dignity."

In his despatch of December 22/January 3, 1855, Gorchakov explained his action by the fact that there were two ways in which Russian control of the Black Sea could be reduced: either by weakening the stronger power, or by strengthening the weaker one; either by improving its own forces, or by admitting others as a counterweight. The Emperor Nicholas had ruled out the first method, as had Franz Joseph. If, however, the Allies sought to obtain naval bases on Turkish territory, Russia would not oppose them, except to exclude Batum, which was very close to Russian territory, for reasons of security. Austria would probably agree to this arrangement, and it probably

31. S. M. Goriainov, *Le Bosphore et les Dardanelles* (Paris, 1910), pp. 95–97.

would not want France or Britain to have permanent bases on the Black Sea.[32]

Gorchakov's immediate solution to the problem was to refer it to his cabinet, for which the conference gave him a delay of fifteen days.[33] The Russian willingness to confer took the Allied representatives by surprise, for they had counted on a stern refusal, and indeed they did not want to negotiate. Napoleon and the French army felt that they had little to show for their efforts and wanted to fight until Sevastopol fell and they could have a glorious finish. Moreover, they could not give up their alliance with Austria, for then it would return to the Holy Alliance. Hence they sought to delay the parleys as long as possible. As for the British, Palmerston had insistently demanded stripping Russia of the Caucasus and the Crimea, along with Poland and Finland, and his prestige also required a victory. Thus only if France and Britain took Sevastopol could they sign a peace. Buol, however, was insistent on holding the conferences, and Prussia and the other German states demanded it. Also Russia, which was eager to bring an end to the war, was serious about the meeetings. But Drouyn de Lhuys urged the British to delay as much as possible, and Bourqueney told Lord Westmorland that the French did not want to hold conferences but had to, to placate Europe. Bourqueney even sketched out a whole series of delays to postpone the talks, so that France could have its victory, as well as the Austrian alliance. This dilemma so terrified Napoleon III that he devised a frantic scheme to go to the Crimea himself to win the war by an imaginative strategy.[34]

At the meeting of the delegates in Vienna on December 28 the French, British, and Austrian representatives presented Gorchakov with a statement of policy, which they insisted he accept. The Russian expressed pleasure at receiving a clear-cut statement of the issues, although he asked how Austria, which was not at war with Russia, could have the right to make demands beyond the Four Points—a query that caused Buol no little embarrassment. In his discussion of the Four Points as presented to him by Bourqueney, Gorchakov was

32. Ibid., pp. 97–99.
33. B. H. M. Harcourt, *Diplomatie et diplomates: Les quatre ministères de M. Drouyn de Lhuys* (Paris, 1882), p. 92.
34. Henderson, pp. 209–12; Evelyn Ashley, *The Life of Henry John Temple, Viscount Palmerston, 1846–1865* (London, 1876), II, 294–99; Friedjung, p. 133.

willing to agree to the substitution of a five-power protectorate over the Principalities for Russia's exclusive supervision. He merely objected to the phrasing of the demand. As for the free navigation of the Danube, he was ready to accept the proposal to put it under the rules of the Congress of Vienna concerning navigable rivers, although he refused to agree to territorial cessions in this connection. While he was willing to approve the proposal for revision of the Treaty of 1841 so as to bring the Ottoman empire more completely within the European balance of power, he insisted that he could not accept any provision that would infringe on the sovereign rights of his master, the emperor. Bourqueney and Westmorland delared that they had no such intention, but that their instructions required them to insist on Gorchakov's preliminary acceptance of the objective and the phrasing of the demand. As for the Fourth Point, Gorchakov stated that his emperor would accept a collective guarantee of the religious rights of all the Christians of Turkey, provided that the statement was seriously drafted and that it would offer effective protection. He termed this point the keystone of the treaty and a commitment for the honor and the conscience of all Christian Europe. This principle would not create difficulties, and the peace conference could frame the details of the provision.

During the discussion Westmorland had persistently tried to get Gorchakov to admit that he was rejecting the Allied proposals, but Gorchakov refused, saying that he had accepted several proposals and objected to others. Finally, Buol, who was clearly eager to avoid a breakdown of the talks, suggested that he refer the decision to his court. This the delegates agreed to, providing fifteen days for a reply.[35] All these machinations indicated that the British, especially, wanted the negotiations to fail so that they could continue the war without restriction; and that Napoleon III and his followers wanted to postpone the negotiations as long as possible so that the French could win a dazzling victory. Thus the outlook for a speedy negotiated peace was hardly promising.

CHAPTER 15. THE SEARCH FOR A POLICY

By the first weeks of 1855 all the warring powers, as well as Austria, were desperately trying to devise a diplomatic and military policy that would produce the desired outcome of the conflict that involved them. The Allies, as a result of the disastrous battle of Inkerman and the breakdown of the British military organization after the great November storm, could see no hope of a victory in the war in the foreseeable future. In fact, there seemed no possibility of the capture of Sevastopol by bombardment or by siege and assault, and the Allies had reason to fear a new Russian offensive against them.

The Russians, who had sustained terrible losses in the Inkerman slaughter, had been able to regroup and, while their wounded lacked proper care for weeks after the battle, on the whole, suffered much less from the winter weather than their opponents. But their logistical situation was so impossible that their troops often were not properly fed and their supply of powder and projectiles was always critical. Nicholas I, who learned from the English press and from deserters of the impossible situation of the Allied army, realized that this was a fine opportunity for an attack that would complete its ruin and repeatedly demanded of Menshikov that he should seize this chance. The prince, however, was terribly disheartened by the outcome of the Inkerman battle and could not bring himself to organize a new attack. He did, however, encourage Colonel Totleben, supported by Admirals P. S. Nakhimov and V. I. Istomin, to strengthen the defenses on a large scale by building new batteries and erecting traverses (banks of earth in a fort to protect gun crews from cross-fire). Totleben had dugouts built for the defenders and communications trenches, for safer movement of the reserves to and from the lines. The powder magazines of the batteries and bastions were made much more secure against enemy fire. He used abbatis (brush emplaced before positions with the ends of the branches sharpened to deter attackers) and installed fougasses (land mines with stones on top) and wolf pits to hamper attacking troops. Totleben believed strongly in active defense, which the Russians carried on by means of sorties, large and small. These sallies proved especially effective against the British, whose trench security measures were much less thorough than those of the French. He also used counterapproaches. At night two or three riflemen would move out in front of the defenses and dig riflepits, from which they could trouble the working parties of the besiegers. If the enemy attacked the riflepits, the guns of the fortress could pour a heavy fire on the attackers and drive them back. After the first riflepits were established, more were built alongside them and soon they formed a regular trench system in front of the works. In this way the Russians managed to impose a full check on the French approaches to Bastions 4 and 5, which in October had seemed certain to make them untenable and thus promised to destroy the defenses of Sevastopol. The British forces, who were positioned before Bastion 3 and the Malakhov and the other works extending toward the valley of the Chernaia river, made almost no progress during this period, as they were hastily fortifying their long-exposed flank extending along the Sapun-gora to Balaklava.[1]

Totleben also paid much attention to the Malakhov kurgan, although it was not really threatened at this time. He converted it into a full bastion (named after Admiral Kornilov), with walls, ditch, dugouts, and powder magazine, and large artillery emplacements. Unfortunately, he concentrated his attention on the city sector, which was under heavy attack by the French, and did not develop the defenses in front of the Malakhov. Before the Malakhov lay the Green Hill, which was the key to the sector. In this slack period it would have been fully possible to fortify this elevation, supporting it with batteries walls, and ditches so as to make it almost impregnable. Later on, when it was fortified, the work had to be done hastily, under heavy opposition from the French, who had moved into the sector. Consequently it was not possible to construct the fortification properly, and the defenders could not hold it.[2]

The employment of counterapproaches and sorties also later proved unwise, for after the French had gained superiority in artillery and

1. Totleben, I, 495–55; Auger, I, 152–54, 170–71; Popov, "Zapiski," *RS,* XXI (1878), 517–20; Bestuzhev, pp. 114–17.
2. Khrushchov, pp. 54–58.

manpower, they were able to capture a number of these positions built by the Russians and thus could advance their lines more rapidly. Originally foxholes before the bastions for scouts and sharpshooters, they had been very useful. Totleben, however, was overly ambitious and converted them into regular trench systems from which to fight. This conversion invited heavy French attacks, which cost the Russians dearly and eventually forced them to relinquish these positions, with nothing to show for the bloodshed they had endured. Many of the Russian soldiers felt that Totleben's counterapproaches opened the way to the enemy and enabled them to advance more quickly.

While the Russians engaged in much aggressive action in the first three months of 1855, they did not try another attack on the Allies comparable to the battle of Inkerman. Many of the secondary commanders realized that there was a fleeting opportunity for an offensive, and the enlisted men seemed to have plenty of fighting spirit, but no one proved ready to undertake any decisive action. The administration of the army in the Crimea, which was in chaos, made no significant improvement, and incompetence, corruption, and inertia made any successful move almost impossible. Menshikov, still in command, was thoroughly discouraged and lacking in confidence, and although the emperor repeatedly urged him to act, he could not bring himself to do so. Hence for two months he did nothing, giving the Allies a chance to reorganize and reinforce their armies.[3] The French and British fortified Eupatoria, their original base, and brought in large numbers of Turkish troops, backing the position with the guns of the fleet. Numerous rumors circulated that they were planning to drive from Eupatoria toward Simferopol, the inland transportation center on which Sevastopol's communications depended. Nicholas I, concerned over this possibility, repeatedly ordered Menshikov to attack, although he warned of an assault in the face of naval guns.[4] Menshikov, unwilling to assume his responsibility, ordered Lieutenant General Baron Wrangel, who was stationed near Eupatoria, to reconnoiter the fortress.

Wrangel and Colonel N. K. Batezatul, an able staff officer, surveyed the scene and advised against an attack, as the losses of the Russians would be heavy and the Allied fleet could force them out if they

3. Vasil'chikov to Men'kov, Dec. 27, 1854, as quoted in Men'kov, I, 244–45; Bogdanovich, III, 186, 214; Dubrovin, *Vostochnaia Voina*, pp. 348–54.
4. Dubrovin, ibid., pp. 357–71.

should take the city. General K. A. Khrulev also inspected the situation and agreed that it was hopeless. In secret, however, he reported to Menshikov that he would promise to take Eupatoria if he were given full command there. Hence Menshikov, after issuing an order opposing an attack, four hours later ordered Khrulev to destroy the town. Khrulev made careful, detailed plans for the action and for proper care for the wounded. According to Menshikov's aide A. A. Panaev, the assault was ruined by the desertion of a Polish soldier in a Russian outpost, who betrayed the Russian plans. In any case, the defenders had made effective preparations, putting water into the deep ditch surrounding their stronghold and installing heavy guns in the bastions. As a result, the Russian columns were not able to climb over the wall, and the naval guns of the defenders overpowered the Russian field artillery. Khrulev, realizing that the attack was a failure, halted it. The Russian losses were 768 men killed, missing, and wounded. The defenders lost far less.[5]

Khrulev's failure to take Eupatoria forced Nicholas I to realize that he could not hope for victories under Menshikov's command, for Khrulev was the best fighting general in the Crimea and had the devoted support of the soldiers, who appreciated his consideration and his ability to inspire them. The fiasco plunged Menshikov into deep despair, for well before this he had been profoundly pessimistic. The emperor did not hesitate to remove him from command and to replace him with Prince M. D. Gorchakov, whose troops had recently withdrawn from the Principalities. General Gorchakov and his staff arrived in the Crimea early in March 1855, confident of winning an early success.[6] The Crimean Army, however, received him with indifference, and Gorchakov himself soon realized that he had little chance of victory.[7]

The removal of Menshikov from the Crimea was the last important act of Nicholas I, for he died before Gorchakov took command. He had been greatly disappointed over the failure of his diplomacy and the defeats of his beloved army. These disappointments broke his spirit and, when he fell prey to a severe cold, his failure to take good care of himself caused it to turn into pneumonia, which soon proved fatal. He died on February 18 (O.S.), 1855. Although many people in western and central Europe expected that his death would change the course

5. Ibid., pp. 368–77; Men'kov, I, 273–83.
6. Khrushchov, pp. 76–77.
7. Schilder, *Graf Totleben*, I, 409–11.

of the war, this was not to be the case. His son, Alexander II, while a less rigorous man than his father, insisted that he would follow the latter's policies without change and was sharply hostile toward England, France, and Austria, all of which he regarded as enemies, and was cordial to King Frederick William of Prussia for having refused to turn against Russia under heavy pressure. When Napoleon III showed a willingness to make peace on moderate terms, Alexander was quick to reciprocate, although he never really trusted the emperor of the French, but he remained hostile to England and to Austria.[8]

The Russian army, failing to find a successful policy that would bring victory, settled down to improving its fortifications and troubling the efforts of the Allies. It did, however, achieve striking successes in its mine warfare before Bastion 4 in late 1854 and early 1855. Since his new batteries and lodgements in this area had halted the French drive against the bastion, Totleben suspected that the French would resort to mining to overcome their opposition. He began mine operations about mid-December, and by early January 1855, before a Paris periodical published a map of a mine system under Bastion 4, the Russians already had a network of mines. In spite of the fact that they had so few trained miners that they had to train their men as they worked, aided by ordinary infantrymen, and although they were handicapped by the lack of proper equipment such as ventilators, compasses for guiding the direction of the tunnels, and boring tools for use underground, the Russians did very well. They managed to use large numbers of men working in three shifts, and, unlike the French, they set off their mines with electric current, which was much more reliable than the fuses used by their opponents.[9]

In December 1854, after the Russian miners had reached a stratum of clay, they pushed a series of listening tunnels about thirty feet toward the enemy, starting from pits sunk from the ditch of the bastion and the neighboring batteries. Then they joined these tunnels by a gallery running parallel to the ditch, from which they could push on. By late January they had sunk twenty-two shafts and had 1,560 yards of tunnels around the bastion, as well as listening tunnels. On December 20 they heard the first sounds of enemy work at some distance. Gradually the enemy miner drew closer, and, on January

8. S. S. Tatishchev, *Imperator Aleksandr II, ego zhizn' i tsarstvovanie* (St. Petersburg, 1903), I, 144–45.

9. Frolov, colonel, *Minnaia voina v Sevastopole v 1854–1855 gg.* (St. Petersburg, 1868), pp. 4–9.

21, 1855, after packing the end of their tunnel with powder, a shield, and sandbags, they set off a great explosion, which caused flames and smoke to rise from the French trenches. The Russian artillery now fired on the French lines. Although Totleben expected the French to retaliate forcefully, only several days later they set off a blast well in front of the Russian position, which indicated that they were destroying their galleries, as they believed that they could not defeat the Russian miners.[10]

The Russians continued to advance their tunnels, occupying many of the French diggings and setting off several new explosions to prevent the French from moving ahead, while the latter contented themselves with setting off defensive mines to keep the Russians back. Both sides exploded several countermines, with each losing some miners. The Russians sank a deep shaft to a stratum of clay about forty feet down, where they developed tunnels and galleries, from which they hoped to blow up all the French mines, but the evacuation of the city took place before they could do this. They also built mines in front of the Schwartz Battery and the Malakhov kurgan, but because of the sudden end of the siege they were not used. On the whole, the Russians were very successful in their mining at Bastion 4; in August the French miners were still not as close to them as they had been in January.[11]

Totleben, the chief engineer in Sevastopol, has usually been given credit for the Russian mine operations. Actually he was so busy erecting new batteries and redoubts that he had little time for mining. Captain A. V. Mel'nikov apparently was in charge, for he lived and slept in the mines, training the men and closely supervising their work. He was in the gallery when the first French miner was detected and prepared the explosion that wrecked the French mines. He won the warm admiration of the soldiers, who nicknamed him "Oberkrot [Supermole] Mel'nikov." But he angered Totleben by setting off the blast without waiting for his chief and hence lost his chance for promotion. He also ruined his health by enduring the cold and dampness of the mines and finally had to take sick leave.[12]

10. Ibid., pp. 11–23.
11. Ibid., pp. 145–50; Weigelt, capt., *Osada Sevastopolia, 1854–1856* (St. Petersburg, 1859), pp. 245–46.
12. N. S. Miloshevich, *Iz zapisok Sevastopol'tsa* (St. Petersburg, 1904), pp. 33–34; A. Detengof, "Zabytyi geroi," *RA,* XLIII, pt. 2 (1905), 546–48; "Russkoe voenno-inzhenerskoe iskusstvo v oborone Sevastopolia v 1854–1855 gg.," in *Iz istorii russkogo voenno-inzhenerskogo iskusstva* (Moscow, 1952), pp. 128–30.

The fame of Totleben's achievement in laying out and constructing the fortifications of Sevastopol, almost *de novo,* became legendary. It was based quite as much on the unwilling tribute of the enemy, who repeatedly found themselves blocked from an apparent easy success by the works that he had conceived, laid out, and constructed, as on the delighted praise of the defenders, who more than once saw themselves saved by the miracles that he was able to bring about. This triumph, however, represented much more than professional skill, for the engineer had to perform his work in an atmosphere of suspicions, hostilities, and rivalries that could easily have made it impossible. On his arrival at Sevastopol he had to deal with the envy and suspicion of Menshikov, who regarded everyone favored by St. Petersburg as a personal enemy. The fact that Menshikov learned to trust him and give him practically a free hand proves clearly that his ability to deal with the touchy prince, while getting what he wanted, was worthy of an experienced diplomat. He also won the trust and support of Admirals Nakhimov, Kornilov, and Istomin, who felt neglected and disregarded by the army. In fact, Kornilov and Istomin were his most zealous supporters. Totleben also was able to work with the various generals and to secure their cooperation, whether sincere or grudging, in the vital tasks of defending the fortress. He was the key man of the defense—probably the only one with an all-inclusive view of the situation—and was involved in everything: rifle-pits and counterapproaches; new batteries to support a threatened bastion and traverses to protect the gunners from flanking fire; dugouts in the bastions and batteries to provide safety for the defenders against bombs; mines and countermines; more secure powder magazines in the strong-points; and many other matters.

Totleben, well grounded in the doctrines of the noted A. Z. Teliakovskii, an engineer whose books were well regarded in France, and General K. I. Schilder, who fought brilliantly against the Turks along the Danube in 1854, was opposed to formalism in the defense of major fortresses. He stressed an active defense, using rifle pits and counterapproaches, as well as frequent sorties. He also insisted on defense in depth, with positions behind the main bastions, supporting batteries in the rear or on the flanks, and in the city trenches, barricades, and strong points to repel enemy forces that might break through the main works. Since he could foresee that the foe, after having penetrated the main defense system in one or more places, might turn to attack one of the bastions from the rear, he considered it was essential to close off the rear entrance (the gorge) by a high wall and ditch. Thus the garrison of the bastion would be able to fight off attacks from all sides until help could come from the rear. This concept was hotly disputed by officers who held that the best defense of a bastion was an open gorge through which the guns of batteries in the rear could sweep the interior of the bastion and thus wipe out or force out the attackers. The latter system was advocated by most of the commanders in Sevastopol, and also was approved by Teliakovskii, who advised closing the gorge with portable fortifications only, which would not protect the enemy in the bastion from artillery fire from the rear. Khrulev especially called for an open gorge on the Malakhov, but to no avail.[13]

As stated earlier, Menshikov let slip two precious months when the Russian forces again might have struck telling blows against the enemy. This time was not entirely wasted, for the Russians did a great deal to improve their defenses, as indicated in the preceding pages. But this "no win" policy by no means promised a successful end to the war, for at best it might lead to weariness and disgust with the war on the part of the French and the British, of which strong symptoms had appeared in France and some even in England. By March 1855, however, the French had poured reinforcements into the Crimea and the British had obtained the services of fifteen thousand Sardinian troops and enrolled considerable numbers of volunteers from Canada, Ireland, and even the United States and sent in a number of territorial regiments. Since it was clear that the time for a successful Russian offensive had passed, the cabinet now hoped that skillful Russian diplomacy might keep the Germans, headed by Prussia, from abandoning their policy of neutrality mixed with decided anti-French overtones. Without definite Prussian assistance to halt Russia's probable blows at the Austrian flank, Austria would not risk war with Russia. And if Austria stayed neutral, Denmark and Sweden, which had proclaimed their neutrality, would remain quiet, and probably the Italian states such as the Kingdom of Two Sicilies would also stay out of the war. That would leave France and Britain as Russia's main enemies, and, except at sea, the British could do little against Russia. But the fifteen thousand crack Sardinians would be useful,

13. "Razvitie . . . Sevastopolia," *Iz istorii russkogo voenno-inzhenergnogo iskusstva,* pp. 127–28.

Army Engineer E. I. Totleben. Courtesy
of Sovfoto.

even though they had no proper reasons for fighting Russia. The Turks also had to be counted, although the terrible corruption and inefficiency of their military administration kept them from posing any real threat to the Russians, in spite of active efforts on the part of the British to train and equip their troops in Asia Minor. But at least the Turks had immobilized a substantial force of veteran Russian troops. Finally, Shamil and the Caucasian tribesmen had engaged some 200,000 Russians who could have been used to advantage in the Crimea. So at best the Russian army could not hope for more than a stalemate, which would give the diplomats a chance to improve the terms of peace.

Great Britain, which had entered the war against Russia so blithely, had found it to be an extremely costly and harrowing struggle, marked by dreadful losses in the battle of Inkerman and followed by casualties of disease and hardship after the great storm in November. There were loud protests over the failings of the military system and especially over the scandal of the hospitals, and cabinet resignations took place in an effort to secure a new war ministry headed by Palmerston, which resulted in the collapse of the Aberdeen government in the face of a Radical motion for an inquiry into the conduct of the war. Although there was much opposition to Palmerston, after Russell and Derby could not or would not form a ministry, he was the obvious choice, and Aberdeen magnanimously helped him to form a government including Gladstone, Graham, Sidney Herbert, and Argyll, who wanted a negotiated peace. But before Palmerston could take office he had to pledge his willingness to negotiate. The new ministry was little stronger than that of Aberdeen, as the military situation continued to worsen, and the death of Nicholas I removed the chief target of British wrath. Even Russell began to say that an indecisive end to the war might not be a calamity, and Palmerston hinted that Turkey's security might best be ensured by a European alliance in its favor. Finally, Napoleon's decision in February to go to the Crimea to take command of the armies so frightened the British that a negotiated settlement appeared to be the most hopeful solution.[14] There was still strong national feeling in England in favor of continuing the war, since the conflict had not disturbed the British finances and popular pride was still hurt. But as it was now obvious that Austria was not

14. Schroeder, pp. 246–49.

going to enter the war against Russia and there were sharp and frequent conflicts between the British and French commanders over the conduct of the war, even the British could see that it might be necessary to go through the motions, at least, of negotiating with Russia. They still hoped to avoid meaningful concessions, but it was clear that they must negotiate. If, however, the conference could be delayed, there would be more time for the armies to win a real victory.

In France, however, the war was definitely unpopular, for the French had lost heavily in the fighting and had little to show for it. The public in general could see no real reason for fighting Russia, especially after the death of Nicholas I, who was widely regarded as the personification of Russian tyranny. The French had no territorial objectives, and now that the Holy Alliance had been broken, they could see no further reason to fight. Russia's willingness to compromise on the protectorate over the Principalities and the navigation of the Danube, and its readiness to accept a general guarantee of the rights of the Christians if it were carefully and conscientiously drafted, settled most of the issues involved. The French cared little about the destruction of the Sevastopol fortress and the severe limitation of the Russian Black Sea Fleet, since they felt they were for the benefit of England. Thus the heavy losses the French incurred in the fighting in the Crimea—which apparently were much more severe than Paris admitted— seemed to the public to be blood shed to benefit Britain and not to further the interests of France. Many French citizens felt that France was pulling English chestnuts out of the fire. Since the French troops in the Crimea were far more numerous than the British, they wondered why France should go on fighting to please England. There was therefore an active demand in France for peace at any price, accompanied by real dislike of the English alliance.

In early 1855 the war was not going well, for the French were unable to overcome the Russian defenses at Bastions 4 and 5, and the British were making almost no progress toward the Malakhov. Also, General Canrobert and Lord Raglan were unable to come to an agreement regarding the final assault on the fortress. At first Raglan had refused even to approve the idea of an attack, and in April Canrobert several times rejected the dates suggested by Raglan.[15]

Napoleon III, bitterly disappointed by the costly fighting with the

15. Brison D. Gooch, *The New Bonapartist Generals in the Crimean War* (The Hague, 1959), pp. 187–96.

Russians and the lack of harmony between the commanders, was eager for drastic action to end the war with a great victory. He could clearly see that Canrobert was not ruthless enough to crush the Russians and he had no hopes of success from the English. Hence he sent General Adolphe Niel to the Crimea in January to survey the scene and make recommendations for a new policy. Niel concluded that it would be impossible to break the defenses on the Russian left, where the bastions were still defying the efforts of the French; instead he thought that the Malakhov was the key to the fortress. Deciding that the Green Hill, almost one thousand meters in front of the Malakhov, was the place to center the attack, he proposed to Canrobert that the French should take over the right of the English lines, from the Inkerman heights to the approaches to the Malakhov. Both Raglan and Canrobert opposed this plan, for the Russians held high ground there, and the terrain was rocky, which made it difficult to build trenches and approaches. But since General Niel represented Napoleon III, his proposal was accepted. The British withdrew from the right sector, which they turned over to the French, and concentrated their efforts against Bastion 3 (The Great Redoubt), a difficult objective. Thus the French forces extended from the sea to Bastion 4—the whole city sector. They also occupied the territory from the ship (Caravel) sector to the Chernaia river, with the British lines sandwiched between the two French attacks.[16]

When the Russian commanders saw the change in the Allied objective, they reacted with vigor. On the night of February 1/11 (O.S.) they surprised the French by setting up the Selenginsk redoubt on the extreme left as an active counterapproach. As it would enfilade all their approaches and batteries against the Green Hill, the French attempted to storm it on the night of the 11th, but after heavy fighting resulting in severe losses they were beaten off. The Russians also lost many men, but they were able to throw back the French and quickly installed cannon in the redoubt, from which they directed a telling fire on the French approaches to the Malakhov. Almost at once a new redoubt arose three hundred paces in advance of the first. The new site—the Volhynia redoubt—also received cannon and by March 5 both redoubts were ready to direct a strong fire toward the Green Hill. According to Camille Rousset, "this formidable system of

16. V. M. Anichkov, *Voenno-istoricheskie ocherki Krymskoi ekspeditsii,* pt. 2, *Opisanie osady i oborony Sevastopolia* (St. Petersburg, 1856), pp. 78–82.

counter-approaches spoiled all the plans of the attack. . . ." Now the Green Hill, formerly jutting ahead of the defense line, lay within an obtuse angle, flanked by Bastion 3 (the Great Redoubt) on the one side, and by the new redoubts on the other.[17] At once the French had to construct new batteries to fire on the highly troublesome redoubts. The Russians connected the Selenginsk and Volhynia redoubts with their lines by trenches to the Kilen-balka and dug trenches in front of their works, from which they directed a harassing fire against the French parallels and batteries. New batteries to support the redoubts were also built, so that the French found themselves obliged to begin a formal attack on the new Russian counterattack. Once more the Russians surprised them by building a lunette on the Green Hill, which, protected by the fire of the two redoubts, was rapidly constructed. Repeated French attempts to take it failed. By March 21 the new Kamchatka lunette was completed and its cannon opened fire on the French. Heavy fighting at once broke out and continued for some time. "Each inch of ground before the Mamelon vert (Green Hill) was hotly disputed . . ." and bloody combats took place every night, with large-scale attacks by one side or the other. On March 22–23 the Russians attacked the French approaches with fifteen battalions and penetrated the French and British lines. Although the French claimed that they lost two thousand men, the official report for the Allies was six hundred. As a result of these actions the French seemed further from success than ever, and their losses were great.[18]

Napoleon III was much distressed by these developments, especially since General A. J. J. Pélissier, who had succeeded Canrobert as commander-in-chief, had disobeyed orders by pushing the siege in spite of the losses. The emperor was convinced that Sevastopol would not fall until it was fully invested by Allied troops and deprived of supplies, and in February he decided he would go to the Crimea in April to take command. He planned to leave the British, the Sardinians, and part of the French army to continue the siege, while he led a field army to cut the communications of Sevastopol by marching from Alushta—a tiny port on the south coast of the Crimea—through the coastal mountains to Simferopol, the communications center for the fortress.[19] At other times he had mentioned reaching Simferopol from

17. Rousset, p. 71.
18. Auger, pp. 211–16; Niel, pp. 167–70.
19. Guérin, II, 43.

Eupatoria (Feodosia) or by way of McKenzie Hill through the wooded mountains northeast of Sevastopol, but the generals who had seen the Crimea were by no means convinced of the feasibility of this scheme since the terrain was very rugged and the roads were primitive, which would create a serious logistical problem.

Baron Hübner, the Austrian ambassador at Paris, had a long interview with Napoleon on February 10, 1855, in which the latter discussed his strategy. The emperor was determined to capture Sevastopol and destroy the Russian fleet, as he felt it was the only way to preserve the Turkish empire from a surprise attack on Constantinople by way of the Bosporus. He had no intention of trying to conquer Russia, but hoped for enough success to make a moderate peace. He did not believe that a satisfactory peace would result from a settlement that would leave Sevastopol intact and in Russian hands, for then Russia would be stronger than ever and "the prestige of his name in France and the influence of his government" would be enfeebled.[20]

When the news of Napoleon's intentions leaked out in mid-February, there was general dismay in France and a sharp fall of the Bourse. Almost everyone, whether Bonapartist or pro-Bourbon, was terrified. Napoleon was not an experienced general, and the professional soldiers did not want him to elbow them aside so he could garner the glory of a victory. But would it be a victory? The very difficult terrain, and the problem of logistics in a wild country where there was little food for man or beast, did not promise success. Moreover, the emperor would be in danger of disease, for cholera was still active in the Crimea, and he might be wounded or killed if he took an active part in the campaign. He planned to return to France in two or three months, but how could one be sure that his departure might not be delayed?

Another cause for concern was the problem of his successor, for Napoleon III had brought to the land stability and prosperity, which might not long endure in his absence. His successor was Prince Jerome-Napoleon, son of his cousin, the former King Jerome of Westphalia, although the emperor expressed the hope that in time there would be a direct heir. Jerome was attractive, but he inclined to the radicals and did not fit into the court. Something of a rebel in his morals, language, and etiquette, he was "systematically hostile to religion and especially to the Catholic Church." In short, he was not a promising

---

20. Hübner to Buol, two despatches, Feb. 10, 1855, HHSA, IX, 49.

heir for Napoleon III to leave behind.[21] Another male relative was the Prince Napoleon, Joseph Charles Paul, also a misfit. He was not a soldier, but in order to make him one Napoleon made him a general and sent him to command a division at the battle of the Alma, where he did fairly well. Not long after, however, he took sick and retired to Constantinople. Many of the French suspected Plonplon, as he was nicknamed, of cowardice. He had opposed the siege of Sevastopol and freely predicted its failure. As he was known to be ambitious, Napoleon could not feel comfortable about leaving him behind in France, but could not compel him to go to the Crimea.[22]

The dignitaries of the Napoleonic regime also were much troubled over the emperor's plans, for they realized that they might lead to his death, through assassination, a battle fatality, or disease. In such a case, or if the regime suffered a bad defeat, there would be little to prevent a revolution, in which Napoleon's chief followers might lose their exalted positions and even their lives. Therefore most of the prominent Napoleonic personages, who had until then supported the war, suddenly became ardent advocates of peace—and peace at almost any price, provided it would leave the Second Empire intact. Morny, Persigny, Walewski, Marshal B. P. Magnan, and the veteran diplomat Drouyn de Lhuys—all became eager advocates of a speedy and moderate peace, which would eliminate the reason for the journey to the Crimea.[23]

Lord Cowley, ambassador at Paris and a close friend of Napoleon's, did not know of this plan, although the emperor had hinted at taking command of the army in July 1854. He decided to go, however, only in February, 1855. Baron A. L. Seebach of Saxony, who had heard of it in secret a week before, reported it to his government, adding that the empress would go too and calling the venture incredible. As the rumors became more definite, Cowley reported them to London on February 16. Napoleon by now had become stubborn about the matter, insisting that it was the only way to achieve peace. On February 27 he sent his plan to Palmerston: he would command 77,000 French, Sardinians, and Turks, while the other Allied forces would push the siege. Palmerston, along with most Frenchmen, was much opposed to the plan. Indeed the English were almost as horrified as the French.

21. La Gorce, I, 118–19.
22. Simpson, pp. 270–71, 288–90.
23. La Gorce, I, 364.

They realized that the English alliance was very unpopular in France, where nine out of ten were sure that France was playing England's game at considerable cost to French interests. Cowley reported rising anti-British feeling, even among the close associates of the emperor. He repeated over and over that Napoleon was England's one friend in France, and if he should take sick or die, the alliance would suffer. Any loss of prestige by Napoleon would harm the alliance. Moreover, the English ministers realized that if Napoleon personally won the war, England would lose whatever prestige it had. Clarendon, who was firmly against the Crimean trip, visited Napoleon in his camp at Boulogne and spoke of the matter. While Napoleon promised not to outshine England, Clarendon was by no means reassured. The British also suspected that if Napoleon won the war, he would make friends with Nicholas I, whom he intended to visit. Would the Emperor of the French then sell out his British allies? The English all felt that the Crimean excursion would lead to disaster and did their best to prevent it.[24]

Napoleon, however, would not abandon his plan. For a time the sudden death of Nicholas I seemed to offer hope of peace, as Napoleon had no grudge against Alexander II. But as the young tsar would not deviate from his father's policies, Napoleon refused to change his attitude toward Russia and was unyielding about his Crimean journey. But peace now seemed to offer an alternative to Napoleon's venture. Drouyn de Lhuys had become ardently in favor of peace and would agree to a Russian fleet no larger than that which was still afloat. He even got Buol to agree to this, thus repudiating the restriction of four ships of the line that France and England had agreed to on December 19, 1854. This decision was taken without even notifying England, France's ally.[25]

While Napoleon had agreed to negotiate for peace on the basis of the Four Points, he really was determined on victory. In an interview with Hübner on May 3 he deplored admitting the possibility that his army might be forced to retire from Sevastopol without having gained a decisive success. In spite of the diplomatic achievements of France, the army and the masses would not understand them, and the effect of such an outcome on the country would be "disastrous and fatal." Nevertheless, faithful to his word, he would negotiate,

24. Henderson, pp. 212–18.
25. Puryear, *England, Russia, and the Straits,* pp. 447–49.

although a direct and positive limitation of the Russian naval forces in the Black Sea was the minimum goal he must obtain. He still hoped that Austria would enter the war and would draw in all the other German states except Prussia, and believed Sweden was ready to fight against Russia.[26]

Although the British leaders were strongly opposed to Napoleon's voyage to the Crimea, they heartily agreed with his desire for a victory over Russia and the destruction of Sevastopol and the Russian Black Sea Fleet. Since, however, there was a good chance that Drouyn de Lhuys might get Napoleon to agree to a compromise peace ardently advocated by Buol and Franz Joseph, which would leave Russia with a substantial fleet in the Black Sea and with Sevastopol in Russian hands, the British acted quickly, for they knew that such a settlement might lead to a Franco-Austrian alliance, with Britain isolated. Knowing of Napoleon's keen desire for a state visit to Queen Victoria at London and Windsor, they quickly arranged this, even though Napoleon had to postpone his Crimean journey. On March 13 the queen sent an urgent invitation to Napoleon III and Eugénie to be her guests at London and Windsor on April 16. The trip to the battlefront now seemed somewhat less likely, and in the meantime Drouyn's compromise concerning the Black Sea had taken a less drastic turn.[27]

With Drouyn in Vienna for the conference, his influence with the emperor declined, and that of the British was in the ascendant. The imperial pair received a warm reception in London and at Windsor were highly honored guests, enjoying every mark of favor that the queen and her subjects could bestow. A dazzling military review took place, and as the British were ardent allies, Napoleon believed more strongly than ever in their association. An enormous, emotional outpouring of the people occurred when on April 19 the City of London held a solemn banquet at Guildhall for him. The queen herself convened a chapter of the Order of the Garter and personally bestowed its insignia on her guest.[28] Thus the British leaders used the pomp and glitter of their empire to tie their wavering ally more firmly to them.

Both the British and the French leaders were now firmly convinced of the necessity of a victory over the Russians that would destroy

26. Hübner to Buol, May 9, 1855, HHSA, IX, 49.
27. Henderson, pp. 219–22.
28. La Gorce, I, 364–66.

Sevastopol and the fleet that it sheltered. They differed, however, over Napoleon's plan to go to the Crimea. When Napoleon told Victoria of his fears that his generals would not be sufficiently bold in pursuing the siege, which moved him to go to the war zone, she warned him of his domestic problems, the great distance, and the danger. To this he replied that the distance troubled him. As for the danger, "it is everywhere," he said. On April 18 a joint council took place, with Palmerston, F. M. R. Panmure, minister of war, and Cowley present, all of whom protested greatly against his journey. The emperor's suite, far from objecting to the disapproval of the British, encouraged it, for their forebodings were greater than those of their hosts. When the queen, in a private talk with Marshal Jean-Baptiste Vaillant, admitted that she had dared to make some remarks, the soldier begged her to do so, for if Napoleon should suffer a reversal, the result would be terrible. *"We are all* in the same boat," he added, "and we have to protect ourselves from the same dangers." [29]

The imperial guests returned to France without any definite word from Napoleon concerning his decision. The departure for the Crimea was repeatedly announced and then cancelled, so that all Europe did not know which of the numerous wild rumors to believe. Finally, on April 28, an assassin attacked Napoleon on his ride to the Bois de Boulogne, although his two shots failed to wound him. The attacker proved to be a Roman, who was angry because Napoleon had sent French troops to overthrow the Roman Republic of 1849. This incident, trivial in itself, showed that the Napoleonic regime was by no means secure at home, where he could keep order, and suggested that if he should leave France for a long period the danger might be critical. More than ever the intimates of the emperor had reason to press their objections with greater strength. Their views received more of a hearing than before because the emperor was having difficulties with Prince Jerome, who was demanding wide powers in his absence, and Plonplon, who refused to go to the Crimea, was also causing trouble. When Napoleon's ministers warned of a possible financial crisis and of the danger of cholera in the Crimea, the pressure finally grew too great and Napoleon had to give in. On April 25 he wrote to Queen Victoria that the journey had been cancelled,[30] to the great relief of many in both countries.

29. Ibid., pp. 366–67.
30. Henderson, pp. 223–24.

The search for a suitable policy that occurred among the powers in the spring of 1855 was coming to a close. Although there was a substantial peace movement in England for a time, the British never really considered anything but fighting through to victory in alliance with France. Palmerston, the war leader, pursued this program with vigor, but little success. Russia had renounced its former rights of dominating the Principalities and the mouths of the Danube and was willing to accept five-power control of the supervision of the Turkish promises of rights to the Christians of Turkey. It refused, however, under Alexander II as well as under his father, to agree to limit its fleet in the Black Sea and to destroy its naval base at Sevastopol. Hence it would continue to fight. It managed to avoid war with Austria, in spite of the latter's leanings toward the seapowers, while gaining strong moral support from Prussia, guided by Bismarck, and most of the middle German states. France, after considering an Austrian alliance, had finally given up its hopes of Hapsburg military support and had confirmed its alliance with England for victory over Russia. Napoleon III had reluctantly renounced his plans to take command in the Crimea and left the campaign there to General Pélissier, who, if anything, was even more energetic and ruthless than Napoleon wanted him to be. The monarch vainly demanded that his commander should not continue to assault the Russian defenses, but should attempt a war of movement to cut the communications of the besieged city.

Under the guidance of Bismarck, Prussia, which had originally been rather unfriendly to Russia and sympathetic to England and Austria, had turned against France and Austria and no longer sought good relations with England. Instead, it had come to realize that Russia was no longer a threat to the princes of Germany but was a bulwark against revolutionary France and the pro-French policies of Austria. Finally, Austria, after being pro-Russian in 1853, had moved steadily toward France and in 1854 actually threatened to fight against Russia. Russia, however, showed a highly conciliatory attitude, giving up its special rights in Turkey and eventually evacuating the Principalities. It accepted the Four Points as the final bases for peace, and from August 1854 fought a defensive war, except for some attacks on Turkish positions in Asia Minor. But Austria was so firmly committed to the Allies that it continued to threaten Russia and in December 1854 signed a treaty of alliance with France and England. As, however, it had no further demands on Russia, it refused to go to war and sought a compromise peace based on the Four Points. This angered Britain and to a lesser degree France, which had encouraged Sardinia to enter the war against Russia and had doubtless reached agreement that in the future it would make gains at the expense of Austria. Thus Austria, under Count Buol, had made enemies of Russia, Prussia, and now France and England, and had no friends on which it could count. It had turned against the old Holy Alliance, had also antagonized France and England, and had been unable to devise a workable policy. Its position was already critical.

CHAPTER 16. THE CONFERENCE OF VIENNA

Because of various interruptions, the Conference of Vienna, which the five powers had almost agreed to by the end of December 1854, did not start until the middle of March 1855. In December Lord John Russell pushed a demand for a War Ministry under Lord Palmerston, which Parliament rejected after a long debate. Russell resigned from the cabinet on January 23, and on the 29th the Aberdeen government fell over general dissatisfaction with its conduct of the war. After two false starts by other leaders, Palmerston was able to arrange a cabinet which included several Peelites, among them Gladstone, Graham, Sidney Herbert, and Argyll. Although Palmerston disliked the idea of conferences, the Peelites had insisted on holding them, and as Drouyn de Lhuys, because of the strong desire for peace in France, also demanded them, Palmerston had to agree, especially since the situation in the Crimea had taken a turn for the worse. All this took time because neither the British nor the French leaders were eager for the meetings, for they hoped that a victory in the Crimea would eliminate the need for negotiations. The death of Nicholas I on March 2 (N.S.) seemed to offer hope for a speedy peace, since to many the deceased seemed to be the personification of Russian aggression.

The hope that Alexander would be more pliable than his father proved to be unfounded, for the new ruler quickly issued a bitter manifesto against Russia's enemies in which he declared that he stood firmly by his father's policies. When Emperor Franz Joseph sent a soothing letter of condolence, Alexander responded with a slashing charge that the Austrian's conduct during the past year had broken the heart of Nicholas I, "for instead of finding in you the friend and faithful ally on whom he counted and whom he loved like a son," Franz Joseph had drawn closer and closer to Nicholas's enemies, "which will lead us inevitably, if it is not changed, to a fratricidal war and make you accountable to God!" Alexander declared that he would continue the war even against all Europe rather than submit to a dishonorable peace. "Be convinced," he said, "that this sentiment is shared by all in Russia, and God, who saved us in 1812, will not desert us." [1]

Nesselrode's circular to the Russian diplomats after the accession of Alexander II breathed the same spirit of devotion to the policies of Alexander's father and trust that God's help would enable the new tsar to meet the tests ahead. The emperor recognized two sacred obligations that he had inherited from his father: the duty to exert all the power at his disposal for the defense of Russia, and to continue the quest for peace in Europe. He would seek to support the religious liberties and the well-being of the Christians of the East, no matter what rite they professed; to ensure the immunities of the Principalities under a collective guarantee and to effect the free navigation of the Danube for all nations; to bring an end to the rivalries of the powers in the Levant, in order to prevent new complications; and to achieve a suitable revision of the Treaty of 1841 concerning the Straits. A peace settlement based on these principles, he said, would be welcomed by all Europe. [2]

On March 5/17 Alexander personally revealed his attitude in an address to the diplomatic corps at St. Petersburg, in which he declared firmly that he would remain faithful to the policies and political principles of Nicholas I and of Alexander I. "These principles are those of the Holy Alliance," he said. He was willing to make peace on the terms accepted by his father; but if the Vienna Conference did not produce an honorable result for Russia, "I should fight with my faithful Russia and I shall perish rather than give in." He closed with cordial words of gratitude for the king of Prussia and somewhat less warm regards for Franz Joseph. [3]

Buol, in despatches to Count Valentin Esterházy at St. Petersburg, expressed his satisfaction over the pacific attitude shown by the new tsar and in Nesselrode's circular. [4] On the other hand, he thought the call for a national militia by Nicholas I shortly before his death [5]

1. Hallberg, p. 94.
2. Circular of Nesselrode, Feb. 26/Mar. 19, 1855, HHSA, X, 42.
3. Esterházy to Buol, Mar. 17, 1855, HHSA, X, 41.
4. Two despatches, Buol to V. Esterházy, Mar. 17 and 22, 1855, ibid.
5. Decree of Nicholas I, Jan. 29/Feb. 10, 1855, sent with desp. V. Esterházy to Buol, Jan. 31/Feb. 12, 1855, HHSA, X, 41.

indicated that Russia did not expect peace to be made soon and that the war was far from over. The news of Napoleon III's intention to take command of the French armies in the Crimea in order to win a victory to end the war also was greatly disconcerting, although it stimulated a desire for peace talks rather than working against them.

In the middle of February Lord John Russell set out for Vienna, where he would be the British plenipotentiary. His cabinet expected that he would act to bring a quick end to the conference, so that it could go on with the necessary business of getting Austria to enter the war over the expected conflict concerning the Third of the Four Points. Russell, however, was more receptive to new ideas than most of his colleagues, for, unlike them, he wanted to bring Prussia into the negotiations and above all favored a conciliatory policy toward Austria regarding the Third Point. Lord Clarendon, who was greatly confused over the situation, thought that possibly this policy might be acceptable. Russell, who was much influenced by Buol and other Austrian leaders, had drawn up a series of proposals on the Third Point which were really Austrian. His chief suggestion was for a defensive alliance among Austria, Turkey, France, and England to protect Turkey from Russia, presumably without war. The four allies also should garrison forts on the Bosporus against a possible Russian attack on Constantinople, and with Turkish permission might have the right to bring their warships to the Black Sea if the Turks felt there was danger from Russia. Hübner reported to Buol from Paris that in discussions with Drouyn de Lhuys and Napoleon they had reached a similar solution. Napoleon now admitted that the destruction of Sevastopol was not essential, although it was vital to secure a pledge from Russia that it would limit its fleet on the Black Sea. Hübner suggested that since half of the Russian fleet had been sunk, they should merely ask that Russia promise not to exceed the present size of its fleet. If England would agree, they would ask Russia to limit its fleet to eight ships of the line (six afloat, with two more nearing completion at Nikolaev). Turkey also would not have more than eight ships in the Black Sea. Consuls should be stationed in Russian ports to verify the number of Russian ships. The French and the Austrian envoy proposed amending the Treaty of 1841 to permit each signatory power, with the approval of the sultan, to station ships in the Black Sea equal to half the number of the Russian ships. This arrangement should be made in a manner that would safeguard the dignity and honor of the sultan.[6] It was later called the Austrian ultimatum.

When the conference opened on March 15, the British program simply was to wreck it, in order to compel Austria to carry out its treaty commitment to enter the war against Russia. Drouyn, however, who had long sought a permanent Franco-Austrian alliance, did not want to antagonize Austria.

At the first working sessions of the conference on March 17 and 19 the delegates generally agreed to Prokesch's proposal for a five-power guarantee of the traditional privileges of the Principalities and consultation with the people on modifying the governing statute. These provisions, which would eliminate Russian influence over the government of the Principalities, were readily accepted by A. M. Gorchakov and V. P. Titov, the Russian delegates—a significant concession. Lord Clarendon, however, made a long and bitter attack on the provisions saying they were unfair to Turkey and would bring about a revival of Holy Alliance tyranny in these provinces. The Austrians were careful to maintain a conciliatory attitude, and since the French took a moderate position, the proposals were easily adopted. The Turks, the nominal suzerains of the region, had nothing to say, merely referring the proposals to their government. Lord John Russell, the British plenipotentiary, courageously supported the Austrian proposals against the attack of his own government.[7]

The question of free navigation of the Danube (the Second Point) was settled with no difficulty, again along Austrian lines, with two slight amendments by England and Russia. Russia gave up its special rights according to its treaties relating to the Principalities and the mouth of the Danube, which was a substantial concession. By the agreement on March 21, the Danube would now be under the control of the great powers of Europe, following the rules of the Congress of Vienna of 1815. A European Commission of the Navigation of the Lower Danube, formed of delegates of the riparian states, would have power to remove obstacles to navigation of the river and to make the necessary regulations concerning it.[8]

6. Hübner to Buol, Mar. 14, 1855, HHSA, IX, 49; Schroeder, pp. 262–64.
7. Ibid., pp. 262–63; Protocols of the Conferences, HHSA, XII, 199.
8. Schroeder, p. 265; Henderson, p. 33; Protocols of the Conferences, HHSA, XI, 199; Gorchakov to Nesselrode, Mar. 12/24, 1855, tg., AVP, f. Kants, D. no. 221.

The remarkable success of the Conference in completing work on the first two points, which met the desires of the Austrians and of the Germans in general, then came to an end. The problem of the Third Point, which was next on the agenda, because of the strongly conflicting positions that the powers had taken, would certainly be extremely difficult to solve. Some months before the *Moniteur officiel* had printed an inspired article saying that the Third Point would require the razing of the fortifications of Sevastopol, the limitation of the Black Sea Fleet to four ships of the line, with auxiliaries, and a guarantee of the Turkish empire. While France and Britain had later taken a more moderate attitude, it was clear that the terms cited in the *Moniteur* were what they still wanted. Russia, however, took the position that, while it would agree to eliminate the predominance of Russia in the Black Sea, it would not accept any demand which would infringe on the dignity and rights of the emperor in his domains. This meant that Alexander II would not consider razing the forts at Sevastopol nor accept any limitation on the size of the fleet. Moreover, in an audience with Emperor Franz Joseph, Gorchakov received a pledge from him that Austria would not make war on Russia over the number of ships in the Russian fleet. As Austria was fully satisfied with the action on the First and Second Points and there seemed to be agreement between Austria and Russia on the Fourth, the Russians felt assured that Austria would not declare war on Russia. Austria still hoped to eliminate Russian preponderance on the Black Sea, but sought to do so by other means.[9] The British and the French, however, were determined to obtain satisfaction on the Third Point, for their plenipotentiaries had received orders from their cabinets not to take up the Fourth Point until the Third had been settled.[10] The maritime powers also agreed on the demands they would make of Russia, including limiting the Russian fleet, stationing Allied ships at the mouth of the Danube and in the Bosporus, appointing consular agents in the leading Russian ports in the south, and providing for the sultan to summon the Allied fleets into the Black Sea if he felt a need for them. Russia would have no right to send its ships into the Mediterranean.[11]

9. Hübner to Buol, Mar. 30, 1855, HHSA, IX, 49.

10. Gorchakov to Nesselrode, Mar. 11/23, 1855, tg., AVP, f. Kants., D. no. 221; Titov to Nesselrode, Mar. 21/Apr. 2, ibid.

11. Annex to desp., Buol to Hübner, Apr. 16, 1855, HHSA, IX, 51.

Austria definitely did not want to go to war against Russia, for it felt that St. Petersburg clearly wanted peace and would make it on a satisfactory basis. On February 4 Emperor Franz Joseph wrote a letter to Napoleon III stating that he thought peace was both possible and desirable, because Nicholas I sincerely wanted it, even at the cost of accepting a broad application of the Four Points. The Austrian believed that Nicholas preferred such a solution to a war to the death which would involve all Europe and which would probably go against Russia. Franz Joseph held that peace would be very desirable, for it would mean Russia's abandonment of its traditional policy against Turkey, in the face of the rampart of European solidarity. To demand greater concessions from Russia would signal the beginning of a bloody and desperate war, whose outcome could not be determined. He therefore urged that they negotiate for peace, instead of hoping vainly for German readiness to make war on Russia. The Germans would be even less ready for war if it was evident that the Allies had rejected Russian peace overtures. Only the joint efforts of France and Austria either at the green table, or, if absolutely necessary, on the field of battle, would bring a solid and lasting peace.[12]

While Napoleon was counting on obtaining Austria's entry into the war against Russia, Drouyn was earnestly seeking a Franco-Austrian alliance. In an audience with Franz Joseph at Vienna, Drouyn proposed full neutralization of the Black Sea with a firm alliance of the two powers. But the young emperor stated that while this proposal had obvious advantages, he could best do his duty by making a moderate peace with Russia. The main need was for unity among the powers concerning the conditions for peace. Thus Austria displayed no interest in France's bid for an alliance between them.[13]

On March 15/27, after the settlement was completed on the First and Second Points, the conference turned to the Third Point. The Allied plenipotentiaries politely asked the Russian and Turkish delegates to work out their own proposals for balancing the forces in the Black Sea at their convenience, thus paying homage to the honesty of Russia's intentions. Gorchakov and Titov, however, declared that, while they were ready to discuss any propositions made to them, they could not take the initiative in the matter. Upon the unanimous vote of the conference the Russian members agreed to refer the question

12. Letter, Franz Joseph to Napoleon III, Feb. 4, 1855, HHSA, IX, 51.
13. Friedjung, pp. 153–55.

to their court, with further discussion suspended until the reply should come from St. Petersburg. In the meantime, they would begin discussion of the Fourth Point at the next session.[14]

In the interim Gorchakov jotted down his ideas concerning the course to follow. He stated that the so-called preponderance of Russians on the Black Sea was actually only an outgrowth of the totality of the political relations between the Ottoman and Russian empires. It was from a superiority of authority that Russia derived the dominance that its earlier treaties with Turkey gave it, and not from its naval supremacy. It resulted from the isolated position of Turkey rather than from its inferiority at sea. Turkish maritime inferiority had developed under circumstances that had nothing to do with Russia: the Greek insurrection, Navarino, and the strivings of Egypt for autonomy. This inferiority, which was not caused by Russia, could cease at the pleasure of the Porte, for with its strong fortresses, the defensive topography of the Bosporus, and its ability to group its navy around three adjoining basins, it had the means for regaining naval parity.

Why had the Porte not done this, in view of its obvious distrust of Russia? Perhaps it was because Turkey sensed that it might be helpful to have a Russian fleet nearby, as was the case in 1833 when it called the Russian fleet into the Bosporus. The Russians would not come unless the Turks wanted them to, for their fleet could bring with it not more than ten or twelve thousand men, which would be far too little to conquer Constantinople. As close as the Russian bases were to Turkey, in three weeks Russia could move only about twenty thousand men—not enough to endanger the Ottoman empire. Thus a Turkish fear of the Russian fleet did not make sense.

The real purpose of the Third Point was to bring Turkey under the public law of Europe, thereby protecting it and saving Europe from new troubles. The could be done in various ways, but a respectable Russian fleet should remain in the Black Sea as a factor of European equilibrium. The danger to Turkey could come from other directions as well as from the north. Cutting down the Russian fleet there would leave Turkey to the mercy of Britain and France, whose fleets were each as dangerous to Turkey as Russia's, and while their bases were more remote, they could easily move their ships to Turkish waters. Without the Russians, who would protect Turkey from the Western

14. Gorchakov to Nesselrode, Mar. 15/27, 1855, tg. (secret), AVP, f. Kants., D. no. 221.

fleets? But once Turkey was placed under the general protection of Europe, fear of the Russian fleet would disappear, for Russia would never risk stirring up a new coalition against itself.[15]

Drouyn de Lhuys, who up to that time had chiefly acted as the faithful instrument of Napoleon III, now stepped to the center of the stage with policies of his own which he tried to suggest to his master. Drouyn was horrified at the emperor's plan to go to the Crimea to take command of the armies, as were most of his associates; he also felt dismay at the Napoleonic plans for a revival of Poland and the persistence of his dream of freeing northern Italy from Austrian domination. He therefore sought an alternative to these schemes, which would also gratify the great longing of the French people for an end to the war. His remedy was neutralization of the Black Sea—which meant removal of all fleets, Turkish, Russian, British, and French— from this body of water. To him the equal application of this principle to all the powers appeared to offer hope for success, for Drouyn even seemed to believe that Russia would agree. He also was a strong advocate of a Franco-Austrian alliance as a means of diverting Napoleon III from his revolutionary schemes for Italy and Poland. The minister managed to interest his master in neutralization and an Austrian alliance, although he showed no real enthusiasm for them.[16] Lord Cowley, who had much influence over Napoleon, disliked the trend of Drouyn's thinking and feared that in Vienna he would fall under the pacific influence of Buol and Prokesch and would move away from the maritime powers, as Lord John Russell seemed to be doing. Consequently Cowley induced Drouyn to confer in London with the British before going to Vienna. On March 30 Drouyn attended a meeting in London, with Palmerston, Clarendon, Russell, and other members of the cabinet. The British were very angry with Austria, since Buol had declared that it would not go to war over one or two ships more or less in the Russian Black Sea Fleet. The British leaders were eager to push the war to the limit, with no concessions to Russia. The conference agreed to a joint policy on the Third Point, with neutralization of the Black Sea as the first proposal. If Russia rejected neutralization, the conference would then suggest a strict limitation of the Russian fleet, which was to be presented as an Austrian ultimatum. If Russia refused the second proposal, the powers would then break up the

15. Gorchakov to Nesselrode, Mar. 31/Apr. 11, 1855, ibid., D. no. 222.
16. Hartcourt, pp. 141–47; Henderson, pp. 46–47.

Conference of Vienna and concentrate on winning the war. Drouyn probably hoped that he would persuade the Austrians to support this position.[17]

From London Drouyn went to Vienna about March 6, where he found a strongly pacific atmosphere. Austria, whose position had greatly improved, thanks to the agreements on the first two points, cared little about the size of the Russian fleet in the Black Sea. On March 31/April 12 Gorchakov sent a secret telegram to Nesselrode stating that Franz Joseph had sent a peremptory order to Buol "to resist the urgings of the Anglo-French that Austria should adhere to the Acte signed at London . . . on the neutralization of the Black Sea."[18] The situation appeared to favor the peace efforts, since the Allies had made no significant progress in the Crimea, and in the heavy fighting their losses were severe. Prussia and the Germanic Confederation showed no signs of backing Austria in a war with Russia, for after the repeated Russian concessions many German leaders, with Bismarck at their head, felt that Britain and France, and not Russia, were the real aggressors. Moreover, there was a substantial peace sentiment in England, and in France there was a widespread desire for peace and a feeling that France was losing too many men in order to satisfy British aims, which were by no means to the interest of France. Napoleon's plan to go to the Crimea had aroused intense dismay among the people of both countries. Thus, the war had proved to be costly, unpopular, and dangerous, and the outcome was not in sight.

While the diplomats at Vienna awaited the response about the Third Point that would come from St. Petersburg, Buol had been actively negotiating with Drouyn and Lord John Russell on an agreement concerning the Russian fleet in the Black Sea. The two Westerners had grown steadily more understanding during their stay in Vienna and were opposed to efforts to force Russia to accept limitation of its fleet. Instead, they leaned toward some form of ponderation or counterpoise—helping Turkey by building up its fleet or by sending in Allied squadrons to equalize Russian power. Since this idea was close to Buol's views, the three men found themselves supporting an almost identical position, with Drouyn and Russell in opposition to their own governments' policies. On April 15 Buol produced the final

17. Henderson, pp. 48–50; Schroeder, p. 266; La Gorce, I, 357.
18. Gorchakov to Nesselrode, Mar. 31/Apr. 12, 1855, tg., AVP, f. Kants., D. no. 222.

Austrian proposal, much of which had been derived from earlier Western suggestions, chiefly made by Drouyn. It was a complicated scheme for responding to any apparently aggressive moves by Russia by bringing into the Black Sea half as many ships as Russia had there. If the sultan felt threatened by Russia, he could admit all the Allied fleets, without opening the Straits to the Russians. All the powers would guarantee Turkey's integrity, and Austria, France, and Britain would make a military alliance in its favor, which would go into effect if Russia attacked Turkey or increased its Black Sea fleet above its 1853 level. Finally, the sea powers might station a few vessels in the Bosporus, to show that they were protecting Constantinople.[19]

Buol and Prokesch strongly supported this plan against the objections of Drouyn and Russell, who soon took positions close to the Austrian ultimatum. Both Drouyn and Russell came to advocate some sort of graduated deterrent with which to keep Russia in line.[20]

On April 17 the conference resumed its sessions, with an announcement from Count Buol that Gorchakov had heard from his cabinet. The prince then stated that, while his government greatly appreciated the initiative that the conference had bestowed on it to present propositions concerning the Third Point, it felt that it should not use this opportunity. Its plenipotentiaries, however, had been authorized to discuss seriously, for the purpose of reaching an agreement, any means that would be proposed, provided that they did not infringe on the sovereignty of the emperor of Russia in his lands. Drouyn expressed keen regret that, after a delay of eighteen days, the Russians had returned unused the initiative that had been proffered. Gorchakov stated that he was willing to consider proposals on a limitation of Russia's ships, although he was not authorized to accept them.[21]

At the following session, on April 19, they discussed the third guarantee, chiefly the aspect of attaching the Porte more completely to the European equilibrium. The Turkish plenipotentiary read a formula whereby the powers declared that, in order to have Turkey share in the advantages of the concert established among the different states, "they henceforth consider this Empire an integral part of this concert and engage themselves to respect its territorial integrity and its independence as a general condition of the general equilibrium." The pow-

19. Schroeder, p. 270.
20. Ibid., pp. 270–71.
21. HHSA, XII, 199, Apr. 17, 1855, Protocol X.

ers, with Russia among them, declared that they adhered to this principle. The text of the proposal that the conference formally adopted provided that if a conflict should arise between the Porte and one of the contracting powers, these two states, before resorting to arms, must make it possible for the other powers to settle the dispute by peaceful means.[22]

After thus disposing of one aspect of the Third Point, the Conference then addressed itself to the problem of the elimination of Russian preponderance in the Black Sea. Drouyn declared that as Russia had accepted this principle and as the best way of effecting it would be to reduce Russia's forces there, it should accept the chief means of doing this, which he held would not be derogatory to the sovereign dignity of the Emperor Alexander. Since Russia now had lost control of a part of the Black Sea, it was only reasonable for it to sacrifice some of its rights in order to regain possession of the remainder. He then read a series of proposals to Russia, which he said were perfectly honorable. This scheme called for Russia and Turkey to pledge each other to maintain on this sea only four ships of the line, four frigates, and a suitable number of light vessels and unarmed troop transports. The rule of cloture of the Straits would remain in force, except that France, England, and Austria would have the right, by permission of the sultan, to send half as many ships into the Black Sea as Russia and Turkey had there. If the sultan felt menaced by an aggressive action, he should have the right to open the Straits to "all naval forces of his allies." In addition, both Russia and Turkey should agree to admit Allied consuls to all ports on the Black Sea. Buol and Prokesch both supported this proposal, although Buol warily stated that Austria would not use force to compel its acceptance by Russia.[23]

While the conference was waiting for the Russian cabinet to state its proposals concerning the Third Point, in the unofficial discussion among the delegates Bourqueney of France had tentatively suggested neutralization of the Black Sea by eliminating all warships from it. Prince Gorchakov, however, refused to consider this as a serious proposal, holding that it was a "polite joke." He added that both the Mediterranean and the Black Sea should be neutralized.[24] Although

22. Ibid., Apr. 19, 1855, Protocol XI, Annex A.
23. Ibid., Protocol XI and Annex B; Titov to Nesselrode, Apr. 8/20, 1855, AVP, f. Kants, D. no. 222.
24. Titov, to Nesselrode, Mar. 16/28, 1855, ibid., D. no. 221.

he did not explain his reasoning, the Russian view was that, while Russia, without a fleet on the Black Sea, would be defenseless there, the Turks could still have their fleets in the Bosporus or the Sea of Marmora, only a short sail from the Black Sea, and the French and the British fleets would remain in the Mediterranean, from which they could easily move through the Straits.

Alexander II would not even consider discussing a limitation of the Russian fleet, for in his official audience with Count Valentin Esterházy, the Austrian ambassador, he mentioned that Lord John Russell had spoken of the necessity of a limitation of the naval forces of Russia in the Black Sea. The emperor stated firmly: "This is a condition of which there cannot be a question, which I cannot have imposed on me." [25] Nesselrode had induced the emperor to summon a special council to consider the question, composed of the leading figures of the realm. The conference completed its deliberations at the end of March, and on the following day a courier left for Vienna to carry the decision to Gorchakov. [26]

On April 10/22 Gorchakov revealed the Russian proposals, after first declaring that Russia could not accept the Allied plan to guarantee the territorial integrity of Turkey. He declared without hesitation that Russia rejected the Allied scheme as prejudicial to the rights of the emperor, contrary to the European equilibrium, and dangerous for the independence of Turkey. He then presented as his counterproject the opening of the Straits to all fleets. After a moment of shocked silence, Lord John Russell declared that he was not authorized to discuss this matter, and Drouyn de Lhuys said the same. Aali pasha, from Turkey, and the Austrian representatives declared that they stood by the rule of cloture of the Straits. Gorchakov insisted on putting his counterproposal in the Protocols, claiming that it was better than the Allied plan, for the sultan could still close the Straits if he felt he was in danger.

Drouyn again brought up the proposal of the neutralization of the Black Sea, whereupon Gorchakov asked that the same principle be extended to the Mediterranean.

Finally, Russell announced that his instructions were exhausted and he was leaving, and Drouyn made a similar declaration. Court Buol thereupon closed the session, while hoping that one of the plenipotenti-

25. V. Esterházy to Buol, Apr. 1/13, 1855, HHSA, X, 41.
26. Ibid.

aries would ask for the calling of another session in the name of peace.[27]

On the next day Gorchakov telegraphed to his court that the situation was very strained, as the emperor had not granted the audience that he had requested. He asked if they could not negotiate on the basis of the cloture of the Straits in principle, with liberty to the Porte to open them to foreign powers without reciprocity for Russia, if it should believe itself menaced by the increase of Russian naval forces. He begged for a reply by telegraph as soon as possible. To this Alexander II replied: "The emperor is astonished that you could ask a reply to proposals that you should have rejected on your own responsibility." [28]

Gorchakov also wrote to Nesselrode on April 11/23 expressing regret that Russia had not taken the lead on the Third Point. He stated his view that in the light of the grave crisis, Russia could strengthen its influence for peace by a declaration of the tsar that he did not intend to increase its fleet above the prewar level. This, he believed, would satisfy Austria.[29]

On April 16/28 Gorchakov presented a new scheme, this time for keeping the Bosporus and the Dardanelles closed in time of peace, as provided for by the Treaty of 1841. The second article of the proposal provided that, as "a transitory exception," the sultan should have the power to open these straits to foreign fleets when he believed his security was menaced. The French and British plenipotentiaries at once rejected these suggestions as not fulfilling their demands and declared that their instructions had been exhausted. On the other hand, Buol said that the Russians had been conciliatory, although their plans did not offer enough protection against future crises.[30]

While the formal sessions of the conference were going on, Buol, Russell, and Drouyn had been holding private talks about the situation, which went far beyond their instructions. After outlining his plan on April 15, Buol submitted it to Russell and Drouyn on the 17th, in an effort to prevent the talks from ending, and although it was a gross violation of their instructions, they accepted it. The plan called for closing the Dardanelles except in case of a real threat to Turkey; a

27. Gorchakov to Nesselrode, Apr. 9/21, 1855, tg. (secret), AVP, f. Kants., D. no. 222; Titov to Nesselrode, Apr. 10–22, 1855, ibid.

28. Gorchakov to Nesselrode, Apr. 11/23, tg. (secret), ibid.

29. Letter, Gorchakov to Nesselrode, Apr. 11/23, 1855, TsGADA, f. 3, D. no. 140, pt. 2.

30. Gorchakov to Nesselrode, Apr. 11/23, 1855, AVP, f. Kants., D. no. 222; Titov to Nesselrode, and Annex, Apr. 17/28, ibid.

European guarantee of the integrity of the Ottoman empire; and either limitation of the Russian fleet in the Black Sea or at least some form of counterpoise to build up the strength of Turkey against Russia. While Russell much preferred limitation of the Russian fleet, he believed that it would not be achieved, while counterpoise, although providing less certain protection for Turkey, would bring peace, and since peace was what he ardently wanted, he agreed to the plan, fully realizing that it might destroy his political career. Drouyn, who was not especially high-minded, felt that this scheme was the only way to prevent Napoleon's voyage to the Crimea, which he thought would lead to revolution and chaos in France. Hence he also assumed the risk.[31]

Buol was hoping for the "Austrian ultimatum" to Russia for a counterpoise system, to uphold "the independence and integrity of Turkey," which he hoped would be supported by an alliance of Austria, France, and Britain to restrain Russia in the future, for he believed that Russia would continue to be hostile to the Danube empire. Franz Joseph had stated to Russell that "Russia would long bear ill will to Austria for the part that she had taken," and hence he wished to have an alliance with the maritime powers "with a view to a permanent political system." Drouyn drafted a treaty by which the three powers promised aid to Turkey against any attack. Its third article stated that an excessive build-up of the Russian fleet, even to the prewar level, would be an act of aggression.[32]

While these developments were taking place, Gorchakov was making strenuous efforts to avoid a break. On April 12/24 he telegraphed to Nesselrode that the situation was becoming increasingly serious, with Austria organizing military actions against Russia. He suggested that, while limitation of the fleet by treaty could not be accepted, "a spontaneous declaration of the Emperor to maintain the *status quo ante bellum* for our fleet and not to intend to surpass it in our own interest" would keep Austria from going to war over this issue.[33] Nesselrode promptly replied that the emperor would regard such a limitation "as a gratuitous sacrifice of his rights of sovereignty on his own territory. . . . It follows from this that we cannot take the initiative in this respect."[34]

31. Henderson, pp. 52–53; Puryear, *England, Russia, and the Straits,* pp. 397–99.
32. Henderson, pp. 53–54; Projected Treaty of Alliance against Russia, HHSA, X, 42.
33. Gorchakov to Nesselrode, Apr. 12/24, 1855, tg., AVP, f. Kants., D. no. 222.
34. Nesselrode to Gorchakov, Apr. 15, 1855, ibid., D. no. 226.

At this time the Russian Black Sea fleet apparently had only six ships of the line afloat, with two others nearing completion at Nikolaev. As this was far below the prewar size of the fleet, it might have been wise for Alexander II to voluntarily limit the fleet to eight ships, as it would not have been possible to build it up to the prewar level for several years. Such a declaration might have made peace possible almost at once. The emperor, however, seems to have felt that such a step would be very unwise, and so he refused to agree to it. Thus the war went on.

When Buol's peace proposal, which was supported by Russell and Drouyn, was communicated to the British and French governments, their leaders were horrified. Clarendon declared that it was not the proposal of an ally or friend, and the queen was angry with Russell and Drouyn. The royal government, however, was not united on the issue and at first took no action. Lord Cowley, however, whose views were close to those of Palmerston, undertook to fight the plan to the limit. On April 23 he had a long audience with Napoleon, who in his presence drafted a telegram to Drouyn telling him to stop the negotiations and come home. But when the latter received the emperor's telegram he said that he was more convinced than ever that Buol's scheme was valuable. The governments did not at once make a formal decision, although Palmerston regarded the plan as both dangerous and dishonorable, and Clarendon was eager to wreck it.[35]

British pressure on France increased greatly during the latter half of April, because of Napoleon's triumphant visit to London and Windsor and the great enthusiasm shown there for continuing the war. When Napoleon soon decided against taking command in the Crimea, his intimates, who had become ardent advocates of peace, again became staunch supporters of victory. But while the emperor was again for war until victory, he also wanted to keep on good terms with Austria and hence did not want to offend Buol by rejecting his scheme. British influence was gaining greatly at Paris, especially in the person of Lord Cowley, who played a big part in defeating Buol's proposal. On April 30 Hübner wrote: "The Emperor no longer sees except with the eyes of Cowley," who almost had become the French foreign minister.[36] Thus the contest centered at Paris.

When Drouyn returned to Paris on April 30, he managed to persuade

35. Henderson, pp. 54–55.
36. Ibid., pp. 55–56.

Napoleon to accept his scheme, and at once wrote to Walewski and Russell to urge them to obtain the consent of the British government. Russell was already pressing his cabinet to accept Buol's plan, although he did not propose that Russia should have the right to restore its fleet to its prewar size. He said that the failure to make peace would be the greatest blunder any government had ever made. When the cabinet debated Napoleon's new proposal on May 2, it was surprised, but did not reject it out of hand. Although it did not favor it, it referred the matter to Paris in order to find out more details. Baron Christian Friedrich von Stockmar, an influential adviser of Queen Victoria's and Prince Albert's, and the prince consort were in favor of accepting the plan, and several of the cabinet were for accepting it. Clarendon felt that if he called for an outright rejection, Lord John Russell would resign and bring down the government by taking Aberdeen and Gladstone with him. Palmerston for once seemed subdued and did not lash out arrogantly against the scheme.[37]

At Paris Drouyn and Buol were working hard to convince Napoleon, who, sullen and passive, had accepted the proposal but would not fight for it. If he had, the British cabinet probably would have agreed. But Buol could not wheedle him into approval, for he was relying more and more on Cowley. On May 4 Napoleon sent for Cowley and asked his opinion because, he said, he did not understand the proposal on which he was going to confer with Drouyn. Cowley boldly asked if he might be present at the conference, and Napoleon agreed!

At the private conference Marshal Vaillant, the minister of war, who was also present, was fiercely against the compromise and insisted on victory in the Crimea. While he was warmly seconded by Cowley, it was Vaillant, backed by the influential French army, whose opinion was decisive. The British cabinet expressed its opposition to the Buol-Drouyn scheme only after Napoleon III did, but it was delighted with the outcome.[38]

After Napoleon had decided against the Austrian ultimatum, he ordered Drouyn to wire Walewski, the French ambassador at London, to reject it and to support a real limitation on the Russian fleet. On the following day Drouyn resigned as minister of foreign affairs, since

37. Ibid., pp. 57–59.
38. Ibid., pp. 60–63; La Gorce, I, 371–72; Puryear, *England, Russia, and the Straits*, p. 404; Schroeder, p. 277. Hübner to Buol, May 9, 1855, HHSA, IX, 49, gives Drouyn's account of the developments, which is similar to the one given above.

he felt he had lost authority over the French diplomatic corps and that Napoleon III had adopted a new policy.

Hübner held that Lord Cowley had had much to do with the outcome of the debate and had used the opposition of the French army to defeat the Austrian plan, as well as the opposition of the British cabinet. In Hübner's opinion, Napoleon III, although he very much wanted an alliance with Austria, needed the British even more and, if he were forced to choose, would side with England rather than with Austria.[39]

Gorchakov, who realized that events were leading steadily to a full-scale resumption of the war, could see that it would come at Sevastopol. In his letter of May 3/15 to Nesselrode he said that he had one word to add to his reports to the cabinet: "The Crimea, in the name of heaven, the Crimea!" This would be the decisive spot, and all other moves were merely feints. Everything that Poland and the Central Army could spare should be sent there.[40]

The fact that Austria no longer felt itself bound by commitments to France and Britain greatly aided this program. Now that the sea powers had disregarded Austria's pressing need for peace and had rejected its sensible plan for achieving it, Austria had no interest in fighting Russia. Why should it? Russia had given up its control over the Principalities and the lower Danube, and Austria had no further objectives within reach. It wanted peace and disarmament. On April 14/26 Vienna had sent orders to the divisions of the First Corps to be ready to march, and the staff of the Third Corps and other units were ordered to move from Graz to Vienna, as preparation for a serious demonstration. But Gorchakov wired his cabinet that after conferring with him, the Austrian government had sent counterorders to the units involved to stay where they were.[41]

On May 7 (N.S.) Gorchakov wrote to Nesselrode that to strengthen his position Franz Joseph had had Bourqueney write to Drouyn that he was concerned about the danger of war with Russia, unless he were strongly supported by France. Hence he had demanded a firm agreement that France would provide the following assistance: (1) a French army large enough to keep Prussia in check to take a position

39. Hübner to Buol, ibid.
40. Letter, Gorchakov to Nesselrode, May 3/15, 1855, TsGADA, f. 3, D. no. 140, pt. 2.
41. Gorchakov to Nesselrode, Apr. 15/27, 1855, tg., AVP, f. Kants., D. no. 222.

on the frontier of Bohemia; (2) an effective demonstration in Bessarabia, under a French general, to cover Austria's flank; (3) subsidies to be placed at once in Austria's treasury; and (4) subsidies for Sweden so that it could take part in the war.[42]

In a despatch Gorchakov pointed out that these requirements would be so difficult, if not impossible, for France to meet that merely stating them was an indirect way of indicating that Austria did not intend to join France in the war against Russia.[43]

Buol still had to close the Conference of Vienna, which had been suspended for over a month. In spite of opposition from Britain and France, he decided to summon the conference on June 4, intending to deal with the Third Point by proposing acceptance of the limitation of the Russian fleet to the number of ships still afloat. He had hoped that the Allies would make the gesture of agreeing to this plan, while Russia would not, so that Russia would have to bear the blame for prolonging the war. But Britain and eventually France saw that Russia might accept the terms, which would compel its opponents to accept an armistice and genuine peace talks—the last thing they wanted. Hence their governments reluctantly permitted their ambassadors to attend, but without power to negotiate. Gorchakov, far from rejecting the terms, decided to accept in principle.[44]

Buol's scheme consisted of the following articles:

(1) A pledge to bring the Porte under the public law of Europe, to respect the independence and the territorial integrity of the Ottoman Empire, and to regard all violations thereof as questions of European interest.

(2) Limitation of the naval forces of the two states on the Black Sea, to be made by common agreement between them, with the fleet of each country not to exceed the number of Russian vessels then afloat.

(3) The continuance of the rule of cloture of the Straits provided by the Treaty of 1841.

(4) Authorization by the Porte for each of the other contracting powers to station two frigates in the Black Sea.

42. Letter, Gorchakov to Nesselrode, Apr. 25/May 7, 1855, TsGADA, f. 3, D. no. 140, pt. 2.
43. Gorchakov to Nesselrode, May 28/June 9, 1855, AVP, f. Kants., D. no. 223.
44. Schroeder, pp. 292–93.

(5) The right of the Sultan, in case of aggression, to open the Straits to all the naval forces of his allies.[45]

When the session convened on June 14, Bourqueney, Westmorland, and Aali pasha had to declare that their instructions did not authorize them to discuss this proposal, whereas Gorchakov, who might have kept silent, agreed to reserve it for the knowledge of his court. Gorchakov thought that his court would be willing to guarantee the territories of the Turkish empire in Europe but not those in Asia and Africa, and that it would make no commitments to help suppress internal uprisings in Turkey. He stated as his personal opinion that the limitation of the fleets, which should result from negotiation between Russia and Turkey, was acceptable. As he found nothing to object to in the other articles, he held that the proposals offered the bases for a possible solution of the third guarantee.[46]

The French, and above all the British, had hoped that this last session of the conference would reveal Russia as the party guilty of prolonging the war. But it turned out otherwise, for the Russians showed themselves eager for peace and willing to cooperate in order to achieve it. More and more the British showed that they were determined to continue the war solely for reasons of prestige, with no sound objective and no means of supplying the military strength necessary for victory. It was widely recognized that the French were heartily weary of the war and anxious to bring it to an end, but at the final session of the Vienna Conference they rejected a reasonable proposal for peace, in part to please Lords Cowley and Palmerston, and chiefly to satisfy the French army. It was the fierce professional soldiers like Vaillant, Pélissier, and Bosquet, who had done so much to bring Napoleon III to power and to keep him there, who almost compelled him to turn his back on Buol's sensible peace proposal and to continue the costly drive against Sevastopol. The Russians seemed reasonable and moderate in comparison.

Understandingly, Buol was angry with France for having taken the advice of Cowley, which resulted in the failure of the conference. In a letter to Hübner he stated that Napoleon's rejection of his political proposals was the greatest error he had committed. Buol replied

45. Protocols of the Conference, HHSA, XII, 199, Protocol XIV.
46. Ibid.

he felt sure that they could live through the period of tension, especially if France should show them some consideration out of courtesy and also because of their power. "I authorize you," he said, "to use this language and to say it very loud." [47] Count Walewski, the new French minister of foreign affairs, was annoyed with Austria for agreeing to oppose Russia and then refusing to do so. Now, after the final session of the conference, it declared that it was no longer bound by the engagements and would be guided by its own interests. It even made an "untimely" reduction of its armies, dispersing the army corps in the north that had kept the Russians in check. Walewski insisted, however, that Austria must still be bound by the Four Points.[48]

After the closing of the conference, Austria's demobilization, which the people strongly desired, proceeded. Buol, seeing that it was inevitable, on June 10 asked Russia for a promise not to invade the Dobrudja nor to repudiate its concessions on the Four Points, to which it willingly agreed. On June 11 Buol readily accepted demobilization of 62,500 reservists from the forces in Galicia, to cut the heavy expense and to reduce the losses from disease.[49]

This action increased French coolness toward Vienna, since its reduction of troops on its frontier with Russia made it possible for Russia to send several infantry divisions to the Crimea and to Bessarabia. Unfortunately for the Crimean army, Marshal Paskevich was very reluctant to part with any of the troops under his command, in spite of the orders from the emperor. Hence these forces were slow in moving, reaching the Crimea only at the end of July.[50] Well-informed Russian generals charged that Paskevich was so loath to let the troops go that he repeatedly marched and countermarched them, so that when the divisions arrived they were worn out and prone to disease. "Such diseases appeared in the Grenadier Corps that it definitely overflowed all the hospitals," commented V. I. Vasil'chikov.[51]

In contrast to the coolness between Paris and Vienna, in June and July Nesselrode repeatedly stressed how cordial the relations were between Russia and Austria. On June 15/27 he wrote to Gorchakov

47. Letter, Buol to Hübner, June 6, 1855, HHSA, IX, 51
48. Walewski to Bourqueney, June 22, 1855, HHSA, IX, 51; Schroeder, p. 301.
49. Schroeder, p. 302.
50. Miliutin MS, pp. 290–92.
51. Vasil'chikov, p. 255.

that because of Austrian cordiality toward the envoy and the friendly remarks of Franz Joseph, all friction between the two empires had been eliminated. Nesselrode was especially pleased by Buol's words that Franz Joseph could not admit that anything could force him to abandon his neutral stance. Alexander II's views were exactly the same. The tsar agreed that it was useless to make new moves toward peace, for neither power could succeed in this endeavor at that time. Their achievements on the first two Points remained firm, and as for the rest, they must wait until there might be a favorable moment to renew the negotiations.[52] At the same time Esterházy wrote from St. Petersburg about his warm and friendly relations with Nesselrode.[53] And on July 19 Nesselrode wrote to Gorchakov that the two cabinets were agreed that the results of the first two Points were settled, but on the Third Point nothing had been achieved, and that on the Fourth Point there had been no negotiation.[54]

As this correspondence showed, the relations between the two imperial cabinets was surprisingly friendly, in the light of the strain and tension that had marked them a few months before. It should be noted, however, that in spite of the cordiality, Austria was still leaning toward the West, and its rebuff by France did not cause it to seek the close understanding with Russia that had existed at the outbreak of the war in 1853. As for Russia, it was on very intimate terms with Prussia, which was avowedly hostile to Austria, and both Gorchakov and Nesselrode remained very distrustful of Buol. Hence the apparent friendship between the two empires was largely superficial, and by early 1856 there was considerable hostility between them.

As has been mentioned, the conference took no action on the Fourth Point, and most of the delegates seemed uninterested in the matter. This was not the fault of the Russians, for at the meeting of the four courts Gorchakov raised the issue of the guarantee of the rights and privileges of the Orthodox Christians under Ottoman jurisdiction. He declared that the powers had to take the initiative to protect the rights of the Christians against local abuses, a duty which he declared to be a matter of conscience. He promised that when the Russian emperor was convinced that the joint protection was effective, he would give up his special patronage over the Orthodox. The only comment

52. Nesselrode to Gorchakov, June 15/21, 1855, HHSA, X, 42.
53. Esterházy to Buol, June 15/27, 1855, HHSA, X, 41.
54. Nesselrode to Gorchakov, July 19/31, HHSA, 42.

produced by this statement was a remark by Bourqueney that Gorcha-kov had failed to mention the spontaneous initiative of the sultan in bestowing rights on his Christian subjects.[55]

On January 6/18 Nesselrode had sent Gorchakov his instructions for use in the conference, most of which dealt with the first three points. On the Fourth Point—the religious question—he stated that this was a matter of conscience for the emperor, to which "he attached the greatest importance," and hence the envoy should give it his special attention. It was very important to make sure that the Fourth Point should state clearly the principle of perfect equality between the Greek and the Latin churches. The tsar insisted that this principle be made very precise, to ensure that the Latins did not obtain by subterfuge privileges that the Greeks did not have. Gorchakov should give great care to the matter of the collective guarantee of the religious rights, so that the promised protection would not "be a vain word." It would not matter what circumlocutions would be used to save the dignity of the sultan—the reality was what would count. If the Western powers valued the entry of the Ottoman empire into the general system of Europe, it must be the duty and a matter of conscience for all the monarchs to insist that "henceforth the Sultan should engage himself to treat all his Christian subjects in a Christian manner (chrétienne-ment)." Only under this condition could Turkey be admitted to the states composing the concert of Europe.[56]

Nesselrode indicated the importance that the Emperor Nicholas attached to this Point by a second despatch that same day, in which he expressed the desire that the religious question be placed first when the conference should discuss the order in which the articles of the treaty of peace would be arranged. "In the thinking of Our August Master this question, as Your Excellency knows, dominates all the others," Nesselrode said. The desire to solve it in the interests of the Orthodox Church was the chief motive for bringing His Majesty to join in the transaction in which all the powers had the duty to take part," for the repose and the general well-being of Christianity in the Orient." Such a solution would give the Christians of Turkey relief from the instability that had burdened their lot. As the war had its origin in this situation, "the emperor attaches a just importance to placing the article on the religious question in the first rank." Gor-

55. Gorchakov to Nesselrode, Dec. 27, 1854/Jan. 8, 1855, AVP, f. Kants., D. no. 220.
56. Nesselrode to Gorchakov, Jan. 6, 1855, AVP, f. Kants., D. no. 226.

chakov was asked to devote his efforts to realizing this goal during the peace negotiations.[57]

In a despatch of February 3/15, 1855, Gorchakov told of stressing to Buol that if he would treat the religious question broadly he would greatly help the cause of peace. He added that "for Russia this was the principal interest involved in the struggle," although he would approach it above all as a Christian, and not exclusively as a Russian. Gorchakov emphasized that all the Christian powers" were in honor and in conscience bound to fulfill, without quibbling, the promise made in the face of the world," concluding that the safe way to ensure the survival of Turkey in Europe was "for the sultan to give satisfaction to his Christian subjects, at least in the first need of the human heart." He felt that it would not be difficult to develop this idea in the full conference, although it would be hard to avoid irritating the feelings of the Turks. Probably the Christian powers should meet beforehand and specify what they wanted to keep for the Christians and what they should further receive. They could then leave it to the Turkish delegate to produce the document in the conference, on his own initiative.

Nicholas I was greatly in favor of these proposals. Buol also seemed to like the idea, whereas previously he had never wanted to discuss the collective guarantee of religious rights. Now Gorchakov said that no written pledge of the Porte was worth anything unless the powers had the right to supervise it. Gorchakov, who was insistent on this point, stated that the terms did not matter greatly, if the principle was stated; "if not, we would have a shameful comedy in the face of the world." ("Fort bien," commented Nicholas I.)

For the first time Buol did not deny that there was a great difference between the words and the acts of the Turkish government and that the powers had to perform a serious and effective work. Would he hold to this position?

The Russian told Buol that they had to be sure that Redcliffe did not interfere by getting the Porte to issue a *Tanzimat* (decree of reforms). If he did, they would have to discuss it and not take the matter as a fait accompli. Buol replied that one reason for holding the conference at Vienna was to get away from Redcliffe, and if the

57. Ibid.

sultan signed a Tanzimat, the powers should revise it and get it signed.[58]

On May 15 Nesselrode, in answer to a query from Gorchakov about combining the Third and Fourth Points, replied that Emperor Alexander approved of this, and sent the text of new provisions that might be used in this connection.

Article I provided that the powers would unanimously state their intention to respect the independence and integrity of the Ottoman empire. Hence they wanted to bring Turkey under the public law of Europe and henceforth would regard it as part of the Concert of Europe. They would seek to prevent any conflict involving Turkey from arising by having the other states work to prevent it.

Article II provided that in return for these pledges of security, the sultan, desiring the concert of the powers, recognize that it "was a matter of honor" for him to issue assurances of his solicitude for the entire liberty of faith and the progressive improvement of the lot of his Christian subjects, without distinction as to the rite that they professed.

The documents that His Highness would issue from his sovereign will to confirm the immunities of the Christians, considered as part of the public law of Europe, would likewise be placed at the demand of the sultan, under the collective guarantee of all the contracting parties.[59]

While it is noteworthy that Nicholas I, the Russian diplomats, and perhaps to a lesser degree Alexander II continued to insist on a solid guarantee of the rights and religious immunities of the Orthodox subjects of the sultan, it is perhaps more significant that Count Anton Prokesch von Osten, an Austrian diplomat with long experience in Turkey, strongly emphasized the need for reform there to guarantee absolute equality of the rights of the Christians. Prokesch, a man who had quarrelled sharply with the Russian diplomats, was even more doubtful than Gorchakov and Nesselrode of the pledges of the sultan regarding the Christians. In a memorandum, "Introduction au quatrième point," he stated that the sultans had showed good will toward the Christians, but had not been able to carry out their meas-

---

58. Gorchakov to Nesselrode, Feb. 3/15, 1855, AVP, f. Kants., D. no. 220.
59. Nesselrode to Gorchakov, May 15, 1855, AVP, f. Kants., D. no. 226.

ures. The religious denominations should be fully independent in their development and have the right to appeal to the powers as a last resort. When the Ottoman empire would grant such freedom and equality, it would be a big step forward. Even this, however, would have little value unless it were accompanied by improvement of the administrative and judicial position of the Christians. The best way to strengthen the Ottoman empire would be to bring the Christian populations "out of the state of suffrance, which causes them to place their hopes elsewhere than in their Moslem sovereign."

The good intentions of the Turks by themselves were not enough, for it was essential to have them carried out. Moreover, innovations would have no real value unless they were applied to the country as a whole. The intentions of the Porte might be excellent, but their execution was often deplorable, because of corrupt institutions and unwilling and unworthy officials. A whole series of reforms was needed: the separation of civil and criminal justice; regularization of the right of a profession, of the ownership of property, and of inheritance; abolition of the principle that all land belonged to the sultan; establishment of the right of Christians to apportion taxes among themselves; the substitution of a property tax for the head tax; a military organization that would include Christians; equality of opportunity for entrance into all ranks of the military and civil hierarchy; and equality of all before the law.

These reforms could be achieved only by persuasion of the Turks, and not by compulsion. Moreover, one could not expect the Moslems to accept the Christians as equals, although equality of all before the law was perhaps possible.[60]

When the Conference of Vienna closed on June 4, 1855, it had by no means fulfilled its ostensible purpose. The chief reason for the failure was that the British and the French cabinets really did not want the conference to succeed, for they were determined to win a great victory in the Crimea and rejected a compromise peace. Even Austria was not wholly eager for a moderate treaty, for Count Buol was torn between a desire to join France and England in defeating Russia and the very real need to accept any reasonable peace that would lift the almost unbearable financial and social burdens that the war placed upon Austria, even though it was not a belligerent.

60. "Introduction au quatrième point," HHSA, XII, 199.

Russia definitely wanted peace, although its cabinet refused the concessions that its enemies sought to force it to accept.

And so the war continued, with France and Britain seeking a victory before a second winter would descend upon their forces. Russia had no real hope of winning a military victory, but hoped that by holding on until winter it could outlast the Allies.

The Conference of Vienna had done what it could, thanks largely to Russia's concessions in the Principalities and at the mouth of the Danube. But because Russia would not agree to reduce its fleet to a low level, the Allies pushed on toward victory. The Fourth Point remained untouched, and the statements of the Russian diplomats and the pessimistic analysis of the Turkish situation by Prokesch suggested that agreement concerning it would not be easy.

CHAPTER 17. THE SECONDARY CAMPAIGNS OF 1854–55

While the attention of Europe centered on the fighting in the Crimea and the diplomats were chiefly concerned with the navies on the Black Sea, there were several other theaters of operation of some importance. Of these the most vital was Asia Minor, at the eastern end of the Black Sea, where the Turkish Anatolian armies repeatedly fought with the Russian Caucasus Corps in Georgia and Armenia. As has been mentioned, in 1853 the weak Russian forces had managed to repulse an invasion of the Turks, although without a decisive result, and both contestants prepared actively for the campaign in 1854 by sending in reinforcements. The Turks hoped that under Ahmet pasha, a leader with a good reputation, they would have success. Ahmet, however, proved to be insatiably corrupt, for he kept his troops without proper food, clothing, and medical care, so that his army melted away, with the soldiers dying of cold and hunger. Finally Lord Redcliffe had him recalled and tried by court-martial. The British and the French now undertook to reorganize and train the Turkish army and brought in substantial contingents from Egypt and Tunis, so that in April there were fifty thousand Turkish troops at Kars, with smaller forces at Baiazet and Ardahan. The Russians under Lieutenant General Prince Bebutov had perhaps twenty thousand men, with veteran infantry and effective artillery.

The Turks, who soon quarrelled with the foreign advisers, were reluctant to move, and Bebutov was able to take a good position near the frontier, from which he threatened the enemy. By sending a detachment against the Turks at Baiazet, which defeated them handily, he forced the main Turkish army to move to Kürük-Dar. Bebutov went to meet them. At dawn on July 24, however, he discovered that the Turks, with a considerable force, had stealthily taken up an excellent position, with artillery on high ground overlooking the Russian position and a strong force of infantry in front, while large formations of cavalry and irregulars threatened Bebutov's flank and rear. The Russians sent a considerable body of fine troops on their left to drive the Turks off the heights, while the Russian infantry and artillery met the strong Turkish infantry head on. The Russian right, heavily outnumbered, had to hold off the Turkish cavalry and irregulars as best they could. The skill and discipline of the Russians won the day, forcing the Turks off the heights and then driving back the Turkish infantry in the center. This action made it possible to rescue the right wing, which drove the Turks in headlong flight. The Russians took 2,000 prisoners and fifteen guns and other trophies. The Turkish losses were about 10,000, plus the 12,000 irregulars who deserted. The Russians lost 600 killed and 2,400 wounded. But while the Russians had won a convincing victory, they were not strong enough to move against Kars, and there was no further fighting in 1854.[1]

In November 1854 Nicholas I named General N. N. Muraviev (Murav'ev) viceroy of the Caucasus and commander of the army. Muraviev quickly alienated many of the leaders by his critical and unwise attitude toward them, accusing them of indolence and corruption. As a result there was much ill will toward him, which weakened the morale of the troops. He was haughty to his subordinates and refused to consider the advice of the experienced soldiers under him.[2]

In June Muraviev led his army to Kars, the key Turkish position in eastern Anatolia, but decided not to storm it, although General Ia. I. Baklanov, an experienced commander, reported that the fortifications were far from complete and that it could be readily taken. Muraviev, however, felt that the attack might not succeed and failure would discourage the troops, as well as encourage the Turks and Shamil's mountaineers. He therefore blockaded Kars and began a regular siege, with an assault planned for the autumn. But in September the Russians heard of the fall of Sevastopol (to be described in chapter 19) and the landing of Omer pasha with a sizable army to attack Akhaltsikh and Tiflis. The Turkish commander at Erzerum, who had showed greater strength, also might threaten the Russian supplies of hay and fuel. Hence Muraviev decided to capture Kars quickly, which would

1. Bogdanovich, II, 168–200; Ol'shevskii, 500–510; A. L. Zisserman, "Fel'dmarshal Kniaz' A. I. Bariatinskii," *RA,* XXVI (1888), pt. 3, 225–31.
2. Zisserman, pp. 234–39; A. P. Berzhe, "N. N. Murav'ev vo vremia ego namestnichestva na Kavkaze, 1854–1855 gg.," *RS,* VIII (1873), 610–11; Bogdanovich, IV, 229–32.

make it possible to take Erzerum and then to drive Omer pasha out of the Caucasus.[3]

Kars proved to be no easy objective, for several able British officers had arrived there to help improve the defenses and to train the defenders, to whom they gave better weapons than those of the Russians. Although the Turkish authorities had failed to provide its army with proper food and other supplies, so that they were close to starvation, in all other respects it was a formidable body of soldiers. The attack before dawn on September 17/29 did not take the Turks by surprise, and they at once poured a terrible crossfire into the Russian columns, which were badly cut up. The attackers took part of the defenses, but the Turks retained their main positions and inflicted heavy losses on them. After seven hours of determined effort to storm the Turkish works, Muraviev had to order his forces to withdraw. Four Russian generals were wounded, and a number of other officers were killed or wounded. In all, 7,478 men were put out of action, although many of the wounded soon returned to duty.[4]

Most of the Russian commanders expected their army to retire to winter quarters, but Muraviev decided to continue the siege, for the Turks were near collapse. He arranged for some reinforcements to join his army, provided for food and fodder for his troops, and had the men construct comfortable huts before the cold weather set in. The morale of the soldiers, which had slumped badly, revived, and they again pushed the siege. In early October, with five battalions joining their force, they again felt confident that they could fight off the Turks and take Kars. The position of the Turks was now hopeless, for their food was completely exhausted, and there appeared to be no hope of rescue by Omer pasha or other Turkish forces. General William Fenwick Williams, the British commander in Kars, feeling that it would be impossible to try to fight their way out, proposed that they surrender, and a Turkish council of war agreed. On November 13 Williams conferred with Muraviev and they quickly came to terms. The irregulars were released, while the Turkish regulars became prisoners. Many of these Turks, almost dead with hunger, died of starvation and disease, although the Russians fed them promptly and well. The Russians captured 12 pashas and 665 officers, as well as 136 bronze

3. Ia. I. Baklanov, "Blokada i shturm Karsa," *RS,* II (1870), 572–73; N. N. Murav'ev, *Voina za Kavkazom v 1855 godu* (St. Petersburg, 1876), II, 4–45.
4. Murav'ev, II, 81–95; Bogdanovich, IV, 314–39.

cannon.[5] The English officers, although technically prisoners, were sent to Russia as honored guests. This victory—the last important action of the war—considerably improved the Russian position and lifted some of the gloom caused by the fall of Sevastopol.

The Russian success at Kars partially redeemed the defeat in the Crimea. But while the army in Asia Minor performed very well, there is much reason to believe that it failed to accomplish all that it could have. The failure to take Kars early in the summer, which Colonel Atwell Lake, a British engineer who served in Kars during the siege, admitted could probably have been done,[6] was a bad error. If Kars had fallen then, the Russians could have crushed the whole Turkish position in eastern Anatolia, which might have forced the Allies to transfer substantial forces from the Crimea to check the Russians in Asia. Moreover, M. D. Likhutin, who served in the Erivan force under General A. A. Suslov, in a persuasive account of the campaign of this detachment in 1855, states that Suslov was eager to destroy the force of Veli pasha near Baiazet, but Muraviev refused to permit him to attack. When Suslov was finally allowed to take the offensive, it was too late, for the Turks had made a clean escape toward Erzerum, the main base of the Turks in the region. Suslov pursued the Turks with ease along the fine road to Erzerum and had no difficulty in obtaining plenty of fodder and other provisions. Finally, Muraviev instructed him to cooperate in his march against Erzerum by joining with Prince A. M. Dondukov-Korsakov's force of cavalry from the main army to trap Veli pasha in his camp before Erzerum. But Dondukov, instead of at once attacking, gave his troops a night's rest, during which Veli pasha again made good his escape. Shortly thereafter Muraviev's powerful force of infantry and artillery arrived, but instead of immediately pushing against Erzerum, which was apparently lightly defended, Muraviev ordered both forces to withdraw. While Muraviev knew that he could easily have taken Erzerum, he felt that he could not hold it, since he had to return to the siege of Kars. He reasoned that a mere temporary occupation of this important center would indicate weakness to the Turks, whereas his main task was to take

---

5. Bogdanovich, IV, 372–99.

6. Sir Henry Atwell Lake, *Narrative of the Defence of Kars: Historical and Military* (London, 1857), pp. 95, 103. Lake states that the garrison was very short of ammunition and was poorly supplied with food. Moreover, the defenses of the fortress were too weak to have stopped the Russians.

Kars. So on July 23 (O.S.) he ordered both armies to retire, with Suslov returning toward Baiazet, to keep provisions at Erzerum from reaching Kars. Muraviev refused to permit Suslov's Erivan force to attack Veli pasha, who had again become active, but later, after the failure of the attack on Kars in September, he permitted him to push on toward Erzerum, with Veli pasha fleeing in terror before him. Erzerum could easily have fallen to the Russians, which would have shaken the whole Turkish position in Anatolia and might have induced the British and the French to divert strength from the Crimea.[7] But again Muraviev denied Suslov the opportunity to attack.

According to Likhutin, the Turks were poor fighters, chiefly because of the social and ethnic composition of the Ottoman empire. Whereas the Russian army was largely composed of Russians, who were loyal, patriotic, and eager for battle, the Turkish army included Arabs, Kurds, Tatars, Egyptians, Greeks, Armenians, and other peoples, many of them hostile and disloyal to the Turkish government. The Turks held all the positions of command, and the rank and file, who had no desire to fight for them, often were ready to desert at the first promising opportunity. The once all-conquering Turks had, over the centuries, become lazy, corrupt, and inefficient, and their morale had weakened. Whatever fanaticism the Turks retained was fanaticism to hold their privileges and position against their rebellious subjects, who demanded improvement of their lot—which the Turks could and would not give. Hence, while the Turkish troops might make a creditable stand, they would not fight to the death in hand-to-hand combat nor even face strong hostile fire. "If there is a pretext for running away," Likhutin said, "they will certainly run away." Occasional, partial Turkish successes "could not resurrect a spirit that had fallen for centuries and vitalize a rotting body; the deception was soon revealed." [8]

One last episode of the war south of the Caucasus remained undecided in the autumn of 1855. This was the attempt by Omer pasha, the leading Turkish commander, with some twenty thousand Turkish regular infantry, thirty-seven guns, and a large force of militia, to push against Prince Mukhranskii, who had about nineteen thousand men, almost half of them Georgian militia, and twenty-eight guns.

7. M. Likhutin, *Russkie v Aziatskoi Turtsii v 1854 i 1855 godakh* (St. Petersburg, 1863), pp. 305–98, 413–34.
8. Ibid., pp. 440–44.

The prince had to spread his forces, leaving a considerable number in Guria on the southwest coast, and others at the mouth of the Rion river in the northwest. In September 1855 Omer pasha landed most of his army at Sukhumi, where he was greeted by the ruler of Abkhazia, General Adjutant Prince Michael Shervashidze, and several other notables. Princes Dmitrii and Grigorii Shervashidze, however, remained loyal to the Russians. With about twenty thousand men Omer pushed slowly from Sukhum, where he left about ten thousand, to cross the Ingura river. He sent only a small force into Guria. On October 17 he reached the Ingura, where Mukhranskii, with 5,700 men, held the crossings, aided by 3,000 militia. The river, usually deep and rapid, was unusually low, so that there were two fordable places. Here the Russian infantry made a desperate stand, inflicting heavy losses on the attackers with artillery fire and making bayonet charges. But while Mukhranskii massed much of his strength at one ford, Omer shifted most of his troops to the other, where two thousand Russians, armed with flintlocks and three guns, faced the Turks, who fought with Minié rifles. There was fierce fighting for over four hours, with the Russians driving the Turks back three times, even fighting them in the stream. Three commanders of one Russian battalion were killed in action. But when the defenders regrouped for a last charge, the Turks had already crossed the river into Mingrelia, a province of Georgia, and outflanked the defense line, and the Russians had to retire under great pressure, carrying away their wounded and cannon, at night.[9]

With the Turks across the river and the flanks of his defense line turned, Mukhranskii, who had lost three guns, had to fight a delaying action, as the Mingrelian militia had dispersed. Fresh Russian troops arrived, however, and the Russian position became fairly strong. Omer did not make an active pursuit, so that his advance bogged down. The Turks occupied all of the country, but the rulers hid in the mountains, and the chiefs, who opposed the Turks, insisted that they stay in Mingrelia.[10]

The apparently desperate position of the Russians in the face of Omer pasha's Turks was in large part redeemed by the determined stand of the people of Georgia against the Turks. In response to the

9. Bogdanovich, IV, 346–52; Murav'ev, II, 264–93; K. Borozdin, *Omer-Pasha v Mingrelii* (St. Petersburg, 1873), pp. 27–29.
10. Bogdanovich, IV, 353–56; Borozdin, pp. 30–54.

looting, murder, and enslavement of the population by the Turks, the Georgians formed militia units that gave valiant support to the hard-pressed Russians. In addition, large partisan units sprang up in the countryside, keeping up active warfare against the invaders, attacking their outposts, and exerting solid pressure on them. A partisan attack on the Turkish camp almost captured Omer pasha himself. This factor, which the Turks had apparently not expected, combined with the flow of Russian reinforcements, especially after the capture of Kars, turned the tide.[11]

Omer's position rapidly deteriorated, for he delayed until November, when heavy rains set in, washing out the bridges and the roads. The Russians, whose strength rose to twenty-two battalions, held a firm position behind a torrential river. Finally, with great difficulty, on November 21 (O.S.) Omer approached the Russian position, but the rains and the flooded river made an attack impossible. News of the fall of Kars reached him, and on the 25th he decided to retreat. The Russians, who had destroyed most of their supplies, could not make an effective pursuit, although they harassed the Turkish rear guard. When the Turks reached the coast, the sea was too stormy for them to evacuate, so that they had to winter in Redut-Kale. The Russians planned to attack them early in 1856, but the signing of the peace treaty at Paris intervened.[12]

In the meanwhile, the Russians, who were fighting the Turks on the frontiers, were also continuously fighting the Caucasian mountaineers on both sides of the mighty range of mountains. There was little action in the western sector along the fortified line of the Kuban river from the Black Sea to the Georgian Military Highway through the center of the range. East of it was the active Chechen country along the Terek river to the Caspian Sea, where the numerous and warlike inhabitants had their villages and farmlands in the foothills, from which they often raided Russian posts. The center of opposition to the Russians was Dagestan, where the fierce tribesmen lived precariously on sheep-raising and pillage. Under Shamil, the Imam, or religious leader, these tribesmen had almost driven the Russians out in 1843 and had organized a government with taxes, courts, and a fighting force that included some artillery. The Russians had beaten back Shamil's offensive, in which the Chechens had played an important part,

11. Bestuzhev, pp. 157–58.
12. Murav'ev, II, 299–329; Bogdanovich, IV, 356–66.

and had evolved a policy of cutting the dense forests that protected them. By opening up roads into the Chechen lands the Russians could destroy the inhabitants' villages and crops and force them either to flee further into the mountains or to submit to the Russians and settle under their protection. While the Chechens still hated the Russians, they valued their safety, and many willingly came under the Russian shelter, electing their own judges and establishing a militia to defend their settlements against the punitive raids of Shamil's forces. By 1852 so many Chechens had settled under the protection of the Russians— which sharply reduced Shamil's power—that full Russian control over the whole mountainous region began to seem possible.[13]

South of the main mountain chain the Russians had another defense line to protect the rich lands of Christian Georgia against the Kabardinians and other mountaineers of the western Caucasus; they also had other fortifications to hold back the fiery Lezgians from attacking Tiflis. On the whole the Russian position seemed fairly secure.

When the Turks declared war in 1853 and attacked the Russian outposts, Prince M. S. Vorontsov, the viceroy of the Caucasus, and his advisers were terrified, as they had far too few troops to fight both the Turks and the tribesmen. The Turks encouraged Shamil to intensify his actions against the Russian defenses, and in 1854 the British vainly sought to mobilize the Circassians to join the attacks and sent in good rifles and ammunition for Shamil's followers. In fact, while the Russian regiments in the Caucasus area were still using flintlocks, Shamil's bands were using modern rifles firing Minié balls. But the Russians had veteran troops of great skill and courage, and with powerful artillery and excellent leadership they were superior to the foe.

Dismayed by the coming of war in 1853, the Russians in this area did very little during the winter, which encouraged Shamil's forces to take action. The tribesmen had no significant successes, however, and the Russians continued to cut the forests and wipe out the food supplies of the Chechens. There were many small actions, in which the losses of the Russians were slight. Late in June, however, reports came in that Shamil was massing fifteen thousand men for a powerful strike, although his objective remained unknown. General N. A. Read, the commander, warned all units to be ready to move as soon as

13. A. L. Zisserman, *Istoriia 80-go pekhotnago Kabardinskago . . . polka* (St. Petersburg, 1881), II, 126–27, 143–45.

Shamil's intention was clear, while two of the local commanders made new raids on the Chechens, destroying more villages and much food. Suddenly Shamil crossed over the central chain of the mountains, making a drive directly against Tiflis, hoping to loot and destroy it and to link up with the Turkish army. But his advance was checked by the Georgian peasants, who, forming bands and attacking his forces, held him up enough for the Russians to collect troops, which almost cut his retreat. In September three thousand mountaineers attacked the post of Andreeva, but it held, and other forces rushed to the rescue, so that the enemy fled in panic, sustaining heavy losses.[14]

But Shamil's plans still remained a mystery, and Baron Nikolai kept his small force concentrated at a fort not far from the village of Istisu, where there were a number of resettled Chechens. Suddenly the sound of cannon fire confirmed Nikolai's expectations, for the village and small redoubts of Istisu were under heavy attack by Shamil's bands. Nikolai's forces rushed to the rescue in headlong fashion, at great risk. Since they were completely unexpected, their musketry and cannon fire shocked the attackers, and when the Russian cavalry attacked the other flank, the whole horde fled in panic. The Chechens had fought bravely against their former allies, and the Russians had arrived in the nick of time. This was a decisive action, for Shamil's hopes were dashed and his supporters were dejected. If Shamil had won, the Russian position would have been in grave danger.[15]

By the summer of 1854 the Chechens who had not settled under Russian protection could see no hope for the future. The best lands in the foothills were now fully open to the Russians and were settled by Cossack villagers or, with the trees cut down, were exposed at all times to Russian raiders, who destroyed the Chechens' crops and their food reserves. They were constantly being pushed further and further into the mountains, to less fertile areas, and had to abandon their newly built homes and the fruits of their labors and in new wilderness to hew out fields for planting, never secured against a new attack. Thus many more Chechens, especially those with grievances against Shamil and his henchmen, decided to turn against his cause and to move to areas completely under Russian control.[16] The Russians' en-

14. Ibid., pp. 170–79.
15. Ibid., II, 182–98.
16. A. L. Zisserman, *Dvadtsat' piat' let na Kavkaze (1842–1867)* (St. Petersburg, 1879), pt. 2, 236.

couragement of this resettlement weakened Shamil's authority and substantially reduced the effect of his promises to prevent the Russians from troubling them. The Chechen families who had settled on lands under the Russians were free of taxation and other obligations and, compared to those still exposed to Russian attacks, enjoyed prosperity.[17]

The woodcutting by the Russians continued until late December 1854; seventeen villages along a river were burned, together with vast food supplies, and several miles of impossibly thick forest were cleared, making way for a road over which small columns of troops could move freely. All the Chechen population of the area fled further up into the mountains, where they suffered from cold and hunger. Most of them were ready to resettle under the Russians, with only the fear of grim vengeance by Shamil's chieftains holding them back. Soon some of them asked the Russians for help, and under the protection of a special column of troops that held the main river crossing, scores of families succeeded in making a secret escape and resettled near the Russian fort of Groznaia.[18]

In April 1855 many of the hostile Chechens returned to their ruined villages to start their farm work, since the Russians had apparently gone away and Shamil had sent a force to protect them. But the Russians suddenly began making surprise raids, destroying the rebuilt huts and causing much other destruction. The unfortunate Chechens sadly sent word to Shamil that the Russians were still far from powerless. Other raids were made during the summer, with more of the tribesmen resettling under Russian protection. In July three battalions of infantry and three thousand cavalry pushed into the remote Shali valley, cutting down or trampling on great fields of corn with no real opposition. Some expeditions ran into stiff resistance, which cost them considerably, but the main force moved freely through the Chechen country, wiping out crops and burning villages and farm houses. The felling of the trees continued, and the troops cleaned out the new growth from earlier clearings. Even more than the fall of Kars in November, the actions of the Russians in the heart of the Chechen country showed the tribesmen that the Russians were still powerful and that Shamil could not stop them.[19]

17. Ibid.
18. Ibid., II, 255.
19. Zisserman, *Istoriia,* II, 216–34.

Although the treatment of the Chechens by the Russians was cruel, the Russians had no choice but to continue fighting against an elusive foe or subdue the population and gain control of the territory. They believed the latter course was the only safe one to follow, especially since it cost them relatively few losses in manpower. Hence they presented the Chechens with three options: to be ruined or destroyed by the Russian raids; to flee into the wilderness to try to escape their punitive measures; or to submit and break their ties with Shamil.[20]

In the Caucasian theater of operations, then, the Russians were quite successful, for, contrary to their expectations, they inflicted several defeats on the Turks and at the end of the war had won Kars and had repelled Omer pasha's attempt to capture Tiflis. Moreover, the Russian commanders in Dagestan and Chechnia had beaten back the efforts of Shamil and his followers to break through the Russian cordon and to link themselves with the Turks. Muraviev had failed to take Erzerum, to be sure, but this was because of excessive caution rather than because of the resistance of the Turks. The latter realized fully that the Russians were far superior to them, in spite of British naval power, British supplies, and excellent English commanders to train their troops and command them.

What is especially significant is that in 1853 the Russian situation had looked very bleak. The Turks had captured one of their frontier posts and Turkish forces were harrying the Armenian villages near Erivan. The Russians were desperately trying to stave off disaster until some reinforcements could come, and with much difficulty they evacuated a string of small forts along the Black Sea coast, which would prove very vulnerable to British attack. When France and England declared war on Russia Prince Vorontsov, the viceroy, completely lost heart and was soon replaced by General Read. Read and the staff at Tiflis were far from confident, however, for they wanted to abandon the whole coast, since they believed that the local population would probably make common cause with the Turks if they landed. In February 1854 Read proposed holding off the enemy by fortifying Tiflis and massing his troops there, with no mention of plans for offensive action. Nicholas I flatly rejected this scheme, insisting on holding the whole position with fewer troops and strengthening the army on the frontier with four battalions from Dagestan and part of

20. Ibid., p. 202.

the forces at Tiflis. Again the Caucasian commanders were dismayed. Read now proposed pulling all troops out of the Dagestan mountains and holding the central position around Tiflis. Nicholas would hear none of this, for he felt the Russian forces should hold the entire position and he threatened Read with disgrace if he abandoned anything. On that basis Read and then Muraviev fought the rest of the war with, as has been seen, considerable success.[21]

The British also erred in their plans for the war in the Caucasus, for they had been far too optimistic. Palmerston, Urquhart, and Redcliffe all had expected great things of the Turks, who, they thought, aided by British money, arms, and seapower, would be able to bring in large and powerful armies and to incite the Kabardinians and other tribesmen to help them, thus overwhelming the Russians and driving them from the Caucasus. Palmerston repeatedly talked of conquering all of the Crimea and the mainland to the mouths of the Don and the Volga, which would reduce the Russian territory to its holdings at the time of Peter the Great. But the Turks were vastly weaker than they had been in the early eighteenth century, and the Russians were obviously much more powerful than they had been before. Hence, in 1856 the Russian position in the Caucasus was much stronger than it had been in 1853, and there was no way in which the British could reverse the situation, especially as they could provide no troops of their own.

In their efforts to strike at the Russians the British and the French undertook several ventures, of which one was to conquer Finland and Sweden. As has been mentioned in chapter 11, in 1854 Sir Charles Napier commanded a fleet in the Baltic in an effort to attack St. Petersburg and the Russian position in Finland, but proved unable to cause any material harm. The Swedes, who probably would have been pleased to recover Finland, dared not challenge their powerful neighbor, especially since the Finns were loyal to the tsar. The British and the French did succeed in capturing the fortress of Bomarsund in the Åland Islands but made no attempt to hold it. In 1855 the British again invaded the Gulf of Finland, with a powerful fleet commanded by Admiral Richard Dundas, including mortar ketches, floating batteries, and gunboats, as well as ships, frigates, and steamers. Once more they could accomplish little. They came within sight of

21. Miliutin MS, pp. 84–88.

Kronstadt but did not try to attack it, although they sent in small landing parties to do as much damage as they could. At Hangö a British party was surprised by the Russians, who killed six men and captured eleven, as well as capturing their boat, and later the Russians beat off another landing party at Hangö. At Vyborg and Friedrichshamn British attacks did little damage. Finally, on July 25/August 6 the Allied fleet was in position before Sveaborg, and on August 9 there was a general bombardment, with the fleet engaged and a French mortar battery on a small island near the fort. Some small magazines blew up, part of the town caught fire, and the ship *Rossiia* was badly hit by bombs and almost exploded. But the attackers failed to make landings, and after three days the fleet sailed away. The Russians lost sixty-two men killed and two hundred wounded; the English lost thirty-three.[22]

Although the Allied operations in Finnish waters proved to be fruitless, late in 1855 King Oscar, who had previously clung to his neutral stance, moved toward an alliance with the West. Earlier he had been quite friendly toward Nicholas I, and he apparently had no current grievance. The fact that by this time it seemed certain that the Allies were going to win the war doubtless encouraged the king, and Russia was Sweden's traditional enemy. Whatever the reason, in April 1855 Count Barck, Oscar's envoy, conferred with Napoleon III and with Lord Clarendon. They were both very cordial, but could promise him no military support, although they offered subsidies. After the fall of Sevastopol Oscar was again interested, although he did not consider the matter urgent. Finally, after long delays, he signed a treaty with the Allies promising not to give Russia fishing, pasturage, and other rights in Norway and Sweden. If Russia should demand such concessions, the Allies would support Sweden with their troops and fleets.[23]

Nesselrode mentioned this development, which apparently came as a surprise to the Russian cabinet, in a letter to Gorchakov, saying that it was not serious if there was to be no secret engagement. "Whatever it may be," he said, "it is always very annoying that Sweden has a foot in the western alliance." [24] Valentin Esterházy at St. Petersburg reported that at any other time such an affront to Russia would

22. Cullberg, pp. 291–93; M. Mikhailov, "Istoricheskii ocherk Sveaborga i bombardirovaniia ego Anglo-Frantsuzskim flotom . . . 1855 goda," *VS,* no. 10 (1860), pp. 251–59.

23. Cullberg, II, 43–77.

24. Letter, Nesselrode to Gorchakov, Oct. 13, 1855, TsGAOR, f. 828, D, no 604, opis' no. 1.

have resulted in a diplomatic rupture between the two governments. "Nevertheless," he said, "the Cabinet at St. Petersburg, painful as this treaty must have seemed to it . . . far from showing itself irritated, sent to its envoy at Stockholm a despatch, whose tenor, according to what M. de Nordin assures me, bears a friendly and benevolent character, which he was far from expecting." [25] Nesselrode apparently felt that this treaty was of little significance, and he was probably correct.

Much less important than the Allied foray into Finnish waters was the British action in the remote White Sea—a very isolated part of Russia—in the summer of 1854. As it had no strategic significance, the English ships probably went there to win a cheap victory and to do what damage they could. The frigates *Brisk* and *Miranda* on July 6/18 approached the Solovetskii monastery and after anchoring, fired at the gate and destroyed it, and then bombarded the monastery. There was a shore battery with two three-pound cannon, and eight small guns on the walls and the towers. The battery returned the fire, but fell silent after thirty rounds. On the next day a ship's boat under a white flag delivered a summons to surrender or be destroyed. When the *archimandrite* (abbot) refused, the ships began a bombardment lasting over nine hours, with bombs and round shot. The bombardment did considerable damage, especially to the roof and the walls, but the monastery was not destroyed, and there was apparently no loss of life. On July 8/18 the *Brisk* and the *Miranda* sailed away, without having obtained the surrender of the monastery. [26]

After remaining inactive for about one month, the *Miranda* appeared off the open town of Kola on the Barents Sea. Kola had no cannon and only a handful of old soldiers and a number of armed volunteers, but on August 10/22 it refused to surrender. Hence the ship bombarded it heavily for over four hours, with bombs, shells, hot shot, and incendiary projectiles. Almost the entire town burned. The British made several attempts at a landing, which were beaten off by the defenders. The bombardment was renewed, so that in all it lasted over twenty-eight hours. When the ship sailed away, only eighteen houses were still standing, and there was food for only two months. The Russians suffered no loss of manpower during the encounter. [27]

A much more important episode was the encounter of an Anglo-

25. Esterházy to Buol, Dec. 17/29, 1855, HHSA, X, 41.
26. Tarle, *Krymskaia Voina,* II, 207–08.
27. Ibid., pp. 209–12.

French squadron with the Russians at Petropavlovsk on Kamchatka. The Allied ships had been on the trail of two Russian frigates which they feared would seek to destroy Allied commerce in the Pacific. They chased the frigate *Aurora* from Valparaiso to Hawaii and then followed it to Kamchatka, but they were always too late, for it had reached the harbor several weeks before the Allies finally arrived. And when they finally reached Kamchatka they found that the *Aurora* and the *Dvina* had been there long enough to land seven hundred men and to build seven batteries to protect the port and the ships. Admiral Price, in command of the force, shot himself, apparently fearing court-martial for having bungled the pursuit. Under the French Admiral Depointe the Allied vessels easily silenced two of the batteries, but then they decided to attack Battery 2 by land. A considerable force of French sailors landed to attack it, but by an error a British shell burst in their midst, doing much damage and throwing them into confusion. A Russian bayonet charge completed their dismay, and they fled to their boats.[28] The bombardment of Battery 2 failed, and the Allied forces retired to lick their wounds and quarrel in their council of war about what to do next.

From two Americans the British learned of an easy way to reach the harbor of Petropavlovsk by going overland across the neck of land separating the two bays. This involved climbing the road to the mountain, knocking out an eight-gun battery, and then pushing down into the harbor. At first all went well and the battery was silenced. But when the landing forces, chiefly sailors, sought to storm the heights, the columns got separated, and some of them were lost in the underbrush. At this moment the Russians made a powerful counter-attack with bayonets. Many of the French and British officers were killed, and the Russians drove numbers of the attackers, in a panic, over a cliff. The rest got to their boats, but many were lost in making good their escape. This was a great Russian victory, for while the Russians had lost about 100 men killed or wounded, the Allies lost about 350. The victors celebrated with full solemnity. They had captured as trophies a British flag, seven officers' swords, and fifty-six muskets.[29]

28. Ibid., pp. 213–19; Edmond de Hailly, "Une campagne dans l'Océan Pacifique. L'expédition de Petropavlovsk," *Revue des Deux Mondes, seconde période*, XVI (1858), 687–709; I. P. Barsukov, *Graf Nikolai Nikolaevich Murav'ev-Amurskii* (Moscow, 1891), I, 376–77.

29. Tarle, *Krymskaia Voina*, II, 220–24; Barsukov, *Graf Nikolai*, I, 378–90; Hailly, pp. 710–16.

After the Allies had definitely left, the Russians decided to evacuate Petropavlovsk, since they were sure that in 1855 the enemy would make another, stronger attack. During the winter they retired into the wilds of Kamchatka, and in March the authorities took away almost all the military and naval personnel as well as artillery and other military equipment and moved them to safety on the mainland.[30] By thus stopping the vengeance of the enemy, the Russians achieved a second triumph.

From these accounts of Russia's secondary campaigns during the Crimean War, as well as from the discussion of the major fighting, it becomes clear that Russia was not an easy country to attack. The scarcity of good, deep-water harbors not bound by ice in the winter made it almost impossible to organize a successful seaborne invasion, while the lack of good roads made an overland campaign into the heart of the country almost impossible, as Charles XII of Sweden and Napoleon I had learned by hard experience. There were no railways into the interior of the country. The Crimea was almost the only place where the invaders had favorable communications and the Russians had difficult logistical problems. If the Allies had ventured any distance away from the coast their logistics would have become much more difficult, while those of the Russians would have improved. The Crimean adventure was not a regular field campaign, but a large-scale landing raid, which ended in a protracted siege. The Allies never ventured to invade the broad plains, the endless forests, and the swamps of Russia, and Russia's neighbors—the Austrians, the Prussians, and the Swedes—were much adverse to such an undertaking.

Moreover, the Russian army was not a negligible force. While its tactics and weapons were often backward, its engineering generals, such as Schilder and Totleben, and its sappers and miners, such as Mel'nikov, were highly effective. Also, its artillery was powerful and well handled, according to the repeated comments of British and French officers. The infantry, using inaccurate smooth-bore muskets against troops with rifles and Minié balls, suffered many losses in combat, and its firepower was weak. But the men were stubborn and determined and their bayonet charges were hard to withstand. In good defensive positions the Russian infantry was difficult to dislodge and would endure severe losses without giving way. The men were patriotic

---

30. Tarle, *Krymskaia Voina,* II, 228–30.

and loyal, and under a commander whom they trusted and admired their morale was fiery and they were capable of great feats. Both the French and the British who survived the Crimea had great admiration for the Russian soldier. The regular cavalry, however, on the whole was ineffective, for Nicholas I had stressed fine-looking horses and manège training of the men, who, as a result, knew little of the duties of the cavalryman on campaign.

The army in the Caucasus differed considerably from the regular army, for there was little of the button-polishing, parade-ground training, and the veteran troops prided themselves on their ability to fight under the most difficult conditions and cared little for the formal tactics of the drill manual. The cavalry of the Caucasus was able to fight on even terms or better with the fierce Caucasian tribesmen in the defiles or in ambushes on precipices or in the dense forests of the Chechen country. The troops of the Caucasus Corps were professionals, and because of their skills they could defeat much larger numbers of Turks or overcome and subjugate the mountaineers. Thus the British and the French achieved no real successes in the Caucasian area, and the Russian position in the unpacified mountain region was much stronger at the end of the war than it had been when it started.

CHAPTER 18. THE LAST RUSSIAN OFFENSIVE

The Russian successes against the Turks in Anatolia and Georgia, the victories over Shamil and the Chechens, and the repulse of the British fleet at Sveaborg showed that the Russian defenses were not about to collapse. These achievements, however, were not decisive, for the Allies had committed their main strength in the Crimea, and it was there that the war would be won or lost. And in the first days of April 1855 even here the Russian situation looked fairly promising. With great skill and boldness the defenders had carried the war to the enemy by setting up two strong redoubts on the Inkerman heights near the mouth of the Chernaia river, which outflanked the French approaches to the Malakhov kurgan and enfiladed their batteries and approaches to it. Once the French attempt to storm the new works had been beaten off and the Russians had installed cannon in them, they did an even more daring thing. On the Green Hill, directly in front of the Malakhov, but about eighteen hundred feet from it and only some twelve hundred feet from the French lines, on the night of February 28 the besieged erected the Kamchatka lunette, which once more troubled the flanks of the attackers. Again the French had to defer their advance until they could overcome this new obstacle. Moreover, the Russians built rifle pits and trenches in front of it, from which their marksmen harassed French workers in their approaches. The French did not try to storm the lunette, as it was protected by the fire of Bastion 3 and the two redoubts on the Russian left, but they made numerous attacks on the trenches in front of it, whereupon the Russians reacted vigorously, and there were heavy losses on both sides. These bold strokes of the defenders brought the French advance to a halt and so ably countered their plans that the French leaders believed that the enemy was learning their plans from spies. The fiery General Bosquet said, "It really seems that the Russian engineers respond day by day to our ideas, all our projects as if they had been present at our conferences. . . . I think today especially about spies." [1] And the French historian Colonel Léon Guérin wrote on March 16 (N.S.), "We are attacking an enemy who envelops us and who, by his right, rests on a formidable entrenchment. . . . We came here to deliver a major defeat to the Russians, and for the moment we do not seem to be on the road to this." [2]

Nevertheless, although the Russians had achieved a brilliant success, it was costly in the long run. Because they built the redoubts and the lunette when the French were already massing in this sector, they had to construct the works hastily and could not properly provide them with secure dugouts for the troops, powder magazines that would withstand enemy bombs, and traverses to protect the flanks of the guns. The terrain, which was mostly shale, was hard to dig and did not stay in position, so that walls crumbled under bombardment. It was impossible to dig an effective ditch before the Kamchatka lunette.[3]

The matter of fortifying the Green Hill had been raised earlier. Both Nicholas I and Paskevich had called for occupation of the forward positions, and after Inkerman Admiral Istomin had urged the building of a redoubt there. On March 20, 1855, Alexander II wrote to Prince M. D. Gorchakov, the new commander at Sevastopol, rejoicing over the success in building the new works. He added: "I am sorry only that their conclusion was not accomplished three months before, as our unforgettable benefactor [Nicholas I] *repeatedly pointed out to Prince Menshikov.* At that time the loss would probably not have been so considerable as now." [4] Paskevich had also made a somewhat similar proposal in his letter of November 13, 1854. On November 17 Nicholas replied, "Thy plan of defense is word for word what I repeatedly asked Menshikov to adopt, but up to now without success, and why I do not know." [5] Certainly it would have been wise to build these fortifications earlier. In 1854, however, the chief danger was to Bastion 4; the Malakhov was not under attack. Much had to be done to strengthen the existing works, and during the bad winter weather it would have been difficult to undertake this extensive new construction, especially as the Russians did not have large forces on

1. Schilder, *Graf Totleben,* I, 410.
2. Guérin, II, 129–30.
3. Vasil'chikov, 222–24.
4. M. I. Bogdanovich, ed., "Imperator Aleksandr Nikolaevich v epokhu voiny 1855 goda," *RS,* XXXVII (1883), 118.
5. Dubrovin, *Vostochnaia,* p. 401.

hand. While possibly a really effective commander would have seen the need for this construction and could have found the means, Menshikov, broken by the defeats of the Alma and Inkerman, was not the man to carry it out. Early in February 1855 the tsar removed Menshikov from his command.

When on March 8, 1855, Prince Gorchakov arrived to take charge of the Crimean Army, bringing with him his able staff, he was full of confidence that the war would soon be won. In his order of the day he assured the troops that the most difficult period had passed, since abundant supplies and reinforcements were coming. "Taking command over you," he said, "I am in full trust that soon, with the help of God, final success will crown your efforts and that we shall justify the expectations of our Sovereign and of Russia." [6] Gorchakov himself, however, quickly decided that all was lost, for in his letter of March 9 to the minister of war he wrote that Menshikov's blunders, especially at Inkerman, had made victory impossible. On March 18 he wrote, "It is a deadly heritage that I have received. . . . I am exposed to being turned, cut off, and perhaps broken, if the enemy has a little good sense and decision." And he continued to send other equally dismal letters.[7]

Gorchakov, who in his early life had been an effective and skillful soldier, in 1835 had become chief of staff under Paskevich in Poland, where he was directly responsible to the field marshal. Paskevich, "a man of iron will and unlimited vanity," dominated Gorchakov so completely that the latter lost all confidence in his own judgment and had little trust in others. Hence, when he had to make a decision he wavered, reconsidered, changed his position, and then halted, so that he became incapable of constructive action. He was personally very brave, honorable, and straightforward, but because for so long Paskevich had broken his spirit he was unable to function as an independent general in a position that called for crucial decisions. Now that he found himself faced with extremely difficult problems, he lost his nerve and sought to avoid solutions by endless appeals to St. Petersburg for more gunpowder and more troops. Hence during his period of command at Sevastopol he made a number of incorrect decisions, which helped to bring on the defeat that he foresaw.[8]

---

6. Khrushchov, pp. 76–77.
7. Schilder, *Graf Totleben*, I, 409–11.
8. Bogdanovich, *Vostochnaia voina*, III, 257; Men'kov, I, 24–27; Schilder, *Graf Totleben*, I, 409–12.

Regarding the construction of the redoubts on the left flank, Gorchakov felt that it was extremely risky, although he also stated that it should have been done three months before.[9] Because he held this negative view of the building of the two redoubts and the Kamchatka lunette, he was unwilling to accept the heavy losses that alone would make it possible to retain them. Hence, at the vital moment, as will be seen, he failed to assign enough men to their defense, which resulted in an easy victory by the French, who overran the Russians with a huge force. Similarly, when Totleben wished to set up a strong point at the cemetery on the Russian right, Gorchakov approved the venture, but when he realized how costly it would be to maintain, he wavered, reconsidered, changed his position, and ended by refusing to commit enough men to hold it, so that the French, who also had lost heavily, took the cemetery, with the Russians having nothing to show for their loss of men.

For several weeks in March the action was not excessive, although the French were making increasingly determined efforts to seize the rifle pits and trenches before the left redoubts and the Kamchatka lunette, from which the Russian sharpshooters harassed the French workers in the approaches and batteries. When the besiegers tried to drive off the Russian marksmen by large sorties, the Russians responded with fierce counterattacks, which even pushed well into the French defenses and spiked guns in their batteries. There were many losses in this fighting, but because it was man to man, the Russians could more than hold their own. The French were also making decided efforts to draw closer to Bastions 4 and 5 on the Russian right and the Schwartz battery, which were actively defended by the Russians, supported by the guns of their fortifications. Here again the losses were heavy on both sides, with the Russians troubling the besiegers by their fierce fighting.

Finally, on March 28/April 9 the Allies began their second bombardment by all their batteries, and their warships increased their movements. The Russians replied, although, because of their shortage of powder, they had to restrict their response to one round for every two of the attackers. The bombardment inflicted great damage on the left redoubts, the Kamchatka lunette, and Bastions 4 and 5. At night the defenders worked furiously to repair the damage, reopening

9. Schilder, ibid., p. 412.

the embrasures, cleaning out the ditches, and replacing smashed guns and gun carriages. The enemy kept up a constant mortar fire all night to kill the workers, and rifle fire also continued until morning. But in spite of severe losses the Russians restored their defenses and renewed their fire. The defenders, however, had so little powder that they severely restricted its use; thus the Allied gunners could easily increase their advantage. Moreover, the Allies had 130 mortars, mostly of huge caliber, of which the Russians had very few. The French and the British fired almost three times as many rounds as the Russians. Bastions 4 and 5, the Kamchatka lunette, and the two redoubts were very hard hit. By nightfall, when the redoubts were silenced, Bastion 4 had only two guns still in action. Nevertheless, the Russians, by superhuman exertions, managed to repair all their defenses during the night and to replace almost all the damaged guns. They worked furiously, especially at Bastion 5, since they feared that the French would assault it. They did attack and captured some of the lodgements, but by a heavy fire of grape shot and by counterattacks the Russians finally drove the enemy out of all their defenses.[10]

Although the French were transferring the center of their attack to the Kamchatka lunette and the Malakhov, the heaviest fighting was at Bastions 4 and 5 and at the Schwartz battery, and after several days of intense firing the gunfire directed against the two redoubts on the left and even against the Kamchatka lunette slacked. But the French, who were close to Bastion 4 and using powerful artillery against it, almost knocked it out. They also tried to capture the Russian approaches near Bastion 5 and the Schwartz battery, but were finally driven out.[11]

In general, during the second bombardment the Russians held out very well, for they were able to restore their works even when they were badly damaged. The two left redoubts, which suffered severely, came through the ordeal and eventually became superior to the opposing French batteries. Even the Kamchatka lunette was successful in its resistance, for after April 7 the Allies halted the general bombardment and from then until April 11 concentrated their fire on Bastion 4. The French, however, could not move their approaches close to it, and did not set up a demounter battery against it. Even so, its position was very weak and the French could have stormed and held

10. Totleben, II, 97–118.
11. Ibid., pp. 120–47.

it if they had not been dismayed by the fierce and determined resistance they encountered.

Actually, the Russians had somewhat more cannon installed than did the Allies, although the latter were superior in the caliber of their guns and especially had a much greater number of mortars. The chief superiority of the Allies was in gunpowder and projectiles, so that most of the time they fired two or three shots for one of the Russians. By March 30 the latter, fearing that they would have to cease fire because of a lack of ammunition, took powder from some of the forts that were in no immediate danger and from some of their ships. By April 2 they were so desperate that they broke open small-arm cartridges and used the powder for the cannon, causing the commander-in-chief to order that each gun keep an untouchable reserve of fifty rounds. In the most important batteries 162 guns were limited to fifteen rounds per day, 224 guns were restricted to ten rounds, and 53 guns to only five rounds per day. On April 7 the general bombardment halted, which permitted the Russians to repair all their defenses, except for Bastion 4, which was still under great pressure.

The Russian losses of men were about three times as great as those of the Allies, in part because of the greater firepower of the latter. Moreover, the Russians had to make many repairs to their defenses every night, under heavy fire from mortars and from Allied sharpshooters, at a severe cost. Finally, because of fear of an imminent assault, they kept their reserves close to the main positions, so that the reserve units were often hit by enemy fire. But in spite of these disadvantages the Russians survived the bombardment and the Allies seemed no nearer success than before.[12]

After the second bombardment the French and, to a lesser degree the English, prepared for a new and even greater effort. The French sent in a large force of reserves early in May and with them came General A. J. J. Pélissier who in Algiers had won the reputation of a determined and ruthless commander. On May 7/19, after a council of war, Canrobert announced his resignation, and Pélissier at once took command. Pélissier was convinced that Sevastopol and the war would be won by centering the attack on the Malakhov, after which the fortress would be untenable. New batteries and approaches were

12. Ibid., pp. 149–69; K. Sh., "Kriticheskoe obozrenie sochineniia Ozhe [Auger]," *Voennyi Sbornik,* no. 8 (1860), pp. 416–32. French General Charles Auger's *Guerre d'Orient* is an authoritative account of the French artillery during the Crimean War.

built against the Kamchatka lunette and the two redoubts on the left. Napoleon was pleased with Pélissier's insistence on pushing on to victory, but the emperor was convinced that it was senseless for the French to continue butting their heads against the stone wall of the Russian defense. Instead, he demanded that Pélissier should lead a powerful army to the northeast of the city, in order to cut its communications with Simferopol and thus to starve it out. But the general, while he pretended to be following orders, secretly made great preparations for a massive drive against the redoubts and the lunette, which he hoped to capture before his master could stop him.[13]

There also was heavy fighting at the other end of the line, for the French were pushing the Russians hard at Bastions 4 and 5 and at the Schwartz battery. As stated in chapter 15, the French troops made vigorous attempts to seize the Russian trenches in front of these works, where they met equally stubborn Russian resistance, so that there were losses of two or three thousand men on each side in a single night's fighting. Hence Totleben and Khrulev decided to build a strong Russian battery in the cemetery on the Russian right, from which powerful Russian guns could rake Allied batteries against the lunette and in that way protect the Malakhov. This decision resulted in bloody hand-to-hand fighting, with the rifle pits changing hands five times. On May 23 the French again occupied the position and again clashed ferociously with the Russians. But Gorchakov was troubled by the bloodshed and reduced the forces assigned to the battle, which permitted the French to take over the position. Totleben, who felt that the Russians could have held it without undue sacrifices, was very disappointed, for he regarded the position as vital to the defense of the fortress, and the morale of the troops was still high.[14]

During this period the British were able to accomplish little, largely because their army had never fully recovered from the terrible winter that they had just experienced. The British navy did succeed in making an expedition through the Kerch Strait into the Sea of Azov on May 13/25, forcing the evacuation of the Russian shore batteries and then destroying quantities of wheat and other provisions in the coastal towns. A number of ships were captured or destroyed. This operation increased the difficulties of the Russians in supplying the Crimea, but since the British could not hold the ports that they had captured,

13. Auger, I, 211–16; Niel, pp. 167–70; Guérin, II, 43.
14. Auger, I, 276–80; Schilder, *Graf Totleben,* I, 419–24; Totleben, II, 232.

the effects of the raid were not great.[15] The British army, however, remained weak, for it had few reserves to fill its ranks and it had to seek recruits for a foreign legion, which obtained numbers of Germans, Canadians, Americans, and other volunteers. The British also, by offering considerable financial assistance, obtained from Cavour a Sardinian army of fifteen thousand, which served in the Crimea for part of 1855, although it saw little action. Since the Sardinians had no grievances against Russia, the sending of this force was clearly an effort to gain political influence, which could later be used against Austria.

The Western powers also sought to have Spain take part in the war, although on a limited scale, because of its civil war with the Carlists. They suggested a contingent of perhaps thirty thousand men, commanded by General Zavala and financed by the British. Spanish public opinion opposed this support, since Spain had no interest in the Eastern Question, and it was felt that the subsidy offered was purely for cannon fodder, which was unworthy of Spain. While the scheme fell through ostensibly for diplomatic reasons, the Spaniards never accepted any role for their country except that of strict neutrality.[16]

After May 12 the French built new approaches to the Russian right and increased their artillery, especially against the Malakhov, the Kamchatka lunette, and the left redoubts. The Russians improved their defenses, adding new guns and installing larger ones. They started mining operations at the Schwartz battery, and at Bastion 4 they had considerable success with their mine warfare. They were sparing with the use of powder, for they expected a new bombardment. Along with new reserves, however, more powder was now arriving in Sevastopol, and they now had 140 rounds per gun and 60 rounds for the mortars. But the Allies had five or six hundred rounds per gun.[17]

On May 25 the third bombardment began along the whole line, with greater intensity than before. By evening the Russian left flank was hard hit. The Kamchatka lunette, which was attacked by forty-eight heavy guns, fared the worst, especially from bombs and from demounter batteries. By evening it was out of commission, for all embrasures were closed, part of the wall had collapsed, and many

---

15. Tarle, *Krymskaia Voina,* II, 394–96.
16. Luís Mariñas Otero, "España ante la Guerra de Crimea," *Hispania: Revista española,* XXVI (1966), pp. 438–40.
17. Totleben, II, sec. 1, 273–84.

of the gunners had been hit. The left redoubts, which were also under heavy assault, continued to fire at the enemy with some success. The main Russian defense line did well, except the Malakhov, which was almost silenced. Bastions 3 and 4 were hard hit, but they continued to maintain a good fire. At night the Allies slacked off their direct fire, but their mortars continued all night. The Russians responded as best they could and worked energetically to repair the damage.[18]

On the 26th the intensity of the bombardment was such that the Kamchatka lunette was soon so badly damaged that it could not reply, and in a few hours the Malakhov was in bad shape. The left redoubts also were hard hit, with many of their gunners out of action. Only Bastion 3 held its own. At all points the defenders worked intensively on the repairs, but by nightfall the two redoubts were almost silenced, and the lunette was a mere pile of dirt, although somehow two of its guns kept on firing. The Malakhov was operating at half its former capacity.[19]

Thus the left redoubts and the Kamchatka lunette were in great danger of capture. Totleben asked that the garrison and reserves be increased to at least eight battalions. As a result, eight were sent to the two redoubts and four to the Kamchatka. Later ten battalions went to the left redoubts. General Timofeev, in command of this sector, feeling that the increase in manpower was far too great, put only two companies in each redoubt, with two battalions in reserve. General Zhabokritskii, the elderly local commander of the sector, who was opposed to the use of the counterapproach system as very costly in terms of human life, reduced the garrisons of the redoubts by 50 percent and then left the area, reporting to the northern side as sick. Since Zhabokritskii was a Pole, his action was widely regarded as treason; it was, however, more likely the result of his desire to minimize losses and his belief that the Allies would not attack the redoubts. Count D. E. Osten-Sacken, commander of the garrison, and Prince Gorchakov also felt that keeping large garrisons in the redoubts and the lunette caused unnecessarily high losses.[20]

On the evening of the 26th General Khrulev, who took Zhabokrit-skii's place on the Russian left, noting that the French were preparing to attack, ordered a large increase of the garrisons and the reserve

18. Ibid., pp. 285–87.
19. Ibid., pp. 288–90.
20. Ibid., pp. 290–93; Miloshevich, p. 47.

of the redoubts and the Kamchatka lunette, but by that time it was too late. The French attacked in overwhelming strength and the garrisons, taken by surprise, could offer little resistance. Khrulev rushed up reserves to retake these works, but his forces met a deadly fire from the French and were almost surrounded.

The French assault on the Kamchatka lunette also met with success at the same time, for the enemy attacked from three sides and almost captured Admiral Nakhimov, who had gone there to observe. Nakhimov and the remnants of the garrison, hotly pursued by the French, retreated to the Malakhov, where the French, attacking contrary to orders, met a terrible fire of grape shot and were driven back in disorder. At this point a land mine exploded inside the lunette, terrifying the French, who, said Totleben, "retired pellmell into their own trenches." The Russians made a strong counterattack and occupied the lunette and all the trenches of the counterapproaches. French reserves now entered the fray and although the Russians defended themselves "with ferocity," they were overcome and driven back in confusion, and the French firmly held this key position.[21]

At the same time the British advanced and took the stone quarries and the parallels in front of their lines, although the Russians, fighting desperately, drove them out three times. Finally the British made good their possession. General Lysons, however, who reported these events, said, "Our loss has been very great." [22]

The French losses in their successful attacks were quite high. Pélissier, who had made the assault contrary to orders, reported his success to Paris only after five days, but he received no reply. Finally he demanded to know if the emperor would not congratulate his troops. Napoleon wired back that before he congratulated them on their brilliant success he wished to know how great the losses had been. He had learned the figure from St. Petersburg. While he admired the bravery of the soldiers, "I would observe to you that a battle fought to decide the fate of the entire Crimea would not have cost you more. I persist then in the order . . . to make all your efforts to enter resolutely into a field campaign." [23] Pélissier, however, continued to disre-

21. Auger, pp. 300–307.
22. Daniel Lysons, *The Crimean War from First to Last: Letters from the Crimea* (London, 1895), p. 188.
23. Gooch, p. 217.

gard the emperor's orders and pushed the assault on the Russian fortifications.

While a number of the Russian leaders drew from this failure the conclusion that the counterapproach system was dangerous and facilitated the Allied advance,[24] Totleben presented a convincing argument that the loss of the redoubts and the lunette was caused by the failure to hold them in sufficient strength and to station strong forces of reserves to support them. Whereas previously the Russians had kept six or more battalions in the two redoubts, and even raised the number to eight or ten, after May 22 there were only two on duty by day, and four others much too far off to be helpful. Totleben claims that eight more battalions could have been safely kept in the nearby ravine, where they would not have had heavy losses. If the Russians had been able to hold the redoubts, the French would have suffered so greatly in their attack that they probably could not have held the Kamchatka lunette, and a French failure to take the lunette would have greatly lengthened the siege.[25] A. P. Khrushchov takes much the same position in his excellent *History of the Defense of Sevastopol,* saying that the Allied success was caused by the scantiness of the defenders of this sector and by the failure to take steps to prepare for the attack that should have been expected. Generals Zhabokritskii and Timofeev did not make the proper preparations, and General Osten-Sacken, the commander of the garrison, did nothing to remedy the situation. Gorchakov also was to blame for assigning the incapable Zhabokritskii to this crucial sector.[26]

As soon as the French were firmly in possession of the captured works, they hastened to convert them into batteries against the main Russian fortifications and linked them with the central French position. In addition, new batteries were built to support them and to fire on the Malakhov and other Russian defenses. The French continued their bombardment for some time, and since the Russians as usual had too little powder, they could not prevent them from pushing their construction work. The defenders were not idle, for they built up batteries against the redoubts and the lunette and improved the interiors of their bastions and batteries with trenches, banquettes (shelves

24. Men'kov, I, 369–73.
25. Totleben, II, sec. 1, 309–10.
26. Khrushchov, pp. 109–10.

cut into the inner side of a fortress wall for marksmen to fire from), communications trenches, and entrenchments in the rear. They also prepared barbettes (platforms from which field guns could fire over low parapets) in some of the bastions.

Early in June the Russians learned that the Allies were about to launch a full-scale attack on the Russian defenses, since they now had great superiority in numbers. The besieged made preparations to fight to the end.[27]

The French and the British, encouraged by their successes in taking the Russian advance positions, planned for an assault of the fortress with 44,000 men. On June 5/17 they began a massive bombardment, to which the Russians could not reply effectively. By nightfall the Malakhov and Bastion 2 had had to curtail their fire greatly. The Allied fire smashed sixteen of the Russian guns, closed two hundred embrasures, and wounded sixteen hundred of the defenders. The Allies also bombarded Sevastopol itself with rockets and bombs, and the Allied fleets joined in the attack. During the night, however, the Russians restored most of the damaged fortifications and also built a barbette on the advanced angle of the Malakhov for four field guns to fire directly on enemy storming columns. Shortly after midnight Russian scouts noticed the massing of Allied troops and the defenders prepared to repel an assault. General Khrulev, who had again been put in command of the Russian left, brought up the reserves and had the guns made ready to fire.[28]

While the attack had been planned for 3:00 A.M., General Maillerand, leader of the French forces on the extreme right, either through a mistake or from excessive zeal, began the action about two o'clock by attacking Bastions 1 and 2. French troops, who were at once overwhelmed by a terrible bombardment from the fortifications and from the Russian steamers in the bay, were quickly disorganized and retired in confusion. General Pélissier then gave the signal for a general assault and the French columns charged Bastion 2 and the Malakhov. The defenders met them with a very heavy fire and drove them back with terrible losses.[29] British attacks on Bastion 3 were also a failure, and General Sir Colin Campbell was killed. General Daniel Lysons, who

27. Totleben, II, sec. 1, 318–28.
28. Ibid., pp. 335–39; Khrushchov, pp. 110–11; Anichkov, II, 142–48.
29. Totleben, II, sec. 1, 341–43; Khrushchov, pp. 112–15; Anichkov, II, 149–50; Auger, I, 326–28.

led a storming party against Bastion 3 stated, "We have had a dreadful day." When his party left their trenches "a perfect storm of grape-shot whistled from every side. I had to advance about 800 yards under this fire; my men and officers fell by dozens. . . ." They reached the abbatis before the bastion, but had to lie there. "At last I was left with about five or six men, and then thought it high time to be off; we were the last to go in. They fired at us all the way back. . . ." Lysons cited severe losses, although he said that the estimate of three thousand was probably too high. "I don't think they can call upon us again to storm," he commented. "Some of our regiments have only two officers left; somebody else must take a turn." [30]

The French had some notable success on this grim day, however, for General d'Hautemar's forces carried the Gervais battery, drove back the outnumbered defenders, and broke into houses at the foot of the Malakhov kurgan, where they fortified themselves, hoping that their reserves would join them to storm the city. But Khrulev, with Russian reserves and reformed units, intercepted them, ousted them from the houses, and forced them to retire in disorder to their own lines. Later other Russians arrived and recaptured the Gervais battery.[31]

According to their official reports, the Russians in the bombardment and fighting of June 5–6 lost 4,924, of whom 781 were killed. The British reported a total loss of 1,570, while the French gave a figure of 3,338, of whom almost half were killed. Since, however, the wounded usually were four or five times the number killed, this figure seems unusually low, especially as the Russians took 287 prisoners.[32]

Totleben explained the Allied failure by the fact that the French and British had to start their attacks from positions too far from their objectives, so that they encountered heavy fire. He also stated that if they had concentrated the operation against Bastions 4 and 5, they could have silenced them and then stormed them from their trenches, which were relatively close, with a victory practically assured. With these two central bastions in Allied hands, Sevastopol would have fallen in June.[33]

Napoleon III was angered by the outcome of the attack on June

30. Lysons, pp. 193–95.
31. Anichkov, pp. 150–51; Totleben, II, sec. 1, 343–45.
32. Anichkov, pp. 154–55.
33. Totleben, II, sec. 1, 405–06.

18, for it was directly contrary to his orders and its cost was excessive. He came close to removing Pélissier from command of the army. Marshal Vaillant and the other leading generals, however, persuaded the emperor to keep Pélissier as commander, for he was decisive and persistent, and Napoleon had no one with whom to replace him. Nevertheless, there was much gloom in the French camp over the severe casualties and the extensive illness. But the work went on, although slowly. The British also were much discouraged.[34]

It was some time before Allied morale recovered from the effects of the failure in June. Late in July General James Simpson, the British commander who replaced Lord Raglan, declared that the plateau before Sevastopol could not be held through a second winter, and if the fortress should hold out much longer, the Allies ought to abandon their trenches and retire to better positions. The chief French and British engineers in the Crimea, General Adolphe Niel and General Harry Jones, drew up a memorandum stating that since the Russian field army was still intact and since a full-scale Allied attack was probably dangerous, they had concluded that if the fortress should hold out until winter, the siege should be raised. Pélissier, however, protested vehemently against this view, and he was able to force through his policies, for Napoleon III insisted on victory in the Crimea.[35]

The Russians rejoiced mightily after the repulse of the Allied assault, but many soon realized that their situation was desperate. Generals V. I. Vasil'chikov, P. K. Men'kov, and Kozlianov, the new assistant chief of staff, conferred at great length concerning the fate of Sevastopol and reluctantly came to the conclusion that it was hopeless. The superiority of the enemy fire and the terrible losses of the Russians made it inevitable. They carefully considered the possibilities of a Russian attack from the valley of the Chernaia river on the Allied position on the Sapun-gora, from the Korabel'naia against the French; or from the city side, and agreed that they had no chance of winning in any of these encounters. Hence the only hope was to evacuate the southern side of Sevastopol voluntarily and to hold on to the northern side, in order to save many Russian lives and to preserve a strong Russian army.

In mid-June Men'kov and Vasil'chikov visited Prince Gorchakov at his headquarters. They raised the question of evacuation, but the

34. La Gorce, I, 410–14.
35. Ibid., pp. 393–95; Gooch, pp. 234–35.

prince and P. E. Kotsebu, his chief of staff, rejected the suggestion, although without giving sound reasons.[36]

In his diary Men'kov added that while St. Petersburg constantly "grieved" about the Crimea, it kept the Crimean Army short of powder, small arms, modern cannon, bombs, and other up-to-date weapons. For the protection of the swampy Baltic shore, however, defended by fortresses, they maintained 300,000 of the best troops armed with high-powered rifles and modern artillery, but they never fired a shot! At the same time "the other army dying in the bastions of Sevastopol was not reinforced in time, was constantly in need of powder and projectiles and, armed with sticks [obsolete muskets], fought against the strong Allied enemy, excellently armed, completely ready for war. . . ."[37]

Paskevich, at Warsaw, also did much to keep the Crimea weak, for in June, 1854 he had stated that there was little danger from Allied landings, because Menshikov "has up to 25,000 troops there, and 20,000 sailors. . . ." He added that "to attack 45,000 Russian troops for a landing, perhaps of 50,000 to 60,000, is not so easy."[38] In December 1854 he took exception to a statement that they should hold the Crimea under all circumstances. His comment was: "Should we *not* leave the Crimea? Why do they ascribe such importance to it? The Crimea is Sevastopol and fourteen ships in it. Compare which is better: to sacrifice these ships, or to be deprived of Bessarabia, Volhynia, Podolia, part of Ekaterinoslav, Kherson, Kiev, when Austria will be against us."[39]

In January 1855 Nicholas I sent his new plan of campaign to Paskevich, in which the monarch denied that he was willing to lose Poland in order to keep the Crimea: "I remain of the opinion that, relatively, preservation of the Crimea and the shore of the Black Sea is probably vastly more important, not only in influence on Europe, but also on Asia, and especially on our Transcaucasian areas." He did not, however, propose to abandon Poland without a fight, for he had always held that the Russian position there permitted Russia to hold the right bank of the Vistula and also to threaten Austria if it should dare to invade Russia.[40]

36. Men'kov, I, 385–87.
37. Ibid., pp. 390–91.
38. N. K. Schilder, "Paskevich v Krymskuiu voinu," *RS,* XV (1875), 641.
39. Shcherbatov, VII, 303.
40. Ibid., pp. 259–60.

Gorchakov, who had been hopeful of a speedy victory in the Crimea when he took command, soon decided that the future looked bleak, for by the end of July 1855 the Allies were so close to the Malakhov and Bastion 2 that an assault would probably be successful. Moreover, both Bastions 4 and 5 were in grave danger, for the Allies could probably knock out their artillery and then storm the fortifications. The defenders had the choice between a strong attack to force back the Allies or an evacuation of the southern side of the city. Late in July the 4th and 5th divisions (22,000 men) arrived, and 13,000 Kursk militia were scheduled to arrive in mid-August. There was a general feeling that the Russian public would not accept withdrawal without a last battle, but since the foe would still have superior numbers, the prospect was not promising. By early July Gorchakov was convinced that a passive defense would be best until many more troops should come, and in the meantime the Allies also were pouring in massive reinforcements and quantities of heavy mortars.[41]

While Gorchakov now sought to prove that an attack on the Allied position would be ruinous, many of the Russian soldiers and many in the government felt that the time had come to take decisive action against the Allies. Some of the leaders at Sevastopol wanted an attack; others, like Osten-Sacken and Khrulev, wanted to evacuate the southern side and to fight the enemy in the open. One important factor in this uncertainty was Baron Vrevskii, director of the Chancellery of the Ministry of War and one of the emperor's adjutant generals. Vrevskii had urged aggressive action, holding that the daily losses under passive defense were large and the results were poor. An attack would probably cost no more, and might bring important results. Both Alexander II and the minister of war urged Gorchakov, after holding a council of war, to attack, probably along the Chernaia river, with its precipitous banks.[42]

Gorchakov, vacillating as usual, sought to avoid a decision by conferring with the commanders under him. Osten-Sacken and Khrulev favored immediate evacuation of the southern side and then making a defense of the northern side and the McKenzie heights. Totleben, who was against an attack along the Chernaia, wanted an attack from the Korabel'naia quarter up the Dock and Laboratory ravines to storm

41. Totleben, II, sec. 2, 56–58.
42. Khrushchov, pp. 116–19; Schilder, *Graf Totleben,* I, 445–47; Men'kov, I, 389–93.

the British and French redoubts and force the Allies to retire. Finally, Gorchakov summoned a council of war to discuss the possibilities. At the meeting the majority favored an attack, and most picked the Fediukhin heights on the left bank of the Chernaia as the place for the offensive. Osten-Sacken again called for evacuation of the southern part of the city, and Vasil'chikov and Khrulev were against an attack, favoring the evacuation of Sevastopol and an assault from the high ground north of the bay. But since Gorchakov refused to evacuate, the majority approved making a stand along the Chernaia, although with no specific objective or plan. Gorchakov wrote a despairing letter to the minister of war prophesying defeat, as the enemy position was very strong. If things should turn out badly, it would not be his fault, he said, for the odds had been against him from the time of his arrival in the Crimea.[43]

Gorchakov, with his force anchored on the McKenzie and Inkerman heights, assigned General Read to lead the right wing with twenty-five battalions and sixty-two guns, against the Fediukhin heights. General Liprandi, with thirty battalions and seventy guns, would face Telegraph Hill, held by the Sardinians. Gorchakov had considerable infantry and artillery in reserve. He assigned Liprandi to capture Telegraph Hill and then to line up facing Gasfort Hill. While Gorchakov planned for Read to open heavy artillery fire against the Fediukhin heights, he instructed both commanders not to cross the river without express orders from him. He planned to decide on the objective after the battle had started—either Gasfort Hill or the Fediukhin heights, or possibly to "limit myself merely to a strong reconnaissance" if neither objective seemed promising. Alexander II had repeatedly expressed the opinion that when the three fresh divisions arrived Gorchakov should attack, not committing them piecemeal, but striking a crushing blow at the enemy, either in the trenches or in the field. Gorchakov, however, still wavered, preferring passive defense until the onset of cold weather, although he was not sure that the Allies would wait that long.[44]

On August 4/16 the forces under Read and Liprandi took up their positions at 4:00 A.M. and awaited orders. The Allies had learned

43. Schilder, *Graf Totleben,* I, 445–59; Vasil'chikov, pp. 239–40; Dmitrii Osten-Sacken, "Voennyi Soviet pri oborone Sevastopolia," *RS,* XI (1874), 332–38; Totleben, II, sec. 2, 69–76; Pogodin, *Zhizn' i trudy,* XIV, 78–79.

44. Bogdanovich, *Vostochnaia voina,* IV, 12–18; Muliutin MS, pp. 301–02a.

that the Russians were planning an attack, although they were not sure of the day.[45] Gorchakov, on the McKenzie heights, seeing that neither Liprandi nor Read had made a move, sent an aide to order them "to begin." But before the aide came Liprandi moved against Telegraph Hill, and Read had his artillery bombard the French position on the Fediukhin heights. Hence when the aide brought the order "to begin," Read did not know whether this meant merely to open fire or to attack. He and General Weimarn, his chief of staff, were convinced that they should make their attack, and as the adjutant could not inform them, they moved up the hill against the French. They had some initial success, swarming up the steep bank, after crossing the river and the canal, and capturing an earthwork and a battery. But French reinforcements were thrown in and the Russians, with no effective artillery support, had to retire. Gorchakov, who now realized that the battle was lost, sent in his reserves to support Read. The 5th division now came to his support, but it was put into action one regiment at a time and never had a chance. Liprandi did what he could to help, but his troops were repulsed and driven back to Telegraph Hill, which they had captured in the first moments of the battle. While Liprandi's artillery, firing across the river, gave Read some support, his position was hopeless and he and General Weimarn were both killed. By eight o'clock the Russians were completely driven back across the river and Gorchakov then halted the battle. After holding his troops in position for some time, hoping that the French would attack, finally in the early afternoon Gorchakov had his troops retire to McKenzie Hill. There was no sortie from Sevastopol, since Gorchakov felt that the Allied position was too strong to assault.[46]

This battle was extremely costly for the Russians, for they lost at least eight thousand men, and perhaps ten thousand. Most of their wounded remained in French hands. Generals Vrevskii, Weimarn, and Read, plus 249 other officers were killed or wounded. The Allies lost about eighteen hundred men, chiefly French and Sardinians. Gorchakov explained the disaster by citing the premature attack by Read and claimed that if this had not happened the Russians would have

45. Gooch, p. 241, states that Loftus, British envoy at Berlin, obtained word about the attack, apparently from Prussian generals, who had learned it from St. Petersburg. As a result the Allies heard of it just a few hours before the action. Lysons, pp. 208–09, says that the Allies had four days' warning.

46. I. I. Krasovskii, "Delo na Chernoi," *RA,* XII (1874), pp. 210–13; Totleben, II, pt. 2, 103–25; Bogdanovich, *Vostochnaia voina,* IV, 30–43.

won. Actually, the Russians had no chance of success, for the Allies, in greatly superior numbers, had an impregnable position.[47]

The outcome of the battle horrified many persons in Russia, including Field Marshal Paskevich, who had dominated much of Gorchakov's military life. From his deathbed the aged soldier wrote a devastating letter in which he correctly charged Prince Gorchakov with leading his army into a battle which he had no hope of winning and which he felt would be a calamity. Paskevich, who in 1854 had done the same, although with less deadly results, when to please Nicholas I he had led the Southern Army across the Danube, was merciless in chastising Gorchakov for the same folly. Charging that the prince had made the attack without purpose and without calculation, he was especially indignant that he had stated that he had done so "for the sake of the Emperor and because it was necessary to satisfy public opinion in Russia," although he had "little expectation of success."

Paskevich began his accusations with the statement that it was unforgivable for the commander to state that he had taken the offensive for the sake of the sovereign. Under such circumstances, the field marshal stated, the commander should sacrifice everything for the army and "should not blame the emperor, who was 1300 versts away." Secondly, he said that the emperor, who had entrusted the commander with a large part of his army, had a right to expect him to take action. Neither the monarch nor Russia could foresee, of course, that the attack would send the army to disaster. But even if the sovereign had ordered him to lead his army to what he regarded as certain death, he should have replied that it was impossible for him to perform the will of his master and asked the latter to recall him from the army as a man who did not justify the trust placed in him. If Gorchakov had acted honestly, as he should have, he would not be responsible for the blood of the ten thousand victims of the battle, who were lost on the Chernaia solely "because you did not dare to state frankly your opinion." [48]

The field marshal failed to see why Gorchakov began the attack when he was convinced it would fail. From this he concluded that it was made "without purpose, calculation, and need." On another occasion, however, the commander had stated that he was sure of

47. Totleben, pp. 126–29.
48. I. F. Paskevich, "Kniaz' Mikhail Dmitrievich Gorchakov v Sevastopole," RS, XL (1883), 373.

success when the battle began, but since Read did not carry out his instructions, he was responsible for the failure of the plan and so the battle was lost. This was a real contradiction. Read and Weimarn could not reply from their graves, and history probably would enter on its tablets that they were the culprits of the battle. Thus, Paskevich declared, Gorchakov's main idea must have been to prevent anyone from objecting to his views, so that all that he said "would become a recognized fact." [49]

Paskevich realized that this letter would not become public for some time, and indeed, it was never sent. But handwritten copies of it circulated widely, and eventually it was published in *Russkaia Starina*, a leading historical periodical. It revealed much about both Paskevich and Gorchakov.

The battle of the Chernaia was the last Russian offensive operation in the Crimea, for Russia's manpower was so depleted by the terrible losses that another was out of the question. Moreover, except for Khrulev and a few others, the soldiers no longer had confidence in their leaders. Although the enlisted men still performed their duties, their losses from enemy fire were extremely high and steadily increasing, and they no longer had dreams of driving the enemy from the Crimea. The most that they could hope for was to hold on until the coming of the winter storms, when they expected that the enemy would have to withdraw, and even that was by no means certain. In his letter to Alexander II Gorchakov again raised the possibility of evacuating Sevastopol. [50]

49. Ibid., p. 375.
50. Bogdanovich, "Imperator Aleksandr Nikolaevich," *RS* XXXIX (1893), 213.

CHAPTER 19. THE END OF THE SIEGE

The defeat of the Russians in the battle of the Chernaia river (August 4/16) made it obvious that they were fighting a losing cause, although they by no means gave up. The Allied superiority in artillery fire increased still further, and General Pélissier now could rule out the possibility of a Russian counterattack, for after their heavy losses further Russian offensive action was out of the question. This advantage permitted the attackers to give their full attention to the siege. Pélissier, knowing that Napoleon III had been angered by the severe losses in the attack of June 6/18, now sought to force the Russians to evacuate the fortress by sheer firepower: by making it impossible for them to maintain and hold the fortifications without unbearable losses, he apparently hoped to avoid the casualties that a full-scale assault would probably produce. For this purpose Pélissier obtained a number of huge mortars that fired thirteen-inch shells into the works, to blow up powder magazines, stores of shells, and dugouts. Since these weapons, once they had been properly laid and sighted, could continue to fire for hours without correcting their aim, they were especially effective at night, when the Russian sappers and other workers were doing their best to repair the damage caused by Allied gunfire.[1]

The fact that Napoleon III approved the sending of the mortars, which could not be used during operations in the field, indicated that he had finally accepted the commander's system of overcoming the defense of Sevastopol by overwhelming artillery fire and was no longer anxious to capture all of the Crimea, which would require large-scale operations by mobile forces.

As for the Russians, their position was clearly desperate. Gorchakov, however, after deciding to evacuate the southern side, on August 14/26 wrote to Alexander II that he had decided not to withdraw, but

1. Totleben, II, pt. 2, 159–60.

to hang on until it would be clearly impossible to do so. He recognized that this would entail huge losses. He did mention the possibility of repulsing the enemy and thus ending the siege, although he had no real hope of doing so.[2]

The emperor replied in a tone of resignation, citing his pain "when I think of the heroic garrison of Sevastopol and the dear blood that is shed every minute in defense of our native land. My heart is drenched with this blood . . . ." He did not, however, order the evacuation of the fortress and instructed Gorchakov to prepare for a winter campaign. He also arranged to hasten the arrival of militia units in the Crimea and asked about sending the cadres of disbanded battalions to serve as cores of newly formed units.[3] In the autumn of 1855 Anna F. Tiutcheva, lady-in-waiting at court, spent a gloomy evening with the imperial couple, during which everyone present was troubled by the terrible news from Sevastopol. "We passed the evening in sad and gloomy spirits," she said, "scarcely uttering a few words, and no one [had] the wish nor the boldness to speak. . . . I avoided even looking at the emperor and the empress, so as not to see the very deep dread that was expressed on their faces." [4]

As the Allies increased their armaments and moved their approaches nearer and nearer to the fortress, the Russians were not idle. Totleben drew up a master plan of the defense and entered on it new fortifications. He planned heavy batteries behind the Malakhov, to protect it by the cross-fire of their guns, and ordered mines dug under the Malakhov and other exposed positions. He also planned to blow up the forward part of this bastion when the French should attack. Unfortunately, early in the summer he was wounded in the leg and, forced to retire to the northern side to recover, his ideas were not implemented. Instead, other less vital construction was carried out, and the important operation that probably would have kept the French in check was not attempted. While the Russians did build new batteries, most of them were not in the right places, and they lacked the proper cannon, projectiles, and powder. One vital undertaking, however, was brought to completion before the end of the siege. This was the building of a floating bridge across the bay to the northern side, to improve communications and to facilitate a withdrawal when the end came.

2. "Aleksandr II—Gorchakovu," *RS,* XLII (1883), 214.
3. Ibid.
4. A. F. Tiutcheva, *Pri dvore dvukh imperatorov: Dnevnik* (Moscow, 1929), II, 45.

Gorchakov conceived of this scheme in June, and had Vasil'chikov work out the plans for it in detail. Since the bay was almost eighteen hundred feet across, most of the engineers opposed it, but Lieutenant General A. E. Bukhmeier agreed to build it. Vast quantities of timber were hauled in from southern Russia by long lines of wagons to form the float for the bridge, which was completed and opened for use on August 15/27.[5] Gorchakov had Totleben work out a detailed plan for evacuation of the army, but then, after reinforcements of militia had arrived, he changed his mind, writing to the emperor that he would not evacuate Sevastopol without a fight, in order to uphold the glory of the emperor. While he admitted that such a stand might be a mistake, of the difficult choices open to him it was the most honorable.[6]

After the battle of the Chernaia the Allies started a furious bombardment, which cost the defenders one thousand men per day. On August 15/27 the rate of fire declined considerably, permitting the Russians to repair their defenses and to strengthen their earthworks, although the daily losses were five hundred or more. On August 24/September 5, however, the cannonade mounted with great fury, which seemed to indicate an imminent storm of the works, with the fire centered on the Malakhov and Bastion 2. All the Allied guns were being used, and no place within the lines was safe, even in the city. Earthworks, guns, gun carriages, and shells were hit, as the firing continued night and day. The Russians answered vigorously, but the foe fired about seventy thousand round shot and sixteen thousand bombs and shells, which put over two thousand of the defenders out of action. On the Russian right flank on the night of August 24–25 the men worked, repairing the half-ruined walls, making embankments, and removing corpses and smashed guns, in spite of the unceasing, although weaker enemy fire. On the left flank, however, and especially on the Malakhov, the Russians made almost no repairs, because the destruction was so great. A number of fires burned in the city from the morning of August 24 to nightfall, and could not be extinguished, since most of the fire-fighting equipment had been destroyed.

The French also turned their guns on the bay, where on August 24 a transport burned, hit by an explosive shell, and on the following day a frigate went up in flames. On August 26 at a wharf a barge

5. Schilder, *Graf Totleben,* I, 439–45; Totleben, II, pt. 2, 131–51; Vasil'chikov, pp. 236–37.
6. Miliutin MS, pp. 307–09.

holding over six thousand pounds of powder blew up with a terrific roar, and another barge nearby sank at its mooring with its load of powder.[7]

During these days the Russians lost over 3,000 men while the Allies lost only 249. Nevertheless, the Russians built a new battery of four heavy guns to the left of the Malakhov. They also dug mines in preparation for blowing up the kurgan, but the powder needed had been lost when the barge was hit. Mines were also dug under Bastion 2, but they were wired and loaded only on August 25, with the powder taken from the guns. In three days the Russians lost 89 guns and 113 carriages to enemy fire, chiefly in the Malakhov and Bastion 2, and most of this equipment could not be replaced. Thus both of these works were in an almost helpless condition, with their guns unable to fire because the embrasures were filled with dirt. On the Malakhov the gabions and fascines, dry after prolonged lack of rain, often caught fire and threatened to explode the powder magazines. In two days the Allies fired 52,000 rounds, chiefly shells, while the Russians fired about 20,000. The Russian losses during these two days were over 2,500. Those of the Allies were 290. Bastion 2 was especially troubled by a lack of drinking water, for in three days not one pailful was brought in for the wounded and for the soldiers. Most of the gunners had been put out of action.[8]

Because of the Russian inability to keep up a strong fire on the attackers, the French could move their saps rapidly toward the Russian position, so that by August 26 they were only eighty-four feet from the parapet of the Malakhov. They continued their heavy bombardment as before, and in addition threw mines containing 220 pounds of powder into the fortress, where they wrought havoc. Most of the Russian cannon were no longer operating and the dugouts were filled with wounded, whom the defenders could evacuate only at night.[9]

In these last days the defenders constantly expected an assault, and because frequent false alarms wearied them and compelled them to keep their reserves close by, they incurred many losses. For days the men had had no rest or sleep and were losing hope, for they knew of the preparation for the evacuation of Sevastopol. The Russian losses were mounting steadily: from August 5th to the 24th they averaged

7. O. Konstantinov, "Shturm Malakhova kurgana," *RS,* XIV (1875), 576.
8. Totleben, II, pt. 2, 162–71.
9. Ibid., pp. 164–66.

635 per day, but from the 24th to the 27th they were 7,500; and by noon on August 27 2,000 men had been hit. Most of the regiments were reduced to two battalions, and some to only one. Many battalions had only 250 to 400 men. Officers and sergeants especially were lacking. Some battalions were commanded by junior captains, and companies by ensigns.[10]

The position of the defenders grew worse and worse, for the earthworks no longer protected them, and the tattered shields of woven rope hung around the guns would no longer stop rifle bullets. The men continued to work on their repairs during the night, but it was useless, for the stones and the dirt of the embankment were dry and without cohesion, and each enemy shot undid what they had just restored. Thus the Russians had little cover and fell by the thousands, "continuing to stand unwavering under the most deadly fire, awaiting the moment when the foe would throw himself into the assault, in order with their breasts to stop his drive and with their bayonets to throw him back to the ruins of his trenches."[11]

As the situation continued to deteriorate, on August 25 Captain Lieutenant Karpov, commander of the 4th division of the defenses, which included the Malakhov and Bastion 2, notified the staff that the kurgan was in grave condition and asked that they send workers immediately to repair the fortifications and artillerymen to man the guns, stating that if reinforcements did not come, it would fall by August 27. That night the enemy fire against the Malakhov increased to an incredible degree, while against the other works it slackened. Hence it was impossible to make the necessary repairs, as the sappers and workers had always been able to do up to then. "By the morning of August 26," N. V. Berg wrote, "the kurgan was in a worse condition than it had been on the preceding evening. This was the *first* such morning of the whole siege." Worst of all was the fact that of the sixty-three guns of the Malakhov only eight of those directed against the enemy were still intact, and since bombs and round shot were very scanty, by the 26th the Malakhov could fire back only very weakly. Fortunately the neighboring Gervais battery defended it, for its supply of bombs and shot was not as depleted as that of the Malakhov. But the night of the 26th-27th was even more frightful than the one before.[12]

10. Ibid., pp. 173–75, 180–81.
11. Konstantinov, "Shturm," pp. 573–74.
12. N. V. Berg, *Zapiski ob osade Sevastopolia* (Moscow, 1858), II, 33.

Suddenly on August 27/September 8 the Allied fire decreased decidedly and stayed at a low level for several hours. But at eleven o'clock the men at the Russian observation posts on the Inkerman heights noticed an unusual movement of French reserves into the advance trenches before the Korabel'naia side and began to signal the information to Sevastopol. But by a strange mistake, instead of reporting that "enemy columns are moving against the Korabel'naia," it signalled, "Enemy fleet is moving against Korabel'naia." Headquarters at once sent to the telegraph station for clarification, but before the reply arrived the French attack began. Russian scouts from the Malakhov who had seen enemy soldiers in full uniforms issued another report, which was interpreted as meaning that there would be an assault that day, although they did not expect it until later.[13]

At noon three volleys thundered from all the Allied guns and the French soldiers, suddenly rising out of their trenches, dashed for the Malakhov, the curtain wall, and Bastion 2. The defenders, most of whom were in dugouts eating their noon meal, were taken by surprise and could fire only a few shots at the thousands of picked French troops under General Marie Edmé Patrice Maurice MacMahon, who had just arrived from Algeria. The Russians were forced back from the parapet of the Malakhov and tried to fight behind the entrenchment further back. Russian reserves were sent in and the fighting continued for hours.[14]

At Bastion 2 and along the curtain wall the Russians had somewhat more warning and met the enemy at the parapet, where there was fierce hand-to-hand fighting. The superior French numbers quickly drove them out and the attackers then pursued them into the second line of defense. By this time the fire from the Russian reserves, from steamers in the bay, and from the northern side struck the French, costing them heavily and driving them out of Bastion 2 and from the wall, leaving 150 prisoners to the Russians. The French had actually broken through the second line and into some of the nearby houses, but the Russian counterattack under Khrulev repelled them and they retired in disorder to their trenches. The French soon returned with reserves to the attack and sent in a battery of field artillery to support them, but a hurricane of fire from the Russian batteries and the ships knocked out the guns and forced the remaining gunners to retire to

13. Konstantinov, pp. 576–77.
14. Ibid., pp. 491–93; Berg, II, 33–34; Bogdanovich, *Vostochnaia voina,* IV, 95–97.

safety. A second French battery fared no better. Nevertheless, after a renewed bombardment fresh French forces again captured Bastion 2, only to be driven out once more, after a powerful land mine had killed many of them and thrown the rest into confusion.[15]

Thus, on the Russian left, except for the Malakhov, the besieged successfully repelled the assaults in fighting which was very costly to both sides. In like manner, on the Russian right and at the Gervais battery alongside the Malakhov they repulsed all attacks. Then the British concentrated a force of eleven thousand men against Bastion 3, which they attacked in two columns. As their assault came when the French were already in the Malakhov, the Russians were ready and met the columns with heavy musketry fire and grape shot from their artillery, with the redcoats losing many men during their long charge to reach the works. Nevertheless, the British broke into the bastion, spiking guns, smashing gun carriages, and driving off the Russian counterattacks. Russian reserves arrived, however, and, striking from three sides, pushed the British into the ditch and the shell holes. After regrouping, they were driven away and forced to leave the ditch. The Russians captured 8 officers and 120 enlisted men, as well as many wounded. They also stopped British efforts against other Russian positions.[16]

The French, who were also in position on the left of the British, also attacked on this front, against Bastion 5 and the Belkin lunette, with ten thousand men, but were cut to pieces with grape shot at the lunette and hence joined the force attacking the bastion. Here, however, the Russians on the wall received them with the bayonet and forced them to retire to their trenches. Fresh French columns then attacked the Schwartz redoubt, where they penetrated the right side, although they were repelled on the front and the left. There was a bloody fight, which ended with all the French killed, except for 153 prisoners. Another French attempt against this redoubt was driven off by the fire of Bastion 6 and the Belkin lunette. The French made no effort to take Bastion 4, although it was in bad condition, for they knew that it had been mined and feared that the defenders would blow it up if an attack took place. The Allied fleets made

15. Konstantinov, pp. 577–78; Bogdanovich, *Vostochnaia voina,* IV, 98–103; La Gorce, I, 436–38; Guérin, II, 402–03.
16. Bogdanovich, *Vostochnaia voina,* IV, 113–16; Totleben, II, pt. 2, 206–10; Auger, I, 425–26; Konstantinov, p. 581; Lysons, pp. 213–14.

efforts to destroy Bastions 6 and 10, but without any real success.[17]

Thus the Russians were successful at all points, with the sole exception of the Malakhov, where the French established themselves at the onset of the attack. Their victory was by no means certain, however, for the Russians fought stubbornly, even though they were greatly outnumbered. When the French drove them from the breastwork in the front part of the bastion, they retired to the entrenchment in the center of the bastion, fighting there with great determination, with the help of reserves, who soon came to their aid. But the entrenchment was not completed, for the carronades to arm it had not been delivered, no field guns had been brought in, and nothing had been done to provide a clear field of fire. Khrulev was late in coming to the rescue, for with the bastion's flagpole shot down it could not signal that it was under attack, and he led his forces to Bastion 2. When he did arrive at the Malakhov with his troops, the French were already well established and he was soon wounded. General Iuferov, next in line, was killed, and General I. L. Lisenko was wounded soon after. The Russian troops fought fiercely, until they ran out of cartridges and percussion caps, which they had to take from those who had fallen. Lieutenant General de Martineau then arrived with two Russian regiments from the city and led them into the bastion, where Iuferov's regiments were still fighting, with their backs to the gorge. When Martineau also was seriously wounded, the Russians lost hope of retaking the bastion, although they fought on with determination. Finally, at about 3:45 P.M. a tall Russian soldier, with a proud and martial air, "entered the bastion with his column, drums in front and beating the charge, while a terrible artillery fire forced the French to return into the work from the gorge." But the commander was wounded and the men also were shot down. "One would have said that the men had come only to show that the Russians knew how, at the very last minute, to sacrifice themselves passively and to die." The French finally made a bayonet charge at the gorge and drove the remnants from the Malakhov.[18]

During the fighting for this key bastion the French found that some of the Russians were holding out in the remnants of the tower, from which they fired on the attackers. But when they ran out of ammunition

17. Totleben, II, pt. 2, 206–10; Auger, I, 425–27; Bogdanovich, *Vostochnaia voina,* IV, 98–115; La Gorce, I, 436–38.
18. Konstantinov, pp. 577–80; Guérin, II, 412–17, 434.

and the French threatened to wipe them out, they eventually surrendered. The French also found 260 men working in the mines under the advanced part of the bastion and made them all prisoners. They also captured 170 workers who had been assigned to clean out the ditch in front of the bastion.[19]

Finally, after all the Russian attempts to retake the Malakhov had failed, about 4:00 P.M. General Gorchakov went to the second line near it, which was under heavy fire, and saw that it could not be recovered. He therefore ordered all attacks to cease, and decided to evacuate the southern side while the French were still disorganized.[20]

For decades there was a heated debate about the Russian failure to retake the Malakhov, which centered on the effect of having its gorge closed. Totleben insisted that it was essential to keep it closed, holding that if it were open the attackers probably could storm the curtain wall between the bastions and then storm them from the rear. In the meantime the Russian reserves could come to the rescue and drive off the enemy trying to enter from behind. He argued strongly that this system had proved its value during the Allied assault in June, when the French had broken into the Russian rear areas but then had been unable to penetrate the Malakhov because of its closed gorge.[21]

On the other hand, Khrulev, the best fighting general of the garrison, and Vasil'chikov and Men'kov, intelligent and devoted officers of the garrison staff, felt that a closed gorge on the Malakhov would be very dangerous, especially if the French should manage to enter this bastion in force. In June Khrulev and the commanders of the defense sectors all pointed out the danger of the closed gorges, saying that if the French stormed the bastions from the front, the Russian reserves would not be able to enter through the gorges to rescue the garrisons. Only Totleben would not agree. Later Khrulev went to see Totleben, who had been wounded, and tried to get him to agree to opening the gorges, but he refused, and Khrulev was told not to disturb the patient. A month later Khrulev again asked Totleben to open the gorges at Bastion 3 and at the Malakhov, but the engineer again stubbornly refused. At the Malakhov the gorge was kept closed and it had a high wall and a ditch in front, with a narrow bridge over the

19. Guérin, pp. 413–14; Konstantinov, pp. 580–81.
20. Bogdanovich, *Vostochnaia voina*, IV, 120–21.
21. Tarle, *Krymskaia Voina*, II, 419.

ditch. There was an entry fifteen paces wide into it, but it was too narrow to permit large bodies of troops to enter, and above all the Russian artillery in the rear was unable to sweep the interior of the bastion. Russian regiments did manage to enter from the gorge and fought inside the bastion for over two hours, but they were not able to drive the French out.[22]

Léon Guérin, an official French historian, stated that the worst mistake in building the Malakhov was "to give it a closed form, so that if the enemy [i.e., the French] got into it, the Russians could not easily bring up reinforcements, [and] it would become a grave obstacle if it should be necessary to reconquer it." [23]

It is probable that the closed gorge was only one of the factors that caused the loss of the Malakhov kurgan. Foremost of these factors was the overwhelming power of the French siege artillery, which made it impossible for this fortification to defend itself. Also the fact that its garrison was the 15th reserve division of older men and poorly trained recruits, instead of the effective 12th division, urged by Vasil'chikov, made it easy for the French to gain control immediately.[24] The attackers were picked troops, supported by large numbers of fine reserves, which were thrown in as soon as needed, so that they always outnumbered the defenders. Another factor was Khrulev's unavoidable mistake in leading his able reserves at first to Bastion 2, causing him to reach the Malakhov too late to recapture it. In addition, the Russians did not have a properly prepared entrenchment inside the bastion, with cannon mounted and with a clear field of fire; they also failed to prepare their countermines in time to blow up the French as they attacked. Moreover, they did not have strong batteries behind the gorge of the Malakhov to fire into it once the French had taken the bastion, and without such batteries already prepared it would not have been possible to open the gorge. Finally, the Russian leaders were all wounded or killed, chiefly by rifle fire, and the French commanders were not shot down by the Russians.[25] The French, with their overwhelming firepower and the numerical superiority of their infantry, made few errors, whereas the Russians, inferior in cannon fire and in manpower, made several errors, which cost them the Malakhov and with it Sevastopol.

22. Vasil'chikov, pp. 216–17; Men'kov, II, 412, n.
23. Guérin, II, 377–78.
24. Vasil'chikov, pp. 243–44.
25. Schilder, *Graf Totleben*, I, 476–79.

In his detailed *Description of the Defense of the City of Sevastopol* Totleben presented convincing statistics on the combat on the day of the assault. The Allies had 55,700 troops for the attack, of which they used 40,900; the Russians used 24,500 to defend their position. On the Korabel'naia sector the Russians used 53 battalions of 21,100 men; the Allied forces in this part of the attack consisted of 50 French battalions or 21,300 men, and 6,250 British, as well as small forces of Sardinians. On the Gorodskaia (city) sector the French attacked with 24 battalions, or 8,380 men; the Russians used 7½ battalions, or 3,350 men. On this day the Russian losses were 12,913 men, of whom 11,334 fell on the Korabel'naia. The Allies lost about 7,570 French, 2,351 British, and 40 Sardinians. The total Allied losses were 10,067, of whom 7,906 fell on the Korabel'naia.[26]

In all the Allies made twelve attacks, of which only the one on the Malakhov was successful; the Russians repelled the others. "From this," said Totleben, "it is seen that the day of August 27/September 8 cannot at all be regarded as a day of victory for the allies; on the contrary, the honor of this day would completely belong to the Russian arms, if the loss of the Malakhov kurgan had not compelled the commander-in-chief to carry out his long-held thought about evacuating the Southern side. . . ." He held that Gorchakov acted correctly in evacuating the city, because if the Russians had tried to hold it "under the close destructive fire of the siege batteries," the losses would have been too great.[27]

Although the French capture of the Malakhov resulted in a great victory, the Russian soldiers who had fought in the battle all were convinced that they had won. They had long endured dreadful wounds and death at a rate four times that of the enemy with resignation, expressed in the saying, "You can't have two deaths, but you can't escape one." On a visit to one of the most dangerous bastions Gorchakov asked a gunner, "How many of you are there in the bastion?" The answer was, "Enough for about three days more." On August 27 over and over they repulsed the attacks of the foe, taking and inflicting heavy losses, and only those who fought in the defense of the Malakhov tasted defeat. Few of the latter, however, were able to tell their stories, for most of them died in action or, wounded, had to be left in the bastion to the French. Hence at the first-aid points and the hospitals there were triumphant shouts of victory; "offi-

26. Totleben, II, pt. 2, 228–30.
27. Ibid., p. 230.

cers, soldiers, and sailors easily endured the most difficult amputations; with a courageous spirit they died firmly convinced that the assault had been repulsed at all points." During the afternoon of the Allied assault "soldiers of all ages, when they were getting them ready to amputate a leg or an arm, said with enthusiasm how gladly they agreed to endure this, knowing that they had succeeded in beating the enemy." They were sure the Allies had been beaten off with great loss at almost all the bastions and batteries. "The wounded rejoiced like victors, not sensing that with their blood they had not saved Sevastopol; they did not expect that the Malakhov kurgan was taken and that this sole success of the enemy compelled us to leave Sevastopol." [28]

In contrast, the Allies, from Pélissier on down, were by no means sure of the magnitude of their success, for, while they were delighted to have taken the Malakhov, they expected further Russian efforts to retake it. Moreover, they knew of the successes of the Russians at all other points and expected them to give up the rest of the fortress only after a stubborn resistance costly to both sides. Pélissier was happy to have taken and held the Malakhov, but he did not know whether his forces could hold it under the expected Russian effort to win it back. The French were worn out by the extreme exertions that they had made and had almost no fresh reserves left. About seven in the evening French observers noticed a great movement of the Russians from the city, and shortly some pointed out to the generals the passage of enormous masses of troops to the northern side of the harbor. This activity, however, was interpreted by many as the movement of units exhausted by the heavy fighting, which would be replaced by fresh troops. Pélissier himself, seeing the long columns of men and of baggage moving over the bridge, vaguely sensed the evacuation of the fortress, but had taken no measures to cut off a Russian retreat. Indeed, the French were so disorganized by their victory and their tremendous losses that they were in no condition to take action against the Russians. The defenders could have held their position for some time and doubtless could have made the Allies pay dearly for further successes.[29] In his report on the battle Pélissier stated that by his orders "Generals Thiry and Niel were going to

---

28. Ibid., p. 242; Dubrovin, *Materialy,* V, 341; Bestuzhev, p. 143; A. C. von Hübbenet, *Ocherk meditsinskoi i gospital'noi chasti v Krymu* (St. Petersburg, 1870), p. 130.
29. Guérin, II, 437–38; La Gorce, I, 436–37.

Defense of Sevastopol. Courtesy of Tass from Sovfoto.

have taken . . . all the dispositions needed to consolidate us definitely in the Malakhov and on the part of the curtain wall remaining in our power, so as to resist, if need be, a night attack by the enemy and to be in a position to make them evacuate on the following day the Little Redan of the Carenage, the Maison Croix and all this portion of the defenses." [30] Significantly enough, Pelissier did not mention a forced evacuation of the city by the Russians, which he obviously still did not expect.

At 5:00 P.M. on the 27th Gorchakov gave orders for the evacuation of Sevastopol, with all the forces to proceed to the northern side, by the new bridge and by boats. The movement began at 7:00 P.M. and lasted all night, according to the careful plans prepared by Totleben and Prince Vasil'chikov. Five regiments were assigned to man the barricades as rear guards, while volunteers stayed in the works to deceive the Allies by keeping up fire against them. The Allies made no effort to interfere with the evacuation, except for firing a few rounds at the bridge, with almost no effect. At first there was much confusion at the bridge, but Vasil'chikov soon got the situation under control. It proved too difficult to evacuate the field artillery and the wagons, so the latter were burned, and a number of cannon were dumped into the bay. Almost all the wounded were taken to the northern side, except for about five hundred hopeless cases, whom they left with a medical corpsman with a letter to the Allies. At night, after most of the forces were across the bay, a rocket gave a signal to the volunteers and the rear guards, who retired to the crossings. Small units of sappers and sailors left fuses of various lengths to the many powder magazines, of which thirty-seven blew up at intervals. Since fires were set in the city, which burned for two days, the Allies did not at once enter, as they feared explosions. The French raised their flag only after the fires had burned out, on August 30/September 10.[31]

The evacuation, without losses, was a creditable achievement, for the Russian army, between a victorious army and the wide bay, was in grave danger. The Allies, however, had too much respect for the valor of the Russians and the strength of the batteries on the northern side, to try to interfere. Moreover, the French, who had covered themselves with glory, had no real reason to push the attack further. Both

30. Guérin, p. 437.
31. Totleben, II, pt. 2, 242–45; Bogdanovich, *Vostochnaia voina,* IV, 127–32.

Alexander II and General Gorchakov issued pronouncements praising the heroism and skill of their warriors. Major Richard Delafield of the United States, who visited the Crimea, declared: "The same night, unknown and unobserved by their enemies, the Russians evacuated all their defenders . . . and crossed to the northern forts over a temporary bridge . . . having previously carried off all that might be needed in the northern works—a masterly retreat that does great credit to Russian military genius and discipline." [32]

The evacuation, while a skillful performance, was not carried out without some confusion. One of the regiments of the rearguard panicked and swarmed to the bridge, where it joined the other units. This disturbance was quickly subdued. Other unrest took place when the troops heard the order to withdraw, for they were sure that they had won the battle and that it was a disgrace to retreat from a place where so many of their comrades had shed their blood. Many of the soldiers, with tears in their eyes, exclaimed loudly: "Let's die here, boys! Let us lay down our bones, but we won't give up Sevastopol!" "We'll die, but we won't give it up!" their comrades shouted. Some of the troops even rebelled, suspecting that the orders were a betrayal, and even the more moderate soldiers joined in the loud talk, unwilling to believe that they had to concede the fortress to the enemy without a fight. The disorder reached such a peak that Lieutenant General Pavlov, the commander of the bastion, had to issue a categorical order to retire. The sailors, who regarded Sevastopol as their city, were especially outraged by the retreat.[33]

Nevertheless, the retirement continued, and early in the morning the volunteers lit the fuses to the various magazines and then, after igniting the fuses to the shore batteries, rowed to the northern side. By 8:00 A.M. the crossing was complete, and the generals crossed over the bridge to safety. The remaining ships and steamers were burned or sunk, the bridge was then dismantled, and the city was given up.

The Russian forces were now in a secure position on the high ground overlooking Sevastopol, with their heavy guns dominating the bay and the lower reaches of the Chernaia river. With their communica-

32. Khrushchov, pp. 151–53; Richard Delafield, *Report on the Art of War in Europe* (Washington, D.C., 1860), p. 52.

33. Bogdanovich, *Vostochnaia voina*, IV, 126–27; Khrushchov, p. 153; P. Ia. Bugaiskii, *Oborona Sevastopolia (Razskazy)* (St. Petersburg, 1877), pp. 87–88.

tions with Russia proper fairly secure, they regrouped and rearmed their units to withstand any attack. Neither the French nor the British had any desire to push the war to a real conclusion, for even Pélissier was against it, as he held that new attacks on Russia would be progressively harder. There was some small-scale fighting, however. On September 29 (N.S.) General d'Allonville, with three regiments of cavalry and some Egyptian battalions, routed eighteen Russian cavalry squadrons and some Cossacks not far from Eupatoria. Later a Franco-British expeditionary force sailed to the mouth of the Bug river, where on October 17, after a brief siege, they captured the third-rate fortress of Kinburn. But these gestures were not followed up, and there was no sign of a major campaign, although by the end of October 1855 the Allies had almost 200,000 men in the Crimean area. Pélissier, however, secure in his triumph, had no desire to risk his laurels. When urged by Paris to state his views, he said he proposed to hold Kinburn, the tip of the Crimea, and Kerch and to blockade Russia's coasts. He did suggest British or Turkish efforts to weaken Russia south of the Caucasus, but he would not favor a campaign against Kherson or Nikolaev.[34]

Late in 1855 an informal conference in Paris considered plans for a new campaign, but the participants could not agree on a promising objective. Napoleon III suggested a drive from Eupatoria against Simferopol, in order to defeat the Russians and push them back. Once that had been accomplished, he said, the Allies could "abandon the Crimea with honor." But as peace was already in the wind, no steps were taken to implement this scheme.[35]

Thus after the Russian evacuation of the southern side of Sevastopol, the fighting rapidly diminished and the bloodshed that had been so terrible practically ceased. This did not mean an end to the loss of life, however, for wounds and disease continued to exact a heavy toll.

Disease in the mid-nineteenth century was a scourge that hit all armies in the field, with rare exceptions. As has been seen, cholera had struck the French at Varna and their troops carried it to the Crimea, where Saint-Arnaud died of it shortly after the battle of the Alma. It died down during the winter of 1854–55, but it reappeared in the spring of 1855 and in June and July it raged among the troops, with 51,971 cases in those months, of which 1,684 were fatal. Scurvy

34. La Gorce, I, 448–50.
35. Ibid., pp. 450–51.

also was serious, for it attacked chiefly the veterans of the Crimea, who, because of exhausting labor and the absence of vegetables, were vulnerable. An official report stated that "all the old soldiers were scorbutic in varying degrees." Of the 95,000 deaths of the French during the war, 75,000 were from disease.[36] The Sardinians, who escaped most of the fighting, underwent a cholera epidemic as soon as they arrived in the Crimea, and suffered more than two thousand deaths from it. Their battle fatalities were twenty-eight.[37]

As has been mentioned, the British army almost collapsed because of its terrible health problems early in 1855, when twelve thousand of its men were in hospitals in Turkey, while only eleven thousand were in camp near Balaklava. More and more shiploads of sufferers arrived at Constantinople, only to wallow in the filth of the hospitals there. Eventually, because of the indefatigible efforts of Florence Nightingale and a group of parliamentary investigators from London, plus the horrifying disclosures of William Howard Russell, the British public compelled action to remedy the situation. It was many months after the arrival of Miss Nightingale and her nurses, however, before the hospitals at Constantinople were really cleaned up, and those in the Crimea, over which she had no authority, continued to have high mortality rates until late in 1855. When she visited the Crimea in May, she nearly died of "Crimean fever," and in June she returned to Constantinople on a stretcher.[38]

The British soldiers continued to be plagued by disease until late in 1855, with cholera, scurvy, dysentery, and typhus widespread. Not only the enlisted men, but even generals—Brown, Pennefather, Codrington, and Eastland—took sick, and General Eastland died. On June 28, 1855, Lord Raglan, the commander, died of cholera. His successor, General James Simpson, resigned his command shortly before the fall of Sevastopol and went home, suffering from a severe case of dysentery. He was succeeded by Sir William Codrington.[39]

In the light of the medical difficulties of the French and the British, it is not surprising that the Russians too had severe problems. It was not until the war shifted to the Crimea, however, that the medical

36. Ibid., pp. 413–14, 472.
37. Ibid., p. 472.
38. Cecil Woodham-Smith, *Florence Nightingale, 1820–1910* (New York, 1951), pp. 98–147, passim, 150–54.
39. Ibid., pp. 154, 159; La Gorce, I, 414.

crisis became apparent, for under General M. D. Gorchakov the army before Silistria had a well-organized system and had experienced very little fighting, so that the usual methods were sufficient to deal with any problems. With the Allied landing in September, 1854, however, serious difficulties at once arose, for Prince Menshikov, who did not expect an attack until the following summer, had taken no steps to prepare for an active campaign. There were no preparations for the wounded of the battle of the Alma, and when Menshikov's forces retreated to Sevastopol there was no organized effort to collect them. As a result many of them lay untended where they fell and many died.

In the middle of September St. Petersburg ordered the authorities in Simferopol to provide space for at least six thousand wounded and had the commissariat officers send equipment for two thousand patients at once. The situation remained bad, however, since the buildings were not available and the supplies did not arrive until almost two months later. When they did come almost five times as many were needed.[40]

In Sevastopol the commanders organized first-aid stations and expanded the hospitals on the northern side. These measures were far from adequate, however, since in two months the garrison lost 8,466 men killed, wounded, and missing, and the medical personnel such as orderlies was terribly insufficient. There was no chief surgeon and no medical organization.[41]

The battle of Balaklava produced relatively few casualties, but the battle of Inkerman (October 24, O.S.), was terribly costly to the Russians, with twelve thousand men killed, wounded, or missing. Many of the wounded lay in their uniforms untended for two or three days, while the surgeons worked night and day. The famed Dr. N. I. Pirogov, the leading surgeon of St. Petersburg, who arrived not long after, wrote to a friend: "No one who has not seen with his own eyes can form any concept of the filth, the miserable condition in which our wounded lay from October to December." [42]

Early in 1855 the medical situation in Sevastopol improved considerably, thanks to the special efforts of the government and the civilians. Drs. Pirogov and A. C. Hübbenet were joined by other civilian doctors,

40. Hübbenet, pp. 2–7.
41. Ibid.
42. Edekauer, p. 294.

and German and American surgeons arrived. Also the lull in the fighting gave them a chance to deal with the untended cases. But in March Pirogov wrote of the increase in cases of typhus and scurvy, the lack of proper medical buildings, the shortage of linens, the lack of mattresses and even of straw or hay to fill them. A week later he wrote: "The General Staff Doctor is a cipher. . . . In the hospital there is not one extra mattress, no good wine nor quinine bark, nor acid, even in case typhus spreads. Almost half of the doctors lie sick, and the only thing that is really fine is the sisters of mercy." [43] The sisters, with little nursing training, provided bedside care for the patients and looked after their feeding and their medication.

The sisters also helped to combat graft and thieving in the hospitals. The authorities gave sums of fifty to one hundred rubles to amputees, but as they had no place in which to keep the money safely, it was all too likely to be stolen by orderlies or medical assistants. Pirogov assigned some of the more reliable sisters to take care of this money and to keep records of it—no mean assignment.

A more important struggle developed over the dispensaries at the hospitals, caused by complaints that the pharmacists were not carrying out the orders of the doctors. The pharmacists blamed the failures on the alleged failings of the Commissariat, which had not sent the necessary supplies, or had sent items of inferior quality. Moreover, the dispensary office, which had to fill the orders of two first-aid stations and two hospitals, claimed it was understaffed, as it had only one pharmacist and two apprentices. Hence Pirogov entrusted the dispensing of wine, vodka, and dressing materials to the sisters, who issued the proper amounts upon orders from the doctors.[44] In his report to St. Petersburg Dr. Pirogov stated that he had put the best educated sisters in charge of the strong drugs, to be issued as ordered. Thus each hospital had its own dispensary, run by the sisters, who supplemented the meager amounts from the government with substantial issues of donated supplies. There were still difficulties, for at times the supplies were late in coming, which made it impossible to provide the patients with what they needed.

The surgeon strongly supported the sisters in their quarrels with the pharmacists, even when their complaints led to the suicide of one of the offenders. "They are true sisters of mercy—that is what

43. Pirogov, p. 59.
44. Hübbenet, pp. 72–73.

is needed—one crook the less," he said. "It would not be bad if they did the same with Fedor Ivanovich here." The nurses had only brought charges against the pharmacist and had insisted on an official investigation, but Pirogov feared that when his tour of duty ended, "the sisters would catch it," for the chief doctors and commissars were spreading rumors that before the sisters had come "it had gone better." He agreed that for these men it had gone better, for the housekeepers he had appointed had interfered with their thieving.[45]

As the siege continued to its climax the sisters became deeply involved. In June the influx of new casualties and the overcrowding in the Nikolaevskaia battery drove the authorities to ship five hundred amputees, in haste and with difficulty, to an area on the northern side. It turned out that as there was no building for them, they had to put the men in soldiers' tents, with their mattresses on the ground. Soon a three-day deluge drenched the tents and their inmates, who lay in pools of muddy water. The sisters had to work kneeling in the mud, drenched to the bone. Some of them were unable to find living quarters for a time and had to spend several nights in their carriages. Some of the nurses fell sick from the exposure, and a few actually died.[46]

In the last stages of the siege there were several crises. Shortly before the ruinous battle of the Chernaia river on August 4 (O.S.) fourteen of the nurses were assigned to a first-aid station on McKenzie Hill, where the wounded arrived in such numbers that everyone— surgeons, nurses, and medical assistants—worked for days without pause. Only after sixteen days without changing their clothing did the authorities send the sisters to bathe in the sea and finally to return to their camp at Bel'bek.[47]

While most of the sisters were in safe positions outside Sevastopol during the final bombardment late in August (O.S.), a number of them were in the city at first-aid stations, hard at work. They then had to help evacuate the patients from the city to the northern side, over the floating bridge across the bay, under occasional fire. The

45. Pirogov, pp. 60–61.

46. E. M. Bakunina, "Vospominaniia sestry miloserdii Krestovozdvizhenskoi obshchiny, 1854– 1860," *Vestnik Evropy*, CXC, no. 3 (March, 1898), 161–62; Pirogov, p. 203; "Ofitsial'naia chast'," *Morskoi Sbornik*, no. 7 (July 1855), pp. 192–93.

47. N. I. Pirogov, "Istoricheskii obzor . . . ," *Morskoi Sbornik*, no. 4 (1856), pp. 183–84; Alexandra Krupskaia, *Vospominaniia Krymskoi voiny sestry krestovozdvizhenskoi obshchiny* (St. Petersburg, 1861), pp. 32–34.

patients were hastily placed in the fortifications on the northern side and later were moved to the hospitals at Bel'bek or Inkerman. Most of the casualties of the final day were taken to Bel'bek, where they were put in tents, but without cots. The men lay on tarpaulins or on mattresses on tarpaulins. There were from eighty to one hundred operations per day, with the sisters assisting. Unfortunately, the weather turned wet and cold, so that dressings often had to be done in the rain, with the nurses kneeling in mud or on damp ground. By mid-September, the authorities transferred all the patients to hospitals at Simferopol or at Bakhchiserai for their convalescence.[48]

When Pirogov returned to the Crimea in October 1855 a new housecleaning was in order. In a letter of October 6 he spoke of Kartseva, a newly arrived senior sister, whose fine work had put the hospital on its feet again. "Together with her," he said, "we put the supervisor under investigation." [49]

On October 17 he wrote that Kartseva, now directress of the order, and he were rigging "all possible hooks to catch the hospital thieves." They were unable, however, to find out why the chicken soup, "into which ninety chickens were put for 360 men, comes out tasting only of gruel, while when the sisters cook a smaller quantity and put in fewer chickens, it tastes better." Nothing—not even sealing the kettle—had checked the thievery. "Truly, it is sad to see; such a fine quality is supplied that it would be possible to feed them marvelously," but the patients almost never got proper soup.[50]

During the last month of the siege the sisters endured many hardships and dangers. Some of them were under fire in Sevastopol in the first-aid points, and when they crossed the bay, bullets, cannonballs, and bombs fell close by. After they transferred the hospitals and patients to safer places on the northern side, they still found themselves under fire. A number of them developed typhus and other diseases and by December 1856, 17 out of the 160 in the order had died.[51]

After the fighting had ended Dr. Pirogov assigned Ekaterina Bakunina, one of the ablest sisters, to a new and demanding task—accompanying convoys of convalescents on the way to Russia proper. She

48. Pirogov, "Istoricheskii obzor," pp. 186–87.
49. Pirogov, Sebastopol'skie pis'ma, p. 86.
50. Ibid., p. 85.
51. "Ofitsial'naia chast'," Morskoi Sbornik, no. 10 (1855), p. 353; Pirogov, "Istoricheskii obzor," pp. 171–81.

was put in charge of the nurses who saw to the care, feeding, and shelter of the men, often five hundred in number. It was a harrowing experience, for the patients, with their wounds still painful, lay three or four in a narrow, springless wagon, riding over terribly rough roads. The sisters had to prepare the food and warm drinks for the men, bandage their wounds, and see to their shelter in the huts of the villages where they stopped. It took six days to reach Perekop on the isthmus out of the Crimea, and two more days if the convoy went on to Nikolaev or Kherson. While the weather was still warm and sunny, the trip was not too difficult; but in November and December there were storms, followed by sharp cold. At times the wagons bogged down in mud and had to be pulled out by oxen. Occasionally there was ice on the roads, which made travel dangerous. On one occasion Bakunina's convoy experienced severe cold, well below zero Fahrenheit, which killed several men and threatened the lives of many others. Fortunately they soon reached a village and were sheltered in the huts.

Bakunina, as ordered, took note of the failings of the convoy system. The wagons did not have canvas covers, but merely rough mats, which did not keep out the wet. While the men all had warm personal clothing, there were only two sheepskins for four men, which caused hardship and suffering in bad weather. Bakunina noted a shortage of good drivers, a lack of proper forage for the animals, and often a shortage of food and drink for the patients.[52]

The convoy system was a cruel, often agonizing way to move the convalescents from the overcrowded hospitals of the southern Crimea to hospitals on the mainland, where they could receive additional treatment and could complete their convalescence before moving on to their homes. In view of the geography of the Crimea and the scanty resources available, it was one more illustration of the primitive conditions in the outlying parts of Russia. But the system continued to function until well into 1856, when all of the sick and wounded could be discharged and returned to civilian life.

Thus the problem of disease in the Crimea was eventually dealt with by shipping the convalescents from the Sevastopol area to Nikolaev, Kherson, and other cities in southern Russia. Unfortunately, an extremely bad situation developed there, as well. Under Prince

52. Pirogov, "Istoricheskii obzor," pp. 180–91.

M. D. Gorchakov the health problems of the Southern Army were not serious, thanks to good administration and no serious transportation problems, as well as the absence of large-scale military operations. In the warm months and even until November 1854 it was possible to ship out convalescents and to bring in the necessary supplies. As a result, the mortality rate was moderate. But the transfer of General Gorchakov and his able staff to the Crimea led to a rapid growth of corruption in the Southern Army, which meant that the soldiers were deprived of necessary supplies, causing a decline in their health. The wet, cold weather during the winter months also was harmful, for large numbers of men were crowded into quarters with little or no ventilation, and the air was unspeakably foul. In addition, the troops were used for guard duty, which was bad for the health, or for building earthworks, which was exhausting, especially in bad weather.[53]

The living conditions of the soldiers were extremely difficult, for the clothing and boots that they had received had worn out and were not replaced, so that the men wore the clothes until they rotted. And since no baths were available during the cold months, they were filthy with dirt and lice. To make matters worse, the food was of very poor quality, and it was impossible to cook it properly. The rations contained much salt meat, which caused terrible thirst. The local drinking water was brackish, and since little or no fresh water was brought in for the soldiers, there was much digestive disease. Under such dismal conditions the morale of the soldiers declined sharply, which helped to make them prone to disease. The militia, homesick and unhappy, were without hope. Hence disease spread rapidly, with grim consequences.[54]

The calamity came in November 1855, when the inclement weather set in, transportation by water ceased, and the roads were almost impassable. Large numbers of troops came in, as well as many convalescents from Sevastopol, causing severe crowding in the quarters. In three months disease spread rapidly, with almost half the men taking sick at the rate of four to five hundred per battalion. No effective measures were taken during November and December, and up to January from ten to fifteen men in each unit fell sick every day. The illness of the garrison was the chief factor in the epidemic, for as

53. N. Obruchev, "Iznanka Krymskoi Voiny," *Voennyi Sbornik,* no. 4 (1858), pp. 440–47.
54. Ibid., pp. 448–49.

many as 250 patients entered the hospitals daily. In addition, the arrival of new troops brought in many more patients, and with water transport stopped and land hauling impossible, almost nothing could be done to reduce the number of inmates. Vast overcrowding developed, with patients lying on their sides and many actually lying on top of each other to make room for others. They lay on the floor, under the benches or on them, in the corners, everywhere. Naturally the air was deadly foul, so that some men died as they crossed the thresholds. Their clothes were rags, their bodies were covered with filth and eaten by lice.[55]

The hospital personnel were unable to deal with such a state of affairs, for they had only a fraction of the space needed, and their equipment was deplorably insufficient. Their linen, utensils, mattresses, and pillows were enough for only a small number of those they had to care for, and their orderlies and other personnel were far too few. Even dishes and cups were lacking, so that in many cases it was impossible to give water to the sick. There was also a shortage of water in the hospitals. In January 1856 some supplies were obtained, the authorities provided more attendants, and water was purchased. But since the attendants themselves became ill, there was little improvement.

Trained medical personnel also were in very short supply, for by January 1856 ten out of the eleven doctors were sick and of the fifteen nurses, thirteen were sick and unable to work. In December 1855 each doctor had from five to seven hundred patients. The navy sent six doctors, but most of them soon became ill. Moreover, even more doctors, nurses, and medicine would have helped little, for the soldiers lay in filth and suffered so from exhaustion, very bad food, and overcrowding that they were doomed to contract typhus, scurvy, and other infections.[56]

The coming of General I. O. Sukhozanet was the turning point. While in many ways he was a stupid martinet, Sukhozanet dealt with the crisis in an effective manner. He made better arrangements for quartering the soldiers and insisted that they get baths once a week; he provided boots and overcoats for the soldiers; he had fresh meat added to their rations; and he reduced their work load. All this was of much value, although many of the men were so weakened and

55. Ibid., pp. 449–50, 452.
56. Ibid., pp. 453–54.

infected that they still fell ill. It was only in April that the incidence of disease declined significantly.[57]

The commander also dealt with the hospital problem by obtaining more suitable buildings for them and having the hospital supplies put in order. The navy helped by assigning doctors to the hospitals. The death rate, however, remained high and did not decline until the warm weather permitted better ventilation of the wards and the shipment of convalescents toward their homes. Two of the hospitals of Nikolaev, from November 1, 1855, to May 1, 1856, had 9,682 of 22,774 patients die. Among the reasons for these deaths in the rank and file were the severe deficiencies in space, healthful food, and proper sanitation. The commanders had failed to think of the soldiers as human beings who were entitled to decent treatment.[58]

Thus for months after the end of hostilities in the Crimea, and indeed after the ratification of the treaty of peace at Paris, Russian soldiers were still dying as unnecessarily as those who had been led into the hopeless battles of Inkerman and the Chernaia river.

While the Crimean War was still in progress, Count F. V. Rüdiger, Commander-in-chief of the Guards and the Grenadier corps, wrote to Alexander II about the failings of the Russian army during the conflict. While Rüdiger emphatically advised that generals with real talents be given wide scope to take responsibility, he chiefly urged the removal of commanders who were worthless, as had been done in the past. Although lesser commanders had to pay dearly for negligence and failures, he said, "we have had the mortification to see how many almost criminal faults and negligences on the part of some of our generals-in-chief were tolerated with the greatest indulgence." He cited the mismanagement of the Danube campaigns of 1853 and 1854, "the neglect of measures against a *coup de main* at Sevastopol, Eupatoria, Balaklava, Kerch, while the Crimean expedition had been predicted three months in advance. . . ." One of the generals [apparently Paskevich], who, if brought before a council of war, would have been declared one of the gravest causes of all the misfortunes and fatalities that befell Russia, "had the insolence not only to come to St. Petersburg, but also to arrogate to himself the right, while he was staying there, to criticize the conduct of others." [59]

57. Ibid., pp. 450–51.
58. Ibid., pp. 454–55.
59. Russia. Voennoe Ministerstvo, *Stoletie,* N. A. Danilov, *Istoricheskii Ocherk Razvitiia Voennago Upravleniia v Rossii,* Prilozhenie 5, p. 21.

Rüdiger continued his analysis of the failings of the military system with two additional notes to the emperor dwelling on the excessive centralization of authority in the military administration, which deprived the lower officials of all initiative and turned them into mere agencies for forwarding instructions. This in turn convinced many of the subordinate officials that all that was needed for success was blind obedience to the orders of their superiors. From this they developed "distrust of their own strength and knowledge." Apparently this reluctance to display initiative extended all the way to the two ministers of war under Nicholas I, who always stated in their official reports that the military administration was functioning perfectly and needed no improvement. A natural result of this state of affairs was that lower officers subdued their leanings toward initiative and that many men with initiative and a strong will were repelled from military service.[60]

Finally, on June 23, 1855, Count Rüdiger presented a series of proposals for improving the military system along the lines suggested in his notes. He urged elimination of excessive centralization; he insisted on changing the nature of the training of the troops so as to emphasize preparation for battle, including careful individual instruction of the soldiers, with parades and reviews to play a secondary role; he stressed raising the intellectual level of the officers; he proposed the creation of special commissions to solve special problems; and lastly, he urged improvement of the quality of the commanders by requiring strict periodical attestation of their suitability, by the drawing up of lists of candidates for positions, careful selection of the appointees, and the weeding out of the unfit. The emperor read these proposals and by his marginal notations on them indicated his agreement and approval. In July 1855 a special commission was formed under Count Rüdiger to improve the military system. The commission proposed measures similar to those suggested by Rüdiger; these were then carried out.[61] In this way the Crimean War, which brought so much suffering and death to Russia, paved the way for the sweeping reorganization of the Russian military system that would later take place under General Dmitrii A. Miliutin.

For Russia the Crimean War was an extraordinary exertion of its full strength. Before this war the army consisted of 980,000 regular

60. Ibid., pp. 19–24.
61. Russia. Voennoe Ministerstvo, *Stoletie,* I, N. A. Danilov, *Istoricheskii Ocherk Razvitiia Voennago Upravleniia v Rossii,* pp. 383–90.

officers and men, plus considerable numbers of Cossack irregulars. By its end in January 1856, in spite of heavy losses in battle and from disease, it numbered 1,802,500 regulars, as well as 171,000 irregulars and 370,000 militia. In order to fight much of Europe, Russia had in the ranks of its armies 2,343,500 men and, with the navy, about 2,400,000. Precise figures for its casualties in battle and from disease are not available. In his book on the *Defense of the City of Sevastopol* Totleben states that in the Crimea Russia lost 128,669 men, of whom 26,000 fell in action outside Sevastopol. These figures, however, do not include losses from disease,[62] which probably were much higher. No complete figures are available for Russian losses in the Caucasus for these years, both against the Turks or against the mountaineers. The fact is that the data on casualties in almost every case do not include the figures of deaths from disease.

It is possible, however, to take the figures for the army at the outbreak of the war in 1853 and add to it the numbers of men enlisted during the war years, which gives a grand total of 1,992,853 men who were enrolled in the army during the war. From this total 1,585,-953 left its ranks by discharge or desertion, or were missing in action. This leaves the army's overall loss at 406,156 men who were killed in action or died of wounds or disease. This figure is apparently too low, since men listed as missing have usually proved to be dead. Moreover, the total does not take into account the officers and men of the navy, who died in considerable numbers in the Crimea, and to a limited degree, were lost in action in Finnish waters.[63]

The Medical Department of the Ministry of War published its figures on the number of army personnel who died each year, as follows:

1853	43,647	men
1854	73,059	men
1855	157,576	men
1856	175,733	men
Total	450,015	

This figure appears to be the most accurate of all the estimates of the deaths during the war, but it includes only army, not navy personnel. As the first figure cited—406,156 men—did not include the deaths

62. Totleben, II, pt. 2, 319–20.
63. M. I. Bogdanovich, ed. *Istoricheskii ocherk deiatel'nosti voennago upravleniia . . . (1855–1880 g.g.)* (St. Petersburg, 1879–81), I, 171–73.

of the Cossacks and the militia, which the Medical Department listed at 26,832, the discrepancy is small.[64] Therefore it seems safe to say that the number of members of the Russian armed services who lost their lives during the Crimean war was probably somewhat over 450,000. If this is correct, this war was more costly for Russia in terms of manpower than any war between 1815 and 1914.

It is widely believed that Russia had no chance of winning this war, both because of the failings and mistakes and because of the very difficult logistics of the Crimean campaign. There is some basis for this opinion, for the errors of Prince Menshikov at the battle of the Alma and again at Inkerman ruined Russia's chances of winning those engagements. If the Allies had lost either of these battles they probably would have been forced to retire from the Crimea. Moreover, if Field Marshal Paskevich had not hoarded all the troops that he could get, refusing to send them to the Crimea when they were desperately needed there, but had sent sufficient forces to arrive simultaneously to support the defenders of Sevastopol, then "the allies would have barked their shins at the Khersonesus [Crimea] and the rash venture of Saint-Arnaud would have received its just reward." This was the opinion of Prince V. I. Vasil'chikov, chief of staff of the garrison during the siege. Vasil'chikov concluded, however, that divine providence, along with the stupidity of the Russians, had made defeat inevitable.[65]

---

64. Ibid., p. 174.
65. Vasil'chikov, 254–55.

CHAPTER 20. THE ROAD TO PEACE

The loss of Sevastopol to the Allies did not necessarily mean the end of the war, although at first Alexander II felt it would be wise to give up all of the Crimea, since there was no reason to hold it, now that the Russian fleet no longer existed. But in a letter of September 22 (O.S.) to Paskevich he agreed that they should not evacuate it, as their position just north of the former fortress was too strong for the Allies to attack.[1] On September 30 he wrote to General M. D. Gorchakov to be ready to grasp any opportunity against the enemy's left flank, if he thought it possible.[2]

The emperor also expected Austria to enter the war actively against Russia now that Sevastopol had fallen, as he was not convinced by the encouraging reports about the substantial reductions of the Austrian army. While he admitted that he might be wrong, he felt that Gorchakov should take all precautionary measures well in advance.[3] When Vienna sent a friendly despatch asking Russia to propose a solution for the Third of the Four Points, Alexander was by no means flattered. He called a special conference to consider the matter, which suggested that the provision for the free passage of merchant vessels should not be changed at all. Count Nesselrode wanted to add a statement that the tsar was touched by the Austrian attitude, but Alexander said: "I do not want this. I do not want to say that I am touched by the attitude of persons who intended to lure me into a trap. I beg of you, count, to put aside all sentimentality in politics." [4]

While the loss of Sevastopol was a shock to all Russians, most informed persons had expected it. Neither the government nor the general public showed signs of discouragement. Alexander II summoned a council of war, which decided to hold the Crimea at all costs, and shortly thereafter he went to visit the army in the south.

1. M. I. Bogdanovich, "Imperator Aleksandr Nikolaevich v epokhu voiny 1855 goda," *RS,* XXXIX (1893), 229, 309.
2. Ibid., p. 316.
3. Letter to M. D. Gorchakov, Sept. 5, 1855, XXXVII, 130.
4. Tiutcheva, *Pri dvore dvukh imperatorov,* II, 19.

He was warmly welcomed by the troops and easily became convinced that they would continue to defend Russia's honor as Kutuzov's troops had done in 1812. He interpreted France's evident desire for peace as the result of weakness and internal difficulties. The young ruler even went into the Crimea, where he hailed the defenders of Sevastopol and defied the Allies and their hopes of conquering the Crimea. He helped draw up the plan for the campaign of 1856, which included the fortification and defense of Nikolaev. He also urged General Gorchakov to take aggressive action if the opportunity arose. When Baron Seebach, who was Nesselrode's son-in-law and Saxon minister at Paris, sought to suggest Napoleon's view that Russia should accept naval limitation on the Black Sea, Alexander sent word to Seebach that Russia would reject such limitation. The tsar held that the Black Sea should be neutralized, with all foreign fleets excluded. Russia and Turkey should have warships on it, with their number fixed by mutual agreement.[5]

Austrian reports from St. Petersburg also indicated that the spirit of the Russians had not been broken by the loss of Sevastopol. Karnicki, chargé d'affaires at St. Petersburg, stated that there was no visible despair and no one demanded peace at any price. While Nesselrode admitted the seriousness of the defeat, he held that Russia would not make the first overture for peace and that if the Allies wanted it, they should take the initiative.[6] Napoleon III, in a talk with Hübner, the Austrian ambassador, sharply denied that the loss of Sevastopol would cause the Russians to evacuate all of the Crimea. The emperor stated that the Russians would give up the rest of the peninsula only if the Allies compelled them to do so.[7]

General Pélissier, the conqueror of Sevastopol, categorically opposed any attempt to drive Russia out of the Crimea. He told Napoleon that the capture of Sevastopol had taken a very long time and had been very costly, although this was the easiest part of Russia to conquer. An attempt to push further into the country would be extremely difficult and he would not undertake it.[8]

5. François Charles-Roux, *Alexandre II, Gortchakoff, et Napoléon III* (Paris, 1913), pp. 34–35; W. E. Mosse, *The Rise and Fall of the Crimean System, 1855–1871* (London, 1963), pp. 15–16, 19–21.

6. Karnicki to Buol, St. Petersburg, Sept. 2/14, 1855, HHSA, X, 41.

7. Hübner to Buol, Paris, Oct. 20, 1855, ibid., IX, 50.

8. Letter, Gorchakov to Nesselrode, Nov. 25/Dec. 7, 1855, TsGADA, f.3, D. 140, pt. 2; La Gorce, I, 446–49.

The British public, however, did not want peace, for Palmerston, Queen Victoria, *The Times,* and the great majority of other newspapers and a large majority in Parliament felt that Britain, which, after the battles of the Alma and Inkerman, had done poorly, needed another year of fighting. The British hoped that they could invade Asia Minor and deprive Russia of all its lands south of the Caucasus, with the help of the Circassians, whom they wanted to incite to join with Shamil in driving the Russians out of the mountains. The British also were building a huge and powerful fleet to attack in the Baltic. Here, together with the Swedes and the Norwegians, they planned to destroy Kronstadt and the Russian Baltic fleet. Their aim was to force the Russians out of Finland, which should return to the Swedish crown. They also hoped to encourage the Poles to revolt against Russia and to restore an independent Polish kingdom as it had existed at the time of the Congress of Vienna, free from Russia. By achieving these ambitious goals, with the help of the French and probably of the Austrians, the British hoped to weaken Russia so it could no longer be a threat to Europe, and at the same time to restore the military glory of Britain, which was at a very low level.

On February 6, 1855, Alexis de Tocqueville wrote to the British economist Nassau Senior to express pleasure at the good relations between the French and British armies in the Crimea. He added, however, that he was not pleased by the British management of the war, which had clearly diminished their prestige in Europe. On a visit to Paris, where he saw a variety of persons, all praised the "heroic courage" of the British soldiers, but he also found agreement "that the importance of England as a military power had been greatly exaggerated; that she is utterly devoid of military talent, which is shown as much in administration as in fighting; and that even in the most pressing circumstances she cannot raise a large army."

Tocqueville continued that not since childhood had he heard such language: "You are believed to be absolutely dependent on us; and in the midst of our intimacy I see rising a friendly contempt for you, which if our Governments quarrel, will make a war with you much easier than has been since the fall of Napoleon." [9] Since the British army had done very poorly during the last months of the siege of Sevastopol, while the French covered themselves with glory, it is under-

9. Alexis de Tocqueville, *Correspondence and Conversations . . . with Nassau Senior* (London, 1896), II, 90–91.

standable that many Englishmen wanted the war to continue so that their army could redeem itself with new victories.

Palmerston was alive to this aspect of the British war effort, which he sought to deal with by the traditional policy of obtaining soldiers by bounties for enlistment. This method produced substantial numbers of recruits, many of them Irish.[10] They were not enough, however, so that by June 1855 he was very eager to obtain foreign troops. The British success in obtaining fifteen thousand Sardinians encouraged him, but he stated that the army was still forty thousand men short of the authorized strength. "Let us get as many Germans and Swiss as we can," he said, "let us get men from Halifax, let us enlist Italians, and let us increase our bounty at home without raising the standard." He urged disregard of departmental or official and professional prejudices: "The thing must be done. We must have troops." [11] His urgency, however, led to a serious quarrel with the United States, for the British minister at Washington and several consuls had violated American laws by recruiting Americans and sending them to Halifax for enrollment. This argument, together with a clash over the Mosquito Coast in Central America, resulted in the expulsion of the minister and a few preparations for war in the United States. But the crisis early in 1856 soon blew over.[12] By the end of 1855 the British army of fifty thousand in the Crimea was in excellent shape and Palmerston and Cowley were talking of continuing the war with Turkey and Sardinia as allies, even if France and Austria refused to join them. The British cabinet, however, unanimously rejected this proposal.[13]

Napoleon III was in the key position as the first tentative peace feelers began in the autumn of 1855. He had broken up the Holy Alliance, which had been one of his main objectives, and, thanks to the successes of the French army, France was predominant both militarily and diplomatically. The French had important allies, and most Europeans preferred French leadership to that of England, Austria, or Russia. On the other hand, the French, who had suffered heavy losses in the war, were extremely eager for peace, and the powerful emperor had to recognize this fact. France had sent 300,000 men to

10. Woodham-Smith, p. 158.

11. Herbert C. F. Bell, *Lord Palmerston* (London, 1936), II, 125.

12. Ibid., II, pp. 141–44.

13. Charles Cavendish Fulke Greville, *The Greville Memoirs, 1814–1860* (London, 1938), VII, 170, 209.

the Crimea, of whom, because of epidemics of cholera, typhus, and scurvy, little more than one-third would return.[14]

Otto von Bismarck, who spent his August vacation in 1855 in France, remarked on the striking lack of infantry in all the garrisons, except in Paris, Lyon, and Boulogne. The others were mere depots in the real sense of the word. In Strasbourg, Rouen, and Metz the infantry regiments had men with the colors only because of the new recruits in training, and any well-drilled detachment was immediately shipped off to the East. In Strasbourg and Metz the noncombattant craftsmen and workers of the regiments did guard duty, while in Metz this duty was performed by the men of the artillery units in training. Inhabitants told the Prussian that the number of infantry in the towns was between five hundred and a thousand. An adjutant of the emperor told him that the number of men still in the East was eighty thousand less than the number that had been sent. The army was sharply critical of the minimization of the losses in the official press, and every officer was quite ready to charge the *Moniteur* with lies in this respect.[15]

These substantial losses, incurred in a far-off region in which the French had no real interest, were thoroughly disliked in all quarters, and the people had no desire for a big campaign in the Baltic, which seemed even more remote. Moreover, the war had brought hardship from high food prices, and the government had had to borrow 1,500,000,500 francs. Public opinion, both in Paris and the provinces, scolded Napoleon for working only for England, and was hostile to Austria, France's nominal ally. Privation and misery made the poorer classes bitter, and there were two attempts to assassinate the emperor. There was discontent in the villages and riots in some of the cities. Hence the emperor, like the vast majority of the French, was very eager for peace with Russia, with which France had no real quarrel.[16]

But while Napoleon desired peace and was averse to the cruelties of war, he was an ardent believer in encouraging the nationalities of Europe to demand their rights. He was a convinced supporter of Italian nationalism, for which he had fought in 1830. An independent Poland, which was to have the boundaries of the Congress Kingdom of 1815, figured strongly in his schemes. He advocated a more unified Germany, although he also wanted France to have the west bank of the Rhine.

14. Debidour, II, 143.
15. Otto von Bismarck, *Die Gesammelten Werke* (2nd. ed., Berlin, 1924–32), II, 72.
16. Debidour, II, 142–43.

He hoped to induce Austria to relinquish Lombardy and Venetia in exchange for the erection of a Rumanian state, to be ruled by an Austrian archduke. He sympathized with the Magyar desire for independence from Austria, and paid at least lip service to the idea of independence for Circassia. And, if the war continued on into 1856, he was agreeable to encouraging the Finns to break away from Russia and to return to Swedish rule. (On the other hand, Louis Napoleon showed little interest in the aspirations of the Bretons, the Irish, the Croats, the Serbs, the Czechs, and the Bulgars.)

This program of Napoleon's was highly ambitious, as it involved redrawing the map of Europe and infringing on the Austrian and Russian empires. Oddly enough, however, Napoleon did not want to achieve these objectives by war, for he hated its brutality. He had repeatedly rebuked Pélissier for the heavy casualties of his operations in the Crimea, and he had an instinctive feeling that war was contrary to the nature of mankind. General von Willisen, a Prussian envoy, reported to Count Manteuffel in November 1855 "that he detested the barbarism that was indispensable to a war." [17] This same squeamishness was to show itself at the battles of Magenta and Solferino in 1859.

The emperor's solution for this dilemma was to redraw the map of Europe, not on the battlefield, but at the green table of a European congress, to be attended by the rulers of Europe. He had already taken a great stride by winning Austria away from its alliance with Russia, which destroyed the Holy Alliance. Now, in 1855, with peace already a possibility, he sought to transform the peace conference into a European congress, which would not only make peace, but would also deal with the problems that had not been settled at Vienna in 1815.

Even before France entered the Crimean War, Napoleon had mentioned to Duke Ernst II of Saxe-Coburg, brother of Albert, the Prince Consort of England, that he hoped that one result of the war would be a European congress which would grapple with the manifold problems of Europe. When France went to war with Russia the idea of a European Congress lapsed, but after the fall of Sevastopol it again became timely. In September 1855 Duke Ernst had two long talks

17. Willisen to King Frederick William, Paris, Nov. 3, 1855, in Otto Freiherr von Manteuffel, *Preussens' auswärtige Politik, 1850 bis 1858,* ed. Heinrich von Poschinger (Berlin, 1902), III, 165, as cited in Baumgart, p. 52.

with Napoleon, during which the latter declared against continuing the war and urged a peace conference. But before the conference could be a real success it would have to deal with the problems inherited from the Congress of Vienna—especially Poland and Italy. The emperor tried to persuade Duke Ernst and Frederick William IV of Prussia to promote this idea. The latter did so, suggesting that a congress of the princes should meet at Aachen—a proposal that Count Otto von Manteuffel had favored in 1848. Queen Victoria, however, vehemently rejected the scheme.[18]

Napoleon III continued to advocate a congress, using leaflets and pamphlets to spread his views. In December 1855 he had a journalist publish a brochure entitled "The Need for a Congress to Pacify Europe," which, although not over his signature, clearly expressed his opinions. Afterwards he continued to issue similar propaganda to Europe, declaring that one should not settle the major political questions against the will of the people. Before a gathering at the end of the Paris Exposition he appealed to all to decide what was right and what was not. Thus, except for Austria, much of Europe was already prepared to accept a congress, and Prussia openly supported the idea. Napoleon wanted an assembly of all the rulers of Europe, with power to settle all its problems. He was tactful toward Russia and even suggested the possibility of alliances in the future, although he declared that the Anglo-French alliance was "eternal." His chief desire was to destroy the system set up at Vienna in 1815, by means of a new Congress of Paris.[19] Unlike Palmerston, who also wanted to change the map of Europe, Napoleon was able to bring about much of what he wanted.

Still another variant of Napoleon's policies appeared in his steps toward continuing the war. He professed to be greatly interested in extending the war to the Baltic, where the Allies should attack the Russian position in Finland and destroy the powerful naval base of Kronstadt. To this end he built up a strong steam navy and had several "floating batteries"—heavily armored vessels with large-caliber guns, which could venture into position close to the Russian defenses. Even more significant, the emperor of the French sent General Canrobert, former French commander in the Crimea, to Stockholm to negotiate with King Oscar about the entry of the kingdom of Sweden and

18. Baumgart, pp. 41–43.
19. Ibid., p. 132.

Norway into the war. As a result, the king signed an alliance with France and England, by which the latter powers agreed to furnish Sweden and Norway protection against Russia's aggressive designs. Sweden cited as proof of aggression a Russian request for an enclave of two and a half square kilometers on the Waranger fjord as a winter base for Finnish fishermen. Also, as a result of the overgrazing of reindeer pastures in northern Finland by the herds of Norwegian Lapps, in 1852 Prince Menshikov, governor general of Finland, had closed the frontier between Finland and Norway. The Swedish government further alleged that Russia had sought a naval base on Gotland in the middle Baltic, and probably had plans to seize another base in southern Sweden. It did not, however, cite evidence for these claims. Swedish diplomats visited London and Paris, where they talked with Palmerston, Clarendon, Persigny, and Walewski and received encouragement for their anti-Russian views, especially in London. Finally, a defensive alliance was signed on November 21, 1855, with strong secret provisions for joint military action in Finland and the vicinity of St. Petersburg. Count Nesselrode was greatly pained by the news of this treaty, but he and Alexander II responded in very mild fashion, hoping that the former good relations between Russia and its neighbors could continue to exist.[20]

Actually, a secret memorandum drawn up by King Oscar and his aides provided for a large-scale campaign in 1856 and 1857 by some 165,000 Swedish, Norwegian, French, British, and even Danish troops to drive the Russians out of Finland and to destroy the base at Kronstadt.[21] But before this "defensive" treaty could be put into effect, the Austrians presented their ultimatum at St. Petersburg, which was accepted by the Russian government, and on February 25, 1856, the first session of the Paris Peace Conference took place. Thus the plans for a Finnish campaign were nullified. The Swedes were much upset by the Russian acceptance of the peace terms and continued to urge England, France, and Austria to go through with their plans to move against Russia. The English were also eager for the 1856 campaign, but the French were so anxious for peace that they paid little attention to the Baltic, except to ask the Russians not to fortify the Åland Islands. What is significant is that the Russian cabinet and the emperor

20. Carl Hallendorff, ed., *Konung Oscar I: s politik under Krimkriget* (Stockholm, 1930), pp. 56–62, 63–67, 71–72, 87–88, 97–102, 108–12.
21. Ibid., pp. 87–91.

simply were not concerned over Sweden's plans to recover Finland by force of arms and made no attempt to punish it for its hostility.[22]

Another aspect of Napoleon III's statecraft is seen in the secret peace negotiations that went on after the French capture of Sevastopol. Strictly speaking, they began earlier, for Princess Dorothea Lieven, a very patriotic Russian subject, maintained a salon in Paris throughout the war, where she represented the Russian point of view and maintained contact with St. Petersburg. In the summer of 1855 Prince A. M. Gorchakov, at Vienna, took advantage of the departure of General Letang from Vienna, where he had presented a quite different French policy from that of Bourqueney. Gorchakov handed Letang a message for Napoleon III, whom the Russian had known personally in earlier years, proclaiming that Russia was not hostile to France in principle, nor to the emperor himself. Russia had applauded Napoleon as the foe of anarchy in France and the enemy of revolution. If now he wanted peace he should cease trying to impose humiliating conditions on Russia, which it would never accept. Once the monarch understood the conditions for a possible peace between the two countries, Gorchakov would be willing to help as best he could. While he had no authority to make overtures, he was showing his personal confidence in Napoleon III.[23] But with the siege of Sevastopol approaching its climax, this overture had no result.

Suddenly, however, in November, 1855, Gorchakov received a letter from the Duc de Morny, who had earlier suggested dealings between them. Gorchakov, believing that it would be useful to encourage Morny, returned a letter saying that he shared his views on the need for peace and admired his qualities as a statesman. Adding that good dealings between the two countries might lead to peace and further fruitful developments in the future, Gorchakov stated that the present poor relations between France and Russia were unnatural, for they had no real conflicts and their interests tended to draw them together.[24] This communication was followed by another, from one of the two Austrian bankers (Barons Eskeles and Sina) who served as intermediaries between the two men. Stating that he regretted that their effort at developing a peace movement had not succeeded, Morny was quite hopeful that his unofficial dealings with the Russian might help to

22. Ibid., pp. 113–72, passim.
23. Letter, Gorchakov to Nesselrode, Nov. 5/17, 1855, TsGADA, f. 3, D. 140, pt. 2.
24. Ibid.

bring his ideas to the knowledge of Napoleon and thus to prepare the way for an understanding.[25]

Another communication from Morny, attached to Gorchakov's letter to Nesselrode, urged the Russians not to believe that France had to have peace and that Russia could draw it away from England. Napoleon could try to bring the English to make concessions, but he would not break with them. Russia must negotiate sincerely with the Allies and hope for peace. France and Britain still wanted to limit the Russian fleet as before, although now they would use the term "neutralization of the Black Sea," and the regulation probably would not have to be in effect very long. Austria was the best intermediary to conclude peace on these bases.[26] Finally, another unsigned, unaddressed letter, probably from Morny to an intermediary for Gorchakov, strongly warned the prince that Russia must accept the Allied terms or disaster would follow. If the war should continue, it would be deadly for Russia, which could not survive it. Now was the time to seek peace, while the French and the English were not as close as they had been. No better chance of peace would come, and it could be made only by absolute acceptance of the terms.[27]

At length, plans were made for a meeting of Gorchakov and Morny in Dresden. Nesselrode, however, told Gorchakov to break off the talks between them, so as not to impair the chances of success of the current dealings in Paris between Walewski and Seebach.[28]

Apparently the first move toward peace negotiations came from Count Beust, foreign minister and minister-president of Saxony, although communications between Nesselrode and Walewski, French minister of foreign affairs, began about the middle of October, with Baron Seebach of Saxony, Nesselrode's son-in-law, as the intermediary. Shortly thereafter Beust and von der Pfordten, Bavarian minister at Paris, traveled together to the Paris Exposition and engaged in diplomatic soundings. Both diplomats talked with Count Walewski and Morny and were entertained by the emperor Napoleon, who granted them interviews. En route to Paris Beust had had a talk with Baron

25. Unsigned, unaddressed letter, Paris, Nov. 14, 1855 (apparently from Morny), TsGAOR, f. 828, D. no. 604, opis' no. 1, f. 1; Charles-Roux, pp. 49–50.

26. Note, Morny to Gorchakov, attached to Gorchakov's letter to Nesselrode, Nov. 18/31, 1855, TsGADA, f. 3, D. no. 140, pt. 2.

27. Unsigned, unaddressed letter, probably from Morny to an intermediary between him and Gorchakov, n.d., TsGAOR, f. 828, D. no. 604, opis' no. 1, f. 1.

28. Tatishchev, I, 174–77; Charles-Roux, p. 55.

Brunnow at Frankfort, who told him he was authorized to say that Russia wanted peace, but could not agree to pay an indemnity or to make territorial cessions. When the Saxon told this to Napoleon he was reassured that these and other humiliating demands would not be made, provided Russia hastened to accept neutralization of the Black Sea. On his return to Dresden Beust promptly wrote a long letter to Nesselrode containing an urgent suggestion that he make a move toward France along these lines. Beust made the point that any concession that Russia might make would be only temporary, for within ten or twelve years some official would propose its cancellation.[29] Beust also wrote a similar letter to Baron Budberg at Berlin.

In a letter of November 14/26, 1855, Nesselrode thanked Beust for his intelligent proposals, saying that his cabinet wanted peace at least as sincerely as Paris did, although it was not proper for it to reply more explicitly to the Tuileries than he had done in his letter to Walewski by means of Seebach. He told Beust that they both had the same solution for the Third Point and that Russia still rejected the proposal that it had rejected at the conferences of Vienna. There Russia's various proposals had been refused almost without discussion, although they knew that the best peace would be one that would conciliate Russia's honor with the interest of Europe and the independence of Turkey; "is it indeed for us to make new propositions?" Russia was so convinced of the firmness of the Anglo-French alliance that it did not seek facilities for peace from France. Both France and Russia had limits that they were obliged not to pass.[30]

During the resulting inactivity the Austrian cabinet, which had learned of the unofficial peace feelers, decided to present its conditions for peace in an ultimatum to St. Petersburg. Unwisely, Vienna decided to demand a considerable territorial cession from Russian Bessarabia to ensure the security of the navigation of the Danube. But the fact that the suggested frontier would be quite far from the river greatly embittered the Russians, as they knew that the demand had come from Austria rather than from France or England.[31]

Pfordten also talked with Walewski, Prince Jerome, and Bourque-

29. Friedrich Ferdinand, Graf von Beust, *Aus Drei Viertel-Jahrhunderten* (Stuttgart, 1887), I, 200–201.
30. Ibid., pp. 205–06.
31. Ibid., p. 202.

ney, and had two long audiences with Napoleon III. He hastened to send a letter to St. Petersburg stating that the French emperor was ready for peace talks, but would not take the first step, which he felt should come from Russia. He would seek no territorial cessions or other humiliating conditions. The Four Points, more clearly defined, should serve as the basis for the peace. The Third Point should provide for the neutrality of the Black Sea, with no Russian or Turkish warships on it. If Russia would not accept these terms, the Allies would pursue the war to conquer territory, chiefly by getting Austria into the war, and in addition would seek to start insurrections in Italy, Hungary, and especially Poland.

Pfordten also wrote to Bismarck that if peace did not come soon, the powers would act strongly for their special national interests, instead of being guided by the principle of the best interest of Europe.[32]

These reports about Napoleon's readiness for peace reached St. Petersburg late in November 1855. The Russian reaction to them was negative, for Nesselrode, who doubtless spoke for his master, refused neutralization of the Black Sea, which early in 1855 he had decided was contrary to Russian honor. Alexander was still belligerent in tone, for he repeatedly wrote General Gorchakov not to be dejected, since Russia would win as it had in 1812. He was highly impressed by his inspection tour in the south, where he found the army in fine spirit and the defenses formidable. It had plenty of provisions and was building a military road into the Crimea. He said that he would not make a bad peace and that perhaps there would be a revolutionary outbreak in France.[33]

Nesselrode, who was much impressed by France's willingness to talk peace as shown by the Morny-Gorchakov talks and the Seebach parleys, by mid-November was eager to accept the French terms at once. Alexander, however, with his head full of dreams of military glory, refused to give an answer until he had returned to St. Petersburg. Nesselrode felt that by acceptance Russia would pull France away from England and would forestall Austria's schemes. On his return from Nikolaev, Alexander had Nesselrode answer Count Walewski with irritating conditions. He would neither agree to limit his forces nor accept the neutralization of the Black Sea, about which he asked for details. It was now that Gorchakov was instructed to break off

32. Baumgart, pp. 92–93.
33. Ibid., pp. 94–95.

his talks with Morny, although they were at a promising stage. Thus Alexander's military pride would not let him accept France's offer, and the peaceful advice from Bavaria, Saxony, and Württemberg accomplished nothing. Pfordten was much annoyed at the Russian refusal.[34] In the meantime, Gorchakov was reporting the intense consultations under way between Count Buol and Baron Bourqueney of France, which were held under full secrecy and promised nothing good for Russia. When these talks resulted in the text of a proposed ultimatum to St. Petersburg to accept peace terms based on the Four Points, but expanded and made more severe, Alexander had to take this threatening development into consideration.

Like the middle states of Germany, Prussia was also greatly concerned over the future, for it knew that England was very hostile to it and would attack it if the war spread to the Baltic. Prussia's relations with Austria were also severely strained. Now if Napoleon decided on a Baltic campaign in 1856, which would probably include an attempt to resurrect the Polish kingdom, Prussia's position would be highly untenable, with Allied landings in Livonia and Kurland. In addition, a persistent rumor, apparently emanating from Belgium, suggested strongly that Russia, in order to gain a favorable separate peace from France, would be willing to permit Napoleon to seize the west bank of the Rhine. When Napoleon talked with Hübner in mid-January, he told the ambassador, "Russia is making advances to me," but he did not specify what they were.[35] But Hübner, Clarendon, and probably the Prussian king himself felt sure that these concessions included the Rhineland.

Whether or not Russia did offer the Rhine frontier to Napoleon, King Frederick William IV was convinced that Prussia was in grave danger, and the news of Sweden's alliance with France and Britain made the danger seem even more real. On January 6, 1856, the king wrote an urgent letter to Alexander II appealing to him to save Prussia from war by accepting the Allied demands. He stated that Prussia was in danger of being the turkey *(dindon)* at the feast of the Allies, for France wanted the Rhine, Austria was eager to recover Silesia, and England wanted to ruin Prussia's industry. Almost as an afterthought, the king also mentioned the dangers threatening Russia in the next campaign—the peril to Kronstadt and to St. Petersburg, and

34. Charles-Roux, pp. 53–56.
35. Baumgart, p. 106.

the probable insurrection of Poland. His appeal to rescue Prussia from these menaces was so vehement as to have almost the quality of hysteria.[36]

In the meantime Alexander, on returning from the south, was facing reality. He comprehended that there was serious danger of an expanded and intensified war unless Napoleon could be placated, for the British were obviously hoping that the war would continue, so that their army could win the triumphs that so far had eluded them. While Austria showed no signs of taking up the sword, it was definitely aligned with Russia's foes, and if the war took on new dimensions Austria probably would enter. The ultimatum to Russia that Buol and Bourqueney had prepared would doubtless be more unfavorable than the Four Points earlier agreed on, and the British were talking of additional demands to be made in a Fifth Point, regarding the nonfortification of the Åland Islands and other matters, such as a pledge not to fortify the Black Sea coast south of the Caucasus. Finally, the Austrian requirement that Russia should cede much of Bessarabia to the Principalities added a new aspect to an already dismal picture.

Fortunately for the Russians, they maintained their contacts with Walewski and Napoleon III by means of Seebach, and the Morny-Gorchakov communications continued for a time. Unlike Nesselrode, Gorchakov expressed his personal opinion that, while neutralization of the Black Sea was an ill-defined concept, Russia might accept it in the hope that it would be applied fairly. He also said that it would be important for both Russia and Turkey to have enough armed vessels on the Black Sea to meet their needs, and this requirement should be the result of a mutual agreement between the two.[37] In addition, Gorchakov, while unable to learn the content of the probable Franco-Austrian proposal to Russia, had learned enough of Napoleon's thinking from Beust and Pfordten to permit him to make some valuable suggestions to his cabinet, which Alexander strongly approved in his marginal comments. Napoleon seemed to hold strongly to the idea of neutralization of the Black Sea, which Gorchakov had ridiculed at the Vienna Conferences eight months before. Now the prince supported this scheme, but with a nuance that he thought deserved consid-

36. Ibid., pp. 90 and 91.
37. Two reports of the go-between between Gorchakov and Morny, and Morny's second note to Gorchakov, annexed to Gorchakov's letter to Nesselrode, Nov. 27/Dec. 9, 1855, TsGADA, f. 3, D. no. 140, pt. 2.

eration. Both Louis Napoleon and Walewski had said that no military flag whatever should fly over the Black Sea, *"except for forces that Russia and Turkey should judge necessary for defense of their coasts."* (Here the emperor commented: "this clause *changes completely the question* such as it was announced to us up to now, and *I would not see in it an obstacle on my side."*[38]

Gorchakov added that since these forces would be fixed by an understanding between the two coastal powers, with no other power ostensibly involved, his humble opinion was that *"no right of sovereignty, no demand of national honor, would be offended."* Alexander agreed with this opinion and stated that if Napoleon's views in other respects did not prevent renewing negotiations, they should not reject them out of hand. The ambassador felt that this was the only way to settle the question of the Black Sea and that it would leave Russia in the dominant position there. He also suggested that the peace talks should be moved to another location. Austria would oppose this suggestion, but England and France would not.

Finally, the prince stressed the need to have a "serious, durable and conscientious settlement" of the Fourth Point. With its opponents not contesting this matter, Russia should make sure that it would be obtained.[39]

In the meantime, Bourqueney, after returning from consultation in Paris, was conferring daily with Buol. Count Colloredo, Austrian minister to London, wrote that, while Napoleon desired peace, he felt that one more move against Russia on the part of Austria would be the way to achieve it more quickly, and this was what Bourqueney was told to request.[40] In a secret despatch of November 2/14 Gorchakov said that the secrecy maintained by the Vienna cabinet was so complete that he had no positive news of Napoleon's plans for peace, and he could only assume that Bourqueney's efforts were an attempt to line up Austria and Germany against Russia and to throw the blame for war on the latter. The British definitely did not want peace, as they had not gained their objectives and wanted to continue the conflict. The prince did say categorically "that we can count on Austria not leaving its present expectant attitude," because of the personal convictions of Franz Joseph and because of Austria's financial situa-

38. Gorchakov to Nesselrode, Nov. 12/24, 1855 (Secret), AVP, f. Kants., D. no. 225.
39. Ibid.
40. Gorchakov to Nesselrode, tg. (secret), Nov. 1/13, 1855, AVP, f. Kants., D. no. 225.

tion. Austria could squeak by financially until 1857, if it stayed out of war and sold all its railways, although there would still be a big deficit. Any complication, however, would bring collapse. According to highly reliable information, the emperor said that Austria wanted a general peace, but if it did not come during the winter, it would sit tight and let Russia and France fight it out. England and Prussia did not count, and France could not attack in Italy. This was what Bach and Buol had persuaded the emperor to believe, and Bruck also believed it. Gorchakov thought that "this collective obstacle" would foil Bourqueney's efforts to draw Austria into the war.[41]

Finally, on November 5/17 Gorchakov was able to send to his cabinet a telegram indicating the nature of the proposal from Paris of the Four Points with Austrian revisions, which Buol quickly agreed to. Buol and Bourqueney then drew up a memorandum, with a new text of the Four Points, which was sent to Franz Joseph at Trieste and which he approved on November 3/15. That evening Buol and Bourqueney verified the two documents, and on November 4/16, Serres took them to Paris. Austria was committing itself to getting this version accepted by Russia and, in case of refusal, to breaking off diplomatic relations. Gorchakov's informants believed that the documents would be communicated simultaneously in St. Petersburg and to Gorchakov in Vienna. Gorchakov did not know their content, although he thought that it would prove to be a return to the scheme of the alternative and the counterweight. He still held to the belief that Austria would not actively enter the war against Russia, unless it suffered serious reverses.[42]

By November 17/29, however, by some devious means Gorchakov obtained the text of a telegram from Bourqueney to Walewski of November 27 (N.S.), indicating changes in the Austrian ultimatum to Russia that the Emperor Franz Joseph had approved. Russia would be forbidden to maintain or construct naval fortresses on the Black Sea. Cloture of the Straits would be stipulated in the treaty as a condition of the principle of neutralization of the Black Sea. The treaty between the coastal powers would form an additional part of the main treaty. Austria would present the ultimatum only if the powers obligated themselves, in case of acceptance, to sign the preliminaries of peace. "I know the Emperor Franz Joseph: he will not cede anything

41. Gorchakov to Nesselrode, Nov. 2/14, 1855 (Very Secret), ibid.
42. Gorchakov to Nesselrode, tg., Nov. 5/17 (Secret), AVP, ibid.

more," Gorchakov wired Nesselrode, "and if one makes new difficulties, we shall lose the fruit of the concessions obtained with so much trouble and labor." Gorchakov stated that his "intimate accomplices" had had difficulty in reading the end of the text, but they believed that it dealt with the problems raised by the English about the special agreement between the coastal powers, which England apparently wanted to eliminate. The envoy added that his informants "retain doubts as to the acceptance of England." [43]

Prince Gorchakov, however, understandably felt handicapped by his lack of knowledge of the secret talks with Paris and in a letter to Nesselrode of November 23/December 5, 1855, said that he was in ignorance of these talks and that he should know what was happening. He had learned indirectly that Beust's trip to Paris had been inspired by Russia, but that in a message carried by Seebach, Russia refused the proposals that he transmitted. Gorchakov also had learned that Russia had made tentative plans for a direct understanding with France. He believed that he needed to know more, in order to operate more effectively. They had reached a "supremely critical moment"—which could settle the fate of Europe.[44]

On November 23 (O.S.)—too early to have been in response to Gorchakov's appeal—Nesselrode telegraphed the prince in code that Alexander II had approved and adopted the schemes that he had suggested, and was ready to consent to having the Third Point resolved by the following measures: (1) cloture of the Straits; (2) no military flag whatever on the Black Sea, except for forces that Russia and the Porte, in a common accord, should judge necessary to maintain there; (3) the establishment of the quantity of these forces by a direct understanding between the two coastal powers, without ostensible participation of other powers.

Gorchakov was authorized to make use of this information as he felt would be most useful for the reestablishment of peace, and above all to avoid an ultimatum from Austria. Nesselrode informed him that this information had been taken directly to Louis Napoleon, "with whom we are in pourparlers without the intermediary of any other power." [45]

43. Gorchakov to Nesselrode, tg., Nov. 17/29, 1855 (Secret), AVP, ibid.
44. Letter, Gorchakov to Nesselrode, Nov. 23/Dec. 5, 1855, TsGADA, f. 3, D. no. 140, pt. 2.
45. Nesselrode to Gorchakov, tg., Nov. 23 (O.S.?) 1855, AVP, f. Kants, D. no. 226.

On the same day Nesselrode wrote a long letter to Gorchakov telling him "under seal of secrecy" that for six weeks the Russian cabinet had been "in direct pourparlers" with Louis Napoleon, who was immediately informed of the scheme which Alexander II had recommended for the solution of the Third Point. This secret communication settled the question of the initiative, if their adversaries were in good faith and if they really desired peace. "Unfortunately," Nesselrode added, "the absence of the emperor [Alexander II] has not permitted me to reply sooner to the confidential overtures that he made to us."

Nesselrode stated that the clause on the fortifications on the Black Sea coast had not been urged in these pourparlers. It was a new item in that it considerably exceeded the Four Points, which France had offered as the basis of negotiations, and as Beust, Pfordten, and the court of Berlin had understood the intentions of Napoleon. He hoped that Gorchakov had warned Buol about this matter. Whenever he could not eliminate "this odious scheme" it would always be useful for Buol and above all Franz Joseph to be cautioned that the claims would become "an insurmountable obstacle to the conclusion of peace." Gorchakov also should reply to Morny in general terms, stressing the necessity of not demanding anything beyond the Four Points.[46]

A letter from Nesselrode to Gorchakov written on November 28/ December 10, 1855, said that Nesselrode could not send exact instructions. Gorchakov should sound out Buol concerning his agreement with Bourqueney.

The chancellor did not know how Paris had received the Russian proposal on the Third Point. If it were rejected, at least that would edify the neutrals, for in this proposal Russia was offering a measure that Pfordten and Beust had indicated would satisfy Louis Napoleon. It included neutralization of the Black Sea and limitation of the fleets to coastguards. The size of the Russian fleet did not matter much. It would take twenty years to rebuild it to its prewar level, and in twenty years much could happen. As Morny said, many such stipulations were not eternal, for time almost always modified them.

Next, Nesselrode remarked that the Russians were in a bad spot and they must get out of it as quickly as possible. Stackelberg (a Russian military expert then in Vienna) would inform him what a third campaign would hold for Russia; unfortunately, "the chances

46. Letter, Nesselrode to Gorchakov, Nov. 23/Dec. 5, 1855, TsGAOR, f. 828, D. no. 604, opis' no. 1, f. 1.

are not in our favor." In closing, he said he eagerly awaited what would come out of Buol's Pandora's box. "Timeo Danaos et dona ferentes." [47]

A despatch from Nesselrode to Gorchakov of the same date said much the same. Alexander II was pleased with his reporting from Vienna, which on the whole agreed with what Beust and Pfordten had found out in Paris. The question of taking the initiative in the peace talks had been settled and it seemed clear that Napoleon III wanted peace. The only question was what arrangement France would approve for settling the Third Point.

Napoleon seemed to hold to the plan of neutralizing the Black Sea, which Nesselrode said was inadmissible and puerile, and if he insisted on it, there was little chance for success. However, Gorchakov had suggested a new arrangement whereby France might accept a direct understanding between Russia and the Porte about the fleets on the Black Sea, along with cloture of the Straits. If Napoleon would accept this agreement, the problem would be settled, as the British would have to give in to him.

Now there was little for Gorchakov to do, for the peace conference would probably meet in Paris, and Austria would lose its importance. The main thing was to try to prevent Austria from presenting an ill-timed ultimatum, which would complicate the precarious Russo-Austrian relations. The point of departure had been found, and everything now would depend on the reception Russia's proposal on the Third Point would receive. [48]

Although Nesselrode had refused to make the proposal to Walewski that Beust had recommended to him, when both Morny and Walewski, through Baron Seebach, urged the Russian cabinet to make peace proposals, Nesselrode permitted Seebach to go to Paris to talk confidentially with Walewski about peace. The latter insisted, however, that Napoleon III was firmly committed to the British alliance and could not make peace proposals, which should come from Russia. They must be satisfactory and practical, so that France could insist that England accept them. Walewski offered a choice between settling the Third Point by an agreement with the Porte about the size of their fleets, or neutralization of the Black Sea. On the basis of these disclo-

47. Letter, Nesselrode to Gorchakov, Nov. 28/Dec. 10, 1855, TsGAOR, f. 828, D. no. 604, opis' no. 1, f. 1.
48. Nesselrode to Gorchakov, Nov. 28 (O.S.?), 1855, AVP, f. Kants., D. no. 226.

sures, in November 1855 Nesselrode authorized Seebach to communicate to the French government the following three proposals of the Russian court: (1) the Bosporus and the Dardanelles were to remain closed; (2) the navies of all nations were to be barred from the Black Sea, except for the ships that the two coastal countries would regard as necessary to keep there; (3) the number of these ships would be set by a direct agreement with the Porte, without any outside mediation.

To Seebach's astonishment, however, Walewski refused to join him in considering these conditions, because of the fact that the Russian court had already communicated them to Vienna. Walewski therefore insisted that Russia should negotiate with Austria, which was preparing a set of conditions it would impart to St. Petersburg in the name of Austria, England, and France. There was nothing for Russia to do but wait for the Austrian proposal.[49]

By November 14, 1855, Baron Bourqueney and Count Buol had agreed on the proposal to be presented by Austria to Russia in the form of an ultimatum. The substance of the proposal was essentially the Four Points, which had been accepted by the Russian cabinet in November 1854: (1) abolition of the Russian protectorate over the Principalities; (2) freedom of navigation of the Danube; (3) revision of the Treaty of 1841, so as to eliminate Russian preponderance on the Black Sea; and (4) general European supervision over the carrying out of the sultan's pledges of rights and immunities to his Greek Orthodox subjects, instead of the purely Russian guarantee of these rights.

A Memorandum on the Preliminaries of Peace, adopted in Vienna on November 14, 1855, included the following provisions:

Point 1. Complete abolition of the Russian protectorate over the Principalities, with Russia to have no special right to interfere in them. The Principalities would enjoy their privileges and immunities under the suzerainty of the Porte, and would develop their national organization and permanent defense forces. Russia would consent to a cession of Bessarabian territory from near Khotyn to Lake Salzyk.

Point 2. The freedom of the Danube and its mouths would be effectively assured by European institutions in which the contracting powers would be represented. Navigation of the Danube would be regulated

49. Tatishchev, I, 177–78.

according to the principles of the Congress of Vienna in 1815 regarding the navigation of rivers. Each of the powers would have the right to station one or two light warships at the mouths of the Danube.

Point 3. The Black Sea would be neutralized and forbidden to warships except as provided under Point 2. The two coastal powers would agree to maintain in the Black Sea only enough light vessels to protect their coasts and not to have any naval arsenals on the coast. The cloture of the Straits would be maintained, except for the exceptions already mentioned.

Point 4. The immunities of the *rayahs* (Christian) subjects of the Porte should be consecrated, without infringement on the independence and dignity of the Sultan. . . . After the signing of the peace Russia would regain its place in common with the signatory powers in the surveillance of the interests guaranteed by this article.

Point 5. The belligerent powers reserve the right to bring forward, in the interest of Europe, special conditions over and above the four guarantees.[50]

A striking aspect of France's efforts to bring the war to an end is that the most important approaches were made, not to the British ally, but to Austria or to Russia, and apparently the Court of St. James did not know of them until they were well advanced. The fact is that the Anglo-French alliance was weak and there were numerous signs of discord between the Allied governments. They differed sharply over Poland; and at Constantinople, a heated quarrel was raging between Lord Redcliffe and E. A. Thouvenel of the Quai d'Orsay. France, which had grown cool toward the war, had no interest in Circassia and Georgia, whereas London had very ambitious objectives in these areas. So France negotiated about the bases for peace with Austria rather than with England. As a result, on November 17, 1854, Napoleon III and his council decided to have Buol send their peace terms to St. Petersburg from Vienna.

On November 14 Bourqueney signed in Vienna a protocol defining the terms of peace to be presented to Russia, which had been agreed on by France and Austria without British participation. These terms included the Four Points, in a much more drastic form. Russia had to agree to neutralize the Black Sea and to cede to Moldavia land at the mouth of the Danube.[51]

50. Memorandum, "The Preliminaries of Peace," Vienna, Nov. 14, 1855, HHSA, X, 42.
51. Anderson, pp. 138–40.

When the French and Austrian governments had approved this procedure, the proposals were sent to London, which at once caused difficulties. The British cabinet, which disliked the peace negotiations, strenuously sought to make them more rigorous by insisting that the Russians accept their special demands, such as no fortification of the Åland Islands, a pledge not to maintain naval arsenals along the Black Sea, and the razing of the installations and fortifications at Nikolaev, which was well inland from the sea. The British also demanded the right to maintain consuls in the Black Sea ports. An especially sweeping demand of the London cabinet was for compelling Russia to give up Circassia, Georgia, and all holdings south of the Kuban river—a condition that the Russians would not accept unless they were overwhelmingly beaten. The Austrians, however, with reason held that, while the British might make these proposals under Point Five, they would be considered only during the regular sessions of the peace conference. But the British government stubbornly demanded that St. Petersburg accept them beforehand. The Austrians had to make repeated appeals to the French cabinet to combat this British insistence.[52] Only on December 16 did London send word that they had finally accepted the proposals of Austria and France. Clarendon and Palmerston continued to be dissatisfied with the decision, however.[53]

Palmerston had consistently opposed a moderate peace with Russia, and as early as August 25, 1855, had written to his brother that, while the fall of Sevastopol would probably soon come, "our danger will then begin—a danger of peace, and not a danger of war." Austria would still try to draw England into negotiations for "an insufficient peace," for England still would not have obtained "those decisive successes" that would entitle it to impose terms to curb "the ambition of Russia for the future." [54] The noble lord, if anything, was a greater revolutionary than Napoleon III, for his goals included the destruction of Kronstadt in a campaign in 1856 and the winning of Finland away from Russia by Swedish and Allied forces. Palmerston was eager for the restoration of the Polish kingdom and hoped to conquer all of the Crimea and to drive the Russians out of Georgia and their holdings

52. Letter, Buol to Hübner, Jan. 9, 1856, HHSA, IX, 54; Buol to Hübner, Jan. 9, 1856, ibid.; Buol to Esterházy, Jan. 25, 1856, X, 43; Buol to Hübner, tg., Jan. 25, 1856, IX, 54.
53. Hübner to Buol, Dec. 17, 1855, HHSA, IX, 50.
54. Ashley, II, 32.

south of the Caucasus mountains. On January 24, 1856, he wrote to Sir Hamilton Seymour, "We are confident that if the war goes on, the results of another campaign will enable us . . . to obtain from Russia much better conditions than we are now willing to accept." [55] Even when he was congratulating Queen Victoria on the Russian acceptance of the Austrian ultimatum, he kept thinking of what might have been: "It would no doubt have been gratifying . . . that another summer should have witnessed the destruction of Cronstadt by Your Majesty's gallant Navy, and the expulsion of the Russians from the countries south of the Caucasus by Your Majesty's brave Army." [56] If in such a campaign England had attacked Prussia, which the English hated, and encouraged a Polish insurrection, quite possibly all Germany would have been drawn in, and even the United States, which had expelled the British minister from Washington. Palmerston, with his lighthearted readiness for risky adventures, thus might have been the sponsor for a real world war.

This was denied him, however, for the London cabinet, apparently hoping to torpedo the peace talks, added new difficulties to their acceptance. After six hours of talks, it demanded neutralization of the Sea of Azov as well as of the Black Sea, with the cabinet of Vienna to be informed of the special conditions that the Western powers would present. [57] But the Russian cabinet was eager for peace, in spite of the British obstacles. In December Russia sought to gain better peace terms by way of Seebach, who urged France to support Russia's counterproposals, thus isolating Austria. The Saxon declared that Russia was willing to accept all the conditions of the ultimatum, with minor alterations, and even the Bessarabian boundary, if it were presented in a less offensive fashion. [58] Napoleon was disposed to accept this overture, for on January 14, 1856, he wrote a letter to Queen Victoria, saying that Russia had accepted most of the ultimatum except for the cession of part of Bessarabia and the special conditions, which it did not know about. It was ready to exchange Kars and its area for the territory the Allies held in the Crimea and elsewhere.

Strictly speaking, this was not the full acceptance demanded by

55. Ibid., II, 325.
56. Letter to Queen Victoria, Jan. 17, 1856, *The Letters of Queen Victoria . . . between 1837 and 1861*, III, 211.
57. Charles-Roux, p. 61.
58. F. H. Geffcken, *Zur Geschichte des Orientalischen Krieges, 1853–1856* (Berlin, 1881), p. 213.

Austria, which meant that Austria should recall its ambassador from Russia, and France and England should proceed with the war. But why should France and England ask new sacrifices of men and money from their countries "for a purely Austrian interest and for a question that does not consolidate the Ottoman Empire?" [59]

There was, however, no need for great efforts, for Russia was giving up its conquests in Asia Minor, and the Allies should ask only for bridgeheads across the Danube like Izmail and Kilia. France wanted nothing but nonfortification of the Ålands and an amnesty for the Tatars. If Napoleon III attempted to continue the war, public opinion would be against him, since he had won all the objectives of the war—Åland and Sevastopol had been taken, the Russian fleet had been destroyed and would not be rebuilt, and there were no arsenals on the Russian coast. Russia had given up its protectorate over the Principalities, its control over the channel of the Danube, its influence over its coreligionists. "Although you have obtained all that," the French public would say, "not without immense sacrifices, nevertheless you want to continue them, compromise the finances of France, spend its treasures and its blood, and why? To obtain some moors in Bessarabia!!!" The emperor concluded by saying that when he knew he was doing right he felt strong; but he would feel weak if he was not sure of doing right and doing his duty.[60]

Queen Victoria responded that she felt that the matter was too important for her to make a hasty decision, especially as the Austrian deadline was near. Hence it seemed to her wiser to wait until they could see what the situation was before they acted.

During this exchange of letters Alexander II and his advisers were considering their course. The emperor summoned several of the leaders of the realm—Prince Vorontsov and Counts Orlov, Kiselev, Bludov, and Nesselrode—[61] to a council on the evening of December 20 (O.S.). After the tsar's introductory remarks, the members of the council declared the seriousness of the situation. Vorontsov said that if the

59. Letter, Napoleon to Victoria, Jan. 14, 1856, *Letters of Queen Victoria*, III, 205–06.
60. Ibid., 206–07.
61. A. P. Zablotskii-Desiatovskii, *Graf P. D. Kiselev i ego vremia* (St. Petersburg, 1882), III, 3. The author also lists the Grand Duke Konstantin and Prince V. A. Dolgorukov as members. General D. A. Miliutin in his memoirs, however, expressly stated that Dolgorukov was not there, and does not include the Grand Duke in this council (Miliutin MS), cited in I. V. Bestuzhev, "Iz istorii krymskoi voiny 1853–1856 gg.," *Istoricheskii Arkhiv*, no. 1 (1959), pp. 204–05.

Allies would not agree to the conditions suggested by Russia, then Russia would have to accept their terms, before the opening of the campaign of 1856. Once the campaign began, the difficulties of Russia would be much greater, and so would the demands of the enemy. Kiselev, asked for his opinion, said that never before in history had Russia been in such a grave situation, faced by four allied powers with nearly double its population and three times its national income. Since the neutral states were almost all inclining toward Russia's enemies, he felt it highly unwise to risk a new campaign, which would increase the challenges of the foe. Hence they should use caution, accepting most of the demands, while rejecting those that they could not approve, in the hope that the other powers wanted peace and would accept the Russian proposals. Count Orlov spoke in the same vein. Count Bludov, perhaps influenced by his daughter, the wife of the Slavophil poet Tiutchev, made an emotional appeal to fight to the death for Russia's honor and questioned the seriousness of the situation, but he did not actually oppose moving toward peace.[62]

Finally, Nesselrode read the draft of a despatch to Gorchakov at Vienna, informing him that the sovereign had accepted most of Esterházy's demands pure and simple, except for the territorial cession, in regard to which they hoped to use Kars as an object of exchange. He had also rejected Point Five—the additional demands. Alexander II approved the despatch. Nesselrode followed it with a letter to Gorchakov, telling him that he should present his answer as an acceptance of the Austrian ultimatum as it was, except for these two minor points. With a little good will, Buol should regard it as satisfactory. If it were not accepted, Gorchakov should try to keep the door open for further negotiation. Two days later the chancellor sent a second letter, again asking Gorchakov to present Russia's reply as an acceptance: "The details that Stackelberg [Russia's military expert at Vienna] will give you will prove that peace is indispensable to us and all reasonable men with us want it. The greatest service that your patriotism could render to Russia would be to facilitate its conclusion by all means in your power." [63]

On December 30 (O.S.) Gorchakov gave Buol the Russian reply, which Nesselrode had sent on December 21, 1855/January 1, 1856. In it the chancellor stated that the Emperor Alexander had hoped

62. Zablotskii-Desiatovskii, ibid.; Baumgart, pp. 119–23; Miliutin MS pp. 384–85.
63. Tatishchev, I, 184; letters, Nesselrode to Gorchakov, Dec. 24, 1855/Jan. 5, 1856 and Dec. 26/Jan. 7, TsGAOR, f. 828, D. no. 604, opis' 1, f. 1.

that the Four Points could serve as the bases for peace and would lead on to an armistice and the final negotiations. He regretted that this had not proved to be the case. Nevertheless, he sought to meet the Austrian conditions in order to bring about a reconciliation. The proposal of the St. Petersburg cabinet had been designed in order to avoid the reefs on which the earlier proposals had been wrecked.[64] He did, however, make two observations.

On the Fifth Point, he asked how, with its vagueness, the hope of peace could be realized, even if there had been full agreement on the Four Points. Buol had urged Russia to trust that London and Paris would use this right to present new demands "only in the interests of Europe and so as to avoid obstacles in the way of peace." The Fifth Point, however, presented so many uncertainties that it would deprive the preliminaries of peace of their definitive nature. Hence the Russian cabinet insisted on its elimination. Secondly, the terms offered by Austria asked material guarantees of Russia but did not demand any of the Porte. Nevertheless, the Russian court had decided to make no objection to the first four Points. Regarding Point 1, however, it objected to the exchange of Bessarabian territory for the evacuation of Russian territory by the Allies. Russia now had Kars and its area, which could serve as the object of an exchange. Hence Russia had suppressed this paragraph entirely and had substituted another for it, although the final solution could be left to the plenipotentiaries at the peace conference.[65]

The Russian cabinet approved Point 2 without change. With regard to Point 3, it accepted the proposal for a Russo-Turkish convention on the fleets, approved beforehand by the powers. But Russia did make two changes, of which the second dealt with its need to suppress the slave trade on the east coast of the Black Sea. On Point 4 the emperor only sought to speak out, with the other European powers, in favor of his coreligionists and to share in the deliberations that would be held to assure the Christians of Turkey of their religious and political rights.

Nesselrode hoped that the Russian reply would be regarded not as a refusal but as a frank and sincere effort to secure peace. The Russian Imperial Cabinet, having conscientiously fulfilled its duties, "cannot see responsibility for failure fall on it."[66]

64. Nesselrode to Gorchakov, Dec. 21, 1855/Jan. 1, 1856, AVP, f. Kants., D. no. 226.
65. Ibid.
66. Ibid.

When Gorchakov read and delivered a copy of this despatch to Buol, the latter would not discuss it, but at once took it to the Emperor Franz Joseph, with the reply to come the following day. At the next meeting Buol said that the emperor was pleased by the peaceful intentions of the Russian court, but regretted that its reply was not an acceptance pure and simple, "which alone would bring peace." If a satisfactory answer did not come within the time limit, the emperor would have to sever their relations. Gorchakov said that too little time was being given for such an important matter. Buol, however, said that St. Petersburg could communicate by telegraph.[67]

Buol read Gorchakov two despatches to Esterházy at St. Petersburg, one confidential and the other secret. The latter stated a pledge by London and Paris not to demand an indemnity or territory under Point 5. Buol would not leave anything to a European congress. He insisted categorically on redrawing the frontier of Bessarabia, and apparently had full backing from France and England on this Point. Buol also read him a despatch from Walewski denying the intention of dealing directly with Russia and declaring that France was irrevocably committed to all Points of the preliminaries and expressly mentioned the frontier question. Buol said that Austria was so firmly bound on this matter that it had no choice—it was a matter of honor.[68]

Thus the decisive moment had come when Russia would have to accept the ultimatum completely or suffer a break in relations with Austria, with the grim threat of a war with all Europe to follow. But before the Russian court made its final decision, Gorchakov, at Vienna, telegraphed to Nesselrode that during the waiting period they should broaden the question by asking for a European congress. So much had happened since the Congress of Vienna and the coalition of powers were so abusing the words "equilibrium" and "European interests" that a general meeting of the representatives of the great powers was needed to correct these abuses. The meeting should not take place in Vienna, however, but at Paris, and the proposals should be addressed to Louis Napoleon by representatives of all states interested in independence and the European equilibrium.[69] In the *Diplomatic Study of the Crimean War* Jomini gives a different account. He says that Gorchakov wired that St. Petersburg should reject the

67. Gorchakov to Nesselrode, Dec. 31, 1855/Jan. 12, 1856, AVP, f. Kants., D. no. 223.
68. Ibid.
69. Gorchakov to Nesselrode, tg., Dec. 18/30, 1855, AVP, f. Kants., D. no. 225.

Austrian ultimatum by appealing to Napoleon III with proposals that would satisfy France but exclude the Bessarabian cession. Knowing from his communications with Morny that Napoleon was becoming irritated with Austria and eager to move in Italy and also to draw closer to Russia, Gorchakov believed that Napoleon would eagerly seize the moment to supersede Austria and to make peace without it. Nesselrode, so Jomini stated, did not agree with Gorchakov, for he showed the telegram to the emperor but did not show it to the council of war. Later on, Orlov allegedly told Gorchakov that if he had known of his proposal he would have voted against accepting the ultimatum. Nesselrode, however, was so convinced of the risk of such an attempt and of the opportunities that Russia had missed in the past that he refused to try this approach.[70] Tatishchev, in *Imperator Aleksandr II,* gives the same account as Jomini,[71] from whom he may have drawn it. It is possible that Jomini may have heard a vague reference to Gorchakov's proposal, which he reported in this incorrect way, and that later on Tatishchev used Jomini's version. Neither apparently saw Gorchakov's telegram.

When the Russian leaders finally realized that they must make a clear-cut decision on the Austrian ultimatum, Alexander II called a second imperial council on January 3/15, 1856, to consider the vital question. It consisted of the members of the first council, as well as the Grand Duke Konstantin Nikolaevich, minister of marine, Prince V. A. Dolgorukov, minister of war, and Baron Peter von Meyendorff, Buol's brother-in-law and an expert in Russo-Austrian diplomacy. The threatening forces arrayed against them dismayed the members, with Austria clearly committed to their enemies, for although its army was weak, its action would greatly influence the other states of Germany, including Prussia. Also the decision of Sweden and Norway to align with the West was a severe shock, for the Russians had counted on a neutral bloc in the Baltic.

After some brief introductory remarks, Alexander II had Count Nesselrode read a detailed memorandum on the situation. The chancellor, while stating that Russia's power had not been broken and it could continue to fight, showed it would be at a great disadvantage with almost all the German and Scandinavian powers joining its enemies. The struggle in 1856 would be deadly, with the battle extending

70. Jomini, II, 360–61.
71. Tatishchev, I, 184–85.

over 1,800 leagues (4,300 miles or more) and on two seas. The Russian forces would be overextended, for they could not take a central position from which to strike at their foes. The Allies, however, could attack at will, and only in Asia Minor could Russia expect to win victories, with their opportunities limited by the difficult terrain. Any successes of the Allies would permit them to strike at Russia's vitals. Nesselrode urgently advised accepting the Austrian terms, for they were not extremely severe, and there was no prospect of better ones, for the longer the war lasted, the worse the peace terms would be, with Russia's resources draining and no hope for the future.[72]

The opinions of all the other speakers added to the gloom. Prince Vorontsov followed Nesselrode, prophesying that in the future the peace terms, hard as they were, would get much worse and Russia would have to make great sacrifices in men, money, and territory: the Crimea, the Caucasus, Finland, and Poland might be lost to the empire. Since the war would have to end sometime, it would be wise not to wait for the bitter end, but to make peace before being compelled to it by outright exhaustion.

Count Orlov now spoke to refute the possible objections to peace, which would come chiefly from hostile or ignorant people. The mass of the population, however, worn out by the war, would be delighted. The government, which knew best, should decide, for any public outcry would not matter. He voted for peace.[73]

Other speakers warned of possible revolts in Volhynia, Podolia, and Poland, the last of which was termed a powder-keg. Prince Dolgorukov, reading a memorandum prepared by General D. A. Miliutin of the General Staff, spoke of the bad military conditions—in manpower, transportation, commanders, and training—which made it impossible for the army to continue with any chance of success. Baron Meyendorff, citing the minister of finance, said that soon the war would cause national bankruptcy, because of a huge debt, a deficit in production and income, and the drain of much manpower into the army. With a speedy peace, however, Russia would soon recover. Count Bludov was the only member who spoke against peace. But when the vote was taken, all were in favor of accepting the Austrian ultimatum, and the emperor heartily agreed.[74]

---

72. Hoetzsch, III, 214; Jomini, II, 361–63; Baumgart, pp. 112–15.
73. Hoetzsch, III, 215.
74. Ibid., pp. 216–17; I. V. Bestuzhev, "Iz istorii krymskoi voiny 1853–1856 gg.," *Istoricheskii Arkhiv,* No. 1 (1959), pp. 204–08.

As a result of this decision, on January 16 Nesselrode sent a message by telegraph to Gorchakov of the unconditional acceptance of the ultimatum. From there it was telegraphed to both of the other European capitals.[75] A protocol accepting the terms was signed by the powers on January 20/February 1 at Vienna, with a pledge to send their plenipotentiaries to Paris to sign the formal preliminaries, make an armistice, and draw up a final treaty. The Crimean War [76] had finally ended.

75. Nesselrode to Gorchakov, tg., Jan. 16, 1856, AVP, f. Kants., D. no. 226.
76. Jomini, II, 372.

CHAPTER 21. THE PARIS PEACE CONFERENCE, 1856

After the completion of the Protocol of Vienna of February 1, which was signed by the powers on February 6, it was agreed that the plenipotentiaries would assemble in the French capital on February 29. Victorious in war, Paris had become the diplomatic center of Europe, for France, as ally of England and nominally of Austria, was on cordial terms with Russia, as well as with Prussia and the middle states of Germany, and also Sweden and Norway. Austria, which had angered England and France by refusing to enter the war and infuriated Russia by turning from it to the West and by presenting the ultimatum, including a demand for the cession of much of Bessarabia, had few friends. With Sardinia an avowed enemy, and Prussia a less open one, Austria was isolated. Russia, now bitterly hostile to it, and conciliatory and ready to make concessions for peace, made overtures to Napoleon III and agreed with his policy.

When the Russian plenipotentiaries came to Paris in 1856, they received an amazing welcome. The French, thoroughly opposed to the war that had cost them so many men and so much wealth, felt that they had no grievance against the Russians, who had fought with great bravery. Instead, the French believed that the war had been essentially for British interests, which were not theirs, and the British insistence on continuing the conflict was abhorrent to them. Since the Russians, by their willingness to make peace, would rescue them from the war, the French regarded them as honored guests.

Baron Brunnow arrived in Paris early in February to prepare for the conference. An experienced diplomat, with long service in England and Germany, he knew most of the leading figures of Europe and was on friendly terms with many of them. His pleasant, ingratiating manners and his tact made it easy for him to establish good relations in Paris. His report to Count Nesselrode of February 7/19 spoke of the great cordiality with which he was received by the French ministers and the generals. General Niel, who had commanded the French engineers in the Crimea, spoke to him warmly of the skill of Totleben, "before the whole court in the Tuileries, before the appearance of the Emperor." "In the salons, in public, on the street, everywhere, general sympathy for us appears. On the road in Strasbourg and in the station in Paris, the day of my arrival, friendly demonstrations were held for me." He assured the chancellor that those Russians who felt that their peaceful policy had lowered public opinion of Russia, would be convinced of the opposite if they came to Paris. Even in the best years of his career, he said, "I never felt myself stronger . . . than now, which it has pleased the Sovereign Emperor to call me for signing the peace." [1]

In his interview with Walewski, who had been eager to have him come to Paris, Brunnow expressed the hope that his coming would not expose him to a setback. "God forbid!" he answered. "The blow would not strike you alone—I should share it together with you. For me this would be even more important. Hence you understand that I shall do all that I can to prevent a failure." [2]

Louis Napoleon, who wanted peace as quickly as possible, was greatly pleased by Alexander II's advice to move the peace talks to Paris; he put great stress on their success and sought to avoid all difficulties that would slow them up or prevent success. These obstacles would come, not from France, but from England and Austria. The British, who wanted to continue the war for another year in order to redeem their tarnished military glory, were fearful that an early peace, which would be unpopular north of the Channel, might weaken Palmerston's government and bring it down. The French had been working on the British cabinet to overcome these fears and had persuaded Lord Clarendon to agree. The emperor was very fearful of British public opinion and the press and was highly suspicious of a Franco-Russian rapprochement, which he felt might be a threat to the Anglo-French alliance. Walewski strongly emphasized this. "The Emperor Napoleon," he told Brunnow, "definitely wishes to maintain the ties that bind him to England. Of necessity he had to be extremely careful in dealing with it." He urged the Russians to bear this in mind during the negotiations. [3]

1. Brunnow to Nesselrode, Feb. 7/19, 1856, AVP, f. Kants., D. no. 147.
2. Ibid.
3. Ibid.

Brunnow also sent Nesselrode a lengthy survey of the problems to be faced in the conference. In the interest of gaining time he suggested to Walewski that they proceed directly to the main peace negotiations without bothering to work out the preliminaries of peace, which might give the impression that they wanted to avoid the chief problems. Brunnow suggested that they deal first with the main question—Kars, and the compensation Russia would receive for returning it. If this agreement proved satisfactory, the whole problem of the peace would be settled. While this matter would be left for Count Orlov to decide, it would be an approach that he might like to consider. Walewski was favorable to this idea and suggested that they could use the Protocol already signed at Vienna as the preliminaries of peace, which could be attached to the Protocol of the first session of the conference, and the armistice could then follow.[4]

In his appraisal of the situation Brunnow saw no obstacles to be expected from France, for Napoleon and his cabinet were so committed to peace that they would do everything possible to achieve it, in order to meet the demand of the people. The emperor, however, did not have a free hand, for he felt it essential to maintain his English alliance by soothing the British cabinet, which was approaching the peace table with reluctance. This would call for great tact on his part, for he would have to induce the British to accept unfavorable decisions without wrecking the conference.

The minister of court confirmed Walewski's statement, saying in a private chat with Brunnow that the emperor would function as mediator in the negotiations, although he would not be present at the sessions. The minister suggested that the Russians should bring to the emperor's attention all incidents that his personal intervention might help to settle. He would be readily accessible to them.[5]

Brunnow listed the various difficulties that the British would probably produce:

The Åland Islands, with demands that no fortifications be erected. The French cabinet would support this position.

Russia's frontiers in Asia. The British would oppose all Russian schemes to establish permanent possession of Kars and its district. The French would support the British in this matter.

4. Brunnow to Nesselrode, Feb. 7/19, 1856, AVP, f. Kants., D. no. 147; Orlov to Nesselrode, Feb. 19/Mar. 2, 1856, ibid.

5. Brunnow to Nesselrode, Feb. 7/19, 1856, ibid.

Cherkassia (Circassia). The British government would insist on giving some moral support to the tribes among whom it had tried to incite an uprising during the war, and would seek to avoid the impression that as soon as peace came, it would desert and betray them. Brunnow gained the impression that the British would use simple diplomatic reproaches which, however, would not prove a real threat to peace. Walewski said that the French cabinet would not take part in this debate and would not support the British. He added that England would not be stubborn on this point.

The Black Sea. So far there had been no mention of Nikolaev, and Brunnow had carefully avoided it. He felt, however, that the British ministers would raise the question of not rebuilding forts on the Asian coast of the Black Sea. Count Orlov would probably have to deal with this matter.

Delimitation of Bessarabia. The Viennese court very cleverly secured the support of the British cabinet on this matter. In a way, the proposed frontier had been confirmed by being accepted by the Russian court in principle in the first article of the preliminary conditions, which would make it difficult for Russia to change this obligation. The capture of Kars and its pashalyk to some extent strengthened the Russian case, by giving it a claim to compensation for Kars. Probably the French would weakly support the British demands in Asia and of Austria in Bessarabia. Much would depend on the position taken by Napoleon III.[6]

When Count Orlov arrived in Paris he saw Walewski, who greeted him warmly and said that the emperor would grant him a special audience on the next day, followed by a talk in his cabinet. So on the following day he went to the Tuileries, where all the court officials showed him great courtesy and led him at once to the emperor. Napoleon III received Orlov very graciously and they exchanged statements concerning their mutual desire to achieve the peace that all Europe so ardently wanted. Orlov said that the Emperor Alexander shared the wish to establish, by united efforts, good relationships between their courts and to strengthen the sympathies between the two great empires and close relations between the sovereigns. Napoleon, after agreeing warmly, dismissed his suite and invited Orlov into his cabinet, where they at once began a political talk.[7] Orlov, feeling that frankness

6. Ibid.
7. Orlov to Nesselrode, Feb. 19/Mar. 2, 1856, no. 18, f. Kants., D. no. 147.

was the best way to approach the emperor, ventured to state openly what he could agree to and what he could not.

On Point 1 he said that Russia agreed that the mouth of the Danube should remain free and open for the trade of all. The obstacles to navigation should be removed, and the islands of the delta should be neutral and remain unoccupied by anyone. Russia would raze its fortifications there if the Turks would do the same. The entire expanse of the Black Sea, as already established under Point 3, would be declared neutral. The frontier line between Moldavia and Bessarabia would be established only after detailed discussion and general agreement, as Alexander wanted to carry out his obligations fully. But, on the other hand, it should be remembered that Russia had taken the fortress of Kars and its district, which its army in Asia had occupied. This fact, which had not been dealt with in the negotiations to date, should be seriously considered from the point of view of compensation. If Russia should give up Kars and its environs, the Allied powers in reciprocity should renounce the proposed cession of Bessarabia and leave the existing frontier without change. Orlov said he hoped he had done right in setting forth frankly the actual Russian position, without diplomatic verbiage or explanations. He had tried to give Napoleon proof of his trust, as he was sure that if he would be pleased to give full support to his proposals, peace would be made very quickly.[8]

After listening carefully and attentively, Louis Napoleon suddenly asked: "But Bomarsund—are you agreed not to restore it?" Orlov answered that he knew the emperor's keen interest in this question and that his master would be quite ready to settle it. It should, however, be made the subject of a special agreement, which should not be included in the final treaty of peace. This reply seemed to satisfy his host, who now spoke of his feeling of admiration and esteem for the deceased Emperor Nicholas I, over whose death he had continued to grieve. Then he asked Orlov's opinion about the Treaty of Vienna, in regard to which time had brought changes. In case its revision should come up, he would like to know Orlov's opinion on it. Orlov hastened to say that this was a question of such vast extent that it touched the interests of all Europe, and he had no instructions regard-

8. Ibid.

ing it. Hence he did not feel he could speak about it, to which Napoleon replied that this was just an informal talk.[9]

The emperor continued: "This poor Italy! Surely in reality, it can't remain in its present calamitous position. Can't something be done for it?" He added that he had spoken to Buol about it, but he did not answer a word.

Then, "this poor Poland, whose religion is persecuted. Could not the Sovereign in his mercy put an end to those restrictions that the Catholic Church suffers, could he not soften somewhat the fate of the many unfortunates who . . . had let themselves be drawn into political mistakes?"

Orlov replied with some sharpness that Poland's sufferings were its own fault. The tsars had given it "all possibilities for its full well-being," but it did not know how to make use of them. The Poles had lost their freedom because they violated their oath and did not keep their promises. As for freedom of confession, Alexander II had taken measures to quiet their consciences, by carefully reconsidering the concordat with the Holy See. He had already been merciful to the Poles and Orlov expected him to moderate the punishment of the guilty at the time of his coronation.[10]

Napoleon thanked Orlov for the frank expression of opinions, and they parted amicably. The Russian expressed the belief that the emperor was already thinking about a future congress to revise the Congress of Vienna and "that at present it is the chief subject of his thinking." He concluded that under a mask of sincerity Napoleon concealed a "deep and at times flexible and keen mind." [11]

After these amenities, the conference settled down to work. Orlov helped to speed matters by getting the delegates to consider the definitive peace terms, instead of preparing formal preliminaries of peace. They also adopted an armistice, although Clarendon, who apparently did not want to seem too lenient, insisted that it should last for only four weeks, when it might be renewed. He also wanted the naval blockade of ports to continue. While the Russians did not object, as in winter there was almost no trade movement, they urged that, to avoid senseless hostilities, the Allied fleets be removed some distance

9. Ibid.
10. Ibid.
11. Ibid.

from the Russian ports and should agree not to attack them. Thus the armistice would last until March 31.

Orlov stated in his report that Walewski "was imbued with the spirit of conciliation" and performed his duties as president in this manner. While there were idle polemics by the English, Austrian, and Sardinian delegates, these arguments had no significance.[12]

On February 14/26, however, in a secret dispatch, Orlov seemed less confident, for he reported that the British had rejected the plan of compensation for the cession of Kars, and the revision of the boundary of Bessarabia probably could not be avoided. Orlov held firm and obtained an adjournment of the session in order to let Napoleon know what was happening. If, however, Napoleon did not help, then the Russians would follow their instructions and accept the Allied demands rather than break up the negotiations.[13]

At the second session the plenipotentiaries reviewed the first four articles, although their final phrasing would be reserved to the definitive treaty. The naval convention would be discussed directly between the Russians and the Turks. The latter desired that the religious article should not figure in the treaty, but the Russians insisted on it and the conference adhered to the Russian view. Aali pasha, however, would refer the matter to the Porte by telegraph. The discussion on the crucial Point Five was adjourned until the following day, with stormy confrontations expected, in view of the British demands. Orlov stated that he and Brunnow would hold firm up to the point of a threat of a rupture of the conference. He added: "I see the Emperor this evening." [14]

Buol's report on this session showed that the Russians were seeking a solution "everywhere except in an understanding with us." The Russian attitude was marked "by a profound resentment, which will be lasting. Austria must accept it as a new situation and take account of it." The treaty of alliance with England and France that had been agreed on in principle by the memorandum of November 14 would be "an infallible means to avoid the inconvenience and danger of the new situation." [15]

12. Ibid., Feb. 19/Mar. 2, no. 19.
13. Ibid., Feb. 14/26, no. 14 (Secret), AVP, f. Kants., D. no. 147.
14. Ibid., Feb. 16/28, 1856, no. 15 (Secret); Conference of Paris, Feb., 1856, Reports of Buol and Hübner, no. 3A, HHSA, XII, 219.
15. Ibid., Reports of Buol and Hübner, no. 3a.

A long report from Orlov to Nesselrode of February 28/March 11, sheds much light on the course of the negotiations, which already had made much progress. By mutual consent, the conference took up the most troublesome matter—Point 5 of the preliminary conditions, whose content was termed the Special Conditions. It had been formulated in ambiguous and undefined terms, which gave Russia's adversaries the opportunity to present extraordinary demands, perhaps in the hope that Russia would refuse them, thus breaking up the conference. Austria had orally told Russia that these terms would not go so far as to threaten peace, but as this understanding had not been acknowledged by the other powers, it meant little. The French had frankly said that their proposals were limited to the Åland Islands and to a decision on the territory east of the Black Sea. The British cabinet, however, had expressly insisted on the importance of Point 5, in order to present demands that Russia could not accept, which might ruin the peace talks. Russia had to face this threatening question, in order to show that it was ready to confront it, and also so as to make clear how the interests of the French and the British diverged. Out of this came an "extraordinarily important discovery," for Walewski revealed to the Russians that Clarendon wanted to throw doubt on the Russian right to any territory between the Kuban river and the Turkish boundary at Batum and Kars. The British wanted to make Russia recognize the independence and neutrality of the countries of this area, or to put them again under nominal Turkish sovereignty. Napoleon III refused to accept this British position, which gave the Russians valuable aid.[16]

Now that the Russians realized France's position, they had little difficulty in refuting the British argument, for neither France nor Austria gave the British any support. In the discussion, which began on March 1, Russia, equipped with the treaties on the question, firmly established that the Russian possession of these Asian territories was clearly supported by its treaties with the Porte, especially Article IV of the Treaty of Adrianople and Article I of the Convention of St. Petersburg of 1834, so that there was no ground for any dispute whatever. Thus the Russians had a great advantage over Lord Clarendon, who "wandered off into hazy utterances, now about Mingrelia, now Abkhazia, and now the Circassians." The Russians refuted him at

16. Orlov to Nesselrode, Feb. 28, 1856, no. 31, Progress Report, AVP, f. Kants., D. no. 147.

all points and even "appealed directly to the Turkish envoys to state whether it was true or not that the frontiers were established by direct treaties." The Grand Vizir did not try to dispute the line as defined by the Convention of 1834, but he did claim that in some places there might be deviations from the correct boundary and that the Porte wished to propose that the conference correct these errors. The Russian delegation agreed to such a study of the frontier, although it pointed out that it should not lead to any cession of territory without recompense. As a result, a mixed commission of Russians and Turks, with French and British commissars also included, was agreed to by the conference. It would not meet until after the Peace Conference had ended its work.[17]

In his report Orlov referred to the great stubbornness of Clarendon, who tried repeatedly to get the Russians to agree not to rebuild their forts on the Black Sea coast. Orlov categorically refused, as he maintained that the Emperor Alexander II had a full right to build forts on his territory or not, as he saw fit, under the principle of sovereign authority. Clarendon, after very lively altercations, which he sometimes reopened, ended by abandoning his position, which the French did not support at all.[18]

When the conference considered the touchy point of Kars, however, Russia did not fare so well, for the French and the British acted together, declaring that their obligations to the Porte compelled them to support the integrity and inviolability of the Ottoman empire. Orlov's instructions required him to use the occupation of Kars as a bargaining point to gain compensation regarding the preliminary conditions. Thus he declared his willingness to return to the matter of Kars, but he expected that it would be considered in relation to other points. He expressed a similar position about Bomarsund, which he stated should not be an article of the main treaty, but should be a separate document between Russia and France and England. This last provision was agreed to. So the discussion on Point 5—originally the main obstacle—was ended, and the way was cleared for discussing the four main Points.[19]

The Russian plenipotentiaries agreed with this procedure, in the

17. Ibid.
18. Ibid.
19. Ibid.

interest of eliminating useless digression, shortening the conference, and bringing it to an end, if harmony could be achieved among the conflicting interests.

On March 4, the delegates dealt with the neutralization of the Black Sea, under Point 3 of the preliminaries. While there was no real disagreement on this matter, some of the conditions required a more precise wording. The discussion chiefly centered on the provision against naval arsenals on the shores of the Black Sea. During the debate Orlov informed Clarendon that this provision did not apply to Nikolaev, which was some distance from the sea, and Russia's feeling of dignity did not permit it to extend the provision to a town in the interior. He did say, however, that the Emperor Alexander II declared that the naval arsenal at Nikolaev would be used for the real needs of the country, building only war vessels for protecting and watching the coast, which was permitted by the treaty. He added that the emperor had said that the two ships of the line nearing completion there would be taken to the Baltic. This statement made a strong impression on the gathering, with Clarendon especially impressed by the frankness of the tsar. In answer to a question from Clarendon, however, Orlov said that the neutralization of the Black Sea did not include the Sea of Azov, and this judgment was confirmed by the conference.

Orlov agreed to the provision for stationing foreign consuls in Russian Black Sea ports, according to the principles of international law, and with full reciprocity of rights of the Russian and the foreign consuls.

The principle of cloture of the Bosporus and the Dardanelles to flags of war would remain in force. A special convention on this matter would be worked out, to replace the London Convention of 1841.[20]

Point 2 of the preliminaries, on the freedom of navigation of the Danube, was taken up next, with no objections from Russia to the wording of the article, most of which Walewski had written. There were heated arguments, however, between Walewski and Buol over the admission of Bavaria, as a Danube state, to membership in the Danube River executive commission. Orlov took no part in this polemic.

Among the questions still unsettled was the Bessarabian frontier

20. Ibid.

line, which was part of Point 1 of the preliminaries. When Walewski proposed to discuss it at a special session before the Principalities, Orlov at once agreed, for he held that the Russian willingness to confront the difficult questions made a good impression.[21]

The issue of the Bessarabian frontier produced the real crisis of the conference, for both Russia and Austria had taken strong positions, and Clarendon, who had failed to unseat Russia in Asia Minor, apparently sought to win a victory here at its expense. In addition, Louis Napoleon had accepted the Five Points, including Bessarabia, although in his eagerness to have the Russians agree to the Austrian ultimatum he had privately hinted that they might use Kars as a bargaining point in return for concessions on Bessarabia. When the debate on this question began, Orlov tried earnestly to get his opponents to show the proposed line clearly on the map, so that he could try to change it later. But they stubbornly refused, saying that the line, from Khotyn, along a chain of hills, would run to the southeast to Lake Salzyk, which had been agreed on in the preliminaries and was not subject to discussion. The Russians objected, saying that they had accepted the preliminaries in general and had asserted the right to receive concessions in return for Kars and Bomarsund. A heated discussion followed, with Clarendon and Buol showing obvious malice and Walewski abstaining.[22]

Finally, since the Russians were getting the worst of the argument, they asked to postpone the session, so that Orlov could appeal to Napoleon. The latter agreed, although he said that his pledges would not permit him to go as far as he wished. But he would do his best. Orlov had Brunnow show Walewski three Russian proposals, with the first two offered by Orlov, but without support from Walewski, who would support the third plan. But before the conference session Walewski had a heated meeting with Clarendon and Buol, at which they gave up their claims to Khotyn but would not agree to the rest of the third Russian proposal. Instead, they suggested two new plans, with the line running southeast of Lake Salzyk.

Walewski told Orlov that the first Austrian plan was an attempt to have Khotyn and its vicinity given to Moldavia, in order to separate Russian territory from Bukovina in Austria, and thus to protect the Austrian domains from Russia. The other Austrian plans would have

21. Ibid.
22. Orlov to Nesselrode, Mar. 11/28, no. 32, AVP, f. Kanto., D. no. 147.

cut the main trade route to Kishinev, which would have impaired Bessarabia's economic life and removed most of the colony of Bolgrad, home of Bulgarian refugees from Turkey.[23]

When Napoleon learned of this, he stated his displeasure in forceful terms, and wrote out to Walewski an order to support the third Russian proposal. In a private chat with Orlov on March 9 he told of his intentions, and that night he imposed them on Buol and Clarendon, who after this took a "softer position—almost a humiliated one." Both sides made some small concessions, but at the official session on March 10 Orlov stated that he would accept the line as then indicated, subject to the approval of the tsar. The envoy was much pleased by the outcome, for by hard work and persistence he and Brunnow had kept most of their frontage on the Pruth facing Bukovina. They also had retained the main trade route and the range of hills on which the Austrian military men had wanted to establish a chain of fortresses linked with the Austrian defenses running to the Danube. The new boundary preserved most of the Bulgar area, including Bolgrad, and all of a substantial German colony. By it Russia kept two-thirds of the territory that the Allies had hoped to detach from Russia.[24]

The settlement of the Bessarabian frontier, in which the influence and intervention of the French monarch played a decisive role, made it evident that Napoleon was determined on peace and would not permit the British and the Austrians to prevent the conference from reaching a reasonable solution. It also may have made Russia's two main opponents realize that if Napoleon were unable to gratify the ardent demand of the French people for a speedy peace, he might turn against his alliance with England and form a new one with Russia, Prussia, and other states, which would be a real threat to both England and Austria. Napoleon had already spoken of the possibility of such an alliance to Count Orlov and other Russians, and if it should come to pass, this new coalition would be sufficiently strong to dominate all Europe, and Britain and Austria would be the losers. Certainly from this time forward the British were less aggressive in their opposition, and Buol also moderated his tone.

Another question that soon arose was that of the size of the Russian and Turkish armed squadrons on the Black Sea, whose numbers should be set by consultation between the two coastal states. Early in March

23. Ibid.
24. Ibid.

Aali pasha came to Orlov to discuss the situation, but his instructions from the Porte were scanty. Orlov thereupon conferred with Walewski, who had Admiral Hamelin prepare a study. This memorandum provided for steamers, to protect the coasts, and unarmed transports, either sailing or steam ships. Orlov also wanted additional vessels to protect and police the ports. By this time, however, the size and numbers of the proposed fleets were so large that the British would be sure to raise a storm over the proposal. As a result, the two states agreed on six armed vessels, fifty meters long, and six unarmed transports, either sail or steam. Each state might have an unlimited number of other vessels that were unarmed and not under a naval flag. All this had taken considerable time and much arguing, often quite heated; but finally on March 7/19 the agreement was initialed.[25]

Not long after, Lord Clarendon sent an apologetic note to Orlov to explain his opposition, which stemmed, he said, not from him personally but from his cabinet. Neither he nor it wanted to present conditions that would be disagreeable, "but we have masters much more severe than yours and our responsibility is so much greater. We have Parliament, the Press, public opinion, finally, which we have to take account of and, worst of all, the spirit of the party, which will make the defense of the treaty . . . a truly severe task." [26]

Point 4, dealing with the protection of the religious and civil rights of the Christians of Turkey, proved to be another stumbling block, for the Russians, as at the onset of the Eastern Question, insisted that not only must this protection be specified and pledged by the Turks, but the powers must have the collective duty and responsibility to ensure that the pledges be carried out. The Turks, who were lavish with their promises, realized clearly that honest enforcement of these provisions would destroy the privileged position of the Moslems of Turkey, for the Christians—especially the Greeks and the Armenians—were more energetic and better educated than the Turks. Hence if they received full equality of opportunity, the unbelievers would quickly gain control of the chief administrative, military, and legal positions, with the Turks reduced to inferior status. The Moslems, who had been told by the Koran that the Christians and the Jews were *rayahs*—cattle—who must remain completely inferior to the dom-

25. Orlov to Nesselrode, Feb. 28/Mar. 11, 1856; Feb. 29/Mar. 11, tg., Mar. 2/14, tg.; AVP, f. Kants., D. no. 147; ibid., Mar. 7/19, tg. (Secret), no. 41, AVP, f. Kants., D. no. 148.
26. Ibid., Orlov to Nesselrode, Mar. 21, 1856, AVP, f. Kants., D. no. 148.

inant Ottomans, would never accept the loss of their superior position, but would revolt and depose any sultan who permitted the Christians to enjoy full equality with them. All the Western leaders, including Palmerston, Gladstone, Thouvenel, Buol, and Prokesch, believed that it was essential for the Turks to introduce a modern regime with equal rights for Christians and Moslems. They realized, however, that to do so would undermine the whole basis of the Ottoman regime, for the Christians, with their ability and superior numbers, would soon dominate Turkey. And since the Christians in their vast majority looked to the Russians as their friends and protectors, the inevitable result of a basic reform movement in Turkey would be to weaken Turkey and to increase Russian influence in the Balkan peninsula.[27] Both the British and the Austrians were horrified at the prospect.

As the peace conference organized to write the treaty, in Constantinople the Allied diplomats (chiefly Redcliffe, Thouvenel, and Prokesch) induced the sultan to issue a solemn proclamation declaring sweeping reforms of Turkish law and administration, which would provide equality for all, irrespective of nationality or religion. All positions in the army and the administration henceforth should be open to all. Non-Moslems might freely sell property and inherit it. Mixed courts would be established with Moslem and Christian judges, in which the testimony of both Moslems and rayahs would be accepted equally. The Christian patriarchs lost much of their power over their followers, and the central authority of the empire increased substantially. There were extensive reforms of the police; of the administration of local affairs; of taxation, banks, and public instruction. The proposed measure was finally promulgated by the sultan on February 18, 1856, several days before the opening of the peace conference at Paris. It was known as the Hatt-i-humayün.[28]

The Turks and their supporters had hoped that the publication of this far-reaching decree would satisfy the Paris Peace Conference and eliminate attempts to supervise its enforcement. Russia, however, was still keenly interested in the lot of the Orthodox within the sultan's domains and made vigorous attempts to make the Hatt-i-humayün a binding document under the public law of Europe. The Porte, however, strongly opposed the proposal, and it was only the determination

27. Ashley, pp. 313–14; Baumgart, pp. 211–16; A. D. Kyriakos, *Geschichte der Orientalischen Kirchen von 1453–1898* (Leipzig, 1902), pp. 20–22.
28. Baumgart, pp. 216–17.

of Count Orlov that prevented the British, with Austrian backing, from making the measure ineffective. Orlov sought the support of Napoleon for his plans, even running the risk of a rupture of the Conference by proposing the adoption of a passage stating that the powers, "accepting the voluntary decision of His Majesty the Sultan" . . . wished to reserve "the rights of the Christians, in the interests of all the Christian world." This proposal failed, because of "insurmountable opposition" from the British cabinet, with Clarendon terming Orlov's proposal "ten times worse than the note of Prince Menshikov" and Count Walewski saying it would be *"impossible"* to get the Turkey plenipotentiary to sign such a document. At length, seeing that his efforts were useless, Orlov accepted the French draft with minor changes, which finally settled the question.[29]

While this solution of Point 4 ended the main negotiations and made possible the signing of the Treaty of Paris, it by no means ended the trials of the Christians in Turkey. A number of the reforms remained dead letters, and many of the Turkish Moslems reacted with fury against the Christians. There were massacres of Christians in the Hedjaz in 1858, and in 1860 there was a fierce onslaught by the fanatical Druses of Lebanon against the Maronites, which became an attempt to wipe out all Christians in Syria. In 1860 some twelve thousand French troops landed in Syria to restore order after much of Damascus and many villages had been destroyed. Other massacres of Serbs, Bulgars, Armenians, and Cretans came in later decades.[30]

As the plenipotentiaries settled the major problems of the peace, thus bringing the end of the congress rapidly nearer, the powers still had to deal with the question of Prussia. It was one of the major powers, with a fine army and a rising industry, and it had played a significant role in defeating the first Napoleon. Its king, Frederick William IV, was brother-in-law of Nicholas I of Russia and, largely out of fear of France and dislike of Austria, he was a devoted member of the Holy Alliance—the league of the three Eastern monarchs. Many of the Prussians, however, detested Russia for its domineering tactics in forbidding Prussia to create a league of princes to unify Germany in 1850, with Prussia's king as emperor. Prussia had rather close connections with England, and Baron Bunsen, Prussia's minister to the

29. Orlov to Nesselrode, Mar. 20/Apr. 1, 1856, no. 57, AVP, f. Kants., D. no. 148; Tatishchev, I, 196–97; Charles-Roux, pp. 95–96.
30. Kyriakos, pp. 22–23.

court of St. James, strongly urged Prussia to ally itself with Britain against Russia. But Frederick William, with the backing of Bismarck, clung rather shakily to Russia against both England and Austria, which angered these powers. Prussia's unwillingness to support Austria in a war with Russia did much to keep Austria neutral, to the delight of Russia, and the British were especially angry with Prussia for its pro-Russian leanings and also because Prussia permitted munitions to enter its ports en route to Russia. But since Prussia had a sizable army, neither France nor Austria wanted it as an active enemy. And because Prussia strongly urged Russia to accept the Austrian ultimatum in January, 1856, it managed to remain neutral to the end.

Because of Prussia's pro-Russian stance, however, the Allies refused to admit it to the Paris Peace Conference, although Austria felt that it was unwise to snub the Prussians, as any stimulus to their resentment would throw them into the arms of Russia. Baron Hübner at Paris wrote to Buol that by excluding Prussia from the conference to please England they would be playing the game of Russia. "You throw the king of Prussia into the arms of Russia," he said. Moreover, sooner or later, when Palmerston left power, Prussia would placate the British, and then it would restore its firm ties with Russia, thus reviving part of the old Northern alliance and strengthening Russian influence in Berlin.[31] Russia still valued Prussia's friendship, for in February 1856, after signing the Protocol of preliminaries, Gorchakov in the name of his cabinet urged that Prussia take part in negotiations on questions of European equilibrium and in the revision of treaties to which Prussia had been a party.[32]

The real opposition to Prussia's admission to the peace negotiations came from England, where public opinion was highly inflamed against it. From Vienna Gorchakov reported that he had learned on good evidence that Clarendon had tartly rejected the arguments used by Count Albrecht Bernsdorff urging its admission. In sarcastic rejoinders he had snubbed the envoy, claiming that Prussia had failed to use its influence with Russia when it would have helped the cause of peace. Napoleon III motivated his refusal of Prussia by saying that it would surely support Russia against the Western powers, although he did not show any animus against it. In fact, late in 1855 Napoleon had told Duke Ernst of Saxe-Coburg that "he hoped to be able to

31. Hübner to Buol, Feb. 6, 1856 (Secret), HHSA, IX, 52.
32. Buol to Hübner and Colloredo, Feb. 1, 1856, ibid., IX, 54.

replace his alliance with Austria by one with Prussia, and certainly at the cost of Austria." [33]

As for Alexander II, he wrote to his uncle, the king: "I shall be eternally grateful to you for the so excellent position that you have been able to maintain during all this crisis and which has been so useful to us. May God reward you for it." [34] In harmony with his cabinet's attitude, Orlov reported to Nesselrode on February 28/March 11, 1856, that from his arrival in Paris he had done everything possible to show regard and friendship for Prussia by trying to get it invited to the peace conference. At last England's resistance ended, and the conference decided to send Prussia a formal invitation to take part in the revision of the Treaty of 1841, which it had signed. Prussia now would attend the conferences and take part in the deliberations until the end. Orlov added that it would do so in spite of the English plenipotentiaries, who displayed ill will against it but were not able to prevent Russia "from claiming for Prussia the rank that is due it" at a meeting that considered questions of European interest.[35]

In a survey of European politics Nesselrode, stressing the value of the favor of Napoleon III, which Orlov had used so successfully, added that it would be enhanced by improving relations between France and Prussia. "Russia," he wrote, "cannot forget that Prussia was the only great power that was not hostile to Russia. It was tied to Russia by its direct interests." The chancellor expressed the view that France would gain if it rested on this alliance.[36]

The Russian court also sought to strengthen its favor with Napoleon III by approving Orlov's hints that Russia should end the ban on the Bonaparte dynasty. Alexander II would act on the matter immediately, or later, and would not object if Orlov, in agreement with the other powers, should sign a declaration on this matter before he left Paris.[37]

On the Polish question, however, Russia was not disposed to be conciliatory. The Russian view was that both Alexander I and Nicholas I had been very generous to the Poles, only to have them become

---

33. Ernst II, Duke of Saxe-Coburg, *Aus Meinem Leben und aus Meiner Zeit* (Berlin, 1887–89), III, 283.
34. Baumgart, p. 211.
35. Orlov to Nesselrode, Feb. 28/Mar 11, 1856, no. 34, AVP, f. Kants., D. no. 147.
36. Letter, Nesselrode to Orlov, Apr. 5/17, 1856, TsGADA, f. 15, D. no. 325.
37. Ibid.

hostile, and finally they had treacherously attacked the Russian troops in 1830. The Russian army had to invade Poland and take Warsaw by storm in August 1831. When the Poles failed to submit, the Russians inflicted harsh punishment on them, which continued until the Crimean War. Many Poles had fled to Paris and London, where they continued to agitate for Polish freedom.

The British and the French governments sympathized with the Poles, but gave them no real support. Louis Napoleon, who was a believer in the national principle as a means of solving Europe's problems, repeatedly raised the question of a revival of Poland. In the summer of 1854 he told Duke Ernst of Saxe-Coburg that he dreamed of restoring Poland—perhaps as the limited Grand Duchy of Warsaw. Later, in a talk with Lord Cowley, he asked whether England would object to the restoration of the Kingdom of Poland. Cowley, however, was cool toward this scheme, as he feared that the Prince Napoleon would be its king.[38]

In March 1855, with the Allies in grave trouble in the Crimea, Drouyn de Lhuys suggested a revival of Poland with the boundaries of 1815, but Clarendon termed the suggestion inopportune. In the spring and summer of 1855 the French made much of demonstrations of Polish exiles in France who, under the aged Prince Adam Czartoryski, urged active measures to liberate Poland. On September 15 Walewski wrote to Clarendon, "The moment is come to prepare to make the reestablishment of the Kingdom of Poland one of the essential objects of peace negotiations. . . ." Clarendon agreed that the objective was very desirable, but he rejected it as a *sine qua non* for peace, as during the negotiations they wanted "to achieve only what was possible." [39]

After the fall of Sevastopol the British had great hopes for inducing the French to mount a new offensive in the Crimea and to invade the Russian lands south of the Caucasus. Napoleon and Pélissier, however, knowing the intense French desire to end the war, were much against any further shedding of blood. But the British, who had fared poorly in the war, wanted it to continue, in the Baltic, if not in the south, as they hoped to make a great attack against the Russian defenses before St. Petersburg. In this undertaking they counted on the support of the Swedish-Norwegian kingdom to invade Fin-

38. Simpson, p. 269.
39. Geffcken, p. 196.

land and tear it away from Russia. In such a case a Polish insurrection would be very useful to weaken Russia and to undermine its internal stability. Prince Czartoryski vowed that large numbers of oppressed people in Russia's dominions would eagerly fight for their freedom if they were given arms and leadership. In a memorandum of September 1855 Czartoryski stressed to Louis Napoleon the untapped resources of the peoples of southern Russia, the Ukrainian provinces, White Russia, Abkhazia, and the Don and Kuban Cossacks. Along with the Poles, who were thirsting for freedom, they would provide numerous recruits. By this time, however, Napoleon wanted no more war. He would use the call for national uprisings to terrify the English, the Russians, and the Prussians, as well as Austria. Through Premier von der Pfordten of Bavaria Napoleon sent word to Alexander II that if by the spring of 1856 no understanding for peace existed, "I will appeal to the nationalities and in particular to the nation of Poland." [40]

Whether Napoleon III was serious about these suggestions is unclear. He does seem, however, to have troubled the British, for Clarendon decided that they should wait to see whether Alexander would spontaneously redress the grievances of the Poles. Similarly, when Napoleon, in his audience with Orlov early in March 1856, raised the question of doing something "for this poor Poland, whose religion is persecuted"—Orlov reacted strongly to declare that the Poles had themselves to blame for their troubles. They should trust the benevolence of the new emperor, who was already planning to revise the concordat with the papacy and to make other concessions at his coronation.[41] Louis Napoleon also spoke to Buol about helping Poland by means of a European congress after the peace conference. Buol, however, believed that they could not accomplish anything as a European transaction, but should rather rely on the understanding of Alexander II and the influence of friendly suggestions, as he believed that Alexander's character and inclinations would probably bring about concessions in religion and in administrative matters.[42]

The Polish problem would not disappear, for the Poles in Western Europe and their friends were eager to do something to show their

40. Simpson, pp. 337–41; Geffcken, pp. 268–69; Baumgart, pp. 33–35.
41. Simpson, pp. 341–44; Geffcken, pp. 269–70; Orlov to Nesselrode, Feb. 19/Mar. 2, 1856, no. 18, AVP, f. Kants., D. no. 147.
42. Buol to Franz Joseph, Feb. 24, 1856, HHSA, PA XL, 49.

sympathy. Palmerston and Clarendon wanted to make some gesture that would indicate to the Poles that they sympathized with them in their troubles. Clarendon, the more moderate, felt that if they could arrange for some sort of declaration in the documents of the congress, that would satisfy English public opinion. On April 2, 1856, Clarendon mentioned this matter to Napoleon, who was ready to speak to Orlov about it, if Clarendon would tell him what he wanted. The latter said that the Poles would probably be satisfied if they might set up some sort of national institution, if Russia would treat the Catholic church with respect, and if they might use the Polish language for instruction in the schools. Napoleon spoke to Orlov, but obtained no satisfaction. Next Clarendon himself spoke to Orlov. Orlov replied that Alexander intended to adopt a new Polish policy, which would meet with the approval of Napoleon III and should calm the Poles. It was not possible, however, for the Russian envoy to announce this to the congress, as it would appear to be a surrender to outside pressure. He strongly advised Clarendon to be patient, since it would anger the emperor and his supporters if they tried to exert pressure on him. Clarendon finally urged his cabinet to let the matter drop.[43] Alexander was well pleased with Orlov's handling of the matter. After the sessions of the congress had ended, however, Count Walewski, who was half Polish, in a private talk urgently asked Orlov, in the name of his emperor, to make a statement favorable to Poland, probably to encourage the Polish emigrants in France. Although Walewski was very polite in his request, Orlov felt that he had to refuse it. He did so by telling him that he had refused a similar appeal from Louis Napoleon himself and hence he could not gratify his minister. Orlov had a farewell audience with Napoleon, who parted with him with real emotion, begging him to gain for him the friendship of Alexander II. "Such is the wish of my heart," said the emperor with tears in his eyes. Napoleon also discussed Poland with him, but in terms that harmonized fully with the intentions of Alexander. Orlov felt that the French sovereign was sincere in his utterances. He ended his report with the claim: "I am fully pleased that I did not hear the name of Poland uttered at the sessions in the presence of the delegates of the great powers." [44]

By the signing of the Treaty of Paris on March 30, 1856, it was

43. Geffcken, pp. 268–69.
44. Tatishchev, II, 203–04.

clear that Russia's relations with France would decide the future of Europe for some time to come. Neither Prussia nor Austria was powerful enough to play a major role, and England, in spite of its wealth, its vast empire, and its navy, could not be a decisive factor on the continent unless it could obtain powerful allies. Certainly there was no reason for Russia to hope for an alliance with England, for British hostility toward Russia was so strong that it seemed out of the question. Moreover, the Russians had little respect for England's army and they distrusted its parliamentary system, which produced instability and irrational conduct. Probably no one in either country thought that they might be allies.

France, however, seemed to have no real grounds for hostility to Russia, and during the peace conference the French displayed toward the Russian delegates remarkable cordiality, which was warmly reciprocated. Napoleon III had personally make it possible for the peace talks to take place and during them he had continually shown his benevolence to Russia, to the great annoyance of his British allies. Orlov had repeatedly pointed this out in his reports to his cabinet. In his long despatch of February 28/March 11 he stated that Napoleon III, by his utterances and in his conduct, had made clear his striving for a speedy peace. If he had not wanted peace, he would not have worked to restrain England regarding Point Five, and if the British had not been checked, the conference would have failed, for Russia's refusal to meet the British demands would have caused the collapse of the negotiations.

Napoleon had actively intervened to moderate the special claims of the British and the selfish schemes of Austria. He did this, not only to bring peace, but also to satisfy Russia's direct interests.[45] Because of the benevolent conduct of the French emperor, Russia obtained a peace far more favorable than it had reason to expect. Moreover, Napoleon repeatedly went out of his way to be cordial to the Russians. Orlov, wishing to return the favor, dropped a hint to Walewski that he wanted to do something personally for the emperor by removing from past treaties provisions that had lost their significance. What he meant was a removal of the ban on the Bonaparte dynasty, a gesture he was authorized to make. Buol had already spoken to Orlov about this, but he felt that the formal announcement should

45. Orlov to Nesselrode, Feb. 28/Mar. 11, 1856, no. 31, AVP, f. Kants., D. no. 147.

come only after the signing of the Treaty of Paris. Louis Napoleon doubtless understood the significance of the gesture, for the Russian noted the increasing signs of attention and good will "which the Emperor shows me more and more every day." A striking example of this cordiality was the postponing of a great review, which was scheduled to be held just before the signing of the treaty. The monarch was especially eager to have Orlov with him on the reviewing stand, but Orlov felt that since the two countries were still technically at war, Russia's military position would not permit him to attend. The emperor thereupon postponed the parade until April 1—a mark of favor that Parisian society widely noticed.[46]

Count Walewski had followed his master's example, although in the sessions of the conference he often had to support the British position. But in his confidential talks with Orlov he maintained a peace-loving, even friendly attitude toward Russia. His attitude toward the Russian delegates was not that of an enemy, but of an "auxiliary." He even used this term and acted as such during the negotiations.[47]

Thus the relations of these two cabinets, whose troops seven months before had been killing each other with sound and fury, in March 1856 were on excellent terms, even cooperating against the English and Austrian allies of the French. But the very skill and flexibility of Louis Napoleon, which led him at times to support contradictory policies, had the effect of arousing doubts about his reliability. While he was on excellent terms with the Russians, he also remained an ally of the British, Russia's greatest foe, and at times seemed to be playing one off against the other. His strong support for the Turks, which had involved France in the war against Russia, turned out to be largely a maneuver, for he gave them little support in the peace conference, and that largely to please the British. He made energetic overtures to the Austrians to enter the war, but during the negotiations over the Bessarabian frontier he sided with the Russians rather than with Buol and Franz Joseph. Moreover, after his victory in the Crimea he joined with England in encouraging Sweden and Norway to take an active part in the war in order to reconquer Finland from Russia, and built up French armaments to prepare for a new campaign in 1856. Yet, while doing so, he was also engaged in direct but secret negotiations with the Russian court through Morny, Seebach, Fried-

46. Ibid., Mar. 20/Apr. 1, 1856, no. 61, D. no. 148.
47. Ibid., Feb. 28/Mar. 11, 1856, no. 31, AVP, f. Kants., D. no. 147.

rich Ferdinand Count von Beust, and Pfordten. And at the same time he actively supported the Austrian scheme to present an ultimatum to Russia, whose rejection would bring on an expansion of the war. Napoleon's intentions in Italy also were fairly obvious, for he was eager to get Austria out of Lombardy and Venetia, by a scheme to trade these two Austrian provinces for the Danubian Principalities under an Austrian archduke. His schemes for a revolutionary movement in Italy and in Hungary troubled the Austrians, just as his efforts to encourage Polish nationalism made Nesselrode and Alexander II suspicious of his reliability.

Hence the Russian emperor and his diplomats, notably Counts Orlov and Nesselrode, Prince A. M. Gorchakov, and Baron Meyendorff, all of whom realized the value of the cooperation of Louis Napoleon, warned of forming an outright alliance with France, because it might involve Russia in unforeseen and dangerous conflicts. They urged close relations with France, to prevent the formation of a new coalition against Russia, but they felt it essential to reserve freedom of action rather than to make advance commitments.

On April 15, 1856, the Russian diplomats received a striking illustration of the unreliability of Louis Napoleon. Although he was still very cordial to them, Europe was amazed to learn that he had just signed a treaty with Britain and Austria pledging support for the Turks, with an infraction of the Treaty of Paris to be a *casus belli*. Although it did not mention Russia, the new agreement was obviously aimed at it. In fact, Austria, the real sponsor of the treaty, probably was using it to ensure itself protection against its huge neighbor.

Not only was there no special reason for such an engagement, now that the peace had been made to the general satisfaction, but the Russian cabinet was annoyed to have had no advance warning of it. Only on April 18/30 did Orlov send the news to Nesselrode, after receiving the information from Count Walewski. According to Orlov, the French cabinet would have acted in a more seemly fashion if it had informed Russia of this demarche at least two weeks earlier. Orlov did not, however, regard Napoleon as the moving spirit behind this development, which he ascribed to the desire of England and Austria to compromise the French emperor before the Russians, and thus to spoil their increasingly warm relations.

Alexander II was annoyed by this disclosure, for his comment on Orlov's despatch stated: "This conduct of France in regard to us is not very loyal and should serve us as a measure of the degree of trust that Louis Napoleon can inspire in us." [48]

On the following day Orlov reported that Walewski had told Brunnow of the guarantee treaty of April 15 and its antecedents. Apparently the idea took shape in the summer of 1855 and on November 15, when, since there appeared to be no hope of better Franco-Russian relations, the three powers adopted a memorandum concerning an ultimatum to Russia on the conditions of peace. It was also agreed that after signing a final peace treaty, the three courts would pledge themselves to sign a special convention to guarantee the maintenance of the Ottoman empire, and to regard any violation of the terms as a *casus belli*. As a result of this memorandum, Austria delivered the ultimatum to Russia, which resulted in Russian acceptance of the preliminaries and the peace conference in Paris in February and March 1856. After the Treaty of Paris was signed, Austria and Britain pressed the Tuileries to complete the last part of the Vienna memorandum. Although Napoleon was very reluctant to do this, the French cabinet felt it must accept the obligation incurred on November 14, although it had it written in general terms without mentioning Russia. Finally, to show good faith with St. Petersburg, the cabinet sent it information about this treaty. [49]

Two days later Orlov was invited to an audience with Napoleon III, which he had not sought. The emperor himself brought up the secret treaty, about which he was very apologetic. He had incurred the obligation through the Vienna memorandum of November 14, which he now regarded as useless, as the Treaty of Paris provided for all possible cases. He was displeased that the agreement had not been communicated to Orlov, since this looked too much like trickery, "to which I am not inclined." He had instructed Walewski to show him all the documents involved. [50]

Finally, on April 22/May 4, Prince A. M. Gorchakov, the new minister of foreign affairs, informed Orlov that Alexander II had marked the incident closed, although his impression of it was not favorable. He did not intend to make "useless reproaches" because of it. He did, however, take it as a warning, since it provided a motive for greater restraint and caution in dealing with France. It also pro-

48. Orlov to Nesselrode, Apr. 18/30, 1856, no. 86, AVP, f. Kants., D. no. 148.
49. Ibid., Apr. 19/May 1, no. 91, with annexes.
50. Ibid., Apr. 21/May 3.

vided an advantage, since, if Louis Napoleon tried to involve Russia in adventurous schemes, a reminder of this convention would make him hesitate, and the Russian envoy at Paris would have at his disposal an argument from the French government itself.[51]

Even before the Russian court had learned of this treaty, in March 1856 an anonymous memorandum on Russia's future foreign policy came to the attention of Alexander II, who noted that he had read it and found it very intelligent. There was no indication of its authorship. Probably Nesselrode did not write it, for in several places he took issue with the author. It does not seem to have come from the pen of Count Orlov, because the author was quite sharp and critical of the reign of Nicholas I, of which Orlov had been a key figure. Perhaps the author was Prince A. M. Gorchakov, whom Alexander appointed minister of foreign affairs in April 1856 and who later became chancellor.

The memorandum dealt with Russia's new position in Europe, after it had been defeated by France and had lost prestige. Many people throughout Europe were delighted to see Russia humbled. Actually it had a much better position than had been expected, for its losses at the peace conference were trifling. Although it was without allies, the bravery of its army was highly regarded, and it was far from crushed. Obviously the course for Russia to follow was to assume a withdrawn, unpretentious position and to concentrate on building up its resources and power. It should not be eager to seek allies until it had restored its strength and moral influence, which would facilitate the making of alliances. Russia thus would gain in influence because it had no ambitions and would have real freedom of choice.[52]

It was impossible for Russia to return to the old order, marked by tight control and binding power. This attitude had brought it little advantage, for while the conservatives still favored Russia, others were hostile and blamed it for all failures. It was the focus of hatred, like Spain at the peak of its power. Instead, it should strive for moral influence, for it had no strong ambitions. Certainly Russia could not again ally itself with Austria, for the very thought of that was "morally monstrous." Also, after its experiences with England, Russia had nothing to gain from that quarter.

51. A. M. Gorchakov to Orlov, St. Petersburg, Apr. 22/May 4, 1856, no. 86, as cited in "K istorii Parizhskogo mira 1856 g.," *Krasnyi Arkhiv,* no. 2 (75) (1936), pp. 56–57.
52. "K istorii Parizhskogo mira," pp. 45–46.

Should Russia even seek a new alliance system? There was a strong tendency toward alignment with France, but it would have no real value, for its sole purpose would be for revenge, and if made hastily and without care it would be a bad mistake. Nesselrode wrote that they should not ally with Louis Napoleon, although they should try to keep him away from Britain and from moving against Russia. Alexander II wrote that they should beware of his adventurous tendencies, of which they already had seen examples. Russia should let France take the lead and let events take their course, without seeking an alliance with France or any other power. Nesselrode objected, however, that Russia should not become isolated; he favored a "good and serious agreement," which would give hope of cooperation, but without firm pledges. (Alexander's comment was *"Oui."*) At that time there was no purpose for an alliance and Russia should not become the tool of France. It had no obligations, even to Prussia, which, while less hostile to Russia than the other powers, actually had done nothing concrete for it during the war.[53]

Russia, which had lost the war on moral grounds, should remain patient and let others come to it, for if it had the support of public opinion, it could accomplish much. Let it try to be always on the side of justice and truth, and then it would be in a sound position. It must await opportunities to assert moral leadership. Such opportunities would probably soon arise, as the political situation was complicated.

Thus at this time Russia should not declare for any political system or an alliance policy but should cling to its freedom of action. It should try always to be on the side of righteousness, and then in the long run it would win. (To this statement, both Nesselrode and Alexander commented that it would be hard for Russia to be always right.)[54]

As for Austria, it had lost heavily in the war. Buol, who at Paris had lost the key position that he had enjoyed at the Vienna Conference, seemed bitter over the decline of his influence. "Moreover," wrote Orlov, "the respect that appears . . . for our representatives at court, in society, and in the army, evidently irritates him. This worries him and creates uncertainty as to the future. It seems to him that this is an augury of more intimate rapprochement between Russia and

53. Ibid., pp. 47–49.
54. Ibid., pp. 50–51.

France," and he realized that Austria would gain nothing from it. This premonition was "a fully deserved punishment for his mistakes. He both repents the past and fears for the future." [55]

Austria had made gains during the war, by forcing Russia from the Danube and by the elimination of its fleet from the Black Sea. The cost, however, was high, for most Russians were bitter over what they regarded as Austria's betrayal. According to Hamilton Seymour, British minister to Vienna in 1856, on one occasion Orlov said to Walewski: "We have torn each other like the brave mastiffs that we are. But now we must bring it to pass so that our conflict does not benefit this cur Austria." Orlov, who was sympathetic with France, charged Emperor Franz Joseph with duplicity and perfidy, after the untiring kindness and personal tenderness of Nicholas I toward him. Many Russian officers were indignant at Austria's "betrayal" and sent back Austrian decorations that they had worn. Russian regiments of which Franz Joseph or an Austrian archduke had been honorary colonels ceased to bear their names.[56] Prince A. M. Gorchakov, who became minister of foreign affairs early in 1856, termed Buol's conduct "unbelievable and indescribable" and said frankly to Austrian diplomats that he dreamed of revenge. Orlov and other Russian diplomats spoke of Austria with the greatest bitterness.[57]

Franz Joseph was troubled by Buol's reports about the isolation of Austria at Paris. "It is only sad that on the most important questions we have only England, or indeed, only Turkey, on our side. . . . The enmity and hatred of the Russian plenipotentiaries exceed my expectations." While France was nominally an ally of Austria, the Kaiser felt that it was far too Russophil and he did not trust Napoleon.[58] England was definitely hostile to Austria, and Prussia was clearly pro-Russian. Furthermore, Austria's economic situation was bad, for it had cost so much to keep its army on a war footing that it had had to sell its national railways at a bargain price and had serious annual deficits.

As before, England remained very hostile to Russia after the war, and its setbacks at Paris and its failures in the Crimea and the Baltic

55. Orlov to Nesselrode, Feb. 28/Mar. 11, 1856, no. 31, AVP, f. Kants., D. no. 147.

56. Germain Bapst, *Le Maréchal Canrobert: Souvenirs d'un siècle* (Paris, 1904), III, 111.

57. Werner Mosse, *The European Powers and the German Question* (Cambridge, Eng., 1958), pp. 69–70.

58. Hallberg, pp. 102–05; Corti, p. 169.

rankled. But its military prestige had declined greatly, and it obviously was unable to attack Russia without powerful allies, which it could not find. Friction between the two countries continued unabated, but neither could harm the other, for Europe and the mountains and deserts of Asia effectively isolated them.

For Russia the strategic results of this costly war were relatively slight. Although its army had suffered defeat, the Black Sea fleet had been wiped out, and it had lost substantially in prestige, for it no longer could lay down the law to its neighbors, it had lost only a tiny bit of territory and it still retained much influence in southeastern Europe. Because it was still hostile to Turkey, it continued to enjoy sympathy among the Greeks, the Serbs and the Montenegrins, and the Bulgars, although it could accomplish nothing of importance for them. It did have some slight success in the Danubian Principalities, where, in opposition to Austria, England, and Turkey, it supported France's efforts to unify them. Its backing helped make it possible for Alexander Cuza to be elected hospodar in both provinces simultaneously, which was a first step toward unification.[59] Russia still enjoyed some favor among the Balkan peoples because of its opposition to Turkey and Austria and because of its religious and ethnic ties with some of them.

On the whole, however, Russia had lost substantially in prestige, for it was no longer the chief power in Europe, and its army, once regarded as invincible, had proved to be technically backward, unwieldy, and poorly led. Nevertheless, the army was greatly admired for its defense of Sevastopol and its repulse of the attacks on Sveaborg and Kronstadt in the Finnish gulf. The Russian diplomats had done well in the negotiations and the Russian cabinet had been reasonable in accepting the terms of peace. In sum, Russia was generally viewed as a powerful country, but backward and underdeveloped, and far less influential than France. Its industries were primitive, it had almost no railways, and its financial position was weak. It was imposing because of its sheer size and population, but it no longer was a leading power. It would remain backward and underdeveloped for almost a century. The Crimean War had revealed these facts about Russia, but had done nothing to change them.

59. E. E. Chertan, *Russko-Rumynskie otnosheniia v 1859–1863 godakh* (Kishinev, 1968), pp. 55–66; Baumgart, pp. 243–44.

CHAPTER 22. THE SOCIAL EFFECTS OF THE WAR ON THE WORKING CLASS

In spite of the defeat in the Crimean War, its immediate effects upon Russia were slight, for it had to give up only the mouth of the Danube and a small strip of land in Bessarabia. It lost no additional land and did not have to pay an indemnity. The renunciation of its fleet and fortifications on the Black Sea and its surrender of its protectorate over Moldavia and Wallachia mattered little, for these concessions did not weaken it appreciably or harm its economic interests. The loss of manpower was more serious, for probably about half a million men lost their lives during the war, chiefly from disease and other hardships, and a smaller number from enemy action. Russia also had heavy economic losses arising from the use of horses and oxen to haul munitions and supplies to the armies in the field. Many of these animals died of exhaustion and poor feeding and numerous peasant wagons collapsed or were destroyed. Also great quantities of provisions were commandeered from provinces close to the war zone, which ruined many peasant families and impoverished landowners. In addition, the government incurred large debts buying munitions and other war supplies, so that the resulting inflation brought poverty to large parts of the population. But in spite of the hardship that these factors caused to many, most of the country soon recovered from the war, and its economic effects quickly disappeared.[1]

There was, however, much social unrest in Russia during the war, although it was largely directed against serfdom and the landowners, rather than against the war and the government. Although the great peasant uprisings of the seventeenth and eighteenth centuries had ceased, there had been spontaneous outbreaks in 1815 and again in 1847–48. In his jubilee report to the emperor in 1850, Count L. A.

1. W. K. Pintner, "Inflation in Russia during the Crimean War Period," *American Slavic and East European Review*, XVIII (1959), 81–87.

Perovskii, minister of internal affairs, in contrast to his optimistic colleagues, spoke of his troubles with the peasants, who because "of their innate credulity" were surprisingly ready to accept all sorts of wild rumors, which were the chief cause of "disturbances and disorders from time to time." Perovskii had to admit, however, that these actions resulted "from the senseless striving of the peasants for freedom, as a result of their incorrect prejudices about their alleged rights to it." [2]

While the government's exactions through taxes and conscription, which took an increasingly large number of men from productive labor, helped to stimulate peasant unrest, the landowners, by their increasing exploitation of the peasants, were the chief offenders. They were steadily reducing the farmland used by the peasants and adding it to their manorial cultivation. The noted scholar V. I. Semevskii indicated that in much of Russia at the end of the eighteenth century the peasants were using 82.3 percent of the plowland. By the 1850s, however, the peasants were cultivating only 34 percent of the arable land, while the landowner was farming 66 percent of it with the compulsory labor of the serfs. [3] The transfer of so much of the land from peasants to masters over a fifty-year period must have caused great resentment among the serfs.

As the manorial holdings grew, the landowners steadily increased their exactions from the peasants in compulsory field labor and especially in the burdensome duty of hauling their produce and other commodities to market, which seems to have taken about three-fifths of their working time. [4] The greater part of the demand for forced labor came at the height of the farming season, when the serfs urgently needed the time for their own crops.

In northern Russia, where farming was not very productive, the nobles did little of it; rather they obtained their incomes from the money payments that the peasants made to them. While statistics on the subject are very scanty, M. K. Rozhkova, who has studied the matter, concludes that between 1800 and 1850 the amount had increased several times over. [5]

The government also exploited the peasants during the war by inten-

2. S. B. Okun', *Krest'ianskoe dvizhenie v Rossii v 1850–1856 gg.,* vol. 3 of *Krest'ianskoe dvizhenie v Rossii v XIX—nachala XX veka,* ed. N. M. Druzhinin (Moscow, 1962), p. 7.

3. M. K. Rozhkova, "Sel'skoe khoziaistvo i polozhenie krest'ianstva," in *Ocherki ekonomicheskoi istorii Rossii v pervoi polovine XIX veka* (Moscow, 1959), p. 28.

4. Okum', p. 9.

5. Rozhkova, p. 33.

sive conscription. Although usually it took approximately 80,000 men from one half of the country, in 1854 the draft was levied in both halves and in increasing numbers, so that it was a quadruple draft, which took more than 358,000 men.[6]

Russia's finances were in bad condition in 1854, for the indebtedness of the agriculture of the nobles had increased to 600 percent of the amount in 1812, to a total of 398 million silver rubles. The landlords had mortgaged 6.6 million of their serfs, or 61.7 percent.[7] As for the government, its debt rose to 796,770,000 rubles. Moreover, the maintenance of the newly formed militia *(opolchenie)* was charged to provincial revenues, which in 1855 amounted to 7,727,156 rubles. It was somewhat less in 1856. Local taxes of almost one million rubles provided the Southern Army with fuel, candles, and straw during the four-year period.[8] Moreover, in addition to this official debt, the government also drew on Russia's resources in other ways, which cannot be expressed in financial terms. It took over one million men away from their peacetime occupations and also imposed all sorts of demands in kind upon the population, which cost it heavily. The price of this, however, could not be stated with any degree of accuracy, but it all was terribly expensive to the people.

For the peasants the results of these burdensome demands were very severe. An administrator of the extensive Iusupov estates in the steppe region wrote in 1856, "Now almost half go begging to the mir." [9] Thus the outcome was the pauperization of great numbers of the people.

Another indication of peasant misery was given by the decline in their numbers. In 1861 a certain Troinitskii from a study of the tenth census concluded that the number of landlords' peasants had declined by 1.1 percent, while the other categories of the population had increased by 16.8 percent in the same twenty-two-year period. The author was sure that these figures were not the result of voluntary liberation of the peasants by their masters, so that the shrinkage must have come from increased peasant mortality.[10]

When the secret archives of the Ministry of Internal Affairs were

6. Okun', p. 9.
7. Ibid., p. 10.
8. Ibid., pp. 28–30.
9. Okun', p. 10.
10. Ibid., pp. 10–11.

opened during the Revolution of 1917 it became clear that the decline of the serf population had accelerated greatly during the Crimean War. The minister cited considerable mortality from cholera and typhus as one of the causes, as these diseases struck chiefly the adult males and hit the agricultural population hard. He also referred to bad harvests as a constant factor in the decline, chiefly in the western provinces near Poland, where there had been repeated crop failures, in some cases for ten consecutive years. Under such conditions conscription bore heavily on the population. The minister did not mention the exactions of the landowners as a cause of the increased mortality. Nevertheless, it is significant that he admitted that there had been a marked decline in the peasant population, which he estimated as at least 6 percent,[11] and not the 1.1 percent given by Troinitskii.

The number of peasant outbreaks during this seven-year period, based on a chronicle of all peasant incidents over these years, offers further evidence about the conditions of peasant life. Whereas the Ministry of Interior had put their number at 215, and the Third Section of His Majesty's Chancellery had listed 302 (with the year 1854 omitted), the chronicle indicated that there had been 414. In addition, one of the special features of these years was the mass flights of peasants, often from several provinces. Though the precise number involved is impossible to determine, we know that thousands and tens of thousands of serfs took part.

The disasters of these years often had the same symptoms as those of earlier decades: an intense longing for freedom from serfdom, desperation aroused by the impossible exactions of their masters, and fierce resentment against landlords and administrators because of cruel and outrageous treatment. K. D. Kavelin, a prominent jurist of the Crimean War period, stressed the intensity of the peasant hope for freedom:

> There is no likely rumor, no improbable pretext, which has not served for the serfs as sufficient ground for declaring ancient claims for liberation. Moreover, the circumstances that the half-peaceful uprising of the serfs assumes ever wider proportions is an ominous portent. All this can convince the noblest and the blindest person that the people are severely burdened by servile dependence and that under unfavorable circumstances a confla-

11. Ibid., pp. 11–13.

gration may flare up out of this exasperation and a holocaust may break out, whose consequences are difficult to perceive.[12]

The economic demands of the serfowners, which often must have driven the peasants to a frenzy, have already been mentioned. The shrinkage of the plowland held by them, which made it almost impossible for them to pay their taxes and to feed their families, has been cited, and the marked increase in the forced labor required of them left all too little time for the working of the little land they had. For those who paid personal dues, usually in money, the amounts had been raised probably to the limit of their ability to pay. The hopelessness of the peasant situation caused by this series of demands must have reduced many to complete despair.

Moreover, the masters under whom the serfs lived, completely at their mercy, were human beings, of whom some had humane and sensitive instincts, while others revealed all the vices of brutal creatures without kindness and without principles. Drunkenness, sadistic behavior, and unbridled lechery were all too common among the Russian gentry, as they were among other servile societies of the ancient and modern worlds. The Report for 1853 of Count A. F. Orlov of the Third Section of His Majesty's Chancellery, listed a number of fatal attacks of house serfs and peasants upon their masters, as well as other attacks that had failed. These attempts to murder their masters, according to Orlov, had occurred mostly because of abuses that the masters had inflicted on their serfs. The peasants killed twenty-five of their tormentors during 1853 and made thirteen unsuccessful attempts to kill others.[13] The number of peasants who were officially recorded as killed by their masters was substantially larger.

During 1853 some thirty-eight landowners were proved to have mistreated their serfs, and sixty-three managers and village elders on the estates had done likewise. The official statistics, which probably minimized the number of such abuses, reported 111 cases of fatal punishment of peasants by nobles and managers. Among the victims were forty-three women, eight children, and thirty premature infants. Usually the provincial authorities were reluctant to take action against those who performed such deeds, but not all of the guilty went unpunished, for in a number of cases the higher organs of government re-

---

12. K. D. Kavelin, *Sobranie sochinenii* (St. Petersburg, 1897–1900), II, 32–33.
13. Okun', p. 392.

moved the perpetrator from his estate, which was put under an official trustee, and often the guilty person was exiled to a distant province. But the criminals were not sent to Siberia for life, much less hanged on the spot by court-martial, which happened to some of the serf assassins.[14] Furthermore, the officials probably acted against cruel landowners only in extreme cases when their infuriated serfs rose against them. Undoubtedly others whose conduct was only slightly less evil escaped punishment.

In order to illustrate the problems that the Russian government faced during the Crimean War, it seems desirable to present several significant examples. The evidence, which is given in the volume of documents from the official files of the Imperial Russian government, is set forth in S. B. Okun', editor, *Krestian'skoe dvizhenie v Rossii v 1850–1856 gg.,* cited above. It came chiefly from the Ministry of Internal Affairs, the Third Section of the emperor's chancellery, the Department of Executive Police, and other official agencies. Other evidence has been cited in Ia. I. Linkov's *Ocherki istorii krest'ianskogo dvizheniia v Rossii,* cited below.

By the spring of 1854 Russia, at war with Turkey, France, and England, expected a difficult campaign in the Baltic and the Gulf of Finland. In order to hold off the British fleet, Russia decided to create a fleet of galleys that could operate with success among the myriads of islands and rocks on the Finnish coast. The crews for these vessels would be volunteers from the four provinces of the northwest, who might enroll in these units, but only with the permission of their masters. The peasants, who would serve for five months, had to give written pledges that at the end of their service they would return to their masters. The authorities promised to provide for the families of the volunteers. The government, which was worried about the effect of this proposal, ordered the marshals of nobility to instruct the nobles about it, so that they could inform the peasants. But as the nobles disliked this measure, they did little to help.[15]

When word of this decree reached the masses, it had a startling effect, for the news spread rapidly, not only in the four provinces specified, but also in all central and northern Russia and along the upper Volga. Whole villages of the provinces of Moscow, Riazan,

14. Ibid., p. 393.
15. Ia. I. Linkov, *Ocherki istorii krest'ianskogo dvizheniia v Rossii* (Moscow, 1940), pp. 96–97; *Polnoe Sobranie Zakonov,* II, 2nd series, no. 28122.

and Tambov left their work and flocked to Moscow to enroll. By June 24 thousands of applicants were pouring in. In his report of July 19 the governor general of Moscow informed Count Orlov of groups of peasants arriving from five neighboring provinces. One of the generals of Gendarmes reported that the police and local authorities were holding many peasants in the provincial and county towns, where they demanded tickets admitting them to the ranks of the naval militia.[16]

While probably much of this enthusiasm for military service was patriotic, to a much greater degree it seems to have come from the belief that joining the service offered a way to escape from serfdom, for it was a hallowed tradition that a man who served in the armed forces became a free man when he was discharged. All that was needed was a rumor that "the Sovereign Emperor calls all volunteers into war service for a time, as a result of which their families would be freed forever not only from serfdom, but also from the recruit obligation and the payment of state dues." The peasants, extremely eager to obtain their freedom, at once stopped work not only on their own fields, but also on those of the landowners. Peasants of Novgorod sold their cattle, did not sow the fields, and refused to do the forced work for the landowners. A female landowner complained that a group of men had refused to serve the landowners and obey their orders, for they said the landowners had compelled them to work beyond their powers.[17]

These reports caused the government much concern. A landlord of Tambov wrote to Governor General Zakrevskii that the peasants, on learning of the call for the galley flotilla, "were stirred up by evil-minded men" and were troubling many estates. If this situation continued, it would be difficult for the landowners to provide the necessary recruits for the draft call. As reports of this nature came in to Nicholas I from Orlov and the minister of war, the tsar ordered his aides to go out into the provinces to stop the peasants, to explain to them the illegality of their acts, to arrest the instigators, and to return them to their villages. He ordered the minister of interior to take the most active measures, to explain the real meaning of the decrees, and to deal directly with the disobedient. The tsar's aides also were ordered

16. Ibid.
17. Slezinskii, "Morskoe opolchenie," *RS*, CXXIV, no. 2 (1905), p. 721.

to arrest a sexton and a priest who were reported to have stirred up the peasants.

As peasants still came to Moscow, Nicholas ordered his officials to send them home in chains. Thousands thus were sent back under convoy, some of them with shaven heads. Many had to sit for some time in jail in Moscow. Zakrevskii reported that the Moscow prisons were full, so that he had to put the culprits in the Manège and in other public buildings.

As the peasants learned of the dangers ahead, they began to arm themselves with pikes, boar spears, knives, and clubs. In some cases they beat Cossacks, constables, and the like. Many peasants avoided the cities to escape capture.[18]

The officials blamed the disorders on "instigators" whom they tried frantically to catch. Actually, the movement was probably largely spontaneous, for a mere rumor would set it off. There were, of course, occasional agitators—unskilled workers, peasants, or minor clergy. In the province of Tver a village elder urged house peasants and other dissatisfied persons to join the naval militia. A foundry serf in Nizhnyi Novgorod was arrested for attracting peasants to the new naval units. In Tambov a state peasant publicly proclaimed in the bazaar the *ukaz* (decree) about the galley flotilla, "where they get freedom, but the landowners and officials hide it." Talk of this sort had quick results. A Gendarme officer said that this agitation swept the province and the peasants quit their field work and went in crowds to Moscow and Tambov. An artisan of Tambov carried on the same sort of propaganda. Occasionally state peasants and lesser townspeople took part, although they did not themselves seek freedom.[19]

Some of the village clergy also were active—sextons, deacons, and a few priests explained the decree in peasant terms. In the province of Riazan a deacon told peasants to go to the militia, where they would get eight rubles in silver per month and after three years they and their families would be free from serfdom and conscription.

The tsar heard of a sexton who told peasants that the priest of the local church had hidden the decree at the request of the landowner. At a foundry church the priest blessed his parishioners and sent them off to join the militia. Nicholas I had these men imprisoned.

18. Linkov, pp. 99–100.
19. Ibid., p. 101.

These were rare cases, for most of the priests supported the official position. But there were others, whose lives were miserable, and who were close to the peasants and thought as they did. All these incidents indicated that there was a tremendous class feeling in Russia.[20]

Difficult as were the problems resulting from the decree concerning the naval militia, the Russian government soon found itself forced to raise more men through a general militia (opolchenie). This time, however, the minister of internal affairs took the trouble to issue a special instruction to the provincial authorities, in the hope of avoiding trouble with the peasants. He advised the provincial authorities to make sure that false rumors or interpretations of the decree did not appear. The government strictly limited the scope of the levy to eighteen provinces and only to twenty-three of every one thousand males, apparently feeling that it would be dangerous to arm more serfs. While the imperial manifesto had carefully avoided mentioning serfdom, the instruction stated definitely that it would not be affected. The opolchenie, it said, was only a temporary measure, and those who entered it would not change their class, but would remain in the group to which they had belonged and would return to it upon discharge from the levy. Hence the townsman would be a townsman in the same town as before; "the state peasant will be a state peasant in the same volost [township] and village, and the landlord's peasant, of his landlord, all will return to their families, their homes, to their usual status and activities." [21]

The instruction stressed that it was the duty of the governors and other local officials to maintain in their provinces everywhere a correct understanding of the rules in the preceding paragraph as the most important part of the instruction, and in particular they should turn their attention to the landlords' peasants, "for, if anywhere, it is precisely in this class that evil-intentioned men may find a more accessible arena for their activities." If trouble occurred, the governors should summon the nobles themselves to cooperate with the authorities, as they had especially close relations with the peasants and hence might be able to inspire in them feelings "of a sacred duty to faith, Tsar, and fatherland." If, however, in spite of sensible precautionary measures, incorrect interpretations and even more unfavorable attitudes should appear, and an uprising of the landowners' peasants should

20. Ibid., pp. 102–03.
21. II P. S. Z., 28991; Linkov, pp. 117–18.

occur, "then the chiefs of the provinces are obliged to suppress them in the very beginning by decisive and strict measures." [22]

The concern of the minister proved to be justified, for when the Holy Synod's proclamation urging the peasants to join the opolchenie was issued, in the province of Saratov many interpreted it as a call to military service, which would give them substantial pay and would later provide personal freedom to the warriors and their families. In one village a zealous priest had the peasants take the oath and enrolled them for the opolchenie, only to find that so many came from the whole district that he had to end the enrollment. In several counties of the province peasants then went in parties of one to two hundred to the county town demanding that they be enrolled and that all labor on the landlords' lands should stop. By May and June 1855 the movement spread to the neighboring province of Simbirsk, where the peasants went in large parties to the provincial town and sent envoys to explain their purpose to the governor. A village priest encouraged them in their error by stating that the Synod's message promised that volunteers would be discharged with pensions after two years of service. The governor sent out eight experienced priests to explain the mistake to the peasants. Since the source does not mention any further disorders in this case, the efforts of the priests apparently were successful.

The movement also spread to the province of Perm in the Urals. Here the serfs were convinced that the Synod's message promised that they would gain their freedom from the nobles if they would enter the militia, which led twenty-five of the peasants to enlist.[23]

For the Tatars of the middle Volga region, however, the decree was an irritant, for they took it as a move to force them to do military service, from which they had previously been exempt. They rioted furiously when the officials verified the lists of drafted men, beat the village and volost authorities, and tried to beat the former district head. This fracas led to the arrest and imprisonment of twelve Tatar leaders in one volost. Other Tatars also opposed the opolchenie as an effort to force them to change their religion, and many of those who were drafted deserted and hid. They were quickly caught and taken as recruits, and the opposition died down after a time.[24]

22. Ibid., pp. 118–19.
23. Ibid., p. 141.
24. Ibid., pp. 141–42.

A more serious situation developed in the Ukraine, for the people remembered that a century before their forefathers had been free Cossacks. When they heard of the call for the opolchenie, they were immensely excited, especially as a separate decree in May 1855 called "Little Russian Cossacks" to join the militia by forming six cavalry regiments of 6,498 men.[25] The Ukrainian serfs, often misinformed by their clergy (chiefly sextons and deacons), were certain that the emperor was calling them to shed their blood for him and the church, for which they would be freed of bondage and given the status of Cossacks. I. S. Gromeka, apparently a military man, heard of this movement while en route to Kiev in March 1855. The governor general was amused by the news, saying that the peasants had heard of the decree and had demanded that they be enrolled as Cossacks. They had refused to do forced labor for their masters, but when they were admonished by the clergy and by officials they had promised to return to their work. A major general with a force of troops had gone to one county to restore order. Disturbing reports soon came in, however, that the general and his troops had been surrounded by huge crowds of peasants, with more and more coming. As he expected an attack, he demanded more soldiers.[26]

Gromeka and the vice governor went off to deal with the problem, which the latter was sure he could handle. On April 1 they came to the village of Bykova-Greblia, where they found a sapper company under arms, in the square, with a huge crowd of unarmed peasants, kneeling, with their caps off, facing them. They all held up two fingers of the right hand (a sign of loyalty to God and the tsar). In a courtyard the second company was flogging peasants, who were lying on the ground. Gromeka went to the kneeling crowd, asking them if they were obeying the authorities. They said they were and brought out the traditional bread and salt signifying loyalty. He asked if they would work for the lords the next day, which they all refused to do; but all, as one man, wanted to shed their blood for the tsar, and Gromeka's efforts to reason with them were in vain. They would do forced labor only if the tsar sent a resolution demanding it. All, however, wished to serve God and the tsar.[27]

---

25. I. S. Bliokh, *Finansy Rossii XIX Stoletiia* (St. Petersburg, 1882), II, 28.
26. I. S. Gromeka, "Kievskiia volneniia v 1855 godu," *Poleznoe Chtenie*, no. 6 (1863), 650–52.
27. Ibid., p. 653; Linkov, pp. 120–21.

Shortly thereafter the crowd, unarmed, rushed the troops, to rescue those who were being birched. They seized the soldiers' muskets and pushed against the bayonets. Suddenly shots were fired and the crowd scattered, leaving twelve victims, six of them dead. After arranging for care for the wounded, Gromeka talked with the peasants, who proved to be new groups, sent by a meeting of several villages. They did not attack, but knelt and brought out bread and salt. They also held up two fingers, saying that they wanted to serve God and the tsar to the last drop of blood. When more troops arrived, the peasants again knelt, and Gromeka again reasoned with them. This episode ended peacefully, for the crowd permitted the flogging of some of their number, and their elder was put under arrest.[28]

At another village Gromeka found a similar situation: peaceful, submissive peasants, who refused to work for their masters, although they said they were not rebels. They had elected an *ataman* (leader), had kept order, and preserved property by putting guards at warehouses and barns. They had shut the liquor stores and guarded them. Like the others, they were ready to serve the tsar to the last drop of blood.[29]

The most sanguinary drama was at the village of Bereznaia, where the acting governor general found a huge crowd from four villages. Since he could do little with only three hundred men, he moved his force to the square in the center of the village. Here the crowd attacked from several sides, but were met with volleys from the troops. Pursued by the soldiers, the peasants then fled, losing twenty men killed in the encounter, with forty wounded. After the shooting, the authorities inflicted punishment on the serfs.[30]

Another fight took place at the village of Tagancha, where the peasants had come from miles around, having ceased work for their masters. A body of troops, aided by an experienced priest, tried to quiet them, but, although they brought out bread and salt, they insisted that they would not serve their masters. The officials told them that no freedom would be given them. Then, at a shout from their leader, the peasants pulled axes, pikes, and pitchforks from beneath their coats and attacked the soldiers. They fired, killing at least eleven, with thirteen wounded. The peasants then fled to the woods, where they continued to defy

28. Gromeka, pp. 653–56.
29. Ibid., pp. 658–59.
30. Ibid., pp. 660–61; Linkov, pp. 122–23.

the authorities. Finally, cavalry arrived and hunted down the fugitives, who were taken into the village, where they were flogged and beaten. Many of them were still stubborn, but the uprising collapsed.[31]

An official report on the events in the province of Kiev mentioned "the rapid involvement of large numbers of villages in the movement, with the same sort of attitudes, rumors, and expectations. As the peasants were led out of their errors in one place, the misunderstandings penetrated and disclosed themselves in other places of those same counties, which had been part of the former Ukraine." The nature of the peasants' error was almost the same everywhere: they were convinced that someone had concealed the tsar's ukaz from them, by which they were all summoned to serve as Cossacks, which would free them from work for the lords. They then quietly and without causing disorder demanded from their parish priests that they reveal the ukaz to them and enroll them in lists, with a report to the authorities that they wished to enter the tsar's service as Cossacks.

Another disturbing factor was the march of units of the opolchenie from central Russia through the Ukraine. Linkov wrote: "The warriors go with music, dance, and sing—and our peasants are under labor for the lords. 'Let us go also to help the tsar; or are we not such men as these?' " The marching units more than ever convinced the peasants of the reality of the manifesto.[32]

Accounts of what had happened in Kiev soon spread to the province of Voronezh, where one-third of the peasants were Ukrainian. Prince Bagration, an aide of the tsar's, reported that instigators had used the example of Kiev to stir up the peasants of Voronezh—chiefly the Ukrainians—with the immediate cause the proclamation of the Holy Synod, which was read in all the churches. The peasants interpreted it as a summons to enlist, in return for which the tsar would give them freedom. On May 10 some seventy peasants from one county came to the city of Voronezh, where the governor received them, gave them a "fatherly admonition," and flogged five "ringleaders." In the following days many more peasants came, from many estates in several counties. Some of them returned home after the explanations of the officials, but the movement continued into mid-May. Although the government used all means to explain to the serfs the real meaning of the decree—the district police officers, the marshals of nobility, and the clergy—the peasants still believed the widespread reports that,

31. Linkov, pp. 124–26.
32. Ibid., pp. 114–15.

after serving nine months in the opolchenie, the tsar would free them from serfdom. In some villages the priests themselves told the serfs that all men had been summoned into the militia and that they should go to Voronezh or the county town to be enrolled. Some priests even served farewell Te Deums for those who set out. Many peasants stopped their labor for their masters and left, and some even ceased their own plowing as well. Others did not, but sent delegates with requests to accept them all into the militia. In the county of Pavlovsk the serfs of several estates "declared themselves free and asserted their right to possess all the land, which once had belonged to their ancestors." On one estate the serfs demanded the removal of the manager, the reduction of the forced labor, and the apportioning of the meadows and the plowland on an equal basis to the peasants and the landowner.[33]

The movement in Voronezh continued until the end of July, with its most violent form in the village of Maslovka of Bobrovskii county. The Maslovka peasants quit work and sent a peasant as spokesman to St. Petersburg to ask that they be enrolled in the militia. When the priest and the police inspector sought to reason with them, they answered that they did not want to remain in the possession of their lord, they would not perform the orders of their masters, but all wanted to enter military service. They elected eighty of the number to enter the opolchenie as volunteers. On July 3 Prince Iurii Dolgoruki, chief of the province, arrived with 250 soldiers from the garrison of Voronezh. They seized 22 peasants and were about to flog them, when the crowd, with a cry, "We won't give up our comrades," attacked the soldiers. In the melee nine peasants were wounded, five of them seriously. During the fighting some of the peasants, among them six "ringleaders," broke through the soldiers' ranks and hid in the woods, along with a new group of peasants armed with staves. One thousand "witnesses," collected for moral support from various villages of state peasants, ran away, without raising any opposition. After this no further resistance to the authorities took place.[34]

Soon after the Maslovka incident, masses of peasants assembled at the large village of Petrovka, with some 3,500 more from nearby villages also coming. The government sent 350 soldiers to Petrovka, with Dolgoruki following soon after. The officials also collected 2,500 "witnesses," who, however, came with big clubs, although they were

33. Ibid., pp. 136–37.
34. Ibid., pp. 137–38.

supposed to be supporters of the government. They also declared that they would not go against their own people. When told that they should regard the governor as a representative of the Sovereign Emperor himself and unconditionally carry out his orders, the witnesses uttered angry cries, clearly showing that they were on the side of the serfs. They were so hostile to those punishing the disobedient that the floggers "panicked terribly." In his report the Gendarme officer wrote: "In my mind I immediately imagined the terrible consequences of a possible clash of this frightful, ignorant mass, armed with clubs, with the 350 men of the troop command, who might be taken between two fires"—i.e., between the serfs and the witnesses.[35]

When Dolgoruki arrived, he at once realized the danger of the situation and sent home many of the witnesses and then began to punish the ringleaders of Petrovka and other villages. But when the soldiers threw twelve men to the ground to flog them, the witnesses, with a great cry, rushed furiously back. Only the "energetic dispositions" of the Gendarme officer somehow averted a general fracas. The peasants submitted and slowly returned to their homes.[36]

This movement diminished in August of 1855. It was not directed against any specific cases of servile oppression, but against serfdom in general. Several individual groups of peasants stated that they had not suffered from their masters, were not overburdened with taxes, and in general regarded themselves as "completely satisfied." In many cases peasants who were well off played a role in the disturbances. In one village which was active in the movement only five peasants were without horses, and many owned considerable livestock. Even the better-off peasants detested serfdom.[37]

It is significant that the agitators "tried to awaken in the peasants memories of the Free Cossacks and the rights that their ancestors had enjoyed." The Ukrainian peasants were especially active in the disobedience, as their families had been under serfdom only for seventy-five years. Prince Bagration, of a noble family of Georgia, remarked that, while the Great Russians strove to enter military service, they could be reasoned with and soon admitted their errors, while the Little Russians (Ukrainians) were the ones who caused the disorders.[38]

35. Ibid., p. 138.
36. Ibid., pp. 138–39.
37. Ibid., p. 139.
38. Ibid.

Another uprising occurred in the province of Chernigov, where three villages owned by Prince Razumovskii had been living as state peasants after the death of the owner in the late 1830s. They were dissatisfied, however, because, unlike other state peasants, they had been compelled to do forced labor—"lord's work"—for the government, against which they had protested, saying that this was an illegal requirement. They asserted that since the tsar had made them state peasants, they would do only the work of this category. The peasants of the village of Velikii Sambor—the leaders—held a meeting in the woods called a *gromada,* which sent delegates to the other villages to induce the peasants to stop working. At a distillery of this estate several hundred men broke in, forcibly shutting down the operation, and drove the peasants out. The authorities sought to persuade them to return to their duties but failed, after which they sent in two battalions of infantry under the command of the governor of the province and a lieutenant of Gendarmes. The peasants, who gathered in a courtyard, on their knees, replied to the demands of their superiors: "We submit to God, to the tsar, and to your honor, but we do not wish to perform lord's work," and demanded that they be sworn the oath of loyalty to the new emperor. When persuasion failed, the authorities had the troops surround the peasants and begin to flog them. The peasants of Velikii Sambor in a body tried to break through the lines, but were halted, with eight of their number wounded with bayonets. The punishment continued, and gradually the peasants submitted, agreeing at first to do forced labor for one year only. They were unable to maintain this condition, however, and had to perform it indefinitely.[39]

Thus, as one might have expected, the efforts of the peasants to obtain freedom from serfdom cost them heavily in blood and suffering. Even after the war was over and the peace had been signed, in May and June 1856 peasant desperation still drove large numbers to try to flee to the entrance to the Crimea where, according to rumors, a better lot awaited them. They had heard that "on Perekop, in a golden chamber, sits the Tsar, who gives freedom to all who come, but those who do not come or are too late, will remain, as formerly, serfs to the lords." [40] Other rumors stated that the peasants were invited to settle in the ruined cities of the Crimea and would receive five silver

39. Ibid., pp. 134–36.
40. Ibid., pp. 144–47.

rubles, plus two rubles per day for their work. Peasants poured into the area, seizing the property of the nobles as they went and taking it with them. The government sent large forces of troops, largely cavalry, against them, but the peasants put up a stubborn resistance, attacking infantry and trying to wrench muskets out of the soldiers' hands. The soldiers fired and men were killed. There were several instances where peasants actually stood up to the troops and even attacked them. The government called on the clergy of the area to aid it in its efforts to pacify the serfs.

By this time the peasants had no hope of obtaining freedom by serving in the war and had to fall back on a dream of some "promised land," which to them meant the Crimea. Hence, as they had lost all hope and had abandoned their homes and livelihoods, they were willing to fight muskets and bayonets. Their dream was in vain, for by July 1856 the movement was largely suppressed by force or faded away. Even so, in the autumn of 1856, new flights of peasants moved from Kaluga and Orel, but they, too, failed.[41]

Although this belated movement does not fit directly into the period of the Crimean War, it gives evidence of the frantic efforts of the peasants to escape from serfdom. While almost nothing came of these efforts in 1856, they certainly helped to convince the government and the public of the need for the abolition of serfdom, which finally came in 1861.

There is little to say about the role of the factory workers of Russian industry in the movement for better working conditions at this time. Although factories had been developing with great rapidity after 1840,[42] and even though wages and working conditions were extremely bad, there seems to be no evidence of an active labor movement during the period of the Crimean War. The workers were only a small part of the population, many of them were only part-time workers, and few of them thought of themselves as anything but peasants temporarily working in factories. Decades would pass before they would become a powerful factor in Russian life. Even at this time, however, probably very few of the industrial workers could be regarded as loyal supporters of the existing regime.

The peasants, however, presented a very real danger, for as early as 1855 K. D. Kavelin, a liberal professor of St. Petersburg, in a

41. Ibid., pp. 144–47.
42. S. G. Strumilin, *Ocherki ekonomicheskoi istorii Rossii* (Moscow, 1960), pp. 390–450.

secretly circulated pamphlet, *Essay About Freeing the Peasants in Russia,* stated that serfdom was an evil that posed a real danger to the state, "for each day more and more takes away hope of a peaceful solution of this problem and brings us closer to a frightful catastrophe, a weak example of which in Galicia, in Tarnovskii county, quite recently brought all Europe to dismay and horror." He added: "Under serfdom, with each year the position will become more dangerous and irreparable, so that if it stays in its present form, several decades later it will blow up the whole state." [43]

On the other hand, A. J. Rieber, editor of *The Politics of Autocracy,* a collection of Alexander II's letters to Prince A. I. Bariatinskii, holds that Alexander's real motive for freeing the serfs was not fear of an uprising, but a realization that Russia could not have the powerful army it needed until it had achieved emancipation. While he was willing to frighten the fractious nobles with warnings of liberation from below, in his letters to the prince he repeatedly stressed the loyalty of the peasants which he found during his tours of the northern and western provinces. He realized that peasant impatience might touch off local uprisings, but on the whole he was confident that the peasants would continue to accept their status.[44]

Certainly, reports of latent peasant disaffection came from the Third Section of the emperor's chancellery, which strongly opposed emancipation. In November 1857 a staff officer of the Corps of Gendarmes reported from Kazan that "rumors about this have become more and more widespread among the peasants and especially the household people. . . ." Sure that it was coming, but impatient over the delay, in some cases they voiced threats, "which cause landowners to fear grave consequences, if they do not prevent them." A similar report from Nizhnii Novgorod spoke of "the most impatient expectation" and added that, because of the insubordination among their peasants, especially the household serfs, "fear is growing among the landowners of the danger of staying in their villages." [45] Finally, in the official report of the Third Section for 1857, it was stated that rumors of liberation had been spreading for three years and had put lords and peasants under great strain. The conclusion was that "the peace of

43. Kavelin, II, 39–40, 54.
44. Alexander II of Russia, *The Politics of Autocracy: Letters of Alexander II to Prince A. I. Bariatinskii,* ed. Alfred J. Rieber (The Hague, 1966), p. 34.
45. P. A. Zaionchkovskii, *Otmena krepostnogo prava v Rossii* (Moscow, 1960), pp. 84–85.

Russia will largely depend upon the proper distribution of troops according to the circumstances." [46]

Alexander was by no means ignorant of peasant affairs, for as grand duke he had by order of Nicholas I spent much time meeting with the secret committee on peasant affairs and knew that his father had been eager to free the serfs. His concern about the situation was now awakened by an essay by the noted Baron A. von Haxthausen, a noted observer of peasant affairs. Haxthausen stated that Mazzini and his revolutionary associates in England were placing great hopes on a social revolution in Russia, and warning that these men, instead of being idle dreamers, were perceptive and practical, he took alarm. He wrote that Russia could not stop in midcourse and leave the matter to its own development, lest a catastrophe should result. In a notation by Alexander on the margin of this essay the latter wrote: "This is completely correct, and this is my chief concern." Shortly thereafter the tsar discussed the matter with Count N. D. Kiselev, ambassador to France, who wrote in his diary that the monarch had said: "The question about the peasants troubles me unceasingly. It must be carried out. I am more than ever determined. . . ." [47]

It is possible that Alexander undertook to free the serfs in large part because of the need for a new and modern army, in place of the serf-army, with its evident failings. But by 1857 he had come to realize that freedom for the serfs was necessary for Russia's social stability and that once having committed himself to this undertaking, he could not desert it. Whatever the reason for taking up this task, it is obvious that the Crimean War had given impetus to the effort.

46. Ibid., p. 85.
47. Ibid., pp. 78–79.

CHAPTER 23. THE RISE OF POLITICAL OPPOSITION

As the preceding chapter has shown, the rise of violent social unrest in Russia was directed not against the war but against serfdom. Indeed, the peasants who demonstrated and rioted did so, not against the government and the tsar, but for the right to enter armed service, which they believed would win them freedom from servile obligations. To win this freedom they fought against the troops of the tsar, and a significant number paid for their stubborness with their lives. Although they insisted that they wanted to fight *for* the tsar with their last drops of blood, in essence this was a rebellion against constituted authority and the government treated it as such, putting it down with rigor.

In marked contrast was the political opposition to the war that arose among the intelligentsia—journalists, educators, and members of the local nobility or the bureaucracy—who felt dismay over the drift to war, for which they saw no good reason. The quarrel with France over the Holy Places in Palestine had seemed trivial, and when it was settled peacefully in 1853, these men could see no grounds for further demands to the Porte about the rights of the Orthodox church. When Turkey proved defiant, few people realized the seriousness of the Russian break with the Porte, and even the occupation of Moldavia and Wallachia seemed merely a threatening gesture rather than a step toward war. Michael P. Pogodin, the Panslav professor of history at Moscow University, hoped for war with Turkey and its expulsion from Europe, and the liberation of the Bulgars, the Greeks of Epirus and Macedonia, the Serbs and the Bosnians, which would form new Christian states under Russian protection. Nicholas I and Nesselrode, however, realized that war with Turkey would bring war with France, Britain, and Austria, so that, under strong urging by Field Marshal Paskevich, the emperor withdrew his forces from Bulgaria and later moved them back to Russia. This retreat was a grave disappointment for Pogodin and the Slavophils—A. S. Khomiakov, S. T. Aksakov and his sons Ivan and Konstantin, and Alexander Kosh- elev—who had Panslav learnings. For them the war no longer had any meaning and they became more and more critical of a policy that had led Russia into trouble. To make matters worse, the Allies refused to accept Russia's peace gestures and invaded the Crimea, hoping to humble the Muscovite empire by capturing Sevastopol and destroying the Russian fleet. But while these hopes proved vain and the British army almost collapsed during the Crimean winter, the Russians had no success and under ruinous leadership lost heavily in battle and from disease. Only the skill of Totleben and the devotion of the rank and file held off the besiegers and saved the fortress from capture. The death of Nicholas I in February 1855 brought little change, and when Prince M. D. Gorchakov, the new commander, could not cope with the increasing superiority of the Allies in artillery and manpower, all informed men realized that Russia was losing the war. To make matters worse, in the summer of 1855 a huge Anglo- French fleet made a heavy attack on Sveaborg, the fortress before Helsingfors, and although it held out, late in the year Sweden and Norway signed an alliance with the maritime powers, which threatened an unprecedented attack on Russia's Finnish position during the fol- lowing summer. Both Austria, although weak militarily, and Prussia, while not hostile to Russia, also appeared likely to enter the war. If this broadened coalition formed, it would probably be too strong for Russia. By midsummer of 1855 many Russians clearly saw that there was no hope ahead and that disaster might be coming.

The result was disillusionment and anger, for Moscow and other cities had made considerable sacrifices in donations for the war—a form of taxation. Repeated draft calls took large numbers of men for the army, and when these had reached their limit, the nobles had to release numerous peasants for service in the seven battalions of opolchenie (militia) formed in Moscow. The war troubled the course of trade and industry and caused high prices. Moreover, these priva- tions were not mitigated by victories, for the war dragged on with new losses, and the diplomatic defeats and the invasion of the Crimea did not improve the attitude of the people. Small wonder that the secret police reported forbidden talk in the bars and saloons of Moscow. The death of Nicholas hastened the political awakening, for the people felt that Alexander's accession represented not only a change of rulers but also the passing of the old order, which was never to return. The news from the Crimea and the Baltic continued to be bad, with Austria and Sweden apparently moving toward war, and perhaps even Prussia as well. Because of the numerous failings of the old regime, the war seemed lost.[1]

Early in July 1855 General A. A. Zakrevskii, governor general of Moscow, reported the circulation of handwritten copies of verses by P. I. Lavrov, which had come from St. Petersburg. In this widely circulated poem Lavrov roundly condemned the regime of Nicholas I and its failure to deal with Russia's ills—its stupid, ignorant officials and its unexpected and shameful defeats. The poet attacked the whole policy of Nicholas and called on the Russian people to rise against its oppressive, ruinous slavery.

The secret agents of Moscow also uncovered other subversive works "imbued with the poison of rebellion and anarchy"—some brochures printed in London by Alexander Herzen and smuggled into Russia, where the intelligentsia eagerly read them. "Baptized Property" was one title; others were entitled "To Our Brothers in Rus'," "The Development of Revolutionary Ideas in Russia," "The Russian People and Socialism," and "Slavery in Russia." Another clandestine work was a handwritten "History of Emperor Nicholas"—a highly critical essay on the emperor's internal and foreign policy.[2]

In the more relaxed period after the death of the powerful tsar both the Slavophils and the Westerners (those who favored a more modern, rational point of view) made energetic efforts to obtain the right to publish. While both were very critical of the government and wanted basic changes, their fundamental principles remained unchanged and their disagreement grew sharper as the situation grew more tense. In the summer of 1855 Khomiakov wrote to Konstantin Aksakov that the situation was taking a new turn, but not necessarily a safe one. The late tsar had died too soon for the Slavophils. . . . "Now it is a matter of conquering Russia, of mastering society, and it is not impossible for us. It is a matter of giving to society . . . the rudiments of seriousness, to prepare the triumph of our thought. . . ."[3]

1. 1. N. M. Druzhinin, "Moskva v gody Krymskoi voiny," *Vestnik Akademii Nauk SSSR*, no. 6 (1947), pp. 49–50.

2. Ibid., pp. 50–51.

3. A. S. Khomiakov, *Polnoe Sobranie Sochinenii* (3rd ed., Moscow, 1900–1906), VIII, 336.

Each faction petitioned for the right to publish a magazine, with M. N. Katkov, editor for the Westerners, asking for one with a supplement in the form of a chronicle. In October 1855, after T. N. Granovskii of Moscow University had learned of the Slavophil intention, he wrote to K. D. Kavelin: "I am glad, because this faction will have to speak out with full frankness, speak out in all its beauty. Willynilly they will have to remove from themelves the liberal adornments with which they have deceived children—such as you. It will be necesary to say the last word on their viewpoint, and this last word is orthodox patriarchality [*sic*] which is incompatible with any movement forward." [4]

Before the struggle was joined, however, the fall of Sevastopol took place, which, although not entirely unexpected, was a severe shock. Granovskii, probably the best-informed man at Moscow University, for months had been disturbed over the failure of the educated to appreciate the peril of the conflict. "Why are we preparing war with a civilization that is preparing its forces against us?" he asked. He was perturbed by the easy optimism of those who foresaw a happy outcome of the struggle, and also by those who were willing to have Russia defeated so that its people would be taught a useful lesson. When the inevitable happened, Granovskii wrote to Kavelin: "The news of the fall of Sevastopol made me weep. If I were in good health I would have joined the militia, without wishing victory for Russia, but with a desire to die for it. My soul was sick at this time. Here all honorable people, no matter what their opinions, hung their heads." [5] O. M. Bodianskii, a writer from Moscow, stated in his diary: "The people crowded into the bars by the hundreds, in the city they moaned and crossed themselves in horror. The shock was terrible, for it was unexpected, as all had trusted the printed statements about the impregnability of Sevastopol." [6] The Slavophils reacted in the same way. S. T. Aksakov wrote to his son Ivan: "It is gloomy and heavy in my soul as never before, especially because one cannot see a solution, but can only realize that this is just the beginning of our calamities."

This feeling of helplessness, however, soon wore off and there was a return to activity. Pogodin, the aggressive historian and publicist of Moscow, who had deluged the monarch with letters of advice,

4. *T. N. Granovskii i ego perepiska* (Moscow, 1897), II, 457.

5. Ibid., I, 252–53; II, 457.

6. O. M. Bodianski, "Vyderzhki iz dnevnika O. M. Bodianskago," *Sbornik Obshchestva liubitelei rossiiskoi slovesnosti na 1890 god.* (Moscow, 1890), p. 130.

from Panslav utterances to sharp criticism of the regime of Nicholas I, again took up his pen, although in impeccably monarchist terms. When Alexander and his family came to Moscow in the autumn of 1856, the publicist lavished praise on him in a glowing article on the ceremonies in the Kremlin and on the capture of Kars in November. All this delighted the emperor. Pogodin also gave some suave words of advice, calling for reforms in military technique and in education. He added, "We await from Thee kindnesses, privileges, orders. With inner order, no foreign foes are dangerous, no misfortunes are frightful to us." [7]

This article caused much comment. Alexander and his entourage were delighted by its enthusiastic monarchist praise. The moderate progressives of Moscow also approved, for, while their zeal for the monarch was less fervent, they felt that the call for reforms and changes expressed their hopes and dreams. The leading bureaucrats and the aristocracy of Moscow were enraged by Pogodin's unsolicited advice. "The local lords, Zakrevskii, S. M. Golitsyn, and others, are in a rage," wrote Granovskii to Kavelin. He took a skeptical attitude toward "the endless and useless letters" of Pogodin and was concerned over the inconsistency of Moscow society and grieved that there were no signs of a really active social initiative. [8]

Shortly thereafter, however, the public of Moscow made known its views in no uncertain fashion. Professor Granovskii, the idol of the students, revered by his colleagues and educated Muscovites, suddenly died on November 7, 1855, after a brief illness. There was a vast outpouring of liberals at his funeral and activities at the university were at a standstill. Bodianskii went to his residence to pay his respects and found Mrs. Granovskii sitting in a trance beside the coffin. The visitor was so desolated by the loss of his friend that he was unable to utter a word, and for five minutes tears streamed down his face. The university community was crushed by the death; "from morning until night the doors of his residence did not close." There was a massive attendance at the funeral and the professors carried the coffin out of the church and handed it to the students, who carried it four miles to the cemetery. "The way was strewn with flowers and laurel leaves. Moscow had not seen such a funeral for a long time; for a long time it had not honored anyone so gloriously, so unanimously,"

---

7. *Moskovskiia Vedomosti,* 1855, no. 109, cited in Druzhinin, p. 53.
8. Druzhinin, pp. 52–53; Granovskii, II, 455–56.

wrote Bodianskii. It was vastly more imposing than the funeral of Count S. S. Uvarov, former minister of education, a month before. M. N. Katkov, a liberal, beautifully characterized Granovskii in a brief but eloquent eulogy.[9]

After the funeral there were newspaper articles and commemorative notices from one end of Russia to the other. I. S. Turgenev wrote, "The funeral itself was a sort of event, both touching and exalting." Indeed it was much more than a funeral, for a young, new Russia was demonstrating beside the bier, as it buried one of the most consistent and fiery opponents of despotism and slavery. With some reason the university trustee V. I. Nazimov publicly rebuked the professors and the students the next day for the "heathen" casting of laurel wreaths on the grave, and the reactionaries of Moscow were indignant at the public commotion raised by the "panegyrists" of the dead professor.[10]

This demonstration, which expressed both admiration for Granovskii and detestation of the regime, was followed six weeks later by a jubilee banquet held in honor of the fiftieth anniversary of the great actor M. S. Shchepkin of the Malyi Theater. It, too, was a personal tribute and a political demonstration. After Konstantin Aksakov had read the chief eulogy for the guest, written by the senior Aksakov, in which Shchepkin's career and talents were traced, he continued significantly: "The present grim time is unfavorable to peacetime art; our horizon is gloomy; the trial is grave. But there is always time to do justice to merit; there is always time to be grateful. Shchepkin has performed such a service to Russian society, above all that of Moscow." The historian S. M. Solov'ev interpreted this conclusion, speaking of the influence of Granovskii on Shchepkin, of the significance of the creativity of N. V. Gogol and of the métier of the artist— "by the strength of a noble laugh to aid in the cleansing of morals." Letters from literary men of St. Petersburg were then read, from Turgenev, Leo Tolstoi, Nicholas Nekrasov, Ivan Goncharov, Kavelin, and others.[11]

The highlight of the occasion was the toast of Konstantin Aksakov, who in the name of his father thanked Shchepkin for his greeting to him as the senior dramatist and Moscow friend of the actor's. "The

9. Bodianskii, pp. 134–35.
10. Druzhinin, p. 53.
11. Ibid., pp. 53–54.

expression of social sympathy, of social opinion," he emphasized, "is precious, and my father places it highest for all. I cannot better answer your toast, so precious for me, than by proposing a toast in honor of public opinion." Since public opinion had never been permitted a voice in Russia, there were two seconds of silence, followed by shouts and a storm of applause. All rose, clinked glasses, embraced; strangers came up to greet the speaker, and all efforts to restore order to the excited throng were in vain. Finally, after gifts had been presented to the guest, the celebration ended, only to begin again in Shchepkin's home, where the finest actresses of the Malyi Theater met him with flowers and kisses.

Although the ceremony had been approved by Zakrevskii, in the eyes of the authorities the setting and the tone of the jubilee had made it an undesirable political demonstration. Nazimov, the university trustee, forbade the printing of Aksakov's toast, and in St. Petersburg the account of the affair produced real alarm even among the moderate liberals.[12]

At the turn of the year—after the capture of Kars and the Russian acceptance of the conditions of peace, as well as the revelations about the state of the country—public indignation again openly expressed itself. It appeared that either Russia would decay and collapse, or its inner strength would assert itself to surmount the crisis and move along a new route to redemption. Angry with the government and condemning the serf system, the rising liberal elements lavished their sympathies on the heroes of Sevastopol, who by their valor, heroism, and devotion had shown the true value of Russia. First of all they turned to the heroic defense of Sevastopol and the courage of General S. A. Khrulev, in which they saw the life-giving forces which would win over the foul and deadening regime of official Russia. By magnifying Sevastopol as an indication of inner national strength, as against the stupid and ruinous actions of the government, they sought to establish a new manifestation of the social movement. The welcome to the men returning from Sevastopol was an organized demonstration of the new and widespread attitude.

The first gesture was Moscow's banquet in honor of General Khrulev, known for his valor and for the Sevastopol garrison's love for him. The banquet took place in the English Club, with M. P. Pogodin

---

12. Ibid., p. 54.

as speaker. In his florid style Pogodin hailed the eleven-month defense of the fortress as a historic event beyond compare, which "has served for all of us, its participants,—as a lifegiving bath of our existence, refreshing, renewing, raising all our moral forces, lifting our souls. . . ." [13]

On February 18, 1856, naval units from Sevastopol entered Moscow en route to St. Petersburg and were met by V. A. Kokorev, a wealthy taxfarmer, who seized the occasion to show Moscow's reverence for the heroic defenders of the fortress. When the sailors arrived at the city gate, Kokorev and his partner in this gesture, Mamontov, met them with a huge gift of bread and salt. With bared heads they thanked the sailors for their labors and deeds, for their blood shed for the people in defense of their native land. "Receive our heartfelt thanks and our bows to the earth," said the welcomers, dropping to their knees and bowing to the ground before the sailors. Then deputies from the merchants, from the lower middle classes, and from the craft guilds presented their bread and salt.

There followed eight days of honors, entertainment, religious observance, sightseeing, and feasting. The highlight of the occasion was a speech by Kokorev, to the effect that Russia had always been stimulated by its sorrow, not to despair, but to purification and exaltation, which made the nation stronger. Kokorev's utterances greatly pleased both S. T. Aksakov and Kavelin. [14]

Finally, after the heavy drinking at the patriotic entertainment of the sailors, Aksakov asked that Pogodin arrange a dinner in honor of General Adjutant Count D. E. Osten-Sacken, in Aksakov's opinion the only devout and honorable general in the whole army. Pogodin made the speech of introduction, in which he credited the general with performing his duty throughout the siege and hailed him for keeping the soldiers of his command well fed and well clothed, and for always providing them with free access to him and just protection. The address drew repeated applause from the audience and Pogodin received numerous compliments on it. In contrast to this cordial reception of Osten-Sacken, General N. N. Muraviev, the conqueror of Kars, received little attention when he passed through Moscow in November 1856. Konstantin Aksakov wrote to Pogodin that he had called on Muraviev, but solely to add his name to the list of callers. He remarked

13. M. P. Pogodin, XIV, 448–53.
14. Ibid., pp. 470–517.

that in many ways Muraviev was worthy of esteem, but he was a supporter of the regime of Nicholas.[15] Some weeks later Pogodin had a friendly chat with Prince V. A. Dolgorukov, the minister of war, during which the latter remarked to Pogodin: "You really stung us with Sacken, but no matter."[16]

Perhaps even more significant than these surges of public opinion against the regime was the rise of a growing, reasoned literature expressing sharp criticism of the policy of the government and accusing Nicholas I of leading Russia to ruin through his blind, headstrong acts. One of the first of these criticisms was an article circulated in handwritten copies early in 1855 by B. N. Chicherin on the suggestion of K. D. Kavelin, which analyzed how Russia, mighty and influential, in two or three years had arrayed much of Europe against it. It was not a holy war into which Russia was slipping, the author insisted, for while Turkey was brutal and oppressive, Russia had never wanted to reform it, and had even betrayed Turkish reformers to the sultan. Russia also was repressive, harshly dominating Poland and conquering the peoples of the Caucasus. Its main purpose was to extend its influence over the Greeks and the Slavs, but it had done so in an infuriating manner and also had alienated the Turks, the Austrians, and the English. Russia's general policy was also unsound, for Nicholas had remained friendly only to strong conservatives, at a time when the political trend was toward liberalism. Internally the tsar had still supported serfdom and would give no voice to the people. As long as he followed Nesselrode's advice he had pursued a sensible policy toward Turkey, but when the French stirred up the Turks he had decided to dominate them, and when they defied him, had sent his troops into the Principalities. With his rapacious designs revealed during the Seymour conversations, most of Europe had turned against him, with the French and the British supporting the Turks.[17]

The great powers, the article continued, then had tried to compromise the dispute with a Note that would grant Russia some satisfaction while protecting Turkey. Russia, however, had refused to make further concessions to the Turks, who, in turn, backed by France and Britain,

---

15. Ibid., pp. 534–42.

16. Ibid., p. 554.

17. B. N. Chicherin, "Vostochnyi vopros s russkoi tochki zrenia," in S. P. Trubetskoi, *Zapiski* (St. Petersburg, 1907), pp. 125–39; see also Chicherin's *Vospominaniia: Moskva sorokovykh godov* (2 vols, Moscow, 1929), I, 153.

had declared war on Russia. The Turks could do little against Russia in the Principalities, and when they had attacked it in Asia Minor, Russia had beaten them and wiped out a Turkish fleet at Sinop. This victory had infuriated the French and the British, who had demanded that Russia evacuate the Principalities or face war. Russia had refused to evacuate, and instead had crossed the Danube to smash Turkey before the Allies could rescue it. Austria, however, horrified that Russia would incite the Serbs and the Bulgars against Turkey, had mobilized to threaten Russia's rear if it did not retire to its own lands, and Paskevich, much concerned by this threat, had induced Nicholas I to allow him to retreat to Russia. But when Russia had refused to make peace on the basis of the Four Points, the Allies had massed to attack it.[18]

The French and the British, Chicherin wrote, after landing troops in Bulgaria, in midsummer had moved their armies to the Crimea, hoping to capture Sevastopol quickly and to destroy it and the Russian fleet. The Russian army, which was very backward, was equipped only with obsolete muskets, while the Allies had Minié rifles. The Russian military organization was cumbersome; its officers were largely ignorant and corrupt; and at first they had had only 35,000 men in the Crimea, while the Allies had 60,000. With no railways to the south, Russia was never properly supplied with provisions for its men and animals or with gunpowder. The soldiers, who were marched great distances, often in the middle of winter, had died by thousands of cold and exhaustion. Even so, the Russians had held off the Allies and inflicted heavy losses on them, although they had no real hope of victory. This survey, while written several months before the fall of the fortress, indicated the probable result, with the country's resources near exhaustion and much of Europe united against the Russians. The Slavs, who favored the Russians, would not help them lest they should come under even worse despotism, and only if Russia should "raise the revolutionary banner" would they join it. This, however, could happen only if Russia should change its whole system, "free Poland, renounce all our past, and proceed by a completely new road," which seemed impossible, because of Russia's "indolence . . . indifference to all noble striving of mankind, [and] denial of thought and freedom."

Chicherin hoped that Russia's punishment would be a lesson to

18. Chicherin, *Vospominaniia*, I, 147–53.

it, for it was evident that the present regime would lead it to ruin: "Let us hope that Russia, renewed by misfortune, will feel in itself new strength and will be able to come forth out of this degrading condition in which it finds itself." [19]

Chicherin's article was not the only one of its kind, for, after obtaining Kavelin's warm approval of it, the author set to work on an essay, "Contemporary Problems of Russian Life," in which he set forth demands for freedom of conscience, the abolition of serfdom, freedom of social opinion, freedom of the press, freedom in teaching, publicity of governmental actions, and finally publicity and openness of court trials, much of which became the program of the new reign. Chicherin was careful, however, not to call for a change in the governmental system, which he felt would be necessary in the future but should not be mentioned at this time. In another article, "On the Servile Condition," he suggested the steps to be taken for the liberation of the peasants. First, the arbitrary authority of the landowners should be limited; then, in a transitional period, the introduction of some limitation of the exactions of the nobility should be introduced; and finally, the peasants should be fully liberated by means of redemption of the land on which they lived. Next he wrote an essay on the aristocracy, castigating them for their idle, unproductive lives. He also persuaded his brother Vladimir, a retired colonel living on his estate, to produce an article about regimental commanders and their economic activities. (This article was concerned with the practice of colonels' buying the equipment and provisions for their units, usually purchasing articles of poor quality or food in insufficient quantity for their men, so that the commanders could pocket considerable sums out of the amounts allotted for these needs.) [20]

Later the authors sent these articles, which at first had passed secretly from hand to hand, to Alexander Herzen in London, whom they asked to publish them, even though they were very much opposed to Herzen's revolutionary beliefs. Herzen did publish them in separate volumes, as they asked, under the title of *Golosa iz Rossii* (4 vols., London, 1857–58), even though he disagreed with the writers' liberal viewpoint.[21]

Chicherin's close friend, N. A. Mel'gunov, also wrote and circulated articles, three of which were "Thinking Aloud about the Preceding

19. Ibid., pp. 147–53.
20. Chicherin, *Vospominaniia*, I, 161–64.
21. Druzhinin, p. 59.

Thirty Years," "Russia in War and Peace," and "A Conversation of Friends." Mel'gunov's writings were less penetrating than those of Chicherin, but both men had the same Western outlook of Moscow society. The content and the tone of their essays differed from the "Letters" of Pogodin and from the writings of the Slavophils, for they were free of adulation of the monarchy and displayed a distrust of the government and an appeal to social initiative. In addition to an exhaustive criticism of the regime of Nicholas, they condemned the Russian aristocracy for its historical lack of productive accomplishment and its selfishness. Unlike the conservative patriots, they demanded an end to senseless bloodletting and the immediate conclusion of a firm peace. But the political demands of the Westerners were basically identical with the hopes of the Slavophils: "We need space, space! That alone we thirst for, from the peasant to the magnate, as the dried-out land thirsts for the life-giving rain. Our limbs have weakened; we can no longer breathe freely. Space is necessary for us, like the air, like bread, like God's light! It is needed for each of us; necessary for all Russia, for its internal flowering, for its defense and guard from without." [22]

Chicherin cast the same demand in a more concrete and precise form: "We need freedom! Liberalism! This is the watchword of every educated and sound-thinking man in Russia. This is the banner which can rally men of all spheres, of all classes, of all tendencies. This is the word that is capable of forming a mighty social opinion, if only we shake off the indolence that is ruining us and indifference toward the common good." [23]

On the other hand, Chicherin, Mel'gunov, Kavelin, and Nicholas and Dmitri Miliutin, all of whom followed a liberal moderate tradition, were sharply hostile to Herzen's revolutionary radicalism. In a letter to Herzen, Kavelin and Chicherin, who signed themselves "a Russian liberal," stressed the loyal monarchist position and sharply attacked Herzen's revolutionary socialism. "Your revolutionary theories," they wrote, "will never find a response in us, and your bloody banner, waving over the orator's tribune, arouses in us only indignation and aversion." [24]

The liberals soon found an opportunity to display their loyalty to

22. Chicherin, *Vospominaniia*, I, 162.
23. Druzhinin, p. 59.
24. Ibid.

the throne in the press approved by the censor, for early in 1856 both the Westerners and the Slavophils obtained permission to publish journals. In January the Westerners of Moscow published the first issue of *Russkii Vestnik,* in place of Pogodin's *Moskvitianin,* which had become defunct that year. The new paper, edited by M. N. Katkov, along with P. N. Kudriavtsev, P. M. Leont'ev, and E. F. Korsh, represented the interests and opinions of the professors of Moscow University. At that time Katkov was quite liberal, for he opposed autocracy and serfdom and warmly favored freedom "to which belongs the future and to which all history serves only as a gradual realization." [25] Later on Katkov became a fiery reactionary, but in 1856 he held a liberal position.

Pogodin also was changing with the times, for while in his speeches at the banquets he continued to insist on his full loyalty to the tsar, he was moving into a position that united the various elements of Moscow—the nobles, the merchants, and the intelligentsia—expressing their dominant thoughts and feelings. His influence reached its peak in his political letter of January 3, 1856, in which he renounced his former aggressive Panslav views: "We now have no reason to think of Constantinople: it is covered by a cloud. We cannot establish direct dealings with the Slavs: they are far removed from us. We cannot incite the other European nationalities, in order not to anger Austria and Prussia, which could put us into a still more difficult position." The Russians, said Pogodin, must save the fatherland from grim danger by means of inspired defense and internal transformation. Under the old system events now seemed to be going from bad to worse, while what was needed was inspiration. They should leap with joy and "must breathe a living soul into the exhausted, blinded multitude, and sprinkle its dead body with living water. . . ." Russia must arise "with all [its] strength in Europe, to gain a strong ally in freedom." Pogodin specified what his watchword of freedom meant with a series of demands: a constitution and an amnesty for Poland; a political amnesty for Russian political offenders; gradual liberation of the peasants; relaxation of the censorship; and noninterference in the internal affairs of the peoples of Europe and protection of their national movements. [26]

But in spite of his transformation, Pogodin could not become the guide of progressive public opinion, because of his reactionary past

25. Chicherin, *Vospominaniia,* I, 280–81.
26. Druzhinin, pp. 57–58.

and his unattractive personal qualities. His political letters had been overtaken by the underground writings of convinced liberals.[27]

In addition, as has been mentioned, the Westerners now had their legal organ in *Russkii Vestnik* essentially representing Moscow University and the friends and supporters of the late Granovskii: S. M. Solov'ev, Chicherin, Kudriavtsev, D. A. Miliutin, and Nicholas Gogol, Alexander Ostrovskii, Michael Saltykov-Shchedrin, N. P. Ogarev, and other literary men. Shortly thereafter, Koshelev and Khomiakov published the first issue of *Russkaia Beseda,* a fierce rival of *Russkii Vestnik.* But while the two periodicals combatted each other, they were both sharp critics of the existing system and strove for peaceful reform under the aegis of the monarchical power. Moscow had nothing comparable to *Sovremennik,* the St. Petersburg organ of the revolutionary democratic left of Chernyshevskii and Dobroliubov, for in Moscow the influence of the landed nobility and of the merchant and industrial bourgeoisie was vastly stronger than in the northern capital. Because of this influence, the growth in Moscow of an independent liberal opposition to the voices of the more conservative serf-owners and of the revolutionary democrats was possible.[28]

But even though the moderate liberal views dominated the Moscow press, among the working masses of the city there was a great excitement resulting from the war and the peace. In March 1856 Zakrevskii reported with concern to the Third Section a rumor that during the peace negotiations there had been a decision to free the Russian serfs. "This rumor was absurd," added the governor general, "but it flatters the servile classes and hence might have harmful consequences." [29]

In spite of the efforts of the authorities to discredit this report, it proved to be very long-lived, for in April, with the coronation of Alexander II set for August, Zakrevskii felt it necessary to instruct his subordinates that the emperor had declared the rumor to be false and had ordered more intensive surveillance over persons who spread such "harmful reports." It proved impossible for the authorities to stamp out such "anti-servile tendencies," however. When the Moscow opolchenie disbanded, the returning men, especially the serfs of

27. Ibid., p. 58.
28. Ibid., pp. 60–61.
29. Ibid. This information and that cited in note 31 are from Moskovskii gosudarstvennyi oblastnoi istoricheskii arkhiv (MGOIA).

landowners, began to speak of "their freedom and to evade" obedience to their masters. When no proclamation of freedom for the serfs came at the coronation, the rumors subsided somewhat, but soon new tales about freedom spread in Moscow with fresh strength, for they were overheard "in bars, eating places, public-houses, baths, and other public places." The reports current late in 1856 stated that the tsar, understanding the unhappy position of the serfs, had decided to make them all state peasants because "it would be better for all Russia to be under one lord, instead of under different ones, who squandered and lost thousands of souls at cards." [30]

While these democratic attitudes were neither clear nor organized, they did evoke some response among university students. In Penza during the summer of 1856 the police arrested one Mikhail Essen, a part-time student at Moscow University, who had in his possession illegal publications of Herzen and Louis Blanc, along with other incriminating documents, including a poem about a dream of the execution of tsars and other rulers. The police also found among Essen's papers a draft of a proclamation to peasants, in which Essen declared that he had sworn to sacrifice himself and spoke of the uproar that would occur at "the coronation of our khan, when his worthy leaders would fall, mocked and accursed." After the completion of the investigation of this case, a resolution of the emperor ordered that Essen be drafted into the army as a private and taken under convoy to serve for a year on the Caucasus Military Line.[31]

This apparently isolated attempt at revolutionary action thus came to naught, but it was doubtless a part of the threatening atmosphere that brought concern to Alexander II. In March 1856, after the signing of the peace treaty, Alexander went to Moscow, where Zakrevskii, the governor general, speaking for the nobility, asked him to calm their troubled minds. His Majesty sought to do so in an address in which he declared that he did not intend to free the peasants: "This is unfair, and you may say so to right and left; but hostile feeling between the peasants and their landowners unfortunately exists, and from this there already have been several cases of insubordination to the landowners. I am convinced that sooner or later we must come

30. Ibid., pp. 61–62.
31. Tsentral'nyi gosudarstvennyi istoricheskii arkhiv, f. 109, op. 18, 1856, no. 215, cited in Druzhinin, p. 62.

to this. . . . I think even you are of one opinion with me, consequently, that it would be vastly better that this should proceed from above than from below." [32]

This imperial pronouncement, contradictory as it was, was a landmark in Russian history, for it led to the Emancipation of February 19/March 3, 1861, which, in turn, in spite of all Russia's imperfections, made possible the remarkable progress the nation achieved in subsequent decades. But if Russia had won the battle of Inkerman in October 1854 and had driven the French and the British from the Crimea in a great debacle (which almost took place), it would have been highly unlikely that the tsar would have freed the serfs in 1861 or would have granted the remarkably liberal court reform of 1864, or the *zemstvos,* which provided for considerable local self-government. The liberal press reform and a freer administration of the schools also would probably not have come for decades, if at all. In other words, a Russian victory in the Crimea would probably have set back the country's development by a generation or more. One of Russia's finest soldiers, Prince V. I. Vasil'chikov, chief of staff of the Sevastopol garrison, wrote that a Russian victory was not to be: "From on high it was decided otherwise; probably in order that we Russians should not become completely conceited, should look seriously at our internal disorders, and should take thought about curing our failings." [33] What Vasil'chikov was saying was that the interests of the people of Russia were better served by defeat than by victory in 1855. It seems probable that this judgment was correct.

32. A. Popel'nitskii, "Rech' Aleksandra II, skazannaia 30 marta 1856 goda moskovskim predvoditeliam dviorianstv," *Golos minuvshego,* nos. 5–6 (1916), p. 393.
33. Vasil'chikov, p. 255.

APPENDIX 1. TEXT OF THE DRAFT
SENED OF APRIL 23/MAY 5, 1853

ARTICLE 1.

No change shall be made in the rights, privileges, and immunities that have been enjoyed or are in possession *ab antiquo* by the churches, the pious institutions and the Orthodox clergy in the States of the Ottoman Sublime Porte, which is pleased to assure these to them forever on the basis of the *strict* status quo existing today.

ARTICLE 2.

The rights and advantages conceded by the Ottoman Government or that will be conceded in future to other Christian cults by treaties, conventions, or special dispositions, by the Sublime Porte, are considered as belonging also to the Orthodox cult.

ARTICLE 3.

It being recognized and stated by the historic traditions and by numerous documents that the Greek Orthodox Church of Jerusalem, its patriarchate and the bishops who are subordinate to it, have been at all times, since the time of the caliphs and under the succeeding reigns of all the Ottoman Emperors, particularly protected, honored and confirmed in their early rights and immunities, the Sublime Porte, in its solicitude for the conscience and the religious convictions of this cult, as well as of all the Christians who profess it and whose piety has been alarmed by various events, promises to maintain and to have respected these rights and these immunities, both in the city of Jerusalem and outside, without any prejudice to the other Christian communities of native born, or *rayahs* [Christians of Turkey], admitted to the worship of the Holy Sepulcher and of other sanctuaries, whether in common with the Greeks, or in their separate oratories.

ARTICLE 4.

His Majesty the Sultan today gloriously reigning, having found it necessary and equitable to explain his sovereign firman adorned with the Hatti Humayun in the middle of the moon of Rebiul-Akhir 1268 (end of January, O.S., 1852) by a sovereign firman of the . . . . and to order, moreover, by another firman dated . . . . the repairing of the great cupola of the Church of the Holy Sepulcher, these two firmans will be textually executed and faithfully observed, in order to maintain forever the strict status quo of the sanctuaries possessed by the Greeks either exclusively or in common with other cults.

It is agreed that they will come to agreement further on the regularization of some points that are not included in the firmans cited.

ARTICLE 5.

The subjects of the Emperor of Russia, both laymen and ecclesiastics, who are permitted, according to the treaties, to visit the holy city of Jerusalem and other places of devotion, are to be treated and considered as equal to the subjects of the most favored nations, and as the latter, both Catholics and Protestants, have their prelates and their special ecclesiastical establishments, the Sublime Porte pledges itself, in case the Imperial court makes request of it, to assign a suitable location in the city of Jerusalem or its environs, for the construction of a church consecrated to the celebration of Divine service by Russian ecclesiastics, and of a hospice for needy or sick pilgrims, which foundations will be under the supervision of the consulate general of Russia in Syria and Palestine.

ARTICLE 6.

It is understood that there is no derogation of any of the existing stipulations between the two courts and that all the earlier treaties, corroborated by the separate act of the Treaty of Adrianople, conserve all their force and value.

APPENDIX 2. THE NOTE OF VIENNA

The Note of Vienna, which was prepared by the diplomats of Austria, France, Great Britain, and Prussia, under the guidance of Count Buol, was to be urged upon the Turks. It was to be signed by the sultan and sent to St. Petersburg by a special ambassador. Nicholas I, who had promised to accept it, would thereupon agree to withdraw his forces from the Principalities and to restore diplomatic relations with the Porte. The following text of the Note of Vienna was sent by Clarendon to Lord Redcliffe at Constantinople on August 2, 1853. The dates left blank in the text were to be filled in by the Turkish officials.

His Majesty the Sultan, having nothing more at heart than to reestablish between himself and His Majesty the Emperor of Russia the relations of good neighborhood and perfect understanding which have been unfortunately impaired by recent painful complications, has diligently endeavoured to discover the means of obliterating the traces of those differences, and a Sovereign irade dated _____ having made known the Imperial decision, is happy to be able to communicate it to his Excellency the Ambassador of Russia (or to his Excellency Count Nesselrode).

If the Emperors of Russia have at all times evinced their active solicitude for the maintenance of the immunities and privileges of the Orthodox Greek Church in the Ottoman Empire, the Sultans have never refused again to confirm them by solemn acts testifying their ancient and constant benevolence toward their Christian subjects. His Majesty the Sultan Abdul-Medjid, now reigning, inspired with the same dispositions and being desirous of giving to His Majesty the Emperor of Russia a personal proof of his most sincere friendship, and of his hearty desire to consolidate the ancient relations of good neighbourhood and thorough understanding existing between the two States, has been solely influenced by his unbounded confidence in the eminent qualities of his august friend and ally, and has been pleased to take into serious consideration the representations which his Excellency Prince Menshikov conveyed to him.

The undersigned has in consequence received orders to declare by the present note that the Government of His Majesty the Sultan will remain faithful to the letter and the spirit of the Treaties of Kainardji and Adrianople relative to the protection of the Christian religion, and that His Majesty considers himself bound in honour to cause to be observed for ever, and to preserve from all prejudice either now or hereafter, the enjoyment of the spiritual privileges which have been granted by His Majesty's august ancestors to the Orthodox Eastern Church, and which are maintained and confirmed by him; and, moreover, in a spirit of exalted equity, to cause the Greek rite to share in the advantages granted to the other Christian rites by convention or special arrangement.

Furthermore, as the Imperial firman which has just been granted to the Greek Patriarchs and clergy, and which contains the confirmation of their spiritual privileges, ought to be looked upon as a fresh proof of these noble sentiments and as, besides, the proclamation of the firman, which affords all security, ought to dispel for ever every apprehension in regard to the rite which is the religion of His Majesty the Emperor, I am happy to be charged with the duty of making the present notification.

As regards the guarantee that hereafter there shall be no change made as to the places of pilgrimage at Jerusalem, that results from the firman invested with the Hatti-humayoun of the 15th of the month of Rebi-ul-akhir [February 1852], explained and corroborated by the firman of _____; and it is the formal intention of His Majesty the Sultan to cause his sovereign decisions to be executed without any alteration.

The Sublime Porte, moreover, officially promises that the existing state of things shall in no wise be modified without previous understanding with the Governments of France and Russia and without prejudice to the different Christian communities.

In case the Imperial Court of Russia should require it, a suitable spot shall be assigned in the city of Jerusalem or its neighbourhood, for the construction of a church destined for the celebration of divine service by Russian ecclesiastics, and of a hospital for the indigent or sick pilgrims of the same nation.

The Sublime Porte engages now to consent to a solemn Act in this respect, whereby these religious foundations shall be placed under the special superintendence of the Consulate-General of Russia in Syria and in Palestine.

BIBLIOGRAPHY

Manuscript Sources

Archive diplomatique Français, Correspondence Politique, Russie (ADF, Russie). Paris.

Arkhiv Vneshnei Politiki, fond Kantseliarii (AVP f. Kants.). Moscow.

Great Britain, Parliament. British Sessional Papers, Eastern Papers (EP). London.

Haus-, Hof-, und Staatsarchiv (HHSA). Vienna.

Miliutin, D. A. "Moi starcheskie vospominaniia, 1816–1873 gg. Tri goda voiny, 1853–1856" (Miliutin MS). Otdel Rukopisei, Biblioteka im. Lenina. Moscow.

Nederland Algemeen Rijksarchief. 's-Gravenhage.

Tsentral'nyi Gosudarstvennyi Arkhiv Drevnykh Aktov (TsGADA). Moscow.

Tsentral'nyi Gosudarstvennyi Arkhiv Oktiabr'skoi Revoliutsii (TsGAOR). Moscow.

Published Documents

Delafield, Richard. *Report on the Art of War in Europe in 1854, 1855, and 1856.* Military Commission to the Theater of War in Europe. Senate Executive Doc. no. 59, 36th Cong., 1st Sess. Washington, D.C., 1860.

Goriainov, S. M. *Le Bosphore et les Dardanelles.* Paris, 1910.

Great Britain, House of Commons. *British Sessional Papers, Eastern Papers,* vol. LXXI (1854).

———. *State Papers,* vols. LXXII (1854); LV (1854–55); LX (1856).

Great Britain, Parliament. *Hansard's Parliamentary Debates.* 3rd series, vols. CXXIV–CLXII (1853–56). London, 1853–56.

Hallendorff, Carl, ed. *Konung Oscar I: s politik under Krimkriget.* Stockholm, 1930.

Hübbenet, Anton Christian von. *Ocherk meditsinskoi i gospital'noi chasti v Krymu v 1854–1856 g.* St. Petersburg, 1870.

Hurewitz, Jacob Coleman. *Diplomacy in the Near and Middle East, 1535–1914.* 2 vols. Princeton, N.J., 1956.

Jasmund, Julius von, ed. *Aktenstücke zur orientalischen Frage.* 3 vols. Berlin, 1855–59.

Jomini, A. H. *Diplomatic Study on the Crimean War (1852–1856), by a Former Diplomat.* 2 vols. London, 1882.

McClellan, George B. *Report.* U.S. Senate, 34th Congress, 1857, Special Session, Exec. Doc. no. 1.

Martens, F. F. *Recueil des traités et conventions conclus par la Russie avec les puissances étrangères.* 15 vols. St. Petersburg, 1874–1906.

Niel, Adolphe, General. *Siège de Sébastopol: Journal des opérations du génie.* Paris, 1858.

Noradounghian, Gabriel. *Recueil d'actes internationaux de l'Empire Ottoman.* 4 vols. Paris, 1897–1903.

Okun', S. B. *Krest'ianskoe dvizhenie v Rossii v 1850–1856 gg.* Vol. 3 of *Krest'ianskoe dvizhenie v Rossii v XIX—nachala XX veka,* edited by N. M. Druzhinin. 4 vols. Moscow, 1962.

Pankratova, A. M., ed. *Rabochee dvizhenie v Rossii v XIX veke.* 4 vols. Moscow, 1955.

Polnoe Sobranie Zakonov Rossiikoi Imperii. Sobranie vtoroe. St. Petersburg, 1830–84. 55 vols. and index.

Poschinger, Heinrich Ritter von, ed. *Preussen im Bundestag, 1851–1859: Dokumente des königlichen preussischen Bundestags-Gesandtschaft.* 4 vols. in 3. Leipzig, 1882–84.

———. *Preussens auswärtige Politik, 1850–1858; Unveröffentliche Dokumente aus dem Nachlasse Manteuffels.* 4 vols. in 3. Leipzig, 1882–84.

Russia, Voennoe Ministerstvo. *Stoletie Voennago Ministerstva, 1802–1902.* 13 pts., summary, and 2 indexes in 56 vols. St. Petersburg, 1902.

Totleben, E. I. *Opisanie oborony g. Sevastopolia.* 2 vols. in 3. St. Petersburg, 1863–78.

Zaionchkovskii, A. A. *Vostochnaia voina v sviazi s sovremennoi ei politicheskoi obstanovki.* 4 vols. in 5. St. Petersburg, 1908–13.

MEMOIRS, DIARIES, AND COLLECTIONS OF LETTERS

Aksakova, V. S. *Dnevnik, 1854–1855.* St. Petersburg, 1913.

Alexander II of Russia. *The Politics of Autocracy: Letters of Alexander II to Prince A. I. Bariatinskii.* Edited by Alfred J. Rieber. The Hague, 1966.

Argyll, George Douglas Campbell, Eighth Duke of. *Autobiography and Memoirs.* 2 vols. London, 1906.

Bapst, Germain. *Le Maréchal Canrobert: Souvenirs d'un siècle.* 3 vols. Paris, 1904.

Beust, Friedrich Ferdinand, Graf von. *Aus Drei Viertel-Jahrhunderten: Erinnerungen und Aufzeichnungen.* 2 vols. Stuttgart, 1887.

Bismarck, Otto, Fürst von. *Die gesammelten Werke.* 15 vols in 19. Berlin, 1924–32.

Bocher, Charles. *Mémoires.* Paris, 1907.

Calthorpe, S. J. G. *Letters from Head-quarters: or, the Realities of the War in the Crimea, By an Officer on the Staff.* 2 vols. London, 1856.

Chicherin, B. N. *Vospominaniia: "Moskva sorokovykh godov."* 3 vols. Moscow, 1904.

Cowley, Henry Richard Charles Wellesley, First Earl of. *The Paris Embassy during the Second Empire.* London, 1928.

Ernst II (duke of Saxe-Coburg). *Aus meinem Leben und aus meiner Zeit.* 3 vols. Berlin, 1887–89.

Franz Joseph I (emperor of Austria). *Briefe Kaiser Franz Josephs I an seine Mutter, 1838–1872.* Munich, 1930.

Gerlach, Ludwig Friedrich Leopold von. *Briefwechsel des Generals Leopold von Gerlach mit dem Bundestags-Gesandten Otto von Bismarck.* Edited by Horst Kohl. Stuttgart, 1893.

Granovskii, T. N. *T. N. Granovskii i ego perepiska.* 2 vols. Moscow, 1897.

Greville, Charles Cavendish Fulke. *The Greville Memoirs, 1814–1860.* 8 vols. London, 1938.

Hamilton-Gordon, Arthur Charles, Baron Stanmore. *Sidney Herbert, a Memoir.* London, 1906.

Hoetzsch, Otto, ed. *Peter von Meyendorff: Ein russischer Diplomat an den Höfen von Berlin und Wien: Politischer und privater Briefwechsel, 1826–1853.* 3 vols. Berlin, 1923.

Hübner, Joseph Alexandre, Graf von. *Neuf ans de souvenirs d'un ambassadeur d'Autriche à Paris sous le Second Empire, 1851–1859.* 2 vols. Paris, 1904.

Kavelin, K. D. *Sobranie sochinenii.* 4 vols. St. Petersburg, 1897–1900.

Khomiakov, A. S. *Polnoe sobranie sochinenii.* 3rd ed. 8 vols. Moscow, 1900–06.

Kireevskii, V. *Polnoe sobranie sochinenii.* Edited by M. Gershenzon. 2 vols. Moscow, 1911.

Krupskaia, Aleksandra. *Vospominaniia Krymskoi voiny sestry krestovozdvi-zhenskoi obshchiny.* St. Petersburg, 1861.

Lake, Sir Henry Atwell. *Narrative of the Defense of Kars, Historical and Military.* London, 1857.

Layard, Sir A. Henry. *Autobiography and Letters, from His Childhood until His Appointment as Ambassador at Madrid.* 2 vols. London, 1903.

Levin, Sh. M. "Krymskaia voina i russkoe obshchestvo." In *Ocherki po istorii russkoi obshchestvennoi mysli, vtoraia polovina XIX vv.* Leningrad, 1974. Pp. 293–304.

Likhutin, M., Major General. *Russkie v Aziatskoi Turtsii v 1854 i 1855 godakh, iz zapisok o voennykh deistviiakh erivanskago otriada.* St. Petersburg, 1863.

Lysons, Daniel, General. *The Crimean War from First to Last: Letters from the Crimea.* London, 1895.

Martin, Sir Theodore. *The Life of His Royal Highness the Prince Consort.* 5 vols. New York, 1875–80.

Men'kov, P. K. *Zapiski.* 3 vols. St. Petersburg, 1898.

Metternich-Winneburg, Clemens Lothair Wenzel, Fürst von. *Mémoires, docu-*

ments et écrits laissés par le prince de Metternich, chancelier du cour et de l'État. 2nd ed. 8 vols. Paris, 1880–84.

Milosevich, N. S. *Iz zapisok Sevastopol'tsa.* St. Petersburg, 1904.

Murav'ev, N. N. *Voina za Kavkazom v 1855 godu.* 3 vols. in 2. St. Petersburg, 1876.

Nesselrode, K. V. *Lettres et papiers du Chancelier Comte de Nesselrode (1760–1856).* Edited by A. de Nesselrode. 11 vols. Paris, 1904–12.

Persigny, Jean Gilbert Victor Fialin, Duc de. *Mémoires du Duc de Persigny publiés avec des documents inédits.* Paris, 1896.

Pirogov, N. I. *Sevastopol'skie pis'ma i vospominaniia.* Moscow, 1950.

Pogodin, M. P. *Zhizn' i trudy.* Edited by N. P. Barsukov. 22 vols. St. Petersburg, 1888–1910.

Rothan, G. *Souvenirs diplomatiques: La Prusse et son roi pendant la guerre de Crimée.* Paris, 1888.

Russell, W. H. *The British Expedition to the Crimea.* Rev. ed. London, 1877.

Stockmar, Ernst von, Baron. *Memoirs.* 2 vols. London, 1872.

Tiutcheva, A. F. *Pri dvore dvukh imperatorov: Dnevnik.* 2 vols. Moscow, 1929.

Tocqueville, Alexis Charles Henri Maurice Clerel de. *Correspondence and Conversations of Alexis de Tocqueville with Nassau Senior.* 2 vols. London, 1896.

Victoria, Queen of Great Britain. *The Letters of Queen Victoria: A Selection from Her Majesty's Correspondence between the Years 1837 and 1861.* 3 vols. London, 1907.

SECONDARY WORKS: BOOKS

Anderson, M. S. *The Eastern Question, 1774–1923.* London, 1923.

Andriianov, A. *Inkermanskii boi i oborona Sevastopolia: Nabroski uchastnika.* St. Petersburg, 1902.

Anichkov, V. M. *Voenno-istoricheskie ocherki Krymskoi ekspeditsii.* 2 pts. St. Petersburg, 1856.

Ashley, Evelyn. *The Life of Henry John Temple, Viscount Palmerston, 1846–1865, with Selections from His Speeches and Correspondence.* 2 vols. London, 1876.

Auger, Charles, General. *Guerre d'Orient. Siège de Sébastopol: Historique de service de l'artillerie, 1854–1856.* 2 vols. Paris, 1859.

Bailey, Frank E. *British Policy and the Turkish Reform Movement, 1826–1853.* London, 1942.

Bapst, Edmond. *Les origines de la guerre de Crimée: La France et la Russie de 1848 à 1854.* Paris, 1912.

Barker, A. J. *The War against Russia, 1854–1856.* New York, 1970.

Barsukov, N. P. *Graf Nikolai Nikolaevich Murav'ev-Amurskii, po ego pis'mam, razskazam sovremennikov, i pechatnym istochnikam.* 2 vols. Moscow, 1891.

Baumgart, Winfred. *Der Friede von Paris, 1856: Studien zum Verhältnis von Kriegsführung, Politik und Friedensbewahrung.* Munich, 1972.

Bazancourt, César Lecat, Baron de. *L'expédition de Crimée jusqu'a la prise de Sébastopol.* 2 vols. Paris, 1856.

Bell, Herbert C. F. *Lord Palmerston.* 2 vols. London, 1936.

Berg, N. V. *Zapiski ob osade Sevastopolia.* 2 vols. Moscow, 1858.

Bestuzhev, I. V. *Krymskaia voina 1853–1856.* Moscow, 1956.

Bliokh, I. S. *Finansy Rossii XIX Stoletiia.* 2 vols. St. Petersburg, 1882.

Bogdanovich, M. I., ed. *Istoricheskii ocherk deiatel'nosti voennogo upravleniia v Rossii v pervoe dvatsatipiatiletie blagopoluchnogo tsarstvovaniia Gosudaria Imperatora Aleksandra Nikolaevicha (1855–1880 gg.).* 6 vols. St. Petersburg, 1879–81.

————. *Vostochnaia voina 1853–1856 gg.* 4 vols. in 2. St. Petersburg, 1876.

Borodkin, M. *Voina 1854–1855 gg. na Finskom poberezh'e: Istoricheskii ocherk.* St. Petersburg, 1904.

Borozdin, K. *Omer-pasha v Mingrelii: Iz vospominanii o vostochnoi voine 1853–56 godov.* St. Petersburg, 1873.

Borries, Kurt. *Preussen im Krimkrieg.* Stuttgart, 1930.

Bourgeois, Émile. *Manuel historique de politique étrangère.* 3 vols. Paris, 1892–1905.

Bugaiskii, P. Ia. *Oborona Sevastopolia (Razskazy).* St. Petersburg, 1877.

Case, Lynn. *French Opinion on War and Diplomacy during the Second Empire.* Philadelphia, 1954.

Charles-Roux, François. *Alexandre II, Gortchakoff et Napoléon III.* Paris, 1913.

Chertan, E. E. *Russko-Rumynskie otnosheniia v 1859–1863 godov.* Kishinev, 1968.

Chicherin, B. N. *Vospominaniia "Moskva sorokovykh godov."* 3 vols. Moscow, 1929.

Christoff, P. K. *An Introduction to Nineteenth-Century Russian Slavophilism: A Study in Ideas.* Vol. 1: *A. S. Xomiakov.* 's Gravenhage, the Netherlands, 1961.

Conacher, James B. *The Aberdeen Coalition, 1852–1855.* Cambridge, Eng., 1968.

Corti, Egon Cäsar, Count. *Mensch und Herrscher: Wege und Schicksale Kaiser Franz Josephs zwischen Thronbesteigung und Berlin Kongress.* Graz, 1952.

Cullberg, Albin. *La politique du roi Oscar I pendant la guerre de Crimée: études diplomatiques sur les négotiations sécrètes . . . les années 1853–1856.* 2 vols. Stockholm, 1912.

Curtiss, J. S. *The Russian Army under Nicholas I, 1825–1855.* Durham, N.C., 1965.

Debidour, A. *Histoire diplomatique de l'Europe, 1814–1878.* 3rd rev. ed. 2 vols. Paris, 1919–20.

Druzhinina, E. I. *Kiuchuk-Kainardzhiiskii mir 1774 goda (ego podgotovka i zakliuchenie).* Moscow, 1955.

Dubrovin, N. F., ed. *Materialy dlia istorii krymskoi voiny i oborony Sevastopolia.* 5 vols. in 16. St. Petersburg, 1871–74.

——. *Trekh-sot-deviati-dnevnaia zashchita Sevastopolia.* St. Petersburg, 1872.

——. *Vostochnaia Voina 1853–1856 godov.* St. Petersburg, 1878.

Engel-Janosi, Friedrich. *Der Freiherr von Hübner, 1811–1892: Eine Gestalt aus dem österreich Kaiser Franz Josephs.* Innsbruck, 1933.

Fadeev, A. V. *Rossiia i vostochnyi krisis 20-kh godov XIX veka.* Moscow, 1958.

Fedorov, B. G. *Vooruzhenie russkoi armii v Krymskuiu kampaniiu.* St. Petersburg, 1904.

Florinsky, M. T. *Russia: A History and an Interpretation.* 2 vols. New York, 1953.

Friedjung, Heinrich. *Der Krimkrieg und die österreichische Politik.* 2nd ed. Stuttgart, 1911.

Frolov (colonel of Engineers). *Minnaia voina v Sevastopol v 1854–1855 g. pod rukovodstvom Totlebena.* St. Petersburg, 1868.

Geffcken, F. H. *Zur Geschichte des Orientalischen Krieges, 1853–1856.* Berlin, 1881.

Gersevanov, N. B. (major general, general quartermaster of the Crimean troops). *Neskol'ko slov o deistviiakh russkikh voisk v Krymu v 1854 i 1855 g.* Paris, 1867.

Gershel'man, S. K. *Nravstvennyi element pod Sevastopolem.* St. Petersburg, 1897.

Geuss, Herbert. *Bismarck und Napoleon III: Ein Beitrag zur Geschichte der preuschisch-französischen Beziehungen 1851–1871.* Graz, 1959.

Gleason, J. H. *The Genesis of Russophobia in Great Britain.* Cambridge, Mass., 1950.

Gooch, Brison D. *The New Bonapartist Generals in the Crimean War.* The Hague, 1959.

Goriainov, S. M. *Le Bosphore et les Dardanelles.* Paris, 1910.

Guérin, Léon (historien de la Marine). *Histoire de la dernière guerre de Russie (1853–1856), écrite au point de vue politique, stratégique, et critique.* 2 vols. Paris, 1858.

Guichen, Eugène, Vicomte de. *La guerre de Crimée (1854–1856) et l'attitude des puissances européennes.* Paris, 1936.

Hallberg, Charles. *Franz Joseph and Napoleon III, 1852–1864: A Study of Austro-French Relations.* New York, 1955.

Harcourt, Bernard Hippolyte Marie d'. *Diplomatie et diplomates: Les quatre ministères de M. Drouyn de Lhuys.* Paris, 1882.

Haywood, R. M. *The Beginning of Railway Development in Russia.* Durham, N.C., 1969.

Henderson, G. B. *Crimean War Diplomacy and Other Historical Essays.* Glasgow, 1947.

Hopwood, D. *The Russian Presence in Palestine and Syria, 1843–1914: Church and Politics in the Near East.* Oxford, 1969.

Huber, E. R. *Deutsche Verfassungsgeschichte seit 1789.* 4 vols. Stuttgart, 1957.

Iz istorii russkogo voenno-inzhenerskogo iskusstva. Moscow, 1952.

Jomini, A. G. *Diplomatic Study on the Crimean War (1852–1856).* London, 1882.

Khrushchov, A. P. *Istoriia oborony Sevastopolia.* 3rd ed. St. Petersburg, 1889.

Kinglake, A. W. *The Invasion of the Crimea: Its Origin and Account of Its Progress Down to the Death of Lord Raglan.* 6th ed. 9 vols. Edinburgh, 1877.

Kovalevskii, E. P. *Voina s Turtsii i razryv s evropeiskimi derzhavami v 1853–1854 godakh.* St. Petersburg, 1868.

Krenke, V. D. *Oborona Bal'tiiskago Priberezh'iia 1853–1854 gg.* St. Petersburg, 1887.

Kukharskii, P. F. *Franko-russkie otnosheniia nakanuna krymskoi voiny.* Leningrad, 1941.

Kyriakos, A. D. *Geschichte der Orientalischen Kirchen von 1453–1898.* Leipzig, 1902.

La Gorce, Pierre François Gustave de. *Histoire du second empire.* 15th ed. 7 vols. Paris, 1894–1904.

Lane-Poole, Stanley. *The Life of Stratford Canning.* 2 vols. London, 1888.

Levin, Sh. *Ocherki po istorii russkoi obshchestvennoi mysli, vtoraia polovina XIX-nachalo XX vv.* Leningrad, 1974.

Linkov, Ia. *Ocherki istorii krest'ianskogo dvizheniia v Rossii vo vremia Krymskoi voiny 1853–1856 gg.* Moscow, 1940.

Manteuffel, Otto, Baron von. *Preussens auswärtige Politik, 1850–1858: Unveröffentliche Dokumente aus dem Nachlasse Manteuffels.* Edited by Heinrich Ritter von Poschinger. 3 vols. Berlin, 1902.

Martin, Kingsley. *The Triumph of Lord Palmerston: A Study of Public Opinion in England before the Crimean War.* London, 1924.

Martin, Theodore. *The Life of His Royal Highness the Prince Consort.* 5 vols. London, 1875–1880.

Maxwell, Sir Herbert. *The Life and Letters of George William Frederick, Fourth Earl of Clarendon.* 2 vols. London, 1913.

Miller, M. *The Ottoman Empire and Its Successors, 1801–1927.* Cambridge, Eng., 1936.

Miloshevich, N. S. *Iz zapisok sevastopol'tsa.* St. Petersburg, 1904.

Mosely, Philip C. *Russian Diplomacy and the Opening of the Eastern Question in 1838 and 1839.* Cambridge, Mass., 1934.

Mosse, W. E. *The European Powers and the German Question.* Cambridge, Eng., 1958.

———. *The Rise and Fall of the Crimean System, 1855–1871: The Story of a Peace Settlement.* London, 1963.

Napier, Sir Charles. *The History of the Baltic Campaign from Documents and Other Materials Furnished by Vice-Admiral Sir Charles Napier.* Edited by Butler Earp. London, 1857.

The New Cambridge Modern History. Vol. X: *The Zenith of European Power, 1830–1870,* edited by J. P. T. Bury. Cambridge, Eng., 1960.

Niel, Adolphe. *Siège de Sébastopol: Journal des opérations du génie, publié avec l'autorisation du Ministère de Guerre.* Paris, 1858.

Pankratova, A. M., ed. *Rabochee dvizhenie v Rossii v XIX veke.* 2nd enlg. ed. Moscow, 1955. Vol. I, pt. 2.

Petrov, A. N. *Voina Rossii s Turtsiei: Dunaiskaia kampaniia 1853 i 1854 gg.* 2 vols. St. Petersburg, 1890.

Petrovich, M. B. *The Emergence of Russian Panslavism, 1856–1870.* New York, 1956.

Pierce, R. A. *Russian Central Asia, 1867–1917: A Study in Colonial Rule.* Berkeley, Calif., 1960.

Pintner, W. M. *Russian Economic Policy under Nicholas I.* Ithaca, N.Y., 1967.

Pirogov, N. I. *Sevastopol'skie pis'ma i vospominaniia.* Moscow, 1950.

Puryear, V. J. *England, Russia and the Straits Question, 1844–56.* Berkeley, Calif., 1931.

———. *France and the Levant from the Bourbon Restoration to the Peace of Kutieh.* Berkeley, Calif., 1941.

———. *International Economics and Diplomacy in the Near East: A Study of British Commercial Policy in the Levant, 1834–1853.* Stanford, Calif., 1935.

Riasanovsky, N. V. *Nicholas I and Official Nationalism in Russia, 1825–1855.* Berkeley, Calif., 1959.

Rousset, Camille. *Histoire de la guerre de Crimée.* 2 vols. Paris, 1878.

Rozhkova, M. K., ed. *Ocherki economicheskoi istorii pervoi poloviny XIX veka. Sbornik statei.* Moscow, 1959.

Runeberg, C. M. *Finland under Orientaliska kriget.* Helsingfors, 1962.

Schiemann, Theodor. *Geschichte Russlands unter Kaiser Nikolaus I.* 4 vols. Berlin, 1904–19.

Schilder, N. K. *Graf Eduard Ivanovich Totleben: ego zhizn' i deiatel'nost'.* 2 vols. St. Petersburg, 1885–86.

Schoeps, H. J. *Der Weg ins Deutsche Kaiserreich.* Berlin, 1970.

Schroeder, P. W. *Austria, Great Britain and the Crimean War.* Ithaca, N.Y., 1972.

Seton-Watson, R. W. *Britain and Europe, 1789–1914: A Survey of Foreign Policy.* Cambridge, Eng., 1937.

Shcherbatov, A. P., kniaz'. *General-fel'dmarshal Kniaz' Paskevich, ego zhizn' i deiatel'nost': Po neizdannym istochnikam.* 17 vols. in 8. St. Petersburg, 1888–1904.

Simpson, F. A. *Louis Napoleon and the Recovery of France, 1848–1856.* London, 1923.

Solov'ev, Sergei M. *Istoriia Rossii s drevneishikh vremen.* 29 vols. in 6. St. Petersburg, 1893–97.

Southgate, Donald. *The Most English Minister: The Policies and Politics of Palmerston.* New York, 1966.

Stavrianos, L. S. *The Balkans since 1453.* 2nd ed. New York, 1958.

Stavrou, T. G. *Russian Interests in Palestine, 1882–1914: A Study of Religious and Educational Enterprise.* Thessaloniki, Greece, 1963.

Strumilin, S. G. *Ocherki ekonomicheskoi istorii Rossii.* Moscow, 1960.

Tarle, E. V. *Gorod Russkoi slavy.* Moscow, 1954.

———. *Krymskaia Voina.* 2 vols. Moscow, 1944.

Tatishchev, S. S. *Imperator Aleksandr II, ego zhizn' i tsarstvovanie.* 2 vols. St. Petersburg, 1903.

Taylor, A. J. P. *The Struggle for Mastery in Europe, 1848–1918.* Oxford, 1954.

Temperley, Harold. *England and the Near East: The Crimea.* London, 1936.

Thouvenel, Louis. *Nicolas I et Napoléon III: Les préliminaires de la Guerre de Crimée, 1852–1854.* Paris, 1891.

Trubetskoi, S. P. *Zapiski.* St. Petersburg, 1907.

Urquhart, David. *Turkey and Its Resources.* London, 1833.

Ward, Sir Adolphus William, and George Peabody Gooch, eds. *Cambridge History of British Foreign Policy, 1783–1919.* 3 vols. Cambridge, Eng., 1922–23.

Webster, C. K. *The Foreign Policy of Castlereagh, 1815–1822.* London, 1925.

———. *The Foreign Policy of Lord Palmerston, 1830–1841.* 2 vols. London, 1951.

Weigelt (captain in the Prussian artillery). *Osada Sevastopolia, 1854–1856.* St. Petersburg, 1859.

Wellesley, F. A., ed. *The Paris Embassy during the Second Empire.* London, 1928.

Woodham-Smith, Cecil. *Florence Nightingale, 1820–1910.* New York, 1951.

Zablotskii-Desiatovskii, A. P. *Graf P. D. Kiselev i ego vremia.* 4 vols. St. Petersburg, 1882.

Zaionchkovskii, P. A. *Otmena krepostnogo prava v Rossii.* Moscow, 1960.

Zatler, F. K. *O gospitaliakh v voennoe vremia.* St. Petersburg, 1861.

————. *O prodovol'stvii voisk v voennoe vremia.* 4 pts. St. Petersburg, 1860–65.

Zisserman, A. L.. *Dvadtsat' piat' let na Kavkaza (1842–67).* 2 pts., St. Petersburg, 1879.

————. *Istoriia 80-go pekhotnago Kabardinskago general-fel'd-marshala Kniazia Bariatinskago polka (1726–1880).* 3 vols. St. Petersburg, 1881.

SECONDARY WORKS: ARTICLES

"Aleksandr II—Gorchakovu." *Russkaia Starina,* XLII (1883).

Baklanov, Ia. I. "Blokada i shturm Karsa." *Russkaia Starina,* II (1870).

Bakunina, E. M. "Vospominaniia sestry miloserdii Krestovozdvizhenskoi obshchiny, 1854–1860." *Vestnik Evropy,* CXC, no. 3 (March 1898).

Baumgart, Winfried. "Probleme der Krimkriegsforschung. Eine Studie über die Literatur des letzten Jahrzents (1961–1970)." *Jahrbücher für Geschichte Osteuropas* NF, XIX (1971).

Berzhe, A. P. "N. N. Murav'ev vo vremia ego namestnichestva na Kavkaze, 1854–1855 gg." *Russkaia Starina,* VIII (1873).

Bestuzhev, I. V. "Iz istorii krymskoi voiny 1853–1856 gg." *Istoricheskii Arkhiv,* no. 1 (1959).

Bodianskii, O. M. "Vyderzhki iz dnevnika O. M. Bodianskago." *Sbornik Obshchestva liubitelei rossiiskoi slovesnosti na 1890 god.* Moscow, 1890.

Bogdanovich, M. I., ed. "Imperator Aleksandr Nikolaevich v epokhu voiny 1855 goda." *Russkaia Starina,* XXXVII (1883), 117–30; XXXIX (1893), 195–220, 299–330, 597–608.

Bolsover, G. H. "Lord Ponsonby and the Eastern Question (1833–1839)." *Slavonic Review,* XIII (July 1934), 104–05.

————. "Nicholas I and the Partition of Turkey." *Slavonic Review,* XXVII (1948), 115–45.

Chicherin, B. N. "Vostochnyi vopros s russkoi tochki zreniia." In S. P. Trubetskoi, *Zapiski.* St. Petersburg, 1907. Pp. 125–39.

Davis, H. W. C. "The Great Game in Asia." *Proceedings of the British Academy,* XII (1926).

Den' (Dehn), V. I. "Zapiski." *Russkaia Starina,* LXV (1890), 55–90, 551–74, 665–80; LXVI (1890), 49–71, 294–324.

Detengof, A. "Zabytyi geroi: Iz vospominanii starago sapëra." *Russkii Arkhiv,* XLIII, pt. 2 (1905), 542–88.

Druzhinin, N. M. "Moskva v gody krymskoi voiny." *Vestnik Akademii Nauk,* no. 6 (1947), 49–63.

Edekauer, N. F. "Nikolai Ivanovich Pirogov v Sevastopole." *Russkaia Starina,* XLVII (1885).

Enisherlov, M. "Srazhenie pri Al'me." *Voennyi Sbornik,* no. 1 (1859), 1–28.

Goriainov, S. "Les étapes d'alliance franco-russe, 1853–1861." *Revue de Paris,* XIX (1912), 1–29, 529–44, 755–76.

Gromeka, S. "Kievskaia volneniia v 1855 godu." *Poleznoe Chtenie,* no. 6 (1863).

Hailly, Edmond de. "Une campagne dans l'Océan Pacifique. L'expédition de Petropavlovsk." *Revue des Deux Mondes, seconde période,* XVI (1858).

Henderson, G. B. "The Diplomatic Revolution of 1854." *American Historical Review,* XLIII (Oct. 1937), 22–50.

Il'inskii, D. V. "Iz vospominanii i zametok sevastopol'tsa." *Russkii Arkhiv,* XXXI, pt. 1 (1893), 274–83.

K——. "Iz pokhodnykh vospominanii o krymskoi voine." *Russkii Arkhiv,* VIII (1870), 2049–50.

"K istorii Parizhskogo mira 1856 g." *Krasnyi arkhiv,* no. 2 (1936), 10–61.

"Kniaz' Menshikov." *Russkii Arkhiv,* XIX (1877), 59–61.

Konstantinov, O. I. "Shturm Malakhova kurgana 27 i 28 avgusta 1855 g." *Russkaia Starina,* XIV (1875), 568–86.

Kozhukhov, Stepan. "Iz Krymskikh vospominanii o poslednei voine." *Russkii Arkhiv,* VII (1869), 381–96.

Krasovskii, I. I. "Delo na Chernoi, iz vospominanii o voine 1853–1856 gg." *Russkii Arkhiv,* XII, no. 7, pt. 2 (1874), cols. 207–24.

Krylov, A. D. "Kniaz' A. S. Menshikov, 1853–1854." *Russkaia Starina,* VII (1873), 853.

Mariñas Otero, Luís. "España ante la guerra de Crimea." *Hispania: Revista española,* XXVI (1966), 410–446.

Martens, F. F. "Rossiia i Angliia nakanune razryva (1853–1854 gg.)." *Vestnik Evropy* (Apr. 1898), 564.

Menshikov, A. S. "Oborona Sevastopolia. Pis'ma." *Russkaia Starina,* XII (1875), 299–328.

Mikhailov, M. "Istoricheskii ocherk Sveaborga i bombardirovanie ego Anglo-Frantsuzskim flotom . . . 1855 goda." *Voennyi Sbornik,* no. 10 (1860), 251–59.

Murav'ev, N. N. "Iz zapisok." *Russkii Arkhiv,* XXVI, pts. 2, 3 (1888); XXVII, pts. 1, 2, 3 (1889); XXXII, pt. 3 (1894).

"Mysli Fel'dmarshala Kn. Paskevicha po povodu oborony i padeniia Sevastopolia." *Russkaia Starina,* VI (1872), 427–35.

Nicholas I. "Iz pisem imperatora Nikolaia Pavlovicha k I. F. Paskevichu." *Russkii Arkhiv*, XLVIII, pt. 2 (1910), 165–70.

Nikitin, S. "Russkaia politika na Balkanakh i nachalo vostochnoi voiny." *Voprosy Istorii*, no. 4 (1946), 3–29.

Obruchev, N. N. "Iznanka krymskoi voiny." *Voennyi Sbornik*, no. 4 (1858).

"Ofitsial 'naia chast.' " *Morskoi Sbornik*, no. 7 (July 1855), 192–93.

Ol'shevskii, M. Ia. "Russko-Turetskaia voina za kavkazom v 1853 i 1854 gg." *Russkaia Starina*, XLIV (1884), 171–90, 417–32, 497–514.

Osten-Sacken, Dmitrii. "Voennyi Sovet pri Oborone Sevastopolia." *Russkaia Starina*, XI (1874), 330–38.

Panaev, A. A. "Kniaz' A. S. Menshikov v razskazakh ego ad'iutanta A. A. Panaeva." *Russkaia Starina*, XVIII (1877), 290–91.

Paskevich, I. F. "Kniaz' Mikhail Dmitrievich Gorchakov v Sevastopole." *Russkaia Starina*, XL (1883), 369–80.

Pintner, W. M. "Inflation in Russia during the Crimean War Period." *American Slavic and East European Review*, XVIII (1959), 81–87.

Pirogov, N. I. "Istoricheskii obzor deistvii Krestovozdvizhenskoi obshchiny sester popecheniia o ranennykh i bol'nykh, v voennykh gospitaliakh v Krymu i Khersonskoi gubernii. . . ." *Morskoi Sbornik*, no. 4 (1856).

Popov, A. E. "Moi priezd k Kn. A. S. Menshikovu, Sentiabr' 1854 goda." *Russkaia Starina*, XIX (1877), 323–29.

———. "Zapiski o prebyvanii ego pod Sevastopole s i-go Oktiabria po l-e dekabria 1854 g." *Russkaia Starina*, XX, XXI (1878), 305–24, 491–530.

Puryear, V. J. "New Light on the Origins of the Crimean War." *Journal of Modern History*, III, no. 2 (1931), 219–34.

Schiemann, Theodor. "Russische-englische Beziehungen unter Kaiser Nikolaus I." *Zeitschrift für Osteuropäische Geschichte*, III (1913).

Schilder, N. K. "Fel'dmarshal Paskevich v Krymskuiu voinu." *Russkaia Starina*, XV (1875), 606–07.

———. "Priezd E. I. Totlebena v Sevastopol' avguste 1854 g." *Russkaia Starina*, XVIII (1877).

Schmitt, B. E. "Diplomatic Preliminaries of the Crimean War." *American Historical Review*, XXV, no. 1 (Oct. 1919), 33–67.

Schroeder, P. W. "A Turning Point in Austrian Policy in the Crimean War: The Conference of March, 1854." *Austrian History Yearbook*, IV-V (1968–69).

Sergeev, A. A. "Tret'e otdelenie i Krymskaia voina." *Krasnyi Arkhiv*, III (1923), 293–94.

Slezinskii. "Morskoe opolchenie." *Russkaia Starina*, CXXIV (1905).

Solomon, Richard. "Die Annerkennung Napoleons III: Ein Beitrag zur Geschichte der Politik Nikolaus I." *Zeitschrift für Osteuropäische Geschichte*, II (1912).

Stolypin, D. A. "Iz lichnykh vospominanii o Krymskoi voine." *Russkii Arkhiv,* XII, no. 5, pt. 1 (1874).

Temperley, Harold. "Stratford de Redcliffe and the Origins of the Crimean War." *English Historical Review,* XXVII, pt. 1 (Oct. 1933), 601–21; XLIX, pt. 2 (Apr. 1934), 265–98.

Vasil'chikov, V. I. "Sevastopol'. Zapiski nachal'nika shtaba Sevastopol'skago garnizona Kniazia Viktora Ilarionovicha Vasil'chikova." *Russkii Arkhiv,* XXIX, pt. 2 (1891), 167–256.

"Voina Rossii s Turtsiei, v 1853–1854 gg. Doneseniia i zapiski kniazia Paskevi-cha i kniazia Gorchakova." *Russkaia Starina,* XIX, no. 9 (1877), 89–90.

Volkov, Mikhail. "Chto dovelo Rossiiu do nastoiashchei voiny?" In A. A. Zaionchkovskii, *Vostochnaia Voina v sviazi s sovremennoi ei politicheskoi obstanovki, Prilozheniia I.* St. Petersburg, 1908–13. Pp. 175–80.

"Vospominaniia o voine na Dunae v 1853–1854 godakh: Dnevnik otstav-nago." *Voennyi Sbornik,* no. 8 (1860).

"V vidu krymskoi voiny. Zametki diplomata pri Peterburgskom i london-skom dvorakh, 1852–1855 gg." *Russkaia Starina,* LIV (1887).

Zaionchkovskii, A. M. "Vzgliad N. N. Murav'eva na sostoianie nashei armii i sobstvennoruchnye zamechaniia Imperatora Nikolaia Pavlovicha." *Voennyi Sbornik,* no. 2 (1903).

Zisserman, A. L. "Fel'dmarshal Kniaz' A. I. Bariatinskii." *Russkii Arkhiv,* XXVI, pts. 1, 2, 3 (1888), 93–128, 157–227, 497–579.

INDEX